Buck Wild
DOONESBURY

BUCK WILD

DOONESBURY

Recent Doonesbury Books by G.B. Trudeau

Read My Lips, Make My Day, Eat Quiche and Die!
Give Those Nymphs Some Hooters!
You're Smokin' Now, Mr. Butts!
I'd Go With the Helmet, Ray
Welcome to Club Scud!
What Is It, Tink, Is Pan in Trouble?
Quality Time on Highway 1
Washed Out Bridges and Other Disasters
In Search of Cigarette Holder Man
Doonesbury Nation
Virtual Doonesbury
Planet Doonesbury

Special Collections

The Doonesbury Chronicles
Doonesbury's Greatest Hits
The People's Doonesbury
Doonesbury Dossier: The Reagan Years
Doonesbury Deluxe: Selected Glances Askance
Recycled Doonesbury: Second Thoughts on a Gilded Age
Action Figure!
The Portable Doonesbury
Flashbacks: Twenty-Five Years of Doonesbury
The Bundled Doonesbury

A DOONESBURY BOOK

BUCK WILD DOONESBURY

Buck Wild DOONESBURY

BY G. B. TRUDEAU

Andrews McMeel Publishing
Kansas City

DOONESBURY is distributed internationally by Universal Press Syndicate.

Buck Wild Doonesbury copyright © 1999 by G.B. Trudeau. All rights reserved. Printed in the United States of America. No part of this book may be used or reproduced in any manner whatsoever without written permission except in the case of reprints in the context of reviews. For information, write Andrews McMeel Publishing, an Andrews McMeel Universal company, 4520 Main Street, Kansas City, Missouri 64111.

www.andrewsmcmeel.com

99 00 01 02 03 BAM 10 9 8 7 6 5 4 3 2 1

ISBN: 0-7407-0015-4

Library of Congress Catalog Card Number: 99-72690

DOONESBURY may be viewed on the Internet at:
www.uexpress.com and www.doonesbury.com

"When I was young and irresponsible,
I was young and irresponsible."

—George W. Bush

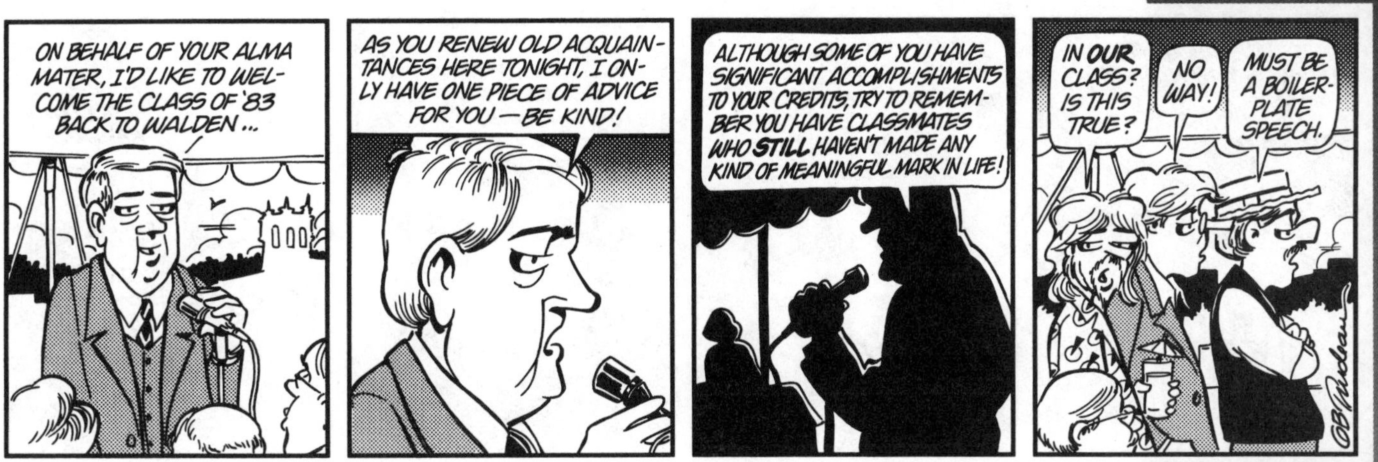
ON BEHALF OF YOUR ALMA MATER, I'D LIKE TO WELCOME THE CLASS OF '83 BACK TO WALDEN...
AS YOU RENEW OLD ACQUAINTANCES HERE TONIGHT, I ONLY HAVE ONE PIECE OF ADVICE FOR YOU — BE KIND!
ALTHOUGH SOME OF YOU HAVE SIGNIFICANT ACCOMPLISHMENTS TO YOUR CREDITS, TRY TO REMEMBER YOU HAVE CLASSMATES WHO STILL HAVEN'T MADE ANY KIND OF MEANINGFUL MARK IN LIFE!
IN OUR CLASS? IS THIS TRUE?
NO WAY!
MUST BE A BOILER-PLATE SPEECH.

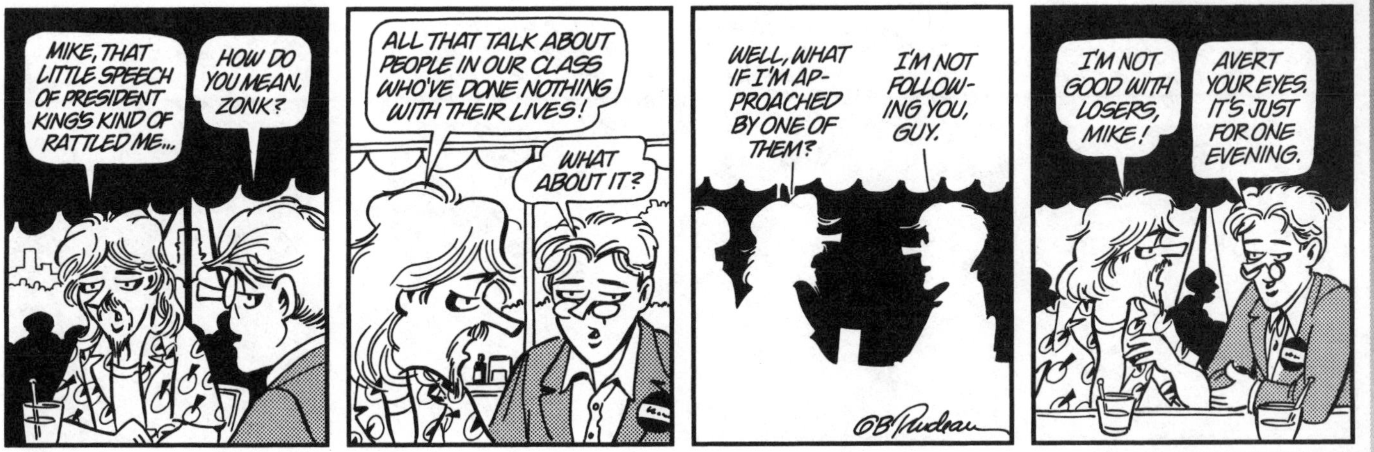
MIKE, THAT LITTLE SPEECH OF PRESIDENT KING'S KIND OF RATTLED ME...
HOW DO YOU MEAN, ZONK?
ALL THAT TALK ABOUT PEOPLE IN OUR CLASS WHO'VE DONE NOTHING WITH THEIR LIVES!
WHAT ABOUT IT?
WELL, WHAT IF I'M APPROACHED BY ONE OF THEM?
I'M NOT FOLLOWING YOU, GUY.
I'M NOT GOOD WITH LOSERS, MIKE!
AVERT YOUR EYES. IT'S JUST FOR ONE EVENING.

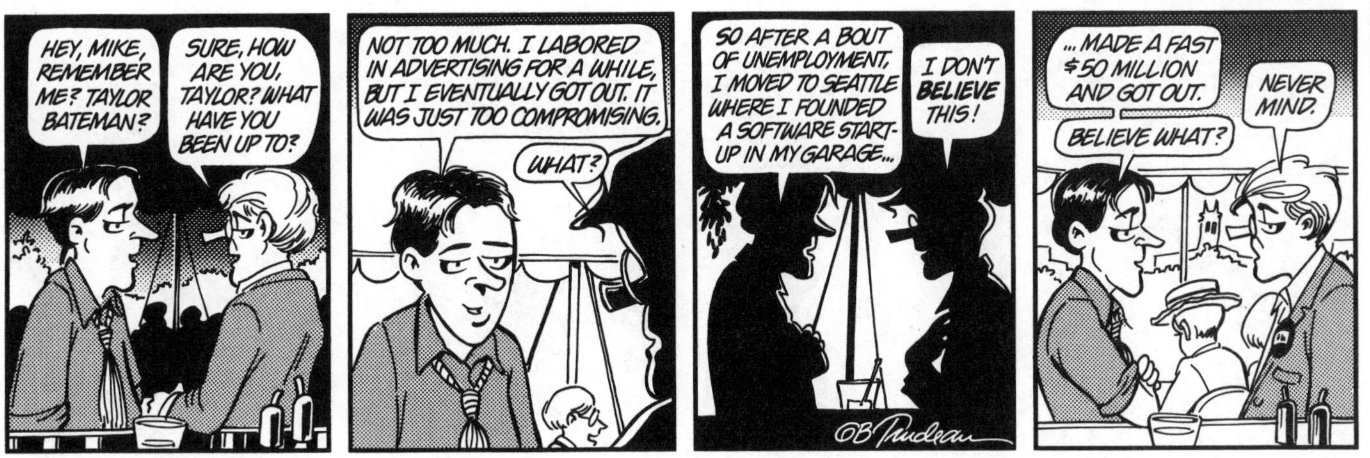
HEY, MIKE, REMEMBER ME? TAYLOR BATEMAN?
SURE, HOW ARE YOU, TAYLOR? WHAT HAVE YOU BEEN UP TO?
NOT TOO MUCH. I LABORED IN ADVERTISING FOR A WHILE, BUT I EVENTUALLY GOT OUT. IT WAS JUST TOO COMPROMISING.
WHAT?
SO AFTER A BOUT OF UNEMPLOYMENT, I MOVED TO SEATTLE WHERE I FOUNDED A SOFTWARE START-UP IN MY GARAGE...
I DON'T BELIEVE THIS!
...MADE A FAST $50 MILLION AND GOT OUT.
BELIEVE WHAT?
NEVER MIND.

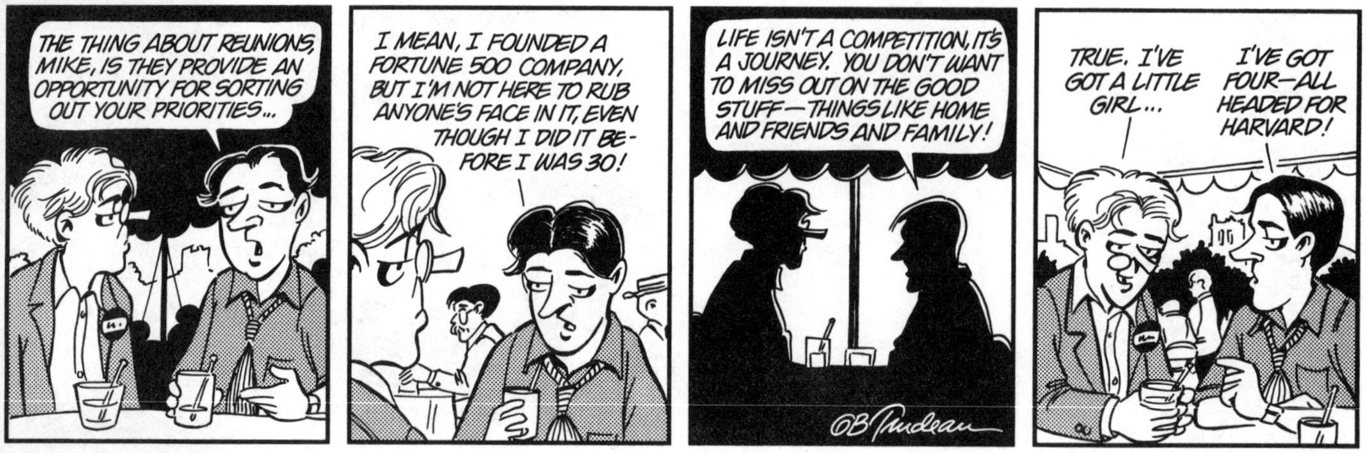
THE THING ABOUT REUNIONS, MIKE, IS THEY PROVIDE AN OPPORTUNITY FOR SORTING OUT YOUR PRIORITIES...
I MEAN, I FOUNDED A FORTUNE 500 COMPANY, BUT I'M NOT HERE TO RUB ANYONE'S FACE IN IT, EVEN THOUGH I DID IT BEFORE I WAS 30!
LIFE ISN'T A COMPETITION, IT'S A JOURNEY. YOU DON'T WANT TO MISS OUT ON THE GOOD STUFF—THINGS LIKE HOME AND FRIENDS AND FAMILY!
TRUE. I'VE GOT A LITTLE GIRL...
I'VE GOT FOUR—ALL HEADED FOR HARVARD!

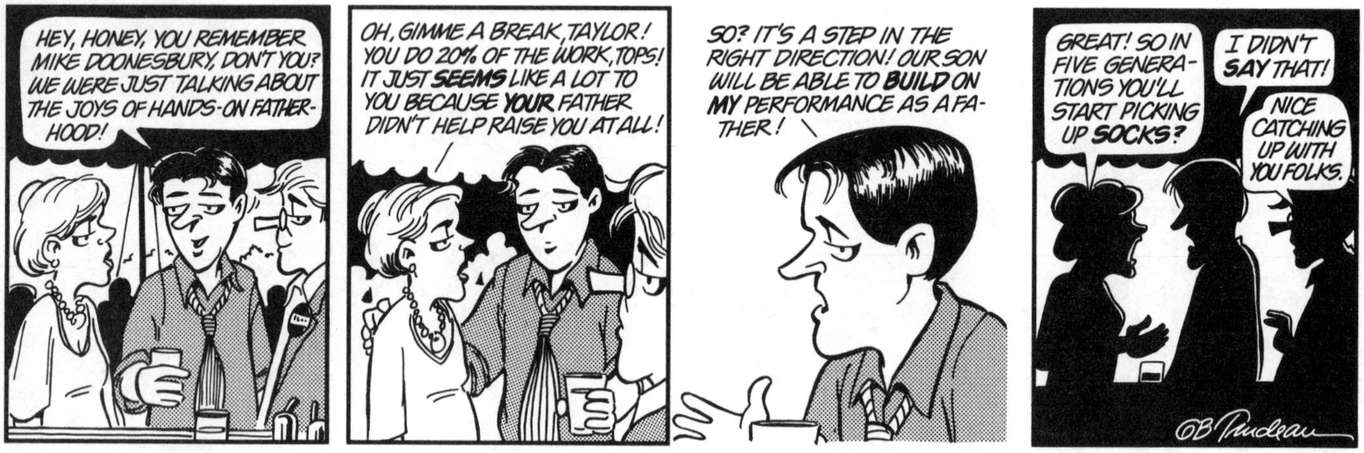
HEY, HONEY, YOU REMEMBER MIKE DOONESBURY, DON'T YOU? WE WERE JUST TALKING ABOUT THE JOYS OF HANDS-ON FATHERHOOD!
OH, GIMME A BREAK, TAYLOR! YOU DO 20% OF THE WORK, TOPS! IT JUST SEEMS LIKE A LOT TO YOU BECAUSE YOUR FATHER DIDN'T HELP RAISE YOU AT ALL!
SO? IT'S A STEP IN THE RIGHT DIRECTION! OUR SON WILL BE ABLE TO BUILD ON MY PERFORMANCE AS A FATHER!
GREAT! SO IN FIVE GENERATIONS YOU'LL START PICKING UP SOCKS?
I DIDN'T SAY THAT!
NICE CATCHING UP WITH YOU FOLKS.

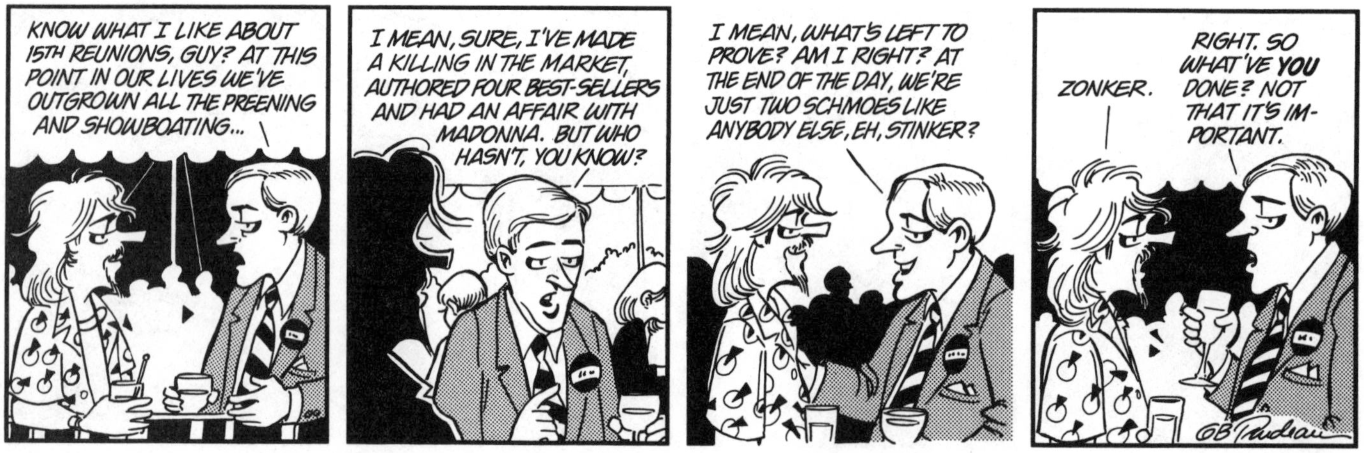
KNOW WHAT I LIKE ABOUT 15TH REUNIONS, GUY? AT THIS POINT IN OUR LIVES WE'VE OUTGROWN ALL THE PREENING AND SHOWBOATING...
I MEAN, SURE, I'VE MADE A KILLING IN THE MARKET, AUTHORED FOUR BEST-SELLERS AND HAD AN AFFAIR WITH MADONNA. BUT WHO HASN'T, YOU KNOW?
I MEAN, WHAT'S LEFT TO PROVE? AM I RIGHT? AT THE END OF THE DAY, WE'RE JUST TWO SCHMOES LIKE ANYBODY ELSE, EH, STINKER?
ZONKER.
RIGHT. SO WHAT'VE YOU DONE? NOT THAT IT'S IMPORTANT.

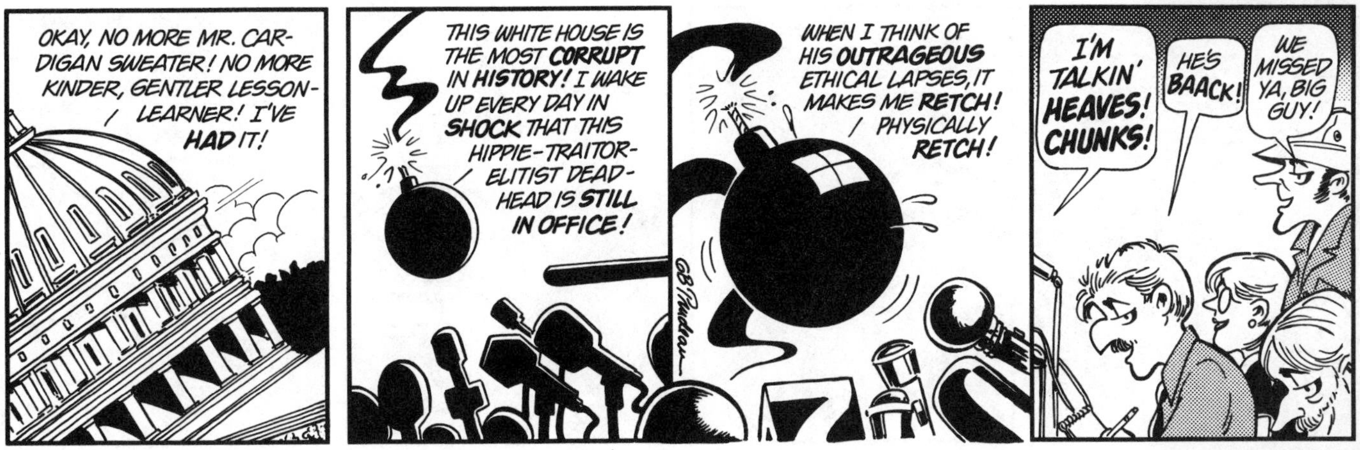
OKAY, NO MORE MR. CARDIGAN SWEATER! NO MORE KINDER, GENTLER LESSON-LEARNER! I'VE HAD IT!
THIS WHITE HOUSE IS THE MOST CORRUPT IN HISTORY! I WAKE UP EVERY DAY IN SHOCK THAT THIS HIPPIE-TRAITOR-ELITIST DEAD-HEAD IS STILL IN OFFICE!
WHEN I THINK OF HIS OUTRAGEOUS ETHICAL LAPSES, IT MAKES ME RETCH! PHYSICALLY RETCH!
I'M TALKIN' HEAVES! CHUNKS!
HE'S BAACK!
WE MISSED YA, BIG GUY!

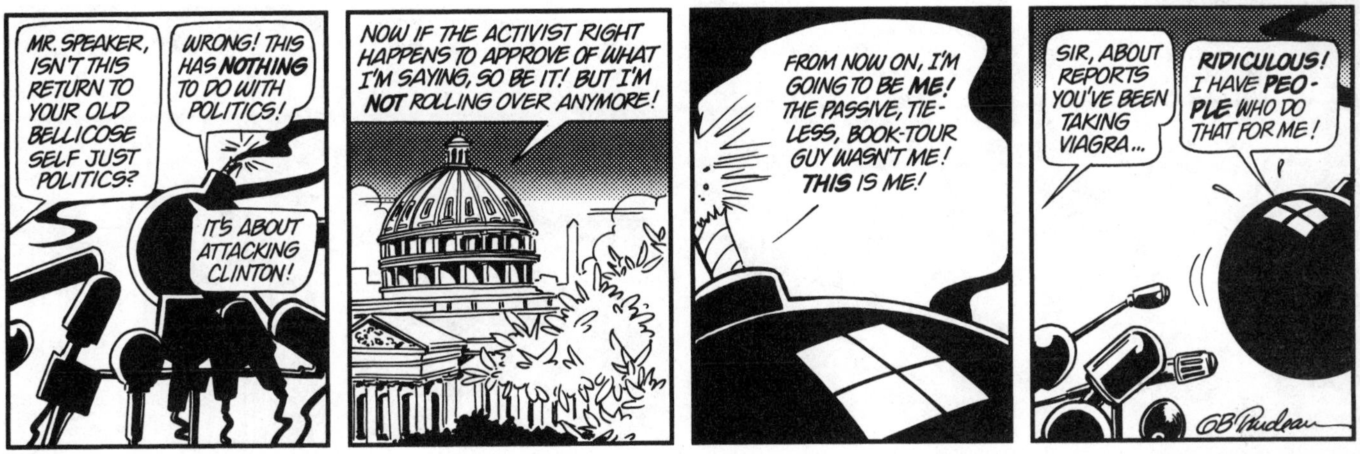
MR. SPEAKER, ISN'T THIS RETURN TO YOUR OLD BELLICOSE SELF JUST POLITICS?
WRONG! THIS HAS NOTHING TO DO WITH POLITICS!
IT'S ABOUT ATTACKING CLINTON!
NOW IF THE ACTIVIST RIGHT HAPPENS TO APPROVE OF WHAT I'M SAYING, SO BE IT! BUT I'M NOT ROLLING OVER ANYMORE!
FROM NOW ON, I'M GOING TO BE ME! THE PASSIVE, TIE-LESS, BOOK-TOUR GUY WASN'T ME! THIS IS ME!
SIR, ABOUT REPORTS YOU'VE BEEN TAKING VIAGRA...
RIDICULOUS! I HAVE PEOPLE WHO DO THAT FOR ME!

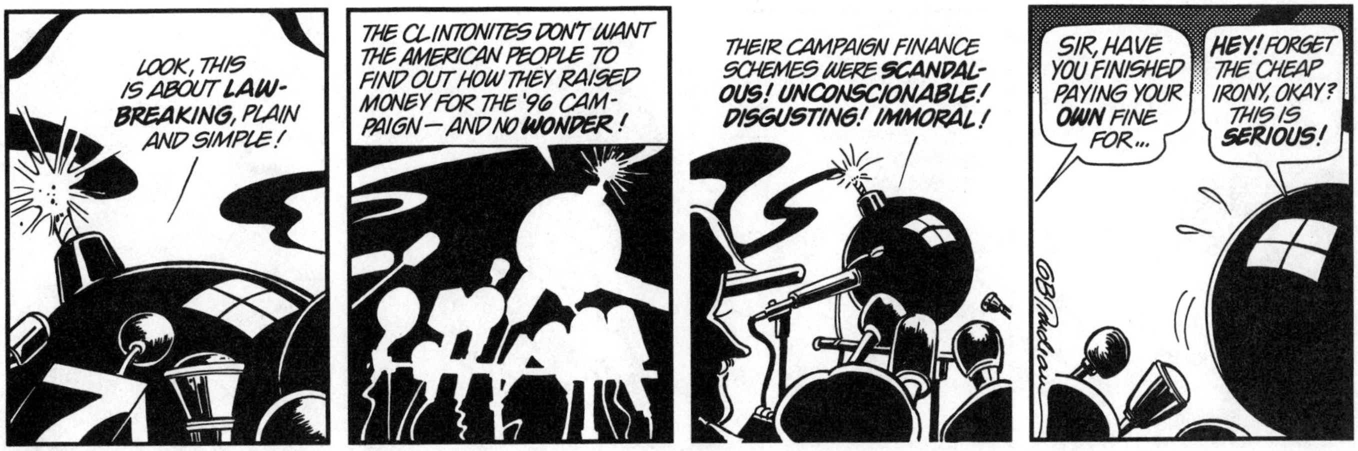
LOOK, THIS IS ABOUT LAW-BREAKING, PLAIN AND SIMPLE!
THE CLINTONITES DON'T WANT THE AMERICAN PEOPLE TO FIND OUT HOW THEY RAISED MONEY FOR THE '96 CAMPAIGN—AND NO WONDER!
THEIR CAMPAIGN FINANCE SCHEMES WERE SCANDALOUS! UNCONSCIONABLE! DISGUSTING! IMMORAL!
SIR, HAVE YOU FINISHED PAYING YOUR OWN FINE FOR...
HEY! FORGET THE CHEAP IRONY, OKAY? THIS IS SERIOUS!

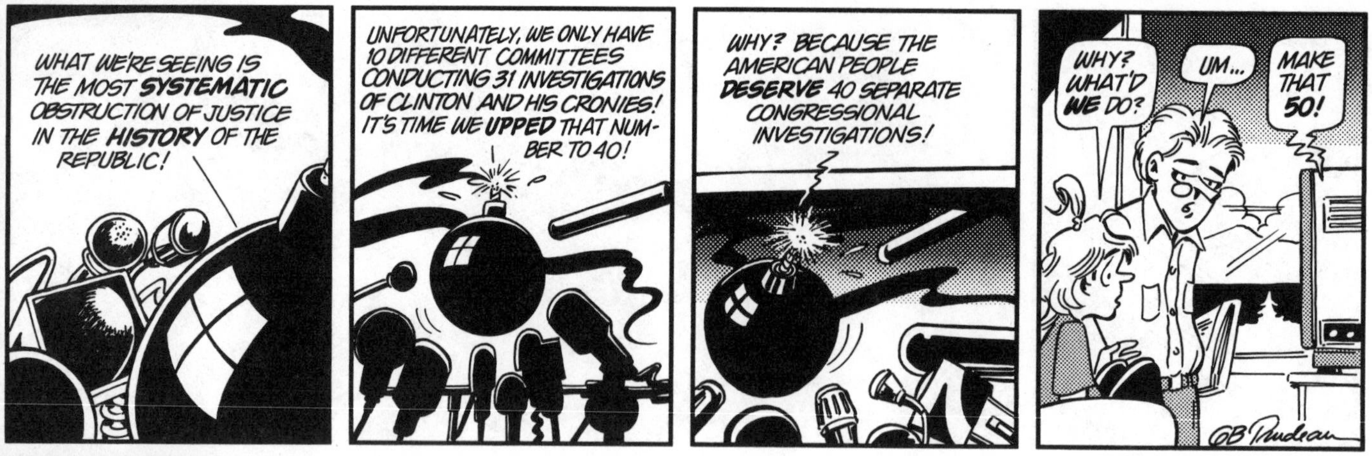
WHAT WE'RE SEEING IS THE MOST **SYSTEMATIC** OBSTRUCTION OF JUSTICE IN THE **HISTORY** OF THE REPUBLIC!
UNFORTUNATELY, WE ONLY HAVE 10 DIFFERENT COMMITTEES CONDUCTING 31 INVESTIGATIONS OF CLINTON AND HIS CRONIES! IT'S TIME WE **UPPED** THAT NUMBER TO 40!
WHY? BECAUSE THE AMERICAN PEOPLE **DESERVE** 40 SEPARATE CONGRESSIONAL INVESTIGATIONS!
WHY? WHAT'D **WE** DO?
UM...
MAKE THAT **50!**

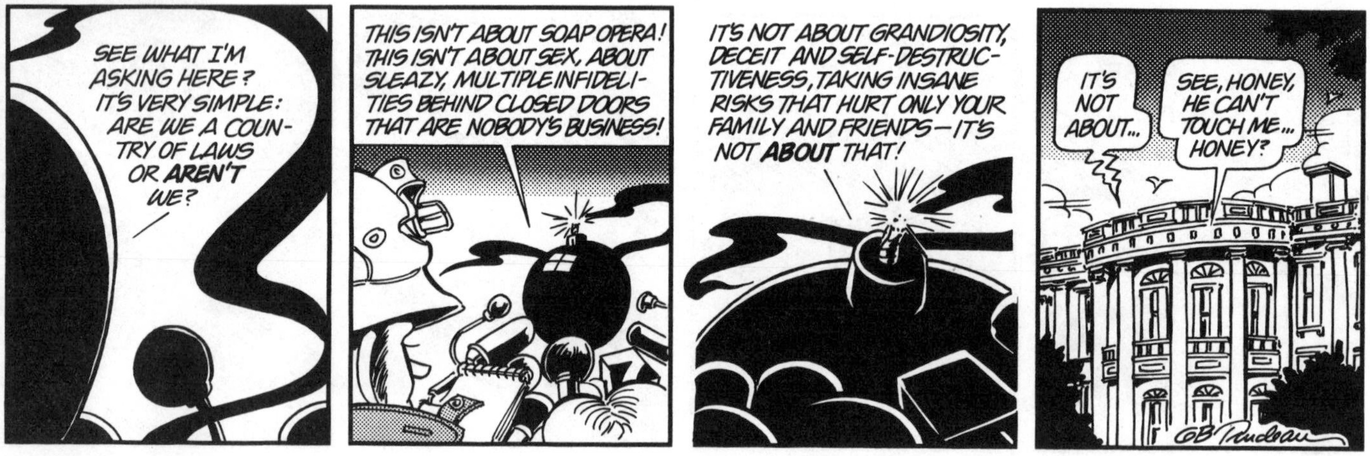
SEE WHAT I'M ASKING HERE? IT'S VERY SIMPLE: ARE WE A COUNTRY OF LAWS OR **AREN'T** WE?
THIS ISN'T ABOUT SOAP OPERA! THIS ISN'T ABOUT SEX, ABOUT SLEAZY, MULTIPLE INFIDELITIES BEHIND CLOSED DOORS THAT ARE NOBODY'S BUSINESS!
IT'S NOT ABOUT GRANDIOSITY, DECEIT AND SELF-DESTRUCTIVENESS, TAKING INSANE RISKS THAT HURT ONLY YOUR FAMILY AND FRIENDS—IT'S NOT **ABOUT** THAT!
IT'S NOT ABOUT...
SEE, HONEY, HE CAN'T TOUCH ME... HONEY?

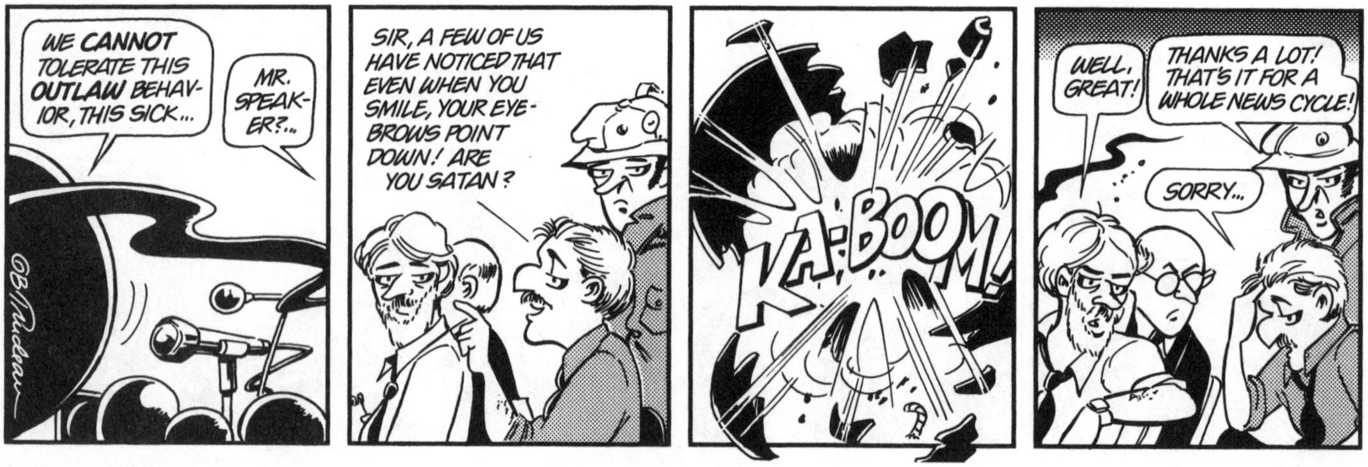
WE **CANNOT** TOLERATE THIS **OUTLAW** BEHAVIOR, THIS SICK...
MR. SPEAKER?..
SIR, A FEW OF US HAVE NOTICED THAT EVEN WHEN YOU SMILE, YOUR EYEBROWS POINT DOWN! ARE YOU SATAN?
KA-BOOM!
WELL, GREAT!
THANKS A LOT! THAT'S IT FOR A WHOLE NEWS CYCLE!
SORRY...

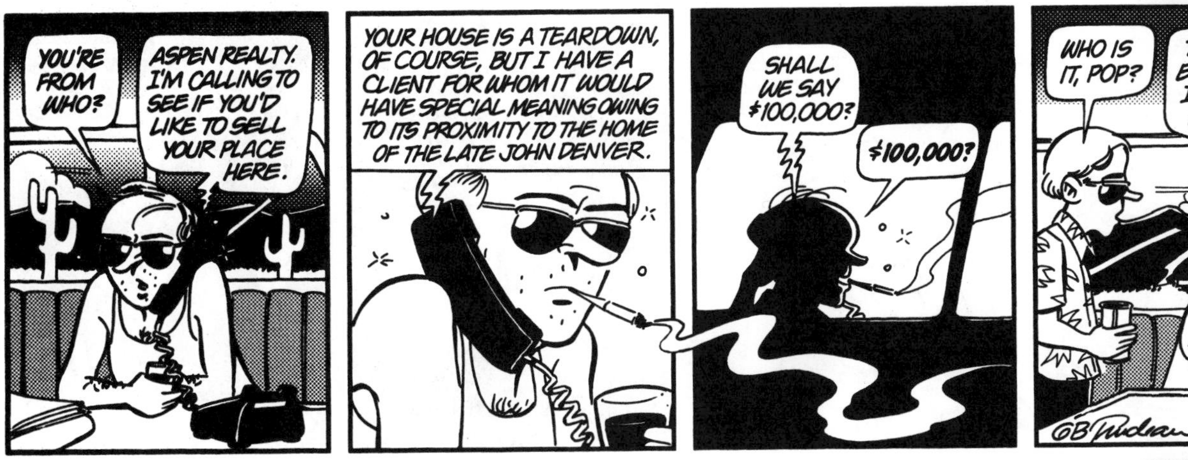
YOU'RE FROM WHO?
ASPEN REALTY. I'M CALLING TO SEE IF YOU'D LIKE TO SELL YOUR PLACE HERE.
YOUR HOUSE IS A TEARDOWN, OF COURSE, BUT I HAVE A CLIENT FOR WHOM IT WOULD HAVE SPECIAL MEANING OWING TO ITS PROXIMITY TO THE HOME OF THE LATE JOHN DENVER.
SHALL WE SAY $100,000?
$100,000?
WHO IS IT, POP?
THE REAL ESTATE FAIRY! I'VE GOT A LIVE ONE!

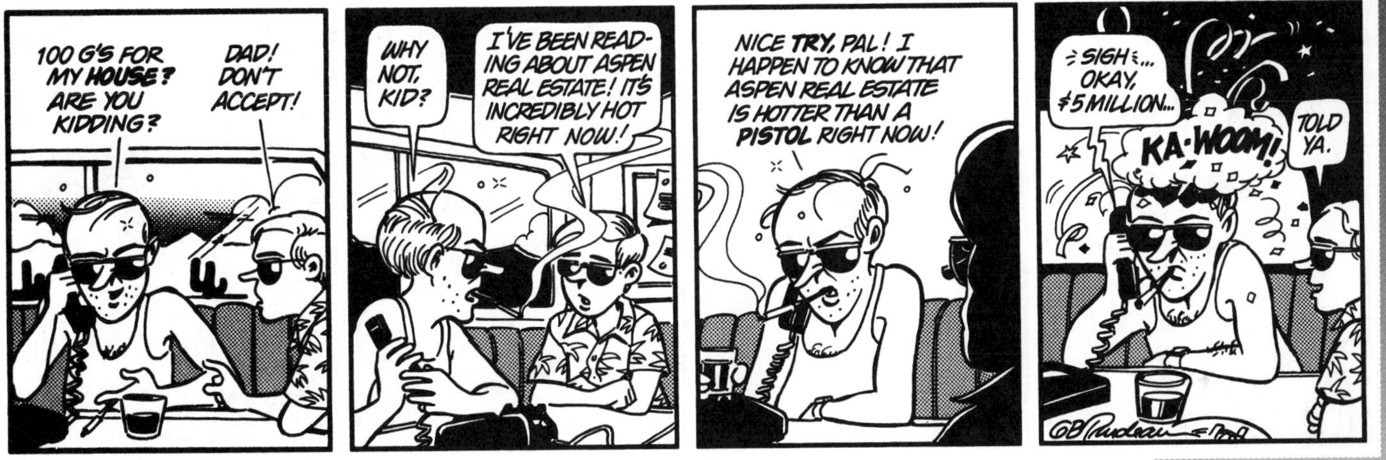
100 G'S FOR MY **HOUSE**? ARE YOU KIDDING?
DAD! DON'T ACCEPT!
WHY NOT, KID?
I'VE BEEN READING ABOUT ASPEN REAL ESTATE! IT'S INCREDIBLY HOT RIGHT NOW!
NICE **TRY**, PAL! I HAPPEN TO KNOW THAT ASPEN REAL ESTATE IS HOTTER THAN A **PISTOL** RIGHT NOW!
SIGH... OKAY, $5 MILLION...
KA-WOOM!
TOLD YA.

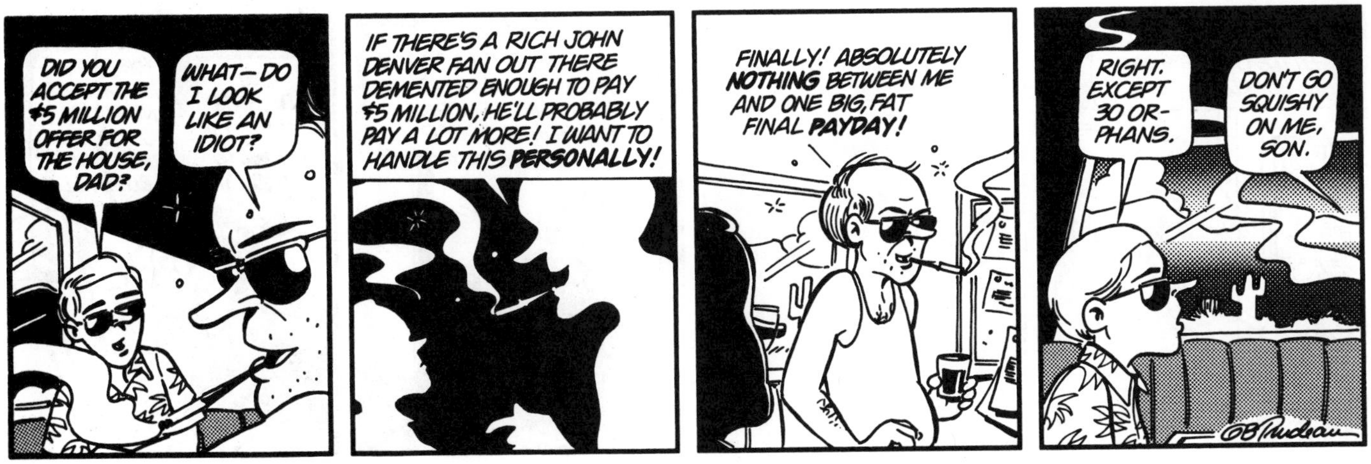
DID YOU ACCEPT THE $5 MILLION OFFER FOR THE HOUSE, DAD?
WHAT—DO I LOOK LIKE AN IDIOT?
IF THERE'S A RICH JOHN DENVER FAN OUT THERE DEMENTED ENOUGH TO PAY $5 MILLION, HE'LL PROBABLY PAY A LOT MORE! I WANT TO HANDLE THIS **PERSONALLY**!
FINALLY! ABSOLUTELY **NOTHING** BETWEEN ME AND ONE BIG, FAT FINAL **PAYDAY**!
RIGHT. EXCEPT 30 ORPHANS.
DON'T GO SQUISHY ON ME, SON.

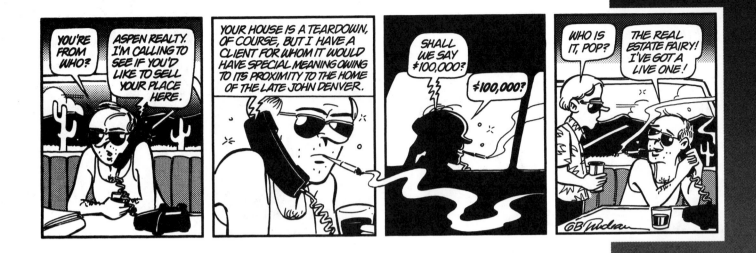

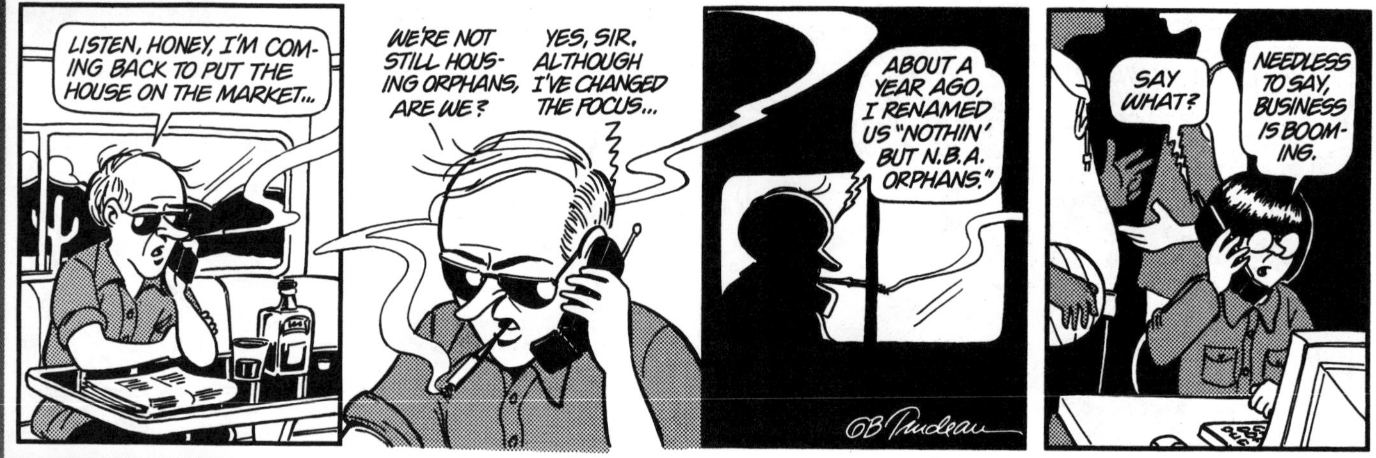
LISTEN, HONEY, I'M COMING BACK TO PUT THE HOUSE ON THE MARKET...
WE'RE NOT STILL HOUSING ORPHANS, ARE WE?
YES, SIR. ALTHOUGH I'VE CHANGED THE FOCUS...
ABOUT A YEAR AGO, I RENAMED US "NOTHIN' BUT N.B.A. ORPHANS."
SAY WHAT?
NEEDLESS TO SAY, BUSINESS IS BOOMING.

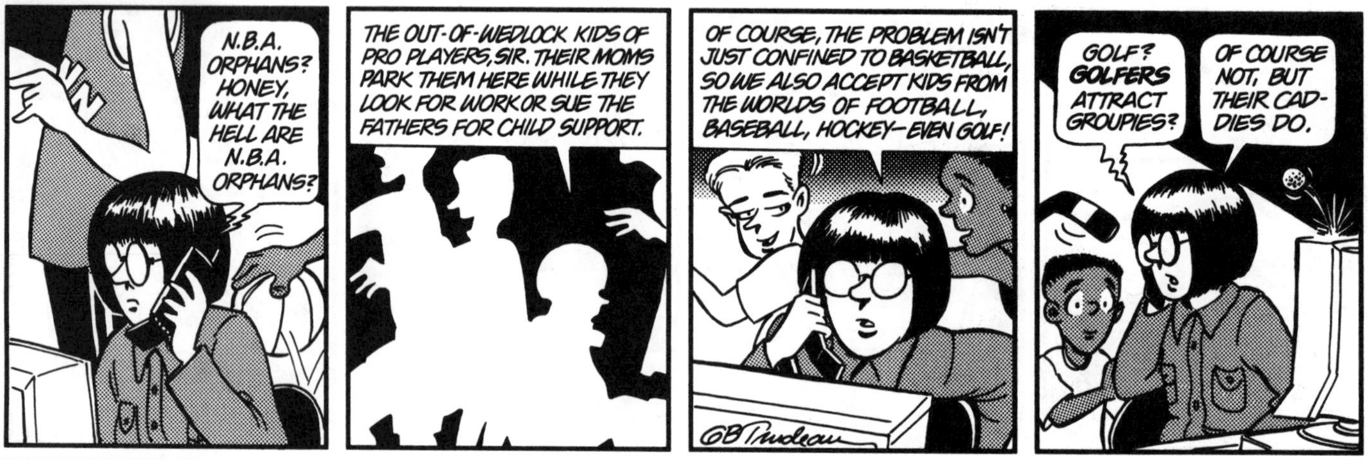
N.B.A. ORPHANS? HONEY, WHAT THE HELL ARE N.B.A. ORPHANS?
THE OUT-OF-WEDLOCK KIDS OF PRO PLAYERS, SIR. THEIR MOMS PARK THEM HERE WHILE THEY LOOK FOR WORK OR SUE THE FATHERS FOR CHILD SUPPORT.
OF COURSE, THE PROBLEM ISN'T JUST CONFINED TO BASKETBALL, SO WE ALSO ACCEPT KIDS FROM THE WORLDS OF FOOTBALL, BASEBALL, HOCKEY—EVEN GOLF!
GOLF? **GOLFERS** ATTRACT GROUPIES?
OF COURSE NOT, BUT THEIR CADDIES DO.

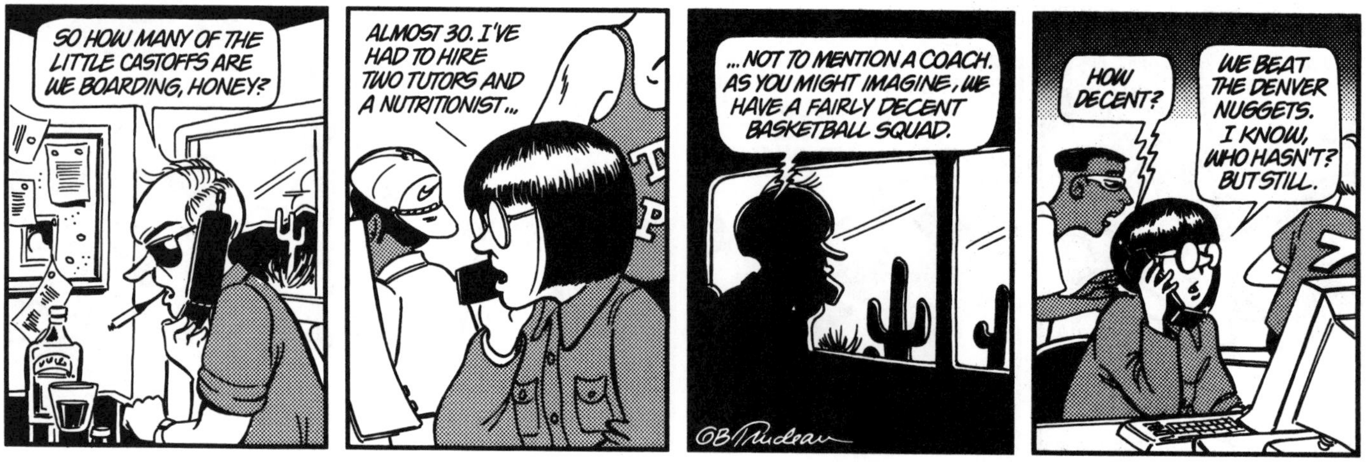
SO HOW MANY OF THE LITTLE CASTOFFS ARE WE BOARDING, HONEY?
ALMOST 30. I'VE HAD TO HIRE TWO TUTORS AND A NUTRITIONIST...
...NOT TO MENTION A COACH. AS YOU MIGHT IMAGINE, WE HAVE A FAIRLY DECENT BASKETBALL SQUAD.
HOW DECENT?
WE BEAT THE DENVER NUGGETS. I KNOW, WHO HASN'T? BUT STILL.

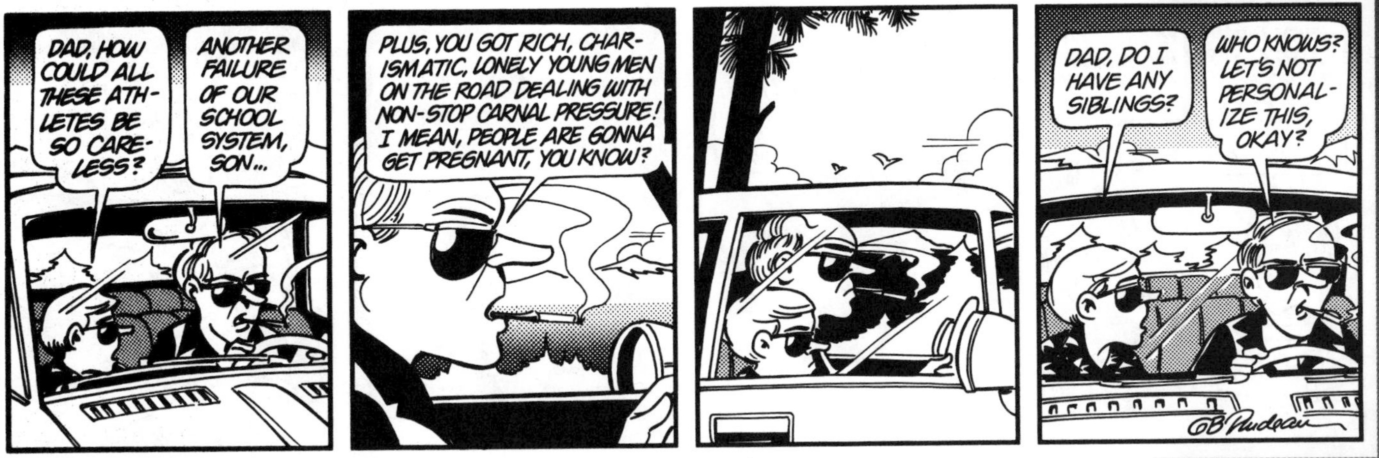
DAD, HOW COULD ALL THESE ATHLETES BE SO CARELESS?
ANOTHER FAILURE OF OUR SCHOOL SYSTEM, SON...
PLUS, YOU GOT RICH, CHARISMATIC, LONELY YOUNG MEN ON THE ROAD DEALING WITH NON-STOP CARNAL PRESSURE! I MEAN, PEOPLE ARE GONNA GET PREGNANT, YOU KNOW?
DAD, DO I HAVE ANY SIBLINGS?
WHO KNOWS? LET'S NOT PERSONALIZE THIS, OKAY?

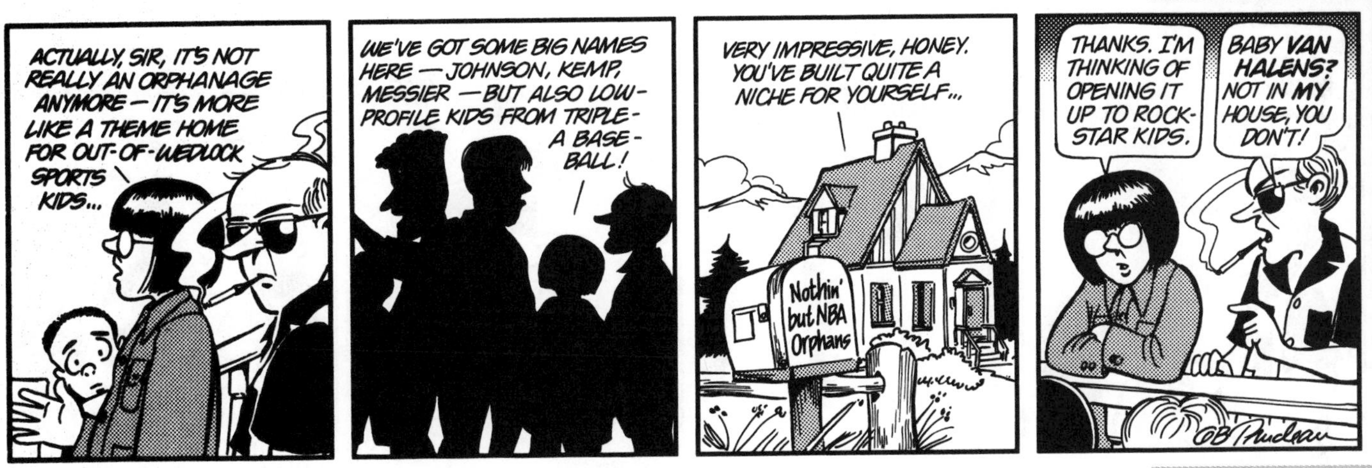
ACTUALLY, SIR, IT'S NOT REALLY AN ORPHANAGE ANYMORE — IT'S MORE LIKE A THEME HOME FOR OUT-OF-WEDLOCK SPORTS KIDS...
WE'VE GOT SOME BIG NAMES HERE — JOHNSON, KEMP, MESSIER — BUT ALSO LOW-PROFILE KIDS FROM TRIPLE-A BASEBALL!
VERY IMPRESSIVE, HONEY. YOU'VE BUILT QUITE A NICHE FOR YOURSELF...
Nothin' but NBA Orphans
THANKS. I'M THINKING OF OPENING IT UP TO ROCK-STAR KIDS.
BABY VAN HALENS? NOT IN MY HOUSE, YOU DON'T!

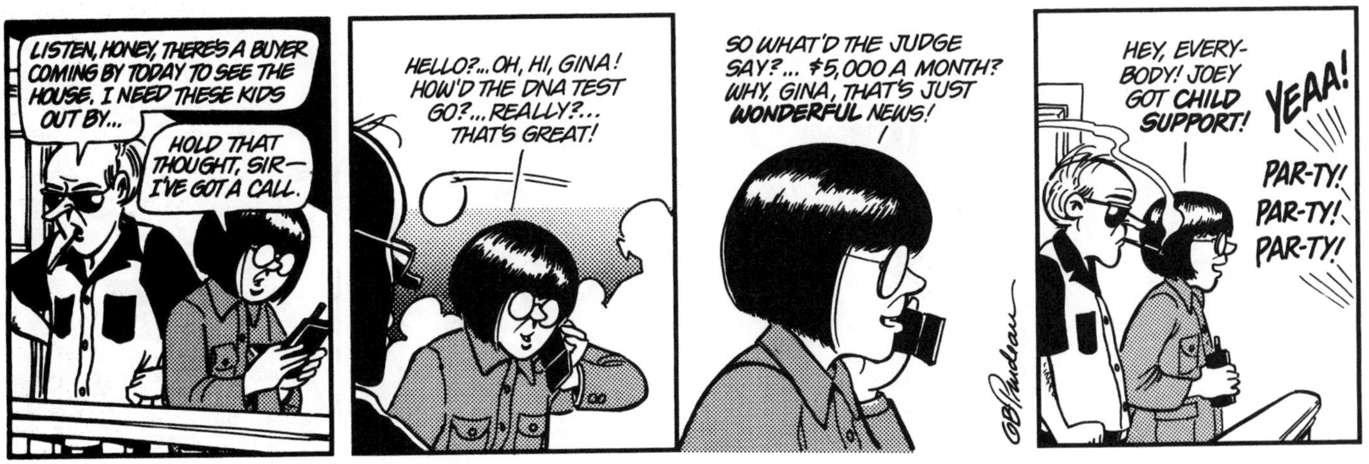
LISTEN, HONEY, THERE'S A BUYER COMING BY TODAY TO SEE THE HOUSE. I NEED THESE KIDS OUT BY...
HOLD THAT THOUGHT, SIR — I'VE GOT A CALL.
HELLO?... OH, HI, GINA! HOW'D THE DNA TEST GO?... REALLY?... THAT'S GREAT!
SO WHAT'D THE JUDGE SAY?... $5,000 A MONTH? WHY, GINA, THAT'S JUST WONDERFUL NEWS!
HEY, EVERYBODY! JOEY GOT CHILD SUPPORT!
YEAA!
PAR-TY! PAR-TY! PAR-TY!

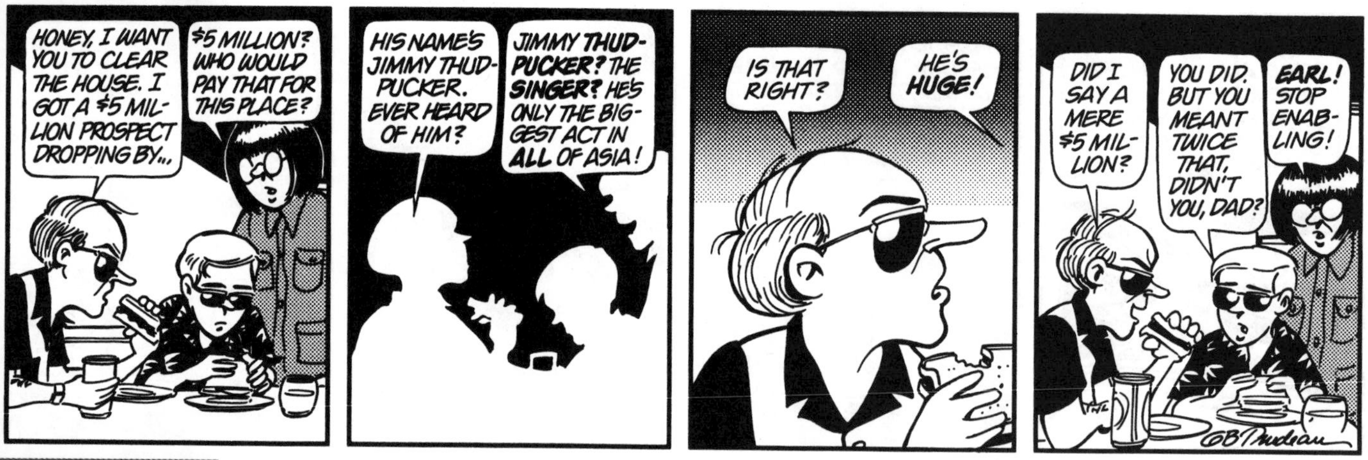
HONEY, I WANT YOU TO CLEAR THE HOUSE. I GOT A $5 MILLION PROSPECT DROPPING BY...
$5 MILLION? WHO WOULD PAY THAT FOR THIS PLACE?
HIS NAME'S JIMMY THUDPUCKER. EVER HEARD OF HIM?
JIMMY **THUDPUCKER?** THE **SINGER?** HE'S ONLY THE BIGGEST ACT IN **ALL** OF ASIA!
IS THAT RIGHT?
HE'S **HUGE!**
DID I SAY A MERE $5 MILLION?
YOU DID. BUT YOU MEANT TWICE THAT, DIDN'T YOU, DAD?
EARL! STOP ENABLING!

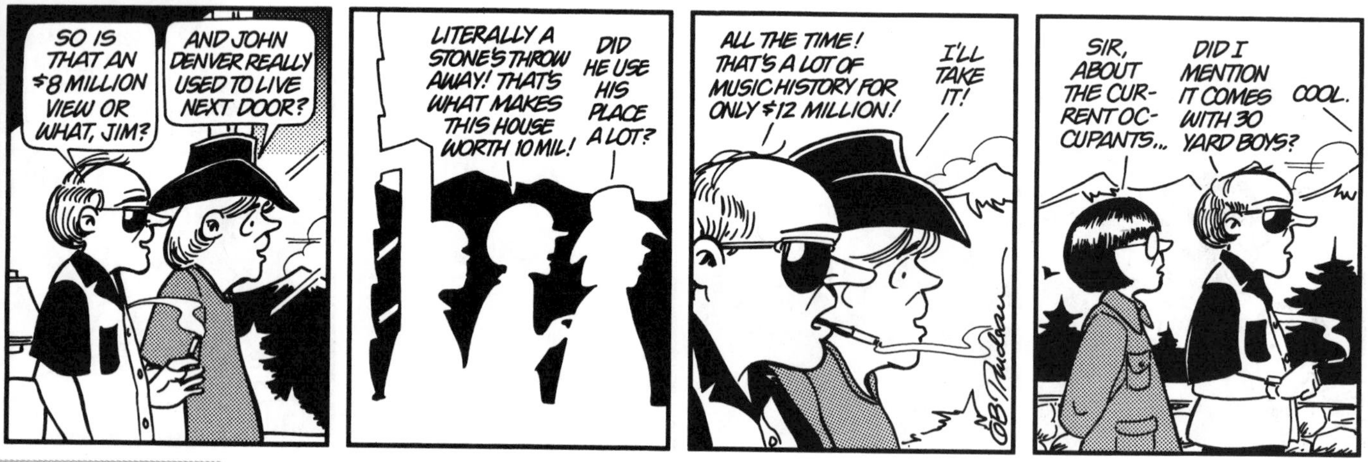
SO IS THAT AN $8 MILLION VIEW OR WHAT, JIM?
AND JOHN DENVER REALLY USED TO LIVE NEXT DOOR?
LITERALLY A STONE'S THROW AWAY! THAT'S WHAT MAKES THIS HOUSE WORTH 10 MIL!
DID HE USE HIS PLACE A LOT?
ALL THE TIME! THAT'S A LOT OF MUSIC HISTORY FOR ONLY $12 MILLION!
I'LL TAKE IT!
SIR, ABOUT THE CURRENT OCCUPANTS...
DID I MENTION IT COMES WITH 30 YARD BOYS?
COOL.

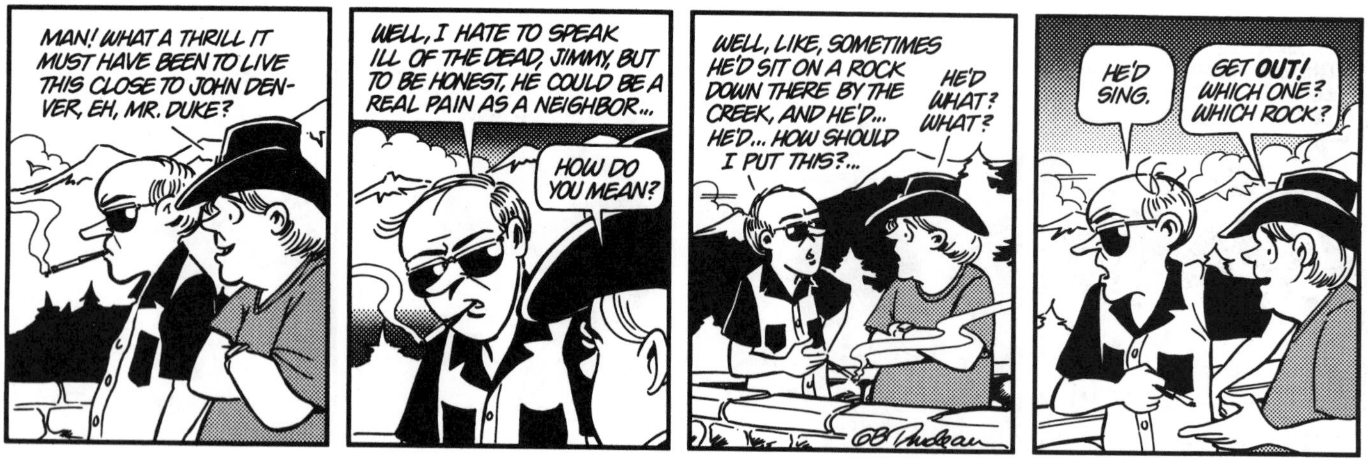
MAN! WHAT A THRILL IT MUST HAVE BEEN TO LIVE THIS CLOSE TO JOHN DENVER, EH, MR. DUKE?
WELL, I HATE TO SPEAK ILL OF THE DEAD, JIMMY, BUT TO BE HONEST, HE COULD BE A REAL PAIN AS A NEIGHBOR...
HOW DO YOU MEAN?
WELL, LIKE, SOMETIMES HE'D SIT ON A ROCK DOWN THERE BY THE CREEK, AND HE'D... HE'D... HOW SHOULD I PUT THIS?...
HE'D WHAT? WHAT?
HE'D SING.
GET **OUT!** WHICH ONE? WHICH ROCK?

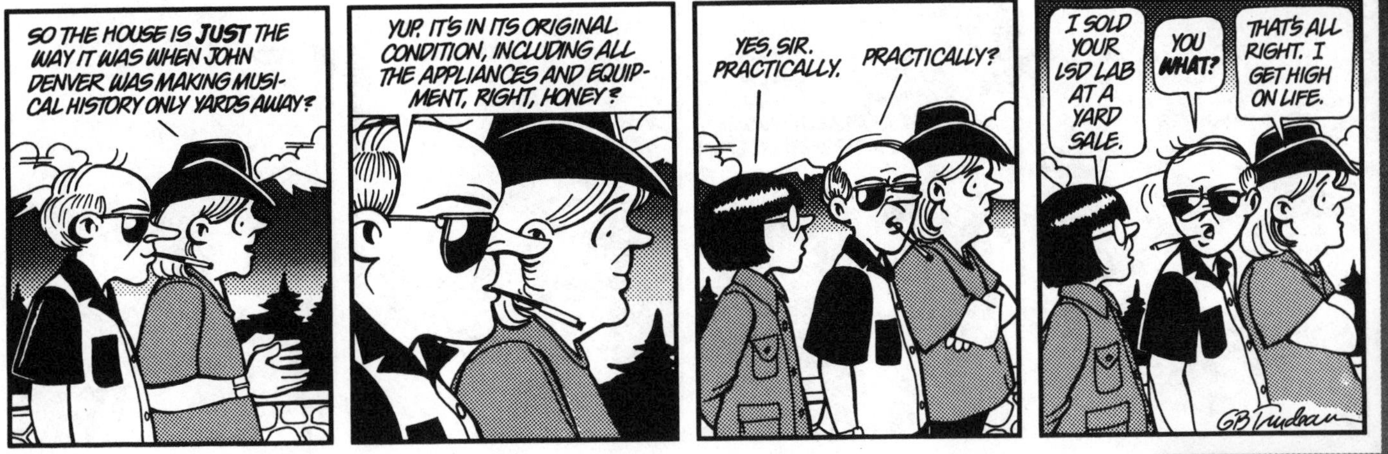
SO THE HOUSE IS **JUST** THE WAY IT WAS WHEN JOHN DENVER WAS MAKING MUSICAL HISTORY ONLY YARDS AWAY?
YUP. IT'S IN ITS ORIGINAL CONDITION, INCLUDING ALL THE APPLIANCES AND EQUIPMENT, RIGHT, HONEY?
YES, SIR. PRACTICALLY.
PRACTICALLY?
I SOLD YOUR LSD LAB AT A YARD SALE.
YOU **WHAT?**
THAT'S ALL RIGHT. I GET HIGH ON LIFE.
GBTrudeau

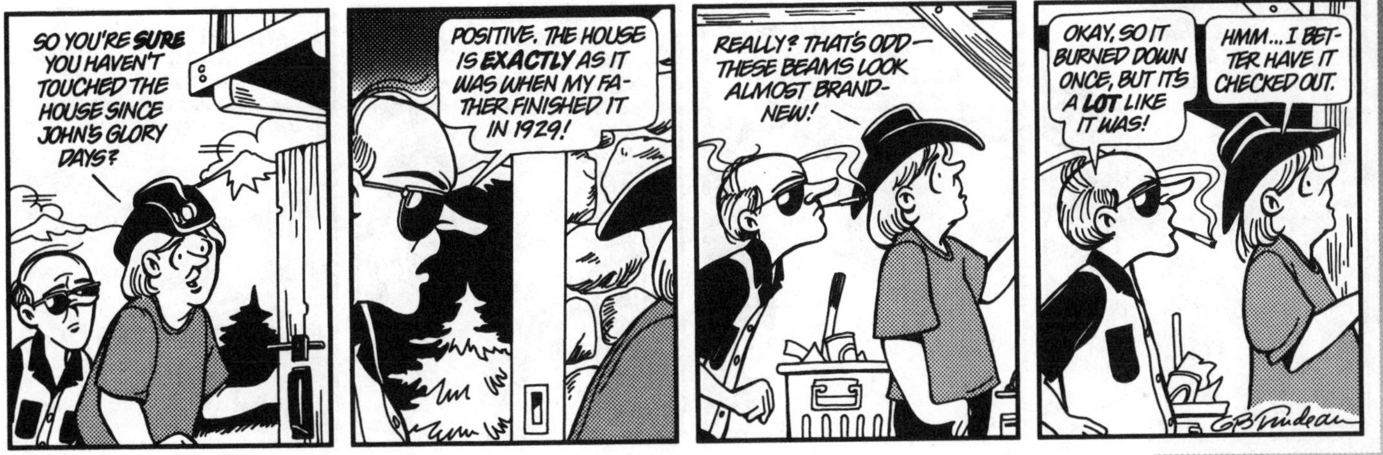
SO YOU'RE **SURE** YOU HAVEN'T TOUCHED THE HOUSE SINCE JOHN'S GLORY DAYS?
POSITIVE. THE HOUSE IS **EXACTLY** AS IT WAS WHEN MY FATHER FINISHED IT IN 1929!
REALLY? THAT'S ODD— THESE BEAMS LOOK ALMOST BRAND-NEW!
OKAY, SO IT BURNED DOWN ONCE, BUT IT'S A **LOT** LIKE IT WAS!
HMM... I BETTER HAVE IT CHECKED OUT.
GBTrudeau

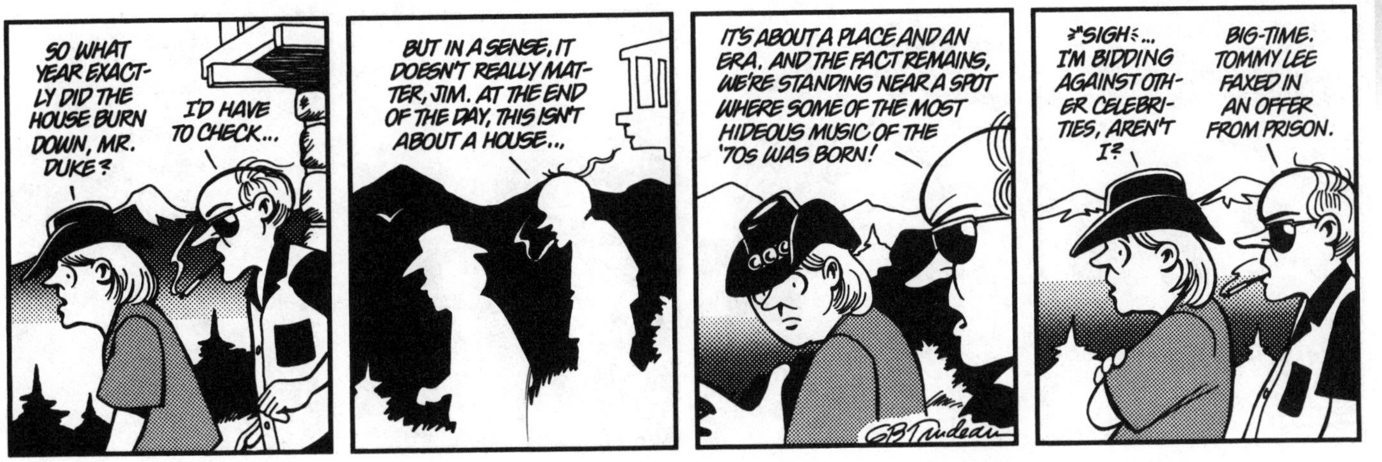
SO WHAT YEAR EXACTLY DID THE HOUSE BURN DOWN, MR. DUKE?
I'D HAVE TO CHECK...
BUT IN A SENSE, IT DOESN'T REALLY MATTER, JIM. AT THE END OF THE DAY, THIS ISN'T ABOUT A HOUSE...
IT'S ABOUT A PLACE AND AN ERA. AND THE FACT REMAINS, WE'RE STANDING NEAR A SPOT WHERE SOME OF THE MOST HIDEOUS MUSIC OF THE '70S WAS BORN!
GBTrudeau
SIGH... I'M BIDDING AGAINST OTHER CELEBRITIES, AREN'T I?
BIG-TIME. TOMMY LEE FAXED IN AN OFFER FROM PRISON.

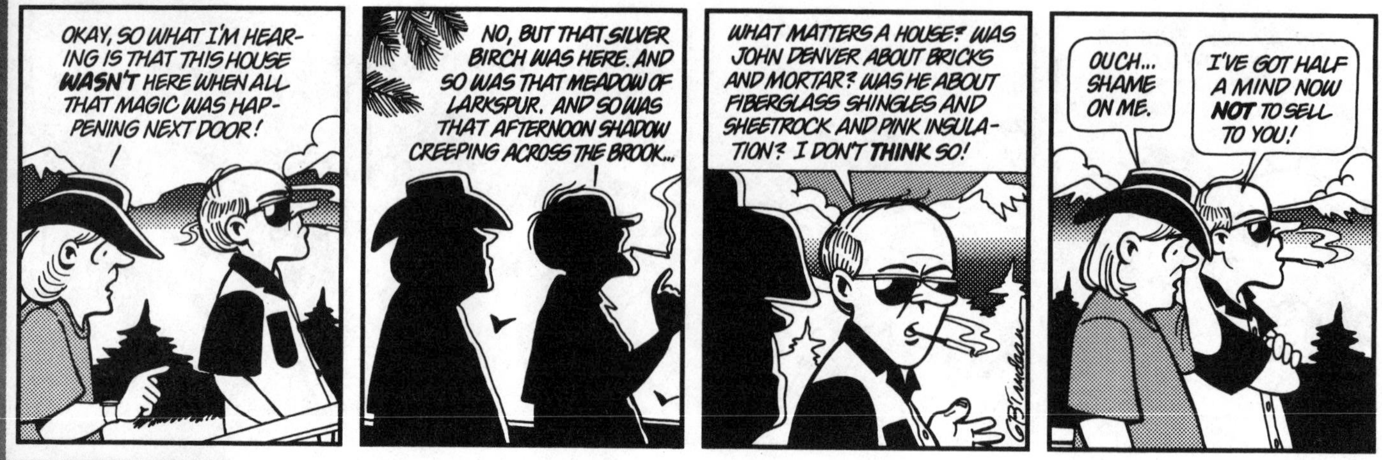
OKAY, SO WHAT I'M HEARING IS THAT THIS HOUSE **WASN'T** HERE WHEN ALL THAT MAGIC WAS HAPPENING NEXT DOOR!
NO, BUT THAT **SILVER BIRCH** WAS HERE. AND SO WAS THAT MEADOW OF LARKSPUR. AND SO WAS THAT AFTERNOON SHADOW CREEPING ACROSS THE BROOK...
WHAT MATTERS A HOUSE? WAS JOHN DENVER ABOUT BRICKS AND MORTAR? WAS HE ABOUT FIBERGLASS SHINGLES AND SHEETROCK AND PINK INSULATION? I DON'T **THINK** SO!
OUCH... SHAME ON ME.
I'VE GOT HALF A MIND NOW **NOT** TO SELL TO YOU!
GBTrudeau

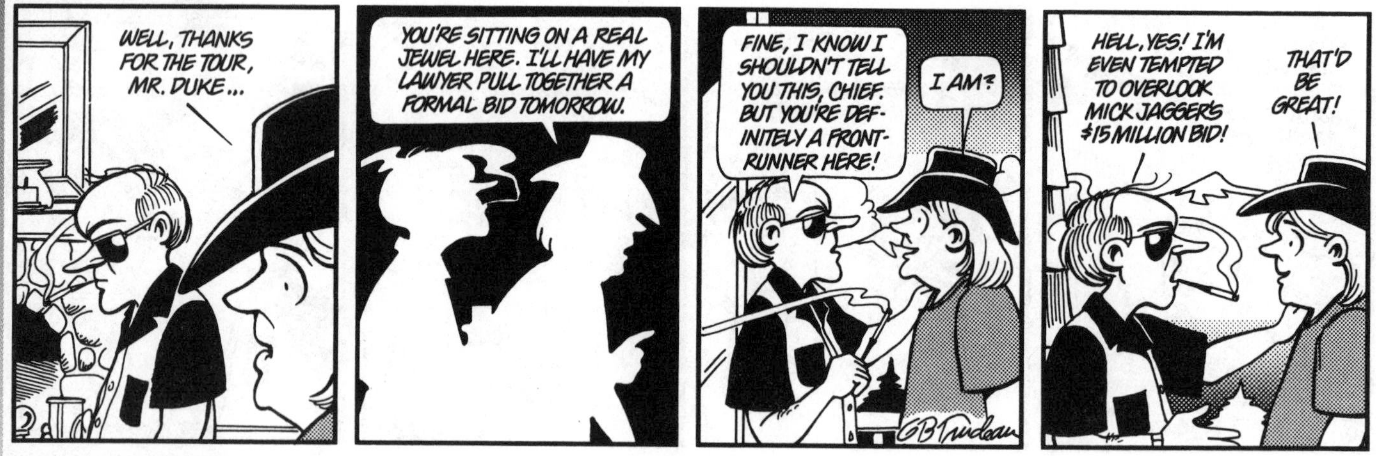
WELL, THANKS FOR THE TOUR, MR. DUKE...
YOU'RE SITTING ON A REAL JEWEL HERE. I'LL HAVE MY LAWYER PULL TOGETHER A FORMAL BID TOMORROW.
FINE, I KNOW I SHOULDN'T TELL YOU THIS, CHIEF. BUT YOU'RE DEFINITELY A FRONT-RUNNER HERE!
I AM?
HELL, YES! I'M EVEN TEMPTED TO OVERLOOK MICK JAGGER'S $15 MILLION BID!
THAT'D BE GREAT!
GBTrudeau

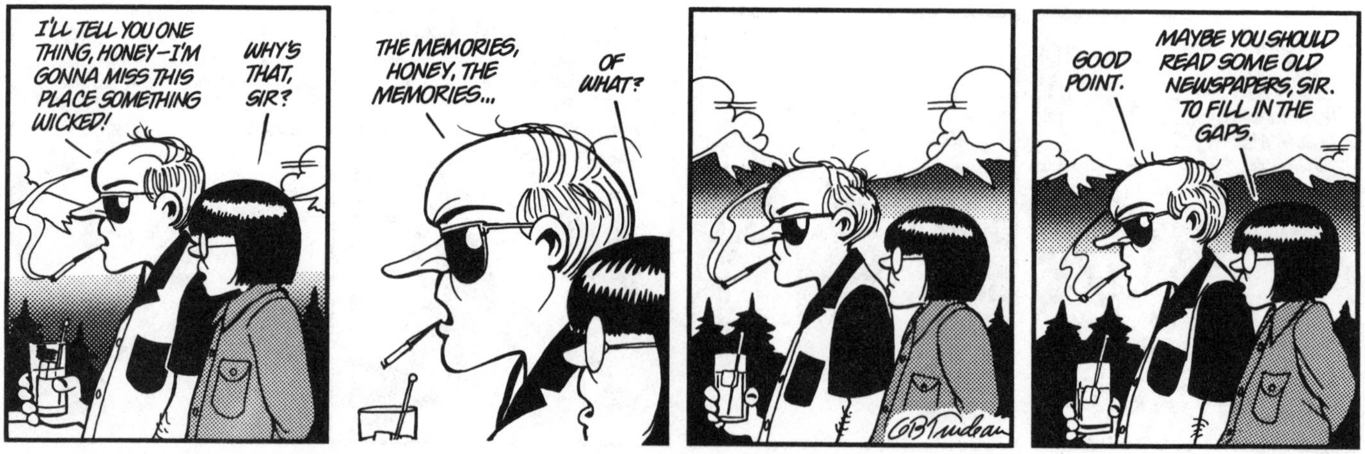
I'LL TELL YOU ONE THING, HONEY—I'M GONNA MISS THIS PLACE SOMETHING WICKED!
WHY'S THAT, SIR?
THE MEMORIES, HONEY, THE MEMORIES...
OF WHAT?
GOOD POINT.
MAYBE YOU SHOULD READ SOME OLD NEWSPAPERS, SIR. TO FILL IN THE GAPS.
GBTrudeau

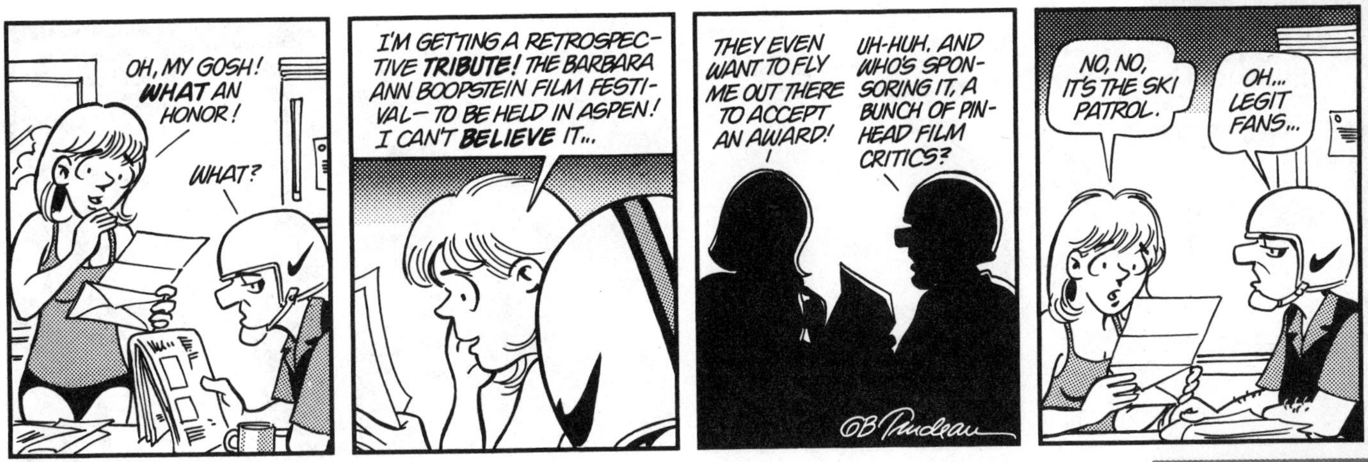
OH, MY GOSH! WHAT AN HONOR!
WHAT?
I'M GETTING A RETROSPECTIVE TRIBUTE! THE BARBARA ANN BOOPSTEIN FILM FESTIVAL– TO BE HELD IN ASPEN! I CAN'T BELIEVE IT...
THEY EVEN WANT TO FLY ME OUT THERE TO ACCEPT AN AWARD!
UH-HUH. AND WHO'S SPONSORING IT, A BUNCH OF PINHEAD FILM CRITICS?
NO, NO, IT'S THE SKI PATROL.
OH... LEGIT FANS...

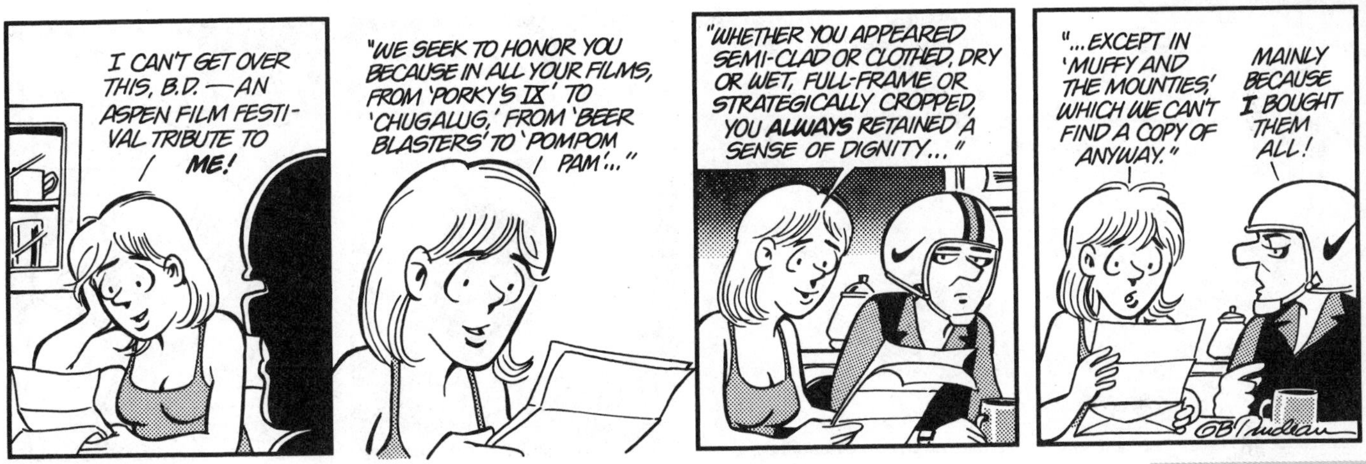
I CAN'T GET OVER THIS, B.D.—AN ASPEN FILM FESTIVAL TRIBUTE TO ME!
"WE SEEK TO HONOR YOU BECAUSE IN ALL YOUR FILMS, FROM 'PORKY'S IX' TO 'CHUGALUG,' FROM 'BEER BLASTERS' TO 'POMPOM PAM'..."
"WHETHER YOU APPEARED SEMI-CLAD OR CLOTHED, DRY OR WET, FULL-FRAME OR STRATEGICALLY CROPPED, YOU ALWAYS RETAINED A SENSE OF DIGNITY..."
"...EXCEPT IN 'MUFFY AND THE MOUNTIES,' WHICH WE CAN'T FIND A COPY OF ANYWAY."
MAINLY BECAUSE I BOUGHT THEM ALL!

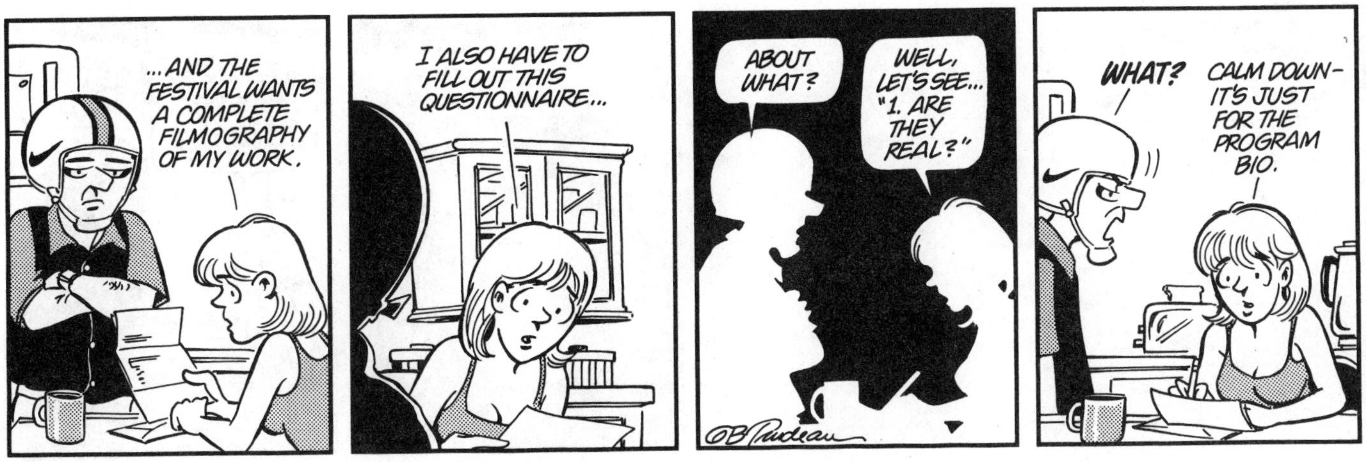
...AND THE FESTIVAL WANTS A COMPLETE FILMOGRAPHY OF MY WORK.
I ALSO HAVE TO FILL OUT THIS QUESTIONNAIRE...
ABOUT WHAT?
WELL, LET'S SEE... "1. ARE THEY REAL?"
WHAT?
CALM DOWN– IT'S JUST FOR THE PROGRAM BIO.

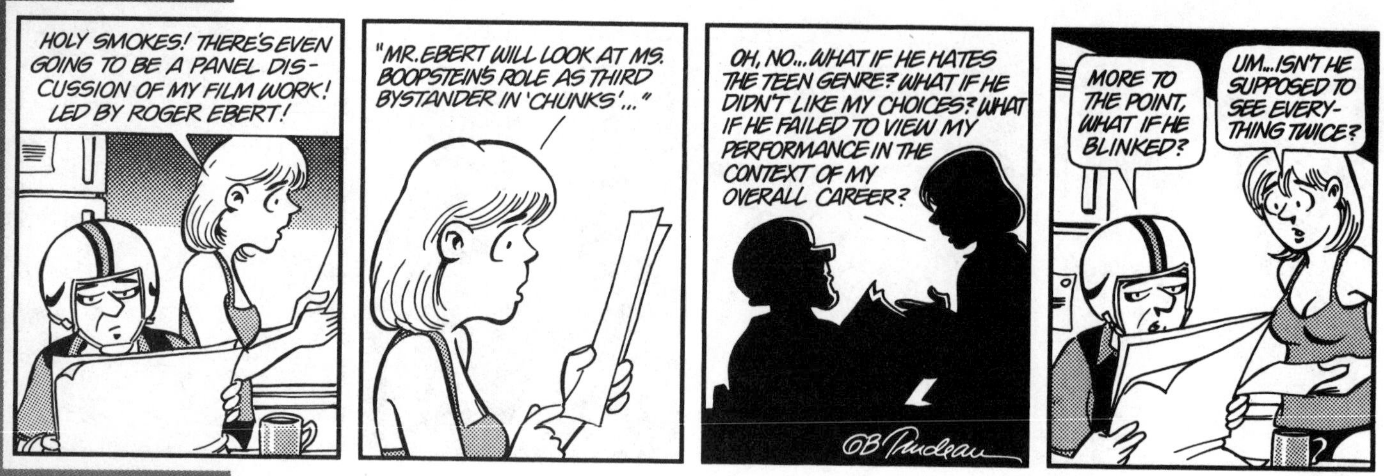
HOLY SMOKES! THERE'S EVEN GOING TO BE A PANEL DISCUSSION OF MY FILM WORK! LED BY ROGER EBERT!
"MR. EBERT WILL LOOK AT MS. BOOPSTEIN'S ROLE AS THIRD BYSTANDER IN 'CHUNKS'..."
OH, NO... WHAT IF HE HATES THE TEEN GENRE? WHAT IF HE DIDN'T LIKE MY CHOICES? WHAT IF HE FAILED TO VIEW MY PERFORMANCE IN THE CONTEXT OF MY OVERALL CAREER?
MORE TO THE POINT, WHAT IF HE BLINKED?
UM... ISN'T HE SUPPOSED TO SEE EVERYTHING TWICE?

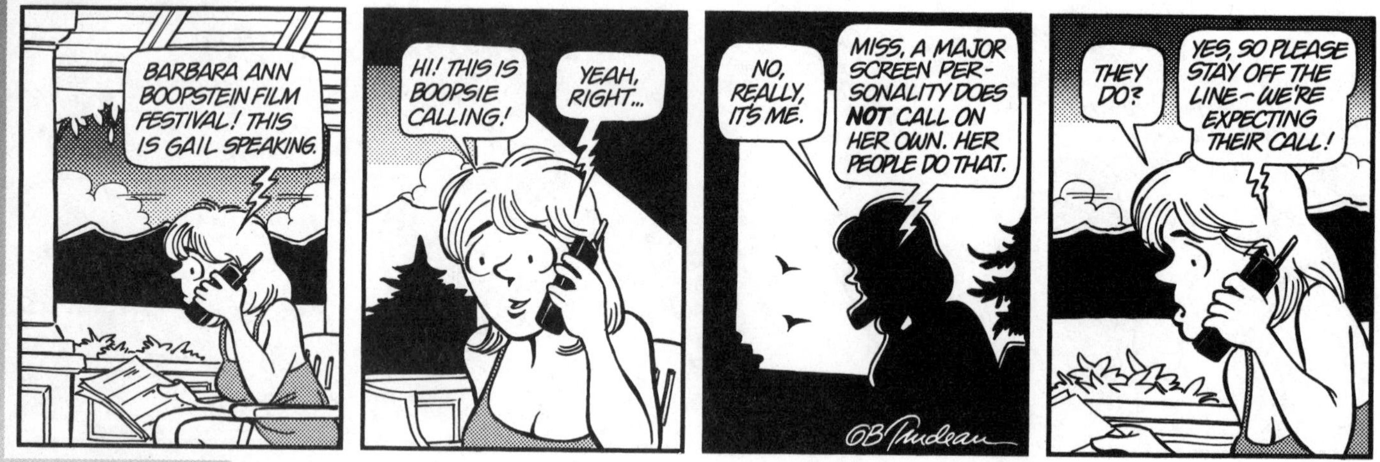
BARBARA ANN BOOPSTEIN FILM FESTIVAL! THIS IS GAIL SPEAKING.
HI! THIS IS BOOPSIE CALLING!
YEAH, RIGHT...
NO, REALLY, IT'S ME.
MISS, A MAJOR SCREEN PERSONALITY DOES NOT CALL ON HER OWN. HER PEOPLE DO THAT.
THEY DO?
YES, SO PLEASE STAY OFF THE LINE – WE'RE EXPECTING THEIR CALL!

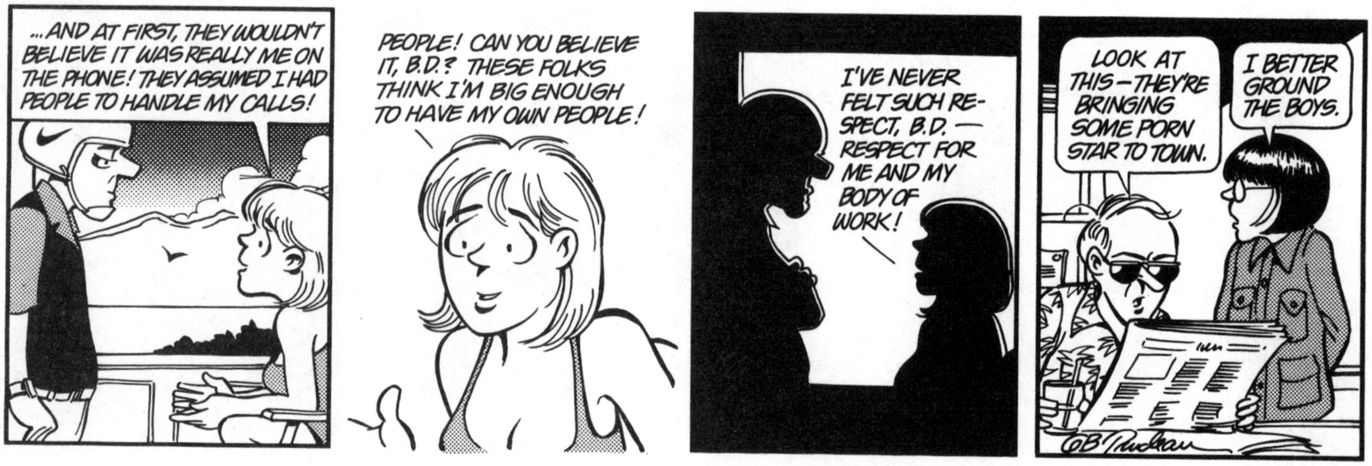
...AND AT FIRST, THEY WOULDN'T BELIEVE IT WAS REALLY ME ON THE PHONE! THEY ASSUMED I HAD PEOPLE TO HANDLE MY CALLS!
PEOPLE! CAN YOU BELIEVE IT, B.D.? THESE FOLKS THINK I'M BIG ENOUGH TO HAVE MY OWN PEOPLE!
I'VE NEVER FELT SUCH RESPECT, B.D. — RESPECT FOR ME AND MY BODY OF WORK!
LOOK AT THIS – THEY'RE BRINGING SOME PORN STAR TO TOWN.
I BETTER GROUND THE BOYS.

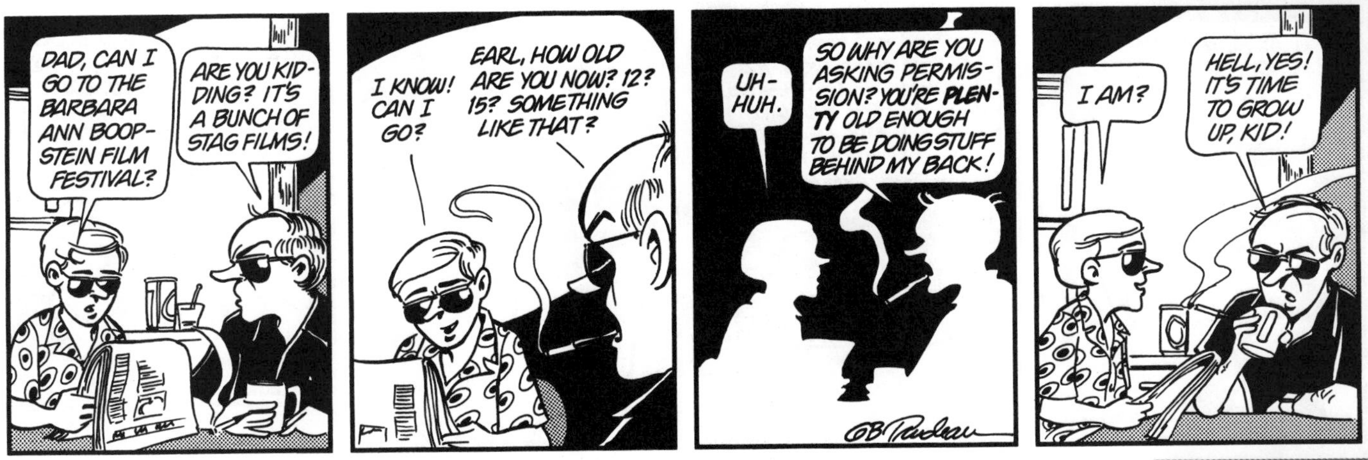
DAD, CAN I GO TO THE BARBARA ANN BOOPSTEIN FILM FESTIVAL?
ARE YOU KIDDING? IT'S A BUNCH OF STAG FILMS!
I KNOW! CAN I GO?
EARL, HOW OLD ARE YOU NOW? 12? 15? SOMETHING LIKE THAT?
UH-HUH.
SO WHY ARE YOU ASKING PERMISSION? YOU'RE PLENTY OLD ENOUGH TO BE DOING STUFF BEHIND MY BACK!
I AM?
HELL, YES! IT'S TIME TO GROW UP, KID!

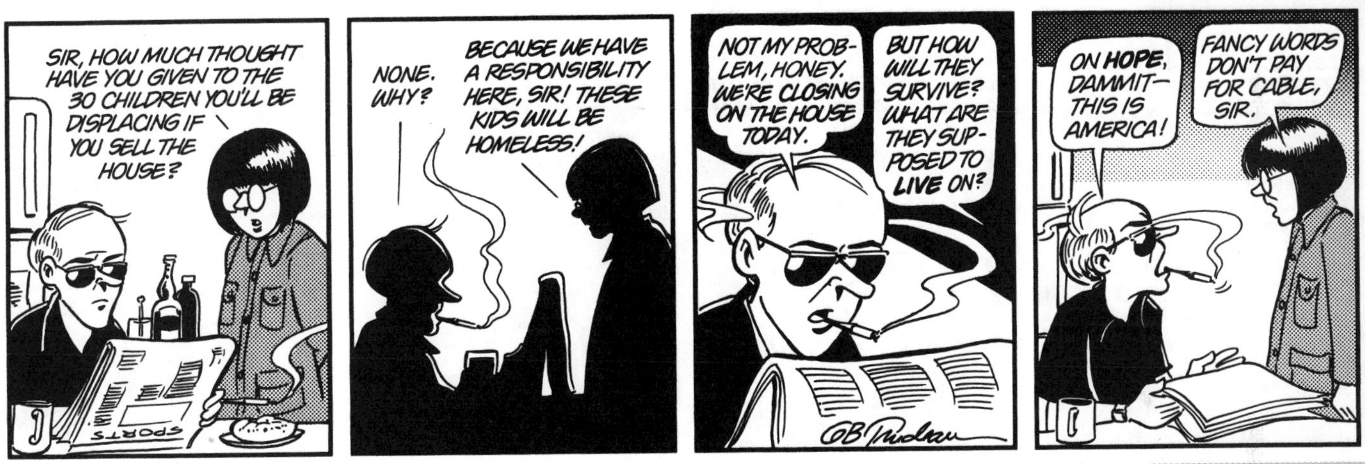
SIR, HOW MUCH THOUGHT HAVE YOU GIVEN TO THE 30 CHILDREN YOU'LL BE DISPLACING IF YOU SELL THE HOUSE?
SPORTS
NONE. WHY?
BECAUSE WE HAVE A RESPONSIBILITY HERE, SIR! THESE KIDS WILL BE HOMELESS!
NOT MY PROBLEM, HONEY. WE'RE CLOSING ON THE HOUSE TODAY.
BUT HOW WILL THEY SURVIVE? WHAT ARE THEY SUPPOSED TO LIVE ON?
ON HOPE, DAMMIT—THIS IS AMERICA!
FANCY WORDS DON'T PAY FOR CABLE, SIR.

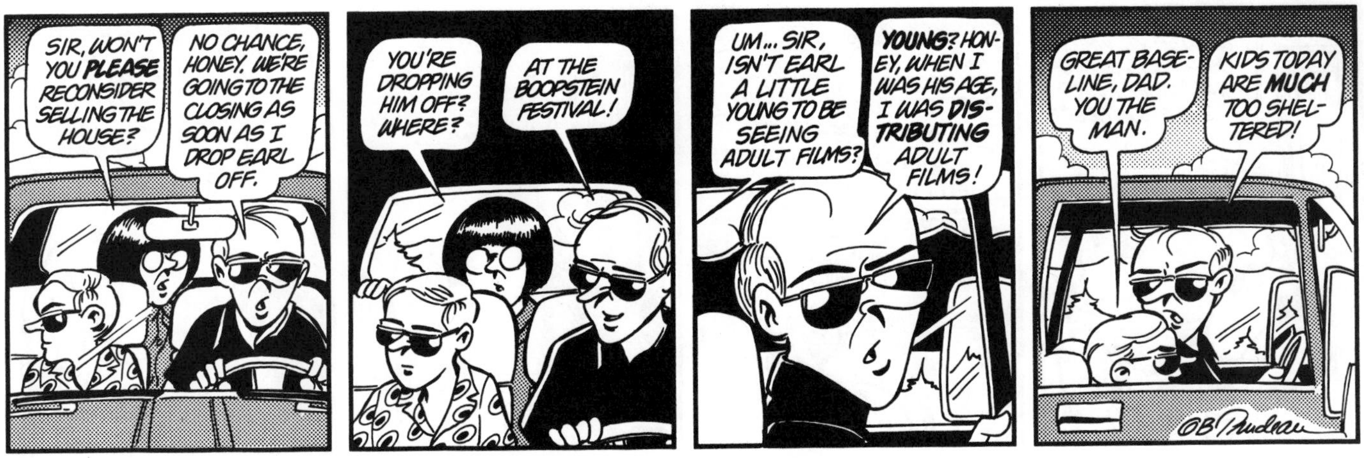
SIR, WON'T YOU PLEASE RECONSIDER SELLING THE HOUSE?
NO CHANCE, HONEY. WE'RE GOING TO THE CLOSING AS SOON AS I DROP EARL OFF.
YOU'RE DROPPING HIM OFF? WHERE?
AT THE BOOPSTEIN FESTIVAL!
UM... SIR, ISN'T EARL A LITTLE YOUNG TO BE SEEING ADULT FILMS?
YOUNG? HONEY, WHEN I WAS HIS AGE, I WAS DISTRIBUTING ADULT FILMS!
GREAT BASELINE, DAD. YOU THE MAN.
KIDS TODAY ARE MUCH TOO SHELTERED!

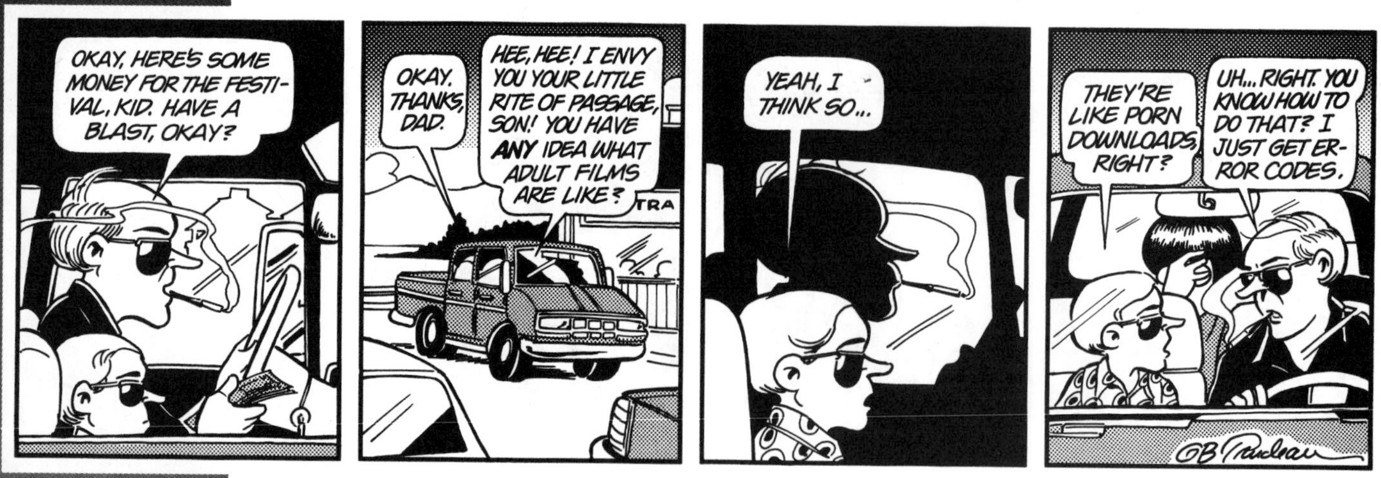
OKAY, HERE'S SOME MONEY FOR THE FESTIVAL, KID. HAVE A BLAST, OKAY?
OKAY. THANKS, DAD.
HEE, HEE! I ENVY YOU YOUR LITTLE RITE OF PASSAGE, SON! YOU HAVE ANY IDEA WHAT ADULT FILMS ARE LIKE?
TRA
YEAH, I THINK SO...
THEY'RE LIKE PORN DOWNLOADS, RIGHT?
UH... RIGHT. YOU KNOW HOW TO DO THAT? I JUST GET ERROR CODES.

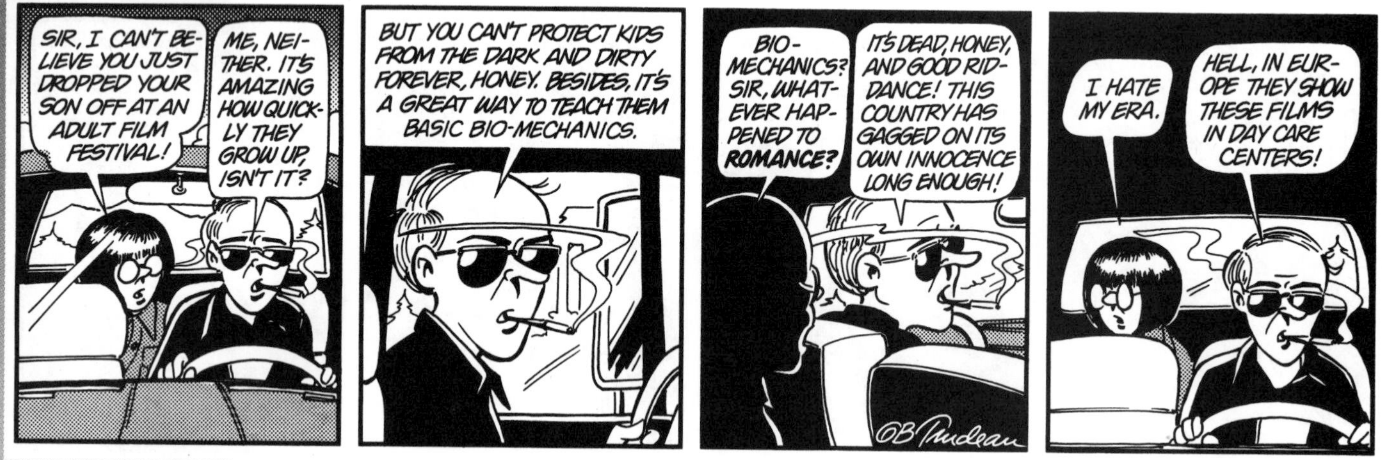
SIR, I CAN'T BELIEVE YOU JUST DROPPED YOUR SON OFF AT AN ADULT FILM FESTIVAL!
ME, NEITHER. IT'S AMAZING HOW QUICKLY THEY GROW UP, ISN'T IT?
BUT YOU CAN'T PROTECT KIDS FROM THE DARK AND DIRTY FOREVER, HONEY. BESIDES, IT'S A GREAT WAY TO TEACH THEM BASIC BIO-MECHANICS.
BIO-MECHANICS? SIR, WHATEVER HAPPENED TO ROMANCE?
IT'S DEAD, HONEY, AND GOOD RIDDANCE! THIS COUNTRY HAS GAGGED ON ITS OWN INNOCENCE LONG ENOUGH!
I HATE MY ERA.
HELL, IN EUROPE THEY SHOW THESE FILMS IN DAY CARE CENTERS!

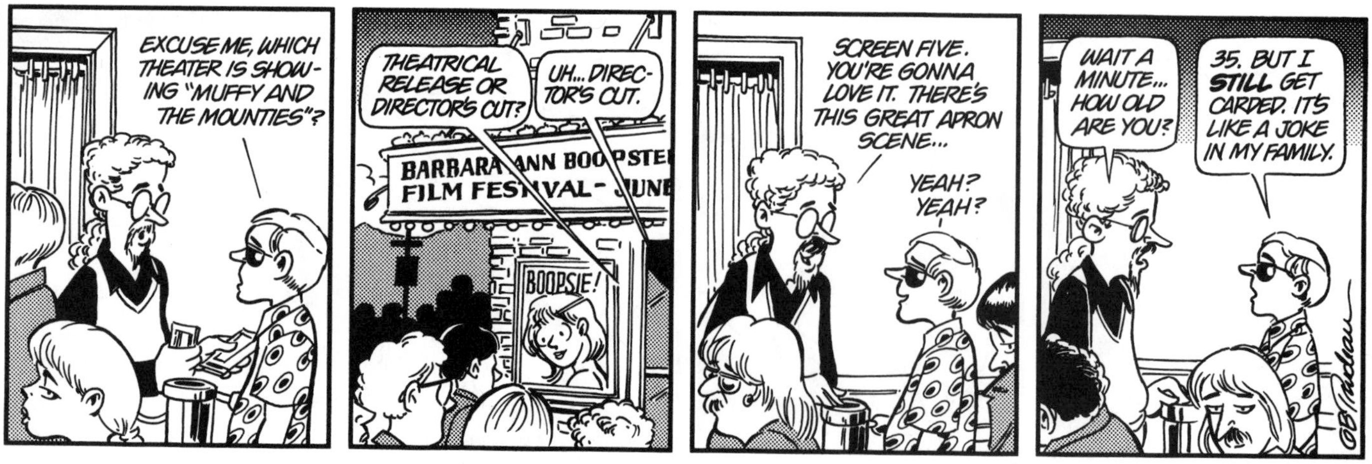
EXCUSE ME, WHICH THEATER IS SHOWING "MUFFY AND THE MOUNTIES"?
THEATRICAL RELEASE OR DIRECTOR'S CUT?
UH... DIRECTOR'S CUT.
BARBARA ANN BOOPSTEI
FILM FESTIVAL - JUNE
BOOPSIE!
SCREEN FIVE. YOU'RE GONNA LOVE IT. THERE'S THIS GREAT APRON SCENE...
YEAH? YEAH?
WAIT A MINUTE... HOW OLD ARE YOU?
35. BUT I STILL GET CARDED. IT'S LIKE A JOKE IN MY FAMILY.

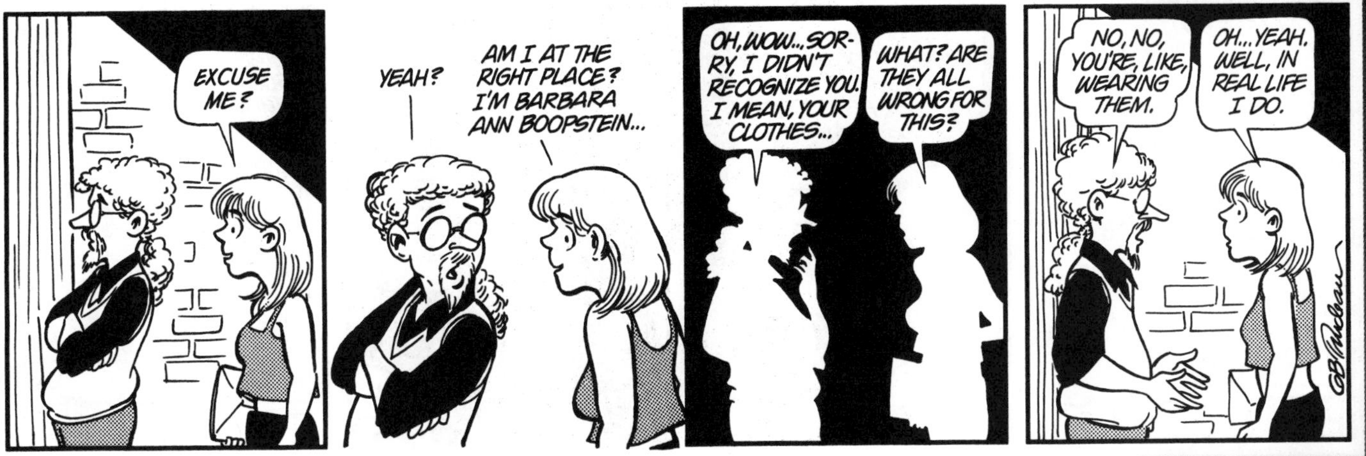
EXCUSE ME?
YEAH?
AM I AT THE RIGHT PLACE? I'M BARBARA ANN BOOPSTEIN...
OH, WOW... SORRY, I DIDN'T RECOGNIZE YOU. I MEAN, YOUR CLOTHES...
WHAT? ARE THEY ALL WRONG FOR THIS?
NO, NO, YOU'RE, LIKE, WEARING THEM.
OH... YEAH. WELL, IN REAL LIFE I DO.
GBTrudeau

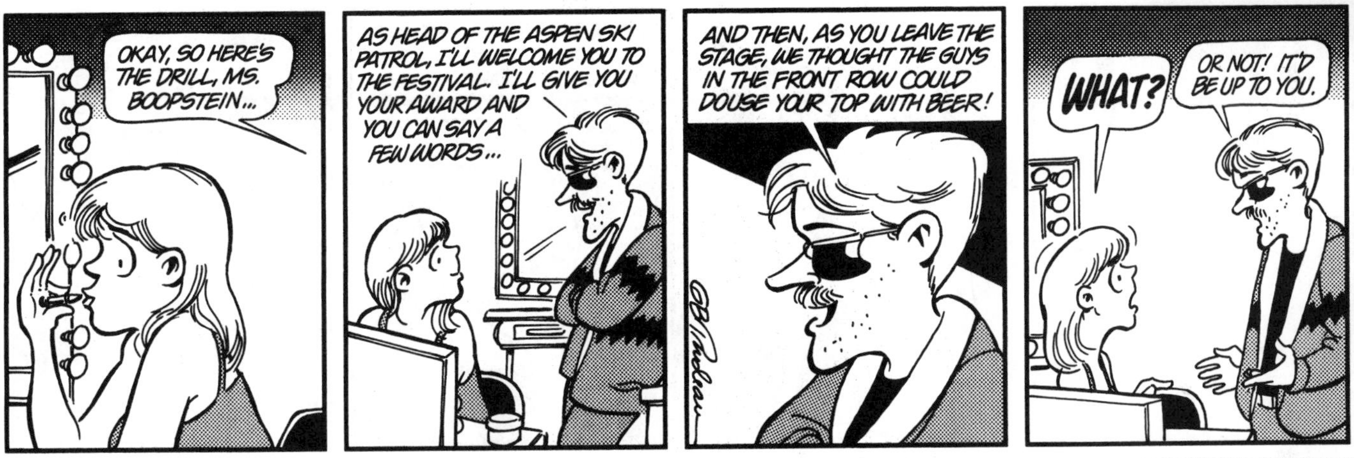
OKAY, SO HERE'S THE DRILL, MS. BOOPSTEIN...
AS HEAD OF THE ASPEN SKI PATROL, I'LL WELCOME YOU TO THE FESTIVAL. I'LL GIVE YOU YOUR AWARD AND YOU CAN SAY A FEW WORDS...
GBTrudeau
AND THEN, AS YOU LEAVE THE STAGE, WE THOUGHT THE GUYS IN THE FRONT ROW COULD DOUSE YOUR TOP WITH BEER!
WHAT?
OR NOT! IT'D BE UP TO YOU.

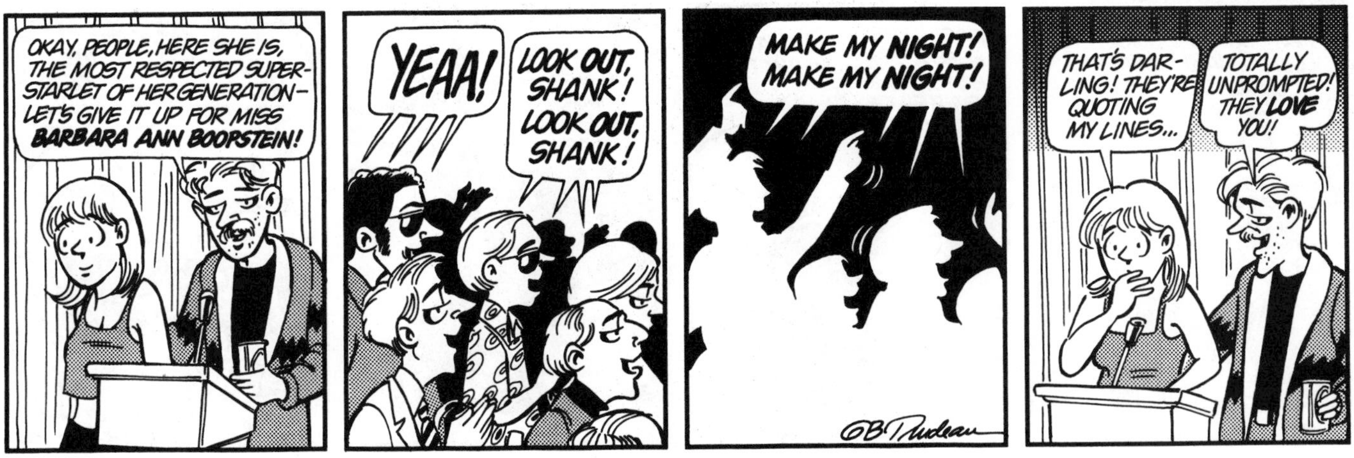
OKAY, PEOPLE, HERE SHE IS, THE MOST RESPECTED SUPER-STARLET OF HER GENERATION– LET'S GIVE IT UP FOR MISS BARBARA ANN BOOPSTEIN!
YEAA!
LOOK OUT, SHANK! LOOK OUT, SHANK!
MAKE MY NIGHT! MAKE MY NIGHT!
GBTrudeau
THAT'S DARLING! THEY'RE QUOTING MY LINES...
TOTALLY UNPROMPTED! THEY LOVE YOU!

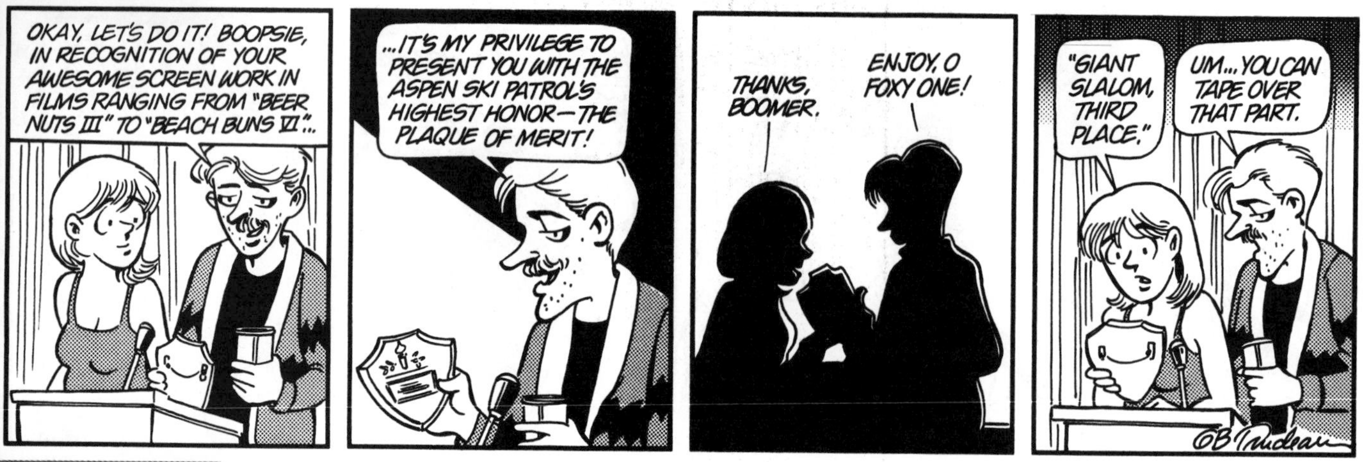
OKAY, LET'S DO IT! BOOPSIE, IN RECOGNITION OF YOUR AWESOME SCREEN WORK IN FILMS RANGING FROM "BEER NUTS III" TO "BEACH BUNS VI"...
...IT'S MY PRIVILEGE TO PRESENT YOU WITH THE ASPEN SKI PATROL'S HIGHEST HONOR—THE PLAQUE OF MERIT!
THANKS, BOOMER.
ENJOY, O FOXY ONE!
"GIANT SLALOM, THIRD PLACE."
UM...YOU CAN TAPE OVER THAT PART.
©B Trudeau

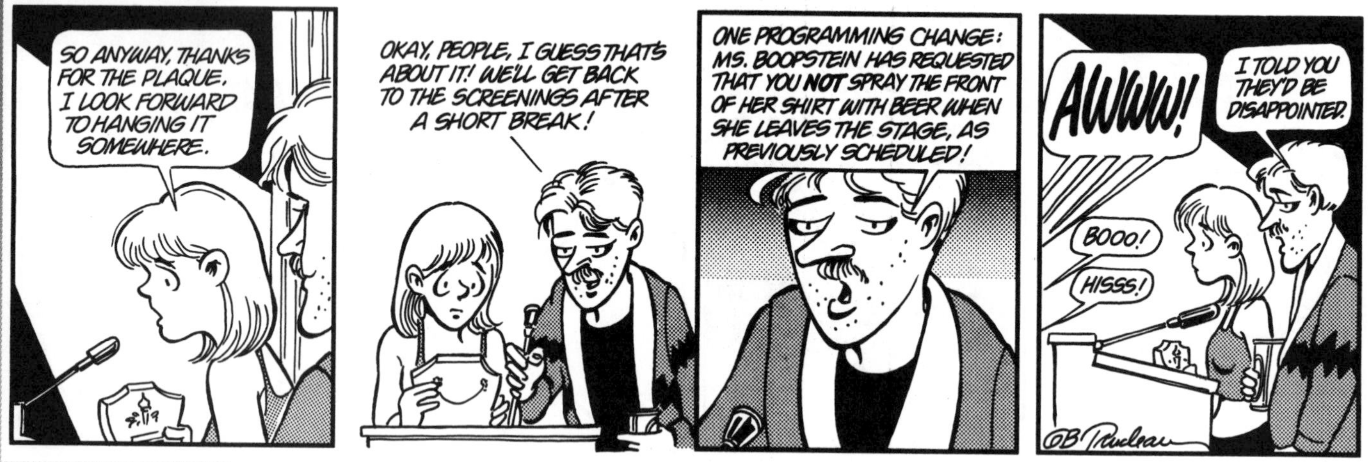
SO ANYWAY, THANKS FOR THE PLAQUE. I LOOK FORWARD TO HANGING IT SOMEWHERE.
OKAY, PEOPLE, I GUESS THAT'S ABOUT IT! WE'LL GET BACK TO THE SCREENINGS AFTER A SHORT BREAK!
ONE PROGRAMMING CHANGE: MS. BOOPSTEIN HAS REQUESTED THAT YOU NOT SPRAY THE FRONT OF HER SHIRT WITH BEER WHEN SHE LEAVES THE STAGE, AS PREVIOUSLY SCHEDULED!
AWWW!
I TOLD YOU THEY'D BE DISAPPOINTED.
BOOO!
HISSS!
©B Trudeau

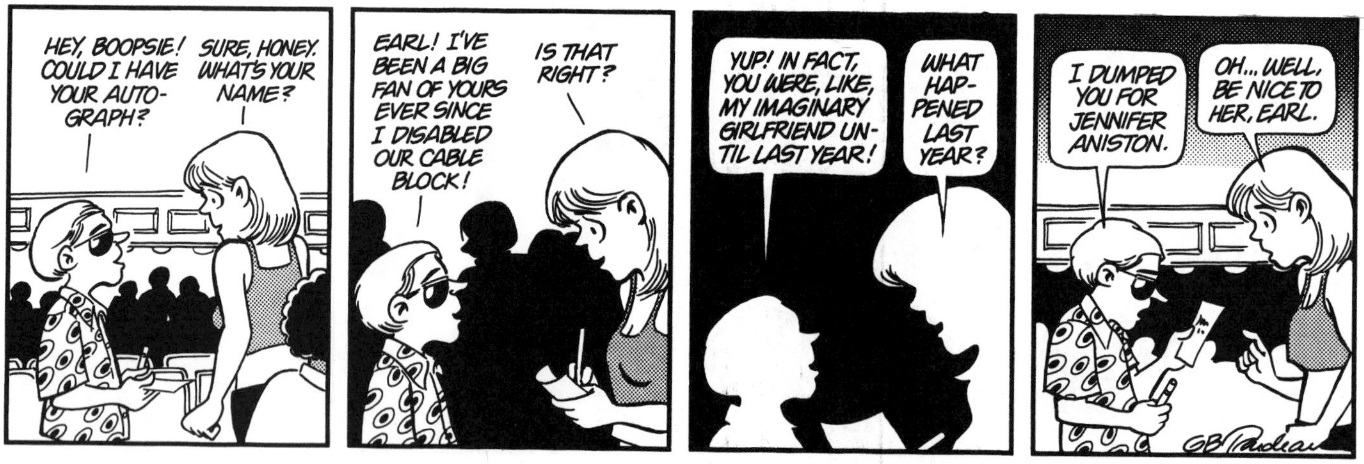
HEY, BOOPSIE! COULD I HAVE YOUR AUTO-GRAPH?
SURE, HONEY. WHAT'S YOUR NAME?
EARL! I'VE BEEN A BIG FAN OF YOURS EVER SINCE I DISABLED OUR CABLE BLOCK!
IS THAT RIGHT?
YUP! IN FACT, YOU WERE, LIKE, MY IMAGINARY GIRLFRIEND UN-TIL LAST YEAR!
WHAT HAP-PENED LAST YEAR?
I DUMPED YOU FOR JENNIFER ANISTON.
OH... WELL, BE NICE TO HER, EARL.
©B Trudeau

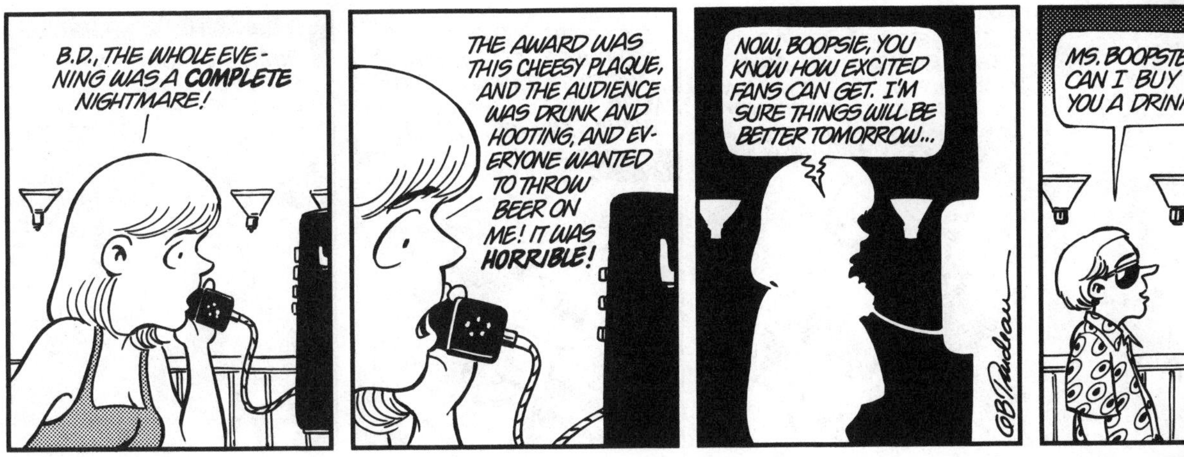
B.D., THE WHOLE EVENING WAS A COMPLETE NIGHTMARE!
THE AWARD WAS THIS CHEESY PLAQUE, AND THE AUDIENCE WAS DRUNK AND HOOTING, AND EVERYONE WANTED TO THROW BEER ON ME! IT WAS HORRIBLE!
NOW, BOOPSIE, YOU KNOW HOW EXCITED FANS CAN GET. I'M SURE THINGS WILL BE BETTER TOMORROW...
MS. BOOPSTEIN? CAN I BUY YOU A DRINK?
I WANT TO COME HOME.

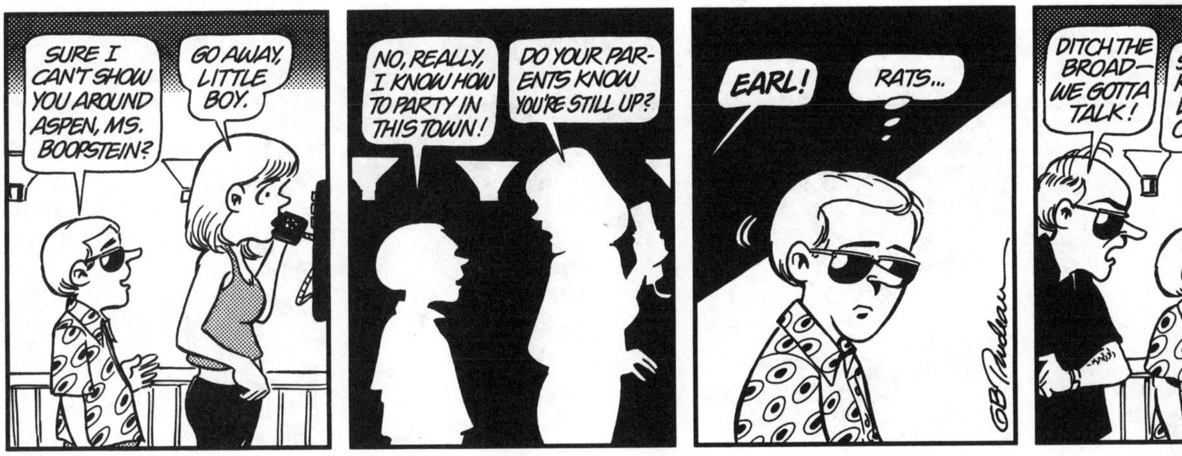
SURE I CAN'T SHOW YOU AROUND ASPEN, MS. BOOPSTEIN?
GO AWAY, LITTLE BOY.
NO, REALLY, I KNOW HOW TO PARTY IN THIS TOWN!
DO YOUR PARENTS KNOW YOU'RE STILL UP?
EARL!
RATS...
DITCH THE BROAD— WE GOTTA TALK!
SORRY, KIDDO, DUTY CALLS!
I'LL GET OVER IT.

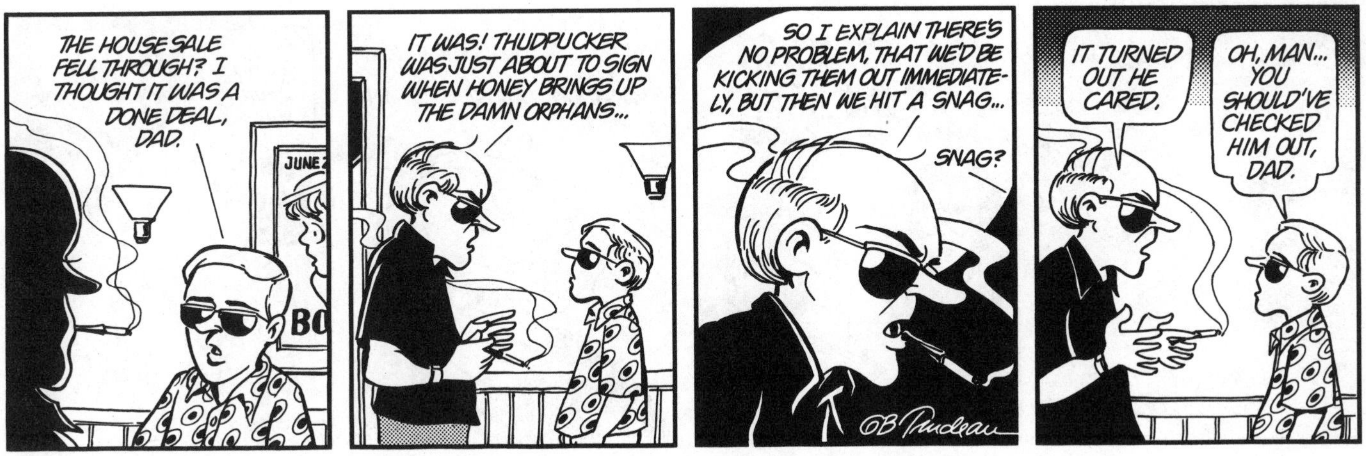
THE HOUSE SALE FELL THROUGH? I THOUGHT IT WAS A DONE DEAL, DAD.
IT WAS! THUDPUCKER WAS JUST ABOUT TO SIGN WHEN HONEY BRINGS UP THE DAMN ORPHANS...
SO I EXPLAIN THERE'S NO PROBLEM, THAT WE'D BE KICKING THEM OUT IMMEDIATELY, BUT THEN WE HIT A SNAG...
SNAG?
IT TURNED OUT HE CARED.
OH, MAN... YOU SHOULD'VE CHECKED HIM OUT, DAD.

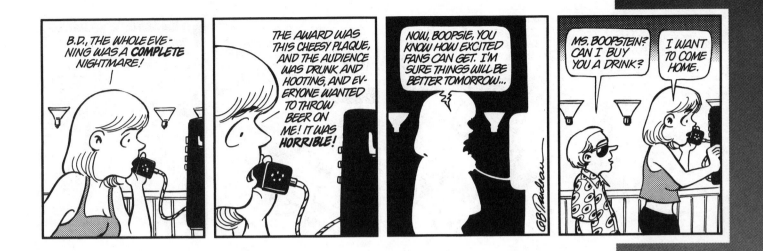

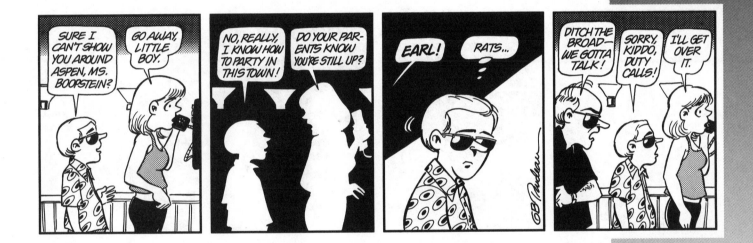

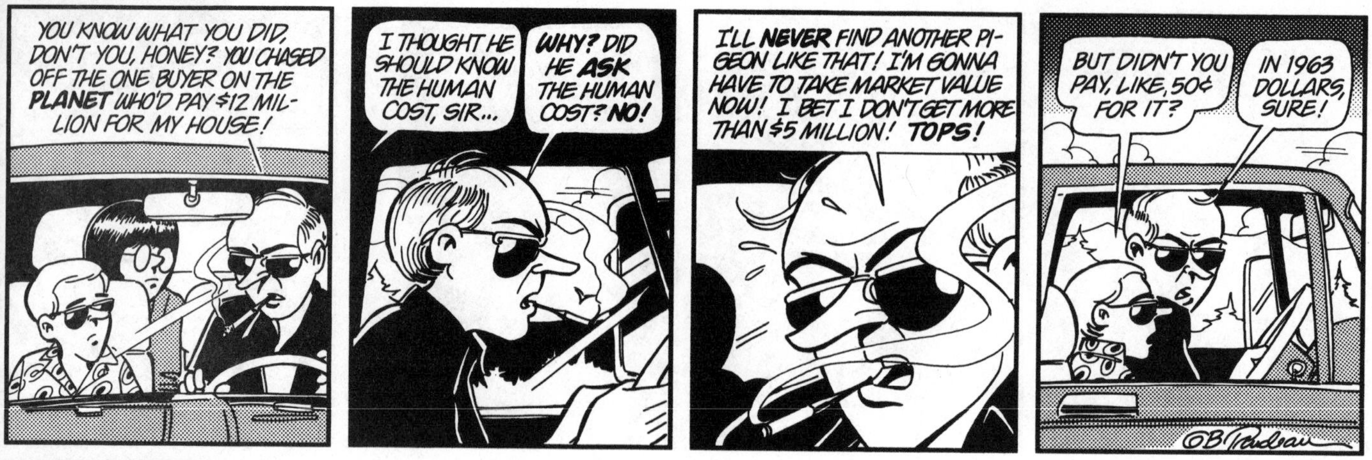

YOU KNOW WHAT YOU DID, DON'T YOU, HONEY? YOU CHASED OFF THE ONE BUYER ON THE **PLANET** WHO'D PAY $12 MILLION FOR MY HOUSE!
I THOUGHT HE SHOULD KNOW THE HUMAN COST, SIR...
WHY? DID HE **ASK** THE HUMAN COST? **NO!**
I'LL **NEVER** FIND ANOTHER PIGEON LIKE THAT! I'M GONNA HAVE TO TAKE MARKET VALUE NOW! I BET I DON'T GET MORE THAN $5 MILLION! **TOPS!**
BUT DIDN'T YOU PAY, LIKE, 50¢ FOR IT?
IN 1963 DOLLARS, SURE!

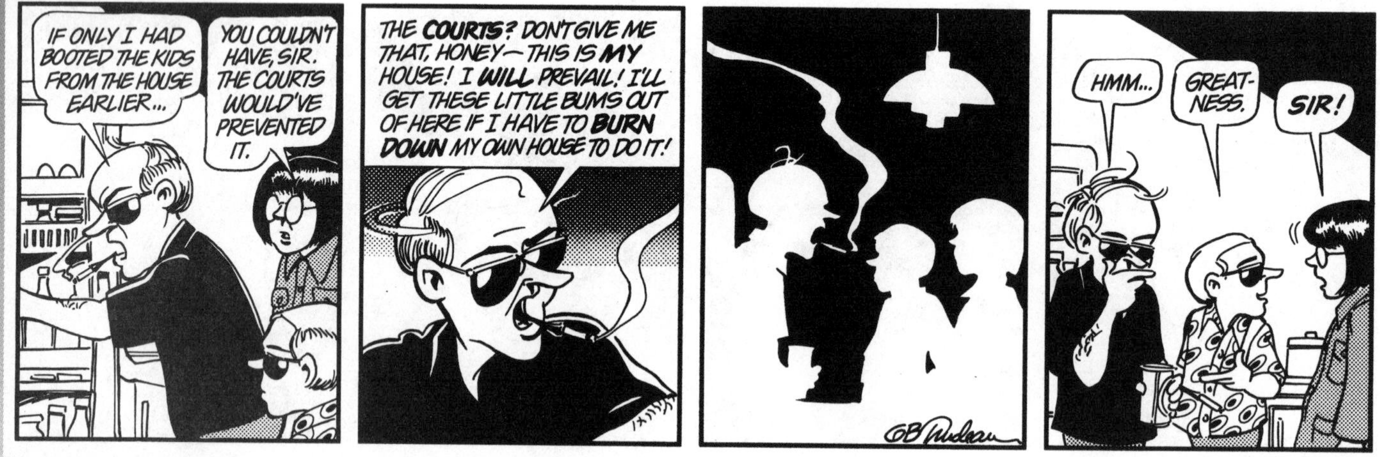

IF ONLY I HAD BOOTED THE KIDS FROM THE HOUSE EARLIER...
YOU COULDN'T HAVE, SIR. THE COURTS WOULD'VE PREVENTED IT.
THE **COURTS**? DON'T GIVE ME THAT, HONEY— THIS IS **MY** HOUSE! I **WILL** PREVAIL! I'LL GET THESE LITTLE **BUMS** OUT OF HERE IF I HAVE TO **BURN DOWN** MY OWN HOUSE TO DO IT!
HMM...
GREATNESS.
SIR!

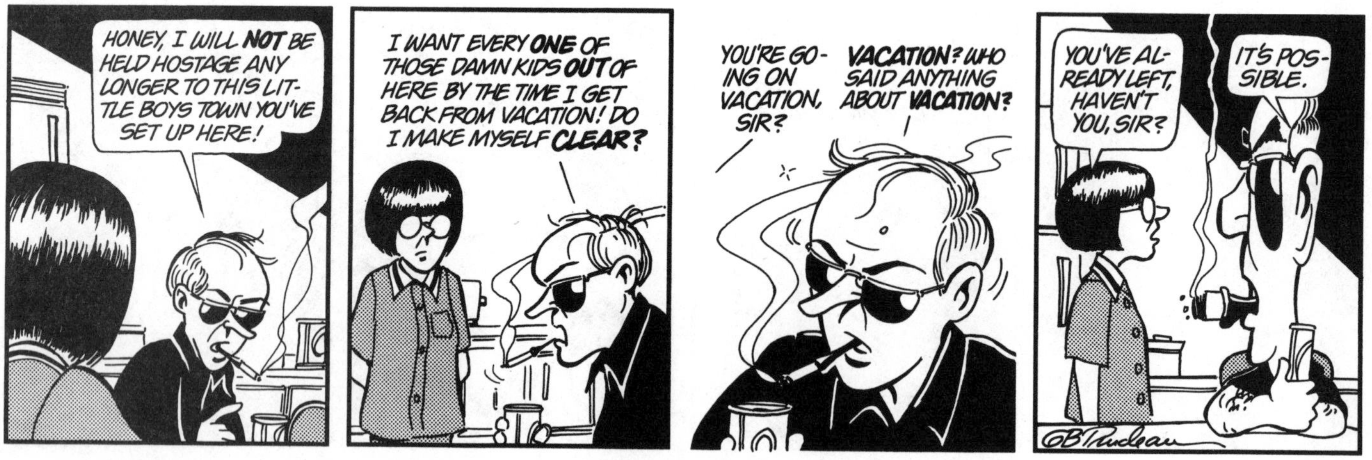

HONEY, I WILL **NOT** BE HELD HOSTAGE ANY LONGER TO THIS LITTLE BOYS TOWN YOU'VE SET UP HERE!
I WANT EVERY **ONE** OF THOSE DAMN KIDS **OUT** OF HERE BY THE TIME I GET BACK FROM VACATION! DO I MAKE MYSELF **CLEAR**?
YOU'RE GOING ON VACATION, SIR?
VACATION? WHO SAID ANYTHING ABOUT **VACATION**?
YOU'VE ALREADY LEFT, HAVEN'T YOU, SIR?
IT'S POSSIBLE.

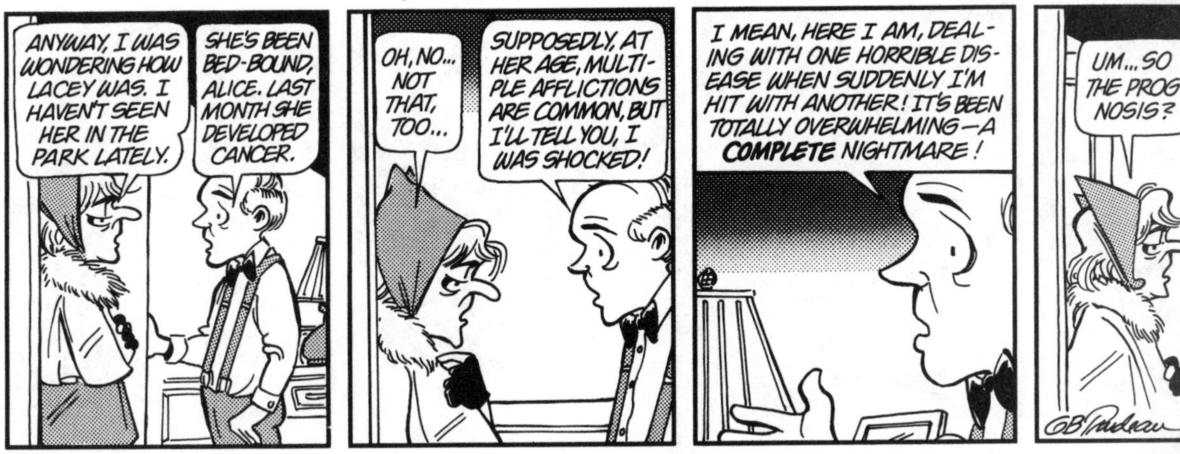
ANYWAY, I WAS WONDERING HOW LACEY WAS. I HAVEN'T SEEN HER IN THE PARK LATELY.
SHE'S BEEN BED-BOUND, ALICE. LAST MONTH SHE DEVELOPED CANCER.
OH, NO... NOT THAT, TOO...
SUPPOSEDLY, AT HER AGE, MULTIPLE AFFLICTIONS ARE COMMON, BUT I'LL TELL YOU, I WAS SHOCKED!
I MEAN, HERE I AM, DEALING WITH ONE HORRIBLE DISEASE WHEN SUDDENLY I'M HIT WITH ANOTHER! IT'S BEEN TOTALLY OVERWHELMING—A COMPLETE NIGHTMARE!
UM... SO THE PROGNOSIS?
OH, I'LL BE FINE. BUT IT'S HARD.

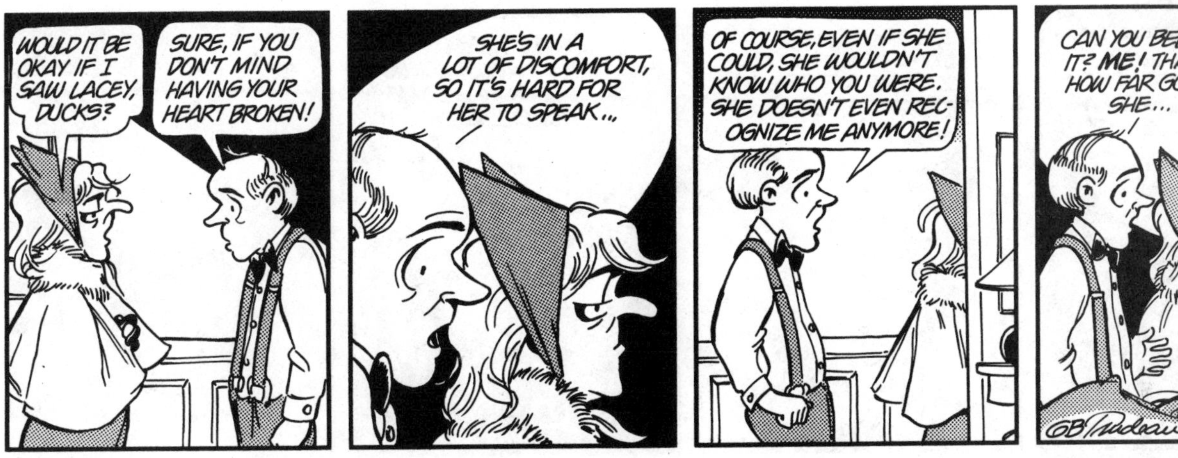
WOULD IT BE OKAY IF I SAW LACEY, DUCKS?
SURE, IF YOU DON'T MIND HAVING YOUR HEART BROKEN!
SHE'S IN A LOT OF DISCOMFORT, SO IT'S HARD FOR HER TO SPEAK...
OF COURSE, EVEN IF SHE COULD, SHE WOULDN'T KNOW WHO YOU WERE. SHE DOESN'T EVEN RECOGNIZE ME ANYMORE!
CAN YOU BELIEVE IT? ME! THAT'S HOW FAR GONE SHE...
PEARL! I'VE MISSED YOU, DEAR HEART!

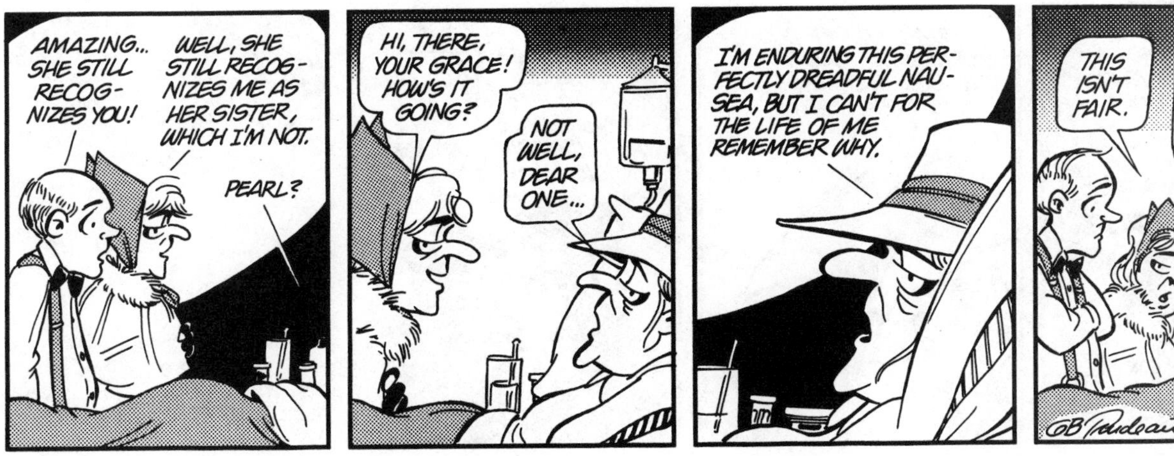
AMAZING... SHE STILL RECOGNIZES YOU!
WELL, SHE STILL RECOGNIZES ME AS HER SISTER, WHICH I'M NOT.
PEARL?
HI, THERE, YOUR GRACE! HOW'S IT GOING?
NOT WELL, DEAR ONE...
I'M ENDURING THIS PERFECTLY DREADFUL NAUSEA, BUT I CAN'T FOR THE LIFE OF ME REMEMBER WHY.
THIS ISN'T FAIR.
IT'S LIKE I HAD BAD OYSTERS AT A FORGETTABLE RESTAURANT.

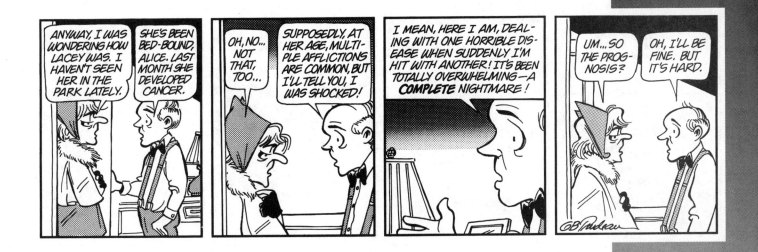

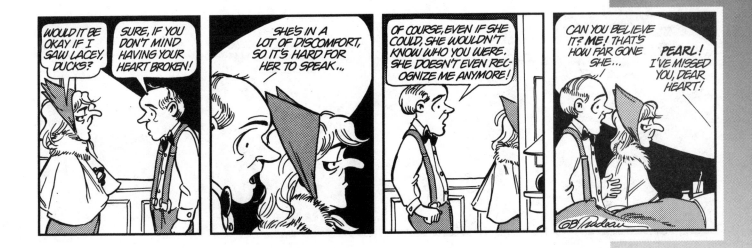

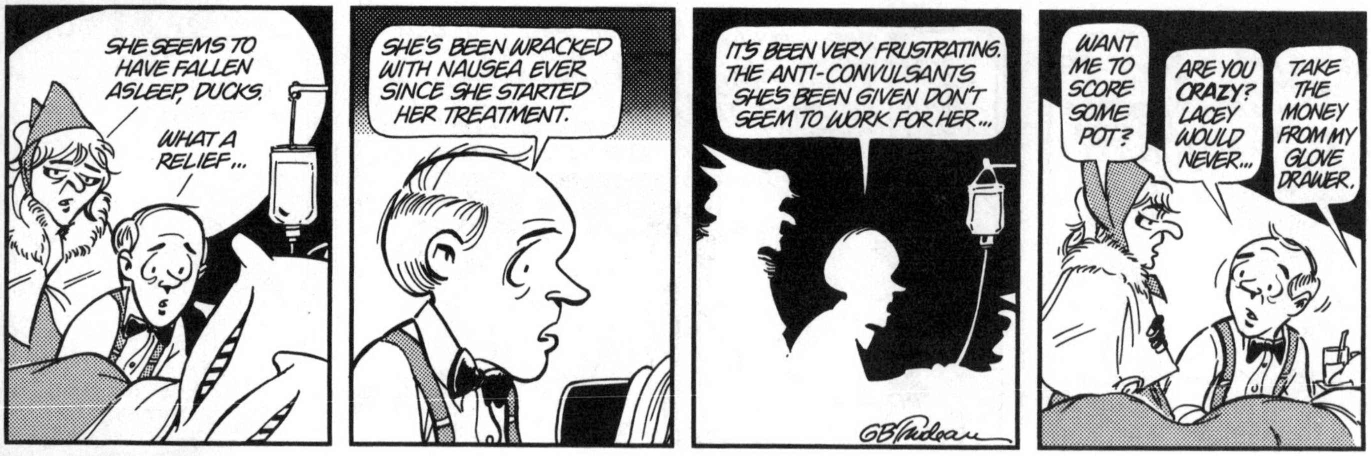
SHE SEEMS TO HAVE FALLEN ASLEEP, DUCKS.
WHAT A RELIEF...
SHE'S BEEN WRACKED WITH NAUSEA EVER SINCE SHE STARTED HER TREATMENT.
IT'S BEEN VERY FRUSTRATING. THE ANTI-CONVULSANTS SHE'S BEEN GIVEN DON'T SEEM TO WORK FOR HER...
WANT ME TO SCORE SOME POT?
ARE YOU CRAZY? LACEY WOULD NEVER...
TAKE THE MONEY FROM MY GLOVE DRAWER.

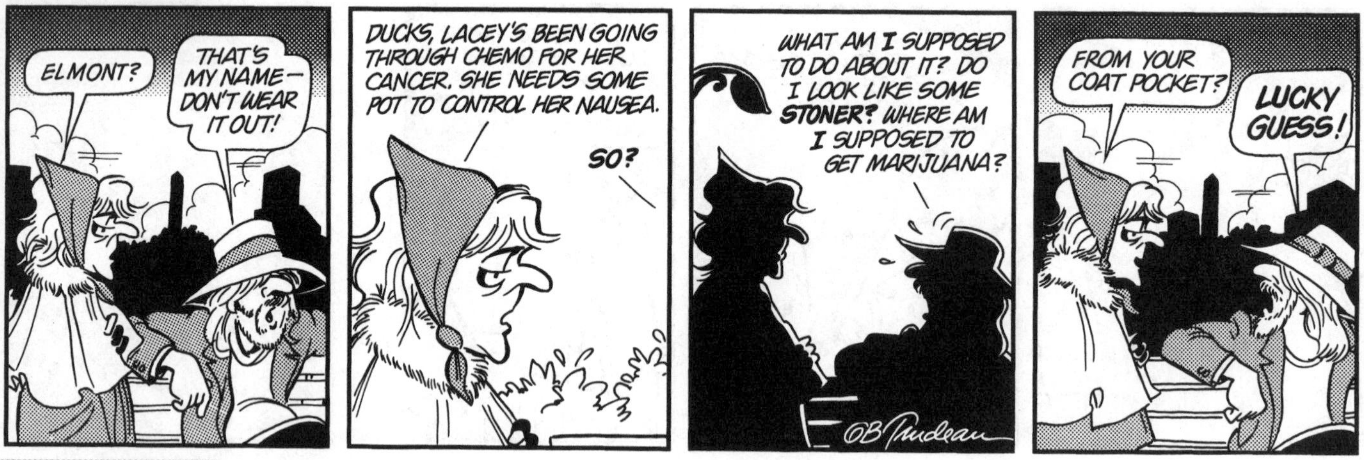
ELMONT?
THAT'S MY NAME— DON'T WEAR IT OUT!
DUCKS, LACEY'S BEEN GOING THROUGH CHEMO FOR HER CANCER. SHE NEEDS SOME POT TO CONTROL HER NAUSEA.
SO?
WHAT AM I SUPPOSED TO DO ABOUT IT? DO I LOOK LIKE SOME STONER? WHERE AM I SUPPOSED TO GET MARIJUANA?
FROM YOUR COAT POCKET?
LUCKY GUESS!

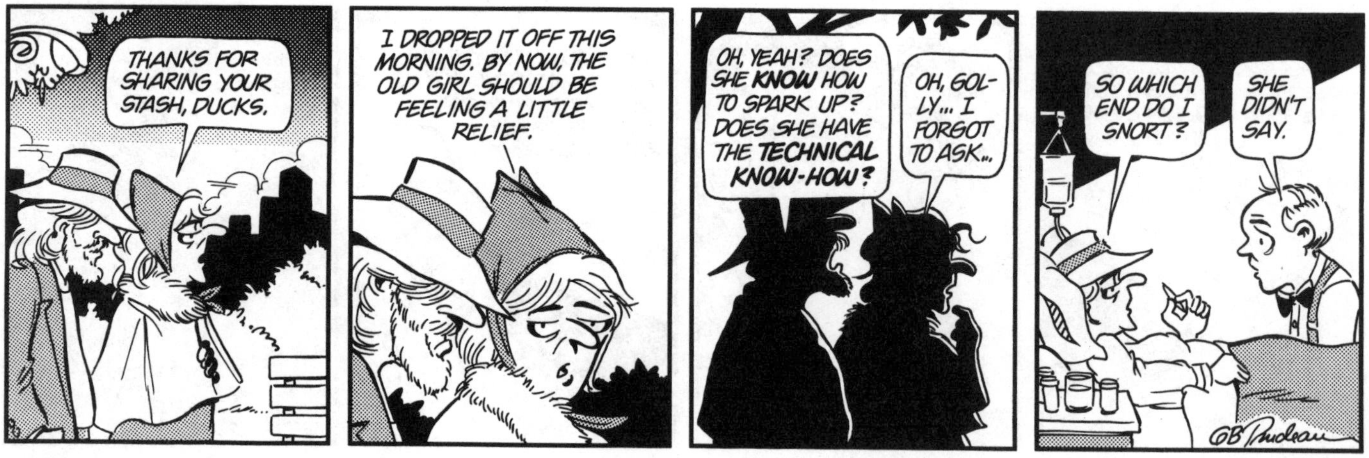
THANKS FOR SHARING YOUR STASH, DUCKS.
I DROPPED IT OFF THIS MORNING. BY NOW, THE OLD GIRL SHOULD BE FEELING A LITTLE RELIEF.
OH, YEAH? DOES SHE KNOW HOW TO SPARK UP? DOES SHE HAVE THE TECHNICAL KNOW-HOW?
OH, GOL-LY... I FORGOT TO ASK...
SO WHICH END DO I SNORT?
SHE DIDN'T SAY.

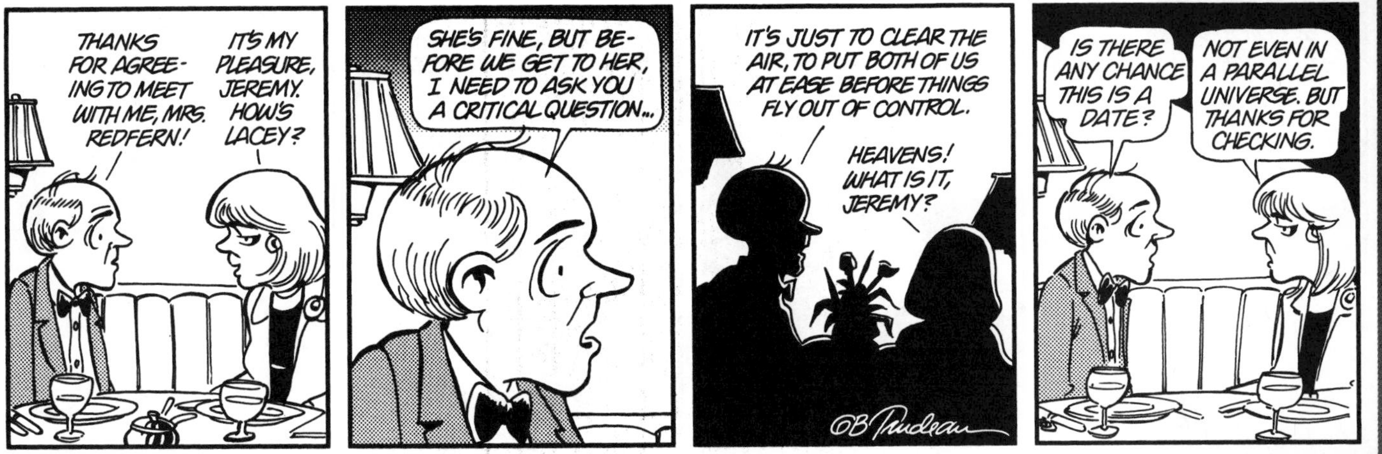
THANKS FOR AGREEING TO MEET WITH ME, MRS. REDFERN!
IT'S MY PLEASURE, JEREMY. HOW'S LACEY?
SHE'S FINE, BUT BEFORE WE GET TO HER, I NEED TO ASK YOU A CRITICAL QUESTION...
IT'S JUST TO CLEAR THE AIR, TO PUT BOTH OF US AT EASE BEFORE THINGS FLY OUT OF CONTROL.
HEAVENS! WHAT IS IT, JEREMY?
G.B. Trudeau
IS THERE ANY CHANCE THIS IS A DATE?
NOT EVEN IN A PARALLEL UNIVERSE. BUT THANKS FOR CHECKING.

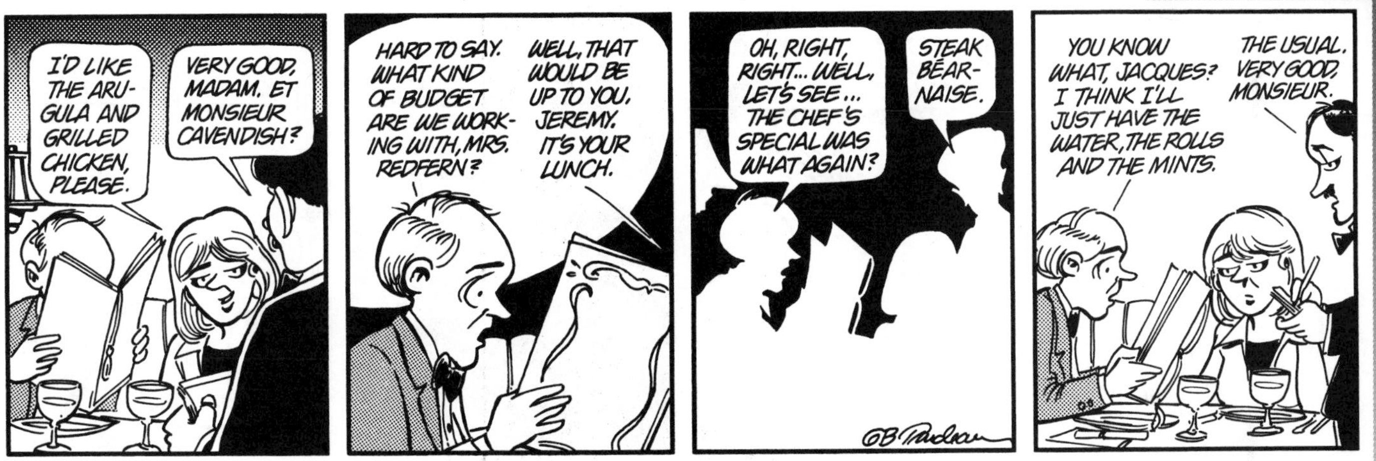
I'D LIKE THE ARUGULA AND GRILLED CHICKEN, PLEASE.
VERY GOOD, MADAM. ET MONSIEUR CAVENDISH?
HARD TO SAY. WHAT KIND OF BUDGET ARE WE WORKING WITH, MRS. REDFERN?
WELL, THAT WOULD BE UP TO YOU, JEREMY. IT'S YOUR LUNCH.
OH, RIGHT, RIGHT... WELL, LET'S SEE... THE CHEF'S SPECIAL WAS WHAT AGAIN?
STEAK BÉARNAISE.
G.B. Trudeau
YOU KNOW WHAT, JACQUES? I THINK I'LL JUST HAVE THE WATER, THE ROLLS AND THE MINTS.
THE USUAL. VERY GOOD, MONSIEUR.

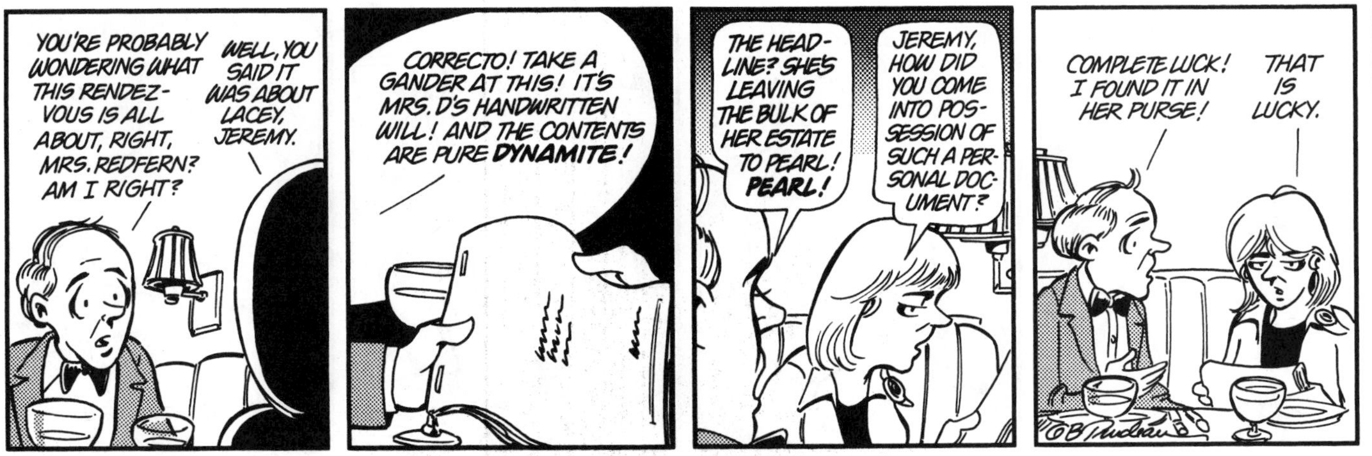
YOU'RE PROBABLY WONDERING WHAT THIS RENDEZVOUS IS ALL ABOUT, RIGHT, MRS. REDFERN? AM I RIGHT?
WELL, YOU SAID IT WAS ABOUT LACEY, JEREMY.
CORRECTO! TAKE A GANDER AT THIS! IT'S MRS. D'S HANDWRITTEN WILL! AND THE CONTENTS ARE PURE DYNAMITE!
THE HEADLINE? SHE'S LEAVING THE BULK OF HER ESTATE TO PEARL! PEARL!
JEREMY, HOW DID YOU COME INTO POSSESSION OF SUCH A PERSONAL DOCUMENT?
COMPLETE LUCK! I FOUND IT IN HER PURSE!
THAT IS LUCKY.
G.B. Trudeau

SEE? LACEY'S LEAVING THE BULK OF HER ESTATE TO **PEARL**! DOESN'T THAT RAISE SERIOUS COMPETENCY QUESTIONS?
WHO'S PEARL AGAIN?
PEARL IS HER DECEASED SISTER. LACEY THINKS ALICE IS PEARL.
WHO'S ALICE?
ALICE IS THE HOMELESS WOMAN WHO'S BEEN SUCKING UP TO LACEY FOR MONTHS!
AND WHO'S THIS "HOUSE BOY" SHE'S LEAVING $10,000 TO?
UH... ME. THAT PART'S LEGIT.
GEE, JEREMY, I DUNNO. THE HOUSE BOY COULD BE DEAD, TOO.

SO WHAT EXACTLY IS THE PROBLEM WITH THIS WILL, JEREMY?
WHAT'S THE **PROBLEM?** LACEY IS BEQUEATHING TO SOME WOMAN SHE MET IN THE PARK MOST OF HER **ESTATE**!
FOR GOOD CAUSE, IT SEEMS.
"I DO SO IN GRATITUDE FOR THE PATIENCE, TENDERNESS AND COUNTLESS SMALL KINDNESSES MY SISTER HAS SHOWN ME IN MY DARKEST DAYS."
BUT SHE'S **NOT** HER SISTER!
NO, BUT ISN'T THAT WHAT YOU'D WANT IN ONE?

WELL, I'LL TELL YOU, JEREMY, I'M SURE YOU COULD FIND A LAWYER WHO WOULD ARGUE THAT LACEY WASN'T COMPETENT WHEN SHE DREW UP THIS WILL...
BUT I'M NOT THAT LAWYER. TO ME, IT'S NOT IRRATIONAL TO WILL YOUR WORLDLY GOODS TO SOMEONE WHO WAS KIND TO YOU.
I'D LEAVE IT ALONE, JEREMY, I'D... HELLO? JEREMY?
OH, SORRY. I ALWAYS KEEP ONE EYE ON THE DOOR FOR JEALOUS HUSBANDS.
A WISE PRECAUTION, I'M SURE.

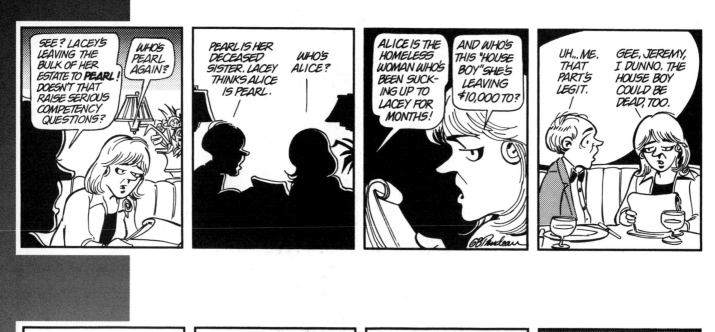

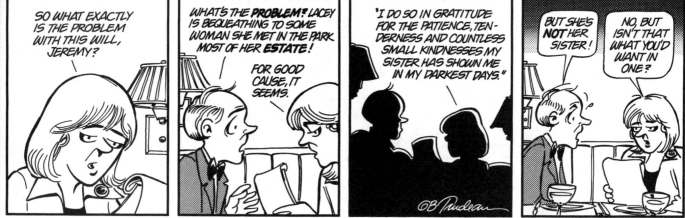

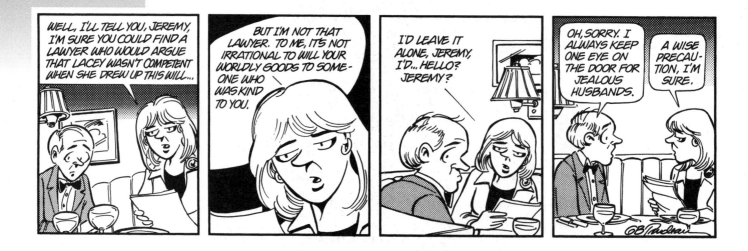

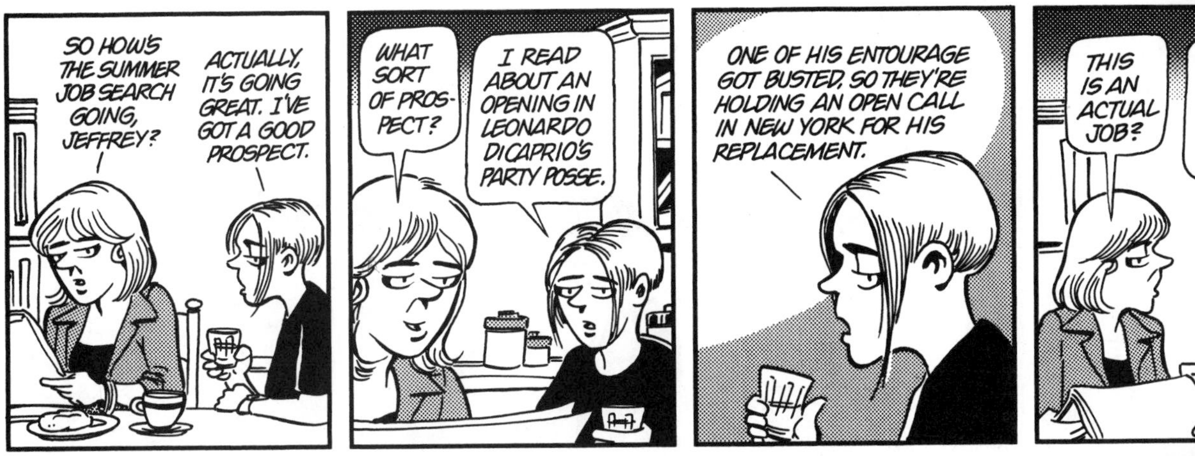
SO HOW'S THE SUMMER JOB SEARCH GOING, JEFFREY?
ACTUALLY, IT'S GOING GREAT. I'VE GOT A GOOD PROSPECT.
WHAT SORT OF PROS-PECT?
I READ ABOUT AN OPENING IN LEONARDO DICAPRIO'S PARTY POSSE.
ONE OF HIS ENTOURAGE GOT BUSTED, SO THEY'RE HOLDING AN OPEN CALL IN NEW YORK FOR HIS REPLACEMENT.
THIS IS AN ACTUAL JOB?
HANGING WITH LEO 24-7? MOM, IT'S PRACTICALLY A CAREER!
GB Trudeau

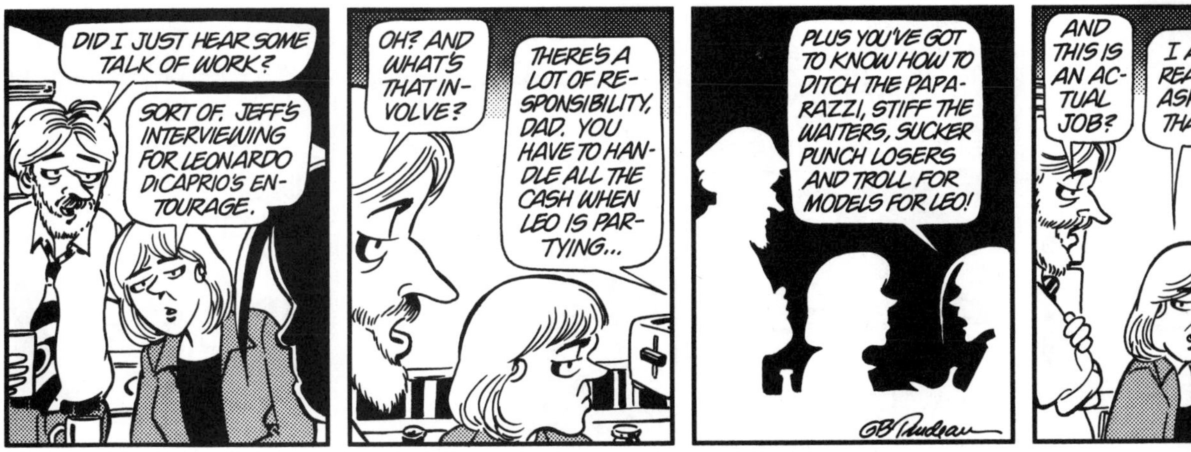
DID I JUST HEAR SOME TALK OF WORK?
SORT OF. JEFF'S INTERVIEWING FOR LEONARDO DiCAPRIO'S EN-TOURAGE.
OH? AND WHAT'S THAT IN-VOLVE?
THERE'S A LOT OF RE-SPONSIBILITY, DAD. YOU HAVE TO HAN-DLE ALL THE CASH WHEN LEO IS PAR-TYING...
PLUS YOU'VE GOT TO KNOW HOW TO DITCH THE PAPA-RAZZI, STIFF THE WAITERS, SUCKER PUNCH LOSERS AND TROLL FOR MODELS FOR LEO!
GB Trudeau
AND THIS IS AN AC-TUAL JOB?
I AL-READY ASKED THAT.
HELL, YES! I MEAN, NOT WITH FULL MED-ICAL OR ANYTHING.

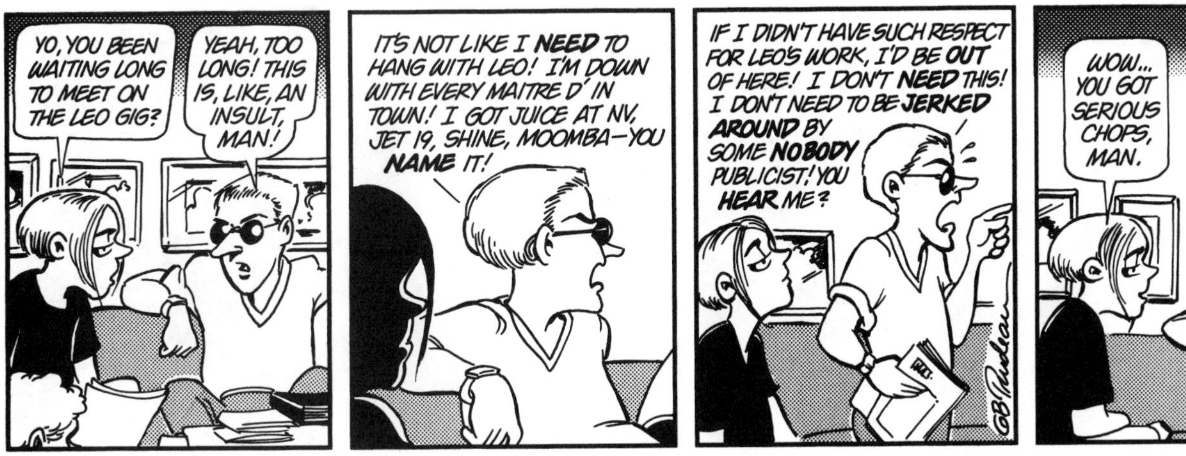
YO, YOU BEEN WAITING LONG TO MEET ON THE LEO GIG?
YEAH, TOO LONG! THIS IS, LIKE, AN INSULT, MAN!
IT'S NOT LIKE I NEED TO HANG WITH LEO! I'M DOWN WITH EVERY MAITRE D' IN TOWN! I GOT JUICE AT NV, JET 19, SHINE, MOOMBA—YOU NAME IT!
IF I DIDN'T HAVE SUCH RESPECT FOR LEO'S WORK, I'D BE OUT OF HERE! I DON'T NEED THIS! I DON'T NEED TO BE JERKED AROUND BY SOME NOBODY PUBLICIST! YOU HEAR ME?
GB Trudeau
WOW... YOU GOT SERIOUS CHOPS, MAN.
THANKS. I DID TWO YEARS WITH MACAULAY CULKIN.

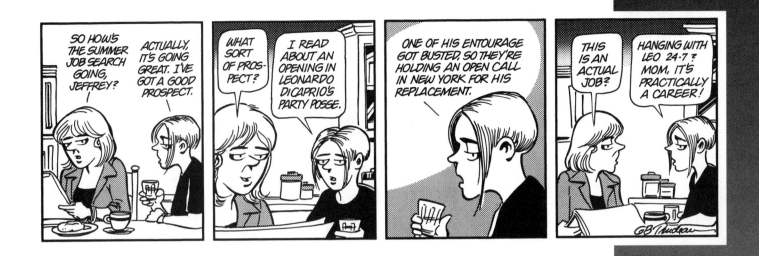

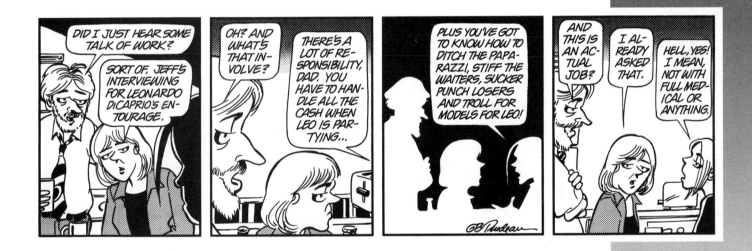

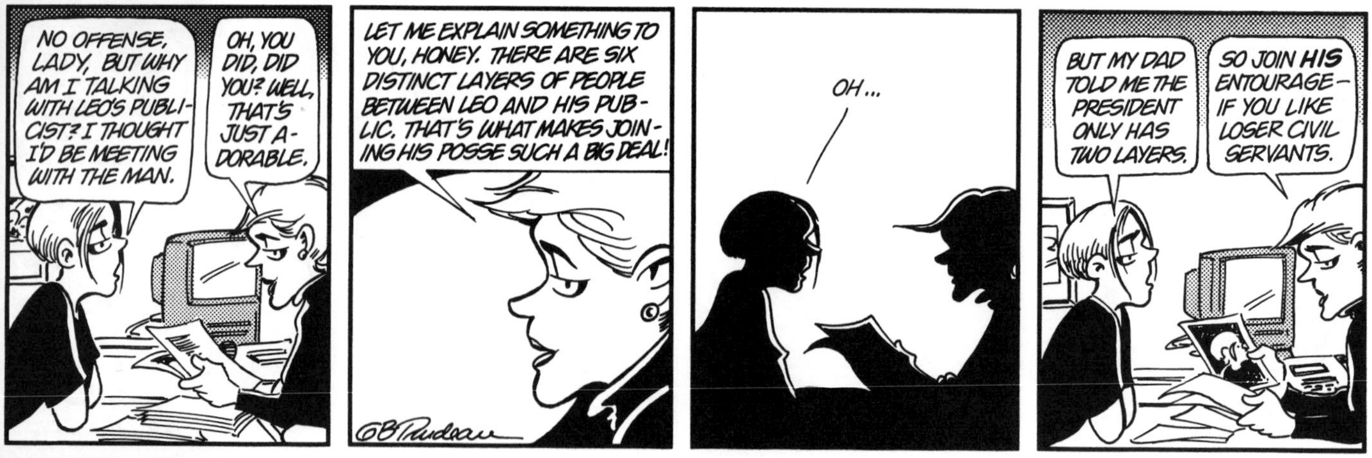
NO OFFENSE, LADY, BUT WHY AM I TALKING WITH LEO'S PUBLICIST? I THOUGHT I'D BE MEETING WITH THE MAN.
OH, YOU DID, DID YOU? WELL, THAT'S JUST ADORABLE.
LET ME EXPLAIN SOMETHING TO YOU, HONEY. THERE ARE SIX DISTINCT LAYERS OF PEOPLE BETWEEN LEO AND HIS PUBLIC. THAT'S WHAT MAKES JOINING HIS POSSE SUCH A BIG DEAL!
OH...
BUT MY DAD TOLD ME THE PRESIDENT ONLY HAS TWO LAYERS.
SO JOIN **HIS** ENTOURAGE— IF YOU LIKE LOSER CIVIL SERVANTS.

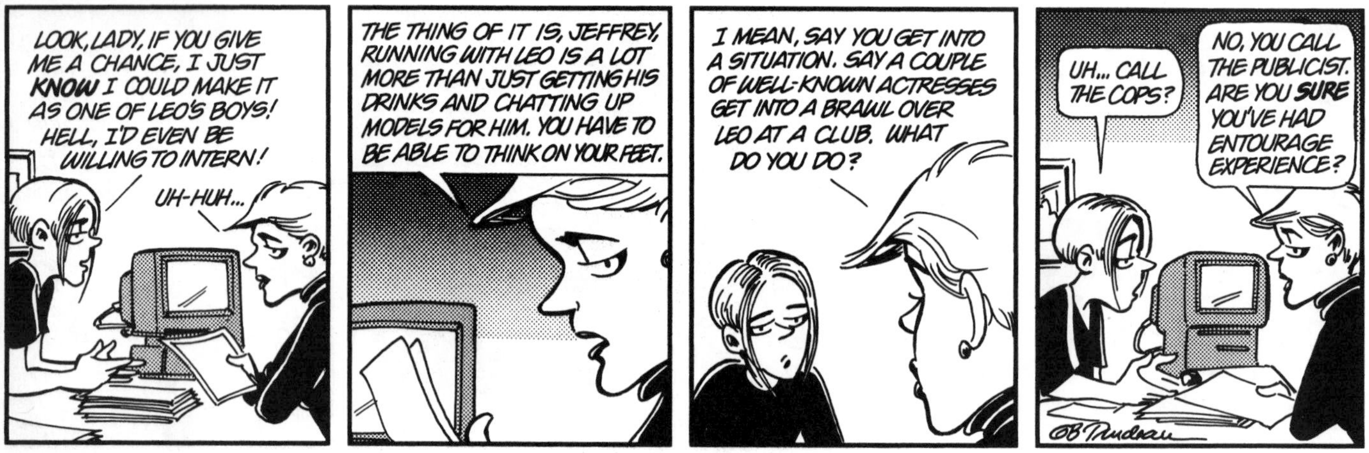
LOOK, LADY, IF YOU GIVE ME A CHANCE, I JUST **KNOW** I COULD MAKE IT AS ONE OF LEO'S BOYS! HELL, I'D EVEN BE WILLING TO INTERN!
UH-HUH...
THE THING OF IT IS, JEFFREY, RUNNING WITH LEO IS A LOT MORE THAN JUST GETTING HIS DRINKS AND CHATTING UP MODELS FOR HIM. YOU HAVE TO BE ABLE TO THINK ON YOUR FEET.
I MEAN, SAY YOU GET INTO A SITUATION. SAY A COUPLE OF WELL-KNOWN ACTRESSES GET INTO A BRAWL OVER LEO AT A CLUB. WHAT DO YOU DO?
UH... CALL THE COPS?
NO, YOU CALL THE PUBLICIST. ARE YOU **SURE** YOU'VE HAD ENTOURAGE EXPERIENCE?

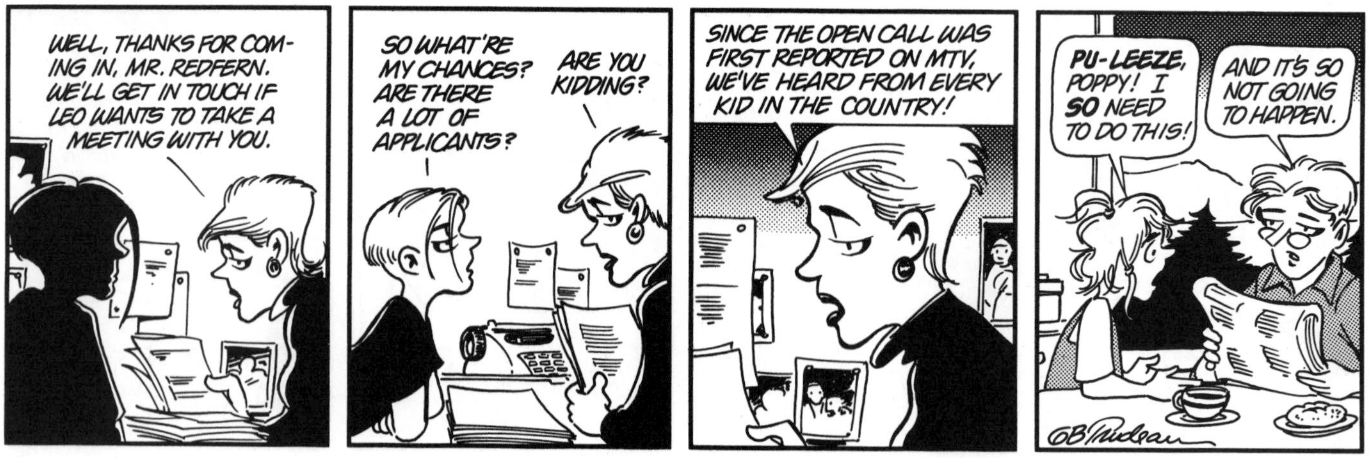
WELL, THANKS FOR COMING IN, MR. REDFERN. WE'LL GET IN TOUCH IF LEO WANTS TO TAKE A MEETING WITH YOU.
SO WHAT'RE MY CHANCES? ARE THERE A LOT OF APPLICANTS?
ARE YOU KIDDING?
SINCE THE OPEN CALL WAS FIRST REPORTED ON MTV, WE'VE HEARD FROM EVERY KID IN THE COUNTRY!
PU-LEEZE, POPPY! I **SO** NEED TO DO THIS!
AND IT'S SO NOT GOING TO HAPPEN.

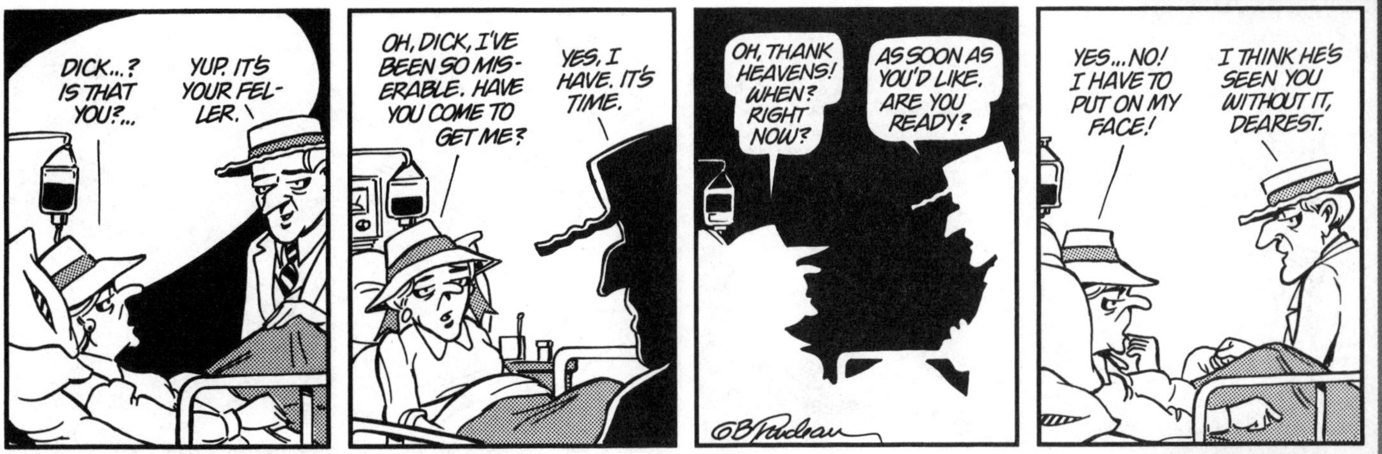
DICK...? IS THAT YOU?...
YUP. IT'S YOUR FEL-LER.
OH, DICK, I'VE BEEN SO MIS-ERABLE. HAVE YOU COME TO GET ME?
YES, I HAVE. IT'S TIME.
OH, THANK HEAVENS! WHEN? RIGHT NOW?
AS SOON AS YOU'D LIKE. ARE YOU READY?
YES... NO! I HAVE TO PUT ON MY FACE!
I THINK HE'S SEEN YOU WITHOUT IT, DEAREST.
©B Trudeau

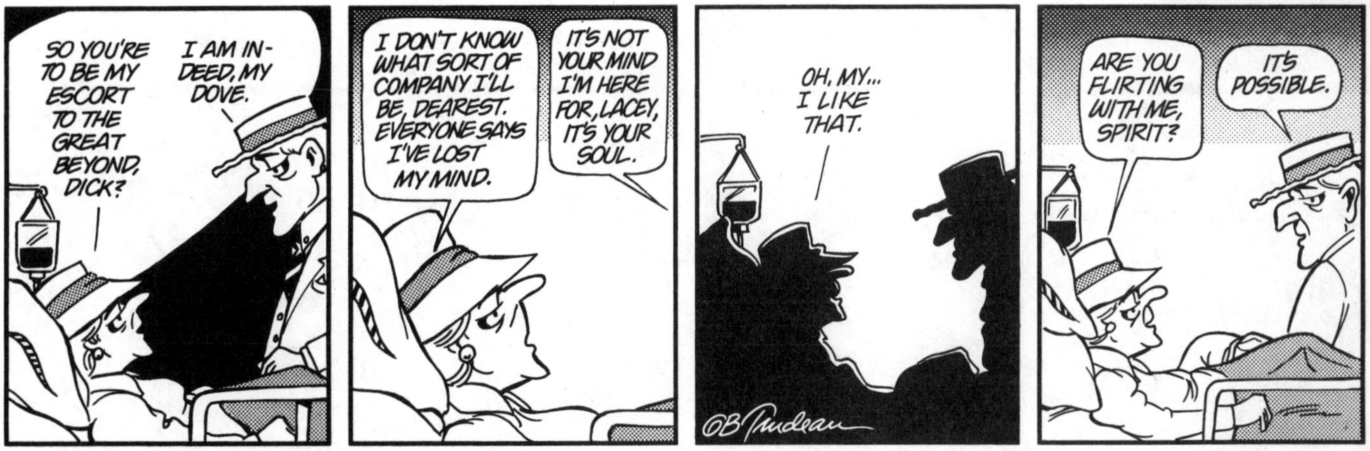
SO YOU'RE TO BE MY ESCORT TO THE GREAT BEYOND, DICK?
I AM IN-DEED, MY DOVE.
I DON'T KNOW WHAT SORT OF COMPANY I'LL BE, DEAREST. EVERYONE SAYS I'VE LOST MY MIND.
IT'S NOT YOUR MIND I'M HERE FOR, LACEY, IT'S YOUR SOUL.
OH, MY... I LIKE THAT.
©B Trudeau
ARE YOU FLIRTING WITH ME, SPIRIT?
IT'S POSSIBLE.

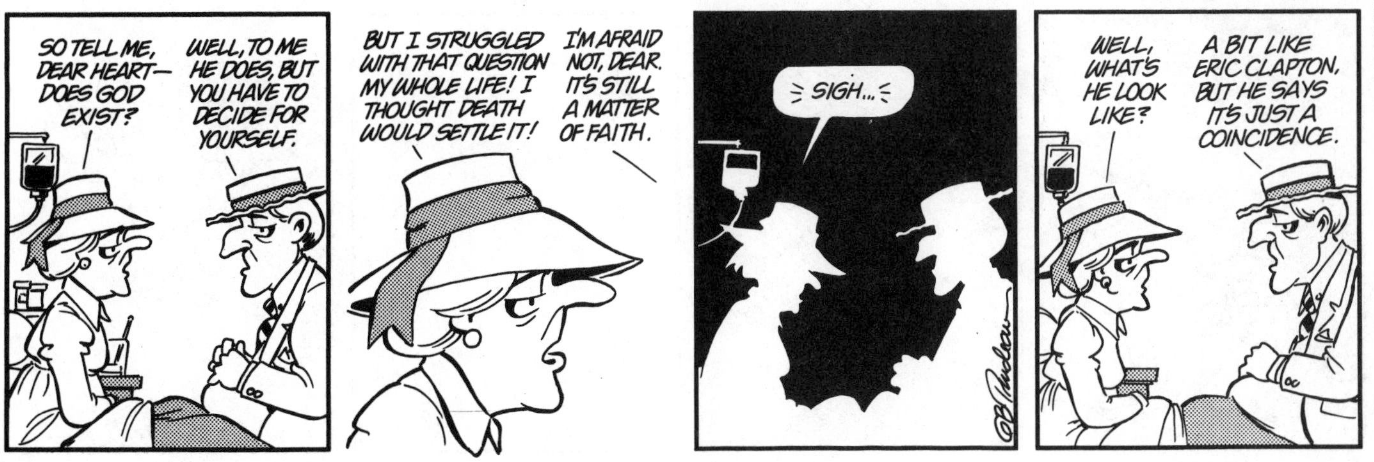
SO TELL ME, DEAR HEART— DOES GOD EXIST?
WELL, TO ME HE DOES, BUT YOU HAVE TO DECIDE FOR YOURSELF.
BUT I STRUGGLED WITH THAT QUESTION MY WHOLE LIFE! I THOUGHT DEATH WOULD SETTLE IT!
I'M AFRAID NOT, DEAR. IT'S STILL A MATTER OF FAITH.
SIGH...
©B Trudeau
WELL, WHAT'S HE LOOK LIKE?
A BIT LIKE ERIC CLAPTON, BUT HE SAYS IT'S JUST A COINCIDENCE.

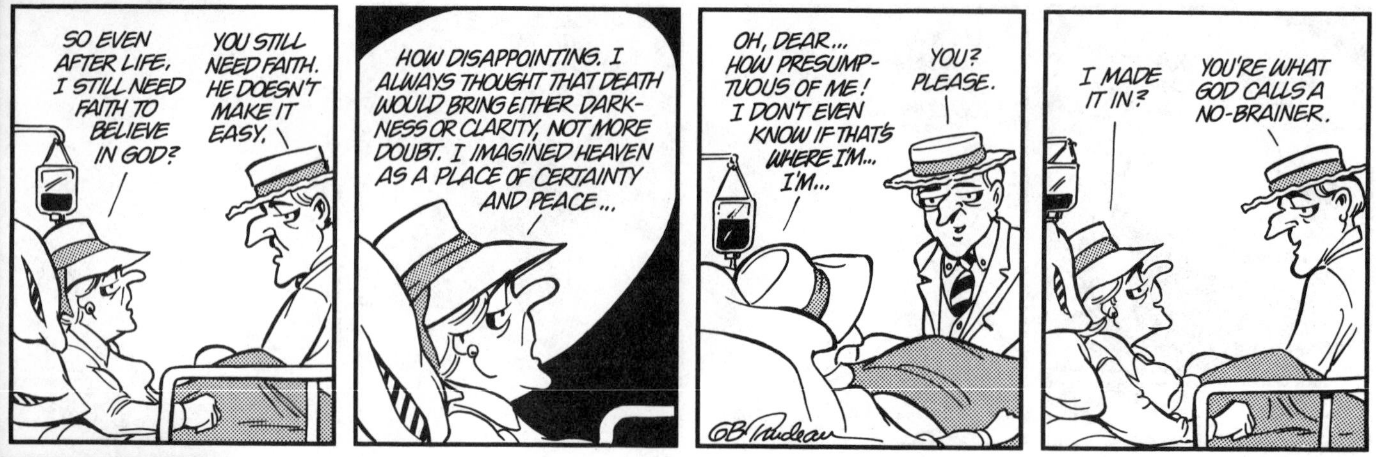
SO EVEN AFTER LIFE, I STILL NEED FAITH TO BELIEVE IN GOD?
YOU STILL NEED FAITH. HE DOESN'T MAKE IT EASY.
HOW DISAPPOINTING. I ALWAYS THOUGHT THAT DEATH WOULD BRING EITHER DARKNESS OR CLARITY, NOT MORE DOUBT. I IMAGINED HEAVEN AS A PLACE OF CERTAINTY AND PEACE...
OH, DEAR... HOW PRESUMPTUOUS OF ME! I DON'T EVEN KNOW IF THAT'S WHERE I'M... I'M...
YOU? PLEASE.
I MADE IT IN?
YOU'RE WHAT GOD CALLS A NO-BRAINER.
©B Trudeau

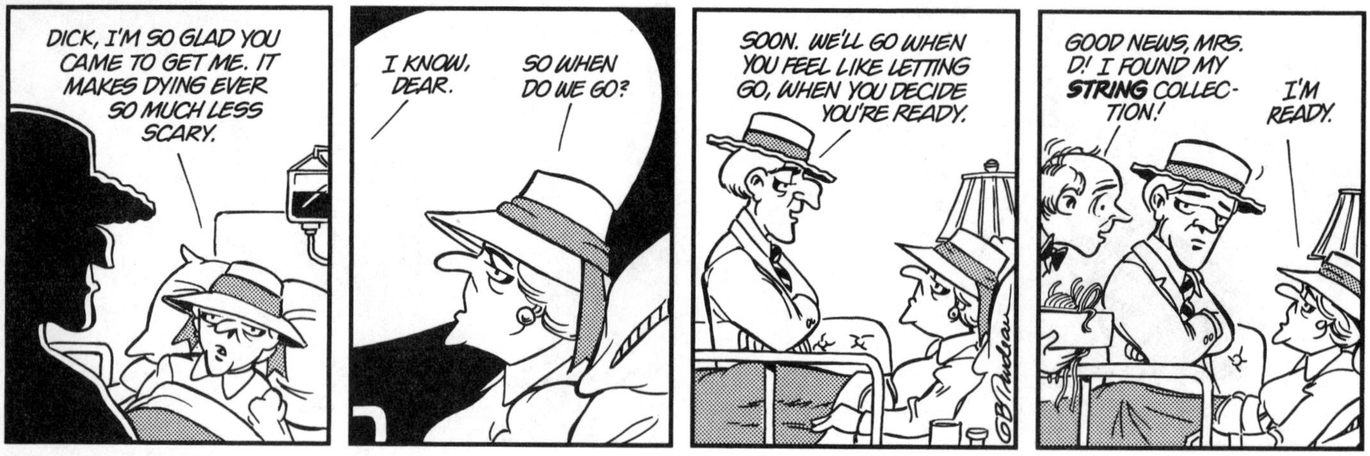
DICK, I'M SO GLAD YOU CAME TO GET ME. IT MAKES DYING EVER SO MUCH LESS SCARY.
I KNOW, DEAR.
SO WHEN DO WE GO?
SOON. WE'LL GO WHEN YOU FEEL LIKE LETTING GO, WHEN YOU DECIDE YOU'RE READY.
GOOD NEWS, MRS. D! I FOUND MY STRING COLLECTION!
I'M READY.
©B Trudeau

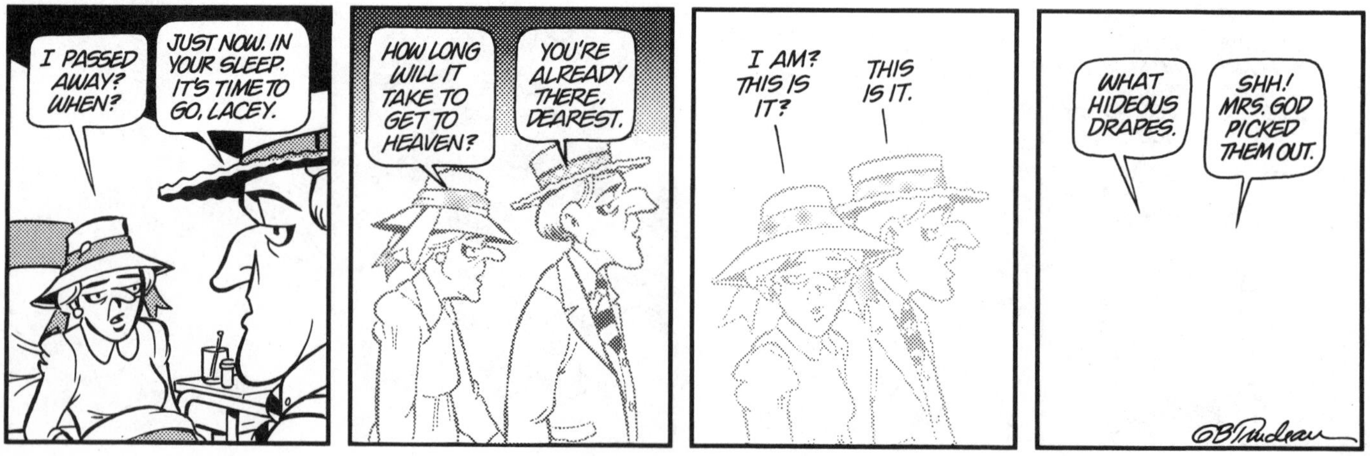
I PASSED AWAY? WHEN?
JUST NOW. IN YOUR SLEEP. IT'S TIME TO GO, LACEY.
HOW LONG WILL IT TAKE TO GET TO HEAVEN?
YOU'RE ALREADY THERE, DEAREST.
I AM? THIS IS IT?
THIS IS IT.
WHAT HIDEOUS DRAPES.
SHH! MRS. GOD PICKED THEM OUT.
©B Trudeau

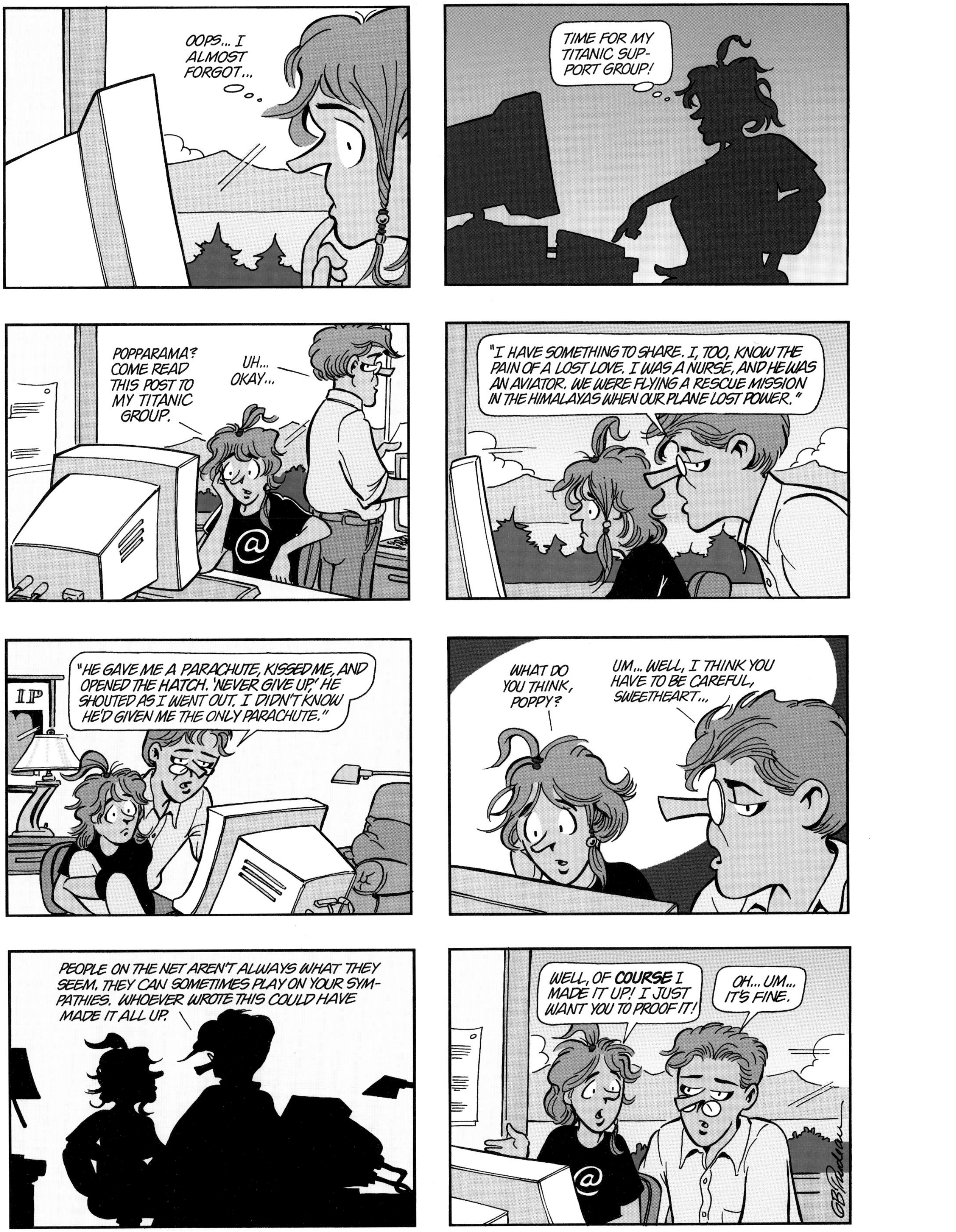
OOPS... I ALMOST FORGOT...
TIME FOR MY TITANIC SUP-PORT GROUP!
POPPARAMA? COME READ THIS POST TO MY TITANIC GROUP.
UH... OKAY...
"I HAVE SOMETHING TO SHARE. I, TOO, KNOW THE PAIN OF A LOST LOVE. I WAS A NURSE, AND HE WAS AN AVIATOR. WE WERE FLYING A RESCUE MISSION IN THE HIMALAYAS WHEN OUR PLANE LOST POWER."
"HE GAVE ME A PARACHUTE, KISSED ME, AND OPENED THE HATCH. 'NEVER GIVE UP,' HE SHOUTED AS I WENT OUT. I DIDN'T KNOW HE'D GIVEN ME THE ONLY PARACHUTE."
IP
WHAT DO YOU THINK, POPPY?
UM... WELL, I THINK YOU HAVE TO BE CAREFUL, SWEETHEART...
PEOPLE ON THE NET AREN'T ALWAYS WHAT THEY SEEM. THEY CAN SOMETIMES PLAY ON YOUR SYM-PATHIES. WHOEVER WROTE THIS COULD HAVE MADE IT ALL UP.
WELL, OF COURSE I MADE IT UP! I JUST WANT YOU TO PROOF IT!
OH... UM... IT'S FINE.

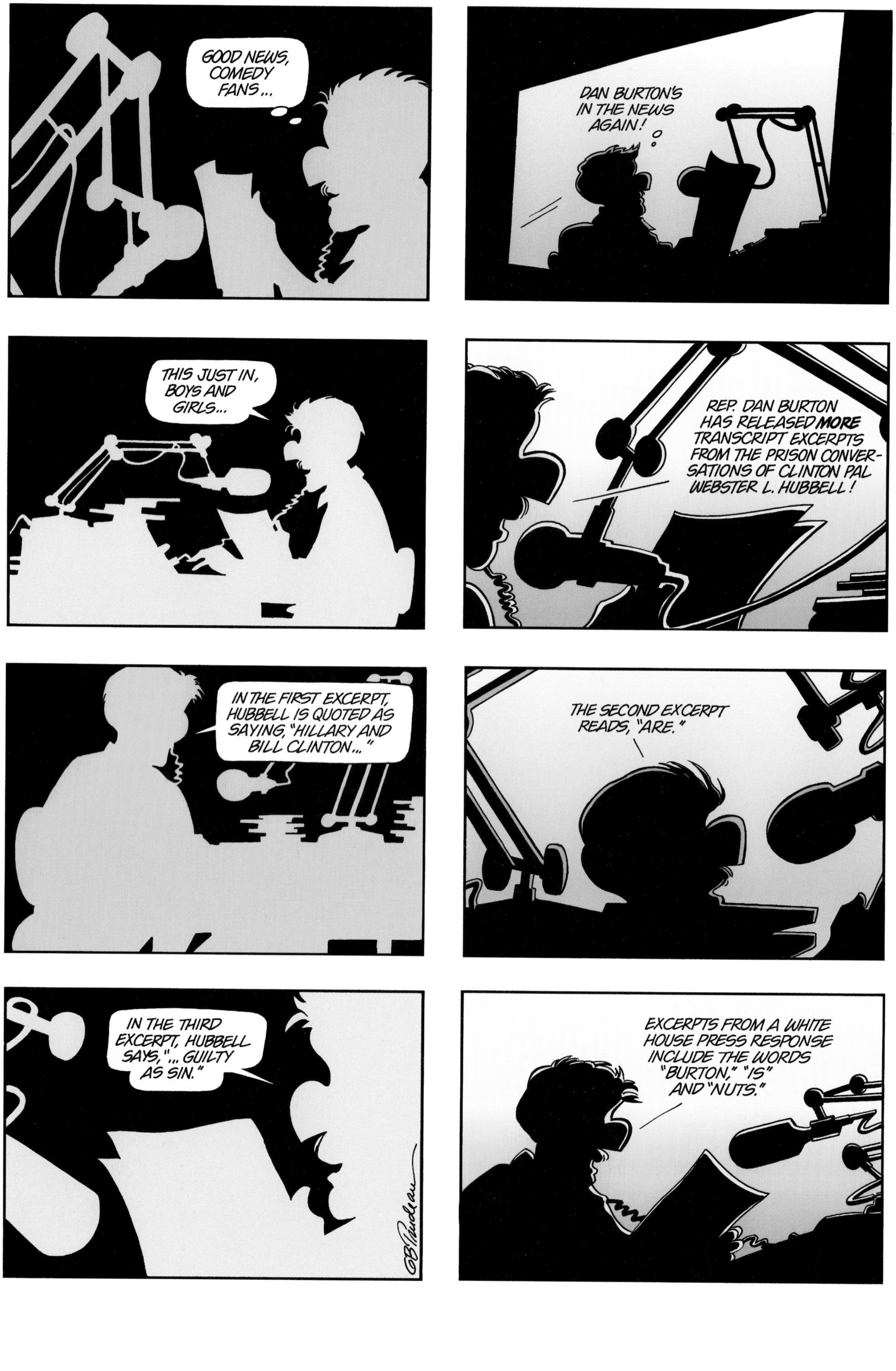
GOOD NEWS, COMEDY FANS...
DAN BURTON'S IN THE NEWS AGAIN!
THIS JUST IN, BOYS AND GIRLS...
REP. DAN BURTON HAS RELEASED **MORE** TRANSCRIPT EXCERPTS FROM THE PRISON CONVERSATIONS OF CLINTON PAL WEBSTER L. HUBBELL!
IN THE FIRST EXCERPT, HUBBELL IS QUOTED AS SAYING, "HILLARY AND BILL CLINTON..."
THE SECOND EXCERPT READS, "ARE."
IN THE THIRD EXCERPT, HUBBELL SAYS, "... GUILTY AS SIN."
EXCERPTS FROM A WHITE HOUSE PRESS RESPONSE INCLUDE THE WORDS "BURTON," "IS" AND "NUTS."

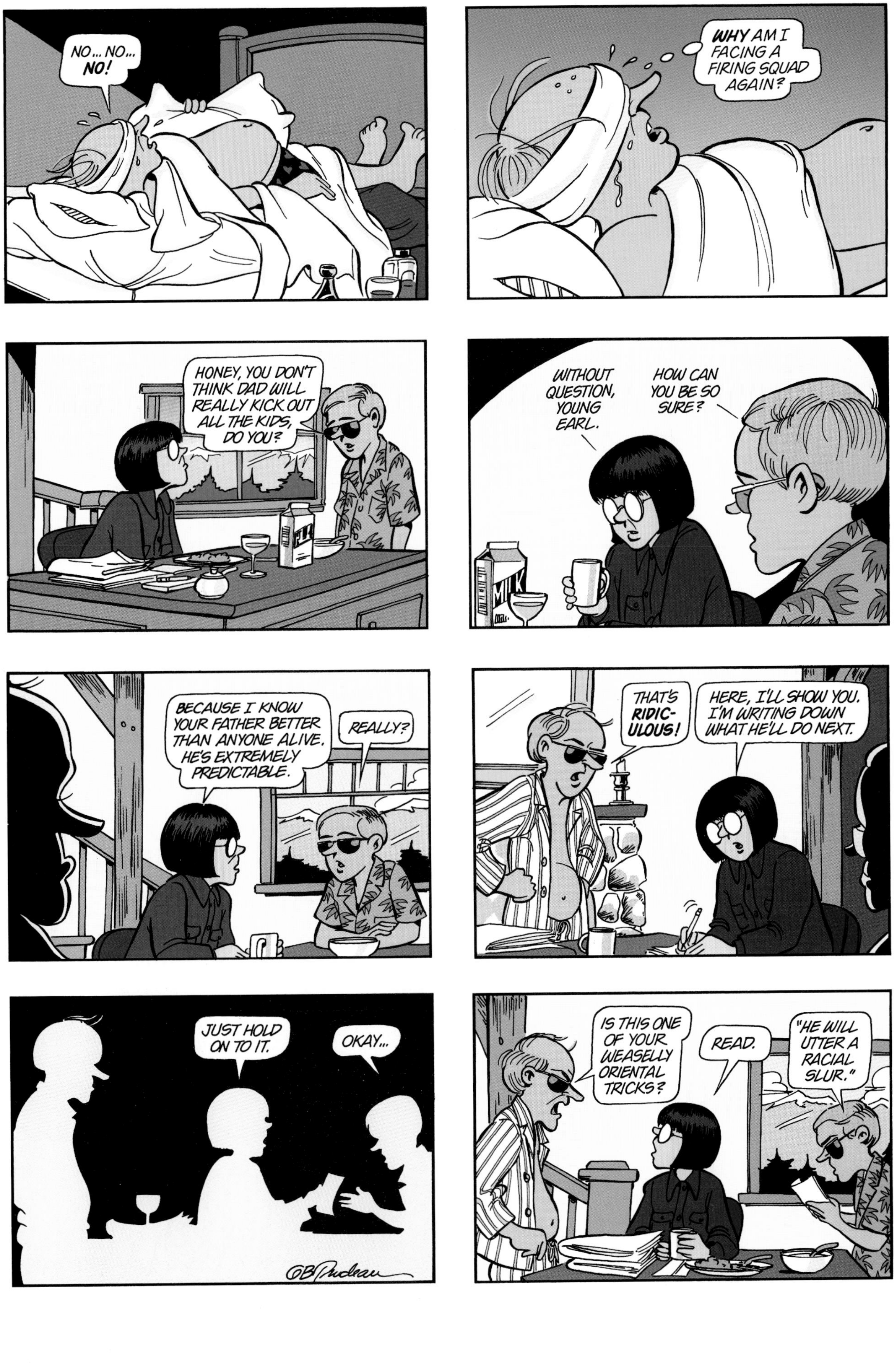
NO... NO... NO!
WHY AM I FACING A FIRING SQUAD AGAIN?
HONEY, YOU DON'T THINK DAD WILL REALLY KICK OUT ALL THE KIDS, DO YOU?
WITHOUT QUESTION, YOUNG EARL.
HOW CAN YOU BE SO SURE?
BECAUSE I KNOW YOUR FATHER BETTER THAN ANYONE ALIVE. HE'S EXTREMELY PREDICTABLE.
REALLY?
THAT'S RIDICULOUS!
HERE, I'LL SHOW YOU. I'M WRITING DOWN WHAT HE'LL DO NEXT.
JUST HOLD ON TO IT.
OKAY...
IS THIS ONE OF YOUR WEASELLY ORIENTAL TRICKS?
READ.
"HE WILL UTTER A RACIAL SLUR."

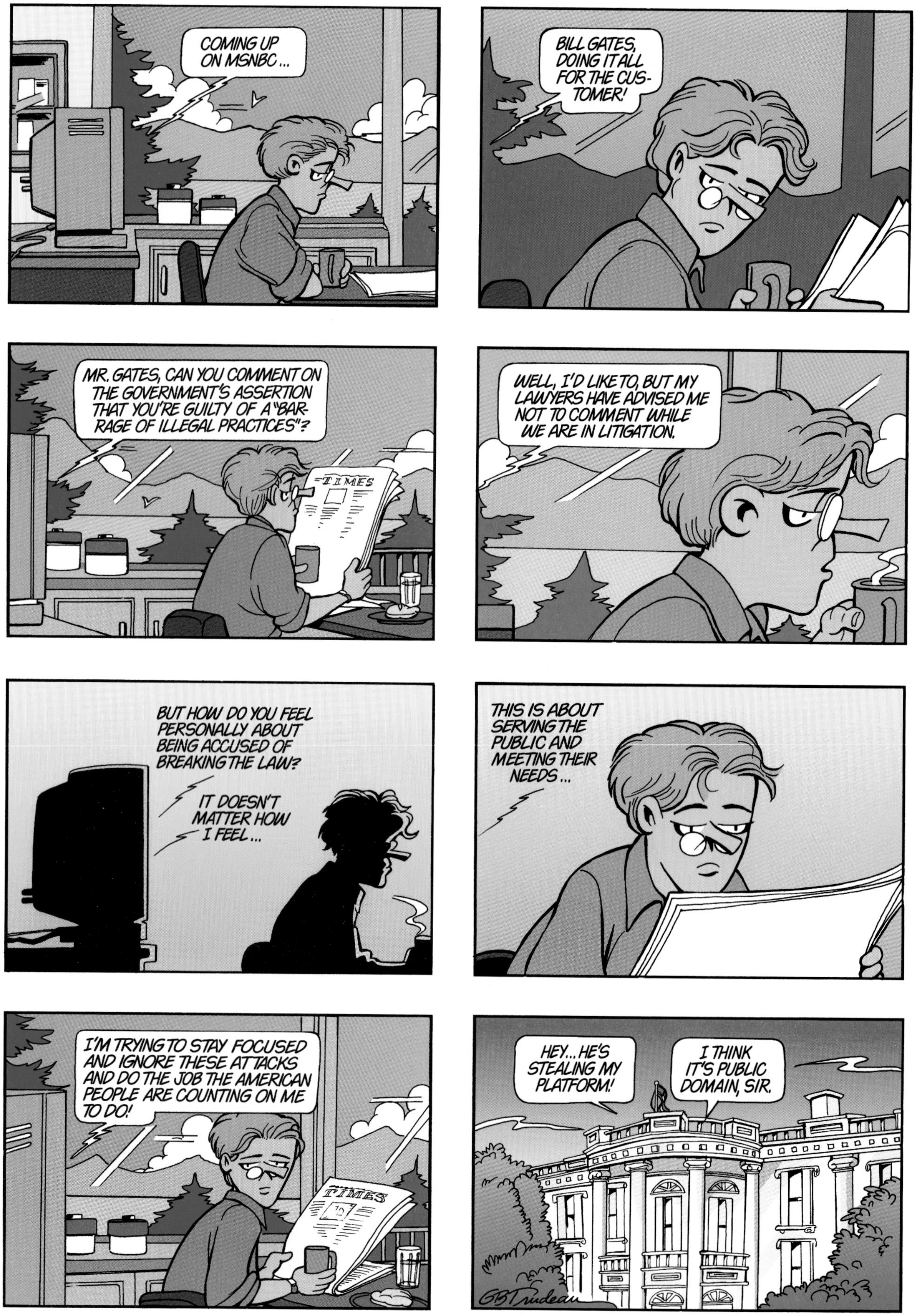
COMING UP ON MSNBC...
BILL GATES, DOING IT ALL FOR THE CUSTOMER!
MR. GATES, CAN YOU COMMENT ON THE GOVERNMENT'S ASSERTION THAT YOU'RE GUILTY OF A "BARRAGE OF ILLEGAL PRACTICES"?
WELL, I'D LIKE TO, BUT MY LAWYERS HAVE ADVISED ME NOT TO COMMENT WHILE WE ARE IN LITIGATION.
BUT HOW DO YOU FEEL PERSONALLY ABOUT BEING ACCUSED OF BREAKING THE LAW?
IT DOESN'T MATTER HOW I FEEL...
THIS IS ABOUT SERVING THE PUBLIC AND MEETING THEIR NEEDS...
I'M TRYING TO STAY FOCUSED AND IGNORE THESE ATTACKS AND DO THE JOB THE AMERICAN PEOPLE ARE COUNTING ON ME TO DO!
HEY... HE'S STEALING MY PLATFORM!
I THINK IT'S PUBLIC DOMAIN, SIR.
GBTrudeau

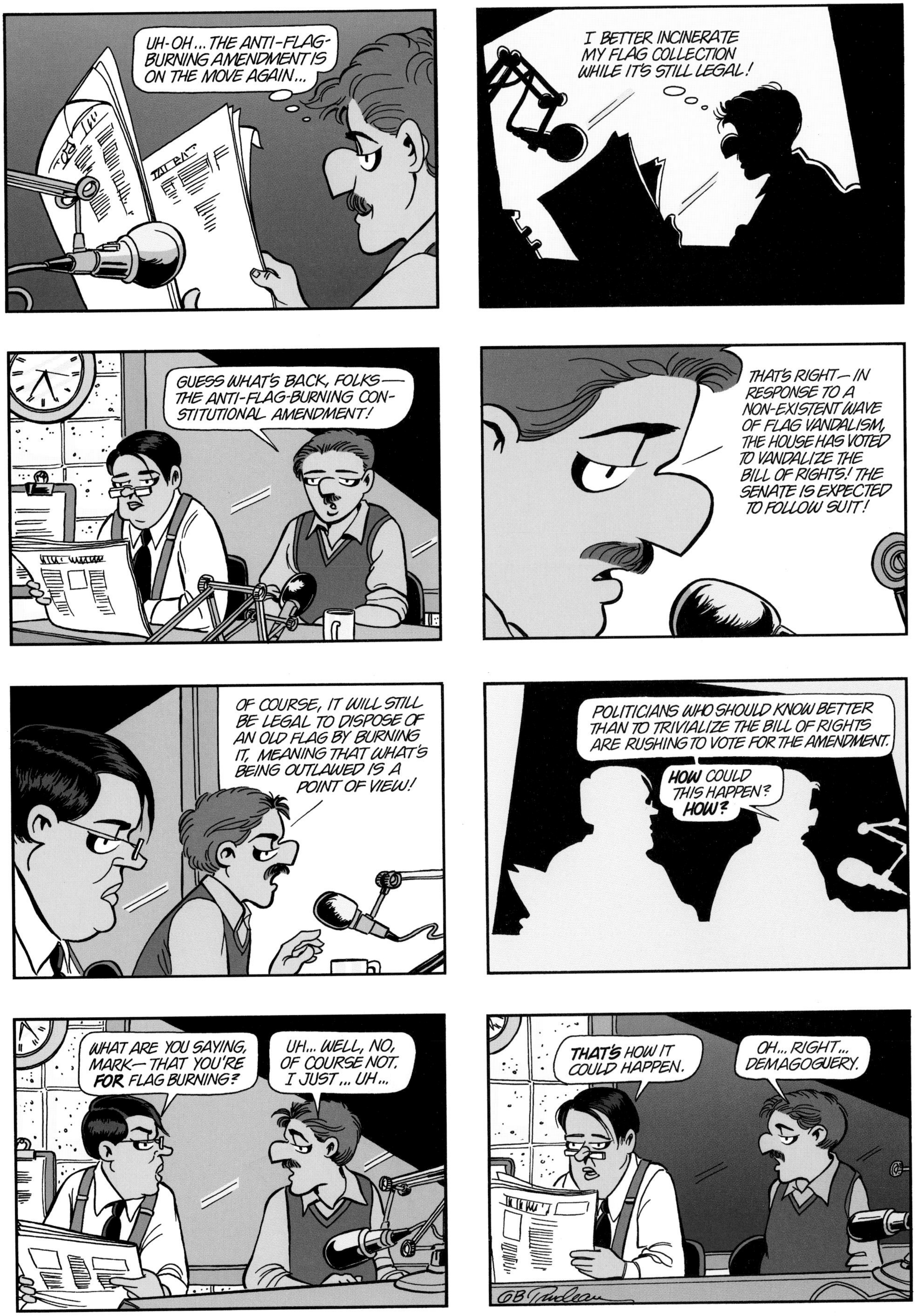
UH-OH... THE ANTI-FLAG-BURNING AMENDMENT IS ON THE MOVE AGAIN...
I BETTER INCINERATE MY FLAG COLLECTION WHILE IT'S STILL LEGAL!
GUESS WHAT'S BACK, FOLKS— THE ANTI-FLAG-BURNING CONSTITUTIONAL AMENDMENT!
THAT'S RIGHT— IN RESPONSE TO A NON-EXISTENT WAVE OF FLAG VANDALISM, THE HOUSE HAS VOTED TO VANDALIZE THE BILL OF RIGHTS! THE SENATE IS EXPECTED TO FOLLOW SUIT!
OF COURSE, IT WILL STILL BE LEGAL TO DISPOSE OF AN OLD FLAG BY BURNING IT, MEANING THAT WHAT'S BEING OUTLAWED IS A POINT OF VIEW!
POLITICIANS WHO SHOULD KNOW BETTER THAN TO TRIVIALIZE THE BILL OF RIGHTS ARE RUSHING TO VOTE FOR THE AMENDMENT.
HOW COULD THIS HAPPEN? HOW?
WHAT ARE YOU SAYING, MARK— THAT YOU'RE FOR FLAG BURNING?
UH... WELL, NO, OF COURSE NOT. I JUST... UH...
THAT'S HOW IT COULD HAPPEN.
OH... RIGHT... DEMAGOGUERY.

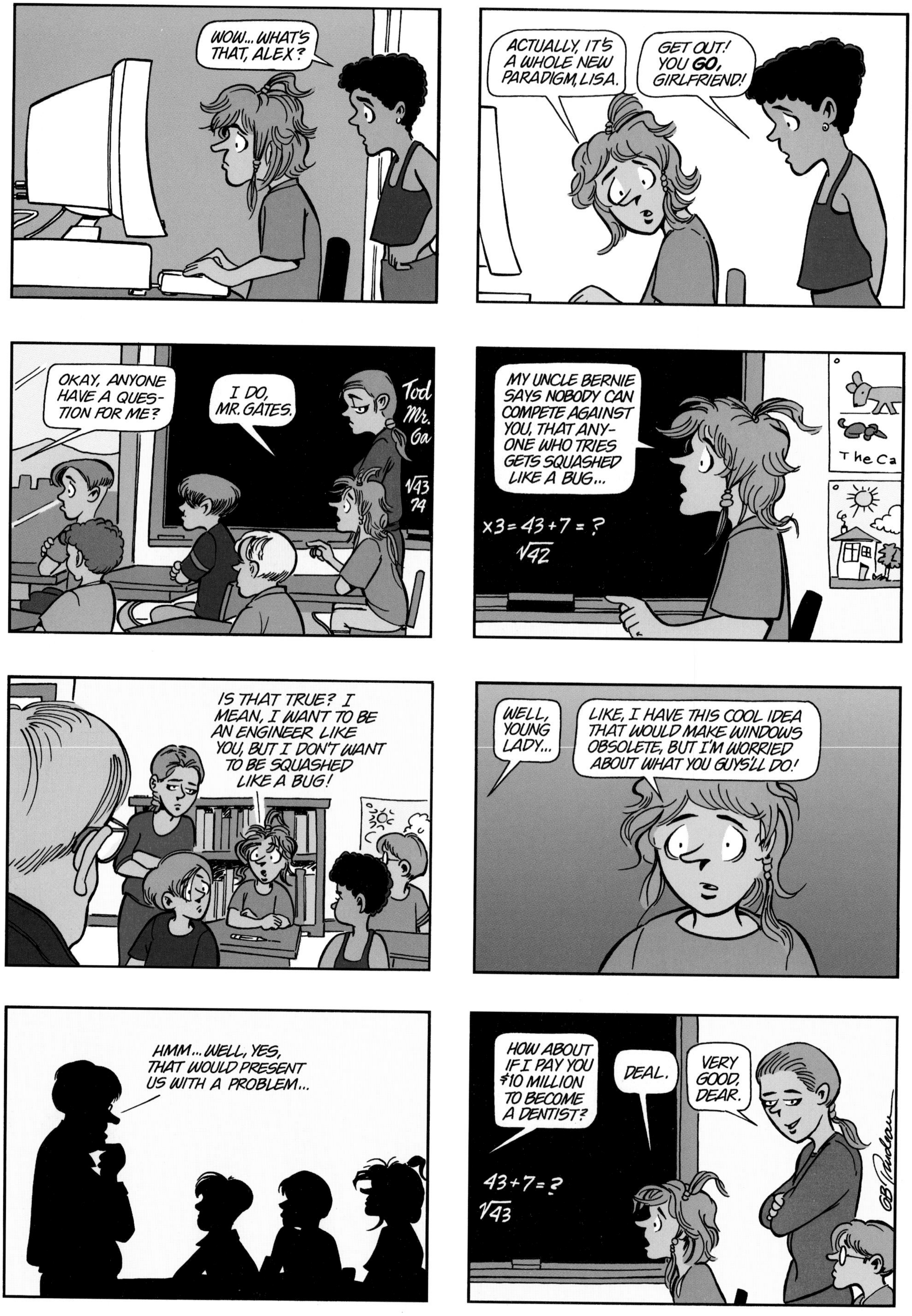
WOW... WHAT'S THAT, ALEX?
ACTUALLY, IT'S A WHOLE NEW PARADIGM, LISA.
GET OUT! YOU **GO,** GIRLFRIEND!
OKAY, ANYONE HAVE A QUES-TION FOR ME?
I DO, MR. GATES.
MY UNCLE BERNIE SAYS NOBODY CAN COMPETE AGAINST YOU, THAT ANY-ONE WHO TRIES GETS SQUASHED LIKE A BUG...
IS THAT TRUE? I MEAN, I WANT TO BE AN ENGINEER LIKE YOU, BUT I DON'T WANT TO BE SQUASHED LIKE A BUG!
WELL, YOUNG LADY...
LIKE, I HAVE THIS COOL IDEA THAT WOULD MAKE WINDOWS OBSOLETE, BUT I'M WORRIED ABOUT WHAT YOU GUYS'LL DO!
HMM... WELL, YES, THAT WOULD PRESENT US WITH A PROBLEM...
HOW ABOUT IF I PAY YOU $10 MILLION TO BECOME A DENTIST?
DEAL.
VERY GOOD, DEAR.

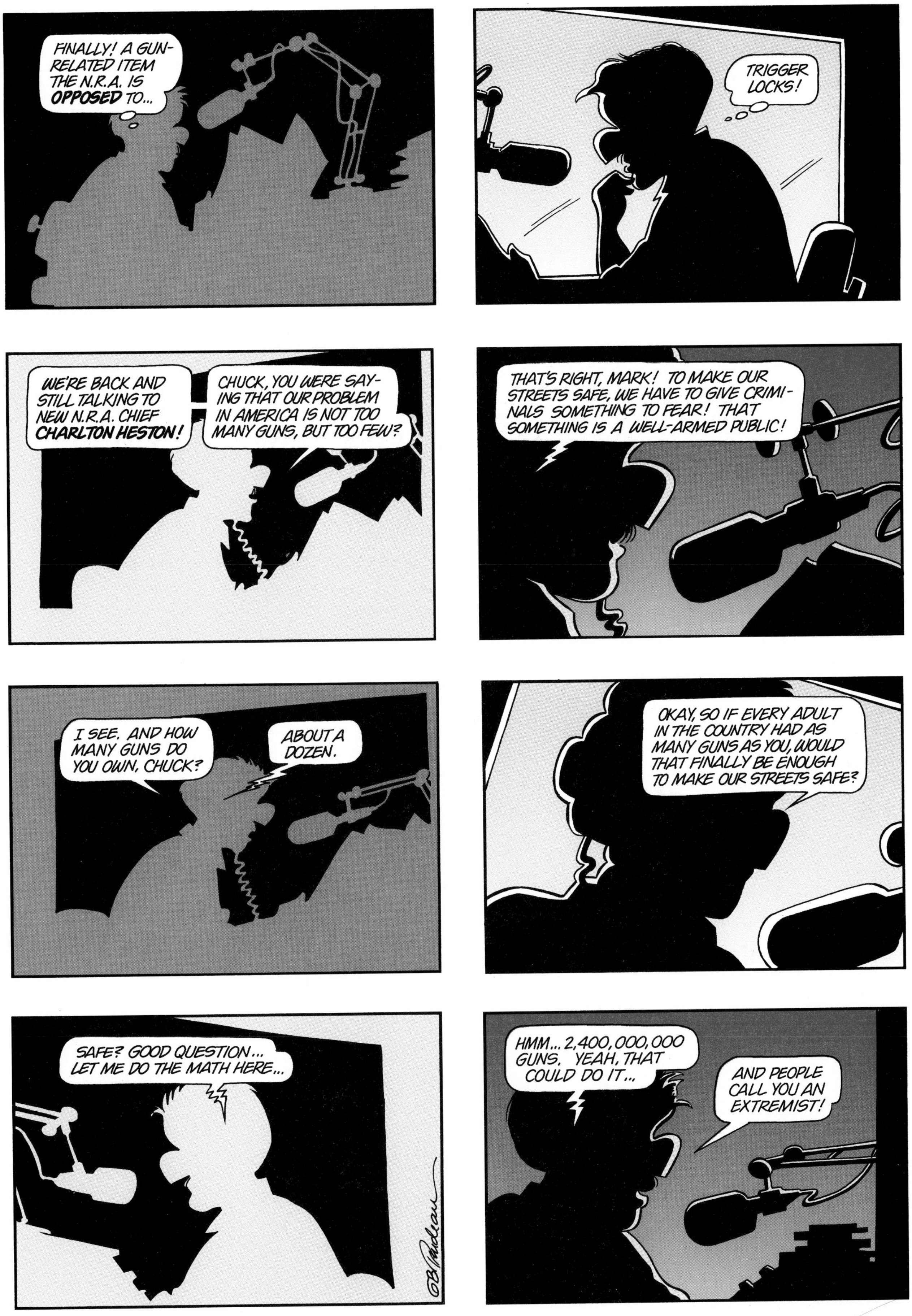
FINALLY! A GUN-RELATED ITEM THE N.R.A. IS OPPOSED TO...
TRIGGER LOCKS!
WE'RE BACK AND STILL TALKING TO NEW N.R.A. CHIEF CHARLTON HESTON!
CHUCK, YOU WERE SAYING THAT OUR PROBLEM IN AMERICA IS NOT TOO MANY GUNS, BUT TOO FEW?
THAT'S RIGHT, MARK! TO MAKE OUR STREETS SAFE, WE HAVE TO GIVE CRIMINALS SOMETHING TO FEAR! THAT SOMETHING IS A WELL-ARMED PUBLIC!
I SEE. AND HOW MANY GUNS DO YOU OWN, CHUCK?
ABOUT A DOZEN.
OKAY, SO IF EVERY ADULT IN THE COUNTRY HAD AS MANY GUNS AS YOU, WOULD THAT FINALLY BE ENOUGH TO MAKE OUR STREETS SAFE?
SAFE? GOOD QUESTION... LET ME DO THE MATH HERE...
HMM... 2,400,000,000 GUNS. YEAH, THAT COULD DO IT...
AND PEOPLE CALL YOU AN EXTREMIST!

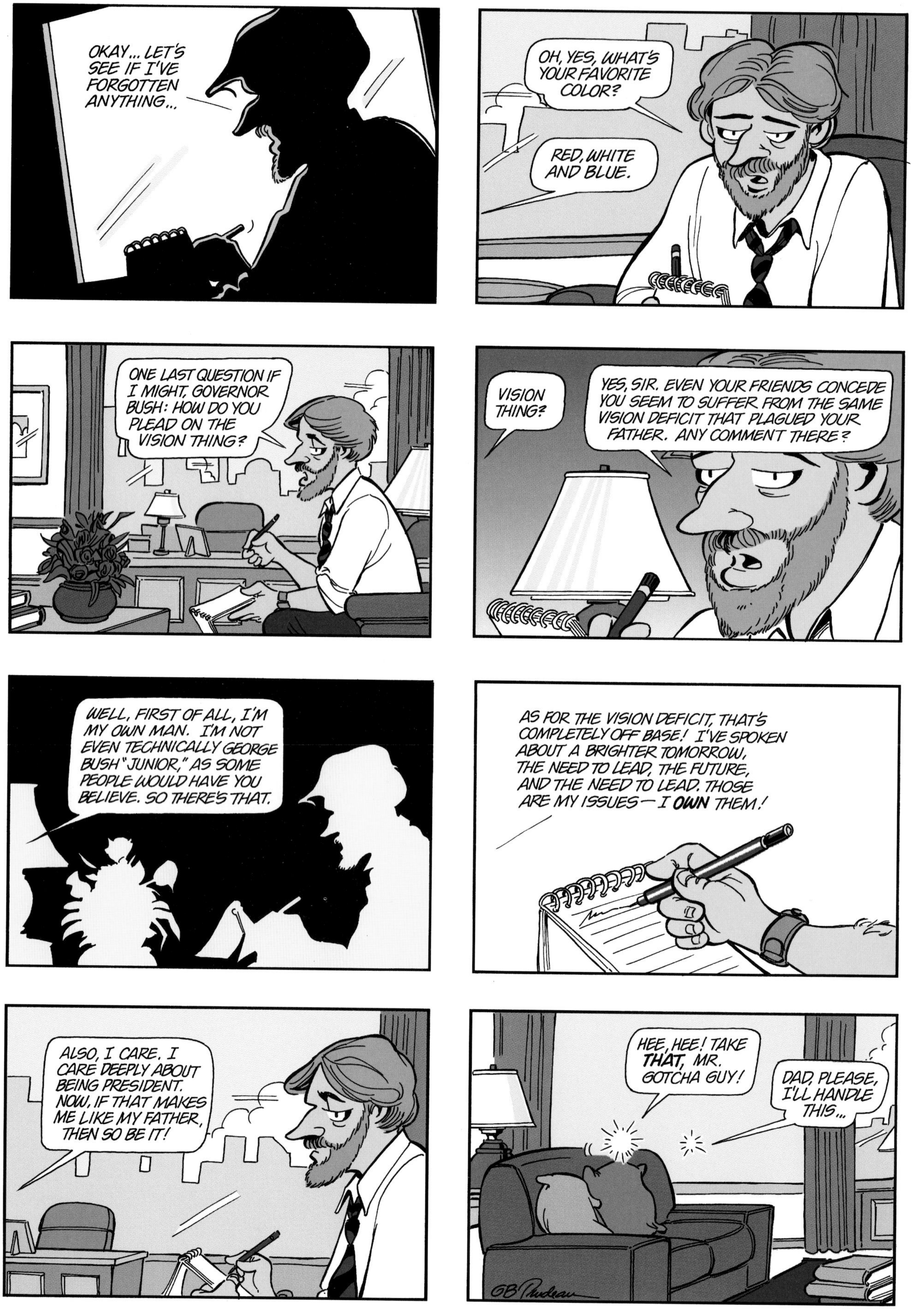
OKAY... LET'S SEE IF I'VE FORGOTTEN ANYTHING...
OH, YES, WHAT'S YOUR FAVORITE COLOR?
RED, WHITE AND BLUE.
ONE LAST QUESTION IF I MIGHT, GOVERNOR BUSH: HOW DO YOU PLEAD ON THE VISION THING?
VISION THING?
YES, SIR. EVEN YOUR FRIENDS CONCEDE YOU SEEM TO SUFFER FROM THE SAME VISION DEFICIT THAT PLAGUED YOUR FATHER. ANY COMMENT THERE?
WELL, FIRST OF ALL, I'M MY OWN MAN. I'M NOT EVEN TECHNICALLY GEORGE BUSH "JUNIOR," AS SOME PEOPLE WOULD HAVE YOU BELIEVE. SO THERE'S THAT.
AS FOR THE VISION DEFICIT, THAT'S COMPLETELY OFF BASE! I'VE SPOKEN ABOUT A BRIGHTER TOMORROW, THE NEED TO LEAD, THE FUTURE, AND THE NEED TO LEAD. THOSE ARE MY ISSUES — I **OWN** THEM!
ALSO, I CARE. I CARE DEEPLY ABOUT BEING PRESIDENT. NOW, IF THAT MAKES ME LIKE MY FATHER, THEN SO BE IT!
HEE, HEE! TAKE **THAT**, MR. GOTCHA GUY!
DAD, PLEASE, I'LL HANDLE THIS...

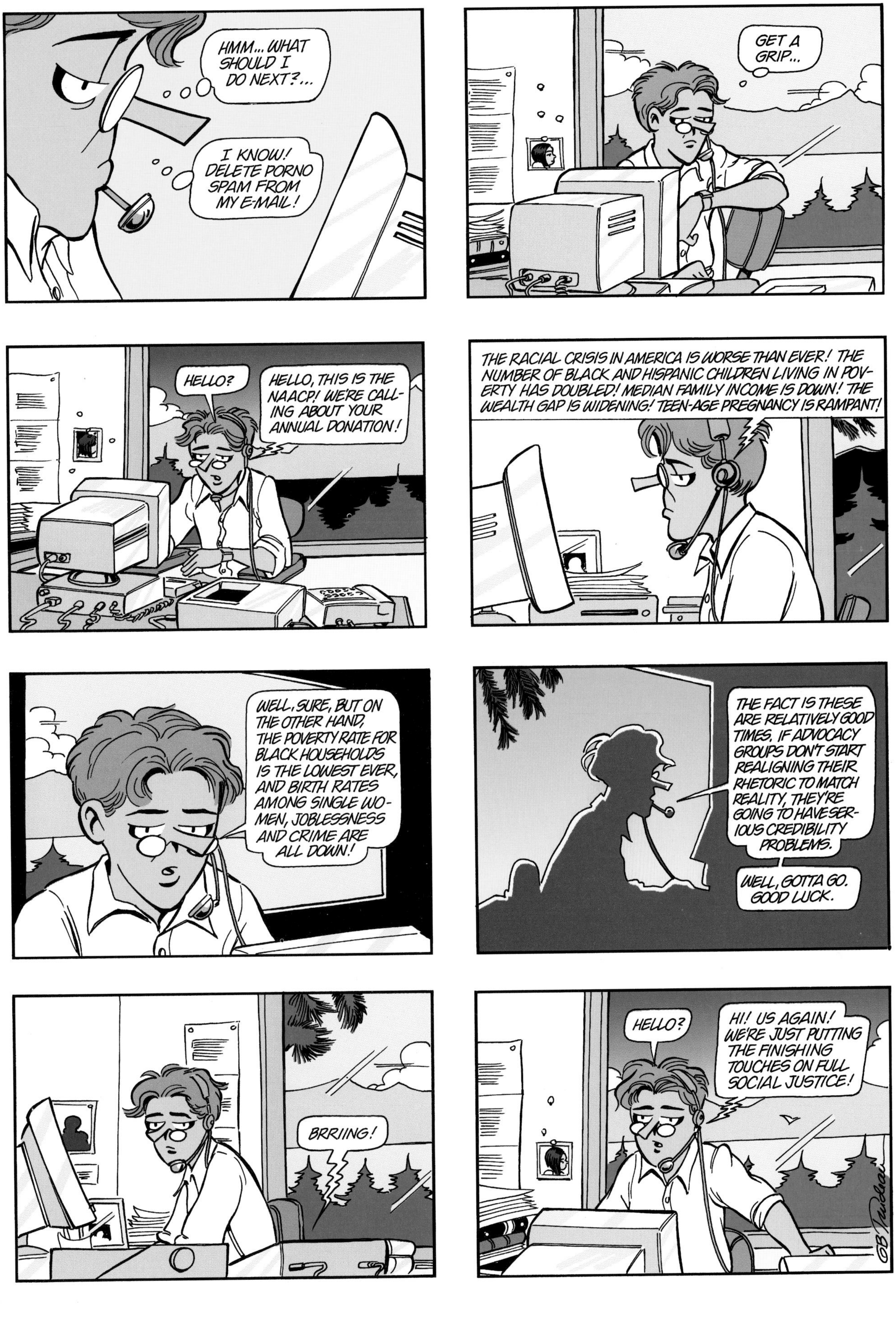
HMM... WHAT SHOULD I DO NEXT?...
I KNOW! DELETE PORNO SPAM FROM MY E-MAIL!
GET A GRIP...
HELLO?
HELLO, THIS IS THE NAACP! WE'RE CALLING ABOUT YOUR ANNUAL DONATION!
THE RACIAL CRISIS IN AMERICA IS WORSE THAN EVER! THE NUMBER OF BLACK AND HISPANIC CHILDREN LIVING IN POVERTY HAS DOUBLED! MEDIAN FAMILY INCOME IS DOWN! THE WEALTH GAP IS WIDENING! TEEN-AGE PREGNANCY IS RAMPANT!
WELL, SURE, BUT ON THE OTHER HAND, THE POVERTY RATE FOR BLACK HOUSEHOLDS IS THE LOWEST EVER, AND BIRTH RATES AMONG SINGLE WOMEN, JOBLESSNESS AND CRIME ARE ALL DOWN!
THE FACT IS THESE ARE RELATIVELY GOOD TIMES. IF ADVOCACY GROUPS DON'T START REALIGNING THEIR RHETORIC TO MATCH REALITY, THEY'RE GOING TO HAVE SERIOUS CREDIBILITY PROBLEMS.
WELL, GOTTA GO. GOOD LUCK.
BRRIING!
HELLO?
HI! US AGAIN! WE'RE JUST PUTTING THE FINISHING TOUCHES ON FULL SOCIAL JUSTICE!

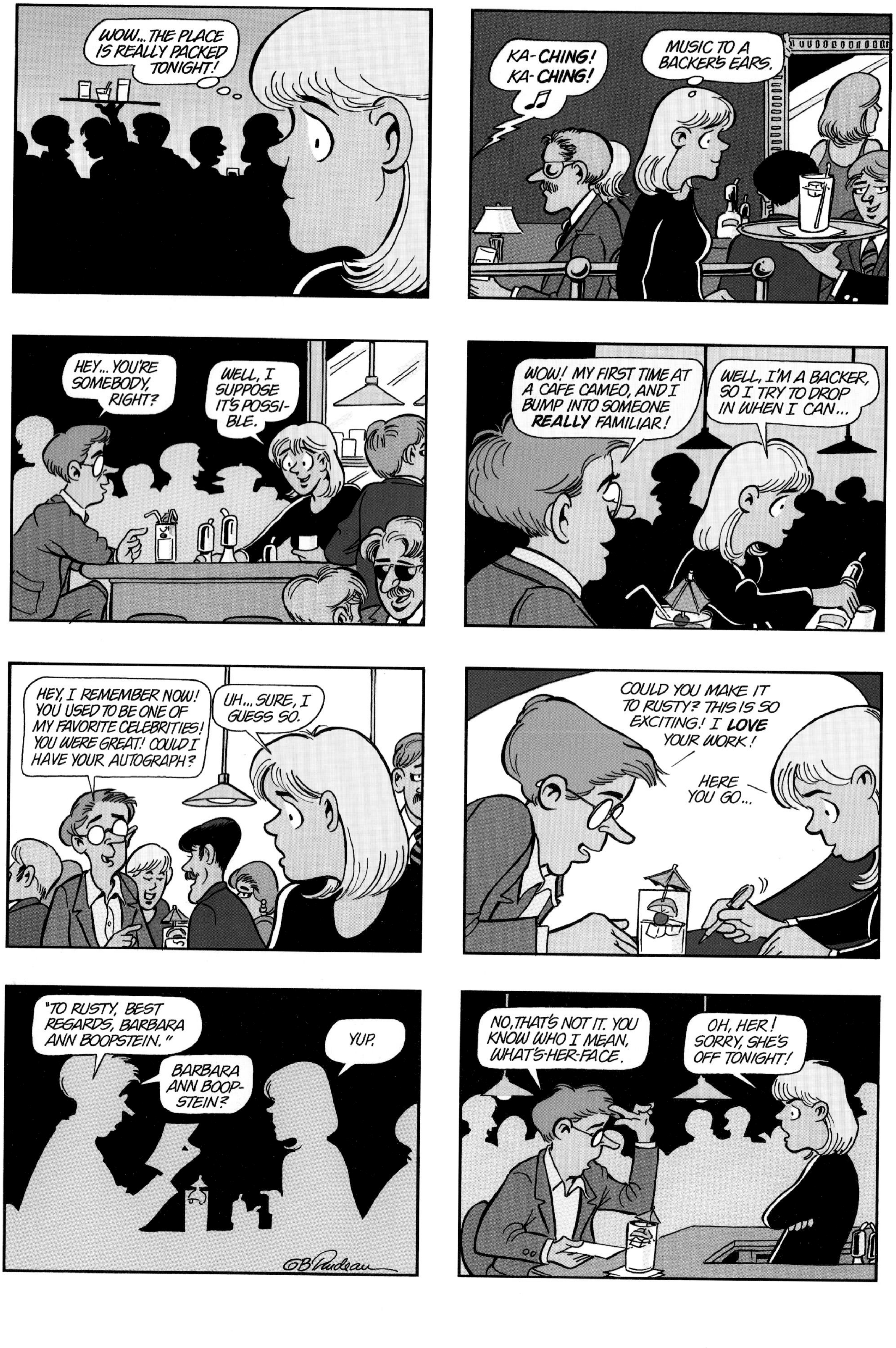
WOW... THE PLACE IS REALLY PACKED TONIGHT!
KA-CHING! KA-CHING!
MUSIC TO A BACKER'S EARS.
HEY... YOU'RE SOMEBODY, RIGHT?
WELL, I SUPPOSE IT'S POSSIBLE.
WOW! MY FIRST TIME AT A CAFE CAMEO, AND I BUMP INTO SOMEONE **REALLY** FAMILIAR!
WELL, I'M A BACKER, SO I TRY TO DROP IN WHEN I CAN...
HEY, I REMEMBER NOW! YOU USED TO BE ONE OF MY FAVORITE CELEBRITIES! YOU WERE GREAT! COULD I HAVE YOUR AUTOGRAPH?
UH... SURE, I GUESS SO.
COULD YOU MAKE IT TO RUSTY? THIS IS SO EXCITING! I **LOVE** YOUR WORK!
HERE YOU GO...
"TO RUSTY, BEST REGARDS, BARBARA ANN BOOPSTEIN."
BARBARA ANN BOOPSTEIN?
YUP.
NO, THAT'S NOT IT. YOU KNOW WHO I MEAN, WHAT'S-HER-FACE.
OH, HER! SORRY, SHE'S OFF TONIGHT!

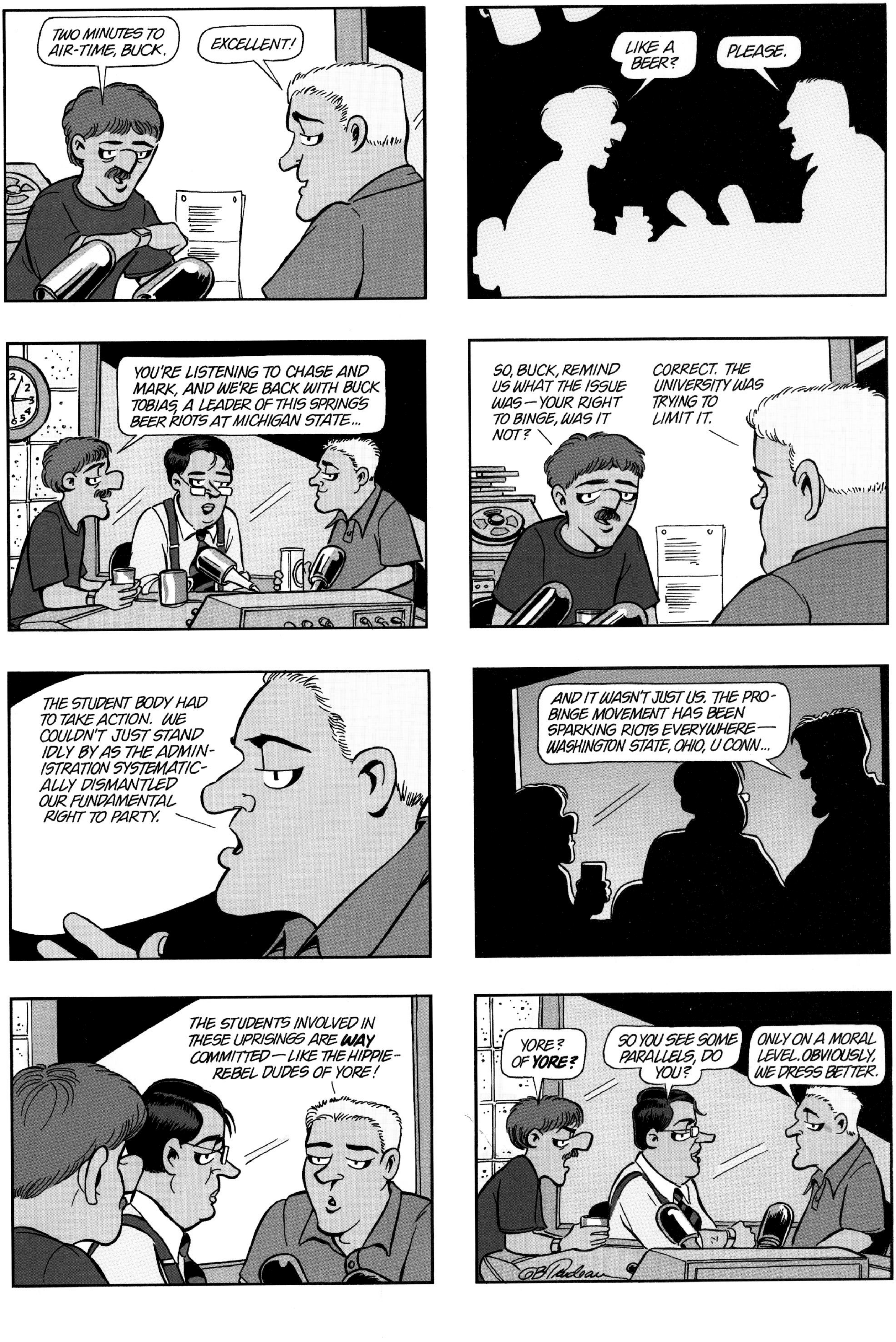
TWO MINUTES TO AIR-TIME, BUCK.
EXCELLENT!
LIKE A BEER?
PLEASE.
YOU'RE LISTENING TO CHASE AND MARK, AND WE'RE BACK WITH BUCK TOBIAS, A LEADER OF THIS SPRING'S BEER RIOTS AT MICHIGAN STATE...
SO, BUCK, REMIND US WHAT THE ISSUE WAS—YOUR RIGHT TO BINGE, WAS IT NOT?
CORRECT. THE UNIVERSITY WAS TRYING TO LIMIT IT.
THE STUDENT BODY HAD TO TAKE ACTION. WE COULDN'T JUST STAND IDLY BY AS THE ADMINISTRATION SYSTEMATICALLY DISMANTLED OUR FUNDAMENTAL RIGHT TO PARTY.
AND IT WASN'T JUST US. THE PRO-BINGE MOVEMENT HAS BEEN SPARKING RIOTS EVERYWHERE—WASHINGTON STATE, OHIO, U CONN...
THE STUDENTS INVOLVED IN THESE UPRISINGS ARE **WAY** COMMITTED—LIKE THE HIPPIE-REBEL DUDES OF YORE!
YORE? OF **YORE?**
SO YOU SEE SOME PARALLELS, DO YOU?
ONLY ON A MORAL LEVEL. OBVIOUSLY, WE DRESS BETTER.

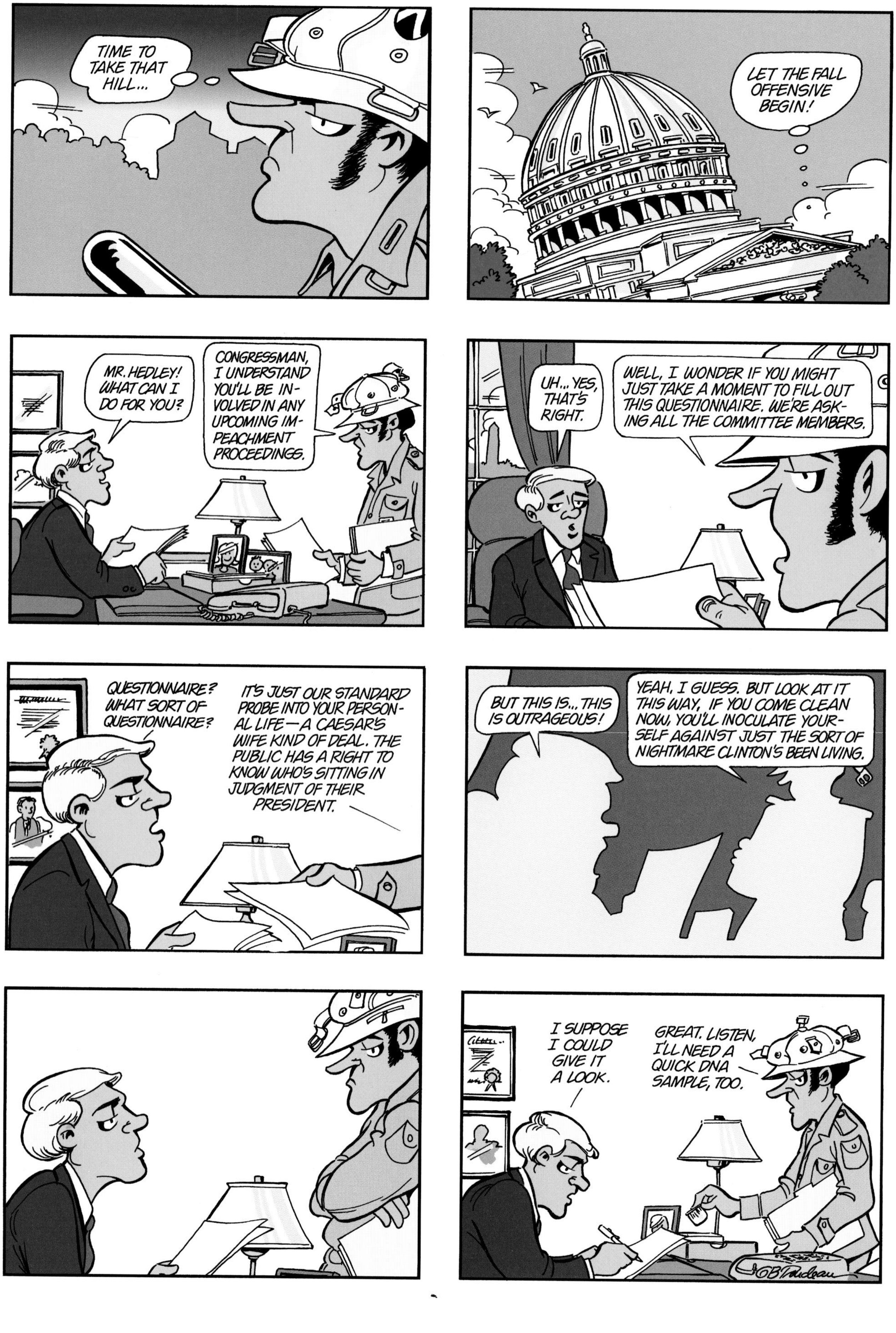
TIME TO TAKE THAT HILL...
LET THE FALL OFFENSIVE BEGIN!
MR. HEDLEY! WHAT CAN I DO FOR YOU?
CONGRESSMAN, I UNDERSTAND YOU'LL BE INVOLVED IN ANY UPCOMING IMPEACHMENT PROCEEDINGS.
UH... YES, THAT'S RIGHT.
WELL, I WONDER IF YOU MIGHT JUST TAKE A MOMENT TO FILL OUT THIS QUESTIONNAIRE. WE'RE ASKING ALL THE COMMITTEE MEMBERS.
QUESTIONNAIRE? WHAT SORT OF QUESTIONNAIRE?
IT'S JUST OUR STANDARD PROBE INTO YOUR PERSONAL LIFE — A CAESAR'S WIFE KIND OF DEAL. THE PUBLIC HAS A RIGHT TO KNOW WHO'S SITTING IN JUDGMENT OF THEIR PRESIDENT.
BUT THIS IS... THIS IS OUTRAGEOUS!
YEAH, I GUESS. BUT LOOK AT IT THIS WAY, IF YOU COME CLEAN NOW, YOU'LL INOCULATE YOURSELF AGAINST JUST THE SORT OF NIGHTMARE CLINTON'S BEEN LIVING.
I SUPPOSE I COULD GIVE IT A LOOK.
GREAT. LISTEN, I'LL NEED A QUICK DNA SAMPLE, TOO.
©BTrudeau

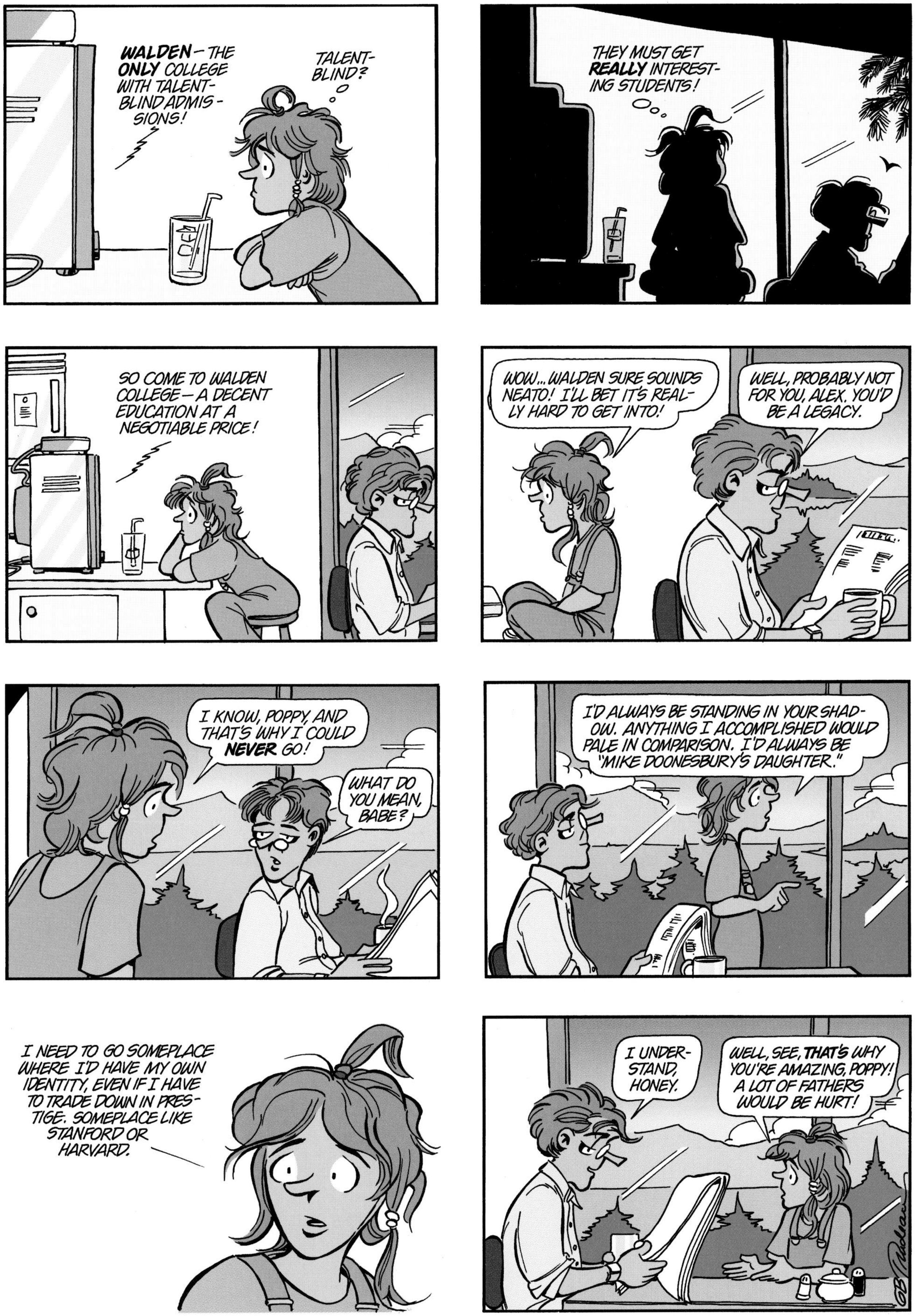
WALDEN – THE ONLY COLLEGE WITH TALENT-BLIND ADMISSIONS!
TALENT-BLIND?
THEY MUST GET REALLY INTERESTING STUDENTS!
SO COME TO WALDEN COLLEGE – A DECENT EDUCATION AT A NEGOTIABLE PRICE!
WOW... WALDEN SURE SOUNDS NEATO! I'LL BET IT'S REALLY HARD TO GET INTO!
WELL, PROBABLY NOT FOR YOU, ALEX. YOU'D BE A LEGACY.
I KNOW, POPPY, AND THAT'S WHY I COULD NEVER GO!
WHAT DO YOU MEAN, BABE?
I'D ALWAYS BE STANDING IN YOUR SHADOW. ANYTHING I ACCOMPLISHED WOULD PALE IN COMPARISON. I'D ALWAYS BE "MIKE DOONESBURY'S DAUGHTER."
I NEED TO GO SOMEPLACE WHERE I'D HAVE MY OWN IDENTITY, EVEN IF I HAVE TO TRADE DOWN IN PRESTIGE. SOMEPLACE LIKE STANFORD OR HARVARD.
I UNDERSTAND, HONEY.
WELL, SEE, THAT'S WHY YOU'RE AMAZING, POPPY! A LOT OF FATHERS WOULD BE HURT!

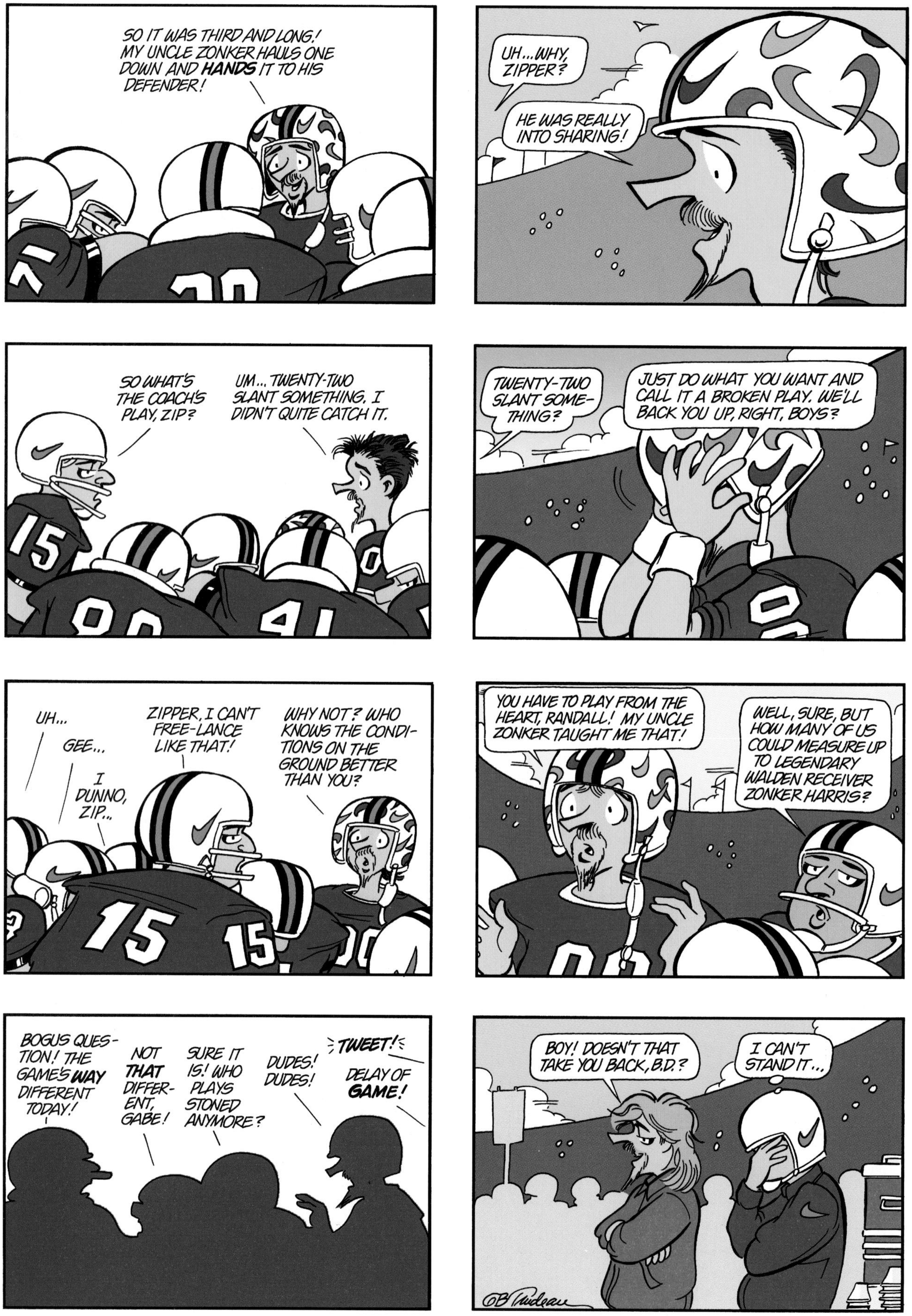
SO IT WAS THIRD AND LONG! MY UNCLE ZONKER HAULS ONE DOWN AND **HANDS** IT TO HIS DEFENDER!
UH... WHY, ZIPPER?
HE WAS REALLY INTO SHARING!
SO WHAT'S THE COACH'S PLAY, ZIP?
UM... TWENTY-TWO SLANT SOMETHING. I DIDN'T QUITE CATCH IT.
TWENTY-TWO SLANT SOME-THING?
JUST DO WHAT YOU WANT AND CALL IT A BROKEN PLAY. WE'LL BACK YOU UP, RIGHT, BOYS?
UH...
GEE...
I DUNNO, ZIP...
ZIPPER, I CAN'T FREE-LANCE LIKE THAT!
WHY NOT? WHO KNOWS THE CONDI-TIONS ON THE GROUND BETTER THAN YOU?
YOU HAVE TO PLAY FROM THE HEART, RANDALL! MY UNCLE ZONKER TAUGHT ME THAT!
WELL, SURE, BUT HOW MANY OF US COULD MEASURE UP TO LEGENDARY WALDEN RECEIVER ZONKER HARRIS?
BOGUS QUES-TION! THE GAME'S **WAY** DIFFERENT TODAY!
NOT **THAT** DIFFER-ENT, GABE!
SURE IT IS! WHO PLAYS STONED ANYMORE?
DUDES! DUDES!
TWEET!
DELAY OF **GAME!**
BOY! DOESN'T THAT TAKE YOU BACK, B.D.?
I CAN'T STAND IT...

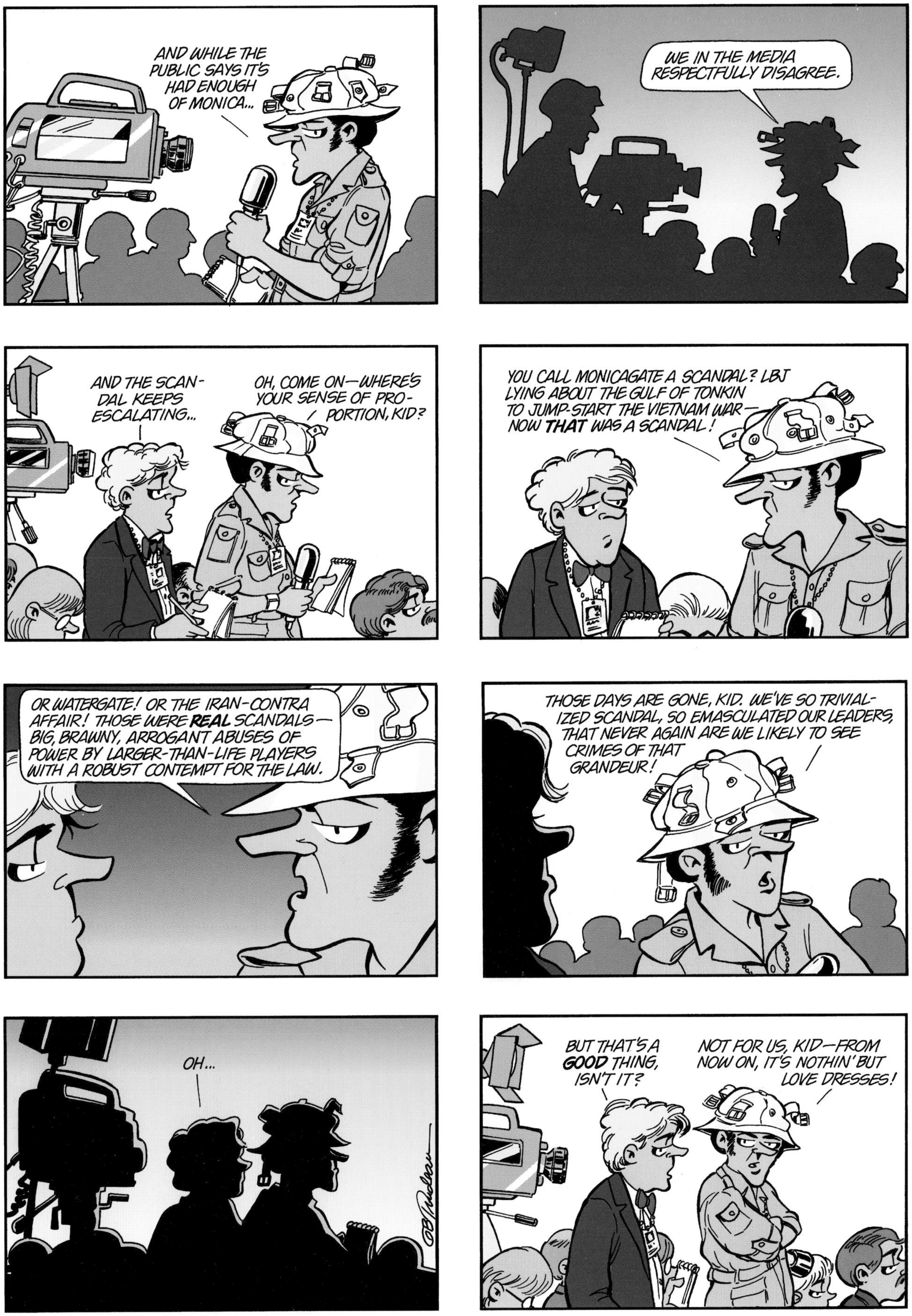
AND WHILE THE PUBLIC SAYS IT'S HAD ENOUGH OF MONICA...
WE IN THE MEDIA RESPECTFULLY DISAGREE.
AND THE SCANDAL KEEPS ESCALATING...
OH, COME ON—WHERE'S YOUR SENSE OF PROPORTION, KID?
YOU CALL MONICAGATE A SCANDAL? LBJ LYING ABOUT THE GULF OF TONKIN TO JUMP-START THE VIETNAM WAR—NOW **THAT** WAS A SCANDAL!
OR WATERGATE! OR THE IRAN-CONTRA AFFAIR! THOSE WERE **REAL** SCANDALS—BIG, BRAWNY, ARROGANT ABUSES OF POWER BY LARGER-THAN-LIFE PLAYERS WITH A ROBUST CONTEMPT FOR THE LAW.
THOSE DAYS ARE GONE, KID. WE'VE SO TRIVIALIZED SCANDAL, SO EMASCULATED OUR LEADERS, THAT NEVER AGAIN ARE WE LIKELY TO SEE CRIMES OF THAT GRANDEUR!
OH...
BUT THAT'S A **GOOD** THING, ISN'T IT?
NOT FOR US, KID—FROM NOW ON, IT'S NOTHIN' BUT LOVE DRESSES!

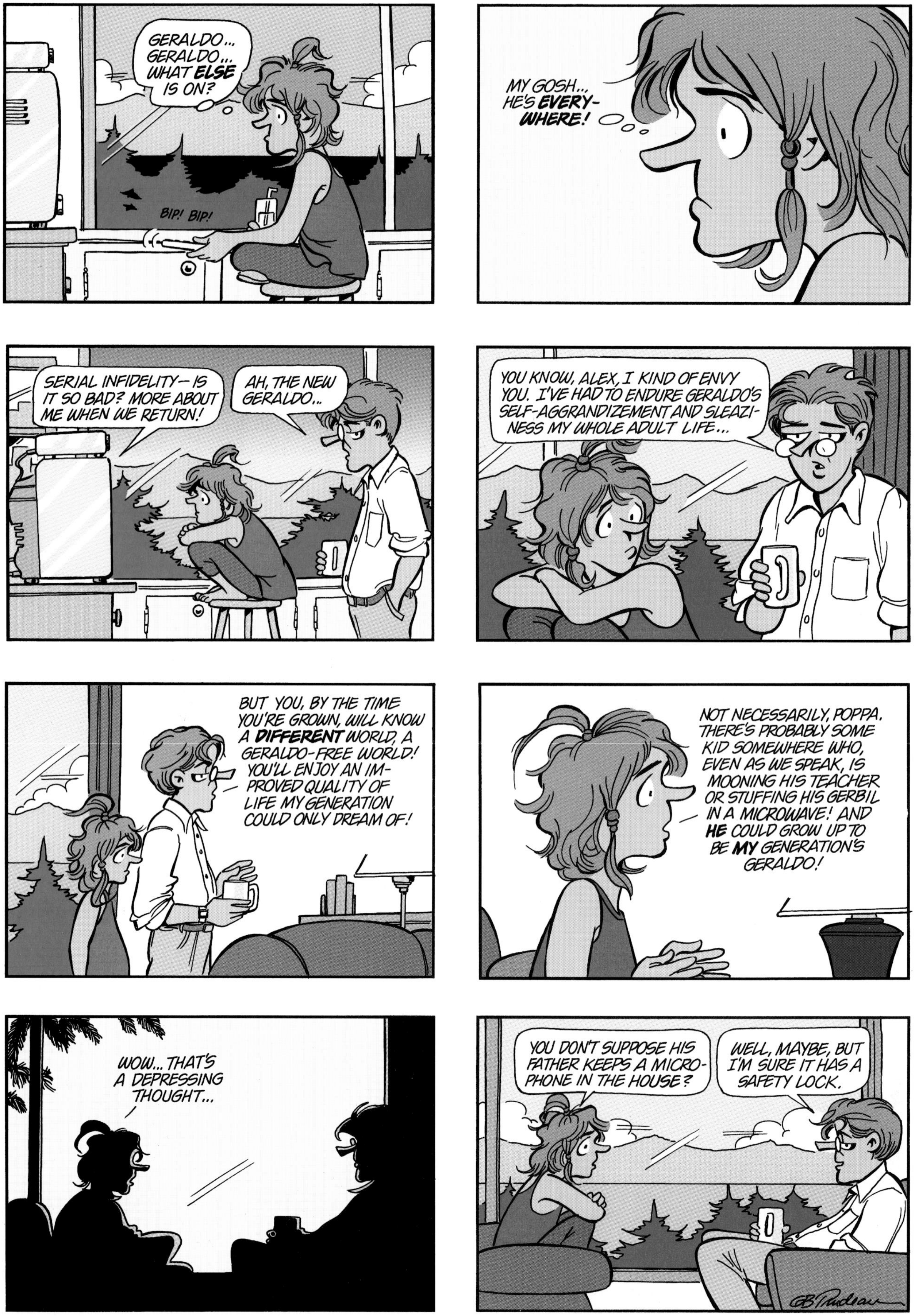
GERALDO... GERALDO... WHAT ELSE IS ON?
BIP! BIP!
MY GOSH.., HE'S EVERY-WHERE!
SERIAL INFIDELITY— IS IT SO BAD? MORE ABOUT ME WHEN WE RETURN!
AH, THE NEW GERALDO...
YOU KNOW, ALEX, I KIND OF ENVY YOU. I'VE HAD TO ENDURE GERALDO'S SELF-AGGRANDIZEMENT AND SLEAZI-NESS MY WHOLE ADULT LIFE...
BUT YOU, BY THE TIME YOU'RE GROWN, WILL KNOW A DIFFERENT WORLD, A GERALDO-FREE WORLD! YOU'LL ENJOY AN IM-PROVED QUALITY OF LIFE MY GENERATION COULD ONLY DREAM OF!
NOT NECESSARILY, POPPA. THERE'S PROBABLY SOME KID SOMEWHERE WHO, EVEN AS WE SPEAK, IS MOONING HIS TEACHER OR STUFFING HIS GERBIL IN A MICROWAVE! AND HE COULD GROW UP TO BE MY GENERATION'S GERALDO!
WOW... THAT'S A DEPRESSING THOUGHT...
YOU DON'T SUPPOSE HIS FATHER KEEPS A MICRO-PHONE IN THE HOUSE?
WELL, MAYBE, BUT I'M SURE IT HAS A SAFETY LOCK.
GBTrudeau

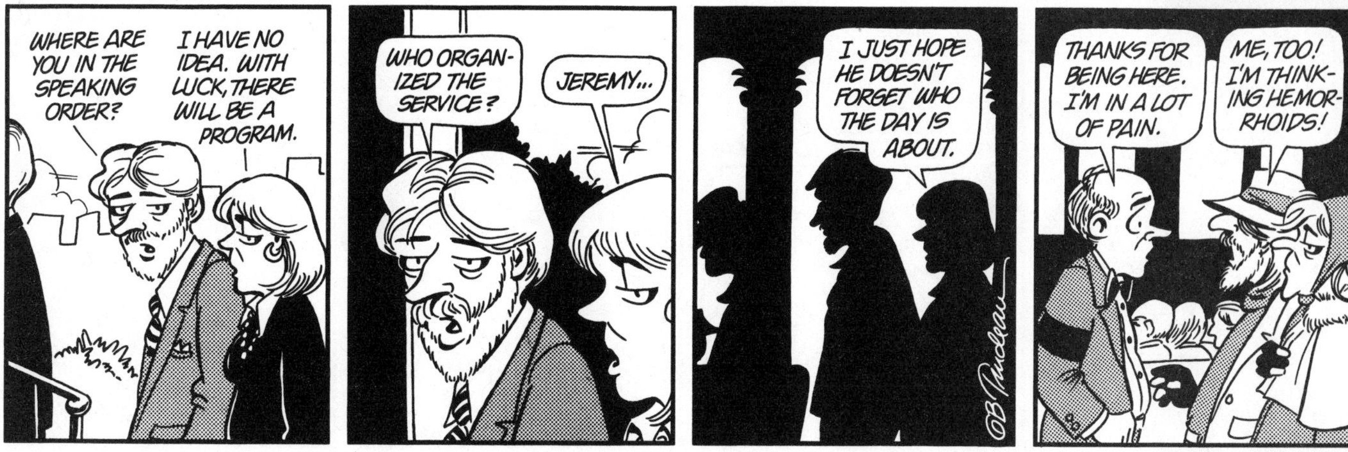
WHERE ARE YOU IN THE SPEAKING ORDER?
I HAVE NO IDEA. WITH LUCK, THERE WILL BE A PROGRAM.
WHO ORGANIZED THE SERVICE?
JEREMY...
I JUST HOPE HE DOESN'T FORGET WHO THE DAY IS ABOUT.
THANKS FOR BEING HERE. I'M IN A LOT OF PAIN.
ME, TOO! I'M THINKING HEMORRHOIDS!

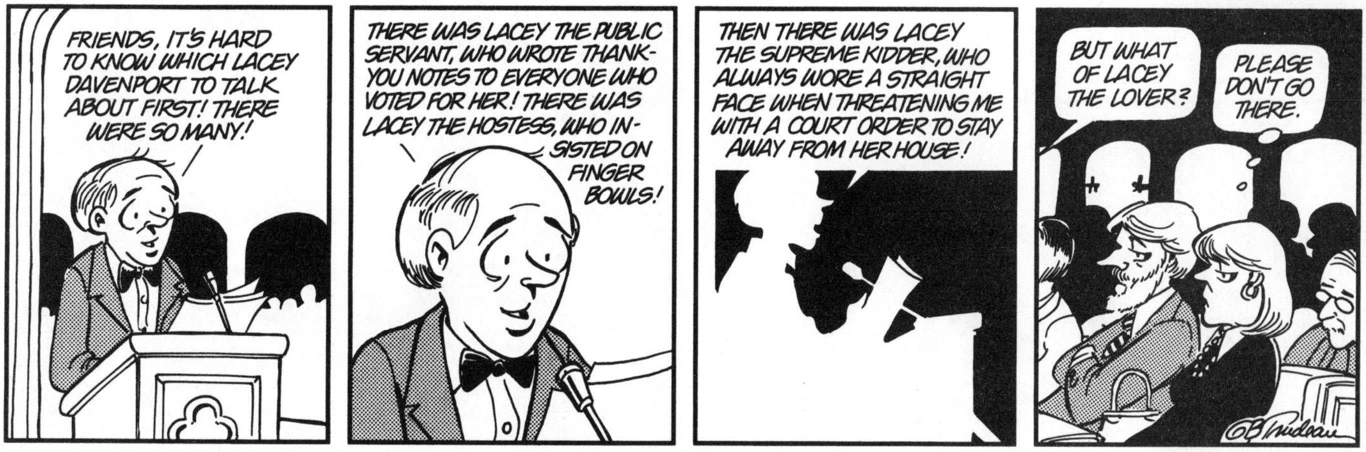
FRIENDS, IT'S HARD TO KNOW WHICH LACEY DAVENPORT TO TALK ABOUT FIRST! THERE WERE SO MANY!
THERE WAS LACEY THE PUBLIC SERVANT, WHO WROTE THANK-YOU NOTES TO EVERYONE WHO VOTED FOR HER! THERE WAS LACEY THE HOSTESS, WHO INSISTED ON FINGER BOWLS!
THEN THERE WAS LACEY THE SUPREME KIDDER, WHO ALWAYS WORE A STRAIGHT FACE WHEN THREATENING ME WITH A COURT ORDER TO STAY AWAY FROM HER HOUSE!
BUT WHAT OF LACEY THE LOVER?
PLEASE DON'T GO THERE.

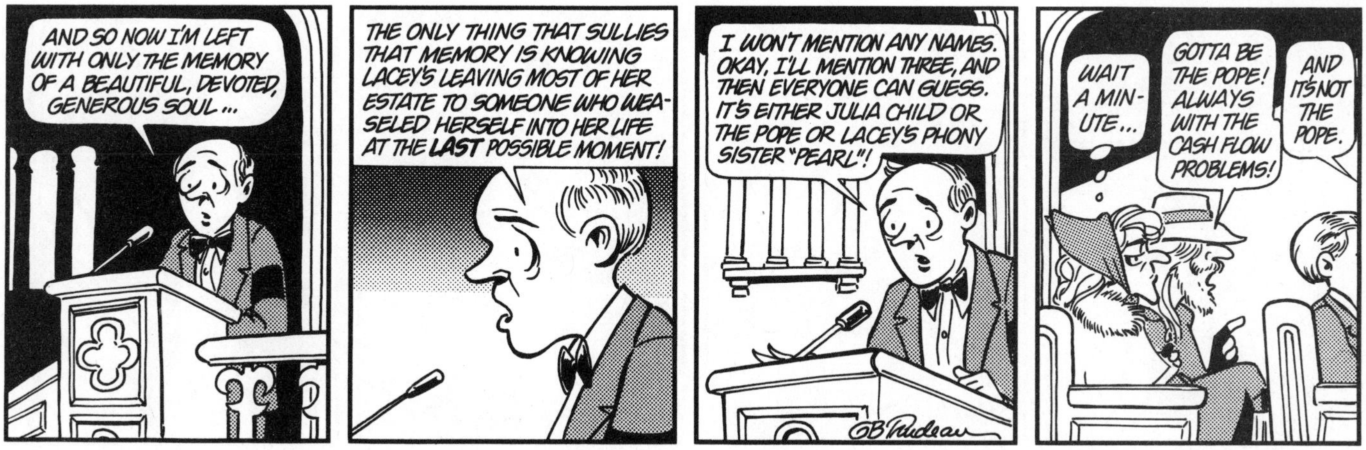
AND SO NOW I'M LEFT WITH ONLY THE MEMORY OF A BEAUTIFUL, DEVOTED, GENEROUS SOUL...
THE ONLY THING THAT SULLIES THAT MEMORY IS KNOWING LACEY'S LEAVING MOST OF HER ESTATE TO SOMEONE WHO WEASELED HERSELF INTO HER LIFE AT THE LAST POSSIBLE MOMENT!
I WON'T MENTION ANY NAMES. OKAY, I'LL MENTION THREE, AND THEN EVERYONE CAN GUESS. IT'S EITHER JULIA CHILD OR THE POPE OR LACEY'S PHONY SISTER "PEARL"!
WAIT A MINUTE...
GOTTA BE THE POPE! ALWAYS WITH THE CASH FLOW PROBLEMS!
AND IT'S NOT THE POPE.

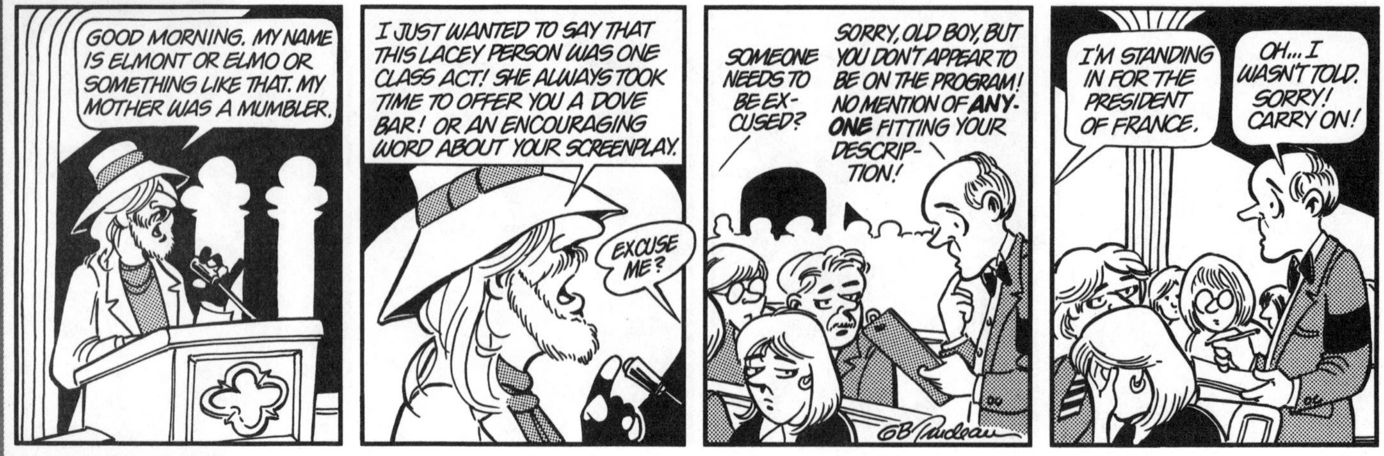
GOOD MORNING. MY NAME IS ELMONT OR ELMO OR SOMETHING LIKE THAT. MY MOTHER WAS A MUMBLER.
I JUST WANTED TO SAY THAT THIS LACEY PERSON WAS ONE CLASS ACT! SHE ALWAYS TOOK TIME TO OFFER YOU A DOVE BAR! OR AN ENCOURAGING WORD ABOUT YOUR SCREENPLAY.
EXCUSE ME?
SOMEONE NEEDS TO BE EXCUSED?
SORRY, OLD BOY, BUT YOU DON'T APPEAR TO BE ON THE PROGRAM! NO MENTION OF ANYONE FITTING YOUR DESCRIPTION!
I'M STANDING IN FOR THE PRESIDENT OF FRANCE.
OH... I WASN'T TOLD. SORRY! CARRY ON!

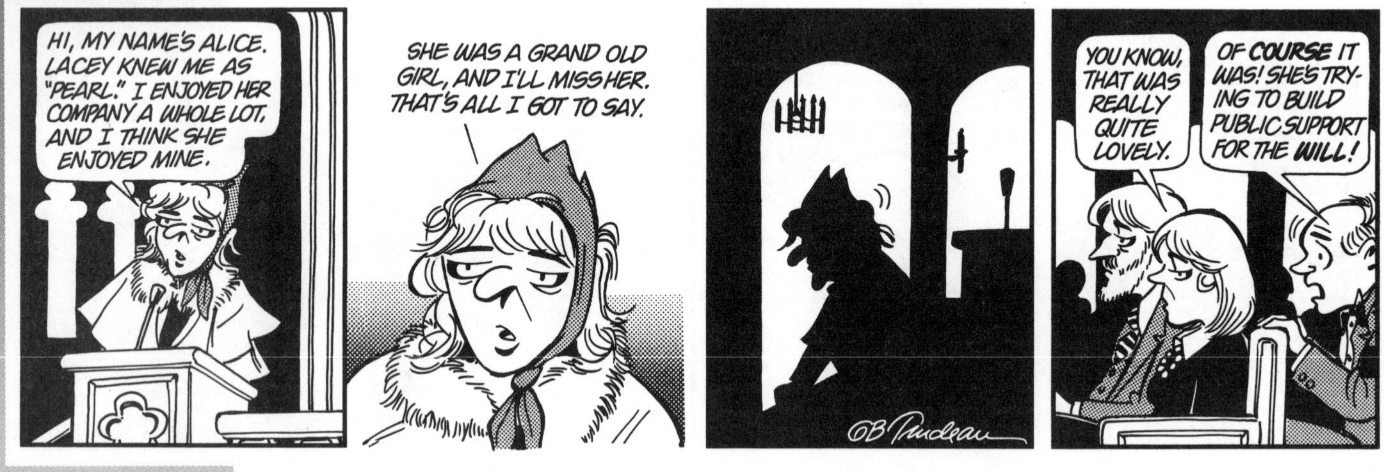
HI, MY NAME'S ALICE. LACEY KNEW ME AS "PEARL." I ENJOYED HER COMPANY A WHOLE LOT, AND I THINK SHE ENJOYED MINE.
SHE WAS A GRAND OLD GIRL, AND I'LL MISS HER. THAT'S ALL I GOT TO SAY.
YOU KNOW, THAT WAS REALLY QUITE LOVELY.
OF COURSE IT WAS! SHE'S TRYING TO BUILD PUBLIC SUPPORT FOR THE WILL!

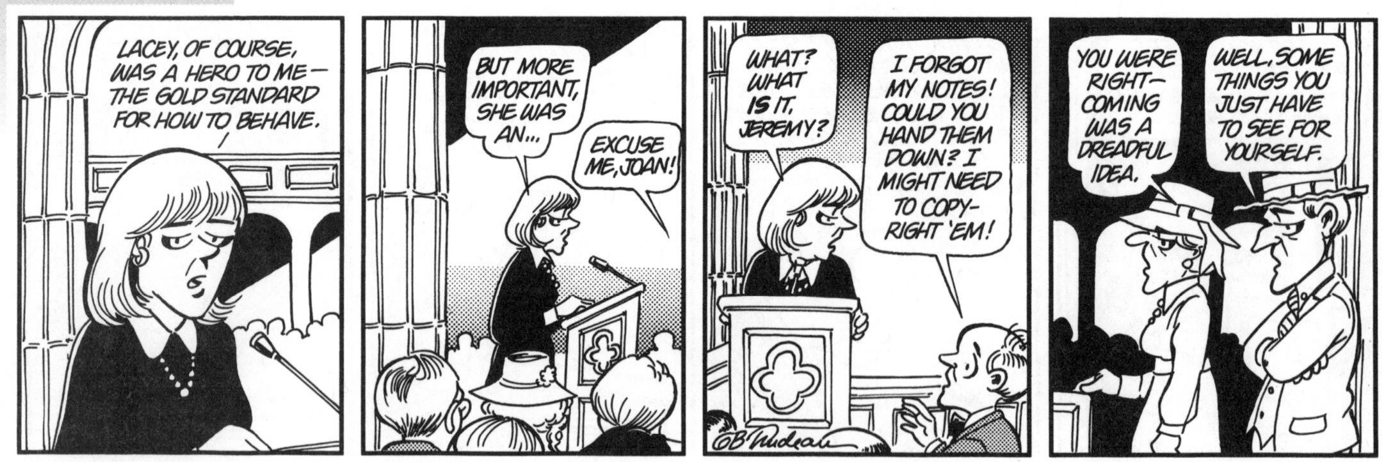
LACEY, OF COURSE, WAS A HERO TO ME— THE GOLD STANDARD FOR HOW TO BEHAVE.
BUT MORE IMPORTANT, SHE WAS AN...
EXCUSE ME, JOAN!
WHAT? WHAT IS IT, JEREMY?
I FORGOT MY NOTES! COULD YOU HAND THEM DOWN? I MIGHT NEED TO COPYRIGHT 'EM!
YOU WERE RIGHT— COMING WAS A DREADFUL IDEA.
WELL, SOME THINGS YOU JUST HAVE TO SEE FOR YOURSELF.

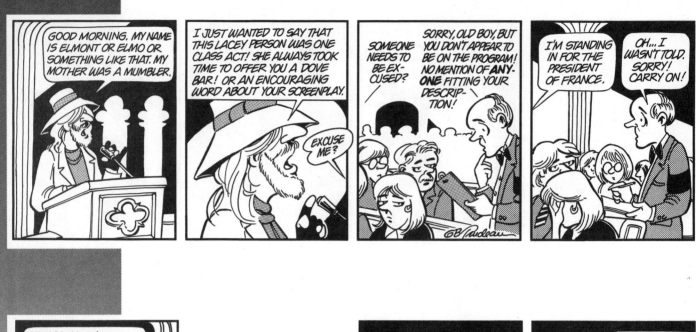

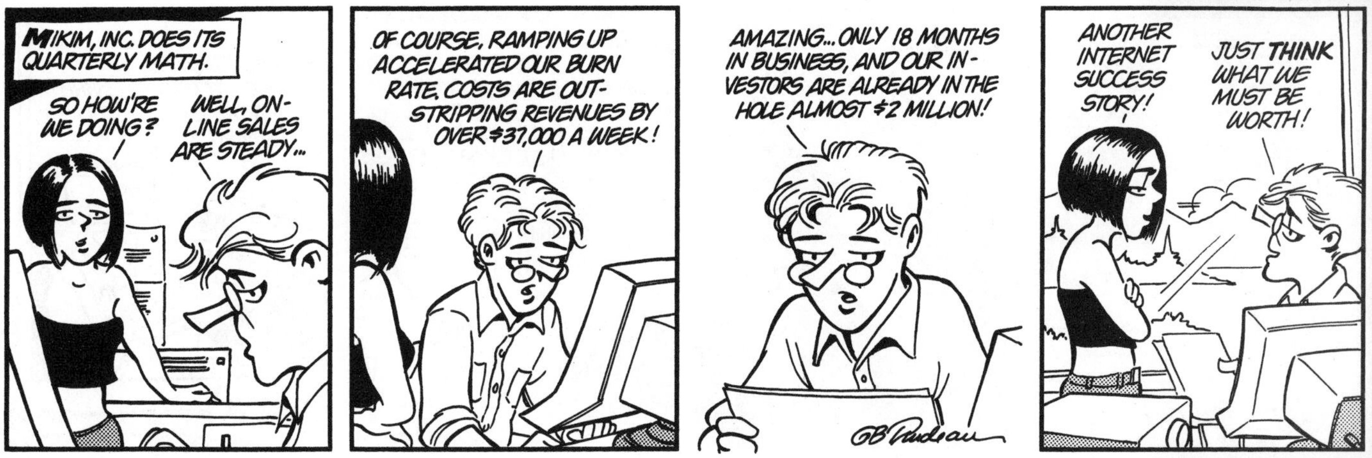
MIKIM, INC. DOES ITS QUARTERLY MATH.
SO HOW'RE WE DOING?
WELL, ON-LINE SALES ARE STEADY...
OF COURSE, RAMPING UP ACCELERATED OUR BURN RATE. COSTS ARE OUT-STRIPPING REVENUES BY OVER $37,000 A WEEK!
AMAZING... ONLY 18 MONTHS IN BUSINESS, AND OUR IN-VESTORS ARE ALREADY IN THE HOLE ALMOST $2 MILLION!
ANOTHER INTERNET SUCCESS STORY!
JUST THINK WHAT WE MUST BE WORTH!

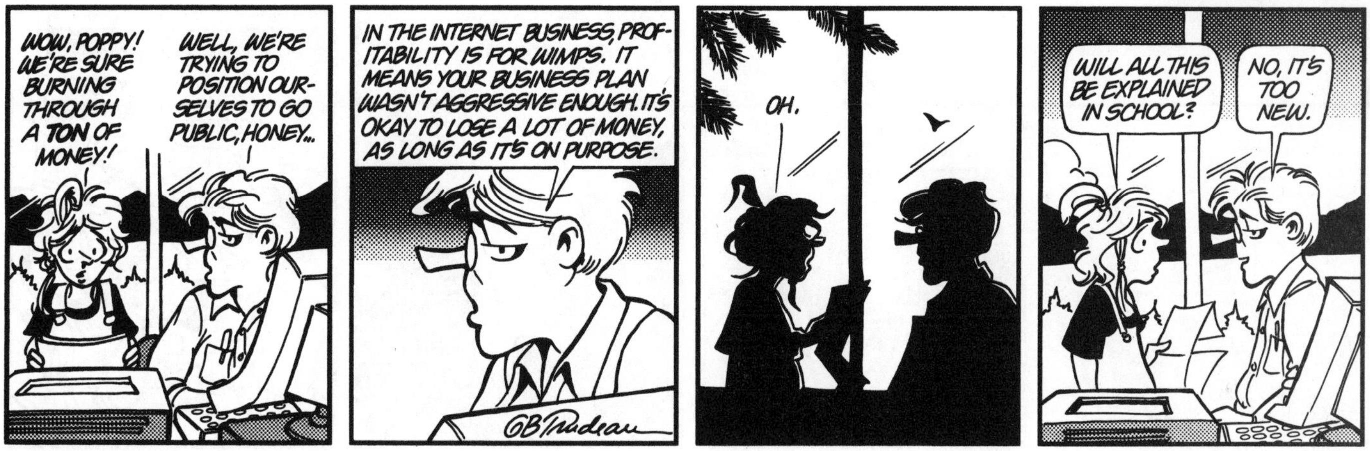
WOW, POPPY! WE'RE SURE BURNING THROUGH A TON OF MONEY!
WELL, WE'RE TRYING TO POSITION OUR-SELVES TO GO PUBLIC, HONEY...
IN THE INTERNET BUSINESS, PROF-ITABILITY IS FOR WIMPS. IT MEANS YOUR BUSINESS PLAN WASN'T AGGRESSIVE ENOUGH. IT'S OKAY TO LOSE A LOT OF MONEY, AS LONG AS IT'S ON PURPOSE.
OH.
WILL ALL THIS BE EXPLAINED IN SCHOOL?
NO, IT'S TOO NEW.

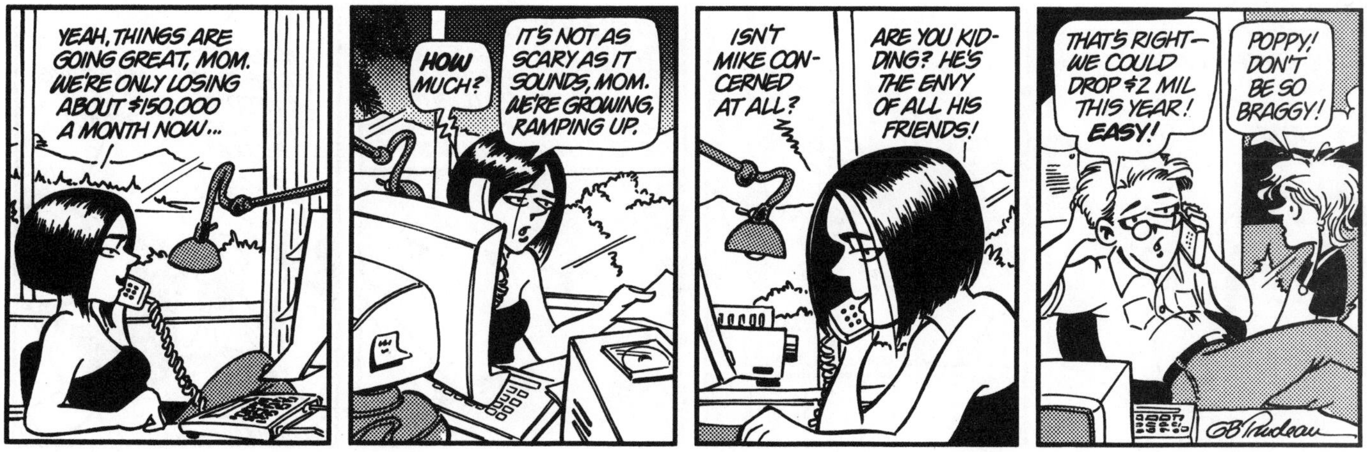
YEAH, THINGS ARE GOING GREAT, MOM. WE'RE ONLY LOSING ABOUT $150,000 A MONTH NOW...
HOW MUCH?
IT'S NOT AS SCARY AS IT SOUNDS, MOM. WE'RE GROWING, RAMPING UP.
ISN'T MIKE CON-CERNED AT ALL?
ARE YOU KID-DING? HE'S THE ENVY OF ALL HIS FRIENDS!
THAT'S RIGHT— WE COULD DROP $2 MIL THIS YEAR! EASY!
POPPY! DON'T BE SO BRAGGY!

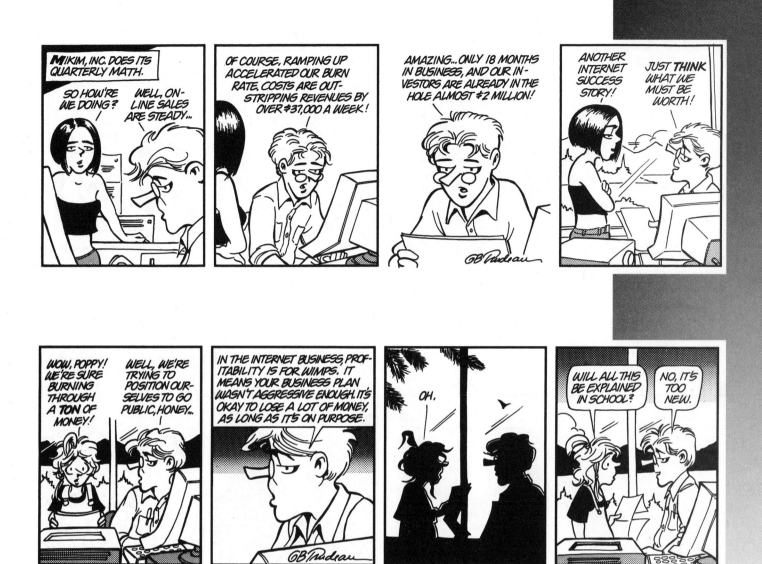

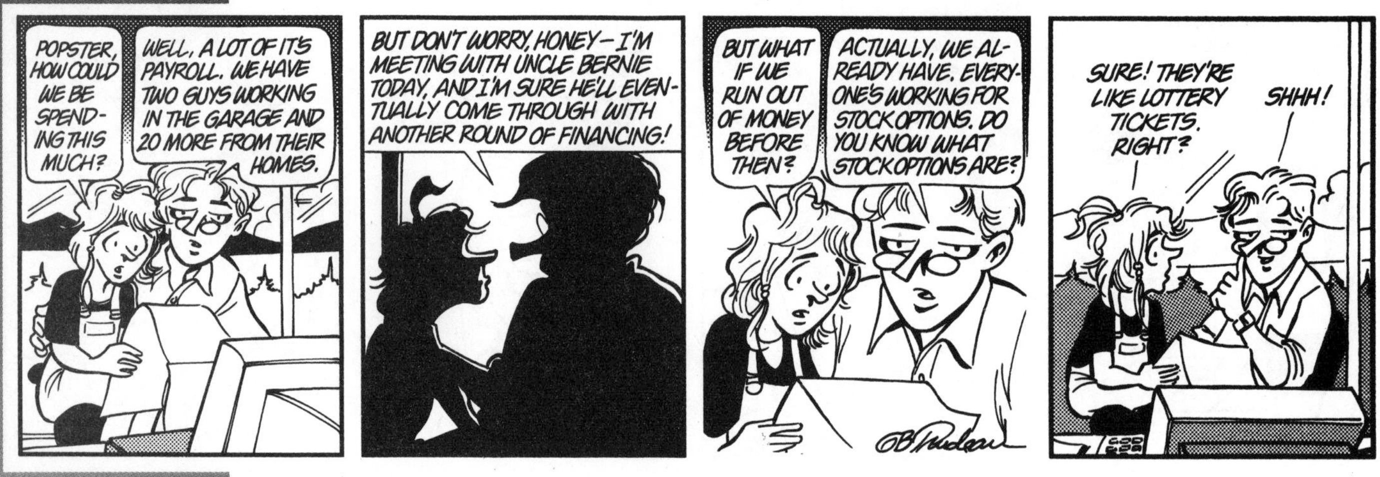
POPSTER, HOW COULD WE BE SPENDING THIS MUCH?
WELL, A LOT OF IT'S PAYROLL. WE HAVE TWO GUYS WORKING IN THE GARAGE AND 20 MORE FROM THEIR HOMES.
BUT DON'T WORRY, HONEY — I'M MEETING WITH UNCLE BERNIE TODAY, AND I'M SURE HE'LL EVENTUALLY COME THROUGH WITH ANOTHER ROUND OF FINANCING!
BUT WHAT IF WE RUN OUT OF MONEY BEFORE THEN?
ACTUALLY, WE ALREADY HAVE. EVERYONE'S WORKING FOR STOCK OPTIONS. DO YOU KNOW WHAT STOCK OPTIONS ARE?
SURE! THEY'RE LIKE LOTTERY TICKETS. RIGHT?
SHHH!

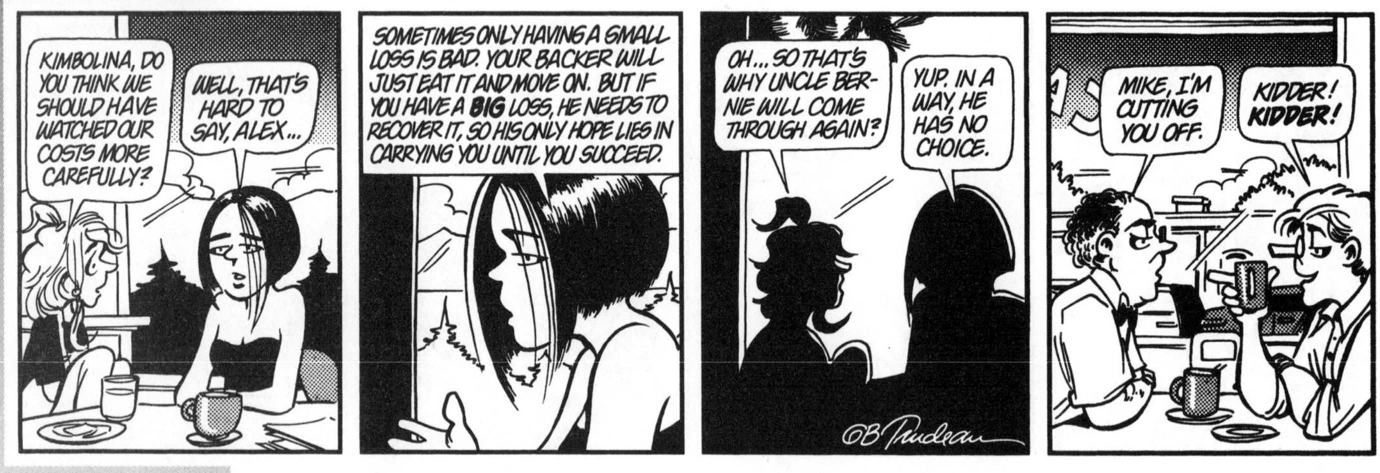
KIMBOLINA, DO YOU THINK WE SHOULD HAVE WATCHED OUR COSTS MORE CAREFULLY?
WELL, THAT'S HARD TO SAY, ALEX...
SOMETIMES ONLY HAVING A SMALL LOSS IS BAD. YOUR BACKER WILL JUST EAT IT AND MOVE ON. BUT IF YOU HAVE A **BIG** LOSS, HE NEEDS TO RECOVER IT, SO HIS ONLY HOPE LIES IN CARRYING YOU UNTIL YOU SUCCEED.
OH... SO THAT'S WHY UNCLE BERNIE WILL COME THROUGH AGAIN?
YUP. IN A WAY, HE HAS NO CHOICE.
MIKE, I'M CUTTING YOU OFF.
KIDDER! **KIDDER!**

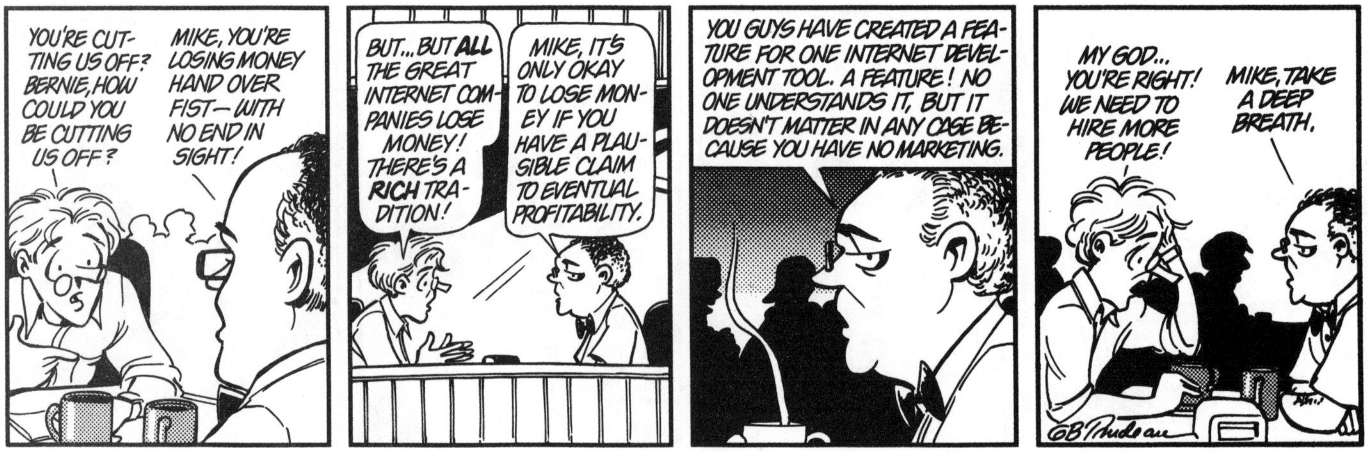
YOU'RE CUTTING US OFF? BERNIE, HOW COULD YOU BE CUTTING US OFF?
MIKE, YOU'RE LOSING MONEY HAND OVER FIST — WITH NO END IN SIGHT!
BUT... BUT **ALL** THE GREAT INTERNET COMPANIES LOSE MONEY! THERE'S A **RICH** TRADITION!
MIKE, IT'S ONLY OKAY TO LOSE MONEY IF YOU HAVE A PLAUSIBLE CLAIM TO EVENTUAL PROFITABILITY.
YOU GUYS HAVE CREATED A FEATURE FOR ONE INTERNET DEVELOPMENT TOOL. A FEATURE! NO ONE UNDERSTANDS IT, BUT IT DOESN'T MATTER IN ANY CASE BECAUSE YOU HAVE NO MARKETING.
MY GOD... YOU'RE RIGHT! WE NEED TO HIRE MORE PEOPLE!
MIKE, TAKE A DEEP BREATH.

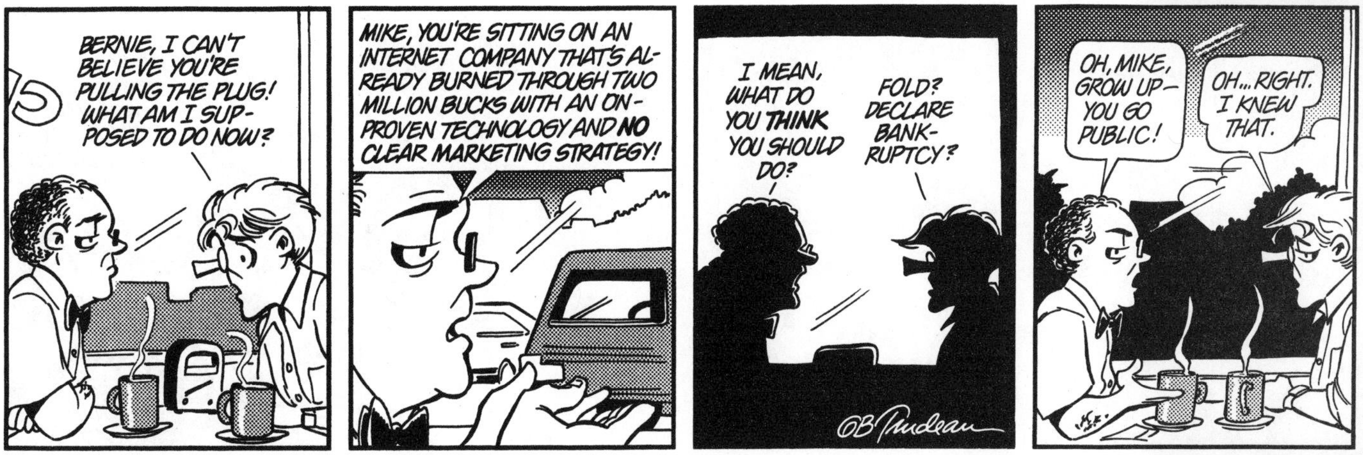
BERNIE, I CAN'T BELIEVE YOU'RE PULLING THE PLUG! WHAT AM I SUPPOSED TO DO NOW?
MIKE, YOU'RE SITTING ON AN INTERNET COMPANY THAT'S ALREADY BURNED THROUGH TWO MILLION BUCKS WITH AN UNPROVEN TECHNOLOGY AND NO CLEAR MARKETING STRATEGY!
I MEAN, WHAT DO YOU THINK YOU SHOULD DO?
FOLD? DECLARE BANKRUPTCY?
OH, MIKE, GROW UP—YOU GO PUBLIC!
OH... RIGHT. I KNEW THAT.

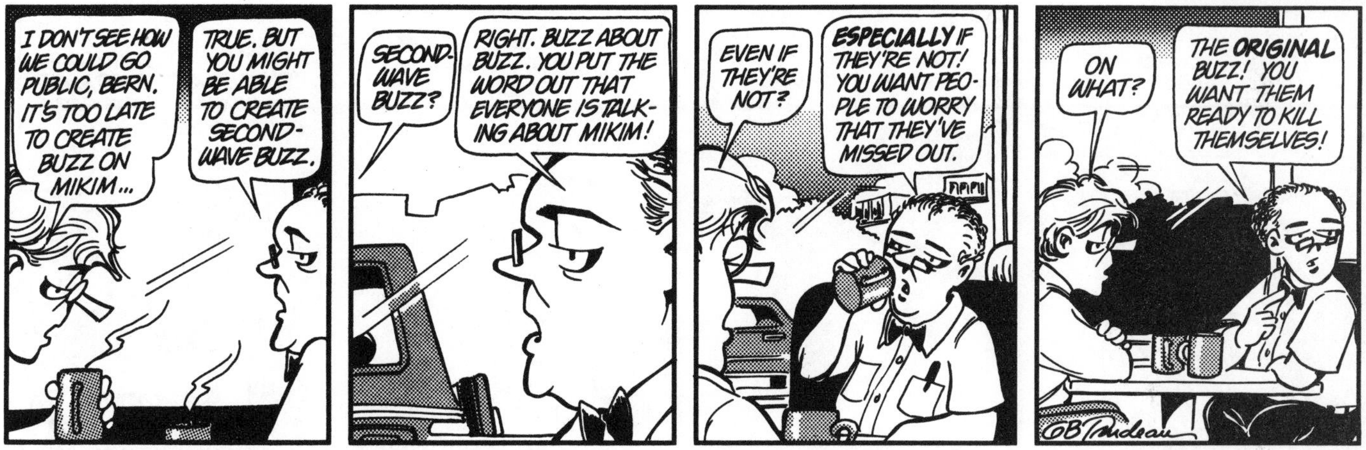
I DON'T SEE HOW WE COULD GO PUBLIC, BERN. IT'S TOO LATE TO CREATE BUZZ ON MIKIM...
TRUE. BUT YOU MIGHT BE ABLE TO CREATE SECOND-WAVE BUZZ.
SECOND-WAVE BUZZ?
RIGHT. BUZZ ABOUT BUZZ. YOU PUT THE WORD OUT THAT EVERYONE IS TALKING ABOUT MIKIM!
EVEN IF THEY'RE NOT?
ESPECIALLY IF THEY'RE NOT! YOU WANT PEOPLE TO WORRY THAT THEY'VE MISSED OUT.
ON WHAT?
THE ORIGINAL BUZZ! YOU WANT THEM READY TO KILL THEMSELVES!

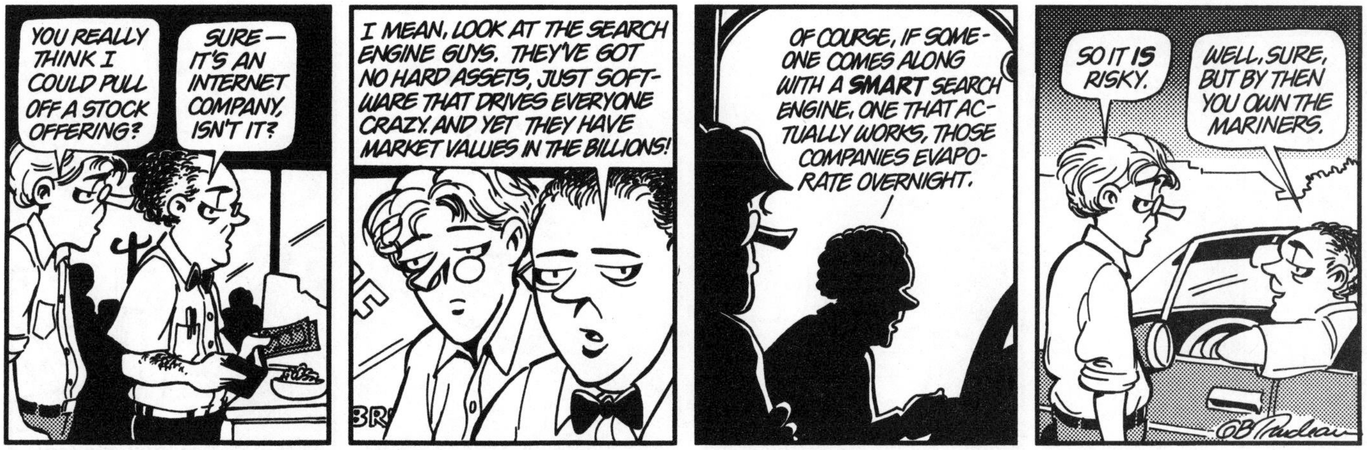
YOU REALLY THINK I COULD PULL OFF A STOCK OFFERING?
SURE—IT'S AN INTERNET COMPANY, ISN'T IT?
I MEAN, LOOK AT THE SEARCH ENGINE GUYS. THEY'VE GOT NO HARD ASSETS, JUST SOFTWARE THAT DRIVES EVERYONE CRAZY. AND YET THEY HAVE MARKET VALUES IN THE BILLIONS!
OF COURSE, IF SOMEONE COMES ALONG WITH A SMART SEARCH ENGINE, ONE THAT ACTUALLY WORKS, THOSE COMPANIES EVAPORATE OVERNIGHT.
SO IT IS RISKY.
WELL, SURE, BUT BY THEN YOU OWN THE MARINERS.

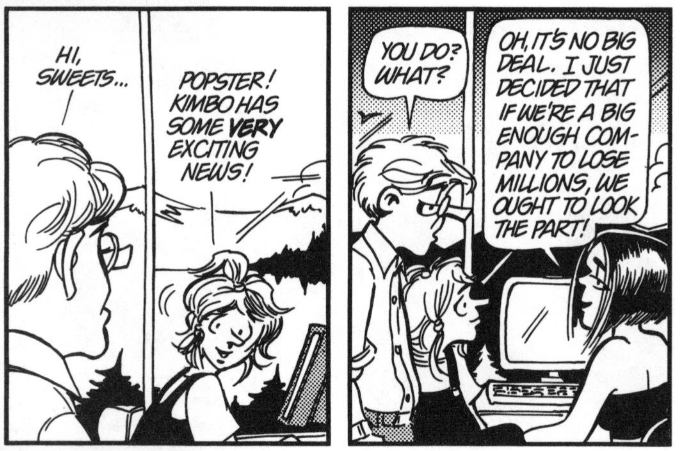
HI, SWEETS...
POPSTER! KIMBO HAS SOME **VERY** EXCITING NEWS!
YOU DO? WHAT?
OH, IT'S NO BIG DEAL. I JUST DECIDED THAT IF WE'RE A BIG ENOUGH COMPANY TO LOSE MILLIONS, WE OUGHT TO LOOK THE PART!
WHAT DO YOU MEAN?
TODAY ALEX AND I WENT INTO TOWN AND BOUGHT A SILVER RANGE ROVER 4.0 SE!
YOU **WHAT?**
DON'T WORRY, POPPA—WE CHARGED IT DIRECTLY TO UNCLE BERNIE.

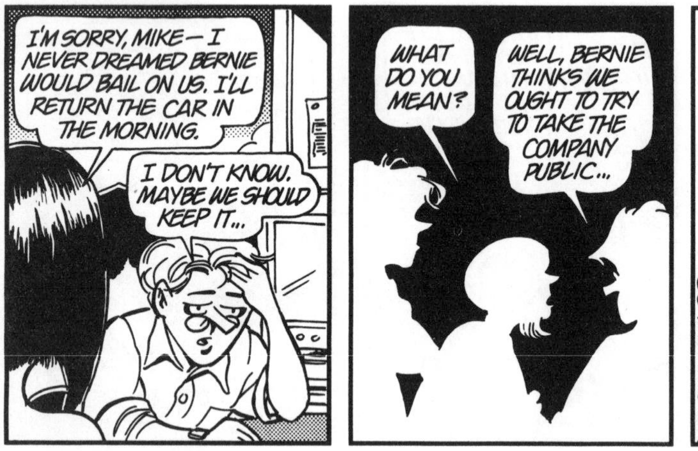
I'M SORRY, MIKE—I NEVER DREAMED BERNIE WOULD BAIL ON US. I'LL RETURN THE CAR IN THE MORNING.
I DON'T KNOW. MAYBE WE SHOULD KEEP IT...
WHAT DO YOU MEAN?
WELL, BERNIE THINKS WE OUGHT TO TRY TO TAKE THE COMPANY PUBLIC...
OUR ONLY HOPE OF ACTUALLY PULLING THAT OFF MAY LIE IN **APPEARING** TO BE SUCCESSFUL. A LUXURY CAR MIGHT HELP...
POPPA? I COULD START WEARING RALPH LAUREN.
THAT'S OKAY, SWEETHEART. THE CAR SHOULD COVER IT.

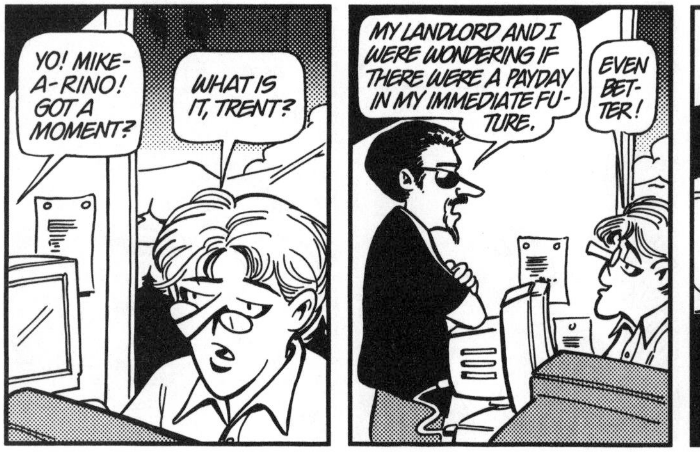
YO! MIKE-A-RINO! GOT A MOMENT?
WHAT IS IT, TRENT?
MY LANDLORD AND I WERE WONDERING IF THERE WERE A PAYDAY IN MY IMMEDIATE FUTURE.
EVEN BETTER!
THIS MONTH, INSTEAD OF SALARY, WE'RE GIVING ALL MIKIM EMPLOYEES MORE **STOCK OPTIONS!**
FABULOUS. WE WERE RUNNING LOW IN THE WASHROOM.
HOW I ENVY YOU, TRENT—GROUND FLOOR CITY, AT **YOUR** AGE!

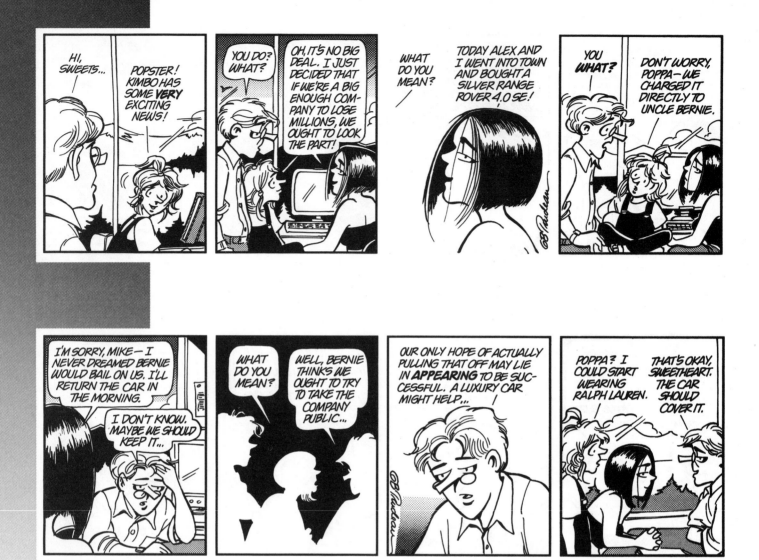

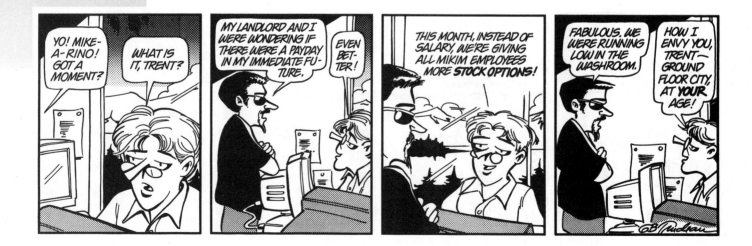

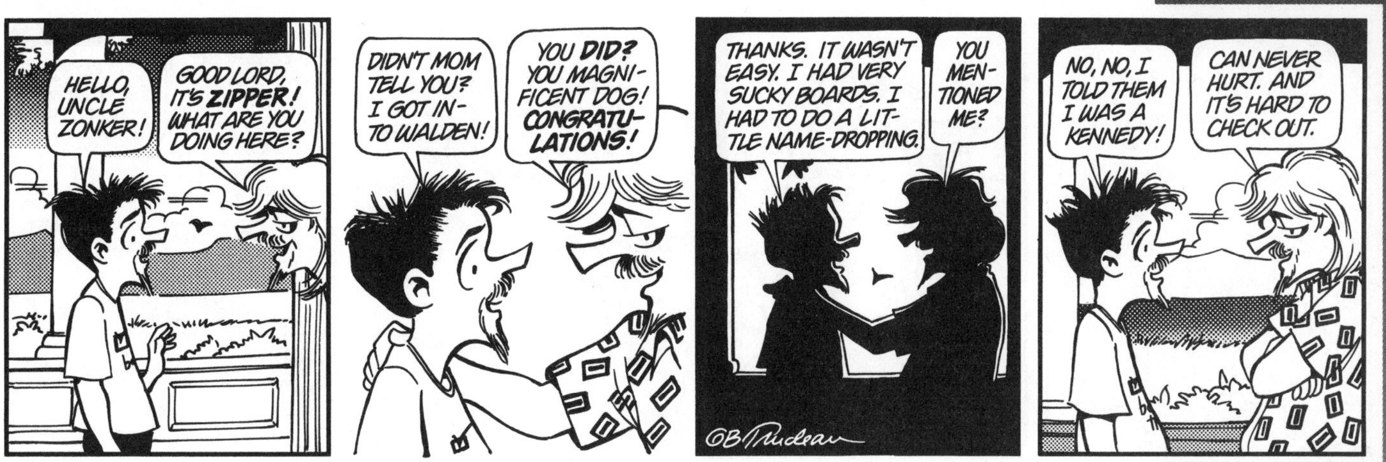
HELLO, UNCLE ZONKER!
GOOD LORD, IT'S ZIPPER! WHAT ARE YOU DOING HERE?
DIDN'T MOM TELL YOU? I GOT INTO WALDEN!
YOU DID? YOU MAGNIFICENT DOG! CONGRATULATIONS!
THANKS. IT WASN'T EASY. I HAD VERY SUCKY BOARDS. I HAD TO DO A LITTLE NAME-DROPPING.
YOU MENTIONED ME?
NO, NO, I TOLD THEM I WAS A KENNEDY!
CAN NEVER HURT. AND IT'S HARD TO CHECK OUT.

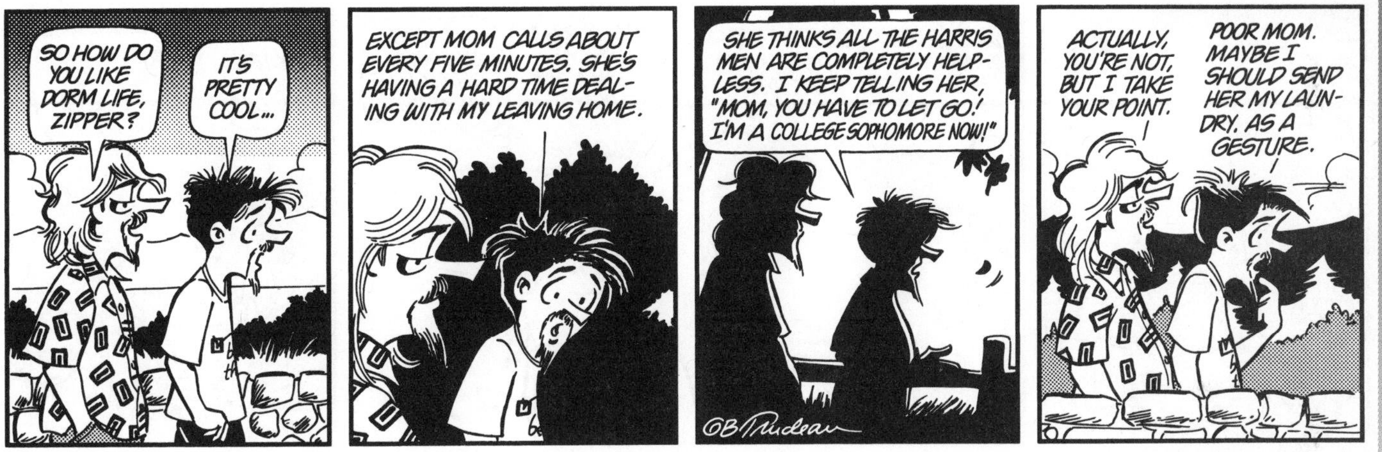
SO HOW DO YOU LIKE DORM LIFE, ZIPPER?
IT'S PRETTY COOL...
EXCEPT MOM CALLS ABOUT EVERY FIVE MINUTES. SHE'S HAVING A HARD TIME DEALING WITH MY LEAVING HOME.
SHE THINKS ALL THE HARRIS MEN ARE COMPLETELY HELPLESS. I KEEP TELLING HER, "MOM, YOU HAVE TO LET GO! I'M A COLLEGE SOPHOMORE NOW!"
ACTUALLY, YOU'RE NOT, BUT I TAKE YOUR POINT.
POOR MOM. MAYBE I SHOULD SEND HER MY LAUNDRY, AS A GESTURE.

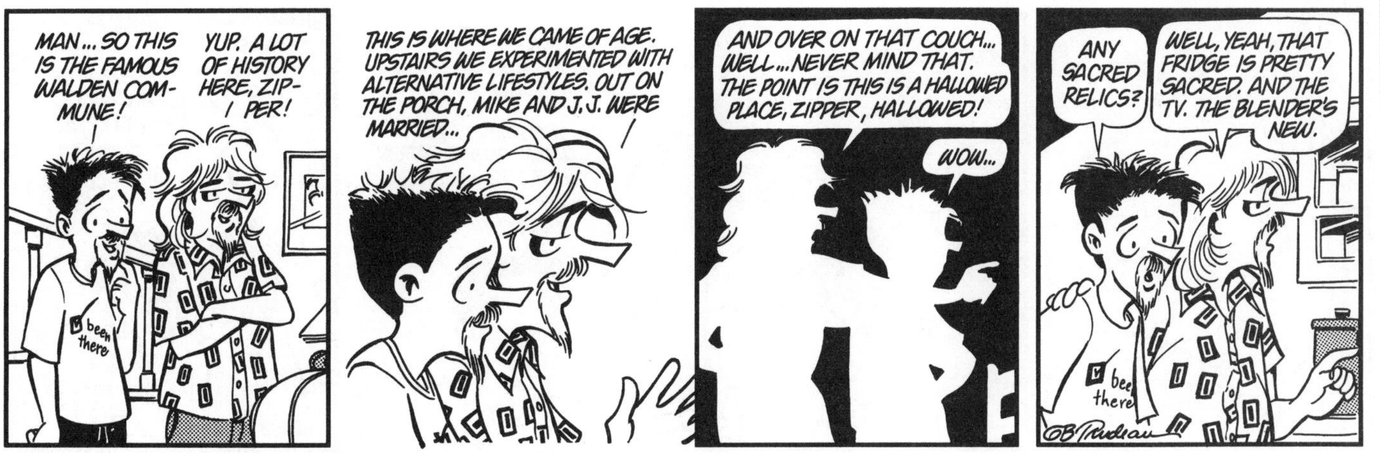
MAN... SO THIS IS THE FAMOUS WALDEN COMMUNE!
YUP. A LOT OF HISTORY HERE, ZIPPER!
been there
THIS IS WHERE WE CAME OF AGE. UPSTAIRS WE EXPERIMENTED WITH ALTERNATIVE LIFESTYLES. OUT ON THE PORCH, MIKE AND J.J. WERE MARRIED...
AND OVER ON THAT COUCH... WELL... NEVER MIND THAT. THE POINT IS THIS IS A HALLOWED PLACE, ZIPPER, HALLOWED!
WOW...
ANY SACRED RELICS?
WELL, YEAH, THAT FRIDGE IS PRETTY SACRED. AND THE TV. THE BLENDER'S NEW.

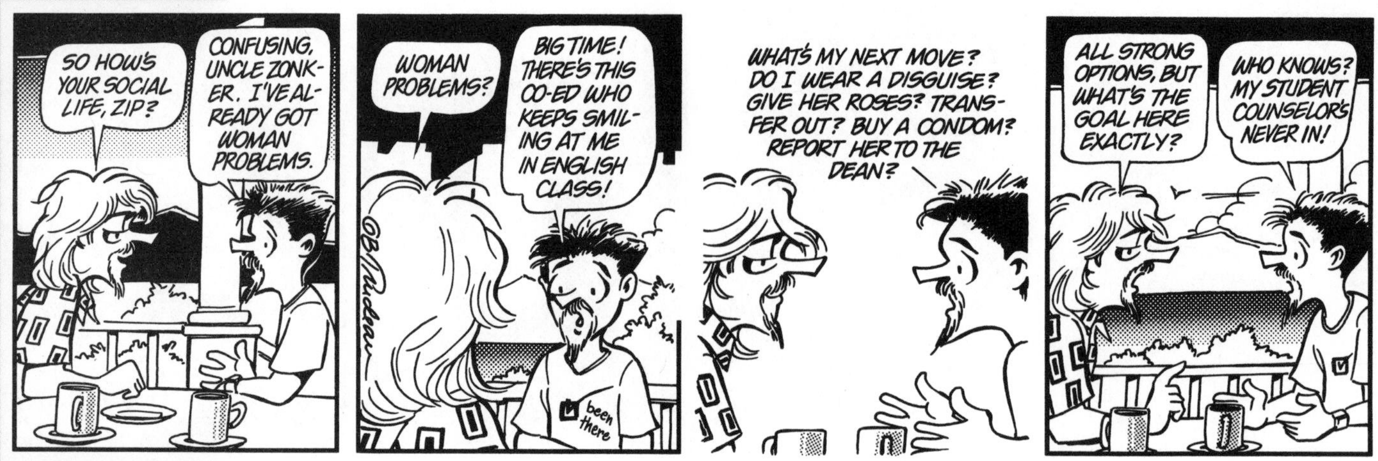
SO HOW'S YOUR SOCIAL LIFE, ZIP?
CONFUSING, UNCLE ZONKER. I'VE ALREADY GOT WOMAN PROBLEMS.
WOMAN PROBLEMS?
BIG TIME! THERE'S THIS CO-ED WHO KEEPS SMILING AT ME IN ENGLISH CLASS!
WHAT'S MY NEXT MOVE? DO I WEAR A DISGUISE? GIVE HER ROSES? TRANSFER OUT? BUY A CONDOM? REPORT HER TO THE DEAN?
ALL STRONG OPTIONS, BUT WHAT'S THE GOAL HERE EXACTLY?
WHO KNOWS? MY STUDENT COUNSELOR'S NEVER IN!

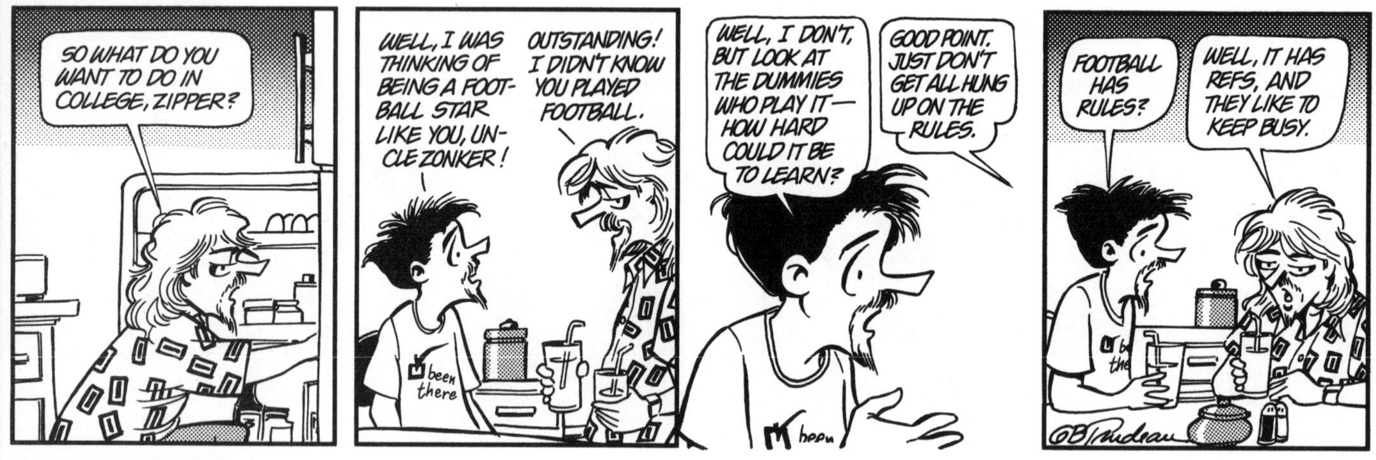
SO WHAT DO YOU WANT TO DO IN COLLEGE, ZIPPER?
WELL, I WAS THINKING OF BEING A FOOTBALL STAR LIKE YOU, UNCLE ZONKER!
OUTSTANDING! I DIDN'T KNOW YOU PLAYED FOOTBALL.
WELL, I DON'T, BUT LOOK AT THE DUMMIES WHO PLAY IT— HOW HARD COULD IT BE TO LEARN?
GOOD POINT. JUST DON'T GET ALL HUNG UP ON THE RULES.
FOOTBALL HAS RULES?
WELL, IT HAS REFS, AND THEY LIKE TO KEEP BUSY.

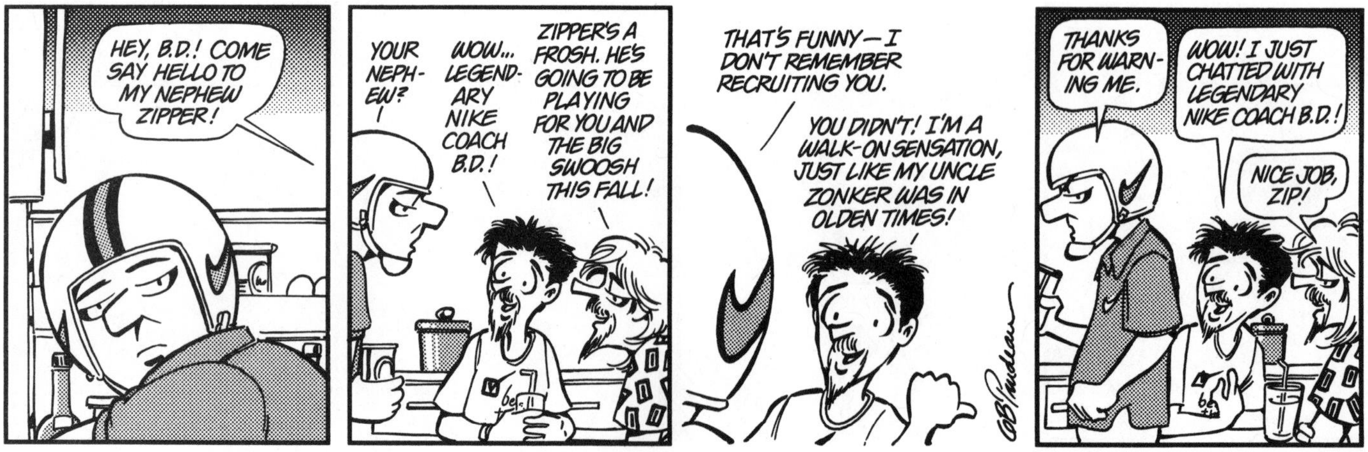
HEY, B.D.! COME SAY HELLO TO MY NEPHEW ZIPPER!
YOUR NEPHEW?
WOW... LEGENDARY NIKE COACH B.D.!
ZIPPER'S A FROSH. HE'S GOING TO BE PLAYING FOR YOU AND THE BIG SWOOSH THIS FALL!
THAT'S FUNNY—I DON'T REMEMBER RECRUITING YOU.
YOU DIDN'T! I'M A WALK-ON SENSATION, JUST LIKE MY UNCLE ZONKER WAS IN OLDEN TIMES!
THANKS FOR WARNING ME.
WOW! I JUST CHATTED WITH LEGENDARY NIKE COACH B.D.!
NICE JOB, ZIP!

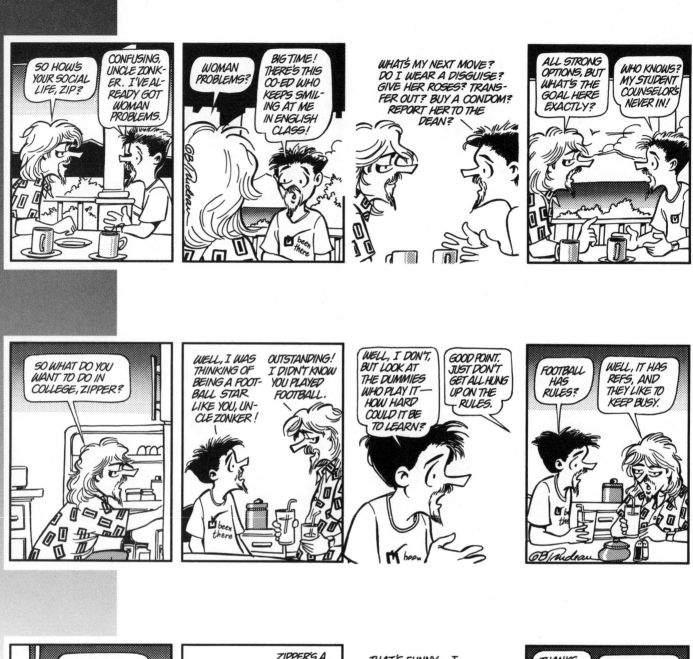

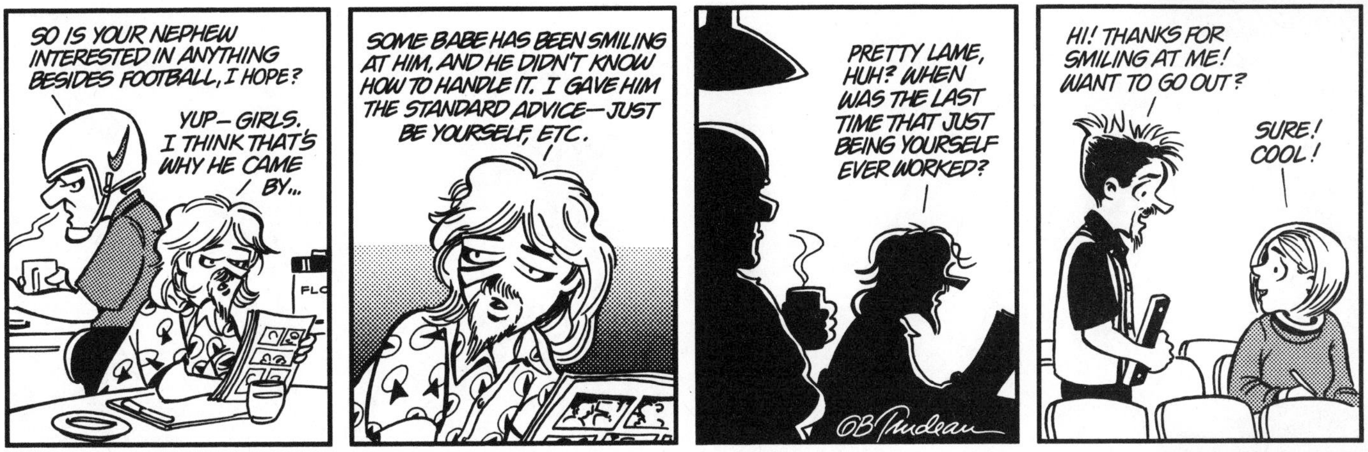
SO IS YOUR NEPHEW INTERESTED IN ANYTHING BESIDES FOOTBALL, I HOPE?
YUP – GIRLS. I THINK THAT'S WHY HE CAME BY...
SOME BABE HAS BEEN SMILING AT HIM, AND HE DIDN'T KNOW HOW TO HANDLE IT. I GAVE HIM THE STANDARD ADVICE – JUST BE YOURSELF, ETC.
PRETTY LAME, HUH? WHEN WAS THE LAST TIME THAT JUST BEING YOURSELF EVER WORKED?
HI! THANKS FOR SMILING AT ME! WANT TO GO OUT?
SURE! COOL!

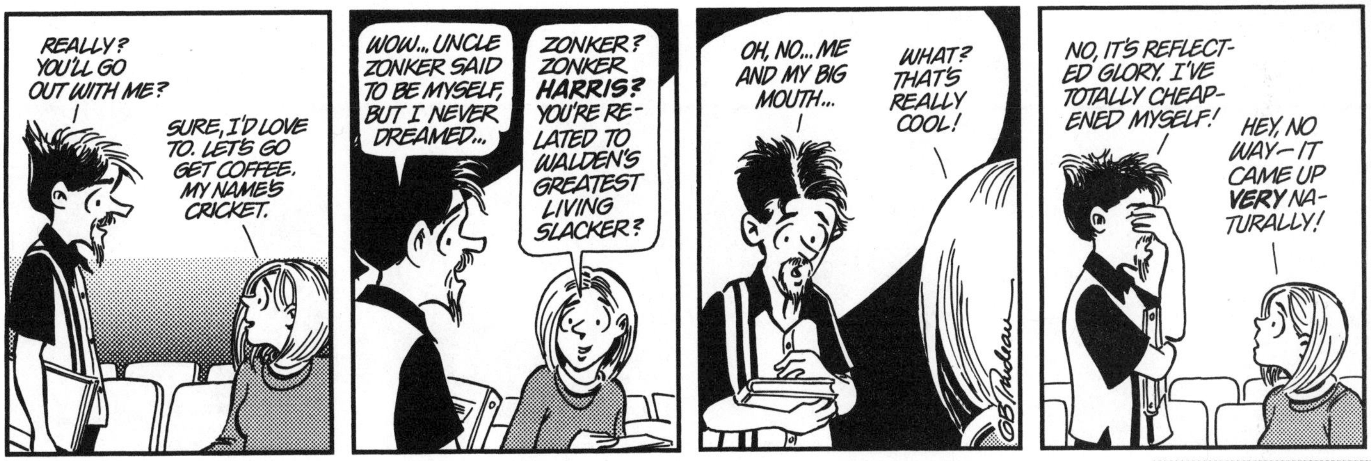
REALLY? YOU'LL GO OUT WITH ME?
SURE, I'D LOVE TO. LET'S GO GET COFFEE. MY NAME'S CRICKET.
WOW... UNCLE ZONKER SAID TO BE MYSELF, BUT I NEVER DREAMED...
ZONKER? ZONKER **HARRIS?** YOU'RE RELATED TO WALDEN'S GREATEST LIVING SLACKER?
OH, NO... ME AND MY BIG MOUTH...
WHAT? THAT'S REALLY COOL!
NO, IT'S REFLECTED GLORY. I'VE TOTALLY CHEAPENED MYSELF!
HEY, NO WAY – IT CAME UP **VERY** NATURALLY!

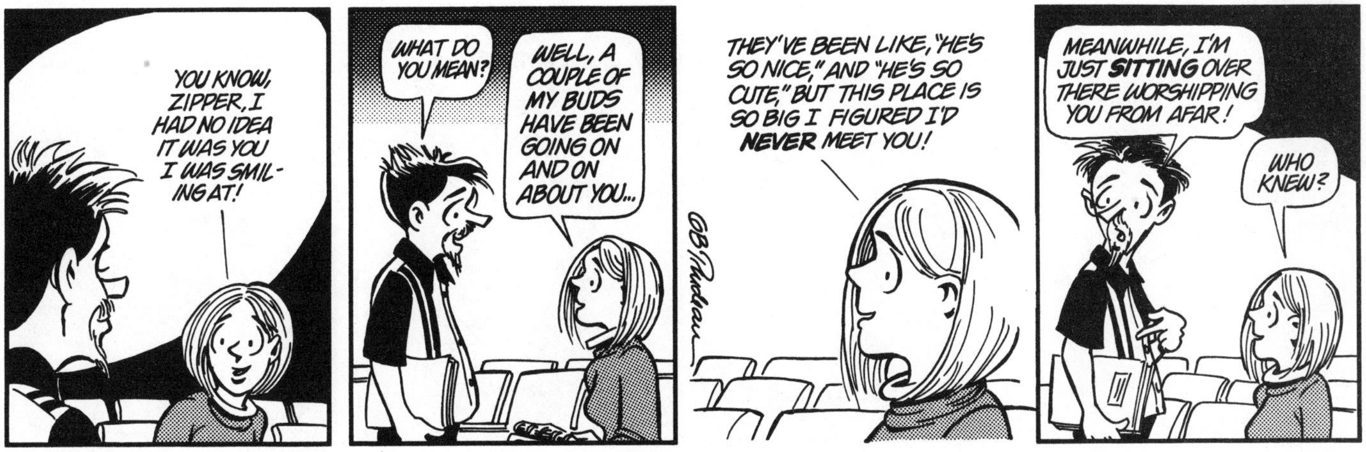
YOU KNOW, ZIPPER, I HAD NO IDEA IT WAS YOU I WAS SMILING AT!
WHAT DO YOU MEAN?
WELL, A COUPLE OF MY BUDS HAVE BEEN GOING ON AND ON ABOUT YOU...
THEY'VE BEEN LIKE, "HE'S SO NICE," AND "HE'S SO CUTE," BUT THIS PLACE IS SO BIG I FIGURED I'D **NEVER** MEET YOU!
MEANWHILE, I'M JUST **SITTING** OVER THERE WORSHIPPING YOU FROM AFAR!
WHO KNEW?

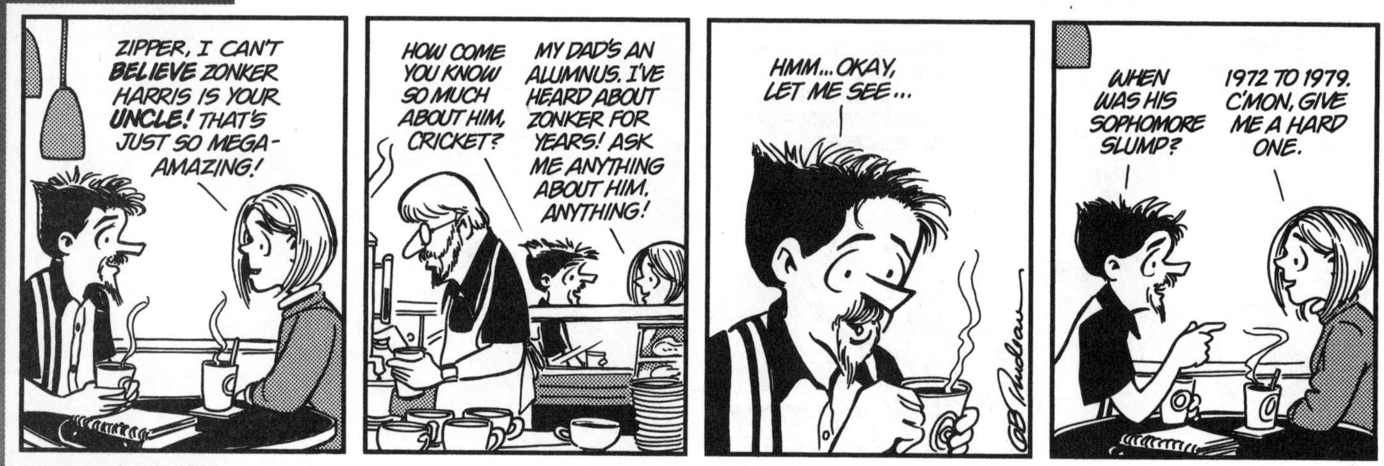
ZIPPER, I CAN'T **BELIEVE** ZONKER HARRIS IS YOUR **UNCLE!** THAT'S JUST SO MEGA-AMAZING!
HOW COME YOU KNOW SO MUCH ABOUT HIM, CRICKET?
MY DAD'S AN ALUMNUS. I'VE HEARD ABOUT ZONKER FOR YEARS! ASK ME ANYTHING ABOUT HIM. ANYTHING!
HMM... OKAY, LET ME SEE...
WHEN WAS HIS SOPHOMORE SLUMP?
1972 TO 1979. C'MON, GIVE ME A HARD ONE.

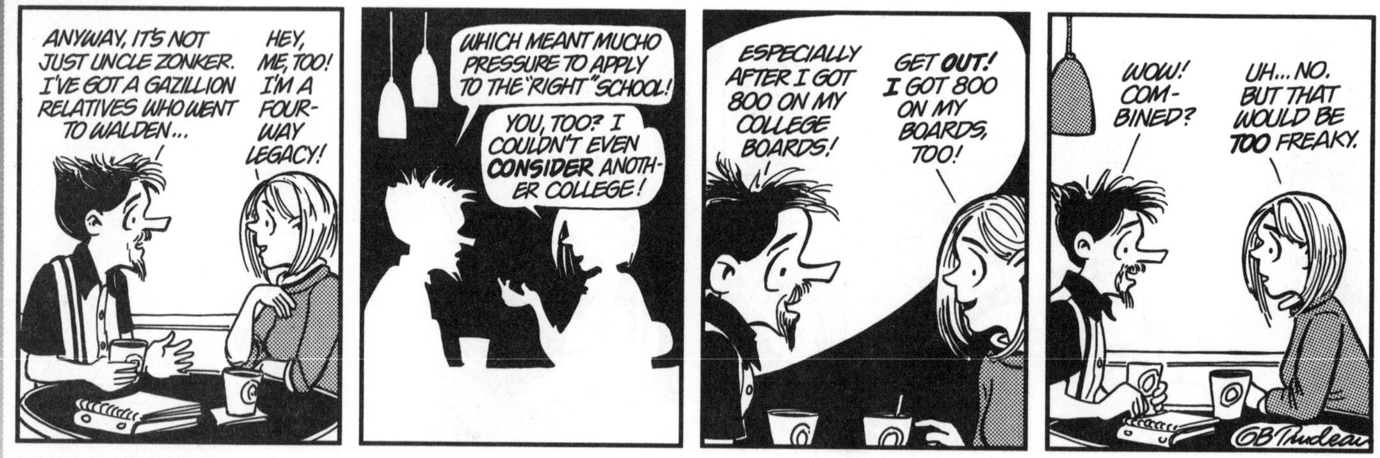
ANYWAY, IT'S NOT JUST UNCLE ZONKER. I'VE GOT A GAZILLION RELATIVES WHO WENT TO WALDEN...
HEY, ME, TOO! I'M A FOUR-WAY LEGACY!
WHICH MEANT MUCHO PRESSURE TO APPLY TO THE "RIGHT" SCHOOL!
YOU, TOO? I COULDN'T EVEN **CONSIDER** ANOTHER COLLEGE!
ESPECIALLY AFTER I GOT 800 ON MY COLLEGE BOARDS!
GET **OUT!** **I** GOT 800 ON MY BOARDS, TOO!
WOW! COMBINED?
UH... NO. BUT THAT WOULD BE **TOO** FREAKY.

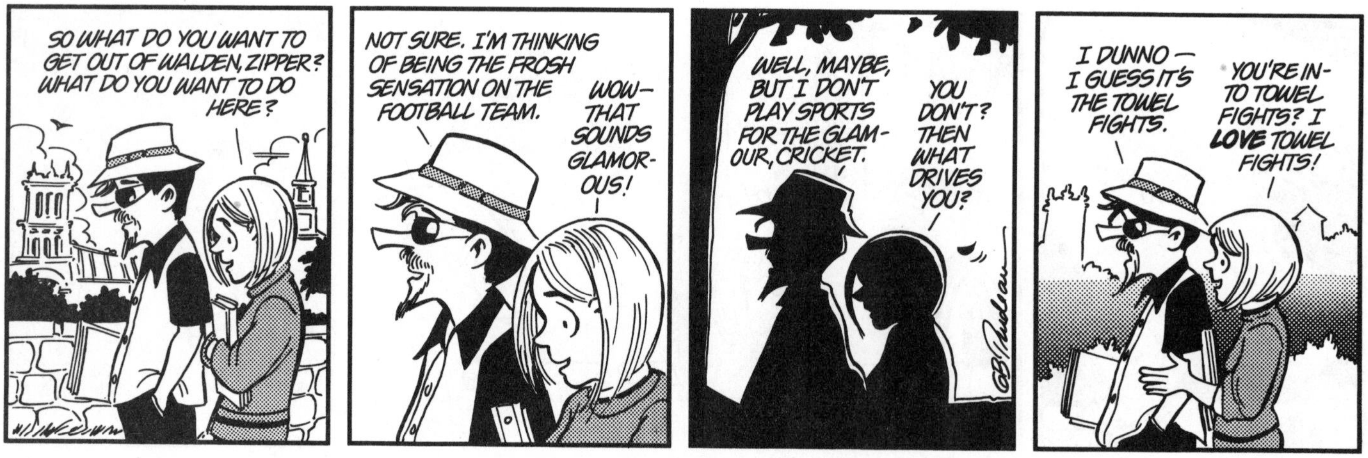
SO WHAT DO YOU WANT TO GET OUT OF WALDEN, ZIPPER? WHAT DO YOU WANT TO DO HERE?
NOT SURE. I'M THINKING OF BEING THE FROSH SENSATION ON THE FOOTBALL TEAM.
WOW—THAT SOUNDS GLAMOROUS!
WELL, MAYBE, BUT I DON'T PLAY SPORTS FOR THE GLAMOUR, CRICKET.
YOU DON'T? THEN WHAT DRIVES YOU?
I DUNNO—I GUESS IT'S THE TOWEL FIGHTS.
YOU'RE INTO TOWEL FIGHTS? I **LOVE** TOWEL FIGHTS!

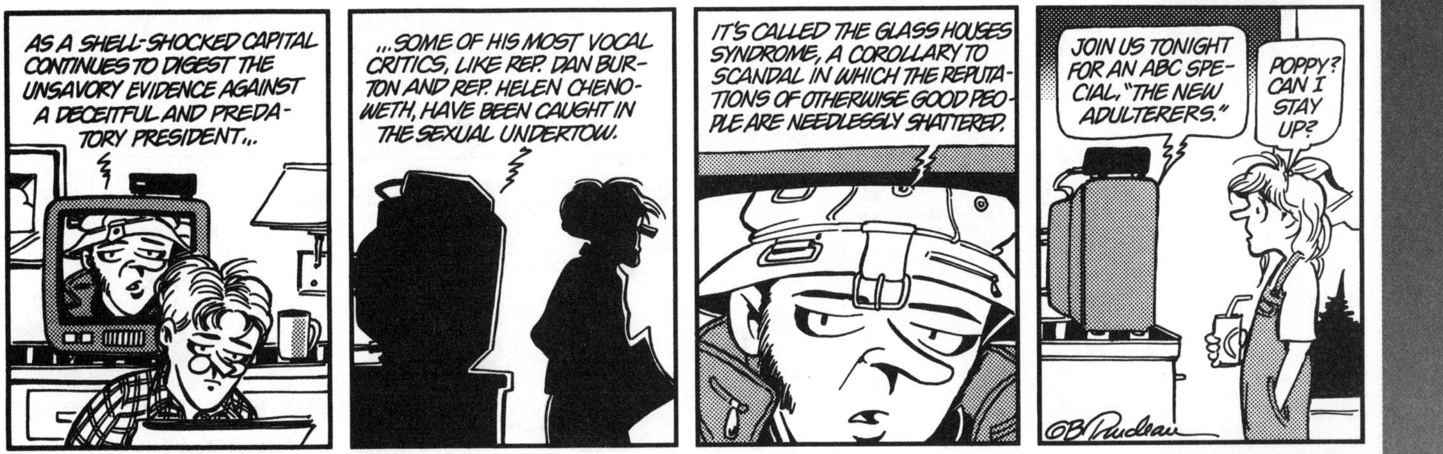
AS A SHELL-SHOCKED CAPITAL CONTINUES TO DIGEST THE UNSAVORY EVIDENCE AGAINST A DECEITFUL AND PREDATORY PRESIDENT...
...SOME OF HIS MOST VOCAL CRITICS, LIKE REP. DAN BURTON AND REP. HELEN CHENOWETH, HAVE BEEN CAUGHT IN THE SEXUAL UNDERTOW.
IT'S CALLED THE GLASS HOUSES SYNDROME, A COROLLARY TO SCANDAL IN WHICH THE REPUTATIONS OF OTHERWISE GOOD PEOPLE ARE NEEDLESSLY SHATTERED.
JOIN US TONIGHT FOR AN ABC SPECIAL, "THE NEW ADULTERERS."
POPPY? CAN I STAY UP?

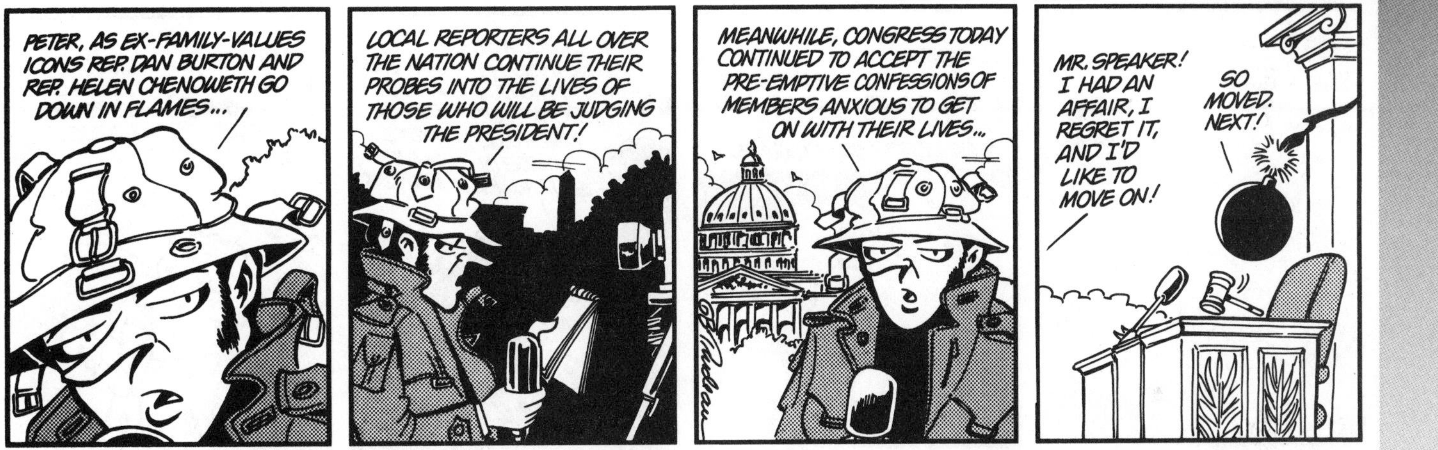
PETER, AS EX-FAMILY-VALUES ICONS REP. DAN BURTON AND REP. HELEN CHENOWETH GO DOWN IN FLAMES...
LOCAL REPORTERS ALL OVER THE NATION CONTINUE THEIR PROBES INTO THE LIVES OF THOSE WHO WILL BE JUDGING THE PRESIDENT!
MEANWHILE, CONGRESS TODAY CONTINUED TO ACCEPT THE PRE-EMPTIVE CONFESSIONS OF MEMBERS ANXIOUS TO GET ON WITH THEIR LIVES...
MR. SPEAKER! I HAD AN AFFAIR, I REGRET IT, AND I'D LIKE TO MOVE ON!
SO MOVED. NEXT!

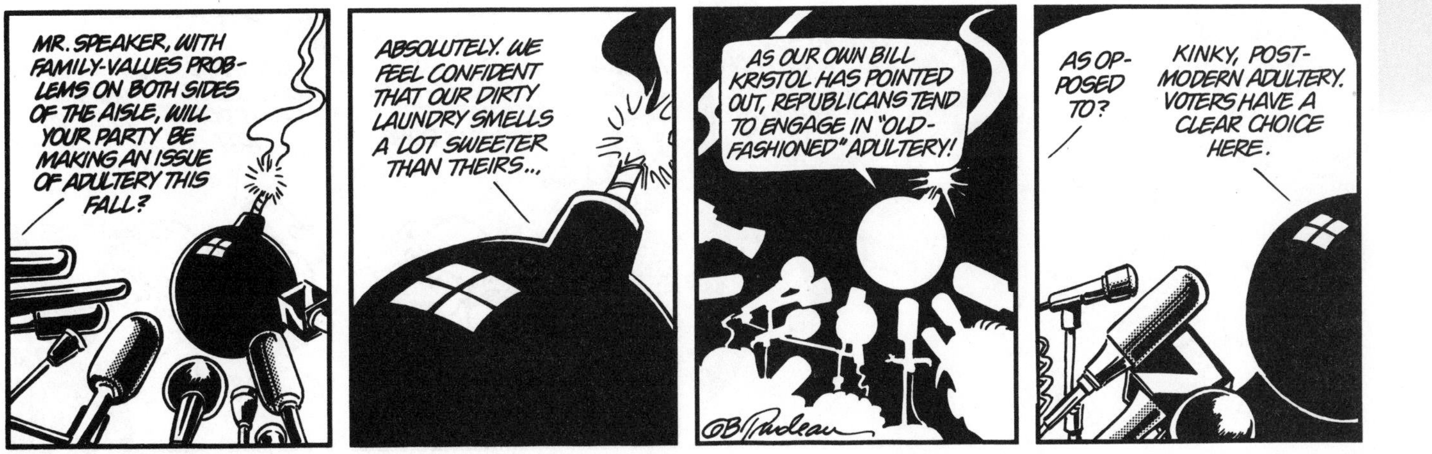
MR. SPEAKER, WITH FAMILY-VALUES PROBLEMS ON BOTH SIDES OF THE AISLE, WILL YOUR PARTY BE MAKING AN ISSUE OF ADULTERY THIS FALL?
ABSOLUTELY. WE FEEL CONFIDENT THAT OUR DIRTY LAUNDRY SMELLS A LOT SWEETER THAN THEIRS...
AS OUR OWN BILL KRISTOL HAS POINTED OUT, REPUBLICANS TEND TO ENGAGE IN "OLD-FASHIONED" ADULTERY!
AS OPPOSED TO?
KINKY, POST-MODERN ADULTERY. VOTERS HAVE A CLEAR CHOICE HERE.

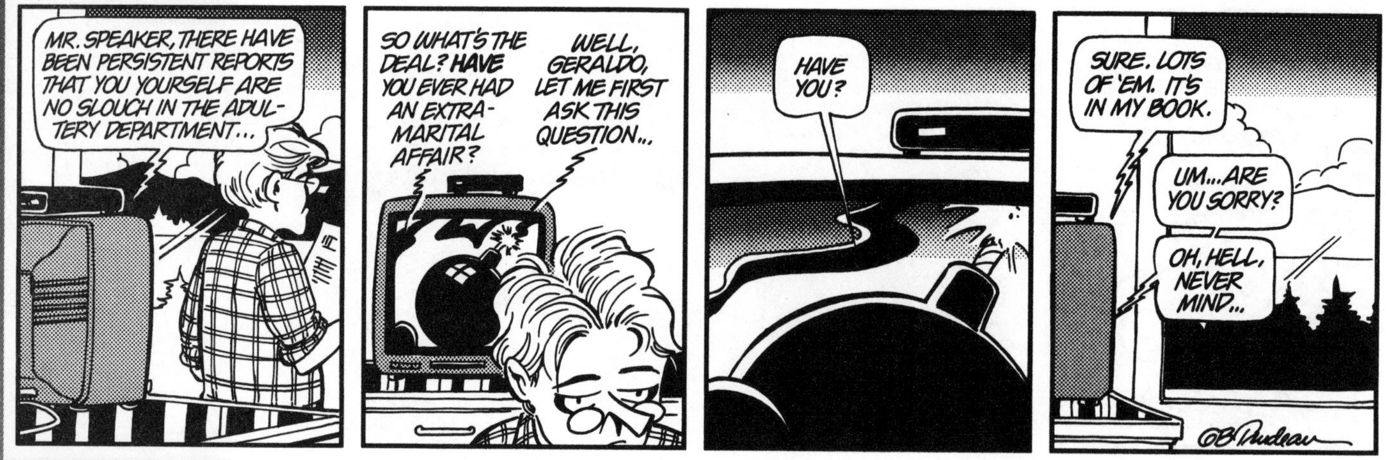
MR. SPEAKER, THERE HAVE BEEN PERSISTENT REPORTS THAT YOU YOURSELF ARE NO SLOUCH IN THE ADULTERY DEPARTMENT...
SO WHAT'S THE DEAL? HAVE YOU EVER HAD AN EXTRA-MARITAL AFFAIR?
WELL, GERALDO, LET ME FIRST ASK THIS QUESTION...
HAVE YOU?
SURE. LOTS OF 'EM. IT'S IN MY BOOK.
UM... ARE YOU SORRY?
OH, HELL, NEVER MIND...

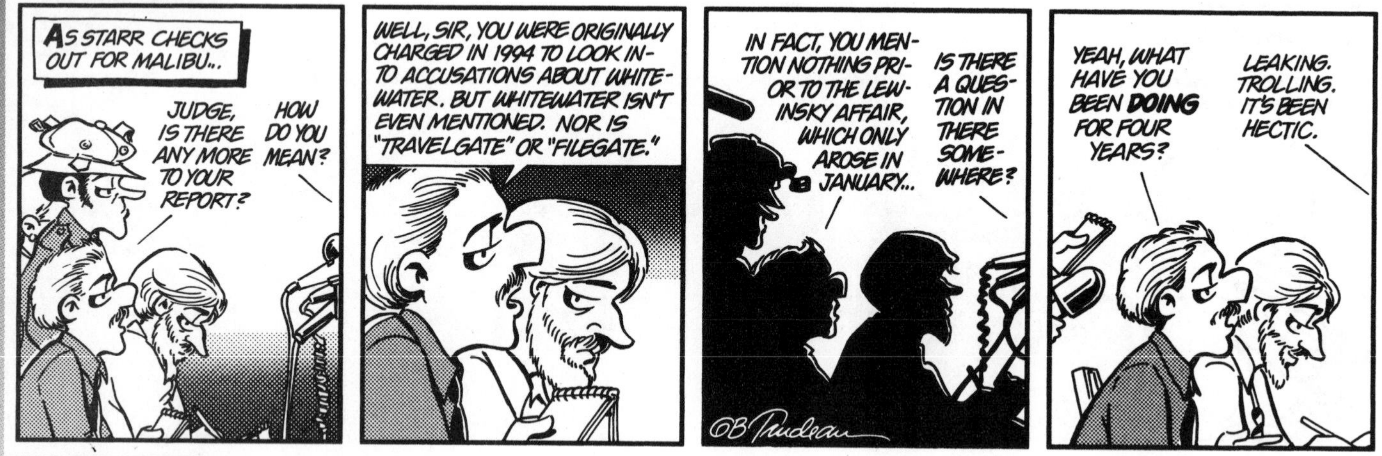
AS STARR CHECKS OUT FOR MALIBU...
JUDGE, IS THERE ANY MORE TO YOUR REPORT?
HOW DO YOU MEAN?
WELL, SIR, YOU WERE ORIGINALLY CHARGED IN 1994 TO LOOK INTO ACCUSATIONS ABOUT WHITEWATER. BUT WHITEWATER ISN'T EVEN MENTIONED. NOR IS "TRAVELGATE" OR "FILEGATE."
IN FACT, YOU MENTION NOTHING PRIOR TO THE LEWINSKY AFFAIR, WHICH ONLY AROSE IN JANUARY...
IS THERE A QUESTION IN THERE SOMEWHERE?
YEAH, WHAT HAVE YOU BEEN DOING FOR FOUR YEARS?
LEAKING. TROLLING. IT'S BEEN HECTIC.

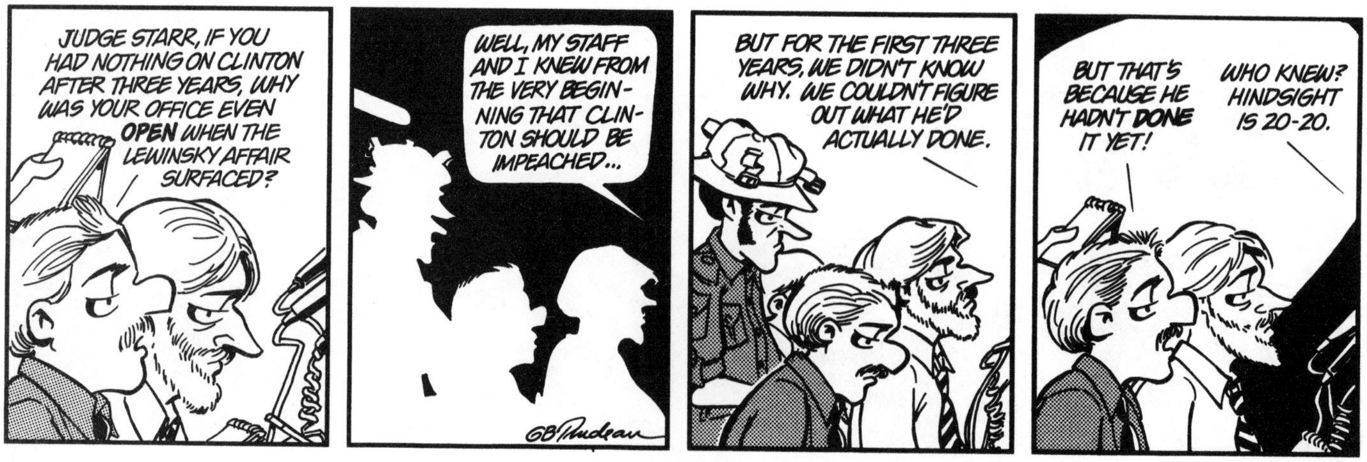
JUDGE STARR, IF YOU HAD NOTHING ON CLINTON AFTER THREE YEARS, WHY WAS YOUR OFFICE EVEN OPEN WHEN THE LEWINSKY AFFAIR SURFACED?
WELL, MY STAFF AND I KNEW FROM THE VERY BEGINNING THAT CLINTON SHOULD BE IMPEACHED...
BUT FOR THE FIRST THREE YEARS, WE DIDN'T KNOW WHY. WE COULDN'T FIGURE OUT WHAT HE'D ACTUALLY DONE.
BUT THAT'S BECAUSE HE HADN'T DONE IT YET!
WHO KNEW? HINDSIGHT IS 20-20.

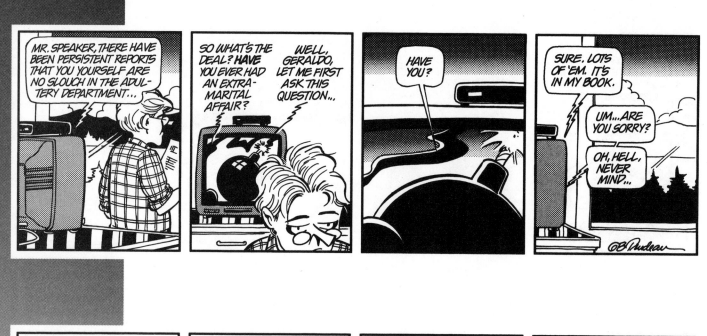

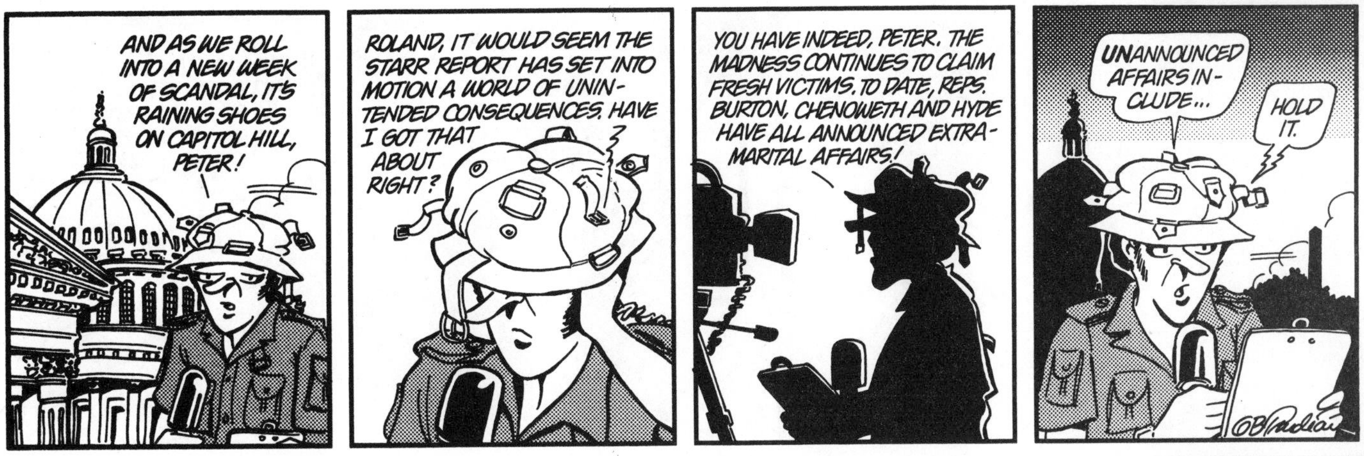
AND AS WE ROLL INTO A NEW WEEK OF SCANDAL, IT'S RAINING SHOES ON CAPITOL HILL, PETER!
ROLAND, IT WOULD SEEM THE STARR REPORT HAS SET INTO MOTION A WORLD OF UNINTENDED CONSEQUENCES. HAVE I GOT THAT ABOUT RIGHT?
YOU HAVE INDEED, PETER. THE MADNESS CONTINUES TO CLAIM FRESH VICTIMS. TO DATE, REPS. BURTON, CHENOWETH AND HYDE HAVE ALL ANNOUNCED EXTRAMARITAL AFFAIRS!
UNANNOUNCED AFFAIRS INCLUDE...
HOLD IT.
©B. Trudeau

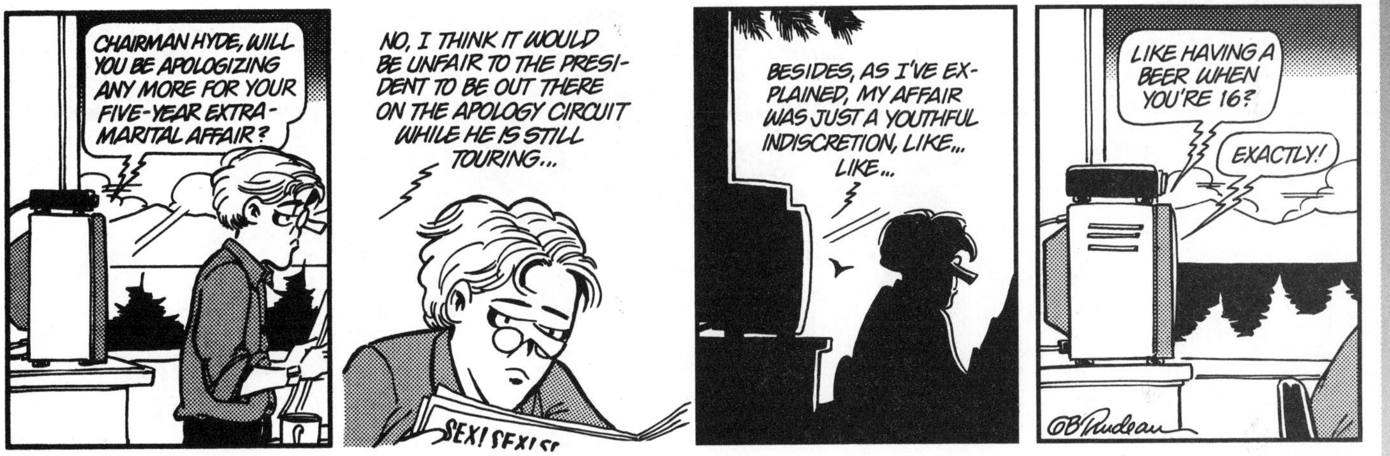
CHAIRMAN HYDE, WILL YOU BE APOLOGIZING ANY MORE FOR YOUR FIVE-YEAR EXTRAMARITAL AFFAIR?
NO, I THINK IT WOULD BE UNFAIR TO THE PRESIDENT TO BE OUT THERE ON THE APOLOGY CIRCUIT WHILE HE IS STILL TOURING...
SEX! SEX!
BESIDES, AS I'VE EXPLAINED, MY AFFAIR WAS JUST A YOUTHFUL INDISCRETION, LIKE... LIKE...
LIKE HAVING A BEER WHEN YOU'RE 16?
EXACTLY!
©B. Trudeau

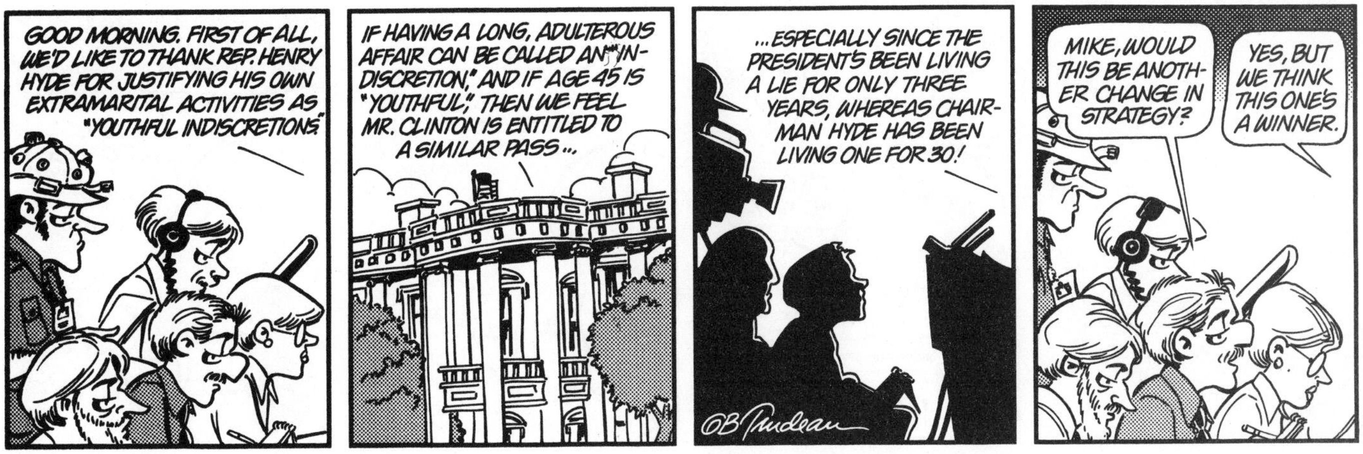
GOOD MORNING. FIRST OF ALL, WE'D LIKE TO THANK REP. HENRY HYDE FOR JUSTIFYING HIS OWN EXTRAMARITAL ACTIVITIES AS "YOUTHFUL INDISCRETIONS."
IF HAVING A LONG, ADULTEROUS AFFAIR CAN BE CALLED AN "INDISCRETION," AND IF AGE 45 IS "YOUTHFUL," THEN WE FEEL MR. CLINTON IS ENTITLED TO A SIMILAR PASS...
...ESPECIALLY SINCE THE PRESIDENT'S BEEN LIVING A LIE FOR ONLY THREE YEARS, WHEREAS CHAIRMAN HYDE HAS BEEN LIVING ONE FOR 30!
©B. Trudeau
MIKE, WOULD THIS BE ANOTHER CHANGE IN STRATEGY?
YES, BUT WE THINK THIS ONE'S A WINNER.

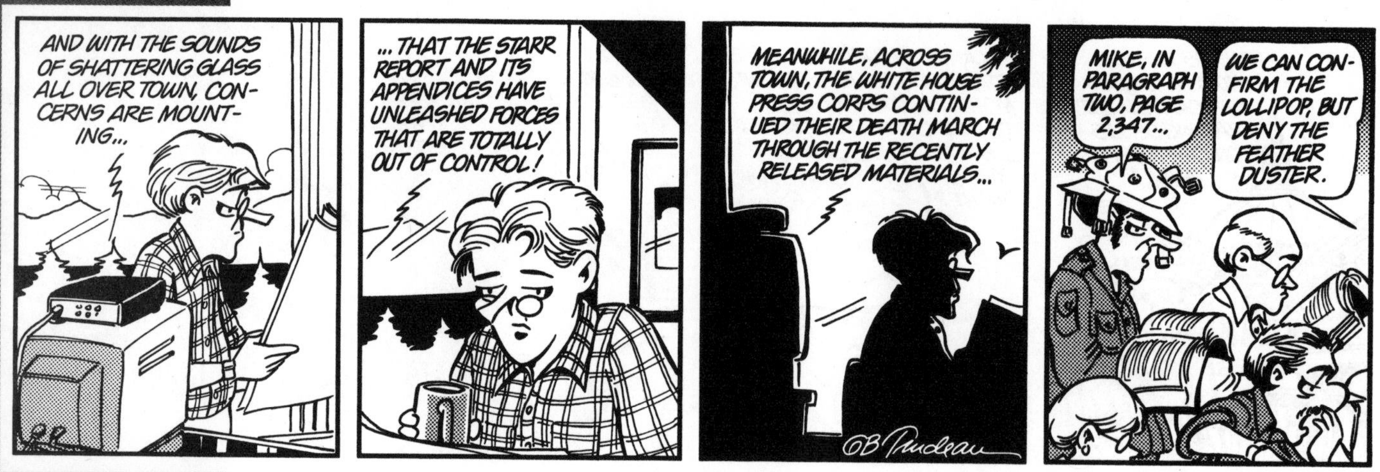
AND WITH THE SOUNDS OF SHATTERING GLASS ALL OVER TOWN, CONCERNS ARE MOUNTING...
...THAT THE STARR REPORT AND ITS APPENDICES HAVE UNLEASHED FORCES THAT ARE TOTALLY OUT OF CONTROL!
MEANWHILE, ACROSS TOWN, THE WHITE HOUSE PRESS CORPS CONTINUED THEIR DEATH MARCH THROUGH THE RECENTLY RELEASED MATERIALS...
MIKE, IN PARAGRAPH TWO, PAGE 2,347...
WE CAN CONFIRM THE LOLLIPOP, BUT DENY THE FEATHER DUSTER.

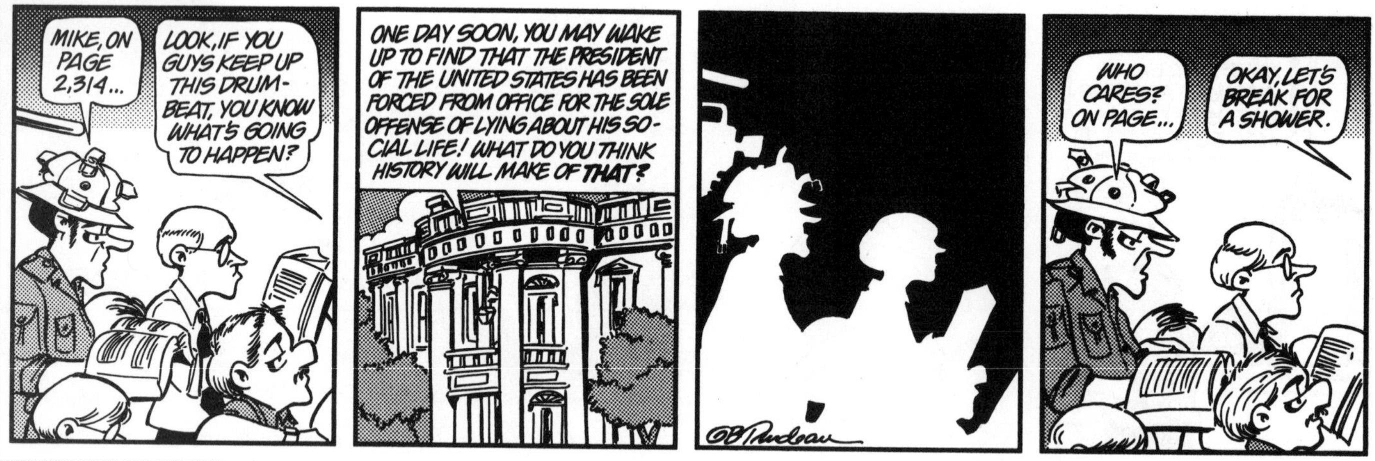
MIKE, ON PAGE 2,314...
LOOK, IF YOU GUYS KEEP UP THIS DRUMBEAT, YOU KNOW WHAT'S GOING TO HAPPEN?
ONE DAY SOON, YOU MAY WAKE UP TO FIND THAT THE PRESIDENT OF THE UNITED STATES HAS BEEN FORCED FROM OFFICE FOR THE SOLE OFFENSE OF LYING ABOUT HIS SOCIAL LIFE! WHAT DO YOU THINK HISTORY WILL MAKE OF THAT?
WHO CARES? ON PAGE...
OKAY, LET'S BREAK FOR A SHOWER.

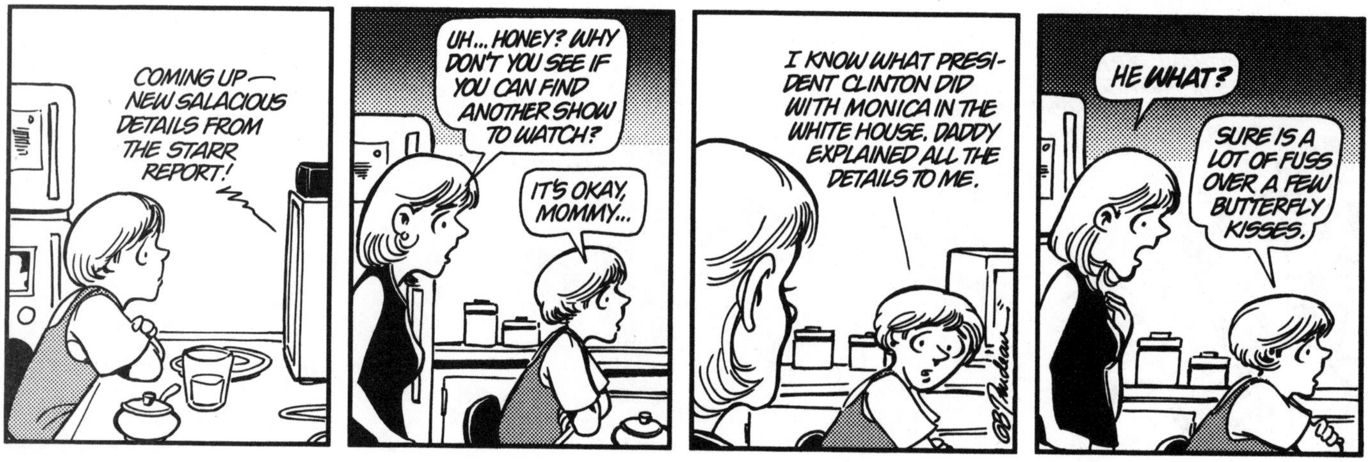
COMING UP— NEW SALACIOUS DETAILS FROM THE STARR REPORT!
UH... HONEY? WHY DON'T YOU SEE IF YOU CAN FIND ANOTHER SHOW TO WATCH?
IT'S OKAY, MOMMY...
I KNOW WHAT PRESIDENT CLINTON DID WITH MONICA IN THE WHITE HOUSE. DADDY EXPLAINED ALL THE DETAILS TO ME.
HE WHAT?
SURE IS A LOT OF FUSS OVER A FEW BUTTERFLY KISSES.

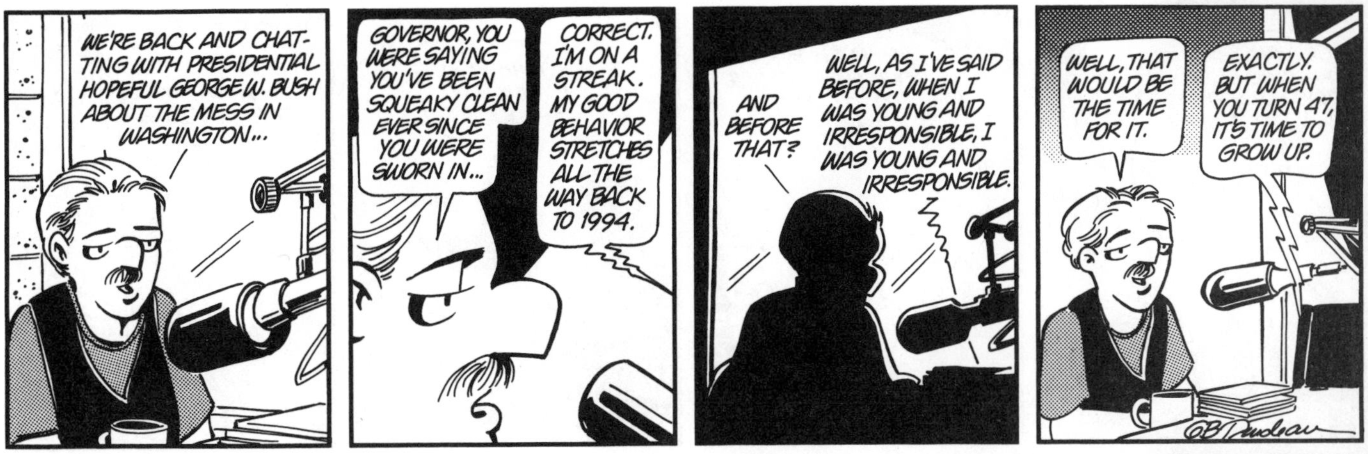
WE'RE BACK AND CHATTING WITH PRESIDENTIAL HOPEFUL GEORGE W. BUSH ABOUT THE MESS IN WASHINGTON...
GOVERNOR, YOU WERE SAYING YOU'VE BEEN SQUEAKY CLEAN EVER SINCE YOU WERE SWORN IN...
CORRECT. I'M ON A STREAK. MY GOOD BEHAVIOR STRETCHES ALL THE WAY BACK TO 1994.
AND BEFORE THAT?
WELL, AS I'VE SAID BEFORE, WHEN I WAS YOUNG AND IRRESPONSIBLE, I WAS YOUNG AND IRRESPONSIBLE.
WELL, THAT WOULD BE THE TIME FOR IT.
EXACTLY. BUT WHEN YOU TURN 47, IT'S TIME TO GROW UP.
©B Trudeau

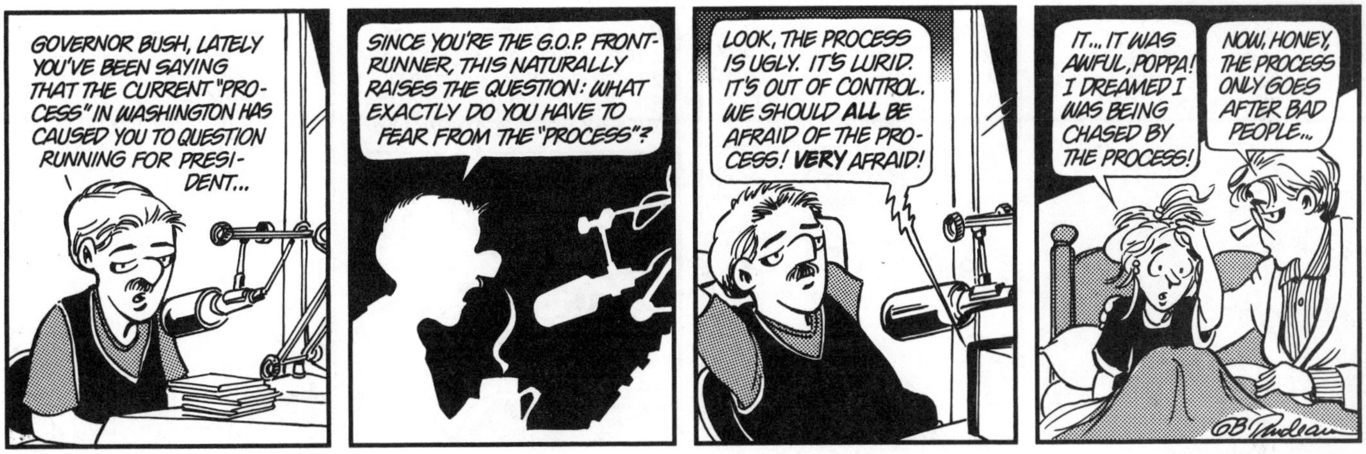
GOVERNOR BUSH, LATELY YOU'VE BEEN SAYING THAT THE CURRENT "PROCESS" IN WASHINGTON HAS CAUSED YOU TO QUESTION RUNNING FOR PRESIDENT...
SINCE YOU'RE THE G.O.P. FRONT-RUNNER, THIS NATURALLY RAISES THE QUESTION: WHAT EXACTLY DO YOU HAVE TO FEAR FROM THE "PROCESS"?
LOOK, THE PROCESS IS UGLY. IT'S LURID. IT'S OUT OF CONTROL. WE SHOULD ALL BE AFRAID OF THE PROCESS! VERY AFRAID!
IT... IT WAS AWFUL, POPPA! I DREAMED I WAS BEING CHASED BY THE PROCESS!
NOW, HONEY, THE PROCESS ONLY GOES AFTER BAD PEOPLE...
©B Trudeau

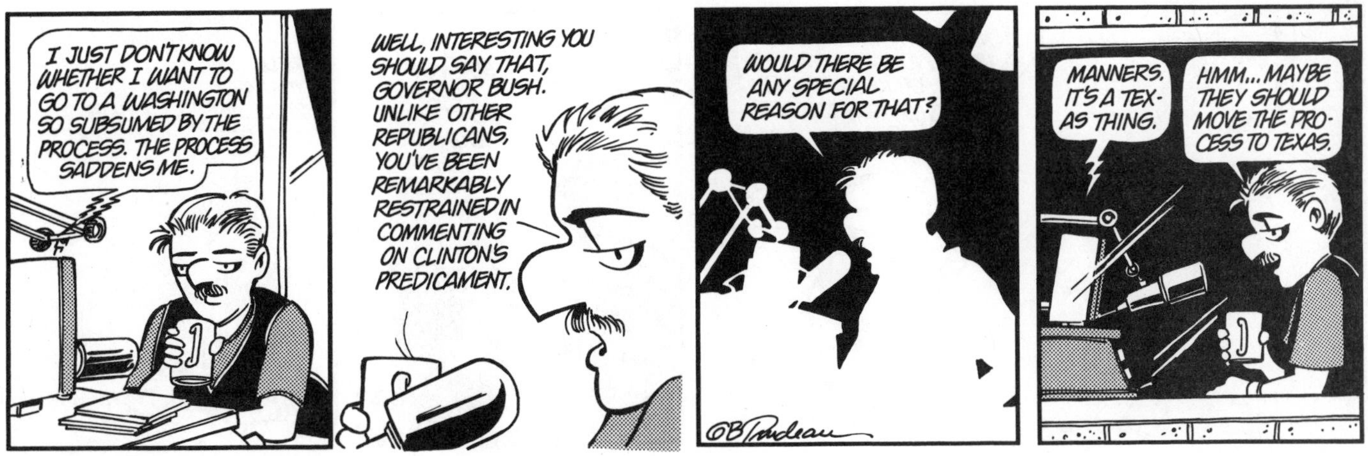
I JUST DON'T KNOW WHETHER I WANT TO GO TO A WASHINGTON SO SUBSUMED BY THE PROCESS. THE PROCESS SADDENS ME.
WELL, INTERESTING YOU SHOULD SAY THAT, GOVERNOR BUSH. UNLIKE OTHER REPUBLICANS, YOU'VE BEEN REMARKABLY RESTRAINED IN COMMENTING ON CLINTON'S PREDICAMENT.
WOULD THERE BE ANY SPECIAL REASON FOR THAT?
MANNERS. IT'S A TEXAS THING.
HMM... MAYBE THEY SHOULD MOVE THE PROCESS TO TEXAS.
©B Trudeau

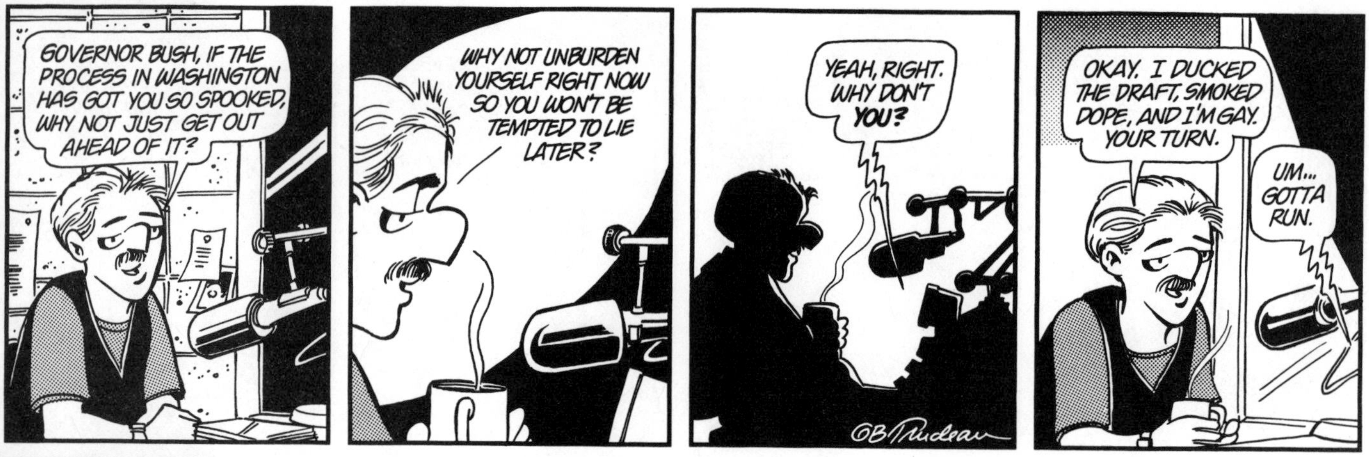
GOVERNOR BUSH, IF THE PROCESS IN WASHINGTON HAS GOT YOU SO SPOOKED, WHY NOT JUST GET OUT AHEAD OF IT?
WHY NOT UNBURDEN YOURSELF RIGHT NOW SO YOU WON'T BE TEMPTED TO LIE LATER?
YEAH, RIGHT. WHY DON'T YOU?
OKAY. I DUCKED THE DRAFT, SMOKED DOPE, AND I'M GAY. YOUR TURN.
UM... GOTTA RUN.
©B Trudeau

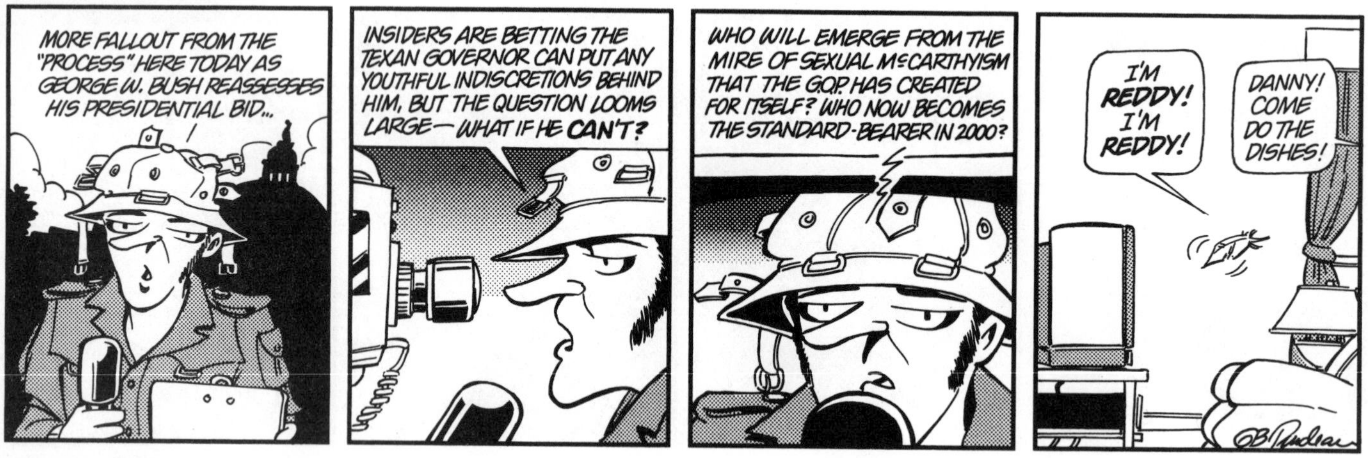
MORE FALLOUT FROM THE "PROCESS" HERE TODAY AS GEORGE W. BUSH REASSESSES HIS PRESIDENTIAL BID...
INSIDERS ARE BETTING THE TEXAN GOVERNOR CAN PUT ANY YOUTHFUL INDISCRETIONS BEHIND HIM, BUT THE QUESTION LOOMS LARGE— WHAT IF HE CAN'T?
WHO WILL EMERGE FROM THE MIRE OF SEXUAL McCARTHYISM THAT THE G.O.P. HAS CREATED FOR ITSELF? WHO NOW BECOMES THE STANDARD-BEARER IN 2000?
I'M REDDY! I'M REDDY!
DANNY! COME DO THE DISHES!
©B Trudeau

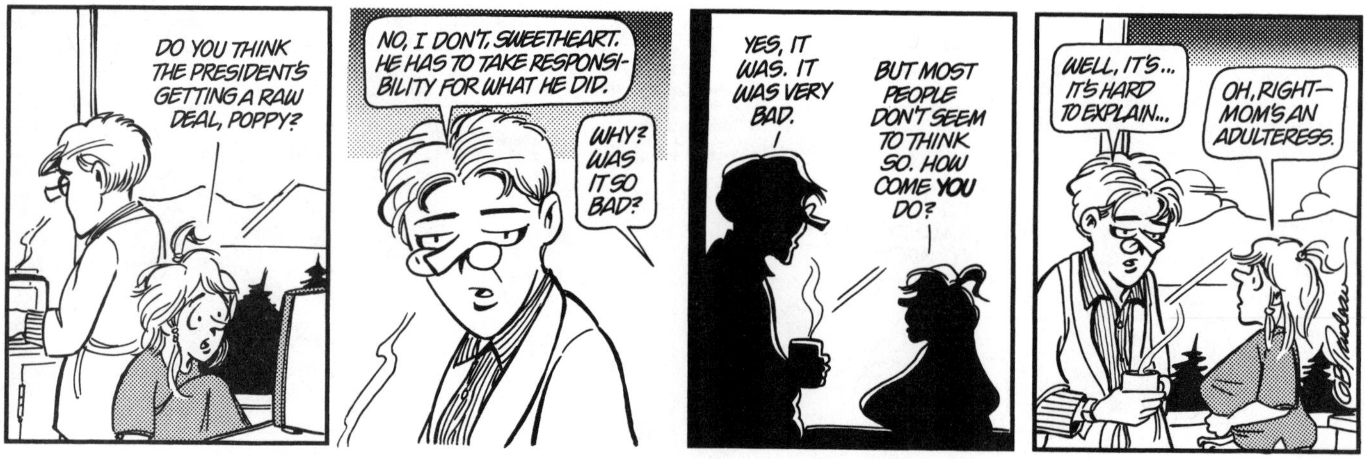
DO YOU THINK THE PRESIDENT'S GETTING A RAW DEAL, POPPY?
NO, I DON'T, SWEETHEART. HE HAS TO TAKE RESPONSIBILITY FOR WHAT HE DID.
WHY? WAS IT SO BAD?
YES, IT WAS. IT WAS VERY BAD.
BUT MOST PEOPLE DON'T SEEM TO THINK SO. HOW COME YOU DO?
WELL, IT'S... IT'S HARD TO EXPLAIN...
OH, RIGHT— MOM'S AN ADULTERESS.
©B Trudeau

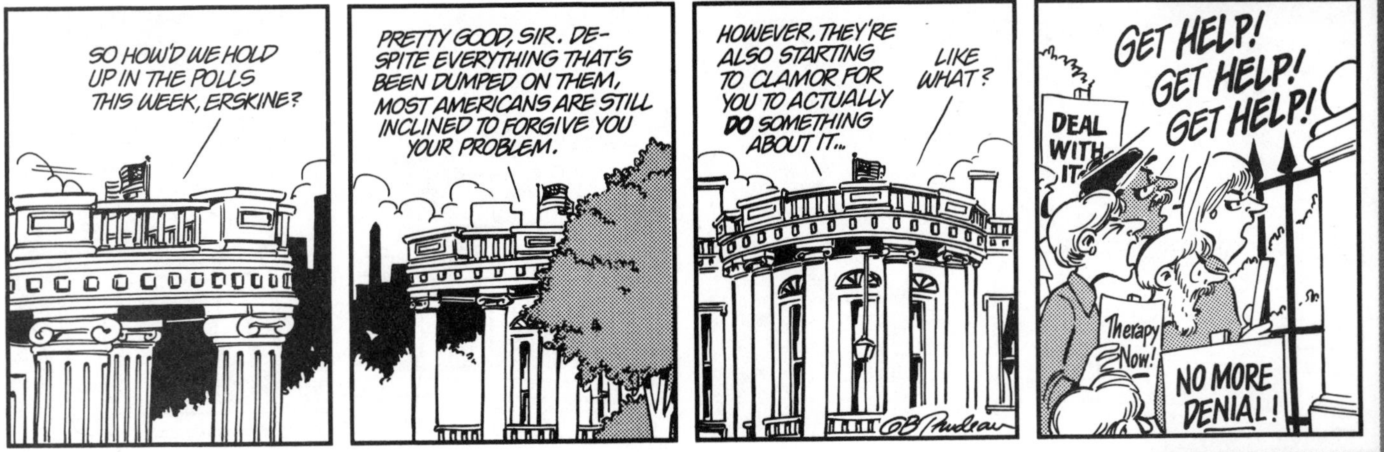
SO HOW'D WE HOLD UP IN THE POLLS THIS WEEK, ERSKINE?
PRETTY GOOD, SIR. DESPITE EVERYTHING THAT'S BEEN DUMPED ON THEM, MOST AMERICANS ARE STILL INCLINED TO FORGIVE YOU YOUR PROBLEM.
HOWEVER, THEY'RE ALSO STARTING TO CLAMOR FOR YOU TO ACTUALLY DO SOMETHING ABOUT IT...
LIKE WHAT?
GET HELP! GET HELP! GET HELP!
DEAL WITH IT
Therapy Now!
NO MORE DENIAL!

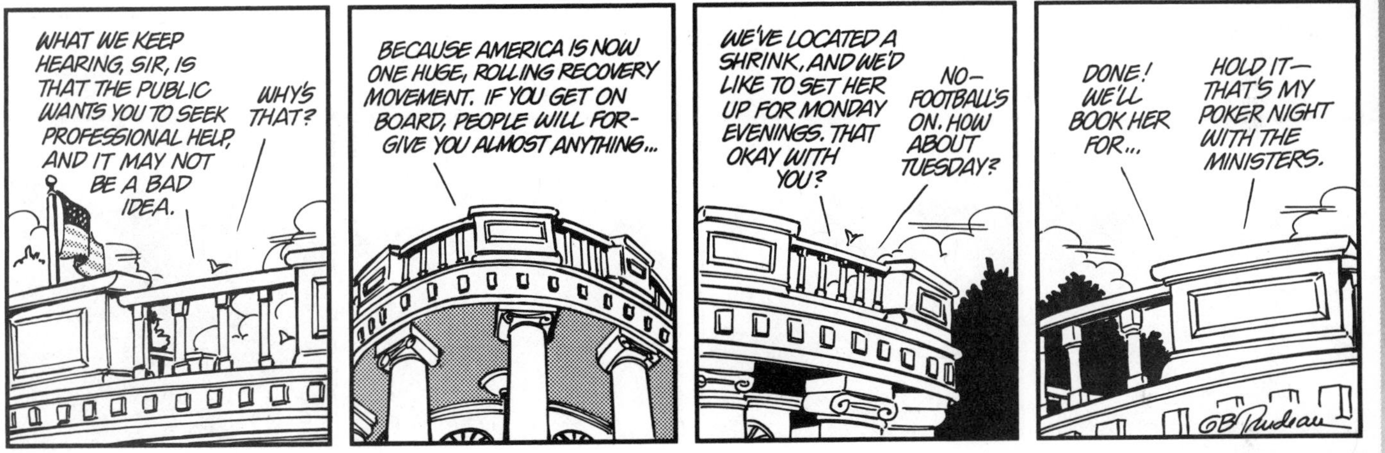
WHAT WE KEEP HEARING, SIR, IS THAT THE PUBLIC WANTS YOU TO SEEK PROFESSIONAL HELP, AND IT MAY NOT BE A BAD IDEA.
WHY'S THAT?
BECAUSE AMERICA IS NOW ONE HUGE, ROLLING RECOVERY MOVEMENT. IF YOU GET ON BOARD, PEOPLE WILL FORGIVE YOU ALMOST ANYTHING...
WE'VE LOCATED A SHRINK, AND WE'D LIKE TO SET HER UP FOR MONDAY EVENINGS. THAT OKAY WITH YOU?
NO-FOOTBALL'S ON. HOW ABOUT TUESDAY?
DONE! WE'LL BOOK HER FOR...
HOLD IT—THAT'S MY POKER NIGHT WITH THE MINISTERS.

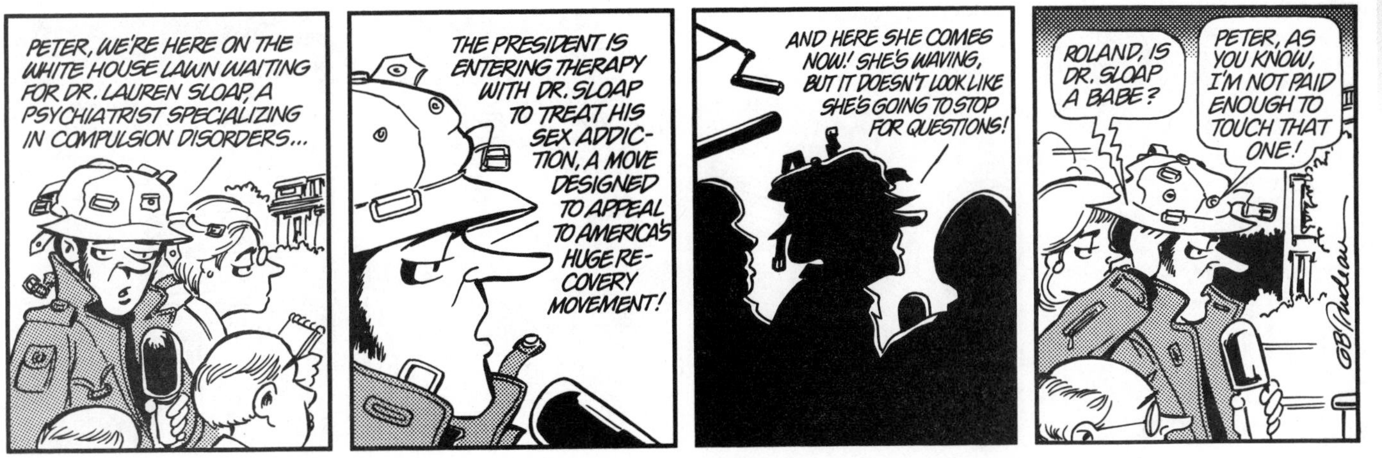
PETER, WE'RE HERE ON THE WHITE HOUSE LAWN WAITING FOR DR. LAUREN SLOAP, A PSYCHIATRIST SPECIALIZING IN COMPULSION DISORDERS...
THE PRESIDENT IS ENTERING THERAPY WITH DR. SLOAP TO TREAT HIS SEX ADDICTION, A MOVE DESIGNED TO APPEAL TO AMERICA'S HUGE RECOVERY MOVEMENT!
AND HERE SHE COMES NOW! SHE'S WAVING, BUT IT DOESN'T LOOK LIKE SHE'S GOING TO STOP FOR QUESTIONS!
ROLAND, IS DR. SLOAP A BABE?
PETER, AS YOU KNOW, I'M NOT PAID ENOUGH TO TOUCH THAT ONE!

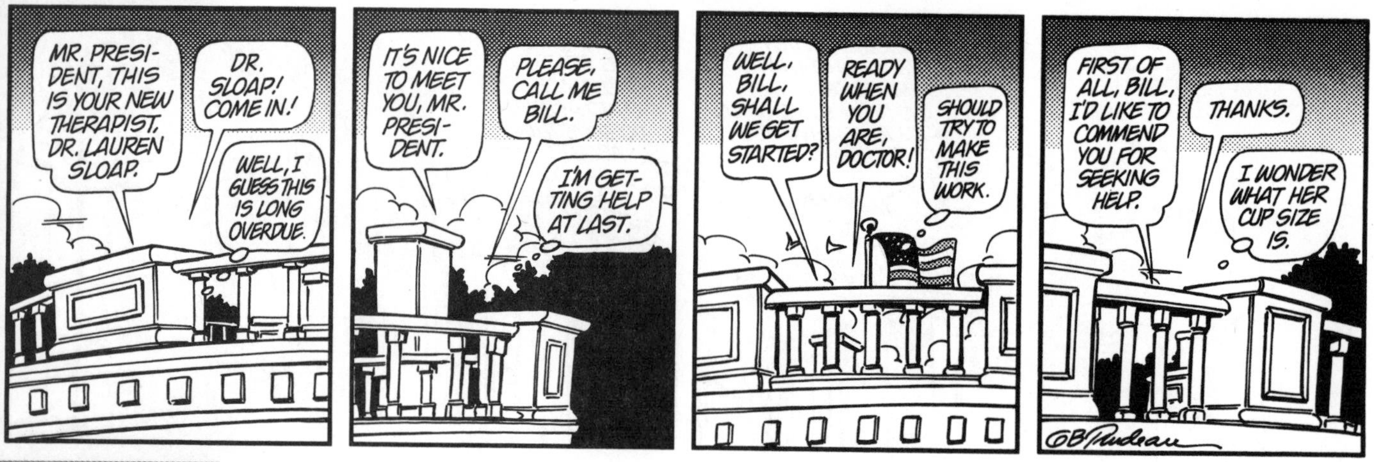
MR. PRESIDENT, THIS IS YOUR NEW THERAPIST, DR. LAUREN SLOAP.
DR. SLOAP! COME IN!
WELL, I GUESS THIS IS LONG OVERDUE.
IT'S NICE TO MEET YOU, MR. PRESIDENT.
PLEASE, CALL ME BILL.
I'M GETTING HELP AT LAST.
WELL, BILL, SHALL WE GET STARTED?
READY WHEN YOU ARE, DOCTOR!
SHOULD TRY TO MAKE THIS WORK.
FIRST OF ALL, BILL, I'D LIKE TO COMMEND YOU FOR SEEKING HELP.
THANKS.
I WONDER WHAT HER CUP SIZE IS.

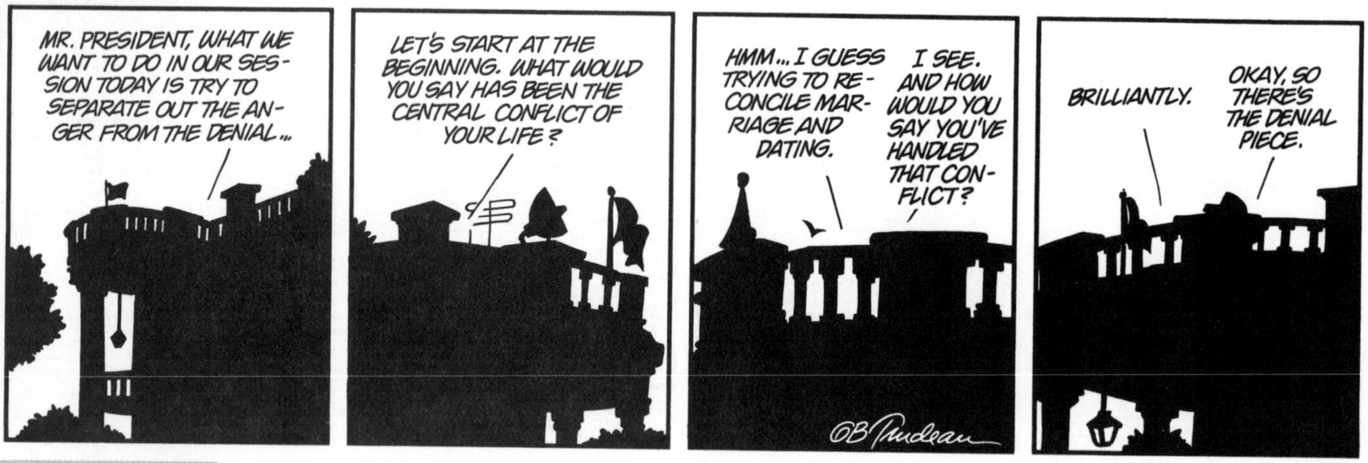
MR. PRESIDENT, WHAT WE WANT TO DO IN OUR SESSION TODAY IS TRY TO SEPARATE OUT THE ANGER FROM THE DENIAL...
LET'S START AT THE BEGINNING. WHAT WOULD YOU SAY HAS BEEN THE CENTRAL CONFLICT OF YOUR LIFE?
HMM... I GUESS TRYING TO RECONCILE MARRIAGE AND DATING.
I SEE. AND HOW WOULD YOU SAY YOU'VE HANDLED THAT CONFLICT?
BRILLIANTLY.
OKAY, SO THERE'S THE DENIAL PIECE.

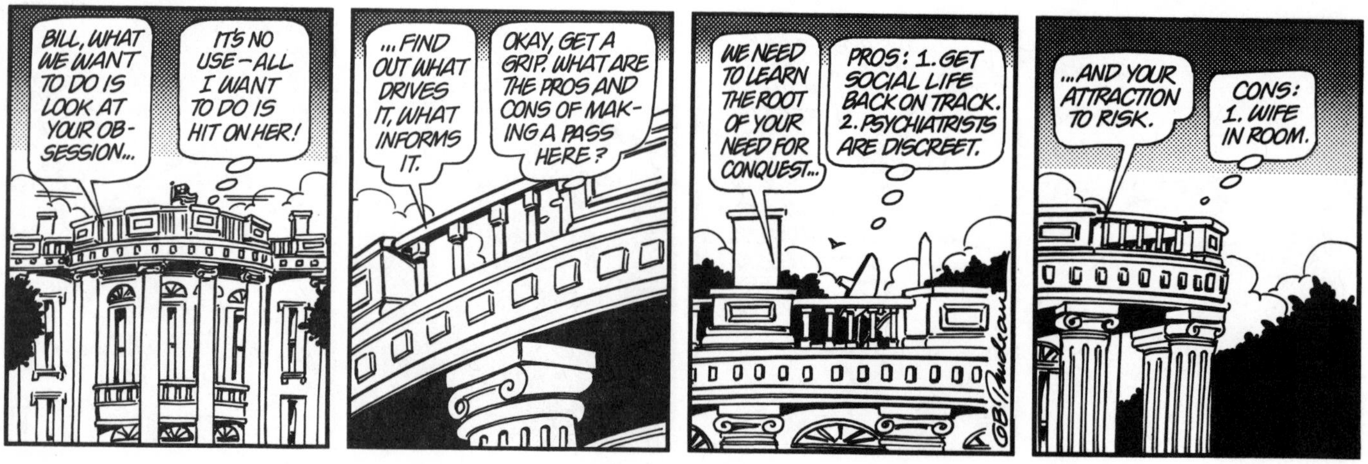
BILL, WHAT WE WANT TO DO IS LOOK AT YOUR OBSESSION...
IT'S NO USE – ALL I WANT TO DO IS HIT ON HER!
...FIND OUT WHAT DRIVES IT, WHAT INFORMS IT.
OKAY, GET A GRIP. WHAT ARE THE PROS AND CONS OF MAKING A PASS HERE?
WE NEED TO LEARN THE ROOT OF YOUR NEED FOR CONQUEST...
PROS: 1. GET SOCIAL LIFE BACK ON TRACK. 2. PSYCHIATRISTS ARE DISCREET.
...AND YOUR ATTRACTION TO RISK.
CONS: 1. WIFE IN ROOM.

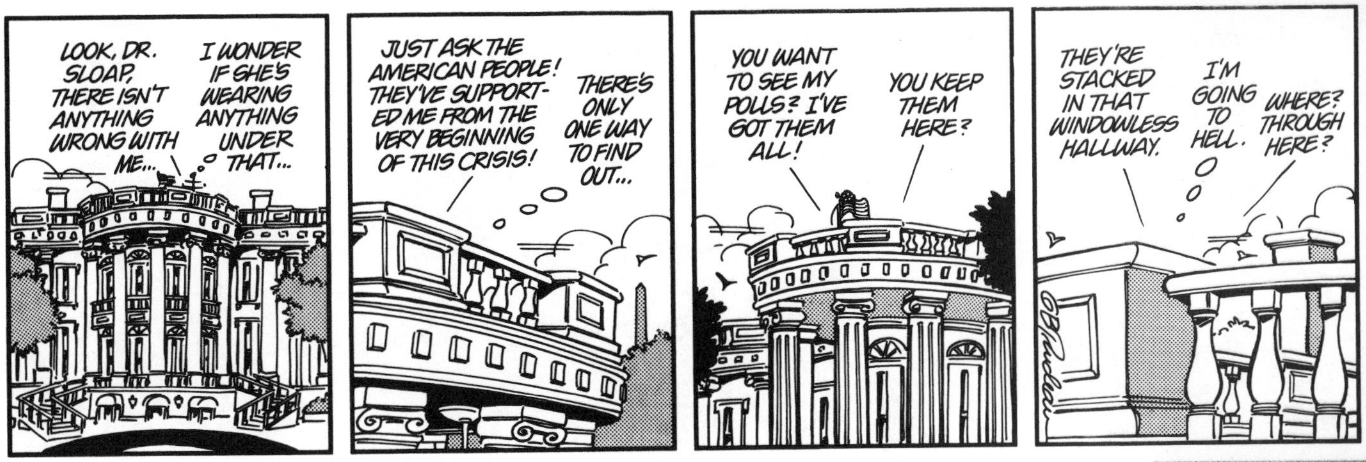
LOOK, DR. SLOAP, THERE ISN'T ANYTHING WRONG WITH ME...
I WONDER IF SHE'S WEARING ANYTHING UNDER THAT...
JUST ASK THE AMERICAN PEOPLE! THEY'VE SUPPORTED ME FROM THE VERY BEGINNING OF THIS CRISIS!
THERE'S ONLY ONE WAY TO FIND OUT...
YOU WANT TO SEE MY POLLS? I'VE GOT THEM ALL!
YOU KEEP THEM HERE?
THEY'RE STACKED IN THAT WINDOWLESS HALLWAY.
I'M GOING TO HELL.
WHERE? THROUGH HERE?

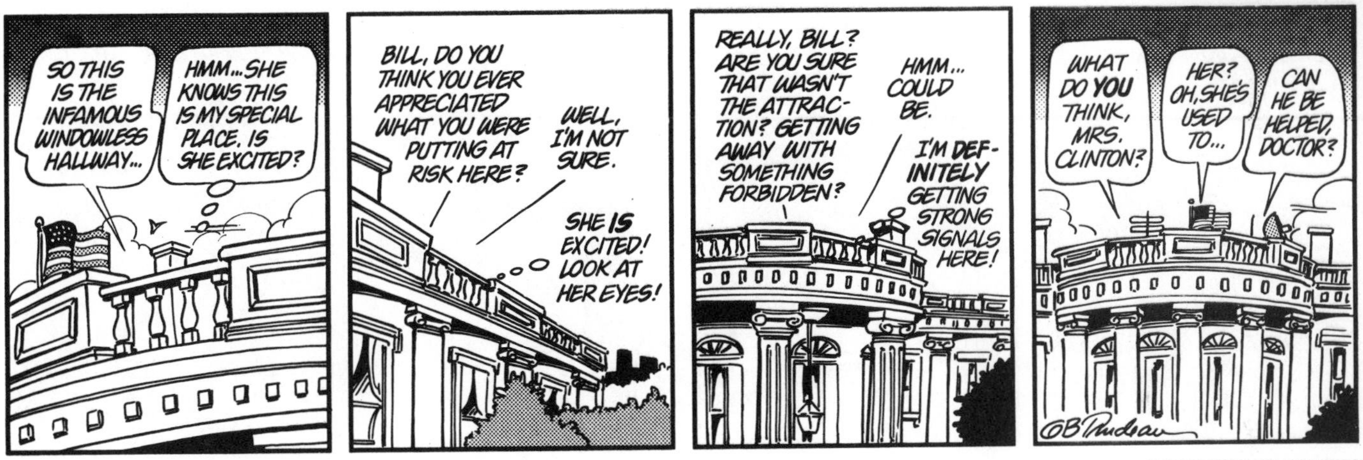
SO THIS IS THE INFAMOUS WINDOWLESS HALLWAY...
HMM... SHE KNOWS THIS IS MY SPECIAL PLACE. IS SHE EXCITED?
BILL, DO YOU THINK YOU EVER APPRECIATED WHAT YOU WERE PUTTING AT RISK HERE?
WELL, I'M NOT SURE.
SHE IS EXCITED! LOOK AT HER EYES!
REALLY, BILL? ARE YOU SURE THAT WASN'T THE ATTRACTION? GETTING AWAY WITH SOMETHING FORBIDDEN?
HMM... COULD BE.
I'M DEFINITELY GETTING STRONG SIGNALS HERE!
WHAT DO YOU THINK, MRS. CLINTON?
HER? OH, SHE'S USED TO...
CAN HE BE HELPED, DOCTOR?

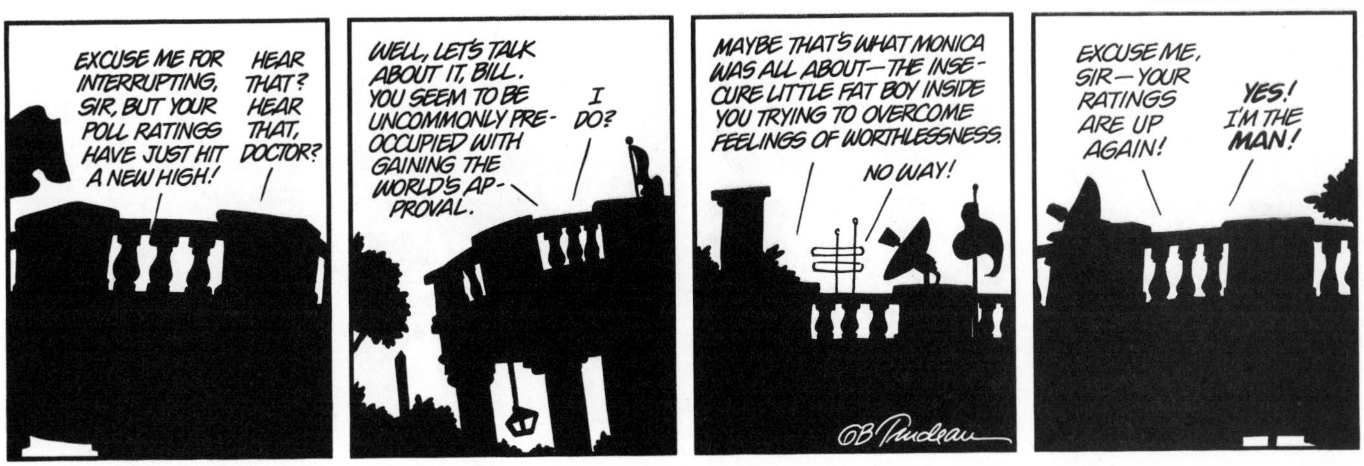
EXCUSE ME FOR INTERRUPTING, SIR, BUT YOUR POLL RATINGS HAVE JUST HIT A NEW HIGH!
HEAR THAT? HEAR THAT, DOCTOR?
WELL, LET'S TALK ABOUT IT, BILL. YOU SEEM TO BE UNCOMMONLY PREOCCUPIED WITH GAINING THE WORLD'S APPROVAL.
I DO?
MAYBE THAT'S WHAT MONICA WAS ALL ABOUT—THE INSECURE LITTLE FAT BOY INSIDE YOU TRYING TO OVERCOME FEELINGS OF WORTHLESSNESS.
NO WAY!
EXCUSE ME, SIR—YOUR RATINGS ARE UP AGAIN!
YES! I'M THE MAN!

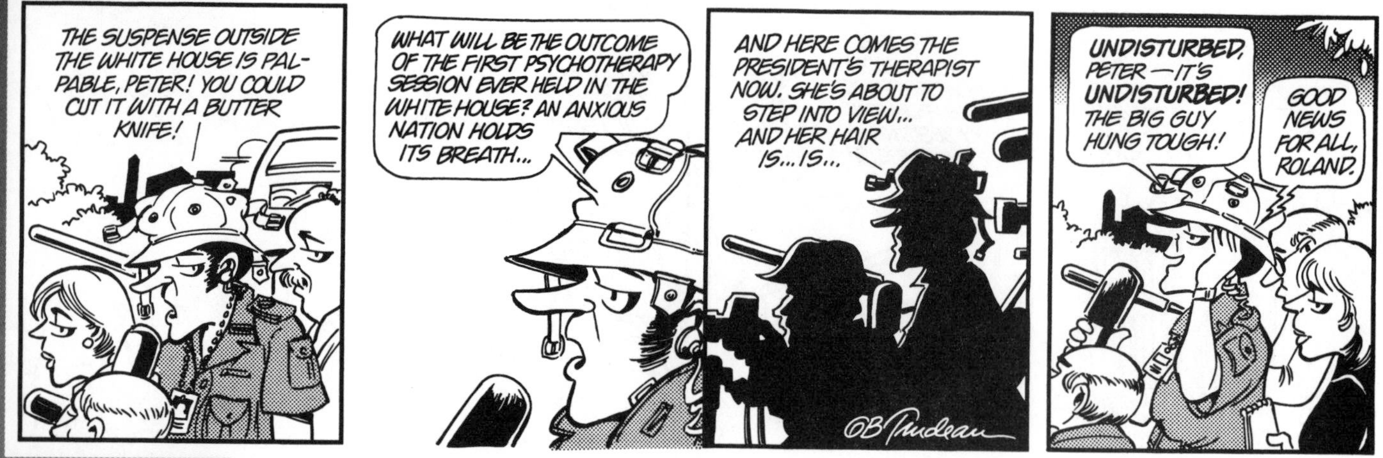
THE SUSPENSE OUTSIDE THE WHITE HOUSE IS PAL-PABLE, PETER! YOU COULD CUT IT WITH A BUTTER KNIFE!
WHAT WILL BE THE OUTCOME OF THE FIRST PSYCHOTHERAPY SESSION EVER HELD IN THE WHITE HOUSE? AN ANXIOUS NATION HOLDS ITS BREATH...
AND HERE COMES THE PRESIDENT'S THERAPIST NOW. SHE'S ABOUT TO STEP INTO VIEW... AND HER HAIR IS... IS...
GB Trudeau
UNDISTURBED, PETER — IT'S UNDISTURBED! THE BIG GUY HUNG TOUGH!
GOOD NEWS FOR ALL, ROLAND.

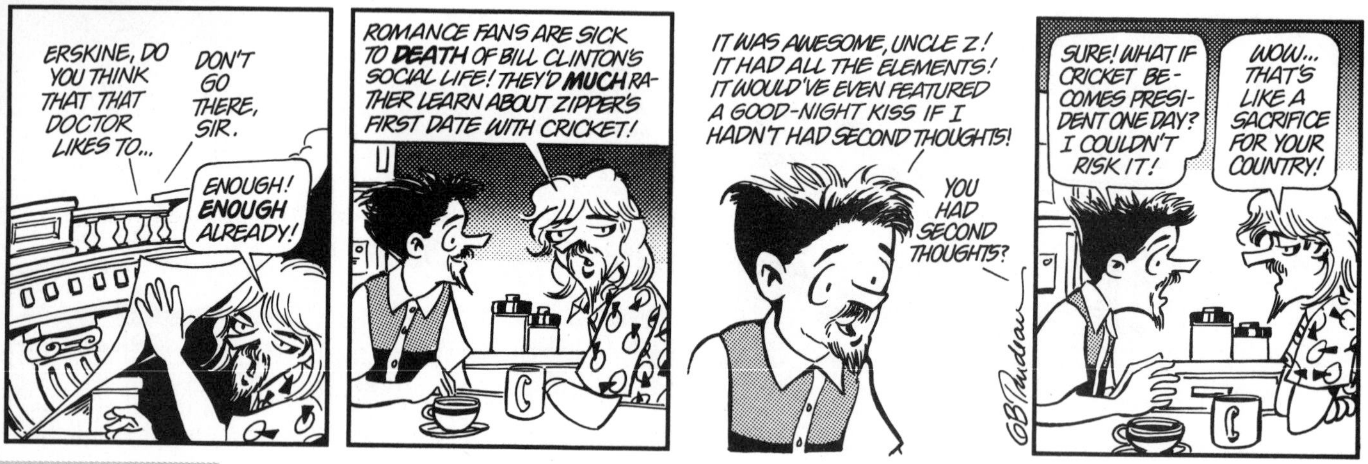
ERSKINE, DO YOU THINK THAT THAT DOCTOR LIKES TO...
DON'T GO THERE, SIR.
ENOUGH! ENOUGH ALREADY!
ROMANCE FANS ARE SICK TO DEATH OF BILL CLINTON'S SOCIAL LIFE! THEY'D MUCH RA-THER LEARN ABOUT ZIPPER'S FIRST DATE WITH CRICKET!
IT WAS AWESOME, UNCLE Z! IT HAD ALL THE ELEMENTS! IT WOULD'VE EVEN FEATURED A GOOD-NIGHT KISS IF I HADN'T HAD SECOND THOUGHTS!
YOU HAD SECOND THOUGHTS?
GB Trudeau
SURE! WHAT IF CRICKET BE-COMES PRESI-DENT ONE DAY? I COULDN'T RISK IT!
WOW... THAT'S LIKE A SACRIFICE FOR YOUR COUNTRY!

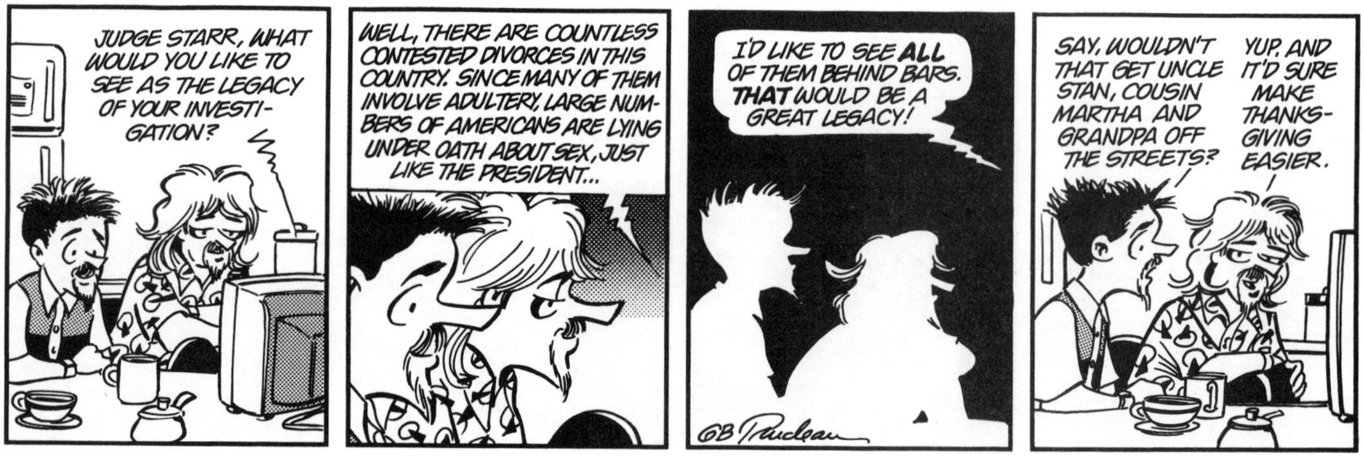
JUDGE STARR, WHAT WOULD YOU LIKE TO SEE AS THE LEGACY OF YOUR INVESTI-GATION?
WELL, THERE ARE COUNTLESS CONTESTED DIVORCES IN THIS COUNTRY. SINCE MANY OF THEM INVOLVE ADULTERY, LARGE NUM-BERS OF AMERICANS ARE LYING UNDER OATH ABOUT SEX, JUST LIKE THE PRESIDENT...
I'D LIKE TO SEE ALL OF THEM BEHIND BARS. THAT WOULD BE A GREAT LEGACY!
GB Trudeau
SAY, WOULDN'T THAT GET UNCLE STAN, COUSIN MARTHA AND GRANDPA OFF THE STREETS?
YUP, AND IT'D SURE MAKE THANKS-GIVING EASIER.

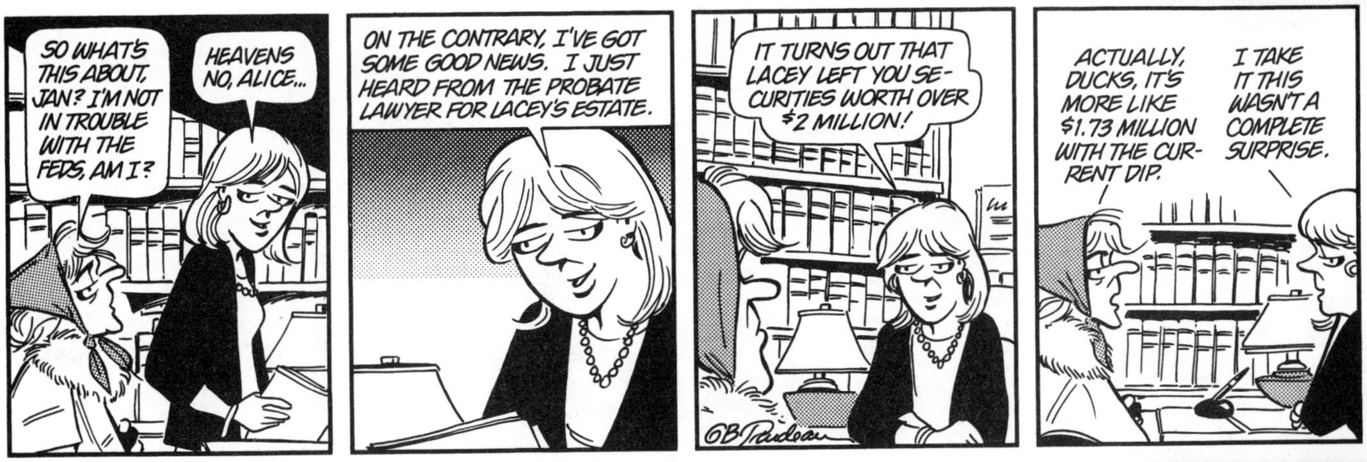
SO WHAT'S THIS ABOUT, JAN? I'M NOT IN TROUBLE WITH THE FEDS, AM I?
HEAVENS NO, ALICE...
ON THE CONTRARY, I'VE GOT SOME GOOD NEWS. I JUST HEARD FROM THE PROBATE LAWYER FOR LACEY'S ESTATE.
IT TURNS OUT THAT LACEY LEFT YOU SECURITIES WORTH OVER $2 MILLION!
ACTUALLY, DUCKS, IT'S MORE LIKE $1.73 MILLION WITH THE CURRENT DIP.
I TAKE IT THIS WASN'T A COMPLETE SURPRISE.

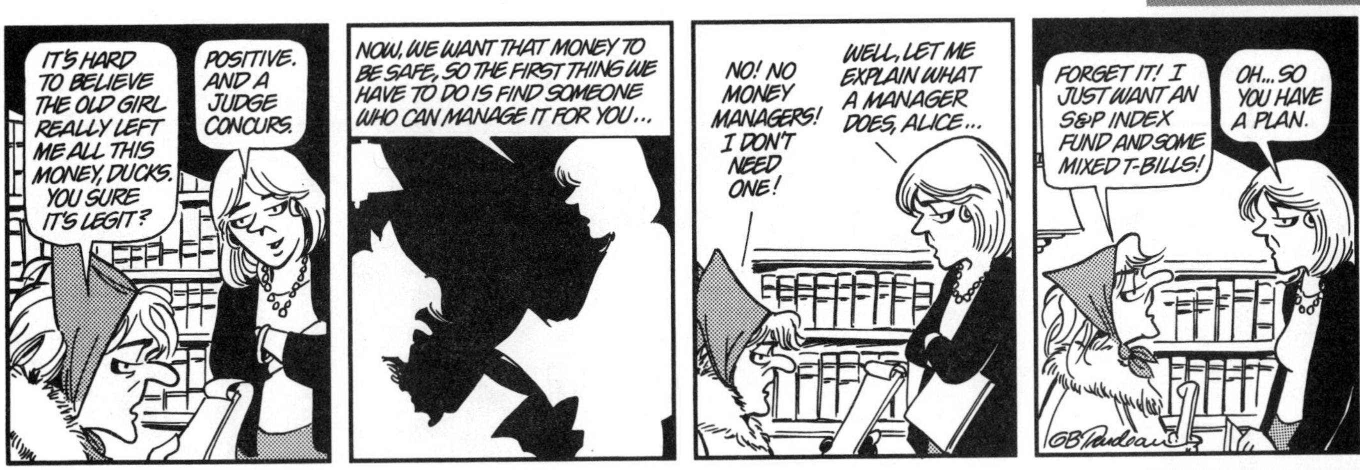
IT'S HARD TO BELIEVE THE OLD GIRL REALLY LEFT ME ALL THIS MONEY, DUCKS. YOU SURE IT'S LEGIT?
POSITIVE. AND A JUDGE CONCURS.
NOW, WE WANT THAT MONEY TO BE SAFE, SO THE FIRST THING WE HAVE TO DO IS FIND SOMEONE WHO CAN MANAGE IT FOR YOU...
NO! NO MONEY MANAGERS! I DON'T NEED ONE!
WELL, LET ME EXPLAIN WHAT A MANAGER DOES, ALICE...
FORGET IT! I JUST WANT AN S&P INDEX FUND AND SOME MIXED T-BILLS!
OH... SO YOU HAVE A PLAN.

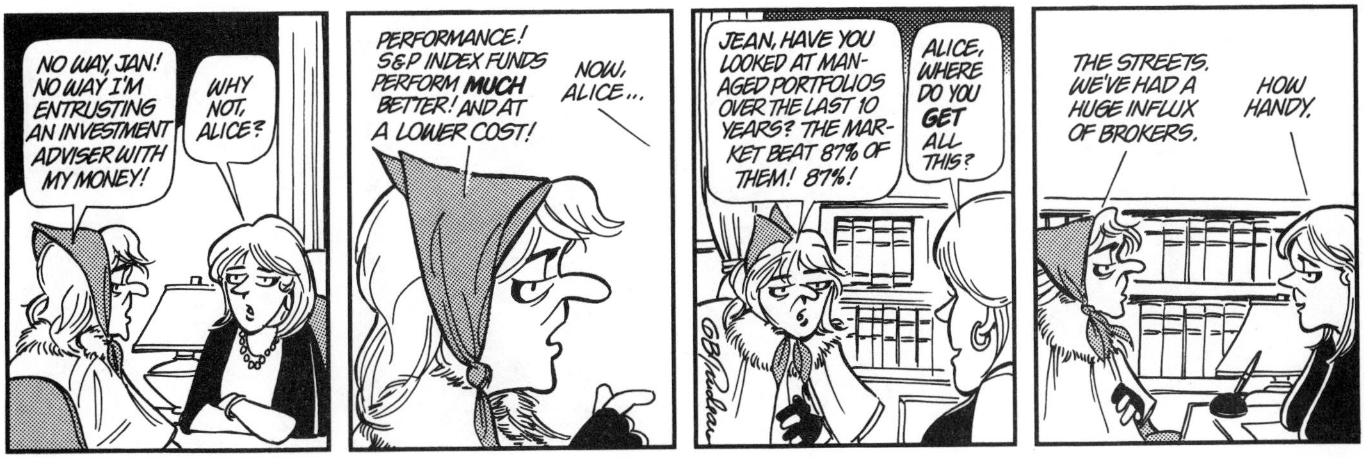
NO WAY, JAN! NO WAY I'M ENTRUSTING AN INVESTMENT ADVISER WITH MY MONEY!
WHY NOT, ALICE?
PERFORMANCE! S&P INDEX FUNDS PERFORM MUCH BETTER! AND AT A LOWER COST!
NOW, ALICE...
JEAN, HAVE YOU LOOKED AT MANAGED PORTFOLIOS OVER THE LAST 10 YEARS? THE MARKET BEAT 87% OF THEM! 87%!
ALICE, WHERE DO YOU GET ALL THIS?
THE STREETS. WE'VE HAD A HUGE INFLUX OF BROKERS.
HOW HANDY.

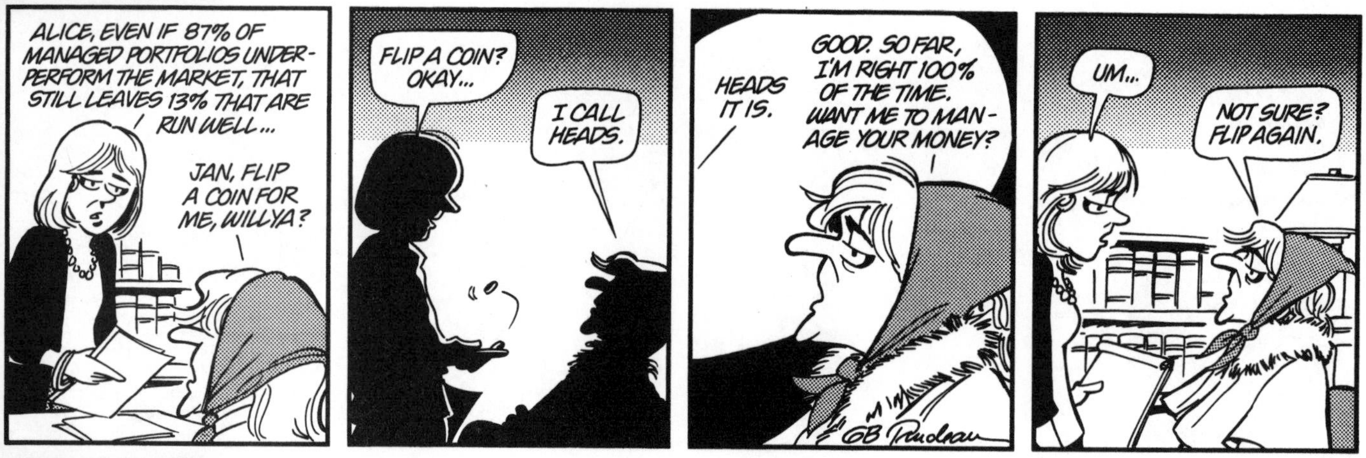
ALICE, EVEN IF 87% OF MANAGED PORTFOLIOS UNDERPERFORM THE MARKET, THAT STILL LEAVES 13% THAT ARE RUN WELL...
JAN, FLIP A COIN FOR ME, WILLYA?
FLIP A COIN? OKAY...
I CALL HEADS.
HEADS IT IS.
GOOD. SO FAR, I'M RIGHT 100% OF THE TIME. WANT ME TO MANAGE YOUR MONEY?
UM...
NOT SURE? FLIP AGAIN.
GB Trudeau

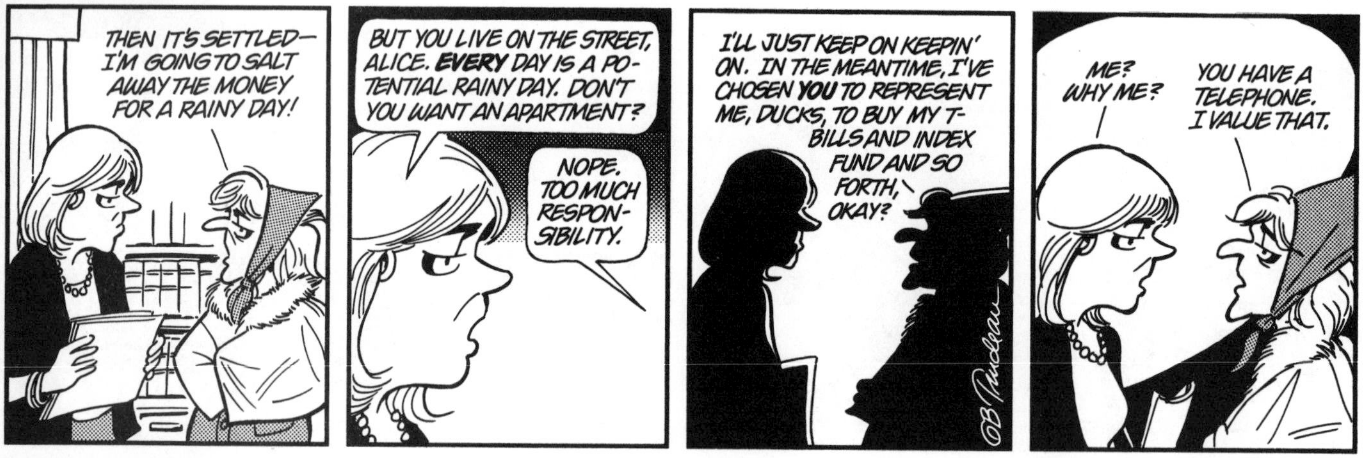
THEN IT'S SETTLED— I'M GOING TO SALT AWAY THE MONEY FOR A RAINY DAY!
BUT YOU LIVE ON THE STREET, ALICE. EVERY DAY IS A POTENTIAL RAINY DAY. DON'T YOU WANT AN APARTMENT?
NOPE. TOO MUCH RESPONSIBILITY.
I'LL JUST KEEP ON KEEPIN' ON. IN THE MEANTIME, I'VE CHOSEN YOU TO REPRESENT ME, DUCKS, TO BUY MY T-BILLS AND INDEX FUND AND SO FORTH, OKAY?
ME? WHY ME?
YOU HAVE A TELEPHONE. I VALUE THAT.
GB Trudeau

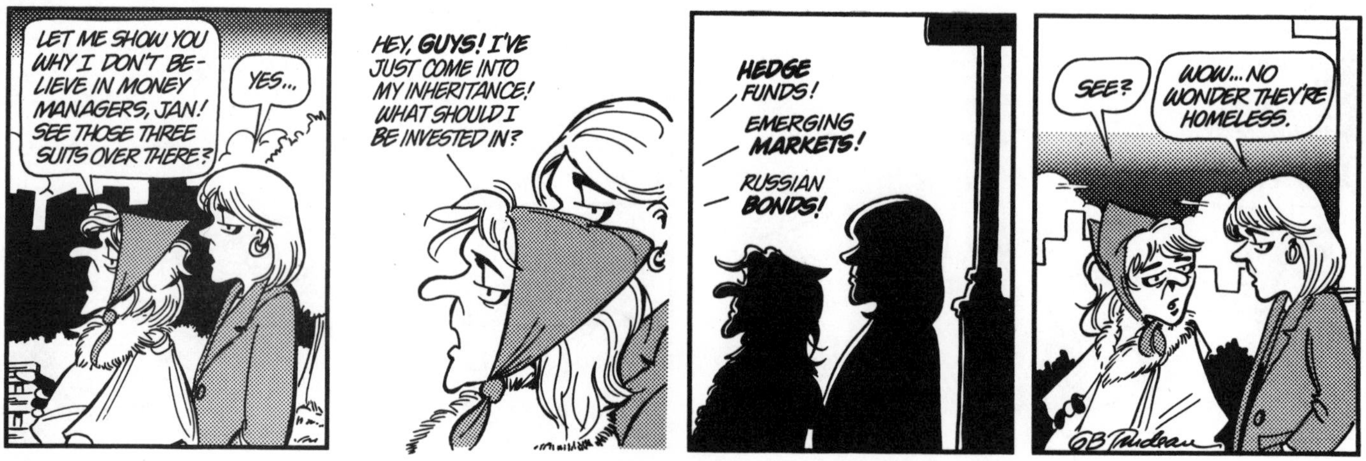
LET ME SHOW YOU WHY I DON'T BELIEVE IN MONEY MANAGERS, JAN! SEE THOSE THREE SUITS OVER THERE?
YES...
HEY, GUYS! I'VE JUST COME INTO MY INHERITANCE! WHAT SHOULD I BE INVESTED IN?
HEDGE FUNDS!
EMERGING MARKETS!
RUSSIAN BONDS!
SEE?
WOW... NO WONDER THEY'RE HOMELESS.
GB Trudeau

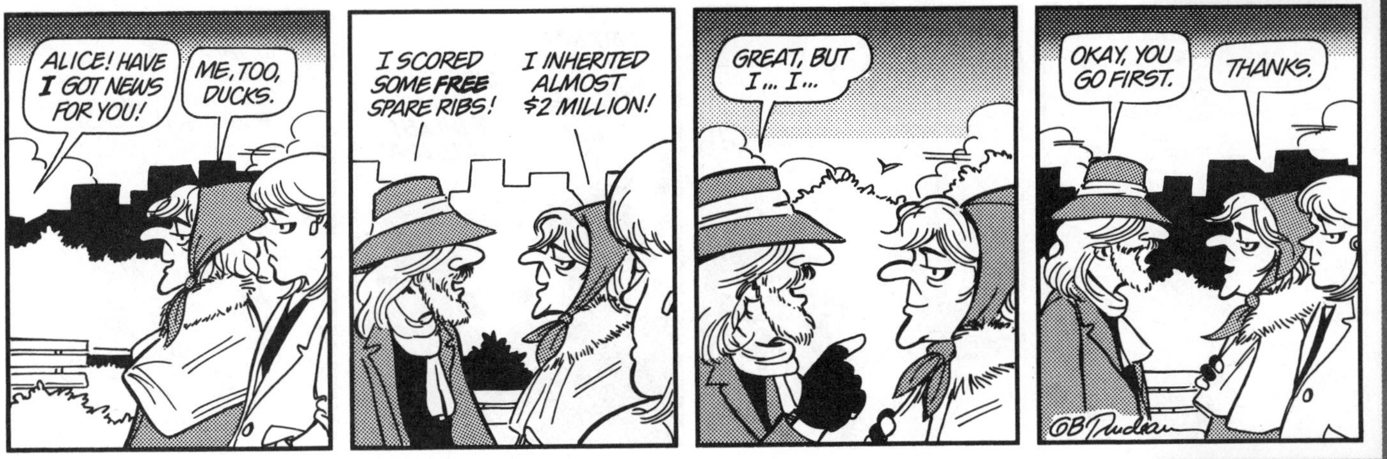
ALICE! HAVE I GOT NEWS FOR YOU!
ME, TOO, DUCKS.
I SCORED SOME FREE SPARE RIBS!
I INHERITED ALMOST $2 MILLION!
GREAT, BUT I... I...
OKAY, YOU GO FIRST.
THANKS.
GB Trudeau

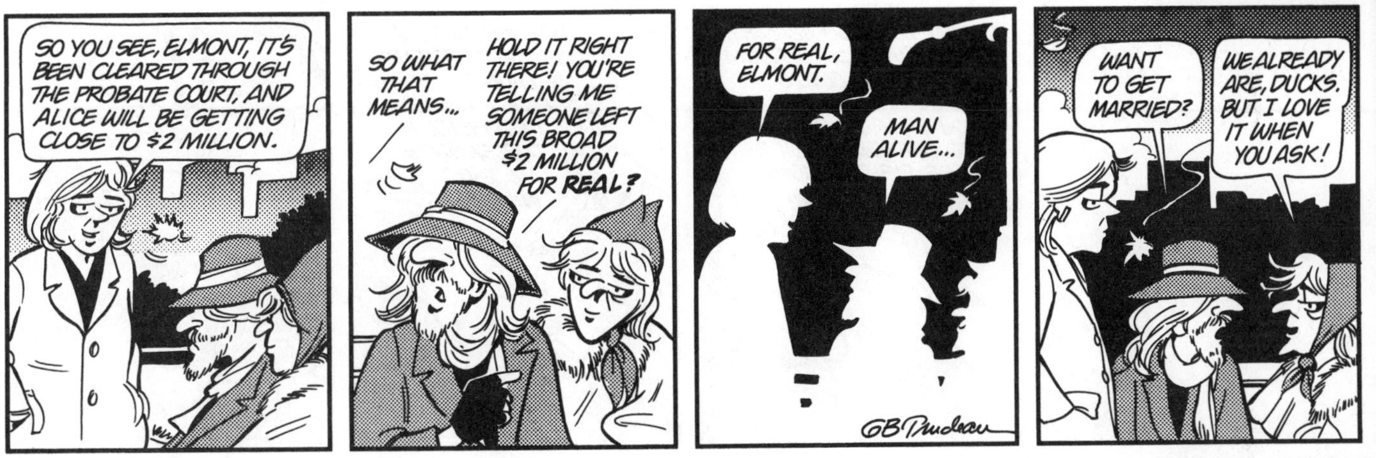
SO YOU SEE, ELMONT, IT'S BEEN CLEARED THROUGH THE PROBATE COURT, AND ALICE WILL BE GETTING CLOSE TO $2 MILLION.
SO WHAT THAT MEANS...
HOLD IT RIGHT THERE! YOU'RE TELLING ME SOMEONE LEFT THIS BROAD $2 MILLION FOR REAL?
FOR REAL, ELMONT.
MAN ALIVE...
GB Trudeau
WANT TO GET MARRIED?
WE ALREADY ARE, DUCKS. BUT I LOVE IT WHEN YOU ASK!

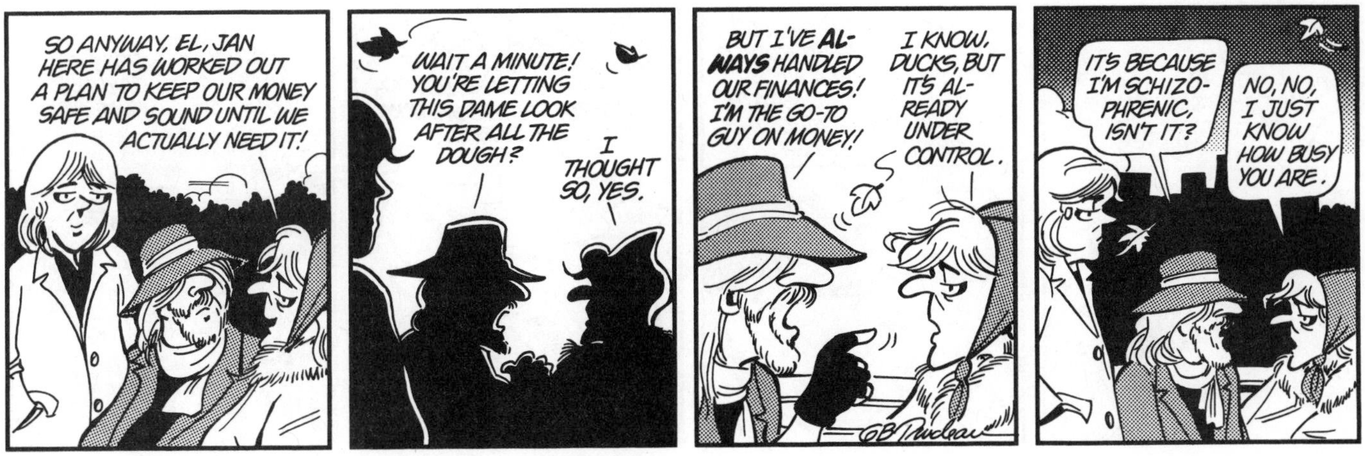
SO ANYWAY, EL, JAN HERE HAS WORKED OUT A PLAN TO KEEP OUR MONEY SAFE AND SOUND UNTIL WE ACTUALLY NEED IT!
WAIT A MINUTE! YOU'RE LETTING THIS DAME LOOK AFTER ALL THE DOUGH?
I THOUGHT SO, YES.
BUT I'VE ALWAYS HANDLED OUR FINANCES! I'M THE GO-TO GUY ON MONEY!
I KNOW, DUCKS, BUT IT'S ALREADY UNDER CONTROL.
GB Trudeau
IT'S BECAUSE I'M SCHIZOPHRENIC, ISN'T IT?
NO, NO, I JUST KNOW HOW BUSY YOU ARE.

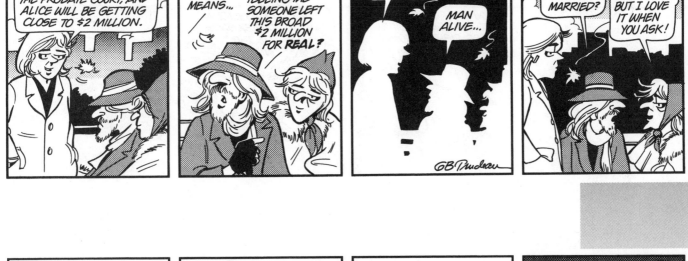

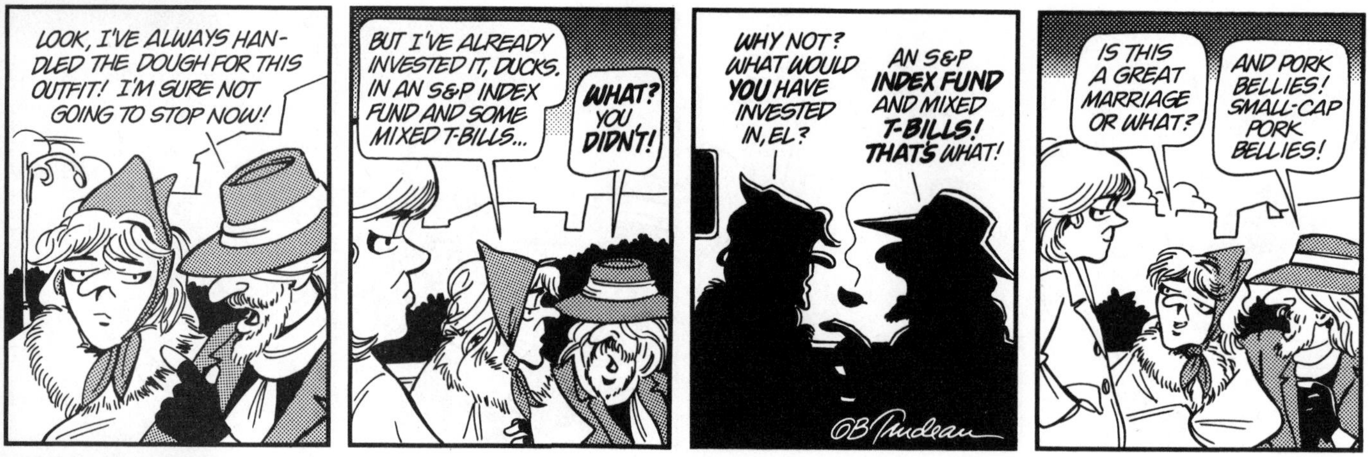
LOOK, I'VE ALWAYS HANDLED THE DOUGH FOR THIS OUTFIT! I'M SURE NOT GOING TO STOP NOW!
BUT I'VE ALREADY INVESTED IT, DUCKS. IN AN S&P INDEX FUND AND SOME MIXED T-BILLS...
WHAT? YOU DIDN'T!
WHY NOT? WHAT WOULD YOU HAVE INVESTED IN, EL?
AN S&P INDEX FUND AND MIXED T-BILLS! THAT'S WHAT!
IS THIS A GREAT MARRIAGE OR WHAT?
AND PORK BELLIES! SMALL-CAP PORK BELLIES!

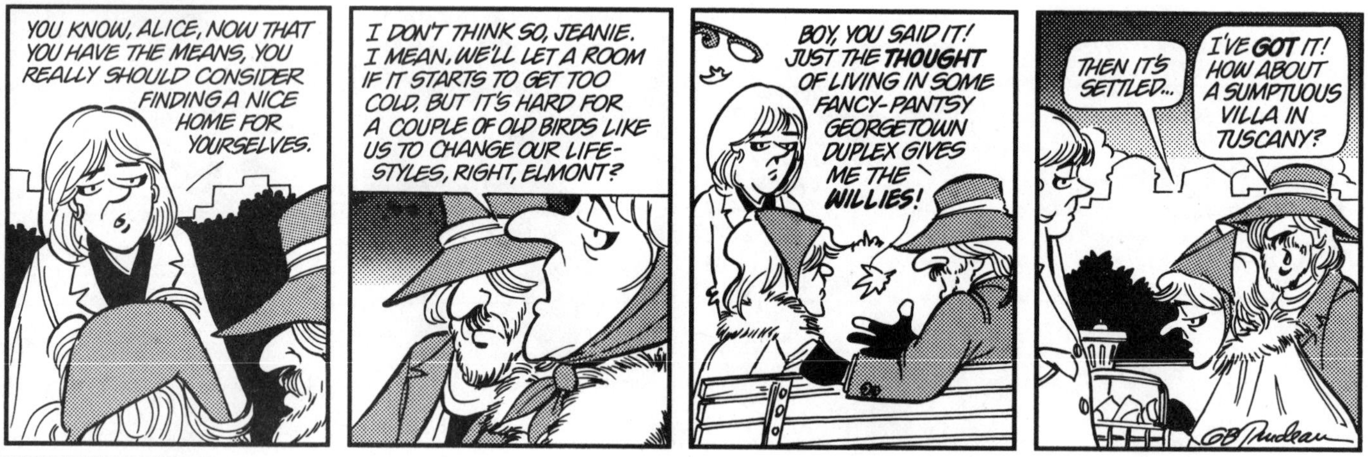
YOU KNOW, ALICE, NOW THAT YOU HAVE THE MEANS, YOU REALLY SHOULD CONSIDER FINDING A NICE HOME FOR YOURSELVES.
I DON'T THINK SO, JEANIE. I MEAN, WE'LL LET A ROOM IF IT STARTS TO GET TOO COLD, BUT IT'S HARD FOR A COUPLE OF OLD BIRDS LIKE US TO CHANGE OUR LIFESTYLES, RIGHT, ELMONT?
BOY, YOU SAID IT! JUST THE THOUGHT OF LIVING IN SOME FANCY-PANTSY GEORGETOWN DUPLEX GIVES ME THE WILLIES!
THEN IT'S SETTLED...
I'VE GOT IT! HOW ABOUT A SUMPTUOUS VILLA IN TUSCANY?

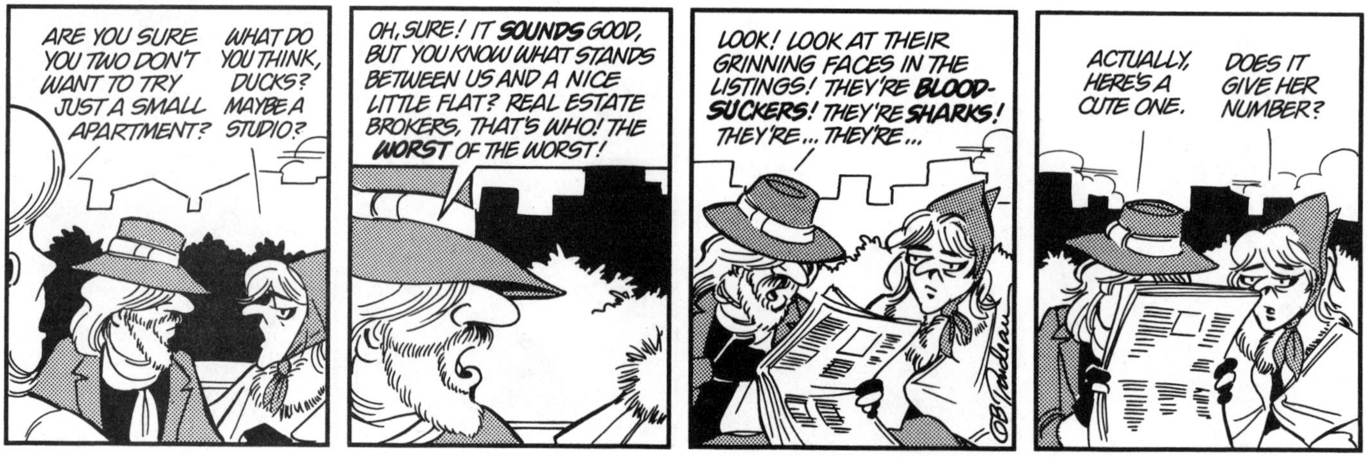
ARE YOU SURE YOU TWO DON'T WANT TO TRY JUST A SMALL APARTMENT?
WHAT DO YOU THINK, DUCKS? MAYBE A STUDIO?
OH, SURE! IT SOUNDS GOOD, BUT YOU KNOW WHAT STANDS BETWEEN US AND A NICE LITTLE FLAT? REAL ESTATE BROKERS, THAT'S WHO! THE WORST OF THE WORST!
LOOK! LOOK AT THEIR GRINNING FACES IN THE LISTINGS! THEY'RE BLOODSUCKERS! THEY'RE SHARKS! THEY'RE... THEY'RE...
ACTUALLY, HERE'S A CUTE ONE.
DOES IT GIVE HER NUMBER?

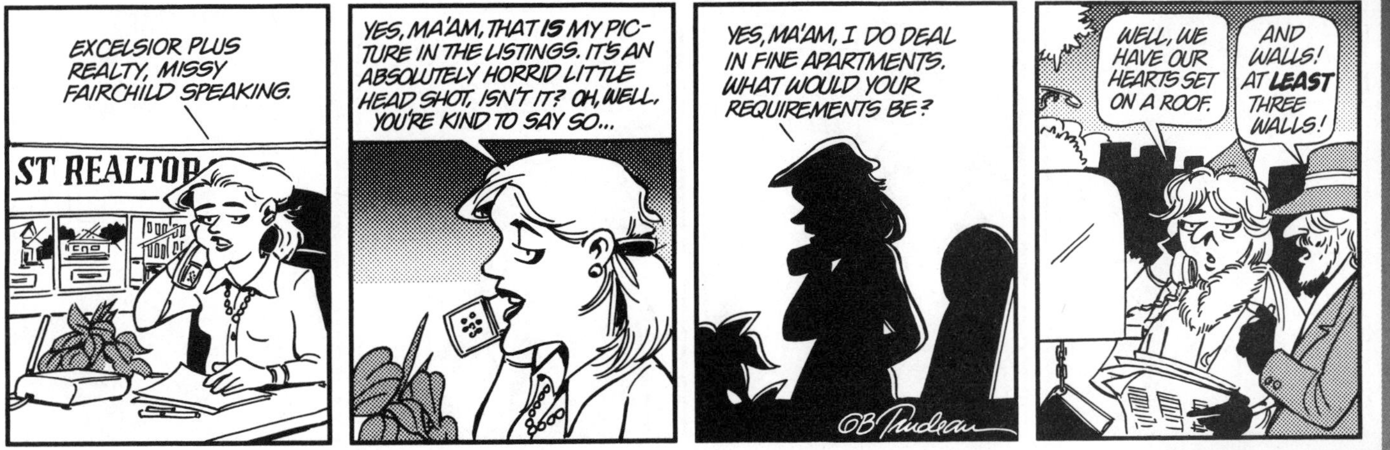
EXCELSIOR PLUS REALTY, MISSY FAIRCHILD SPEAKING.
ST REALTOR
YES, MA'AM, THAT **IS** MY PICTURE IN THE LISTINGS. IT'S AN ABSOLUTELY HORRID LITTLE HEAD SHOT, ISN'T IT? OH, WELL. YOU'RE KIND TO SAY SO...
YES, MA'AM, I DO DEAL IN FINE APARTMENTS. WHAT WOULD YOUR REQUIREMENTS BE?
WELL, WE HAVE OUR HEARTS SET ON A ROOF.
AND WALLS! AT **LEAST** THREE WALLS!

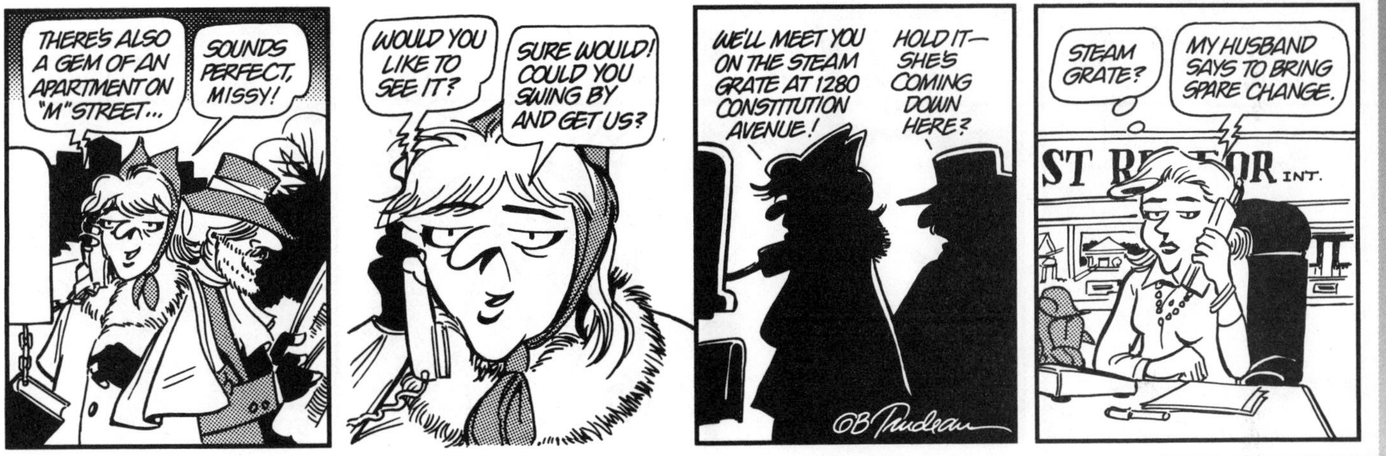
THERE'S ALSO A GEM OF AN APARTMENT ON "M" STREET...
SOUNDS PERFECT, MISSY!
WOULD YOU LIKE TO SEE IT?
SURE WOULD! COULD YOU SWING BY AND GET US?
WE'LL MEET YOU ON THE STEAM GRATE AT 1280 CONSTITUTION AVENUE!
HOLD IT— SHE'S COMING DOWN HERE?
STEAM GRATE?
MY HUSBAND SAYS TO BRING SPARE CHANGE.

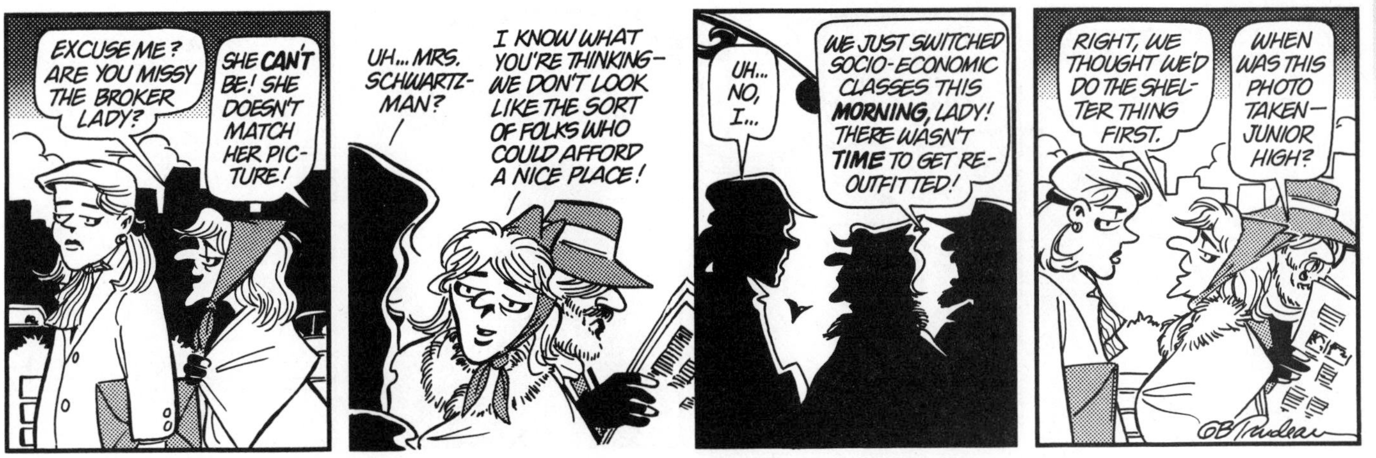
EXCUSE ME? ARE YOU MISSY THE BROKER LADY?
SHE **CAN'T** BE! SHE DOESN'T MATCH HER PICTURE!
UH... MRS. SCHWARTZMAN?
I KNOW WHAT YOU'RE THINKING— WE DON'T LOOK LIKE THE SORT OF FOLKS WHO COULD AFFORD A NICE PLACE!
UH... NO, I...
WE JUST SWITCHED SOCIO-ECONOMIC CLASSES THIS **MORNING**, LADY! THERE WASN'T **TIME** TO GET RE-OUTFITTED!
RIGHT, WE THOUGHT WE'D DO THE SHELTER THING FIRST.
WHEN WAS THIS PHOTO TAKEN— JUNIOR HIGH?

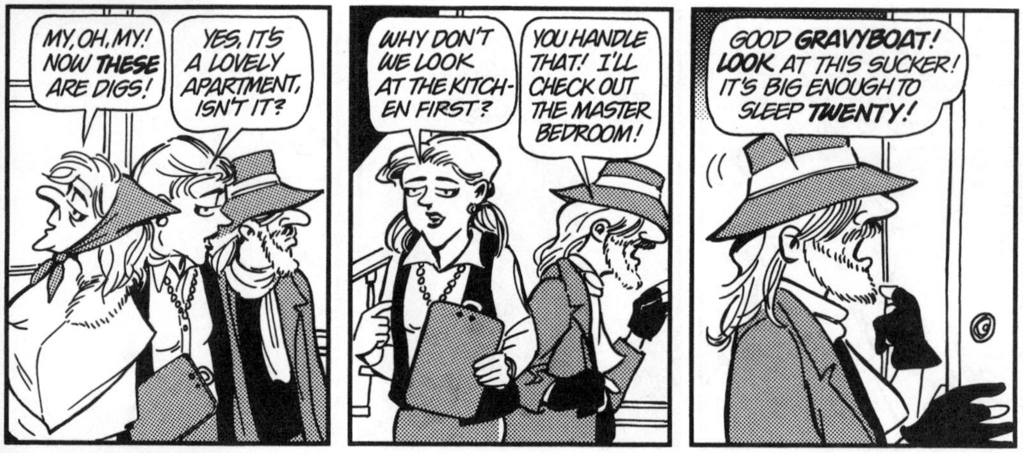
MY, OH, MY! NOW THESE ARE DIGS!
YES, IT'S A LOVELY APARTMENT, ISN'T IT?
WHY DON'T WE LOOK AT THE KITCH-EN FIRST?
YOU HANDLE THAT! I'LL CHECK OUT THE MASTER BEDROOM!
GOOD GRAVYBOAT! LOOK AT THIS SUCKER! IT'S BIG ENOUGH TO SLEEP TWENTY!
ACTUALLY, IT'S A LINEN CLOSET.
IT'S BEAU-TIFUL! I'LL TAKE IT!

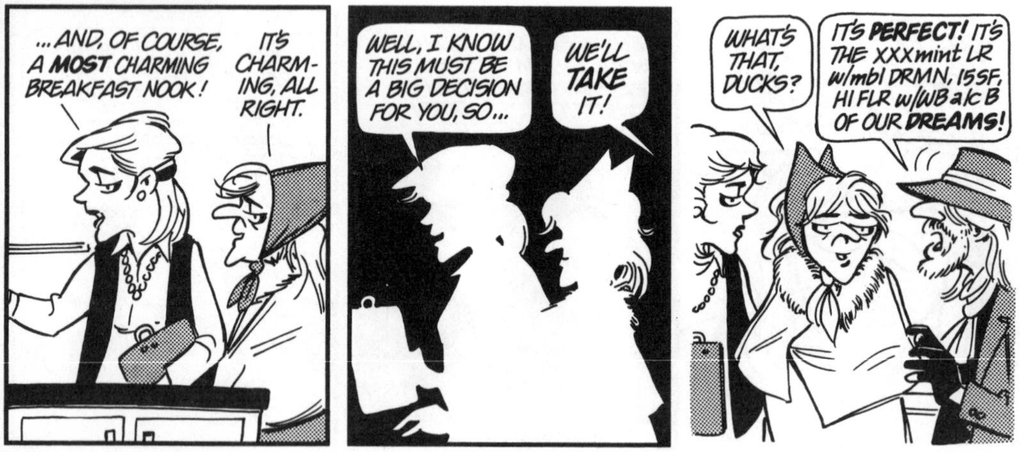
...AND, OF COURSE, A MOST CHARMING BREAKFAST NOOK!
IT'S CHARM-ING, ALL RIGHT.
WELL, I KNOW THIS MUST BE A BIG DECISION FOR YOU, SO...
WE'LL TAKE IT!
WHAT'S THAT, DUCKS?
IT'S PERFECT! IT'S THE XXX mint LR w/mbl DRMN, 15SF, HI FLR w/WB a/c B OF OUR DREAMS!
IT IS?
JUST LOOK AT THOSE hdwd SEP SPAC d/w RENT STABS!
THEY ARE PRETTY DARN GRA-CIOUS.

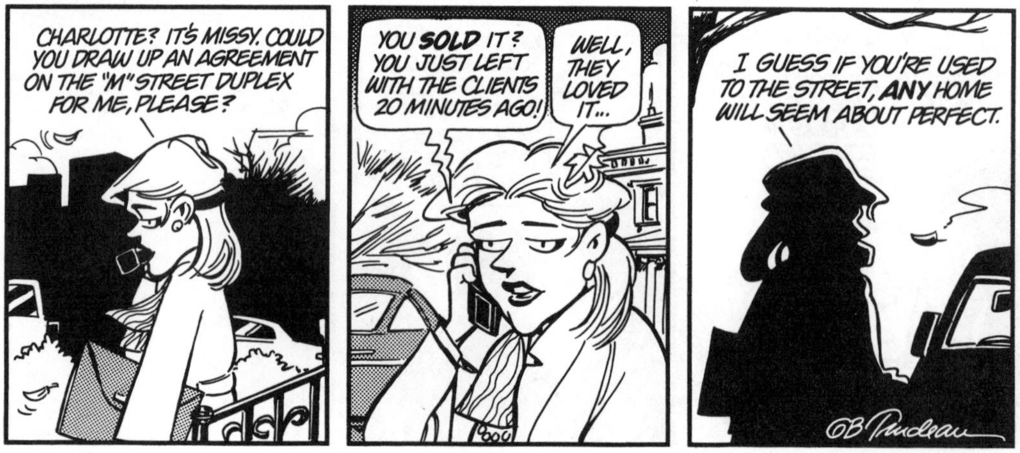
CHARLOTTE? IT'S MISSY. COULD YOU DRAW UP AN AGREEMENT ON THE "M" STREET DUPLEX FOR ME, PLEASE?
YOU SOLD IT? YOU JUST LEFT WITH THE CLIENTS 20 MINUTES AGO!
WELL, THEY LOVED IT...
I GUESS IF YOU'RE USED TO THE STREET, ANY HOME WILL SEEM ABOUT PERFECT.
YOU KNOW WHAT GETS ME GOING? THE SPACIOUS, TREE-LINED, EAT-IN POW-DER ROOM!
ME, TOO, DUCKS!

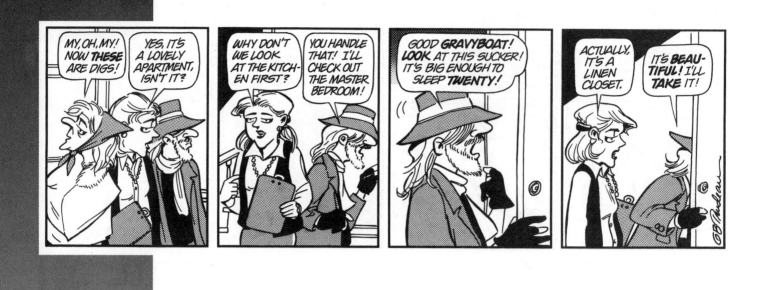

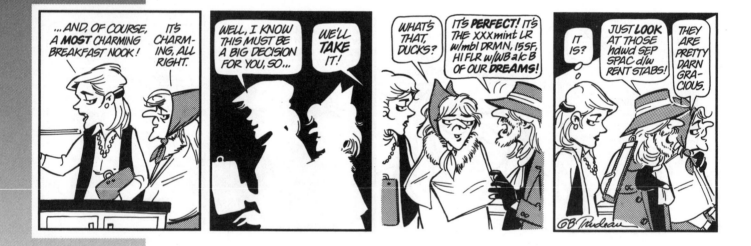

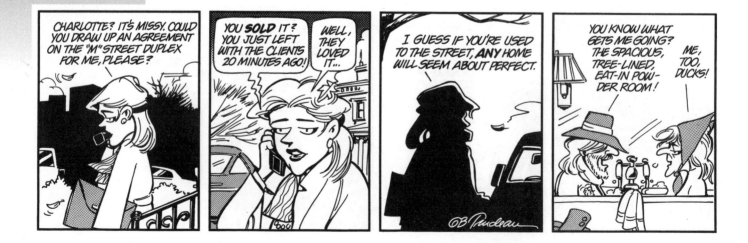

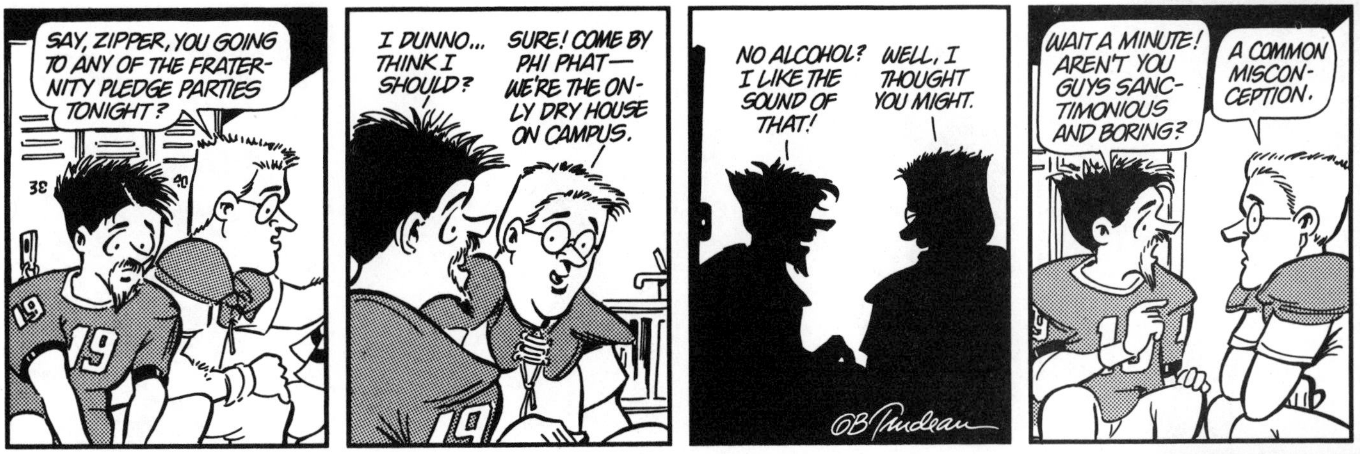
SAY, ZIPPER, YOU GOING TO ANY OF THE FRATER-NITY PLEDGE PARTIES TONIGHT?
I DUNNO... THINK I SHOULD?
SURE! COME BY PHI PHAT— WE'RE THE ON-LY DRY HOUSE ON CAMPUS.
NO ALCOHOL? I LIKE THE SOUND OF THAT!
WELL, I THOUGHT YOU MIGHT.
WAIT A MINUTE! AREN'T YOU GUYS SANC-TIMONIOUS AND BORING?
A COMMON MISCON-CEPTION.

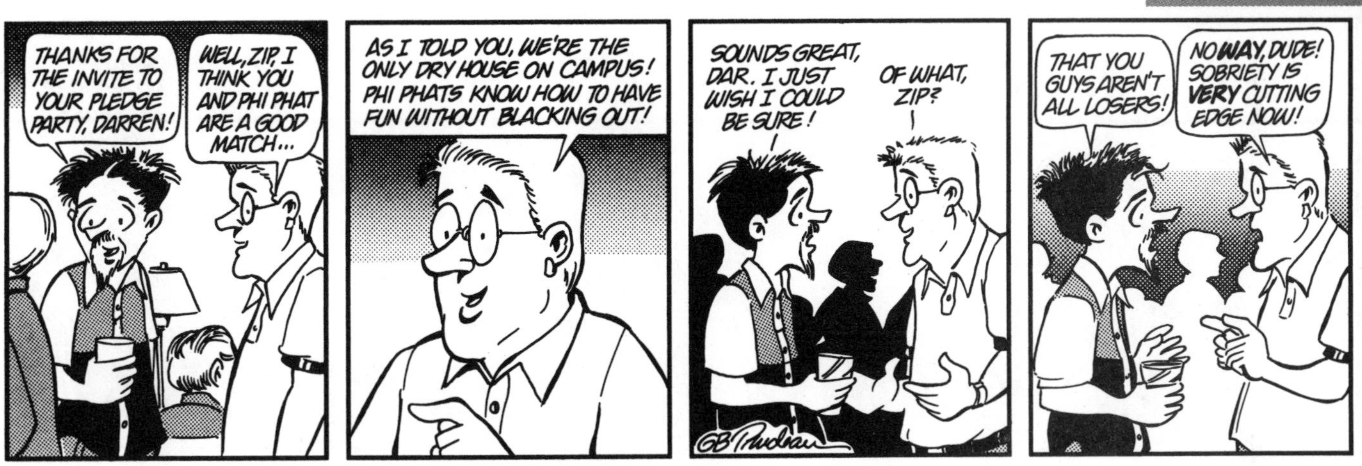
THANKS FOR THE INVITE TO YOUR PLEDGE PARTY, DARREN!
WELL, ZIP, I THINK YOU AND PHI PHAT ARE A GOOD MATCH...
AS I TOLD YOU, WE'RE THE ONLY DRY HOUSE ON CAMPUS! PHI PHATS KNOW HOW TO HAVE FUN WITHOUT BLACKING OUT!
SOUNDS GREAT, DAR. I JUST WISH I COULD BE SURE!
OF WHAT, ZIP?
THAT YOU GUYS AREN'T ALL LOSERS!
NO **WAY**, DUDE! SOBRIETY IS **VERY** CUTTING EDGE NOW!

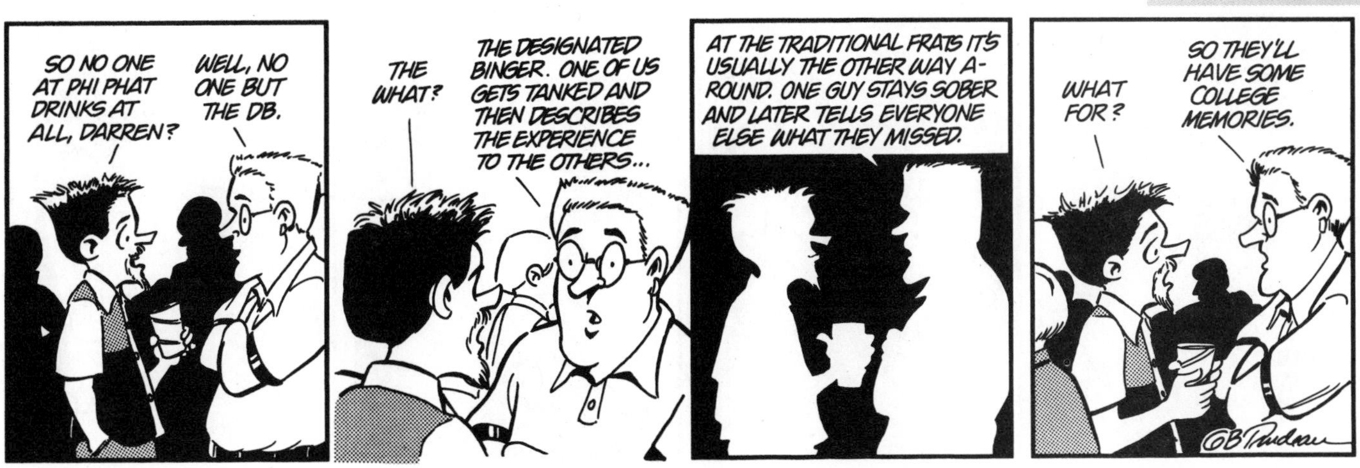
SO NO ONE AT PHI PHAT DRINKS AT ALL, DARREN?
WELL, NO ONE BUT THE DB.
THE WHAT?
THE DESIGNATED BINGER. ONE OF US GETS TANKED AND THEN DESCRIBES THE EXPERIENCE TO THE OTHERS...
AT THE TRADITIONAL FRATS IT'S USUALLY THE OTHER WAY A-ROUND. ONE GUY STAYS SOBER AND LATER TELLS EVERYONE ELSE WHAT THEY MISSED.
WHAT FOR?
SO THEY'LL HAVE SOME COLLEGE MEMORIES.

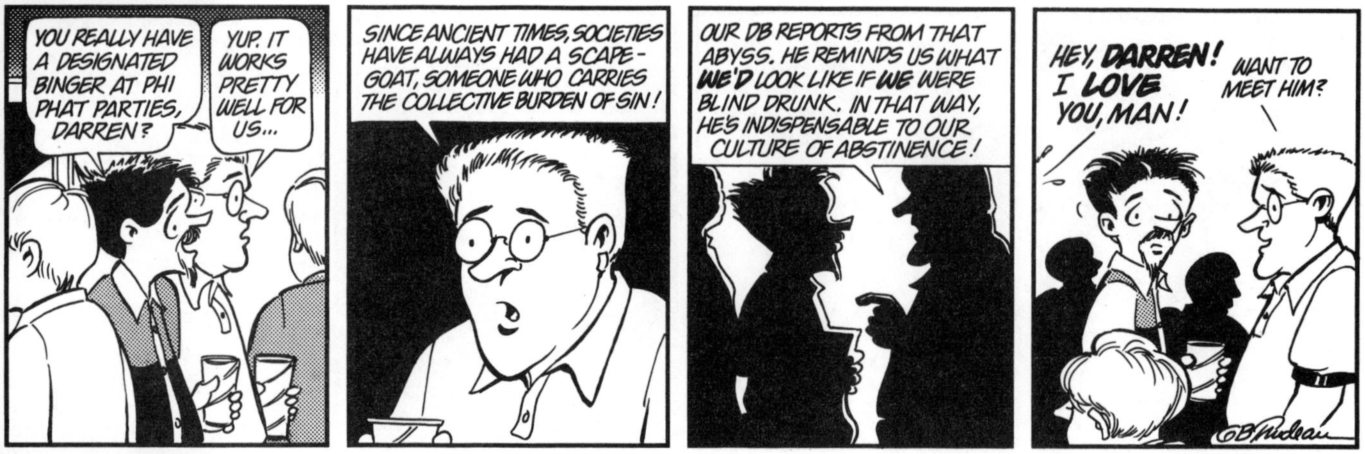
YOU REALLY HAVE A DESIGNATED BINGER AT PHI PHAT PARTIES, DARREN?
YUP. IT WORKS PRETTY WELL FOR US...
SINCE ANCIENT TIMES, SOCIETIES HAVE ALWAYS HAD A SCAPE-GOAT, SOMEONE WHO CARRIES THE COLLECTIVE BURDEN OF SIN!
OUR DB REPORTS FROM THAT ABYSS. HE REMINDS US WHAT **WE'D** LOOK LIKE IF **WE** WERE BLIND DRUNK. IN THAT WAY, HE'S INDISPENSABLE TO OUR CULTURE OF ABSTINENCE!
HEY, **DARREN!** I **LOVE** YOU, MAN!
WANT TO MEET HIM?

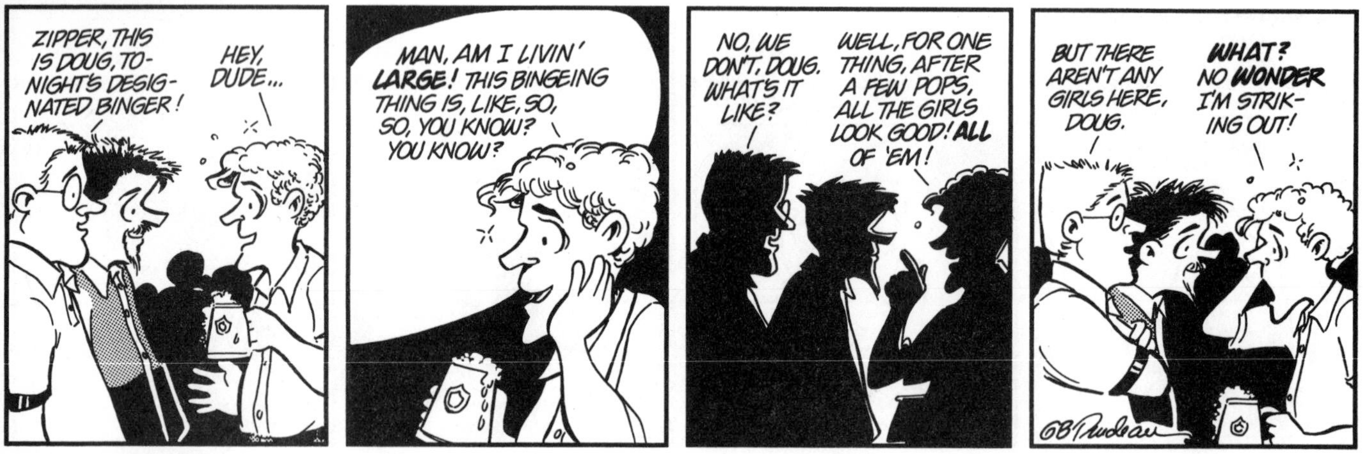
ZIPPER, THIS IS DOUG, TO-NIGHT'S DESIG-NATED BINGER!
HEY, DUDE...
MAN, AM I LIVIN' **LARGE!** THIS BINGEING THING IS, LIKE, SO, SO, YOU KNOW? YOU KNOW?
NO, WE DON'T, DOUG. WHAT'S IT LIKE?
WELL, FOR ONE THING, AFTER A FEW POPS, ALL THE GIRLS LOOK GOOD! **ALL** OF 'EM!
BUT THERE AREN'T ANY GIRLS HERE, DOUG.
WHAT? NO **WONDER** I'M STRIK-ING OUT!

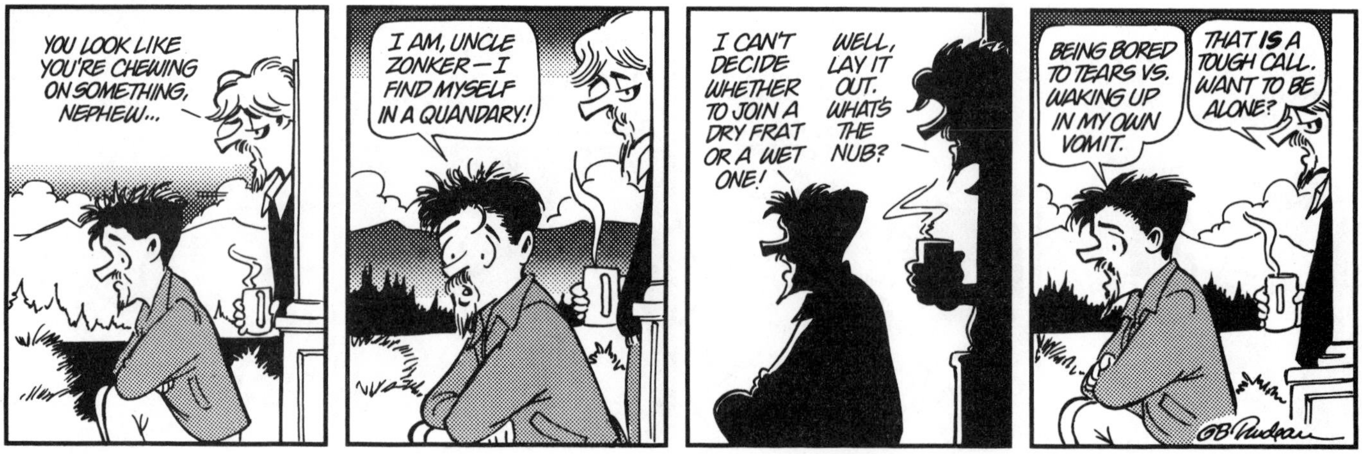
YOU LOOK LIKE YOU'RE CHEWING ON SOMETHING, NEPHEW...
I AM, UNCLE ZONKER — I FIND MYSELF IN A QUANDARY!
I CAN'T DECIDE WHETHER TO JOIN A DRY FRAT OR A WET ONE!
WELL, LAY IT OUT. WHAT'S THE NUB?
BEING BORED TO TEARS VS. WAKING UP IN MY OWN VOMIT.
THAT **IS** A TOUGH CALL. WANT TO BE ALONE?

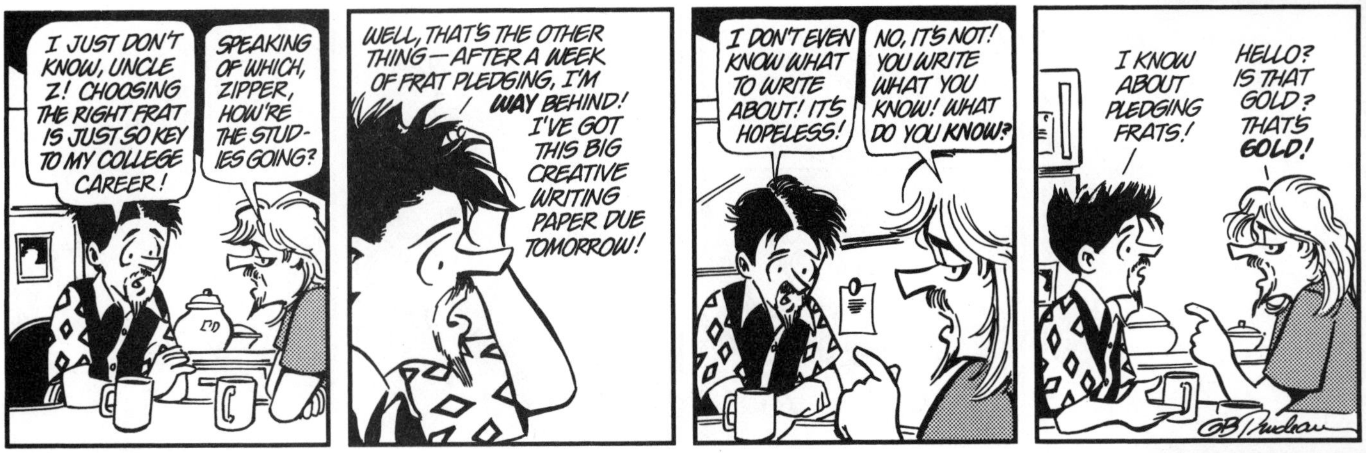
I JUST DON'T KNOW, UNCLE Z! CHOOSING THE RIGHT FRAT IS JUST SO KEY TO MY COLLEGE CAREER!
SPEAKING OF WHICH, ZIPPER, HOW'RE THE STUDIES GOING?
WELL, THAT'S THE OTHER THING — AFTER A WEEK OF FRAT PLEDGING, I'M WAY BEHIND!
I'VE GOT THIS BIG CREATIVE WRITING PAPER DUE TOMORROW!
I DON'T EVEN KNOW WHAT TO WRITE ABOUT! IT'S HOPELESS!
NO, IT'S NOT! YOU WRITE WHAT YOU KNOW! WHAT DO YOU KNOW?
I KNOW ABOUT PLEDGING FRATS!
HELLO? IS THAT GOLD? THAT'S GOLD!

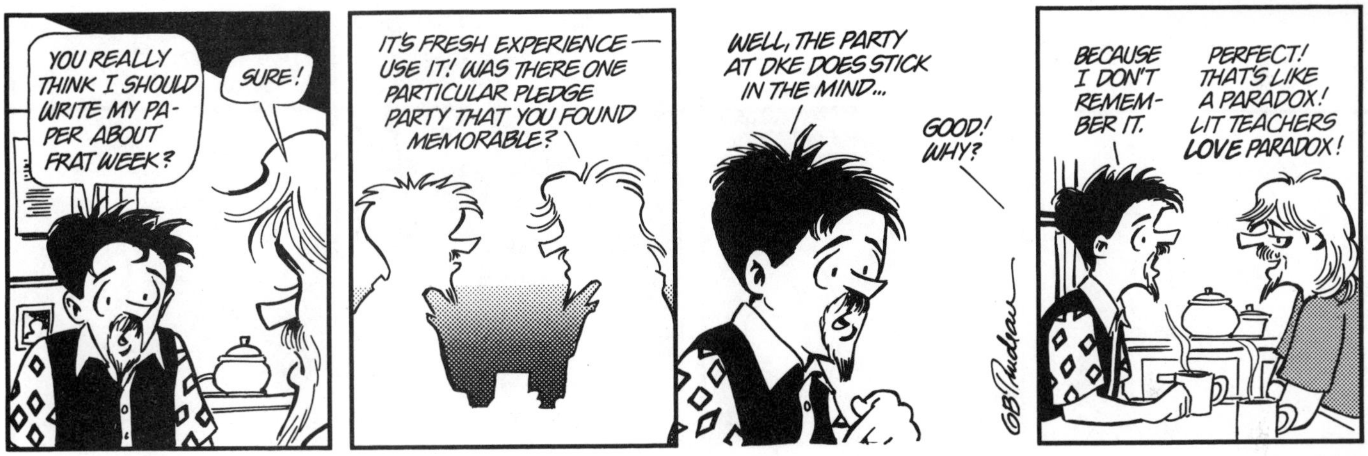
YOU REALLY THINK I SHOULD WRITE MY PAPER ABOUT FRAT WEEK?
SURE!
IT'S FRESH EXPERIENCE — USE IT! WAS THERE ONE PARTICULAR PLEDGE PARTY THAT YOU FOUND MEMORABLE?
WELL, THE PARTY AT DKE DOES STICK IN THE MIND...
GOOD! WHY?
BECAUSE I DON'T REMEMBER IT.
PERFECT! THAT'S LIKE A PARADOX! LIT TEACHERS LOVE PARADOX!

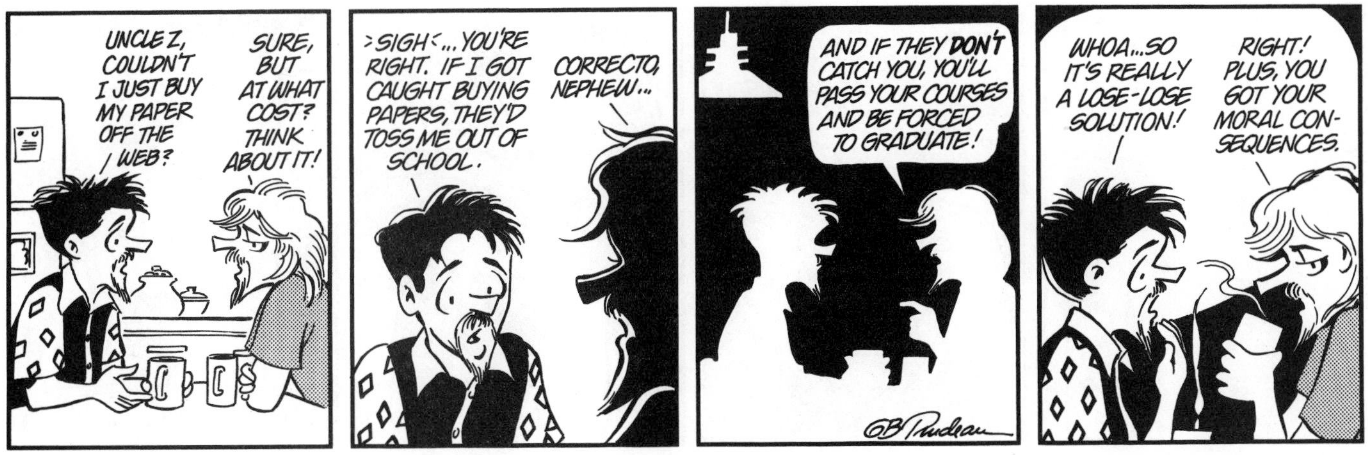
UNCLE Z, COULDN'T I JUST BUY MY PAPER OFF THE WEB?
SURE, BUT AT WHAT COST? THINK ABOUT IT!
>SIGH<... YOU'RE RIGHT. IF I GOT CAUGHT BUYING PAPERS, THEY'D TOSS ME OUT OF SCHOOL.
CORRECTO, NEPHEW...
AND IF THEY DON'T CATCH YOU, YOU'LL PASS YOUR COURSES AND BE FORCED TO GRADUATE!
WHOA... SO IT'S REALLY A LOSE-LOSE SOLUTION!
RIGHT! PLUS, YOU GOT YOUR MORAL CONSEQUENCES.

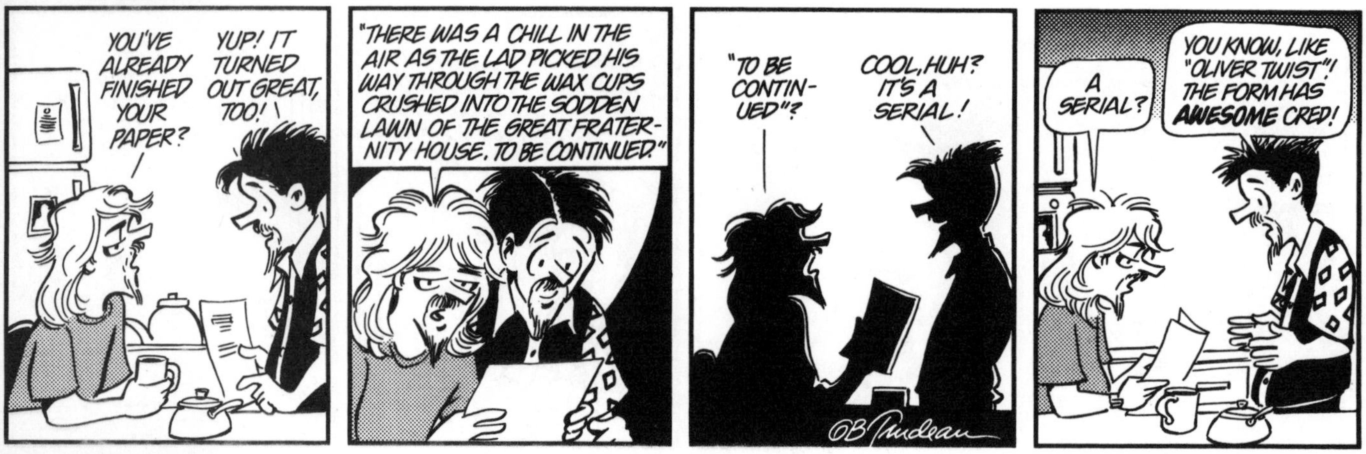
YOU'VE ALREADY FINISHED YOUR PAPER?
YUP! IT TURNED OUT GREAT, TOO!
"THERE WAS A CHILL IN THE AIR AS THE LAD PICKED HIS WAY THROUGH THE WAX CUPS CRUSHED INTO THE SODDEN LAWN OF THE GREAT FRATERNITY HOUSE. TO BE CONTINUED."
"TO BE CONTINUED"?
COOL, HUH? IT'S A SERIAL!
A SERIAL?
YOU KNOW, LIKE "OLIVER TWIST"! THE FORM HAS **AWESOME** CRED!
©B Trudeau

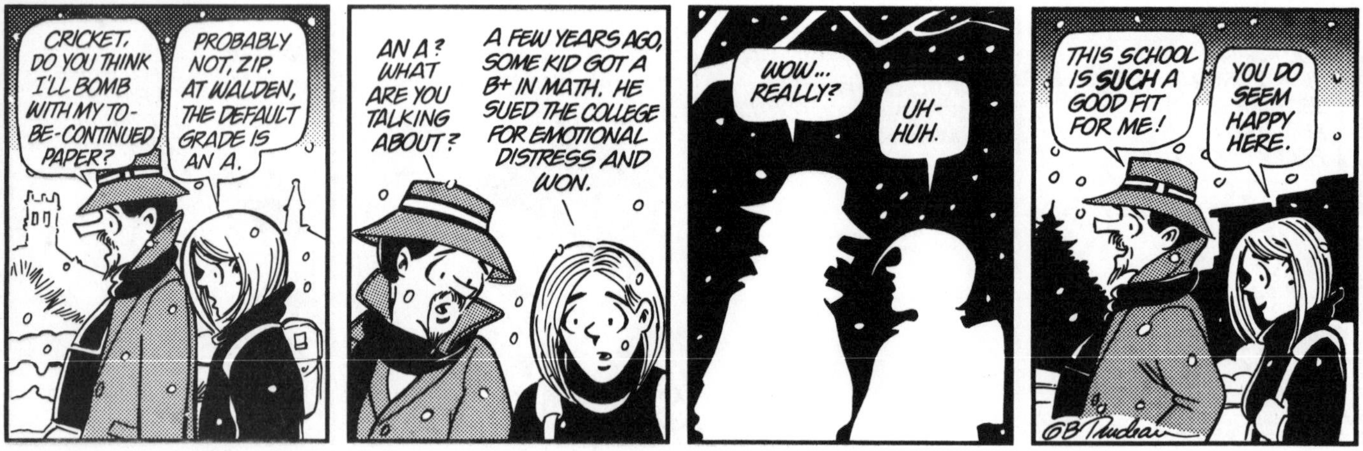
CRICKET. DO YOU THINK I'LL BOMB WITH MY TO-BE-CONTINUED PAPER?
PROBABLY NOT, ZIP. AT WALDEN, THE DEFAULT GRADE IS AN A.
AN A? WHAT ARE YOU TALKING ABOUT?
A FEW YEARS AGO, SOME KID GOT A B+ IN MATH. HE SUED THE COLLEGE FOR EMOTIONAL DISTRESS AND WON.
WOW... REALLY?
UH-HUH.
THIS SCHOOL IS **SUCH** A GOOD FIT FOR ME!
YOU DO SEEM HAPPY HERE.
©B Trudeau

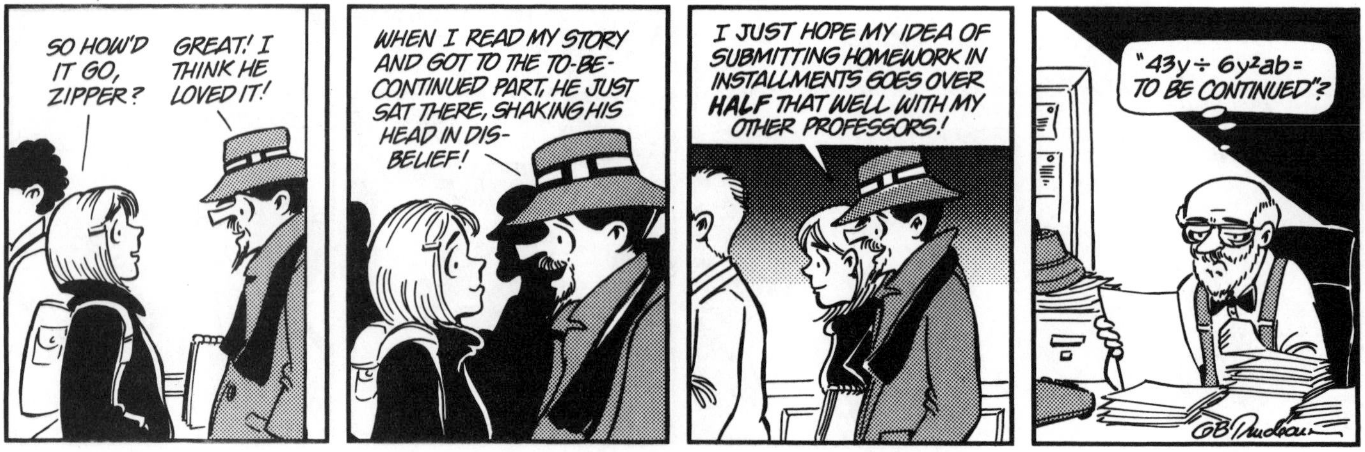
SO HOW'D IT GO, ZIPPER?
GREAT! I THINK HE LOVED IT!
WHEN I READ MY STORY AND GOT TO THE TO-BE-CONTINUED PART, HE JUST SAT THERE, SHAKING HIS HEAD IN DISBELIEF!
I JUST HOPE MY IDEA OF SUBMITTING HOMEWORK IN INSTALLMENTS GOES OVER **HALF** THAT WELL WITH MY OTHER PROFESSORS!
"$43y \div 6y^2ab$ = TO BE CONTINUED"?
©B Trudeau

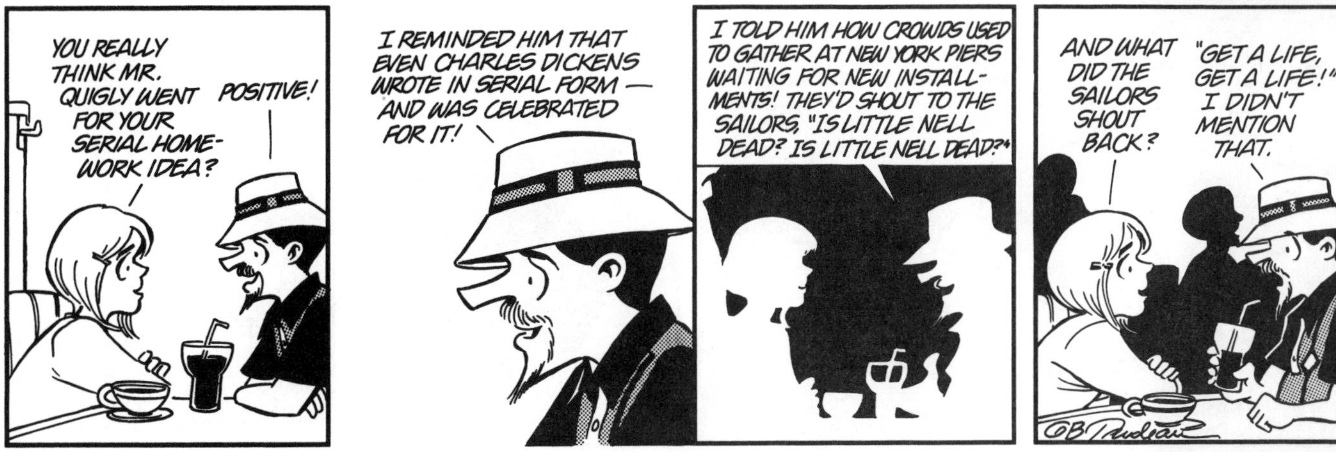
YOU REALLY THINK MR. QUIGLY WENT FOR YOUR SERIAL HOME-WORK IDEA?
POSITIVE!
I REMINDED HIM THAT EVEN CHARLES DICKENS WROTE IN SERIAL FORM — AND WAS CELEBRATED FOR IT!
I TOLD HIM HOW CROWDS USED TO GATHER AT NEW YORK PIERS WAITING FOR NEW INSTALL-MENTS! THEY'D SHOUT TO THE SAILORS, "IS LITTLE NELL DEAD? IS LITTLE NELL DEAD?"
AND WHAT DID THE SAILORS SHOUT BACK?
"GET A LIFE, GET A LIFE!" I DIDN'T MENTION THAT.

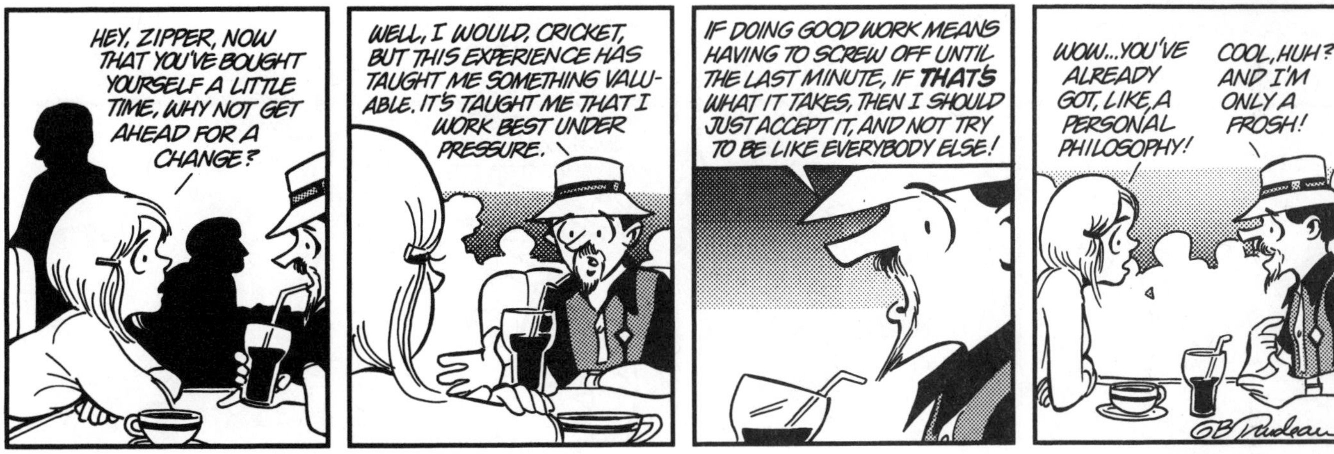
HEY, ZIPPER, NOW THAT YOU'VE BOUGHT YOURSELF A LITTLE TIME, WHY NOT GET AHEAD FOR A CHANGE?
WELL, I WOULD, CRICKET, BUT THIS EXPERIENCE HAS TAUGHT ME SOMETHING VALU-ABLE. IT'S TAUGHT ME THAT I WORK BEST UNDER PRESSURE.
IF DOING GOOD WORK MEANS HAVING TO SCREW OFF UNTIL THE LAST MINUTE, IF THAT'S WHAT IT TAKES, THEN I SHOULD JUST ACCEPT IT, AND NOT TRY TO BE LIKE EVERYBODY ELSE!
WOW...YOU'VE ALREADY GOT, LIKE, A PERSONAL PHILOSOPHY!
COOL, HUH? AND I'M ONLY A FROSH!

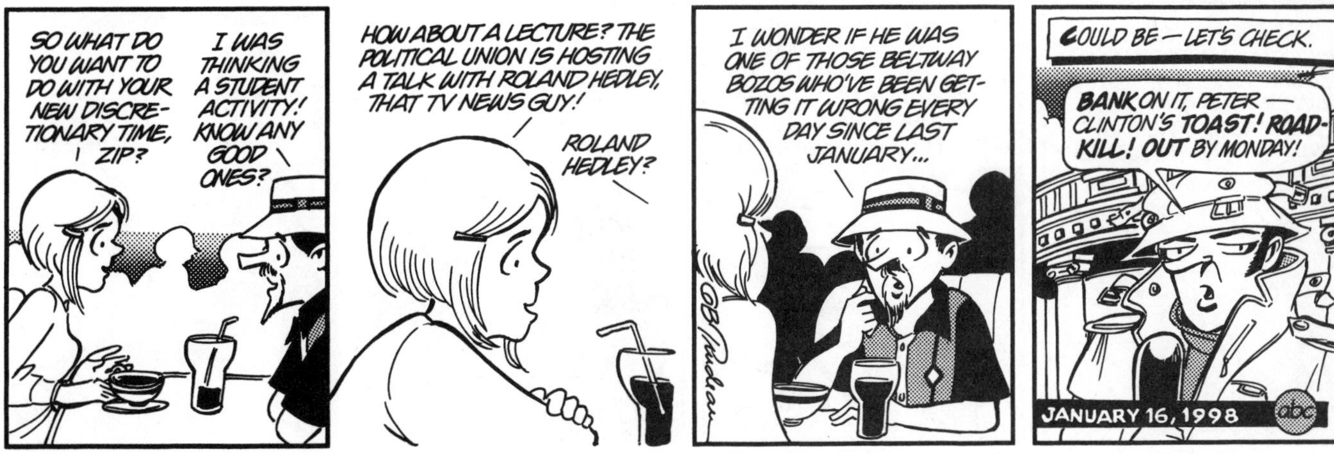
SO WHAT DO YOU WANT TO DO WITH YOUR NEW DISCRE-TIONARY TIME, ZIP?
I WAS THINKING A STUDENT ACTIVITY! KNOW ANY GOOD ONES?
HOW ABOUT A LECTURE? THE POLITICAL UNION IS HOSTING A TALK WITH ROLAND HEDLEY, THAT TV NEWS GUY!
ROLAND HEDLEY?
I WONDER IF HE WAS ONE OF THOSE BELTWAY BOZOS WHO'VE BEEN GET-TING IT WRONG EVERY DAY SINCE LAST JANUARY...
COULD BE — LET'S CHECK.
BANK ON IT, PETER — CLINTON'S TOAST! ROAD-KILL! OUT BY MONDAY!
JANUARY 16, 1998
abc

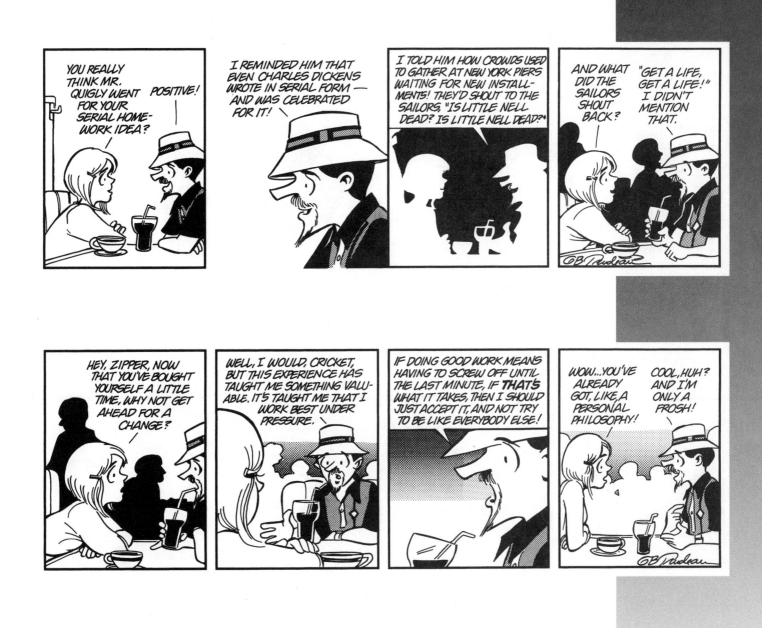

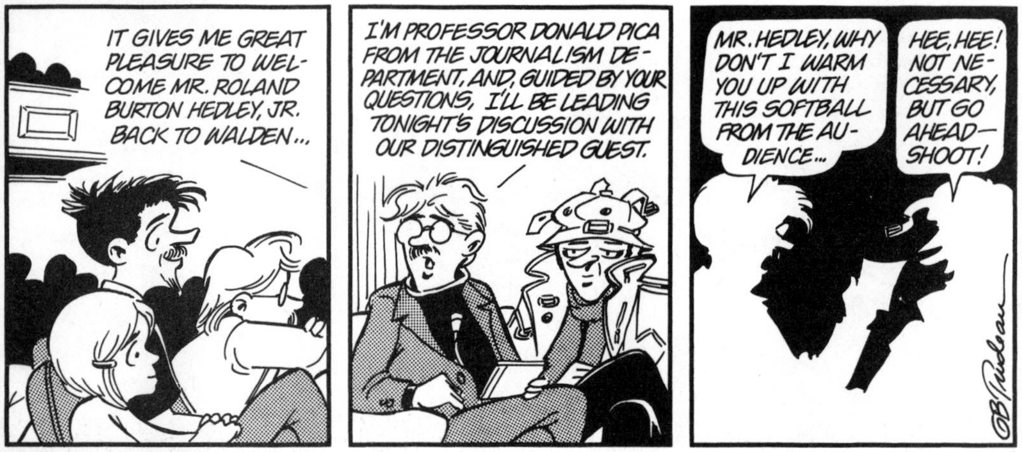
IT GIVES ME GREAT PLEASURE TO WELCOME MR. ROLAND BURTON HEDLEY, JR. BACK TO WALDEN...
I'M PROFESSOR DONALD PICA FROM THE JOURNALISM DEPARTMENT, AND, GUIDED BY YOUR QUESTIONS, I'LL BE LEADING TONIGHT'S DISCUSSION WITH OUR DISTINGUISHED GUEST.
MR. HEDLEY, WHY DON'T I WARM YOU UP WITH THIS SOFTBALL FROM THE AUDIENCE...
HEE, HEE! NOT NECESSARY, BUT GO AHEAD—SHOOT!
"WHEN DID YOU FIRST KNOW YOU WANTED TO BE A BOTTOM-FEEDER?"
WELL, I... THAT'S A SOFTBALL?
©B Trudeau

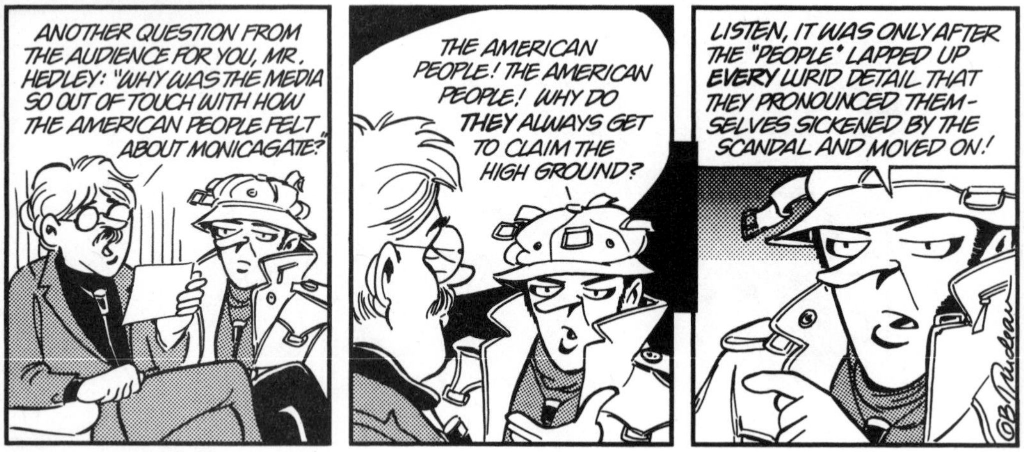
ANOTHER QUESTION FROM THE AUDIENCE FOR YOU, MR. HEDLEY: "WHY WAS THE MEDIA SO OUT OF TOUCH WITH HOW THE AMERICAN PEOPLE FELT ABOUT MONICAGATE?"
THE AMERICAN PEOPLE! THE AMERICAN PEOPLE! WHY DO THEY ALWAYS GET TO CLAIM THE HIGH GROUND?
LISTEN, IT WAS ONLY AFTER THE "PEOPLE" LAPPED UP EVERY LURID DETAIL THAT THEY PRONOUNCED THEMSELVES SICKENED BY THE SCANDAL AND MOVED ON!
SO THE MEDIA FEEL BETRAYED?
WORSE—WE FEEL CHEAP! USED!
©B Trudeau

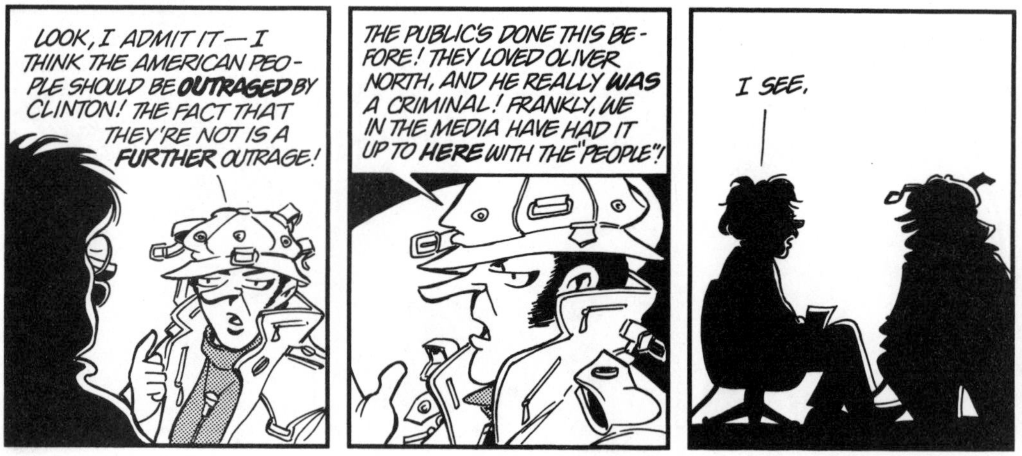
LOOK, I ADMIT IT—I THINK THE AMERICAN PEOPLE SHOULD BE OUTRAGED BY CLINTON! THE FACT THAT THEY'RE NOT IS A FURTHER OUTRAGE!
THE PUBLIC'S DONE THIS BEFORE! THEY LOVED OLIVER NORTH, AND HE REALLY WAS A CRIMINAL! FRANKLY, WE IN THE MEDIA HAVE HAD IT UP TO HERE WITH THE "PEOPLE"!
I SEE.
OKAY, MOVING ON... "DOES NETWORK NEWS STILL HAVE AN AUDIENCE?"
WHO CARES? THEY NEVER LISTEN!
©B Trudeau

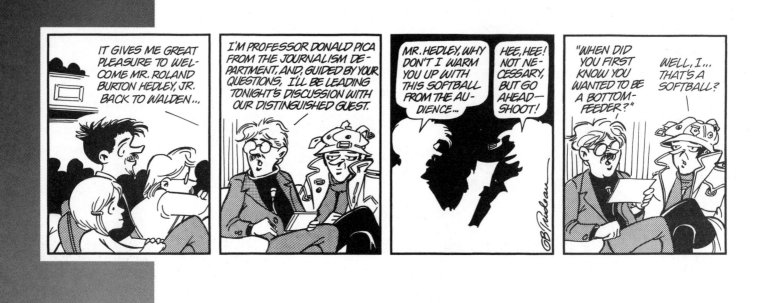

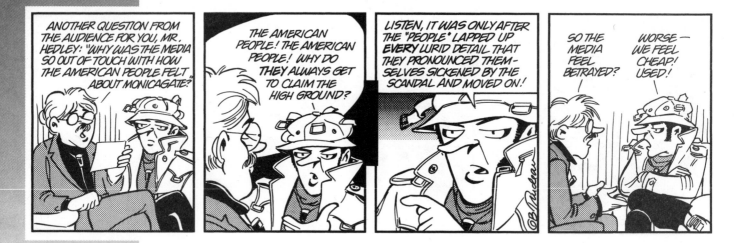

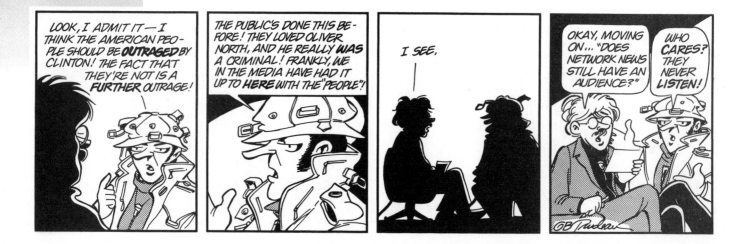

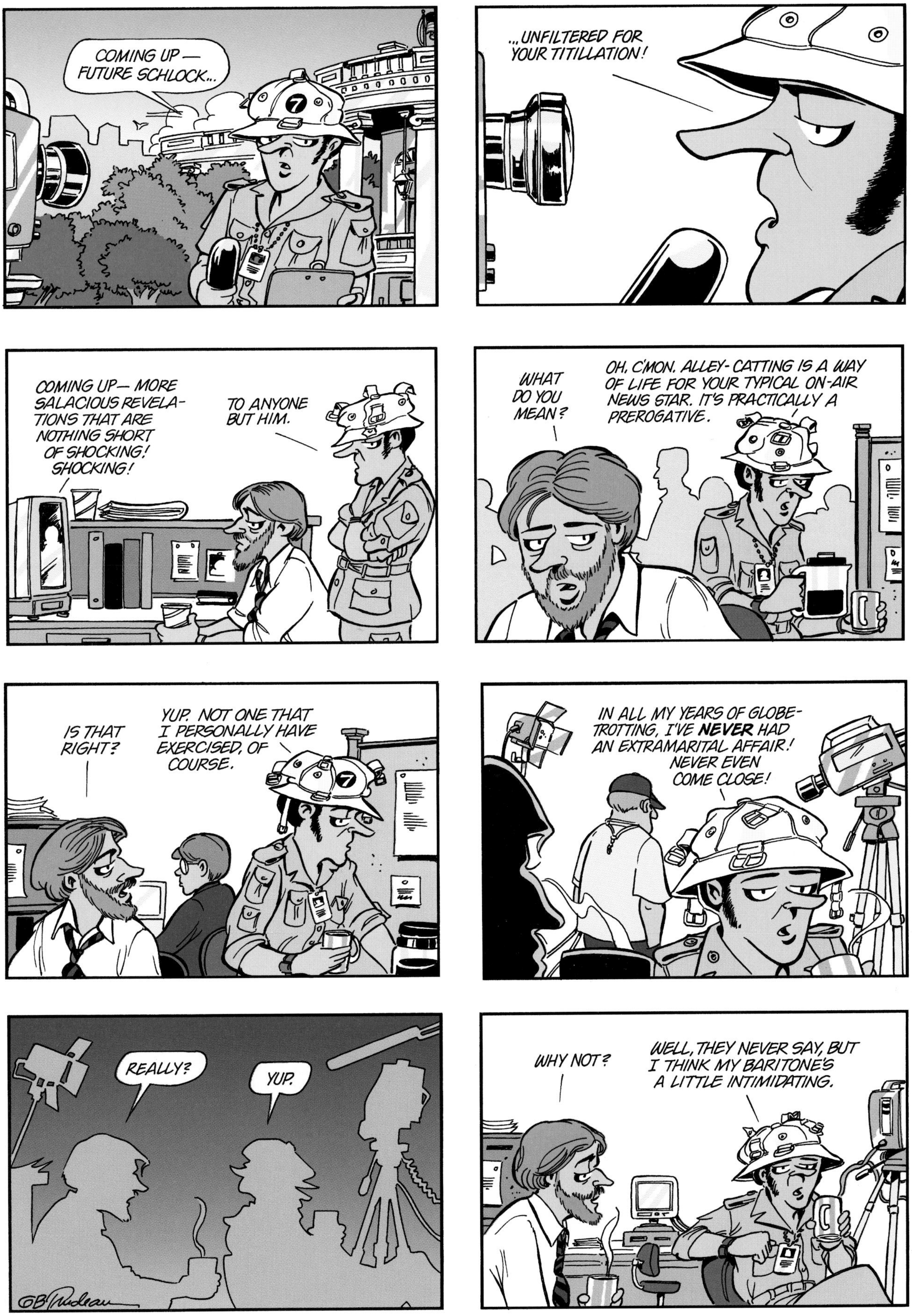
COMING UP — FUTURE SCHLOCK...
...UNFILTERED FOR YOUR TITILLATION!
COMING UP— MORE SALACIOUS REVELATIONS THAT ARE NOTHING SHORT OF SHOCKING! SHOCKING!
TO ANYONE BUT HIM.
WHAT DO YOU MEAN?
OH, C'MON. ALLEY-CATTING IS A WAY OF LIFE FOR YOUR TYPICAL ON-AIR NEWS STAR. IT'S PRACTICALLY A PREROGATIVE.
IS THAT RIGHT?
YUP. NOT ONE THAT I PERSONALLY HAVE EXERCISED, OF COURSE.
IN ALL MY YEARS OF GLOBE-TROTTING, I'VE **NEVER** HAD AN EXTRAMARITAL AFFAIR!
NEVER EVEN COME CLOSE!
REALLY?
YUP.
WHY NOT?
WELL, THEY NEVER SAY, BUT I THINK MY BARITONE'S A LITTLE INTIMIDATING.

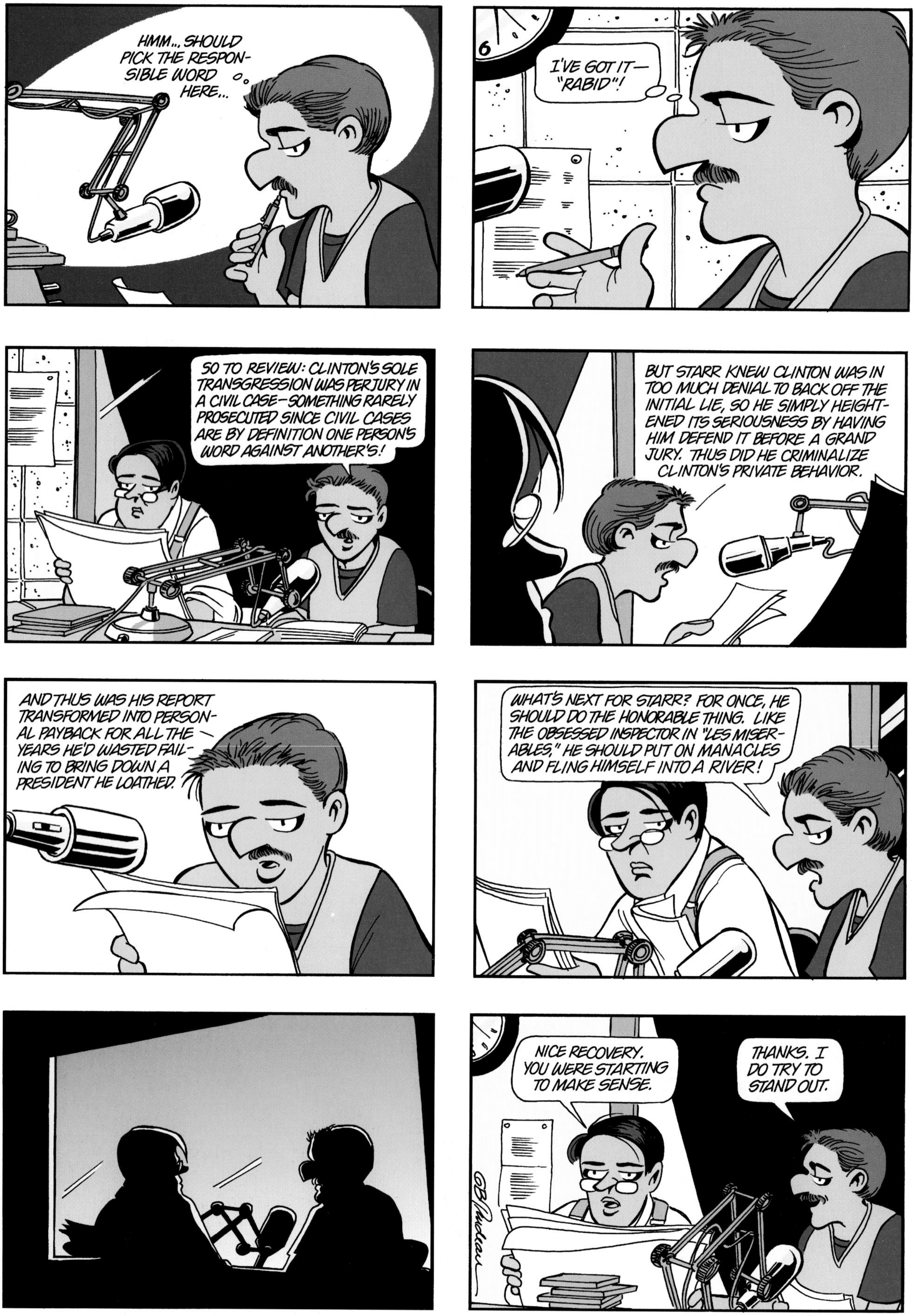

HMM... SHOULD PICK THE RESPONSIBLE WORD HERE...
I'VE GOT IT— "RABID"!
SO TO REVIEW: CLINTON'S SOLE TRANSGRESSION WAS PERJURY IN A CIVIL CASE—SOMETHING RARELY PROSECUTED SINCE CIVIL CASES ARE BY DEFINITION ONE PERSON'S WORD AGAINST ANOTHER'S!
BUT STARR KNEW CLINTON WAS IN TOO MUCH DENIAL TO BACK OFF THE INITIAL LIE, SO HE SIMPLY HEIGHTENED ITS SERIOUSNESS BY HAVING HIM DEFEND IT BEFORE A GRAND JURY. THUS DID HE CRIMINALIZE CLINTON'S PRIVATE BEHAVIOR.
AND THUS WAS HIS REPORT TRANSFORMED INTO PERSONAL PAYBACK FOR ALL THE YEARS HE'D WASTED FAILING TO BRING DOWN A PRESIDENT HE LOATHED.
WHAT'S NEXT FOR STARR? FOR ONCE, HE SHOULD DO THE HONORABLE THING. LIKE THE OBSESSED INSPECTOR IN "LES MISERABLES," HE SHOULD PUT ON MANACLES AND FLING HIMSELF INTO A RIVER!
NICE RECOVERY. YOU WERE STARTING TO MAKE SENSE.
THANKS. I DO TRY TO STAND OUT.

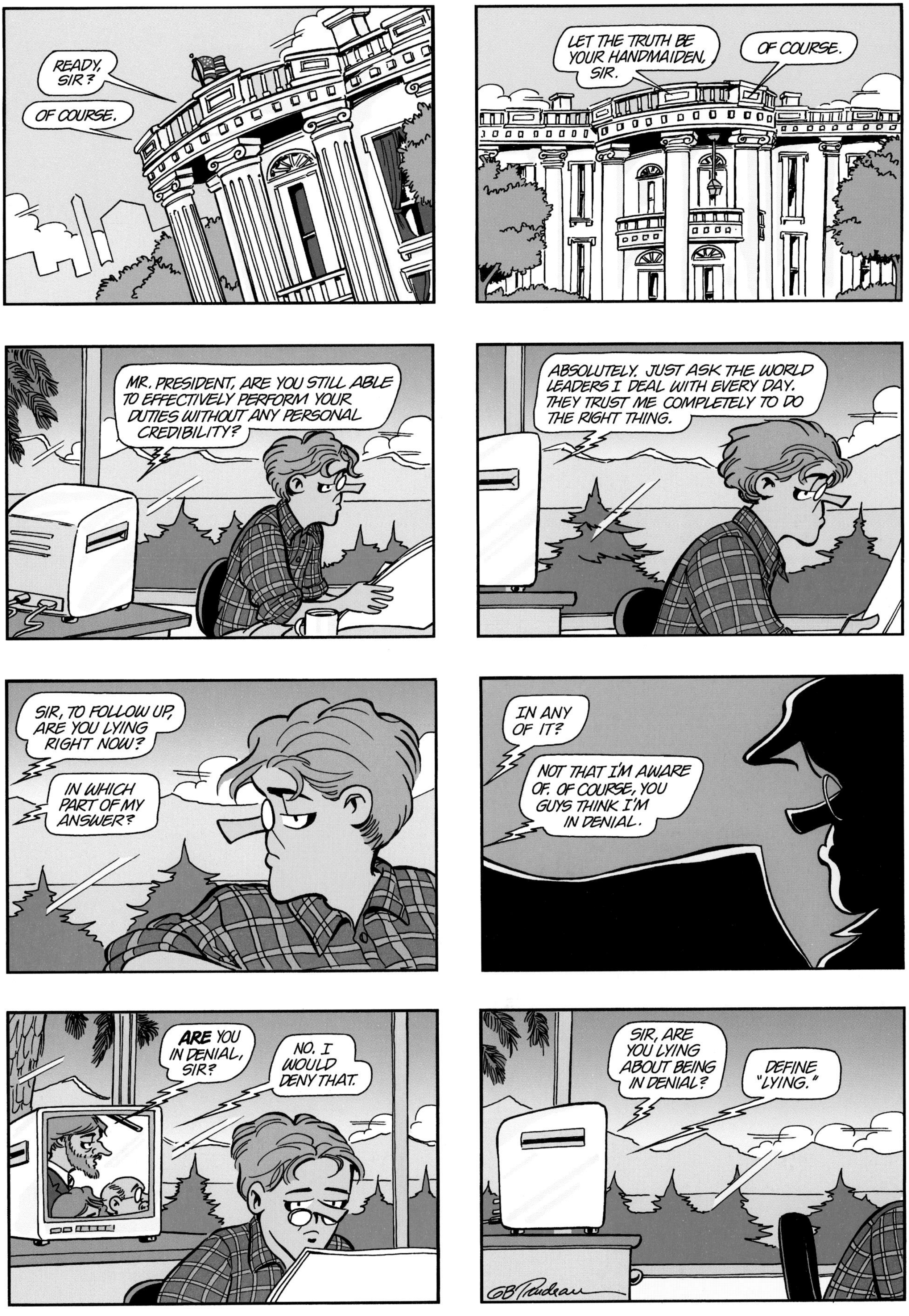
READY, SIR?
OF COURSE.
LET THE TRUTH BE YOUR HANDMAIDEN, SIR.
OF COURSE.
MR. PRESIDENT, ARE YOU STILL ABLE TO EFFECTIVELY PERFORM YOUR DUTIES WITHOUT ANY PERSONAL CREDIBILITY?
ABSOLUTELY. JUST ASK THE WORLD LEADERS I DEAL WITH EVERY DAY. THEY TRUST ME COMPLETELY TO DO THE RIGHT THING.
SIR, TO FOLLOW UP, ARE YOU LYING RIGHT NOW?
IN WHICH PART OF MY ANSWER?
IN ANY OF IT?
NOT THAT I'M AWARE OF. OF COURSE, YOU GUYS THINK I'M IN DENIAL.
ARE YOU IN DENIAL, SIR?
NO. I WOULD DENY THAT.
SIR, ARE YOU LYING ABOUT BEING IN DENIAL?
DEFINE "LYING."
GB Trudeau

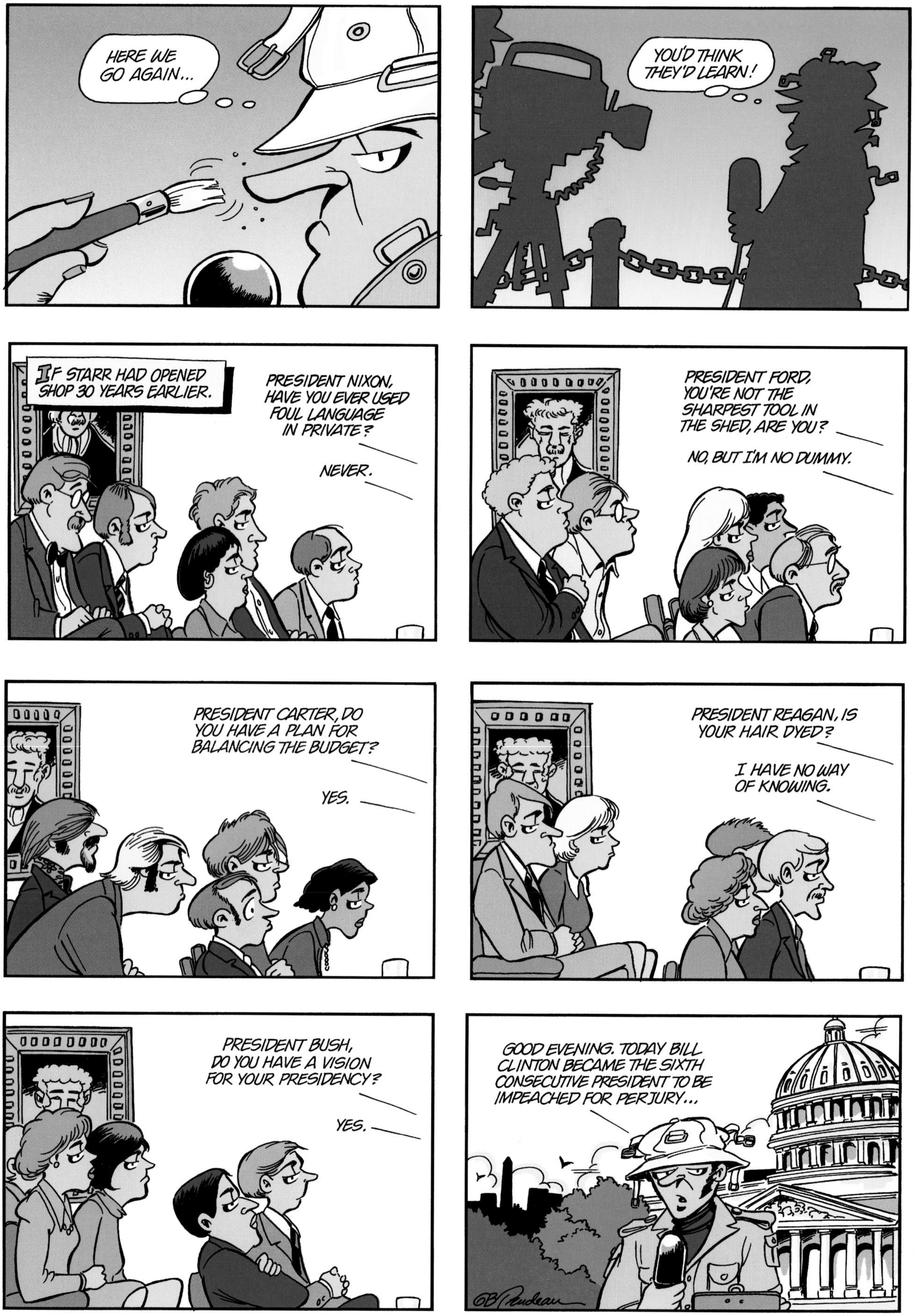
HERE WE GO AGAIN...
YOU'D THINK THEY'D LEARN!
IF STARR HAD OPENED SHOP 30 YEARS EARLIER.
PRESIDENT NIXON, HAVE YOU EVER USED FOUL LANGUAGE IN PRIVATE?
NEVER.
PRESIDENT FORD, YOU'RE NOT THE SHARPEST TOOL IN THE SHED, ARE YOU?
NO, BUT I'M NO DUMMY.
PRESIDENT CARTER, DO YOU HAVE A PLAN FOR BALANCING THE BUDGET?
YES.
PRESIDENT REAGAN, IS YOUR HAIR DYED?
I HAVE NO WAY OF KNOWING.
PRESIDENT BUSH, DO YOU HAVE A VISION FOR YOUR PRESIDENCY?
YES.
GOOD EVENING. TODAY BILL CLINTON BECAME THE SIXTH CONSECUTIVE PRESIDENT TO BE IMPEACHED FOR PERJURY...
GB Trudeau

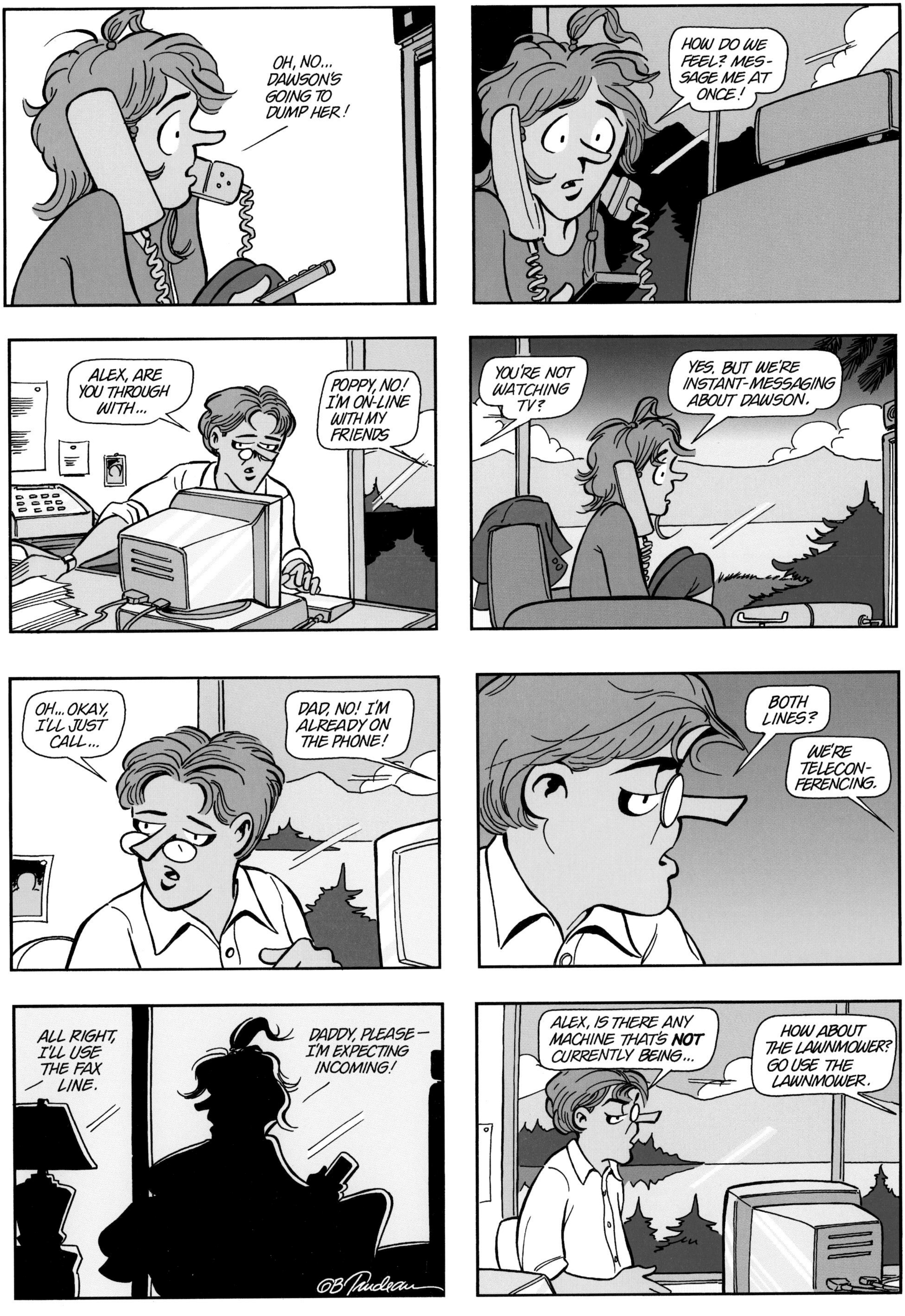
OH, NO... DAWSON'S GOING TO DUMP HER!
HOW DO WE FEEL? MES-SAGE ME AT ONCE!
ALEX, ARE YOU THROUGH WITH...
POPPY, NO! I'M ON-LINE WITH MY FRIENDS
YOU'RE NOT WATCHING TV?
YES. BUT WE'RE INSTANT-MESSAGING ABOUT DAWSON.
OH... OKAY, I'LL JUST CALL...
DAD, NO! I'M ALREADY ON THE PHONE!
BOTH LINES?
WE'RE TELECON-FERENCING.
ALL RIGHT, I'LL USE THE FAX LINE.
DADDY, PLEASE— I'M EXPECTING INCOMING!
©B Trudeau
ALEX, IS THERE ANY MACHINE THAT'S **NOT** CURRENTLY BEING...
HOW ABOUT THE LAWNMOWER? GO USE THE LAWNMOWER.

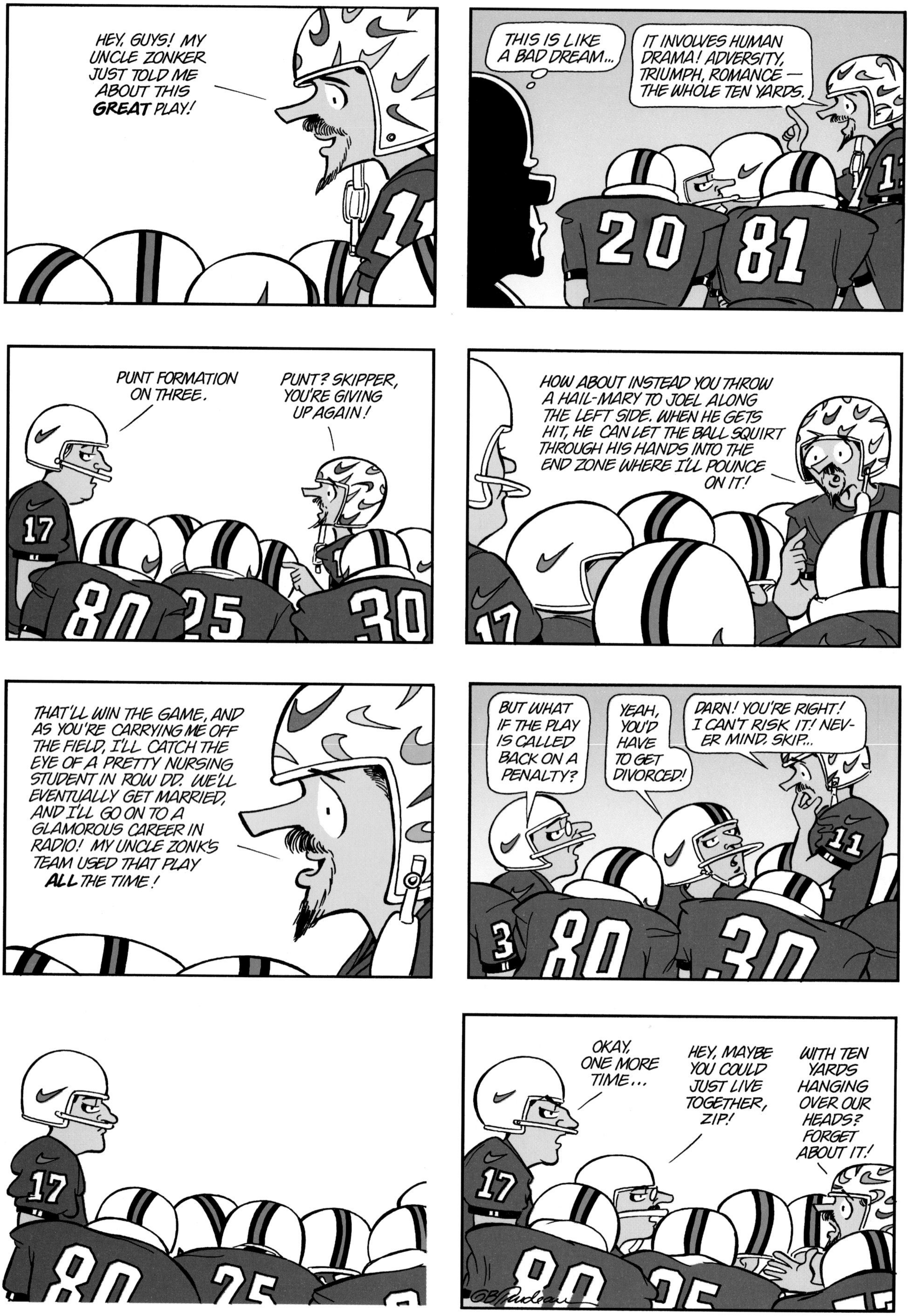
HEY, GUYS! MY UNCLE ZONKER JUST TOLD ME ABOUT THIS GREAT PLAY!
THIS IS LIKE A BAD DREAM...
IT INVOLVES HUMAN DRAMA! ADVERSITY, TRIUMPH, ROMANCE — THE WHOLE TEN YARDS.
PUNT FORMATION ON THREE.
PUNT? SKIPPER, YOU'RE GIVING UP AGAIN!
HOW ABOUT INSTEAD YOU THROW A HAIL-MARY TO JOEL ALONG THE LEFT SIDE. WHEN HE GETS HIT, HE CAN LET THE BALL SQUIRT THROUGH HIS HANDS INTO THE END ZONE WHERE I'LL POUNCE ON IT!
THAT'LL WIN THE GAME, AND AS YOU'RE CARRYING ME OFF THE FIELD, I'LL CATCH THE EYE OF A PRETTY NURSING STUDENT IN ROW DD. WE'LL EVENTUALLY GET MARRIED, AND I'LL GO ON TO A GLAMOROUS CAREER IN RADIO! MY UNCLE ZONK'S TEAM USED THAT PLAY ALL THE TIME!
BUT WHAT IF THE PLAY IS CALLED BACK ON A PENALTY?
YEAH, YOU'D HAVE TO GET DIVORCED!
DARN! YOU'RE RIGHT! I CAN'T RISK IT! NEVER MIND, SKIP...
OKAY, ONE MORE TIME...
HEY, MAYBE YOU COULD JUST LIVE TOGETHER, ZIP!
WITH TEN YARDS HANGING OVER OUR HEADS? FORGET ABOUT IT!
©B.Trudeau

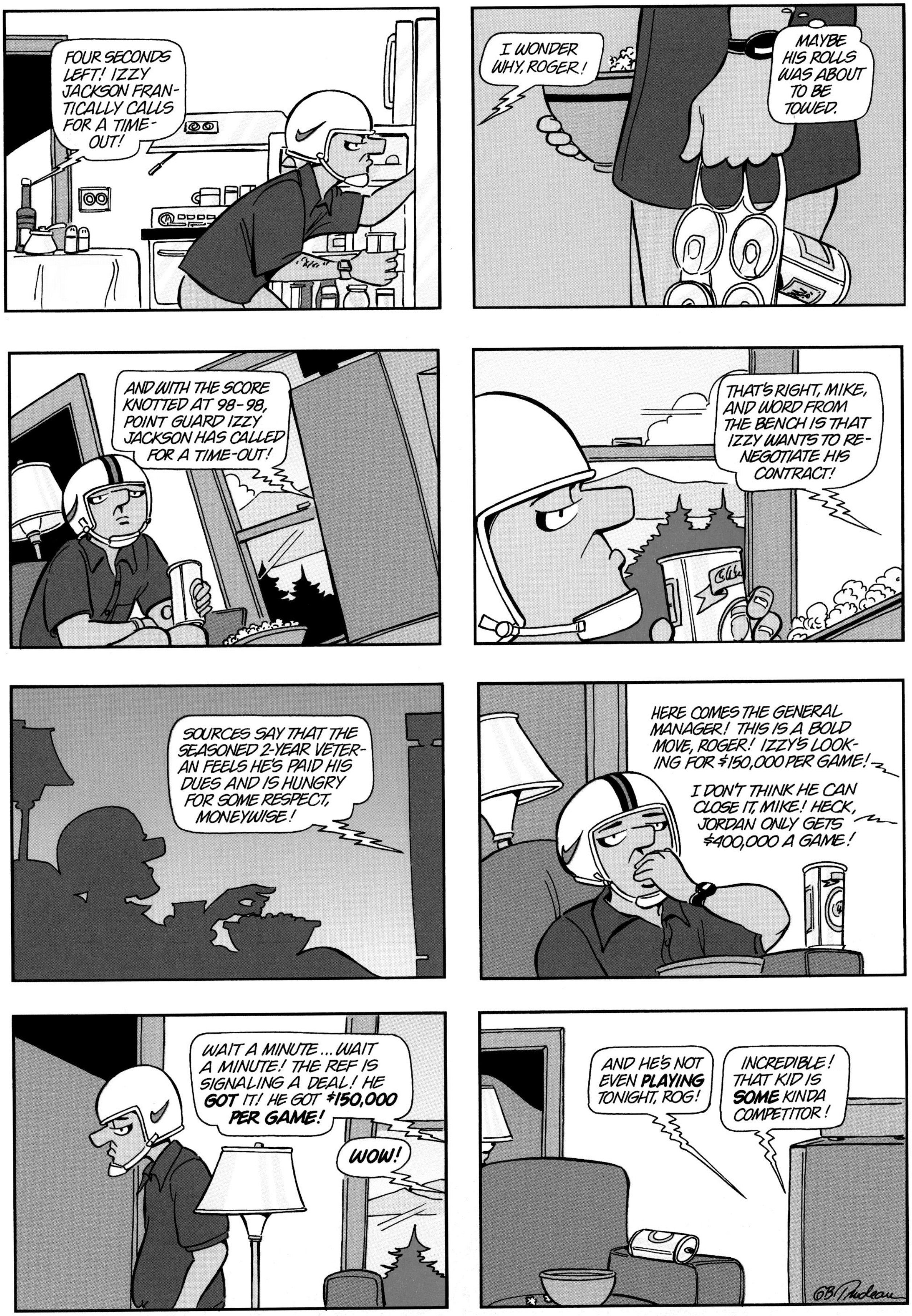
FOUR SECONDS LEFT! IZZY JACKSON FRANTICALLY CALLS FOR A TIME-OUT!
I WONDER WHY, ROGER!
MAYBE HIS ROLLS WAS ABOUT TO BE TOWED.
AND WITH THE SCORE KNOTTED AT 98-98, POINT GUARD IZZY JACKSON HAS CALLED FOR A TIME-OUT!
THAT'S RIGHT, MIKE, AND WORD FROM THE BENCH IS THAT IZZY WANTS TO RENEGOTIATE HIS CONTRACT!
SOURCES SAY THAT THE SEASONED 2-YEAR VETERAN FEELS HE'S PAID HIS DUES AND IS HUNGRY FOR SOME RESPECT, MONEYWISE!
HERE COMES THE GENERAL MANAGER! THIS IS A BOLD MOVE, ROGER! IZZY'S LOOKING FOR $150,000 PER GAME!
I DON'T THINK HE CAN CLOSE IT, MIKE! HECK, JORDAN ONLY GETS $400,000 A GAME!
WAIT A MINUTE ... WAIT A MINUTE! THE REF IS SIGNALING A DEAL! HE GOT IT! HE GOT $150,000 PER GAME!
WOW!
AND HE'S NOT EVEN PLAYING TONIGHT, ROG!
INCREDIBLE! THAT KID IS SOME KINDA COMPETITOR!
GBTrudeau

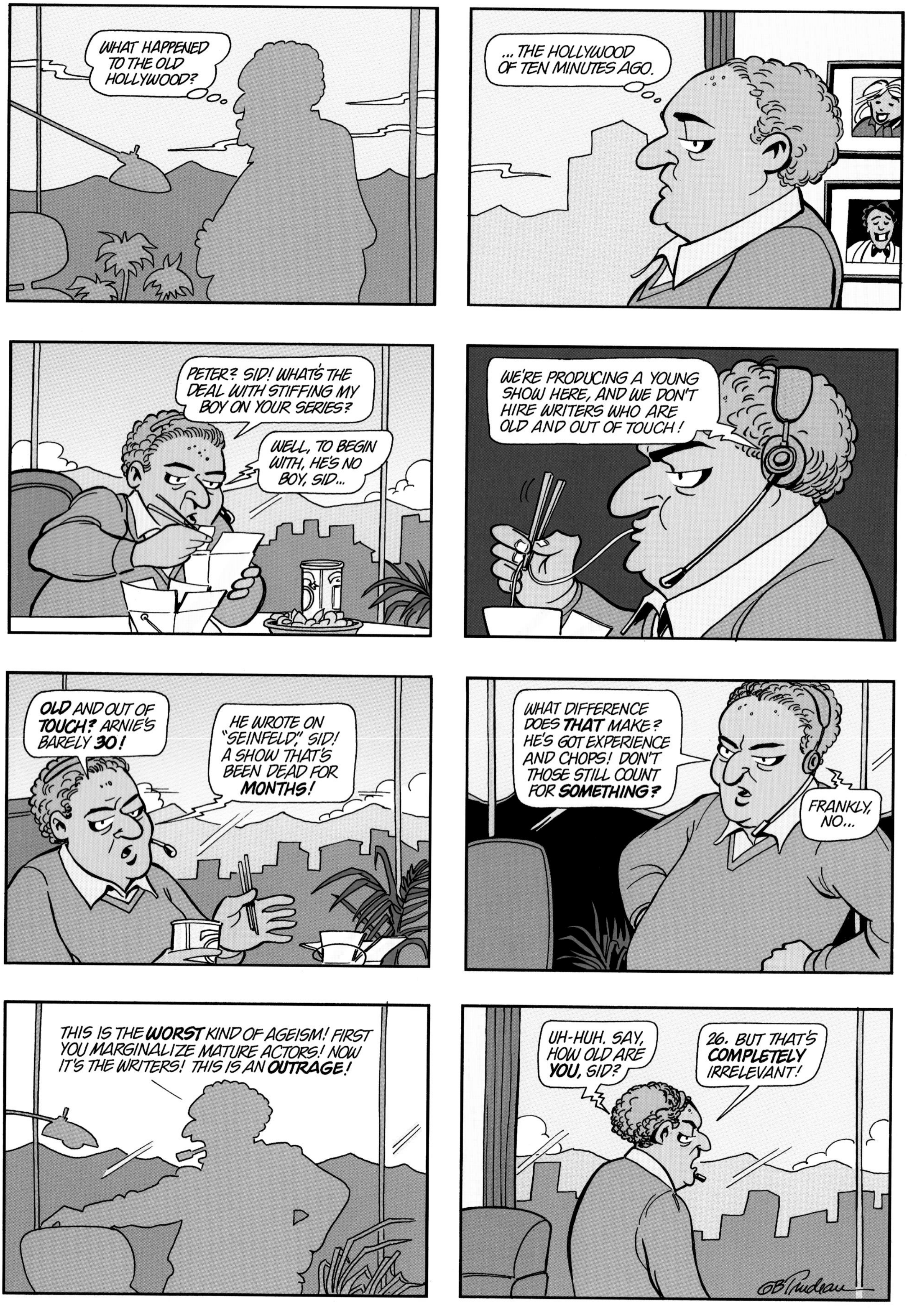
WHAT HAPPENED TO THE OLD HOLLYWOOD?
... THE HOLLYWOOD OF TEN MINUTES AGO.
PETER? SID! WHAT'S THE DEAL WITH STIFFING MY BOY ON YOUR SERIES?
WELL, TO BEGIN WITH, HE'S NO BOY, SID...
WE'RE PRODUCING A YOUNG SHOW HERE, AND WE DON'T HIRE WRITERS WHO ARE OLD AND OUT OF TOUCH!
OLD AND OUT OF TOUCH? ARNIE'S BARELY 30!
HE WROTE ON "SEINFELD," SID! A SHOW THAT'S BEEN DEAD FOR MONTHS!
WHAT DIFFERENCE DOES THAT MAKE? HE'S GOT EXPERIENCE AND CHOPS! DON'T THOSE STILL COUNT FOR SOMETHING?
FRANKLY, NO...
THIS IS THE WORST KIND OF AGEISM! FIRST YOU MARGINALIZE MATURE ACTORS! NOW IT'S THE WRITERS! THIS IS AN OUTRAGE!
UH-HUH. SAY, HOW OLD ARE YOU, SID?
26. BUT THAT'S COMPLETELY IRRELEVANT!
©B Trudeau

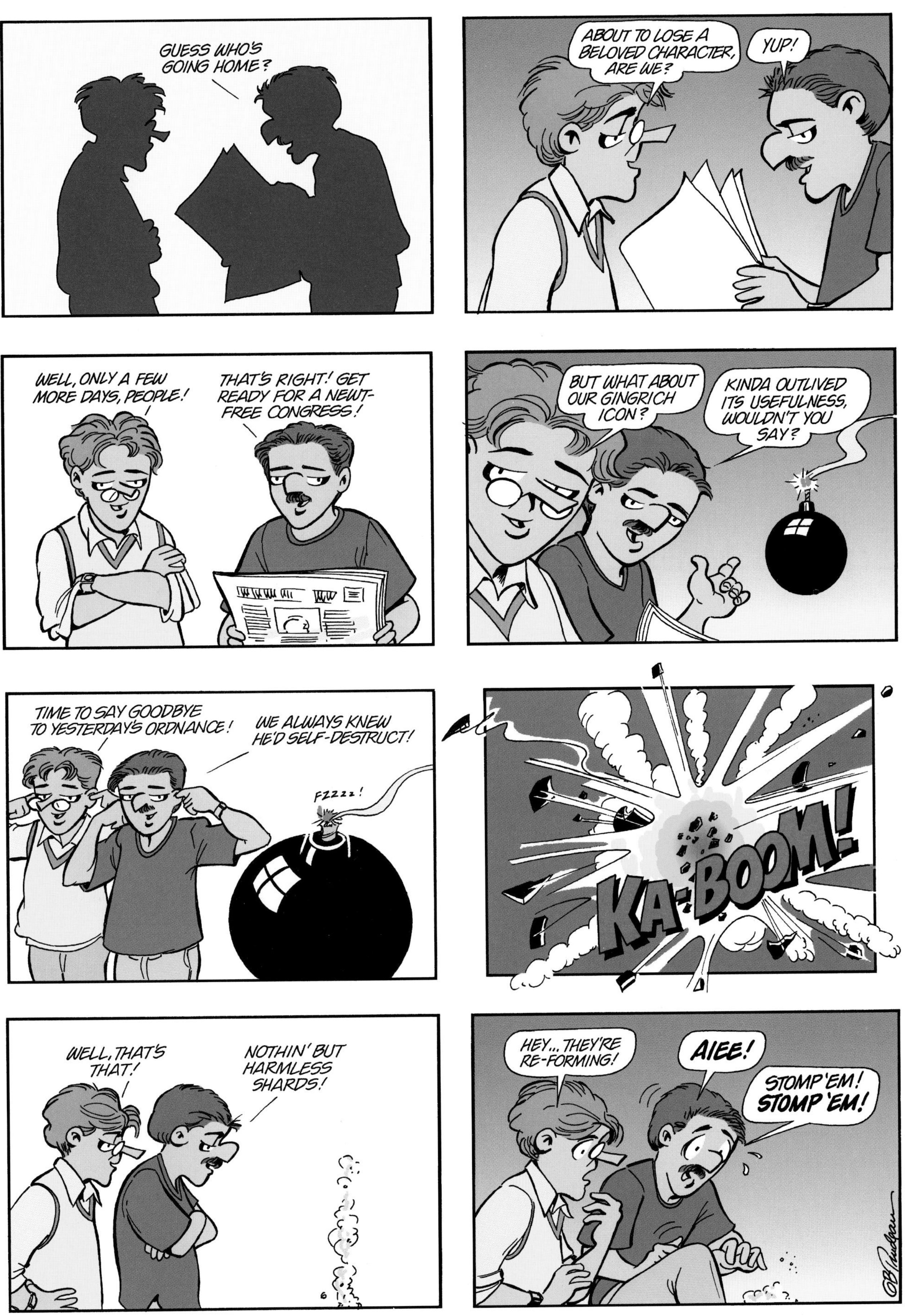
GUESS WHO'S GOING HOME?
ABOUT TO LOSE A BELOVED CHARACTER, ARE WE?
YUP!
WELL, ONLY A FEW MORE DAYS, PEOPLE!
THAT'S RIGHT! GET READY FOR A NEWT-FREE CONGRESS!
BUT WHAT ABOUT OUR GINGRICH ICON?
KINDA OUTLIVED ITS USEFULNESS, WOULDN'T YOU SAY?
TIME TO SAY GOODBYE TO YESTERDAY'S ORDNANCE!
WE ALWAYS KNEW HE'D SELF-DESTRUCT!
FZZZZ!
KA-BOOM!
WELL, THAT'S THAT!
NOTHIN' BUT HARMLESS SHARDS!
HEY... THEY'RE RE-FORMING!
AIEE!
STOMP 'EM! STOMP 'EM!

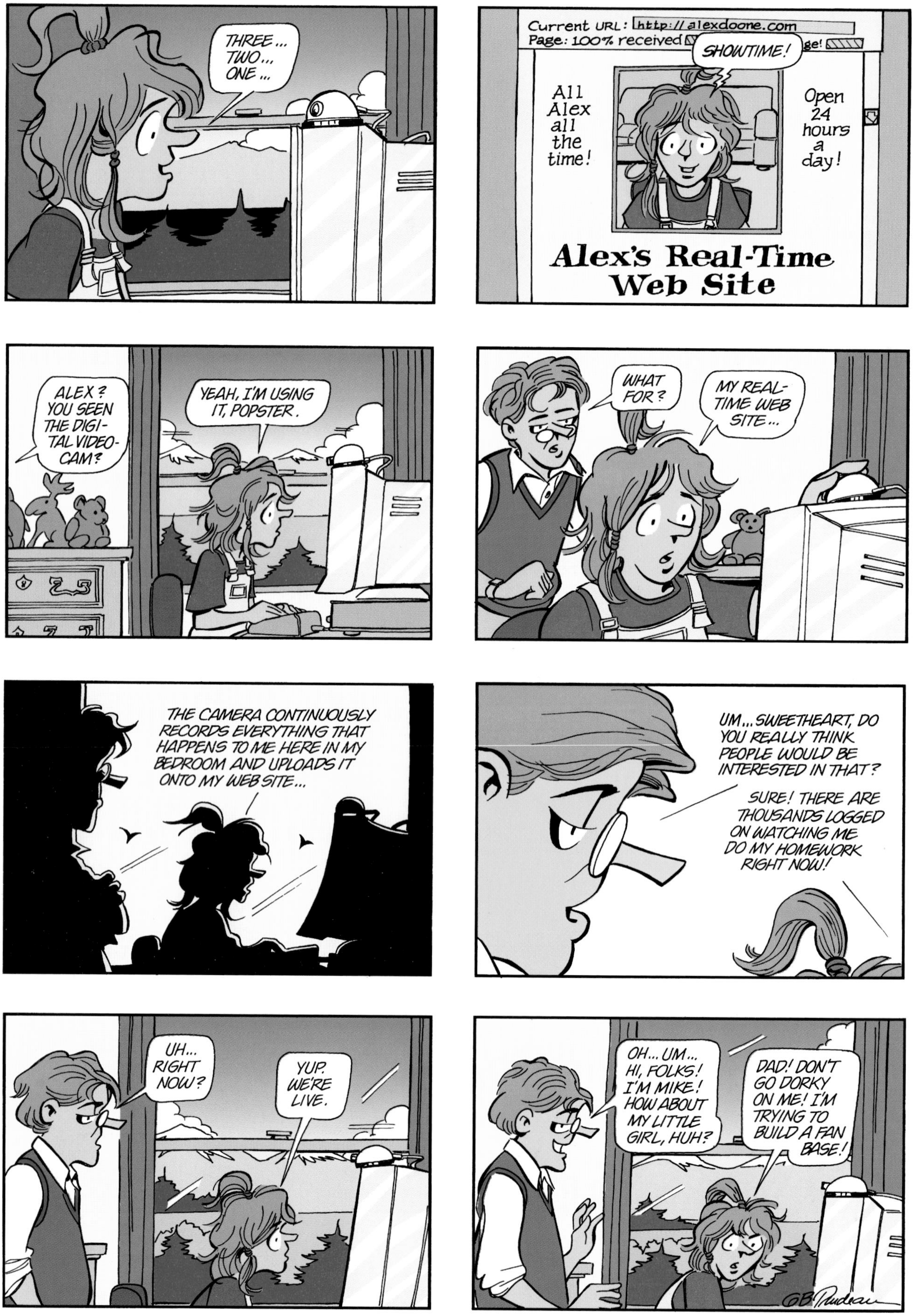
THREE... TWO... ONE...
Current URL: http://alexdoone.com
Page: 100% received
SHOWTIME!
All Alex all the time!
Open 24 hours a day!
Alex's Real-Time Web Site
ALEX? YOU SEEN THE DIGITAL VIDEO-CAM?
YEAH, I'M USING IT, POPSTER.
WHAT FOR?
MY REAL-TIME WEB SITE...
THE CAMERA CONTINUOUSLY RECORDS EVERYTHING THAT HAPPENS TO ME HERE IN MY BEDROOM AND UPLOADS IT ONTO MY WEB SITE...
UM... SWEETHEART, DO YOU REALLY THINK PEOPLE WOULD BE INTERESTED IN THAT?
SURE! THERE ARE THOUSANDS LOGGED ON WATCHING ME DO MY HOMEWORK RIGHT NOW!
UH... RIGHT NOW?
YUP. WE'RE LIVE.
OH... UM... HI, FOLKS! I'M MIKE! HOW ABOUT MY LITTLE GIRL, HUH?
DAD! DON'T GO DORKY ON ME! I'M TRYING TO BUILD A FAN BASE!

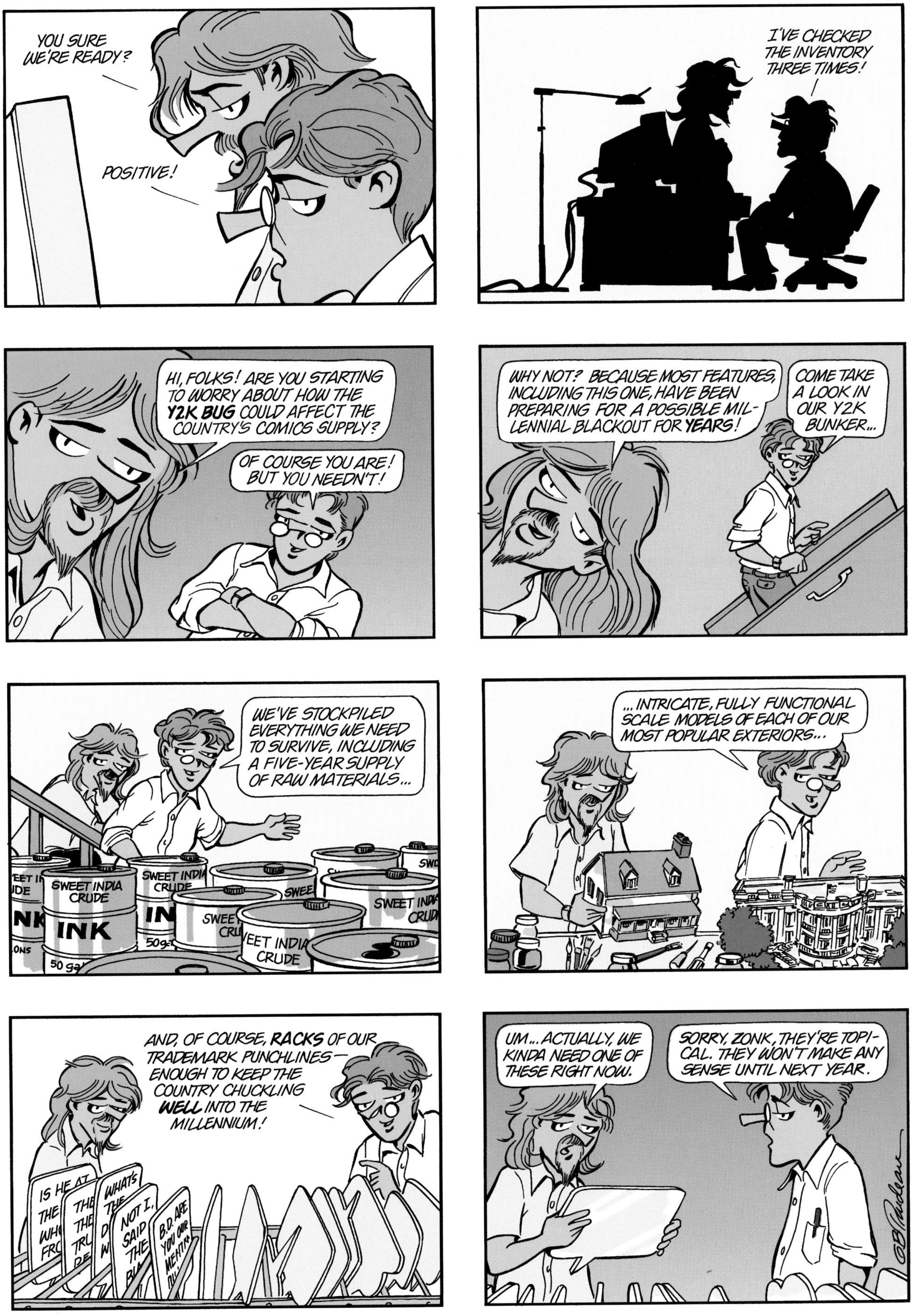
YOU SURE WE'RE READY?
POSITIVE!
I'VE CHECKED THE INVENTORY THREE TIMES!
HI, FOLKS! ARE YOU STARTING TO WORRY ABOUT HOW THE **Y2K BUG** COULD AFFECT THE COUNTRY'S COMICS SUPPLY?
OF COURSE YOU ARE! BUT YOU NEEDN'T!
WHY NOT? BECAUSE MOST FEATURES, INCLUDING THIS ONE, HAVE BEEN PREPARING FOR A POSSIBLE MILLENNIAL BLACKOUT FOR **YEARS**!
COME TAKE A LOOK IN OUR Y2K BUNKER...
WE'VE STOCKPILED EVERYTHING WE NEED TO SURVIVE, INCLUDING A FIVE-YEAR SUPPLY OF RAW MATERIALS...
SWEET INDIA CRUDE
INK
...INTRICATE, FULLY FUNCTIONAL SCALE MODELS OF EACH OF OUR MOST POPULAR EXTERIORS...
AND, OF COURSE, **RACKS** OF OUR TRADEMARK PUNCHLINES— ENOUGH TO KEEP THE COUNTRY CHUCKLING **WELL** INTO THE MILLENNIUM!
UM... ACTUALLY, WE KINDA NEED ONE OF THESE RIGHT NOW.
SORRY, ZONK, THEY'RE TOPICAL. THEY WON'T MAKE ANY SENSE UNTIL NEXT YEAR.
©B Trudeau

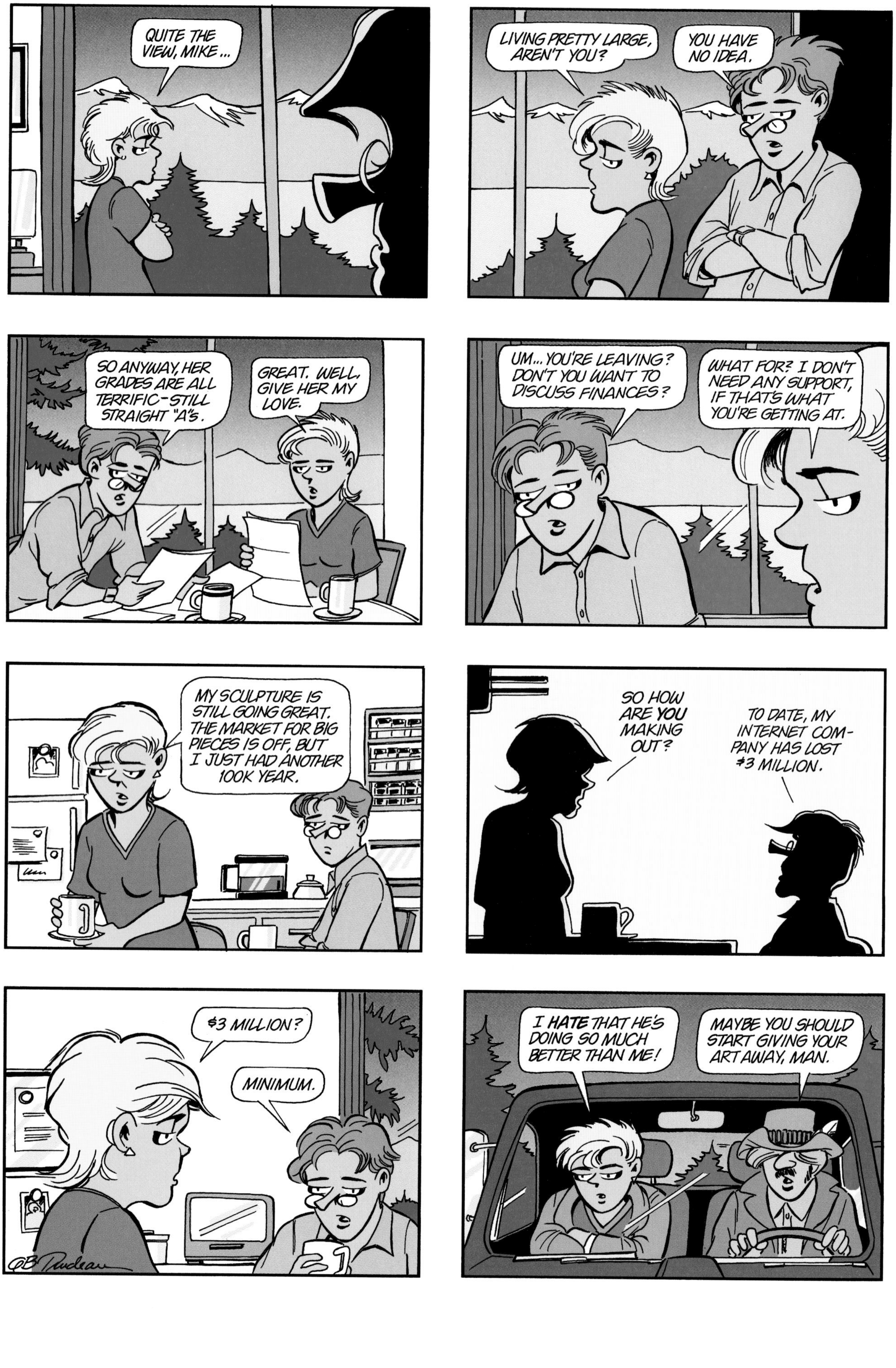
QUITE THE VIEW, MIKE...
LIVING PRETTY LARGE, AREN'T YOU?
YOU HAVE NO IDEA.
SO ANYWAY, HER GRADES ARE ALL TERRIFIC–STILL STRAIGHT "A"S.
GREAT. WELL, GIVE HER MY LOVE.
UM... YOU'RE LEAVING? DON'T YOU WANT TO DISCUSS FINANCES?
WHAT FOR? I DON'T NEED ANY SUPPORT, IF THAT'S WHAT YOU'RE GETTING AT.
MY SCULPTURE IS STILL GOING GREAT. THE MARKET FOR BIG PIECES IS OFF, BUT I JUST HAD ANOTHER 100K YEAR.
SO HOW ARE **YOU** MAKING OUT?
TO DATE, MY INTERNET COMPANY HAS LOST $3 MILLION.
$3 MILLION?
MINIMUM.
I **HATE** THAT HE'S DOING SO MUCH BETTER THAN ME!
MAYBE YOU SHOULD START GIVING YOUR ART AWAY, MAN.

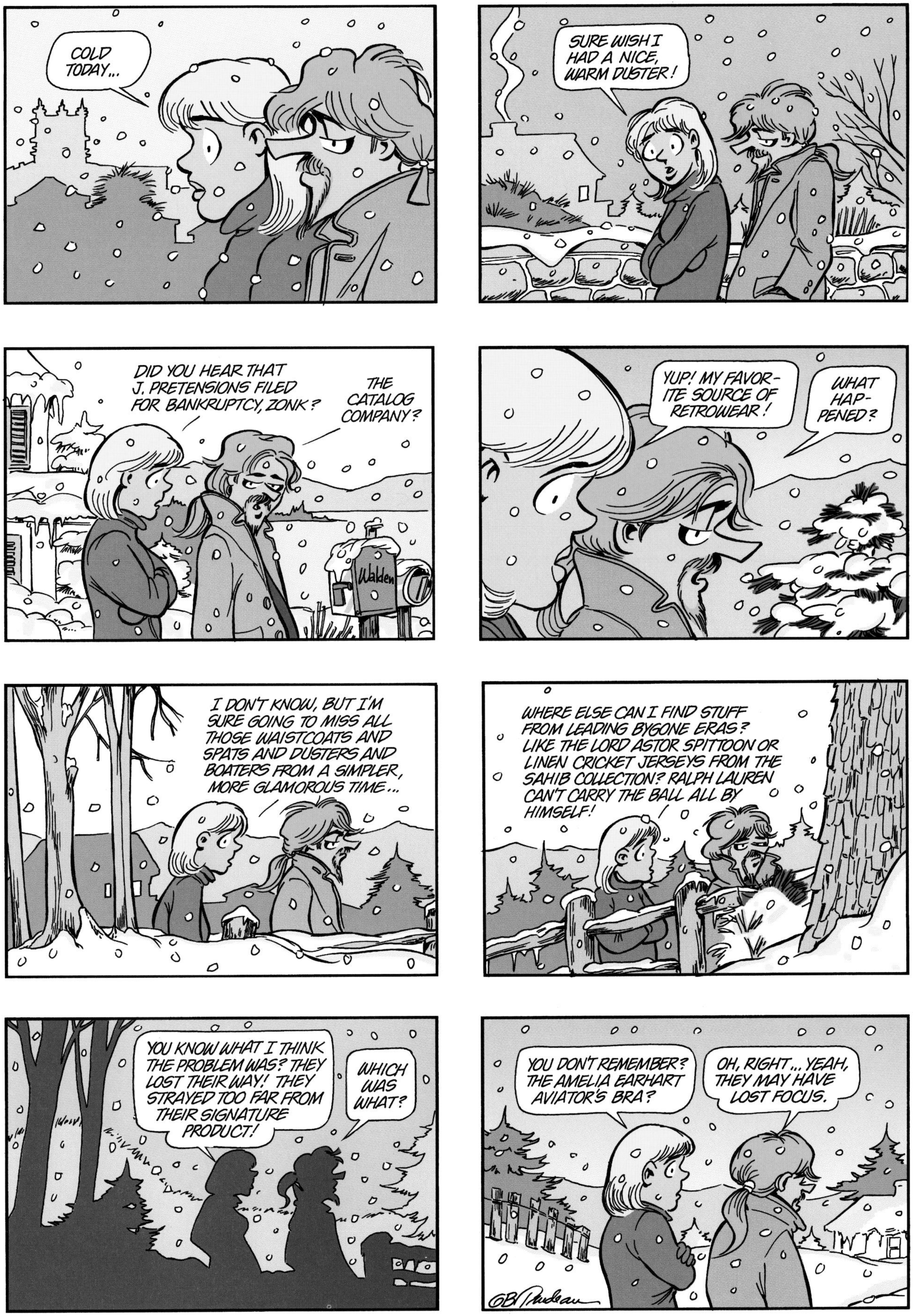
COLD TODAY...
SURE WISH I HAD A NICE, WARM DUSTER!
DID YOU HEAR THAT J. PRETENSIONS FILED FOR BANKRUPTCY, ZONK?
THE CATALOG COMPANY?
Walden
YUP! MY FAVORITE SOURCE OF RETROWEAR!
WHAT HAPPENED?
I DON'T KNOW, BUT I'M SURE GOING TO MISS ALL THOSE WAISTCOATS AND SPATS AND DUSTERS AND BOATERS FROM A SIMPLER, MORE GLAMOROUS TIME...
WHERE ELSE CAN I FIND STUFF FROM LEADING BYGONE ERAS? LIKE THE LORD ASTOR SPITTOON OR LINEN CRICKET JERSEYS FROM THE SAHIB COLLECTION? RALPH LAUREN CAN'T CARRY THE BALL ALL BY HIMSELF!
YOU KNOW WHAT I THINK THE PROBLEM WAS? THEY LOST THEIR WAY! THEY STRAYED TOO FAR FROM THEIR SIGNATURE PRODUCT!
WHICH WAS WHAT?
YOU DON'T REMEMBER? THE AMELIA EARHART AVIATOR'S BRA?
OH, RIGHT... YEAH, THEY MAY HAVE LOST FOCUS.
GBTrudeau

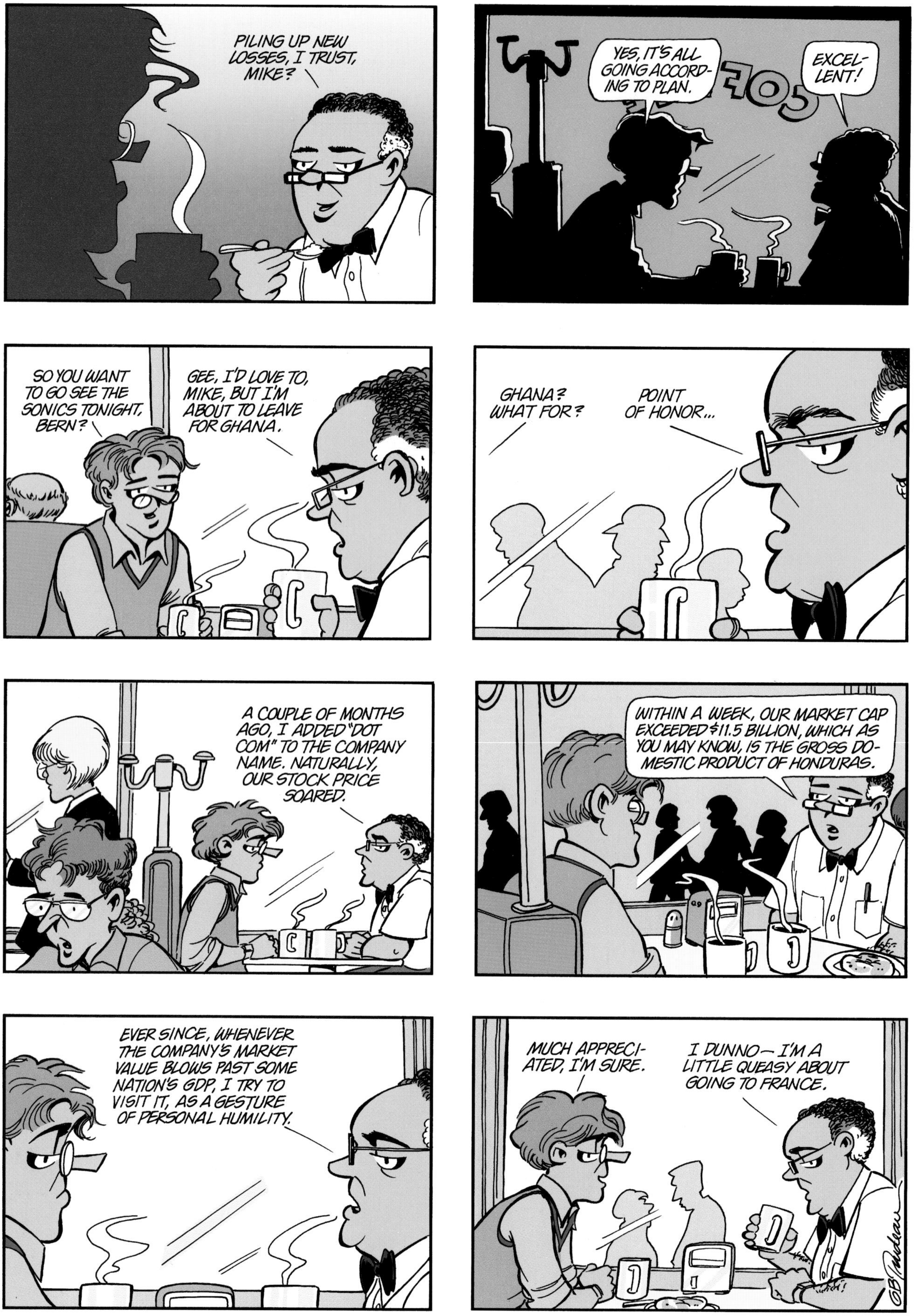
PILING UP NEW LOSSES, I TRUST, MIKE?
YES, IT'S ALL GOING ACCORDING TO PLAN.
EXCELLENT!
SO YOU WANT TO GO SEE THE SONICS TONIGHT, BERN?
GEE, I'D LOVE TO, MIKE, BUT I'M ABOUT TO LEAVE FOR GHANA.
GHANA? WHAT FOR?
POINT OF HONOR...
A COUPLE OF MONTHS AGO, I ADDED "DOT COM" TO THE COMPANY NAME. NATURALLY, OUR STOCK PRICE SOARED.
WITHIN A WEEK, OUR MARKET CAP EXCEEDED $11.5 BILLION, WHICH AS YOU MAY KNOW, IS THE GROSS DOMESTIC PRODUCT OF HONDURAS.
EVER SINCE, WHENEVER THE COMPANY'S MARKET VALUE BLOWS PAST SOME NATION'S GDP, I TRY TO VISIT IT, AS A GESTURE OF PERSONAL HUMILITY.
MUCH APPRECIATED, I'M SURE.
I DUNNO — I'M A LITTLE QUEASY ABOUT GOING TO FRANCE.

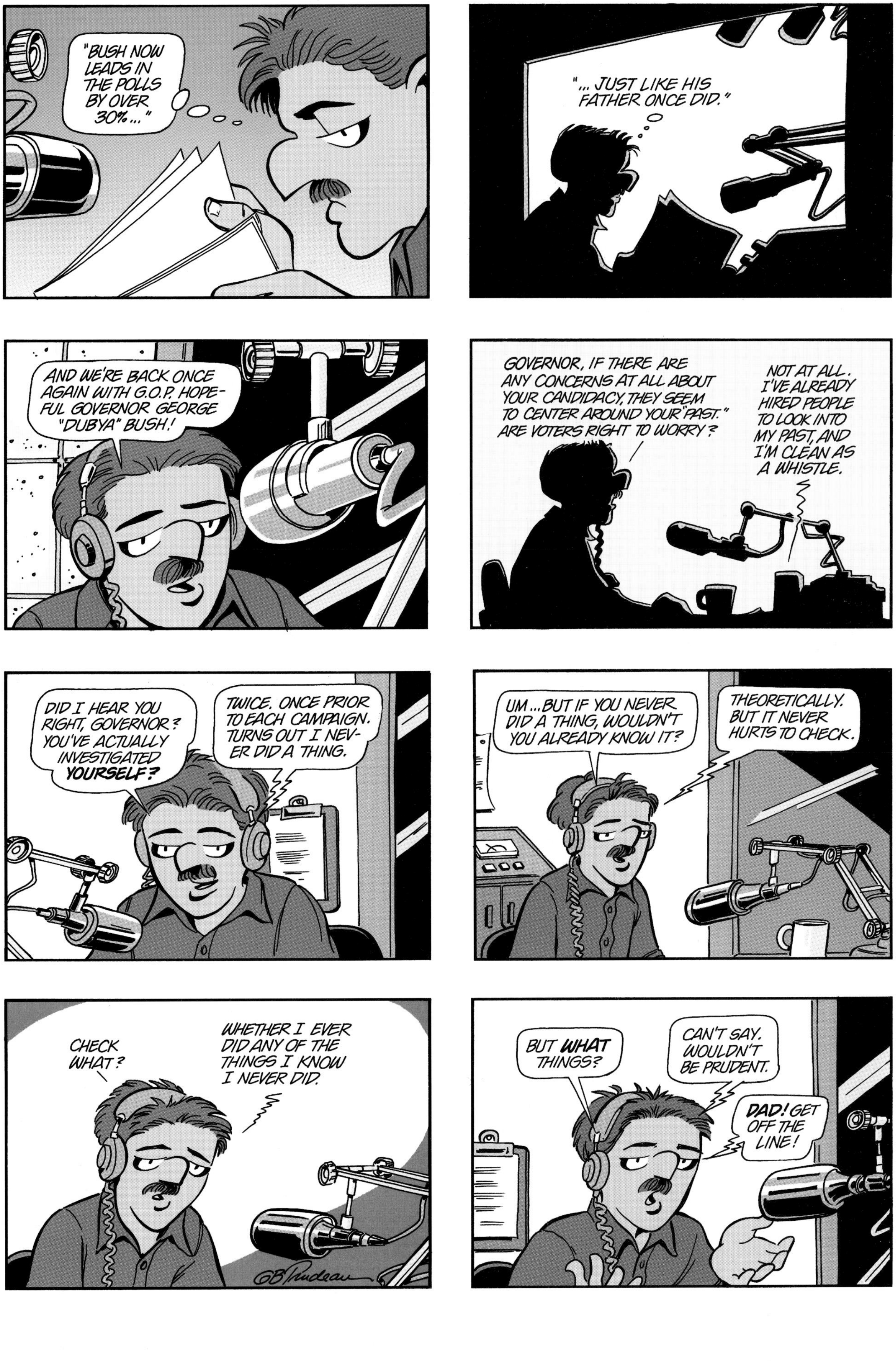
"BUSH NOW LEADS IN THE POLLS BY OVER 30%..."
"...JUST LIKE HIS FATHER ONCE DID."
AND WE'RE BACK ONCE AGAIN WITH G.O.P. HOPEFUL GOVERNOR GEORGE "DUBYA" BUSH!
GOVERNOR, IF THERE ARE ANY CONCERNS AT ALL ABOUT YOUR CANDIDACY, THEY SEEM TO CENTER AROUND YOUR "PAST." ARE VOTERS RIGHT TO WORRY?
NOT AT ALL. I'VE ALREADY HIRED PEOPLE TO LOOK INTO MY PAST, AND I'M CLEAN AS A WHISTLE.
DID I HEAR YOU RIGHT, GOVERNOR? YOU'VE ACTUALLY INVESTIGATED **YOURSELF?**
TWICE. ONCE PRIOR TO EACH CAMPAIGN. TURNS OUT I NEVER DID A THING.
UM... BUT IF YOU NEVER DID A THING, WOULDN'T YOU ALREADY KNOW IT?
THEORETICALLY. BUT IT NEVER HURTS TO CHECK.
CHECK WHAT?
WHETHER I EVER DID ANY OF THE THINGS I KNOW I NEVER DID.
©B Trudeau
BUT **WHAT** THINGS?
CAN'T SAY. WOULDN'T BE PRUDENT.
DAD! GET OFF THE LINE!

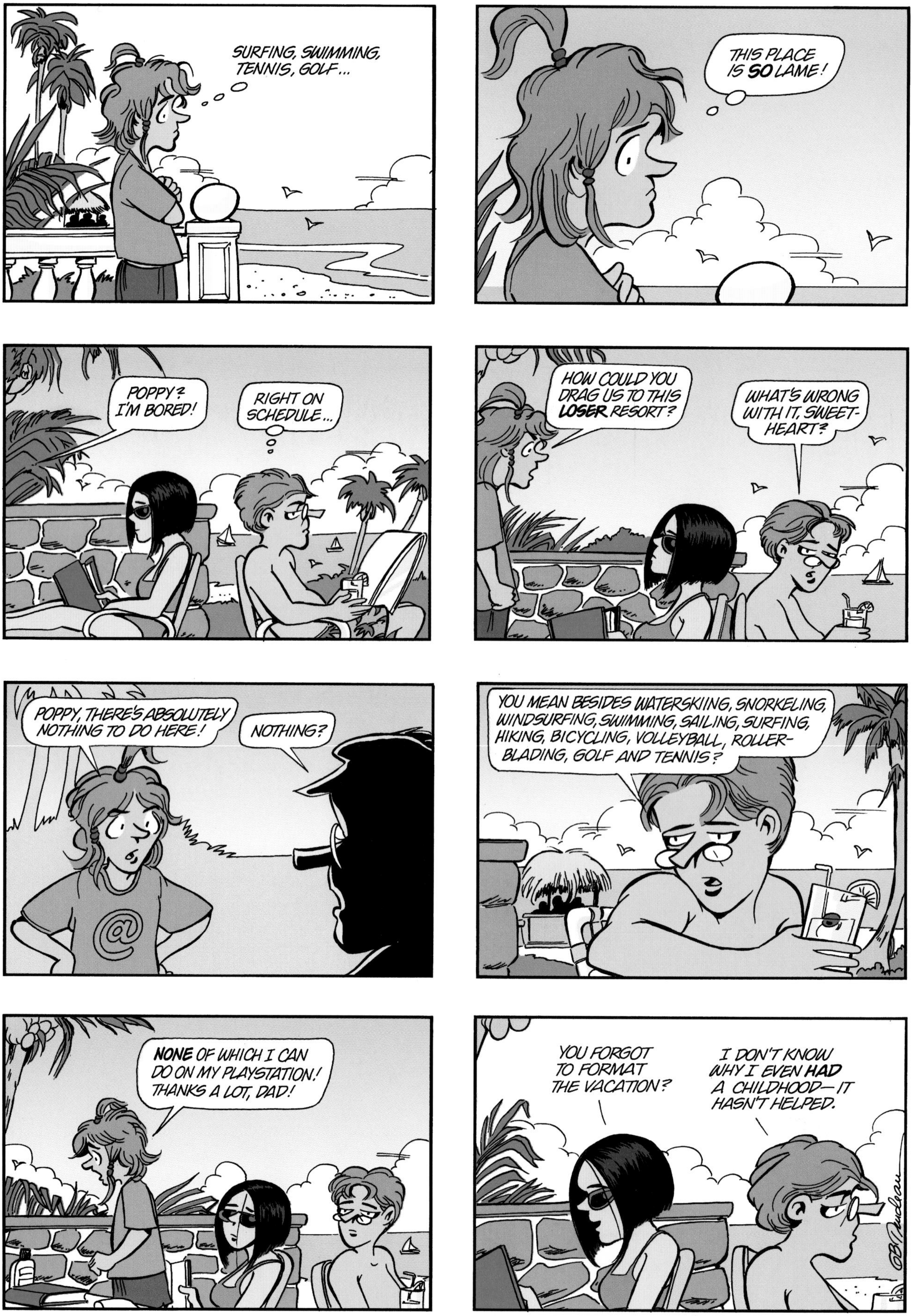
SURFING, SWIMMING, TENNIS, GOLF...
THIS PLACE IS SO LAME!
POPPY? I'M BORED!
RIGHT ON SCHEDULE...
HOW COULD YOU DRAG US TO THIS LOSER RESORT?
WHAT'S WRONG WITH IT, SWEETHEART?
POPPY, THERE'S ABSOLUTELY NOTHING TO DO HERE!
NOTHING?
YOU MEAN BESIDES WATERSKIING, SNORKELING, WINDSURFING, SWIMMING, SAILING, SURFING, HIKING, BICYCLING, VOLLEYBALL, ROLLERBLADING, GOLF AND TENNIS?
NONE OF WHICH I CAN DO ON MY PLAYSTATION! THANKS A LOT, DAD!
YOU FORGOT TO FORMAT THE VACATION?
I DON'T KNOW WHY I EVEN HAD A CHILDHOOD— IT HASN'T HELPED.

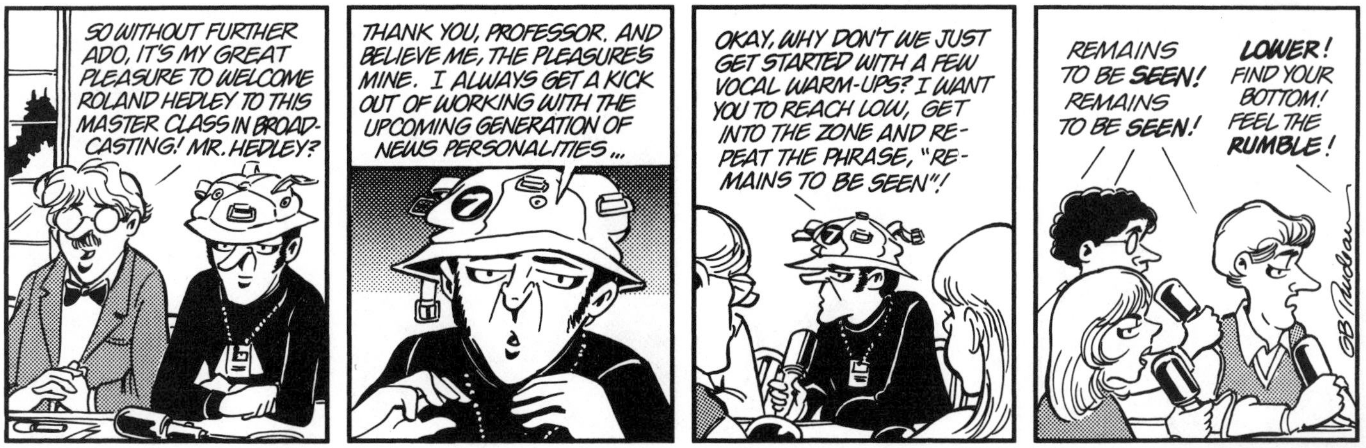
SO WITHOUT FURTHER ADO, IT'S MY GREAT PLEASURE TO WELCOME ROLAND HEDLEY TO THIS MASTER CLASS IN BROADCASTING! MR. HEDLEY?
THANK YOU, PROFESSOR. AND BELIEVE ME, THE PLEASURE'S MINE. I ALWAYS GET A KICK OUT OF WORKING WITH THE UPCOMING GENERATION OF NEWS PERSONALITIES...
OKAY, WHY DON'T WE JUST GET STARTED WITH A FEW VOCAL WARM-UPS? I WANT YOU TO REACH LOW, GET INTO THE ZONE AND REPEAT THE PHRASE, "REMAINS TO BE SEEN"!
REMAINS TO BE SEEN! REMAINS TO BE SEEN!
LOWER! FIND YOUR BOTTOM! FEEL THE RUMBLE!

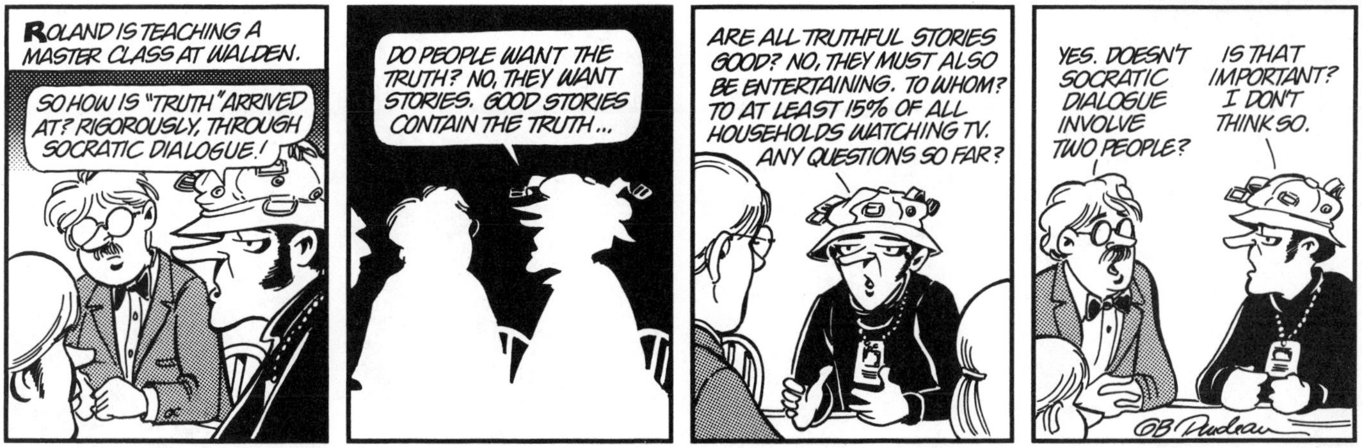
ROLAND IS TEACHING A MASTER CLASS AT WALDEN.
SO HOW IS "TRUTH" ARRIVED AT? RIGOROUSLY, THROUGH SOCRATIC DIALOGUE!
DO PEOPLE WANT THE TRUTH? NO, THEY WANT STORIES. GOOD STORIES CONTAIN THE TRUTH...
ARE ALL TRUTHFUL STORIES GOOD? NO, THEY MUST ALSO BE ENTERTAINING. TO WHOM? TO AT LEAST 15% OF ALL HOUSEHOLDS WATCHING TV. ANY QUESTIONS SO FAR?
YES. DOESN'T SOCRATIC DIALOGUE INVOLVE TWO PEOPLE?
IS THAT IMPORTANT? I DON'T THINK SO.

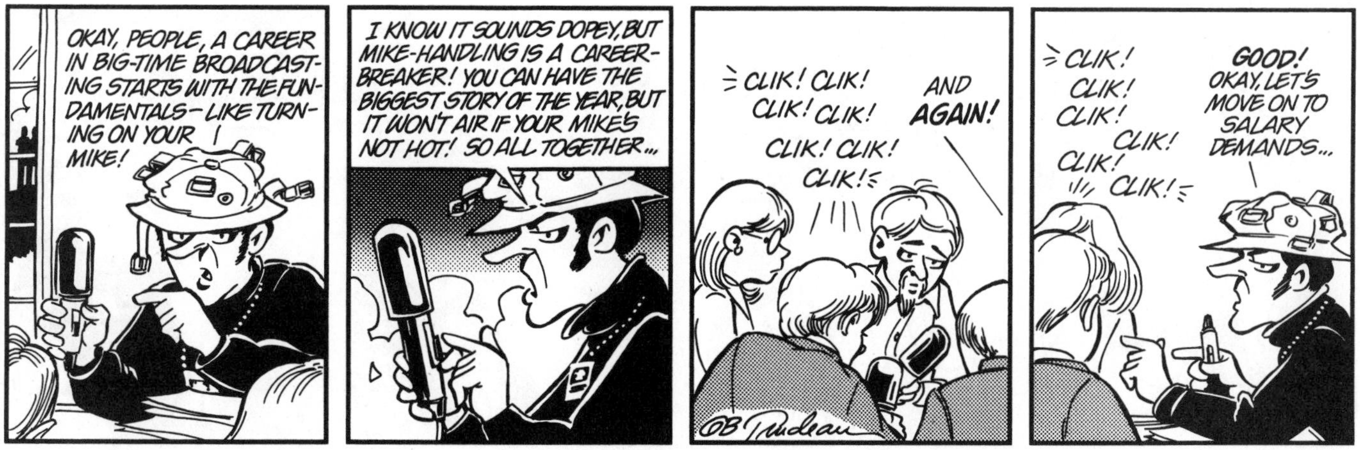
OKAY, PEOPLE, A CAREER IN BIG-TIME BROADCASTING STARTS WITH THE FUNDAMENTALS — LIKE TURNING ON YOUR MIKE!
I KNOW IT SOUNDS DOPEY, BUT MIKE-HANDLING IS A CAREER-BREAKER! YOU CAN HAVE THE BIGGEST STORY OF THE YEAR, BUT IT WON'T AIR IF YOUR MIKE'S NOT HOT! SO ALL TOGETHER...
CLIK! CLIK! CLIK! CLIK! CLIK! CLIK! CLIK!
AND AGAIN!
CLIK! CLIK! CLIK! CLIK! CLIK! CLIK!
GOOD! OKAY, LET'S MOVE ON TO SALARY DEMANDS...

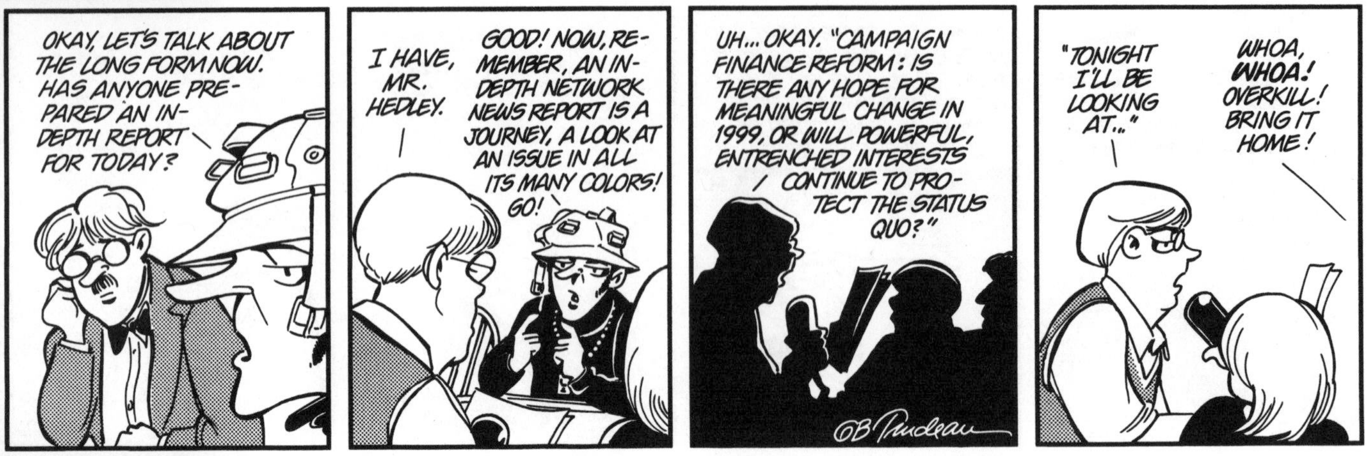
OKAY, LET'S TALK ABOUT THE LONG FORM NOW. HAS ANYONE PREPARED AN IN-DEPTH REPORT FOR TODAY?
I HAVE, MR. HEDLEY.
GOOD! NOW, REMEMBER, AN IN-DEPTH NETWORK NEWS REPORT IS A JOURNEY, A LOOK AT AN ISSUE IN ALL ITS MANY COLORS! GO!
UH... OKAY. "CAMPAIGN FINANCE REFORM: IS THERE ANY HOPE FOR MEANINGFUL CHANGE IN 1999, OR WILL POWERFUL, ENTRENCHED INTERESTS CONTINUE TO PROTECT THE STATUS QUO?"
"TONIGHT I'LL BE LOOKING AT..."
WHOA, WHOA! OVERKILL! BRING IT HOME!

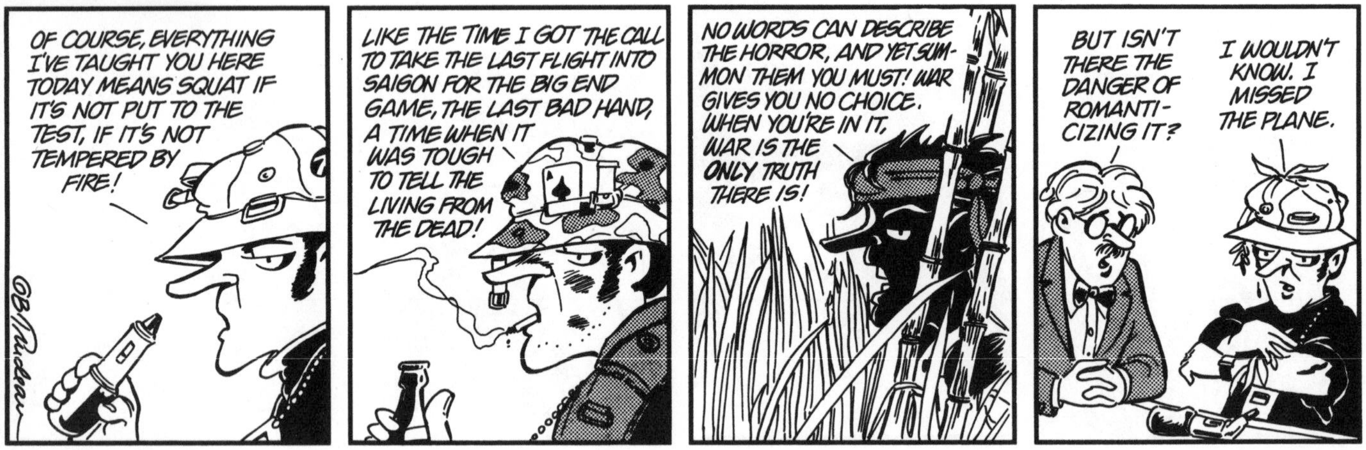
OF COURSE, EVERYTHING I'VE TAUGHT YOU HERE TODAY MEANS SQUAT IF IT'S NOT PUT TO THE TEST, IF IT'S NOT TEMPERED BY FIRE!
LIKE THE TIME I GOT THE CALL TO TAKE THE LAST FLIGHT INTO SAIGON FOR THE BIG END GAME, THE LAST BAD HAND, A TIME WHEN IT WAS TOUGH TO TELL THE LIVING FROM THE DEAD!
NO WORDS CAN DESCRIBE THE HORROR, AND YET SUMMON THEM YOU MUST! WAR GIVES YOU NO CHOICE. WHEN YOU'RE IN IT, WAR IS THE ONLY TRUTH THERE IS!
BUT ISN'T THERE THE DANGER OF ROMANTICIZING IT?
I WOULDN'T KNOW. I MISSED THE PLANE.

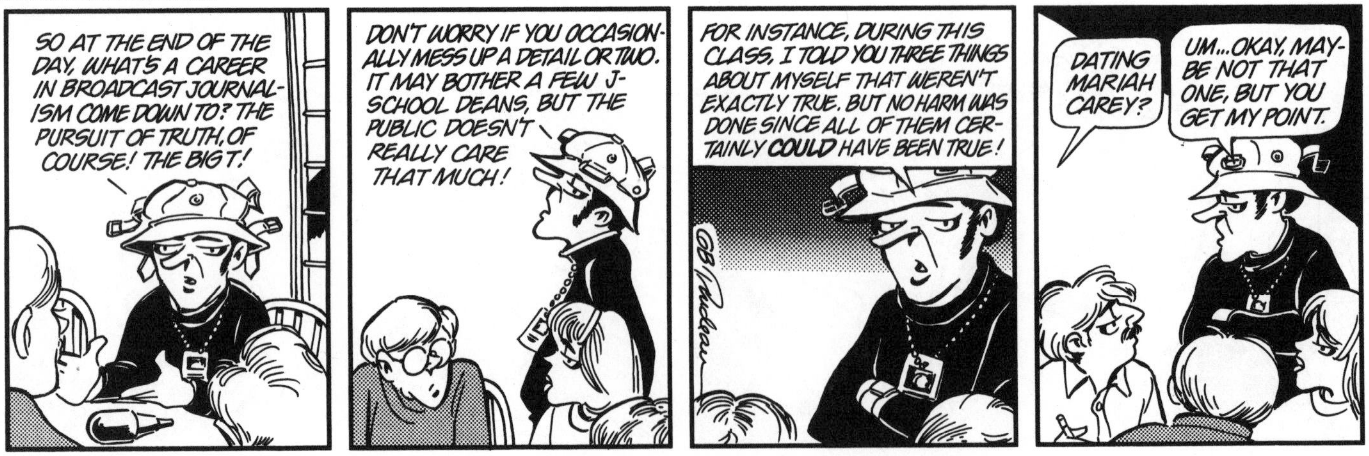
SO AT THE END OF THE DAY, WHAT'S A CAREER IN BROADCAST JOURNALISM COME DOWN TO? THE PURSUIT OF TRUTH, OF COURSE! THE BIG T!
DON'T WORRY IF YOU OCCASIONALLY MESS UP A DETAIL OR TWO. IT MAY BOTHER A FEW J-SCHOOL DEANS, BUT THE PUBLIC DOESN'T REALLY CARE THAT MUCH!
FOR INSTANCE, DURING THIS CLASS, I TOLD YOU THREE THINGS ABOUT MYSELF THAT WEREN'T EXACTLY TRUE. BUT NO HARM WAS DONE SINCE ALL OF THEM CERTAINLY COULD HAVE BEEN TRUE!
DATING MARIAH CAREY?
UM... OKAY, MAYBE NOT THAT ONE, BUT YOU GET MY POINT.

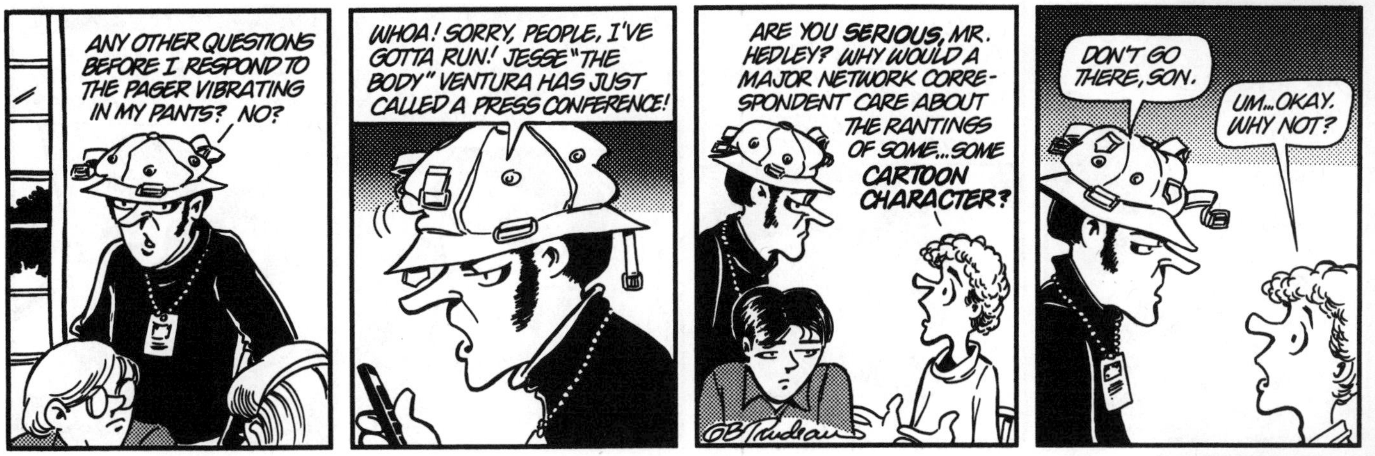
ANY OTHER QUESTIONS BEFORE I RESPOND TO THE PAGER VIBRATING IN MY PANTS? NO?
WHOA! SORRY, PEOPLE, I'VE GOTTA RUN! JESSE "THE BODY" VENTURA HAS JUST CALLED A PRESS CONFERENCE!
ARE YOU **SERIOUS**, MR. HEDLEY? WHY WOULD A MAJOR NETWORK CORRESPONDENT CARE ABOUT THE RANTINGS OF SOME...SOME **CARTOON CHARACTER?**
DON'T GO THERE, SON.
UM...OKAY. WHY NOT?

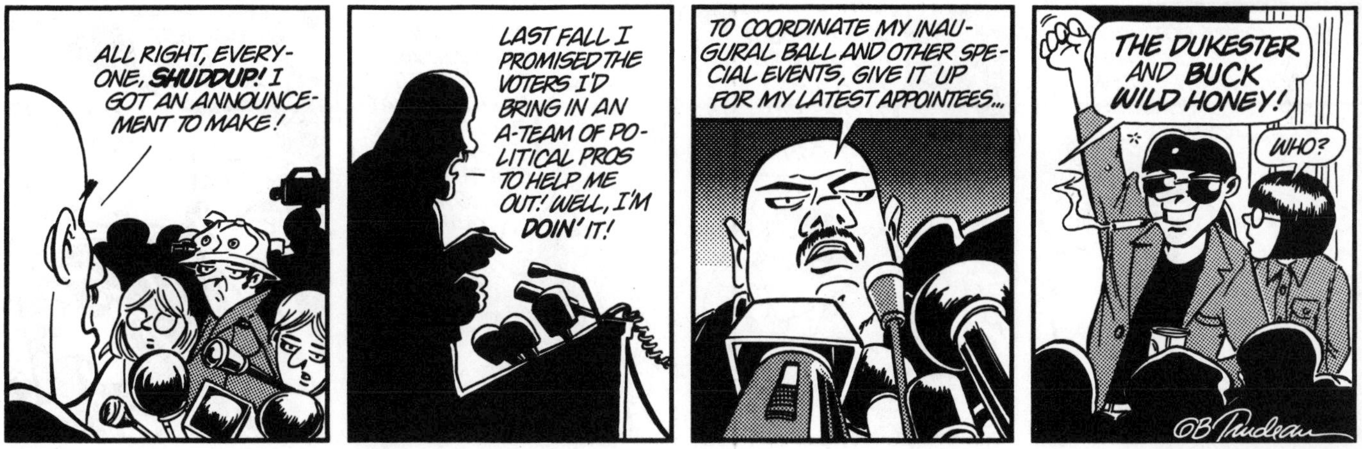
ALL RIGHT, EVERYONE, **SHUDDUP!** I GOT AN ANNOUNCEMENT TO MAKE!
LAST FALL I PROMISED THE VOTERS I'D BRING IN AN A-TEAM OF POLITICAL PROS TO HELP ME OUT! WELL, I'M **DOIN'** IT!
TO COORDINATE MY INAUGURAL BALL AND OTHER SPECIAL EVENTS, GIVE IT UP FOR MY LATEST APPOINTEES...
THE DUKESTER AND BUCK WILD HONEY!
WHO?

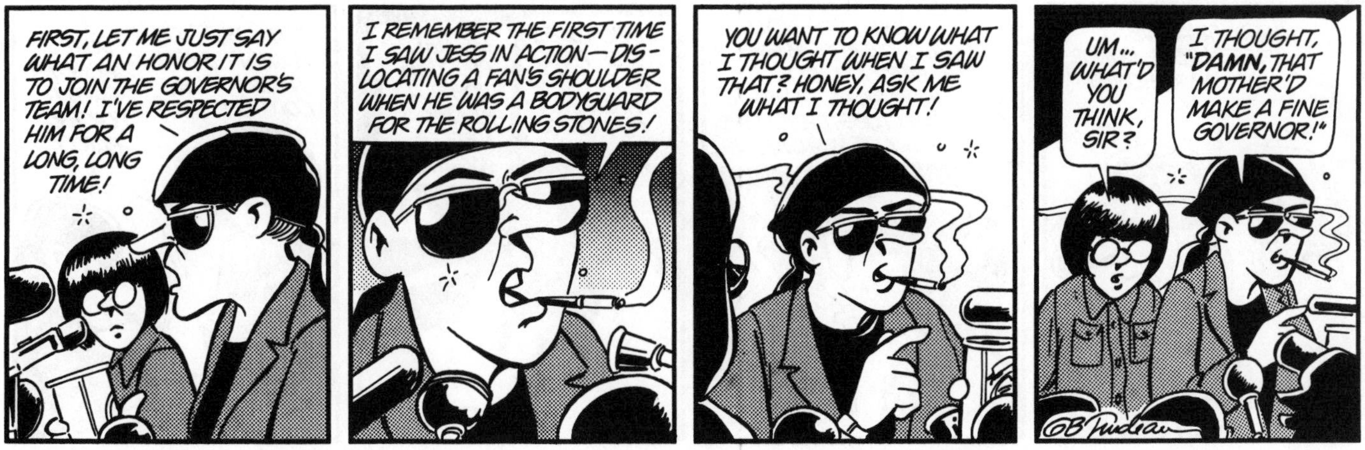
FIRST, LET ME JUST SAY WHAT AN HONOR IT IS TO JOIN THE GOVERNOR'S TEAM! I'VE RESPECTED HIM FOR A LONG, LONG TIME!
I REMEMBER THE FIRST TIME I SAW JESS IN ACTION—DISLOCATING A FAN'S SHOULDER WHEN HE WAS A BODYGUARD FOR THE ROLLING STONES!
YOU WANT TO KNOW WHAT I THOUGHT WHEN I SAW THAT? HONEY, ASK ME WHAT I THOUGHT!
UM... WHAT'D YOU THINK, SIR?
I THOUGHT, "**DAMN**, THAT MOTHER'D MAKE A FINE GOVERNOR!"

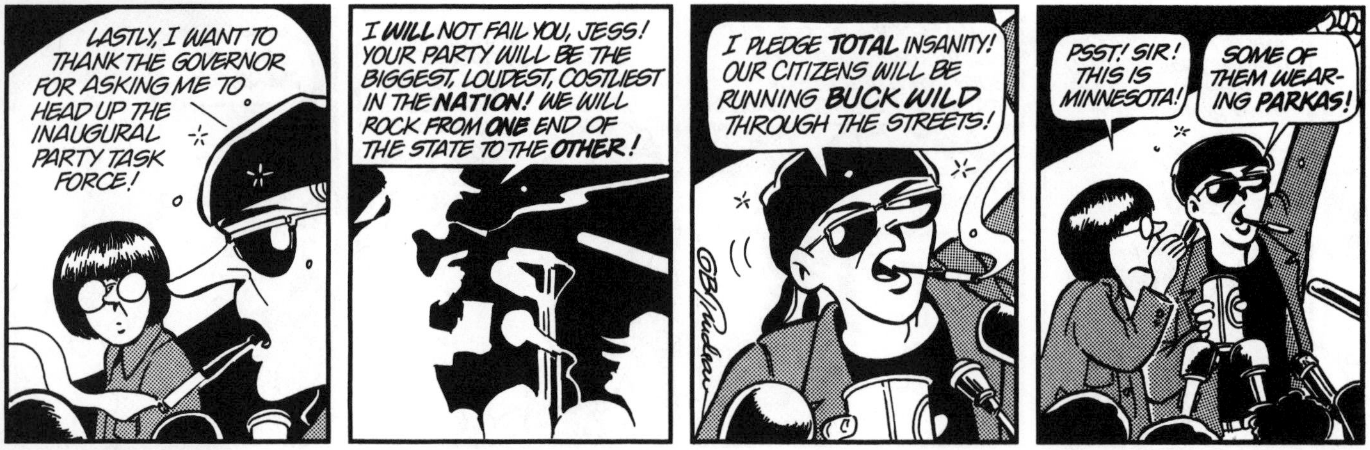
LASTLY, I WANT TO THANK THE GOVERNOR FOR ASKING ME TO HEAD UP THE INAUGURAL PARTY TASK FORCE!
I WILL NOT FAIL YOU, JESS! YOUR PARTY WILL BE THE BIGGEST, LOUDEST, COSTLIEST IN THE NATION! WE WILL ROCK FROM ONE END OF THE STATE TO THE OTHER!
I PLEDGE TOTAL INSANITY! OUR CITIZENS WILL BE RUNNING BUCK WILD THROUGH THE STREETS!
PSST! SIR! THIS IS MINNESOTA!
SOME OF THEM WEARING PARKAS!

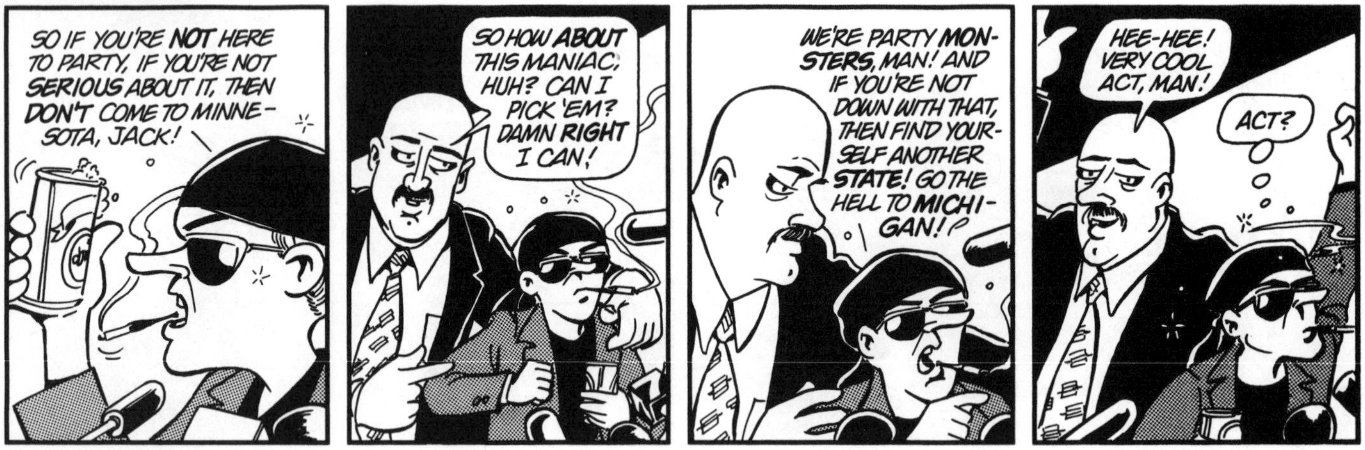
SO IF YOU'RE NOT HERE TO PARTY, IF YOU'RE NOT SERIOUS ABOUT IT, THEN DON'T COME TO MINNESOTA, JACK!
SO HOW ABOUT THIS MANIAC, HUH? CAN I PICK 'EM? DAMN RIGHT I CAN!
WE'RE PARTY MONSTERS, MAN! AND IF YOU'RE NOT DOWN WITH THAT, THEN FIND YOURSELF ANOTHER STATE! GO THE HELL TO MICHIGAN!
HEE-HEE! VERY COOL ACT, MAN!
ACT?

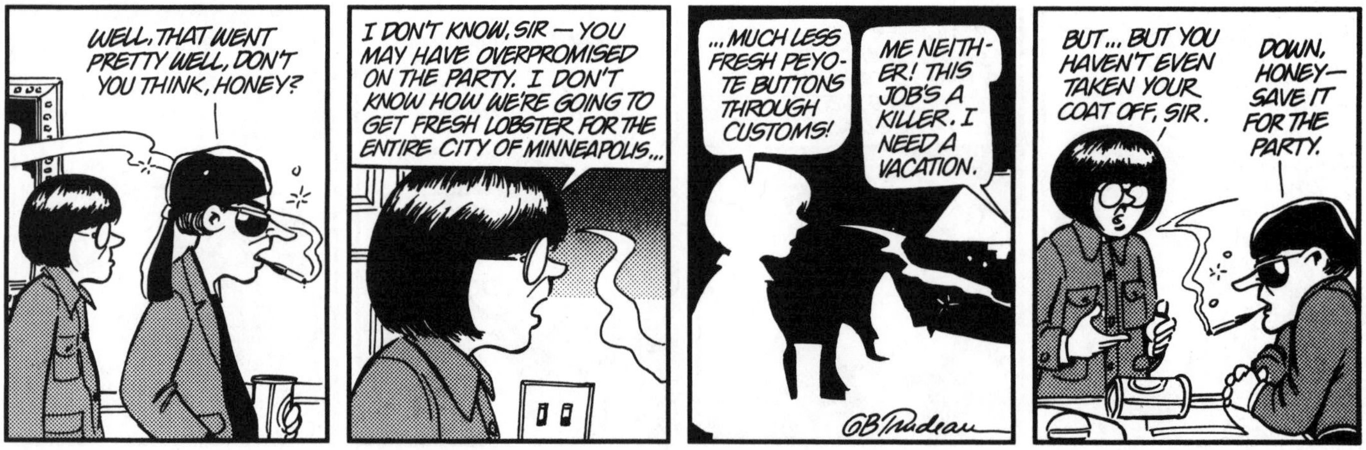
WELL, THAT WENT PRETTY WELL, DON'T YOU THINK, HONEY?
I DON'T KNOW, SIR — YOU MAY HAVE OVERPROMISED ON THE PARTY. I DON'T KNOW HOW WE'RE GOING TO GET FRESH LOBSTER FOR THE ENTIRE CITY OF MINNEAPOLIS...
...MUCH LESS FRESH PEYOTE BUTTONS THROUGH CUSTOMS!
ME NEITHER! THIS JOB'S A KILLER. I NEED A VACATION.
BUT... BUT YOU HAVEN'T EVEN TAKEN YOUR COAT OFF, SIR.
DOWN, HONEY— SAVE IT FOR THE PARTY.

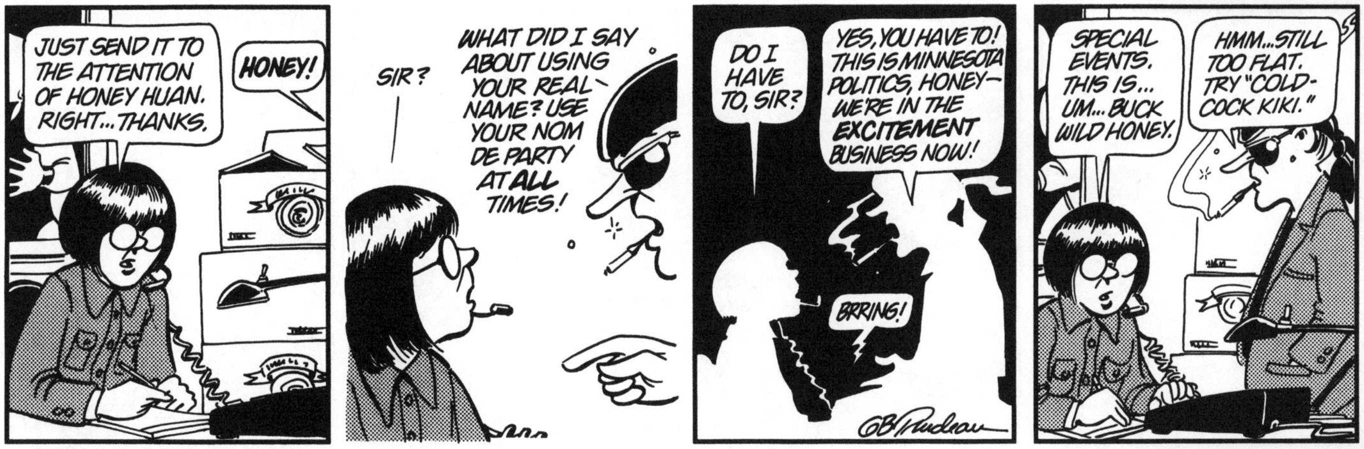
JUST SEND IT TO THE ATTENTION OF HONEY HUAN. RIGHT... THANKS.
HONEY!
SIR?
WHAT DID I SAY ABOUT USING YOUR REAL NAME? USE YOUR NOM DE PARTY AT ALL TIMES!
DO I HAVE TO, SIR?
YES, YOU HAVE TO! THIS IS MINNESOTA POLITICS, HONEY— WE'RE IN THE EXCITEMENT BUSINESS NOW!
BRRING!
SPECIAL EVENTS. THIS IS... UM... BUCK WILD HONEY.
HMM... STILL TOO FLAT. TRY "COLD-COCK KIKI."

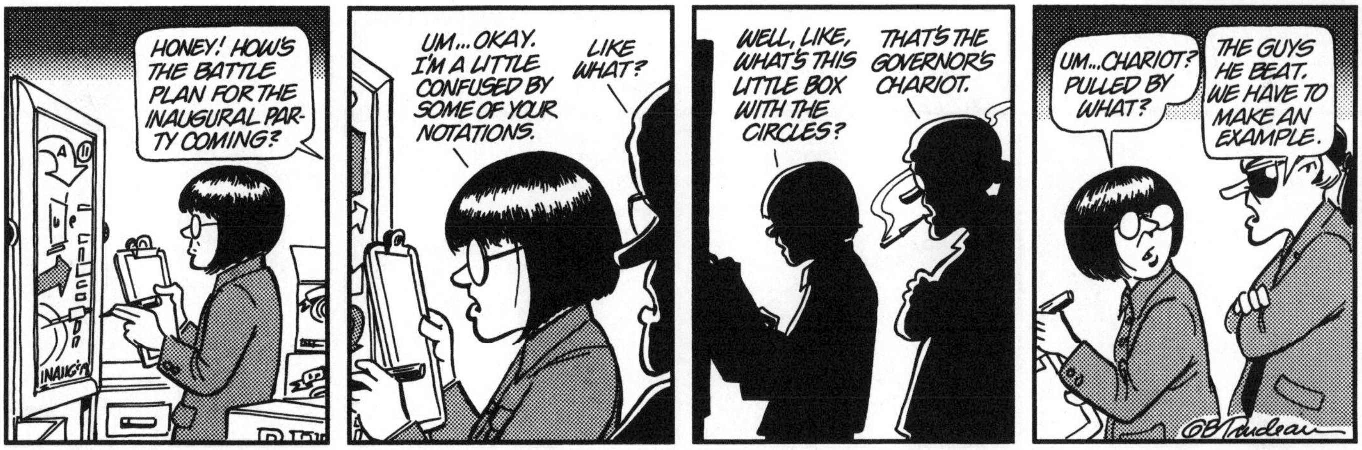
HONEY! HOW'S THE BATTLE PLAN FOR THE INAUGURAL PARTY COMING?
UM... OKAY. I'M A LITTLE CONFUSED BY SOME OF YOUR NOTATIONS.
LIKE WHAT?
WELL, LIKE, WHAT'S THIS LITTLE BOX WITH THE CIRCLES?
THAT'S THE GOVERNOR'S CHARIOT.
UM... CHARIOT? PULLED BY WHAT?
THE GUYS HE BEAT. WE HAVE TO MAKE AN EXAMPLE.

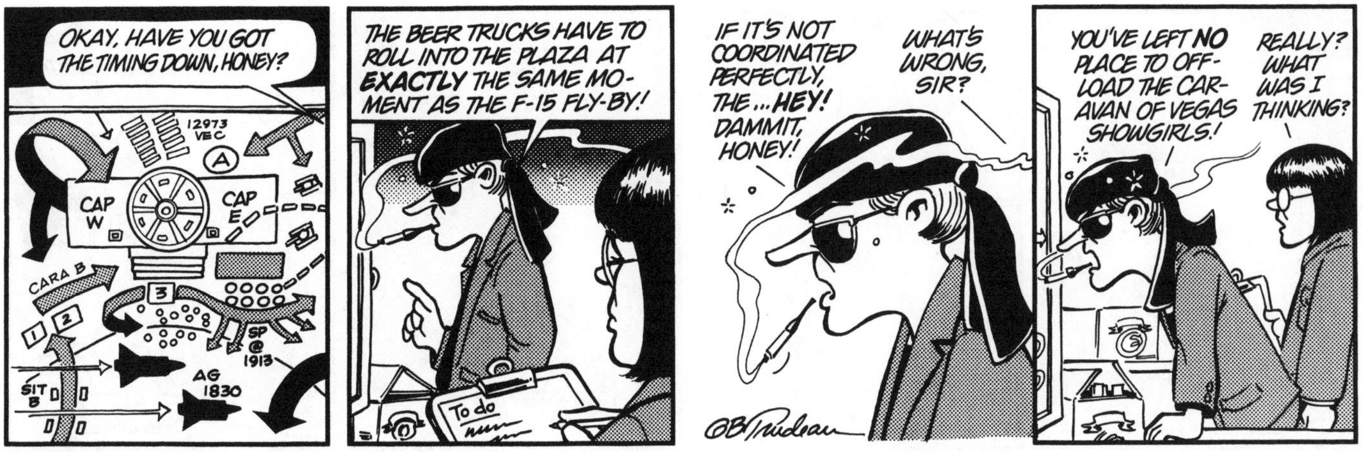
OKAY, HAVE YOU GOT THE TIMING DOWN, HONEY?
12973 VEC
A
CAP W
CAP E
CARA B
1
2
3
SP @ 1913
SIT B
AG 1830
THE BEER TRUCKS HAVE TO ROLL INTO THE PLAZA AT EXACTLY THE SAME MOMENT AS THE F-15 FLY-BY!
To do
IF IT'S NOT COORDINATED PERFECTLY, THE ... HEY! DAMMIT, HONEY!
WHAT'S WRONG, SIR?
YOU'VE LEFT NO PLACE TO OFF-LOAD THE CARAVAN OF VEGAS SHOWGIRLS!
REALLY? WHAT WAS I THINKING?

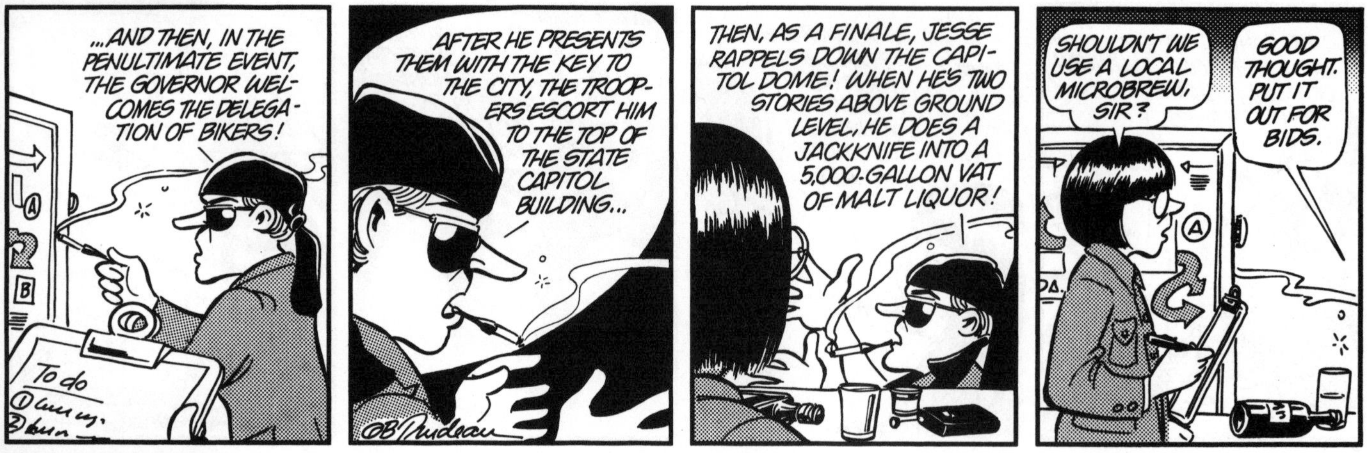
...AND THEN, IN THE PENULTIMATE EVENT, THE GOVERNOR WELCOMES THE DELEGATION OF BIKERS!
AFTER HE PRESENTS THEM WITH THE KEY TO THE CITY, THE TROOPERS ESCORT HIM TO THE TOP OF THE STATE CAPITOL BUILDING...
THEN, AS A FINALE, JESSE RAPPELS DOWN THE CAPITOL DOME! WHEN HE'S TWO STORIES ABOVE GROUND LEVEL, HE DOES A JACKKNIFE INTO A 5,000-GALLON VAT OF MALT LIQUOR!
SHOULDN'T WE USE A LOCAL MICROBREW, SIR?
GOOD THOUGHT. PUT IT OUT FOR BIDS.

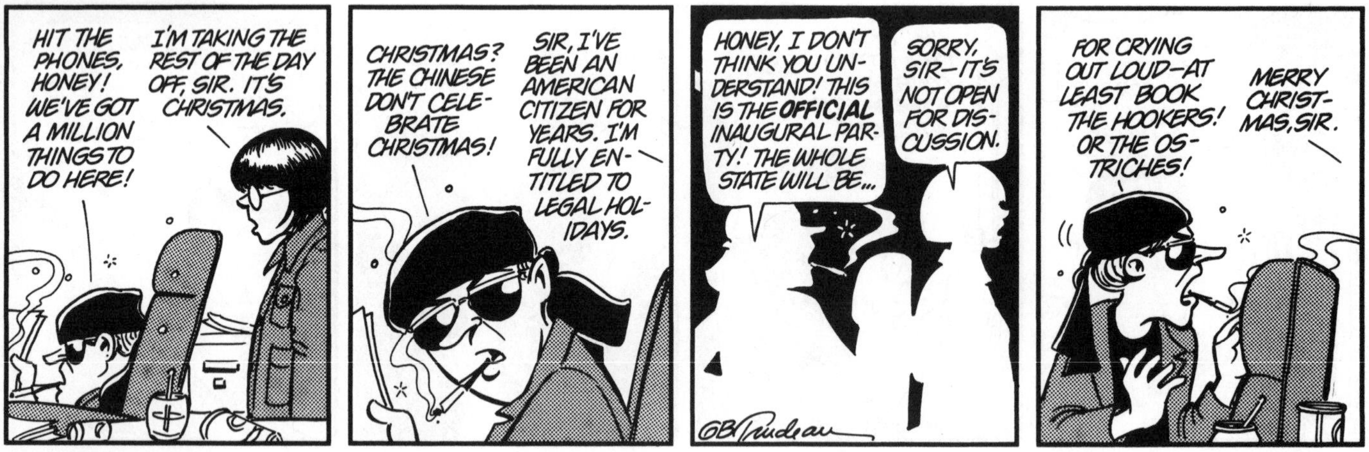
HIT THE PHONES, HONEY! WE'VE GOT A MILLION THINGS TO DO HERE!
I'M TAKING THE REST OF THE DAY OFF, SIR. IT'S CHRISTMAS.
CHRISTMAS? THE CHINESE DON'T CELEBRATE CHRISTMAS!
SIR, I'VE BEEN AN AMERICAN CITIZEN FOR YEARS. I'M FULLY ENTITLED TO LEGAL HOLIDAYS.
HONEY, I DON'T THINK YOU UNDERSTAND! THIS IS THE OFFICIAL INAUGURAL PARTY! THE WHOLE STATE WILL BE...
SORRY, SIR—IT'S NOT OPEN FOR DISCUSSION.
FOR CRYING OUT LOUD—AT LEAST BOOK THE HOOKERS! OR THE OSTRICHES!
MERRY CHRISTMAS, SIR.

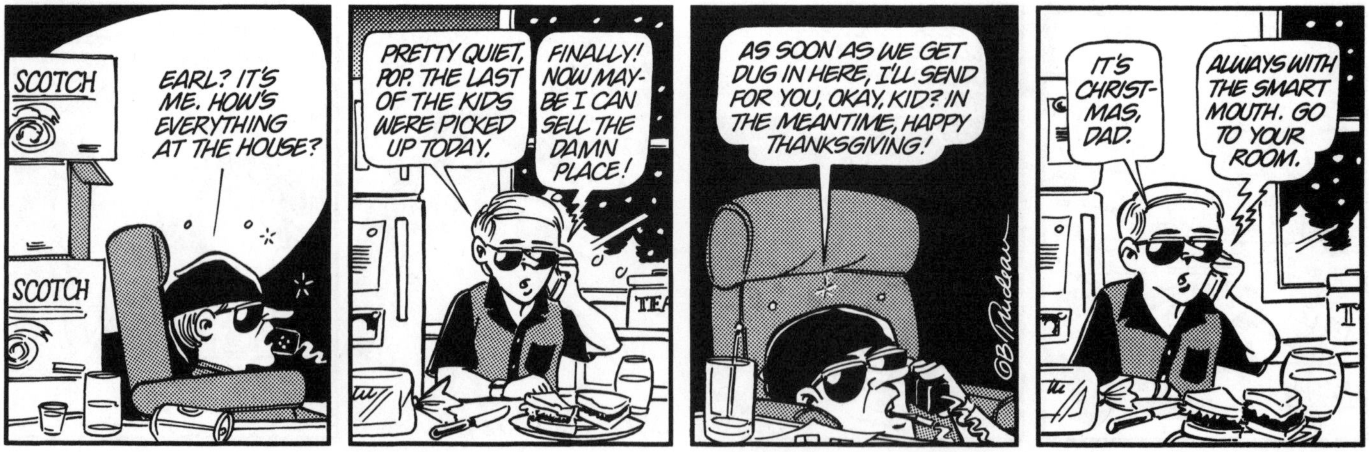
SCOTCH
SCOTCH
EARL? IT'S ME. HOW'S EVERYTHING AT THE HOUSE?
PRETTY QUIET, POP. THE LAST OF THE KIDS WERE PICKED UP TODAY.
FINALLY! NOW MAYBE I CAN SELL THE DAMN PLACE!
AS SOON AS WE GET DUG IN HERE, I'LL SEND FOR YOU, OKAY, KID? IN THE MEANTIME, HAPPY THANKSGIVING!
IT'S CHRISTMAS, DAD.
ALWAYS WITH THE SMART MOUTH. GO TO YOUR ROOM.

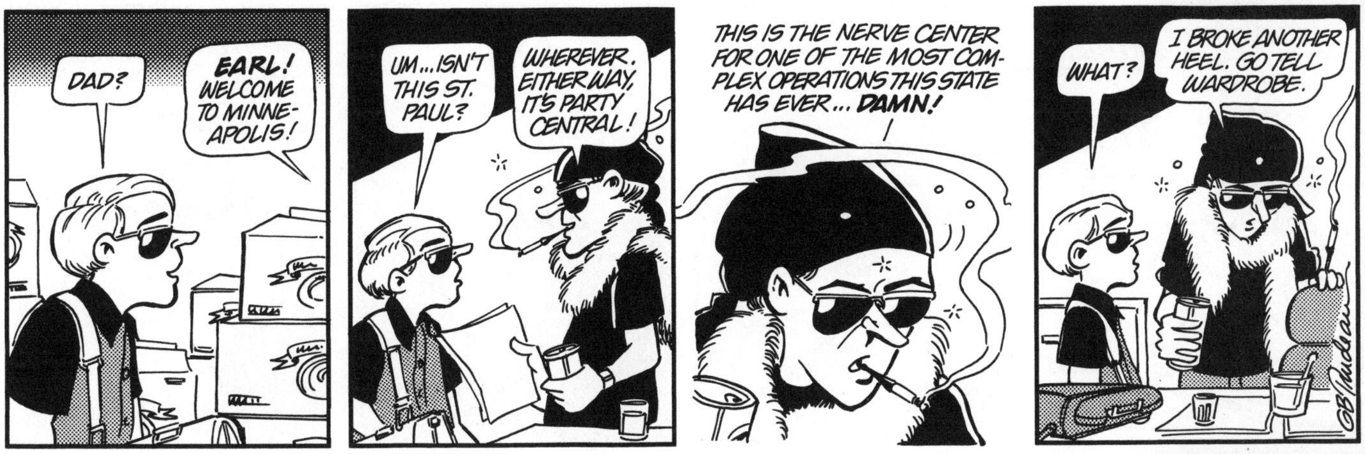
DAD?
EARL! WELCOME TO MINNE-APOLIS!
UM... ISN'T THIS ST. PAUL?
WHEREVER. EITHER WAY, IT'S PARTY CENTRAL!
THIS IS THE NERVE CENTER FOR ONE OF THE MOST COMPLEX OPERATIONS THIS STATE HAS EVER... DAMN!
WHAT?
I BROKE ANOTHER HEEL. GO TELL WARDROBE.

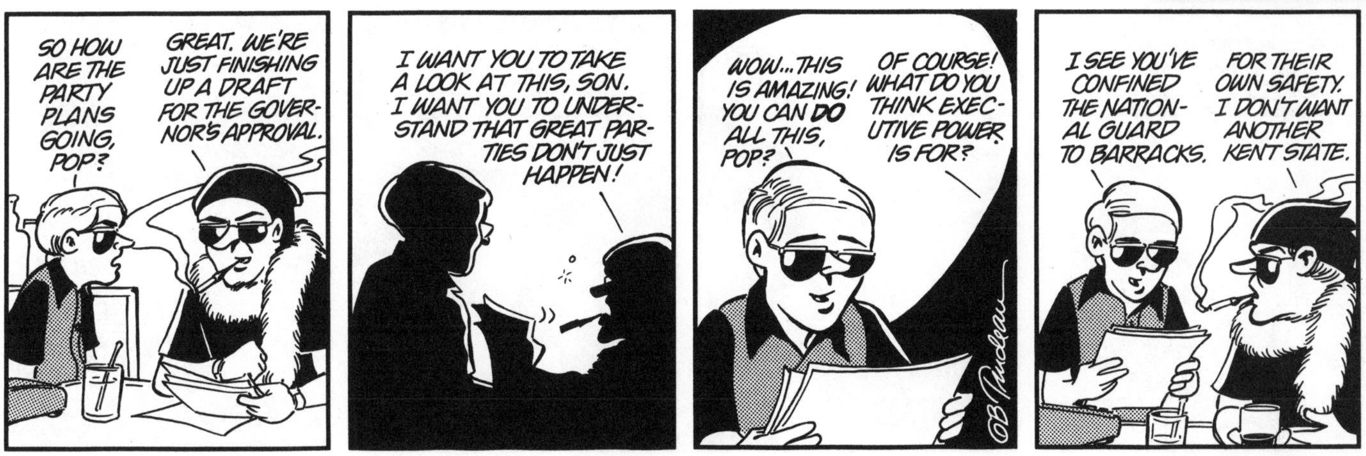
SO HOW ARE THE PARTY PLANS GOING, POP?
GREAT. WE'RE JUST FINISHING UP A DRAFT FOR THE GOVERNOR'S APPROVAL.
I WANT YOU TO TAKE A LOOK AT THIS, SON. I WANT YOU TO UNDERSTAND THAT GREAT PARTIES DON'T JUST HAPPEN!
WOW... THIS IS AMAZING! YOU CAN DO ALL THIS, POP?
OF COURSE! WHAT DO YOU THINK EXECUTIVE POWER IS FOR?
I SEE YOU'VE CONFINED THE NATIONAL GUARD TO BARRACKS.
FOR THEIR OWN SAFETY. I DON'T WANT ANOTHER KENT STATE.

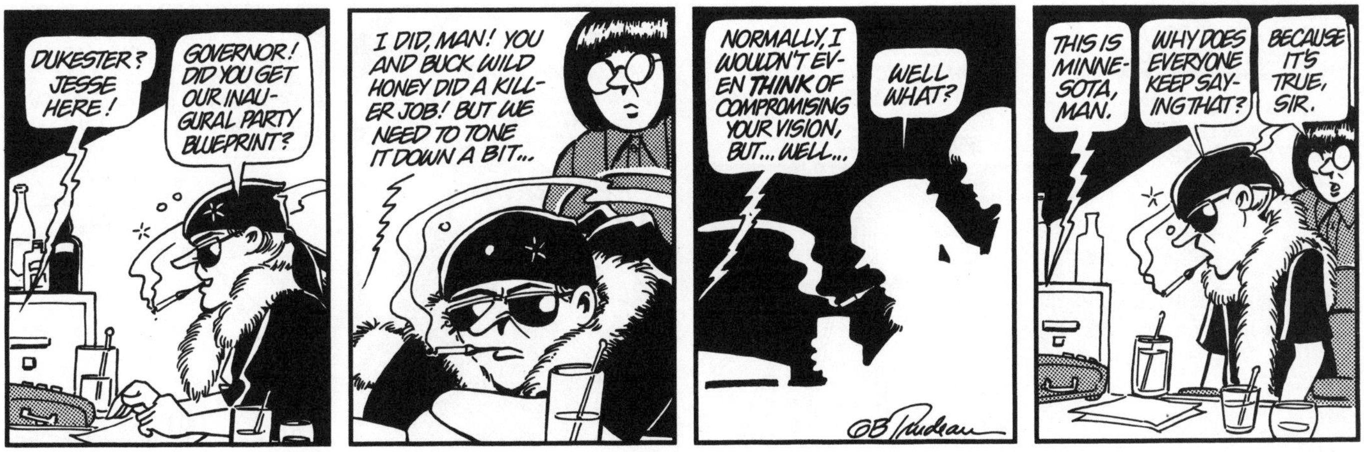
DUKESTER? JESSE HERE!
GOVERNOR! DID YOU GET OUR INAUGURAL PARTY BLUEPRINT?
I DID, MAN! YOU AND BUCK WILD HONEY DID A KILLER JOB! BUT WE NEED TO TONE IT DOWN A BIT...
NORMALLY, I WOULDN'T EVEN THINK OF COMPROMISING YOUR VISION, BUT... WELL...
WELL WHAT?
THIS IS MINNESOTA, MAN.
WHY DOES EVERYONE KEEP SAYING THAT?
BECAUSE IT'S TRUE, SIR.

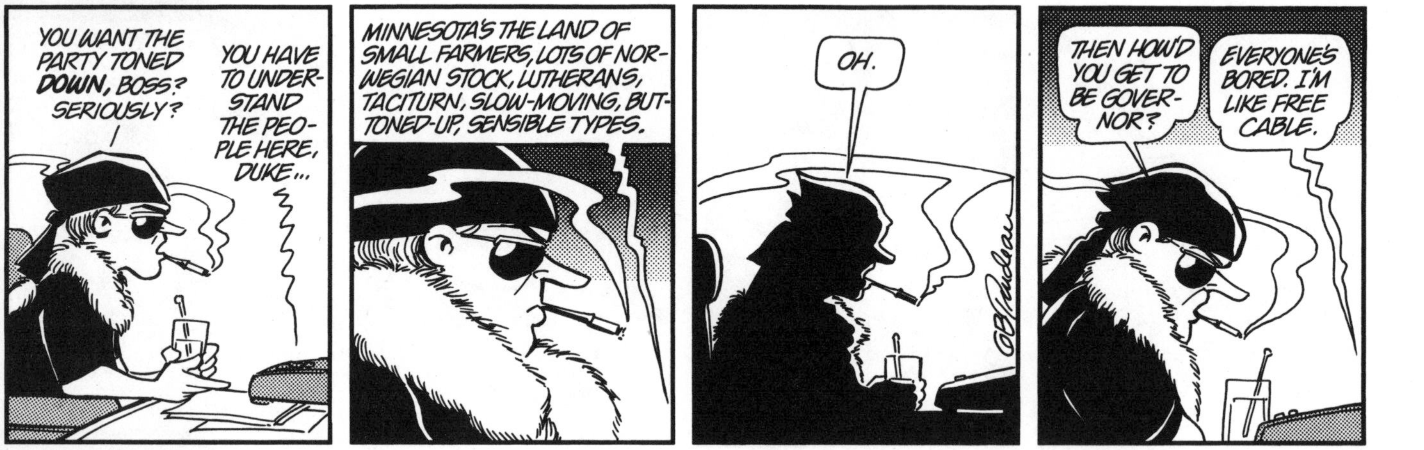
YOU WANT THE PARTY TONED DOWN, BOSS? SERIOUSLY?
YOU HAVE TO UNDERSTAND THE PEOPLE HERE, DUKE...
MINNESOTA'S THE LAND OF SMALL FARMERS, LOTS OF NORWEGIAN STOCK, LUTHERANS, TACITURN, SLOW-MOVING, BUTTONED-UP, SENSIBLE TYPES.
OH.
THEN HOW'D YOU GET TO BE GOVERNOR?
EVERYONE'S BORED. I'M LIKE FREE CABLE.

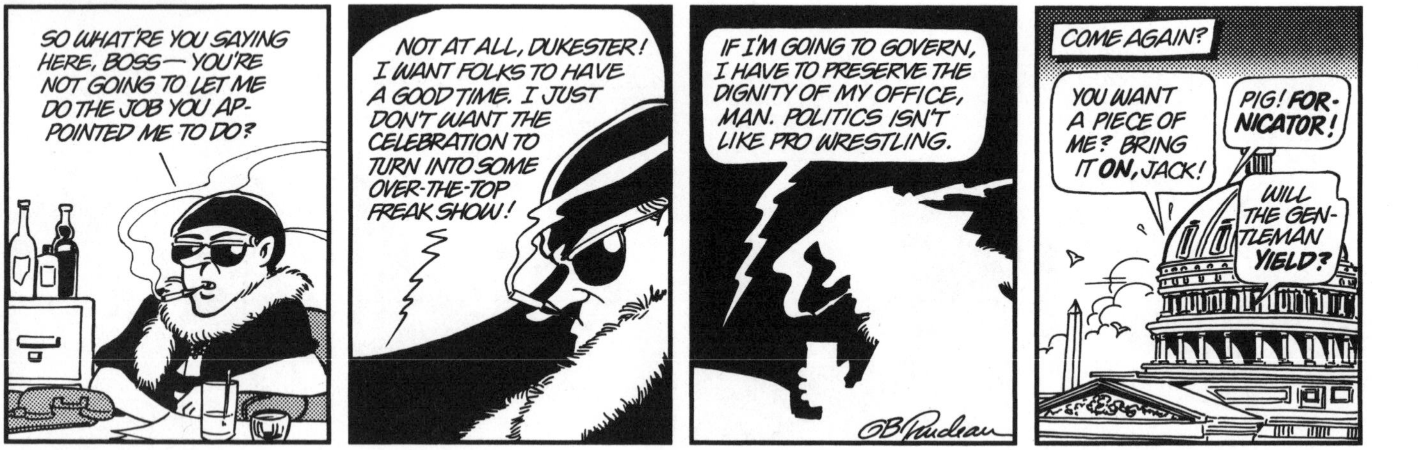
SO WHAT'RE YOU SAYING HERE, BOSS— YOU'RE NOT GOING TO LET ME DO THE JOB YOU APPOINTED ME TO DO?
NOT AT ALL, DUKESTER! I WANT FOLKS TO HAVE A GOOD TIME. I JUST DON'T WANT THE CELEBRATION TO TURN INTO SOME OVER-THE-TOP FREAK SHOW!
IF I'M GOING TO GOVERN, I HAVE TO PRESERVE THE DIGNITY OF MY OFFICE, MAN. POLITICS ISN'T LIKE PRO WRESTLING.
COME AGAIN?
YOU WANT A PIECE OF ME? BRING IT ON, JACK!
PIG! FORNICATOR!
WILL THE GENTLEMAN YIELD?

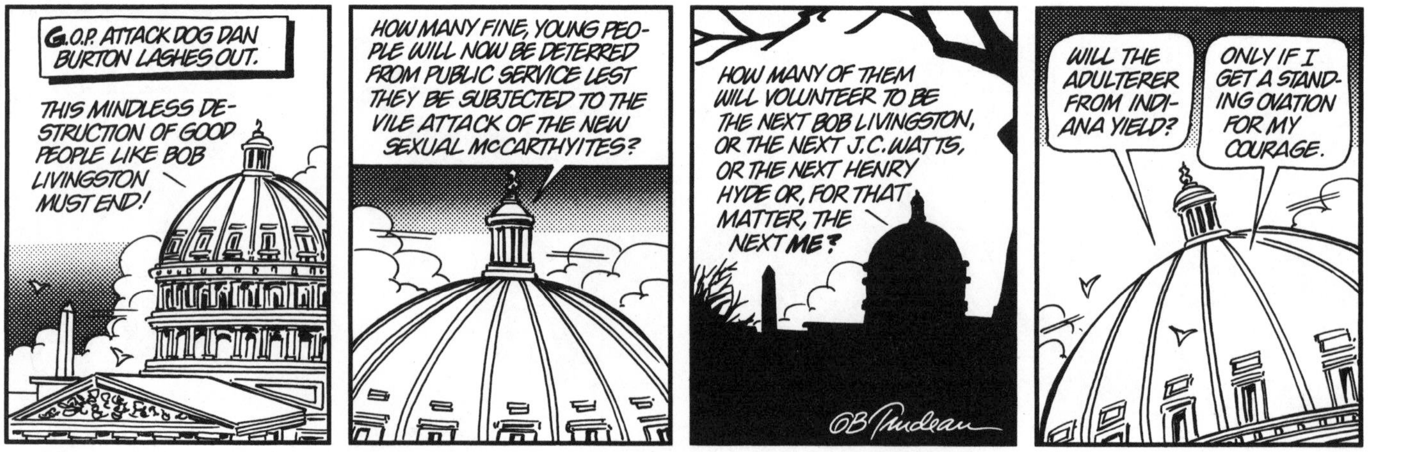
G.O.P. ATTACK DOG DAN BURTON LASHES OUT.
THIS MINDLESS DESTRUCTION OF GOOD PEOPLE LIKE BOB LIVINGSTON MUST END!
HOW MANY FINE, YOUNG PEOPLE WILL NOW BE DETERRED FROM PUBLIC SERVICE LEST THEY BE SUBJECTED TO THE VILE ATTACK OF THE NEW SEXUAL McCARTHYITES?
HOW MANY OF THEM WILL VOLUNTEER TO BE THE NEXT BOB LIVINGSTON, OR THE NEXT J.C. WATTS, OR THE NEXT HENRY HYDE OR, FOR THAT MATTER, THE NEXT ME?
WILL THE ADULTERER FROM INDIANA YIELD?
ONLY IF I GET A STANDING OVATION FOR MY COURAGE.

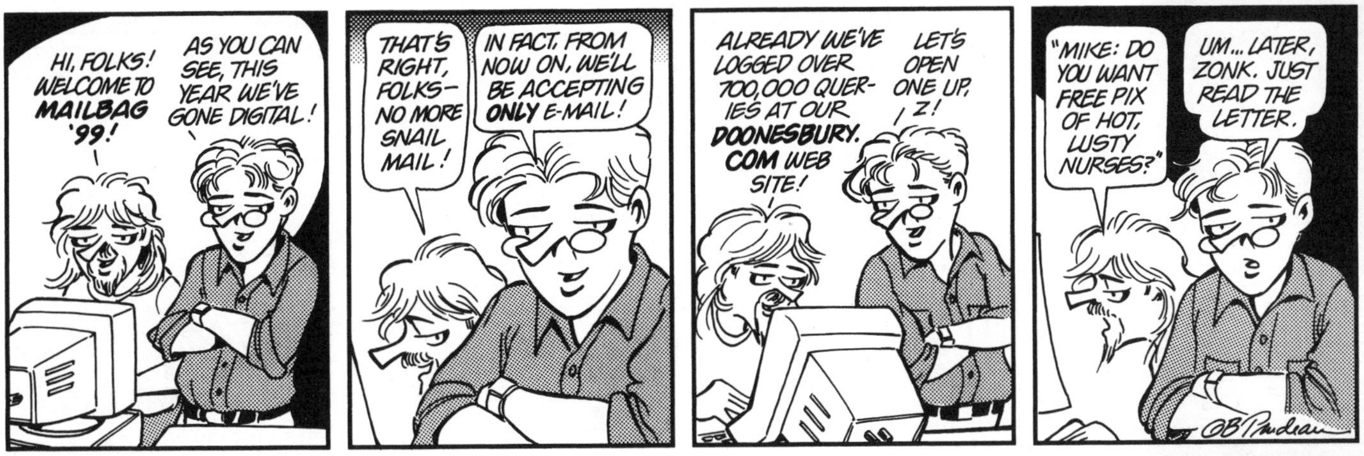
HI, FOLKS! WELCOME TO MAILBAG '99!
AS YOU CAN SEE, THIS YEAR WE'VE GONE DIGITAL!
THAT'S RIGHT, FOLKS– NO MORE SNAIL MAIL!
IN FACT, FROM NOW ON, WE'LL BE ACCEPTING ONLY E-MAIL!
ALREADY WE'VE LOGGED OVER 700,000 QUERIES AT OUR DOONESBURY.COM WEB SITE!
LET'S OPEN ONE UP, Z!
"MIKE: DO YOU WANT FREE PIX OF HOT, LUSTY NURSES?"
UM... LATER, ZONK. JUST READ THE LETTER.
GB Trudeau

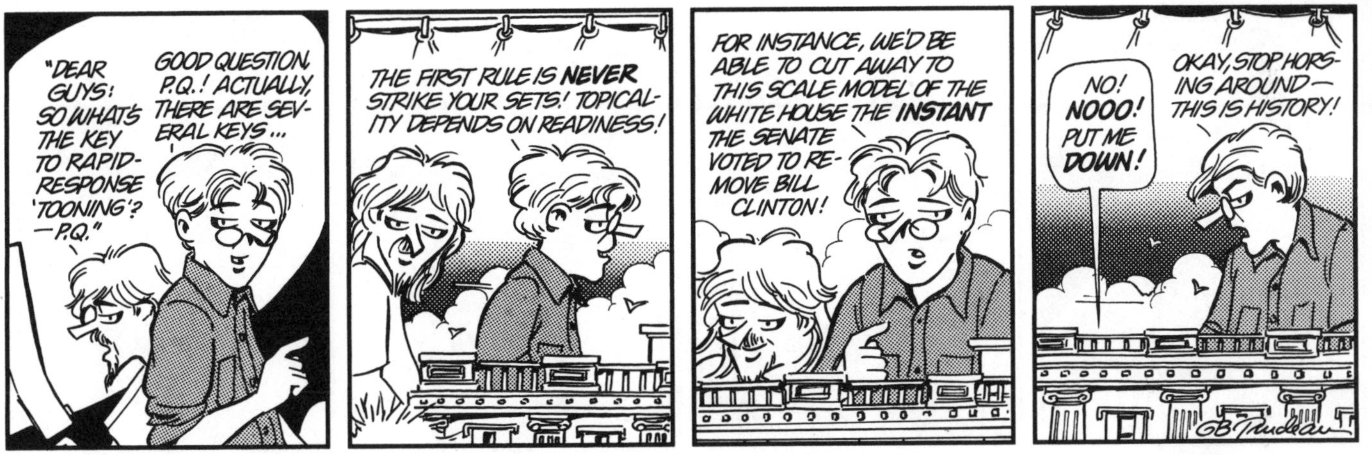
"DEAR GUYS: SO WHAT'S THE KEY TO RAPID-RESPONSE 'TOONING'? —P.Q."
GOOD QUESTION, P.Q.! ACTUALLY, THERE ARE SEVERAL KEYS...
THE FIRST RULE IS NEVER STRIKE YOUR SETS! TOPICALITY DEPENDS ON READINESS!
FOR INSTANCE, WE'D BE ABLE TO CUT AWAY TO THIS SCALE MODEL OF THE WHITE HOUSE THE INSTANT THE SENATE VOTED TO REMOVE BILL CLINTON!
NO! NOOO! PUT ME DOWN!
OKAY, STOP HORSING AROUND— THIS IS HISTORY!
GB Trudeau

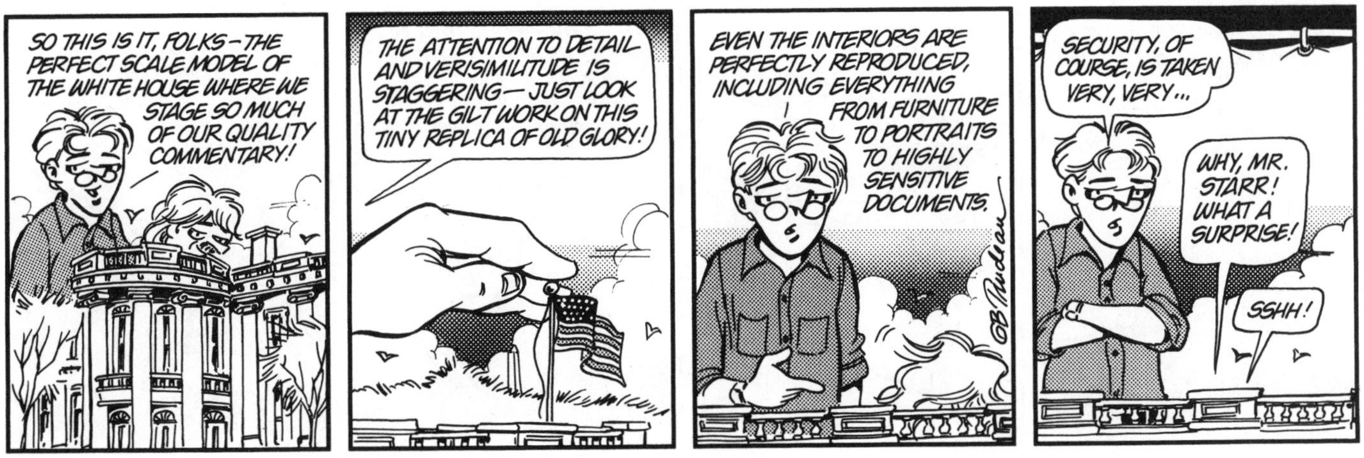
SO THIS IS IT, FOLKS—THE PERFECT SCALE MODEL OF THE WHITE HOUSE WHERE WE STAGE SO MUCH OF OUR QUALITY COMMENTARY!
THE ATTENTION TO DETAIL AND VERISIMILITUDE IS STAGGERING— JUST LOOK AT THE GILT WORK ON THIS TINY REPLICA OF OLD GLORY!
EVEN THE INTERIORS ARE PERFECTLY REPRODUCED, INCLUDING EVERYTHING FROM FURNITURE TO PORTRAITS TO HIGHLY SENSITIVE DOCUMENTS.
GB Trudeau
SECURITY, OF COURSE, IS TAKEN VERY, VERY...
WHY, MR. STARR! WHAT A SURPRISE!
SSHH!

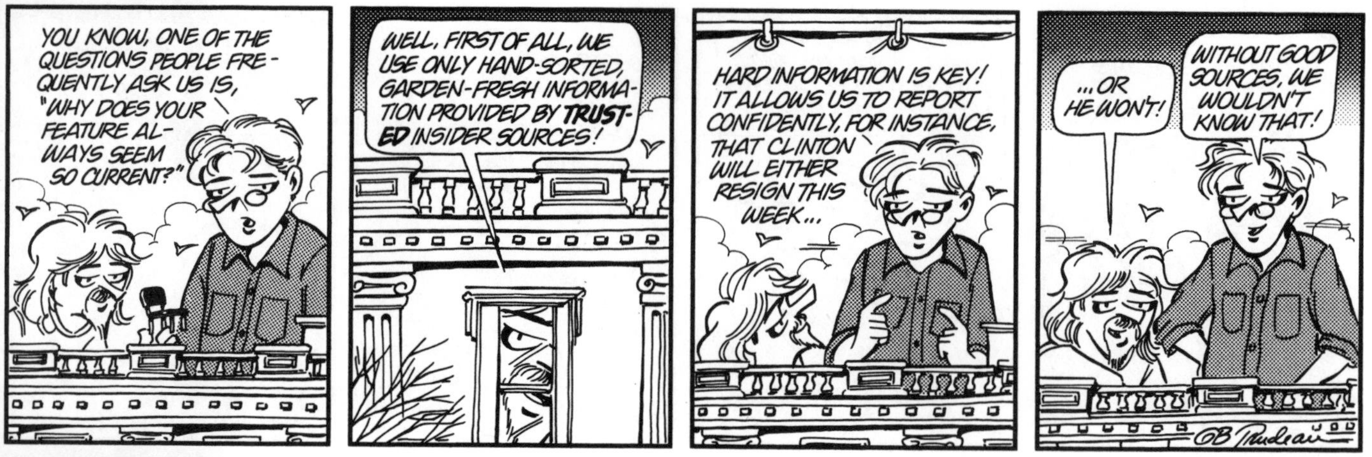
YOU KNOW, ONE OF THE QUESTIONS PEOPLE FRE-QUENTLY ASK US IS, "WHY DOES YOUR FEATURE AL-WAYS SEEM SO CURRENT?"
WELL, FIRST OF ALL, WE USE ONLY HAND-SORTED, GARDEN-FRESH INFORMA-TION PROVIDED BY TRUST-ED INSIDER SOURCES!
HARD INFORMATION IS KEY! IT ALLOWS US TO REPORT CONFIDENTLY, FOR INSTANCE, THAT CLINTON WILL EITHER RESIGN THIS WEEK...
...OR HE WON'T!
WITHOUT GOOD SOURCES, WE WOULDN'T KNOW THAT!

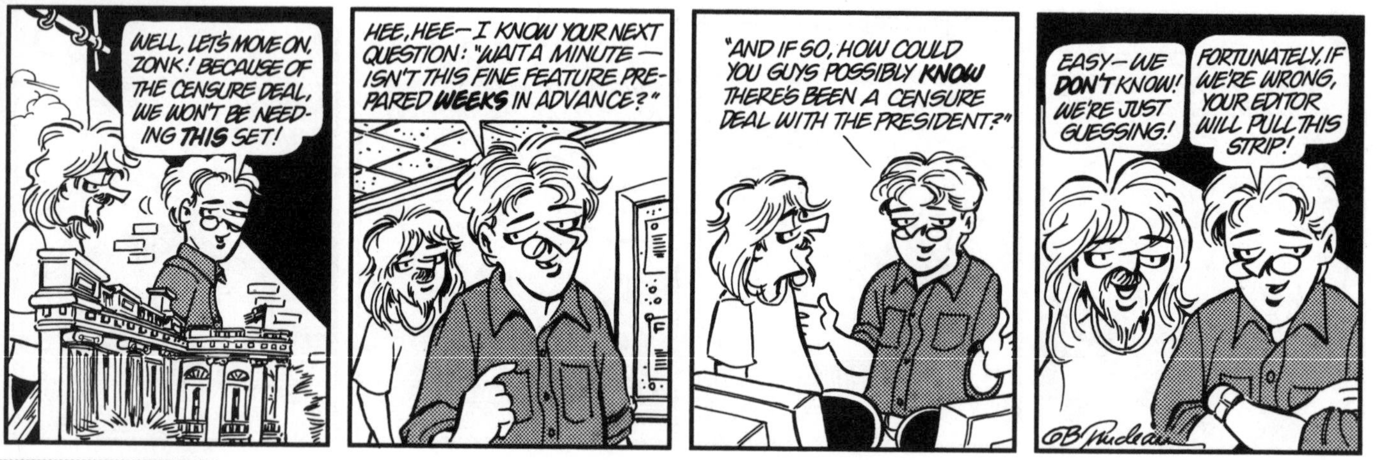
WELL, LET'S MOVE ON, ZONK! BECAUSE OF THE CENSURE DEAL, WE WON'T BE NEEDING THIS SET!
HEE, HEE— I KNOW YOUR NEXT QUESTION: "WAIT A MINUTE — ISN'T THIS FINE FEATURE PRE-PARED WEEKS IN ADVANCE?"
"AND IF SO, HOW COULD YOU GUYS POSSIBLY KNOW THERE'S BEEN A CENSURE DEAL WITH THE PRESIDENT?"
EASY— WE DON'T KNOW! WE'RE JUST GUESSING!
FORTUNATELY, IF WE'RE WRONG, YOUR EDITOR WILL PULL THIS STRIP!

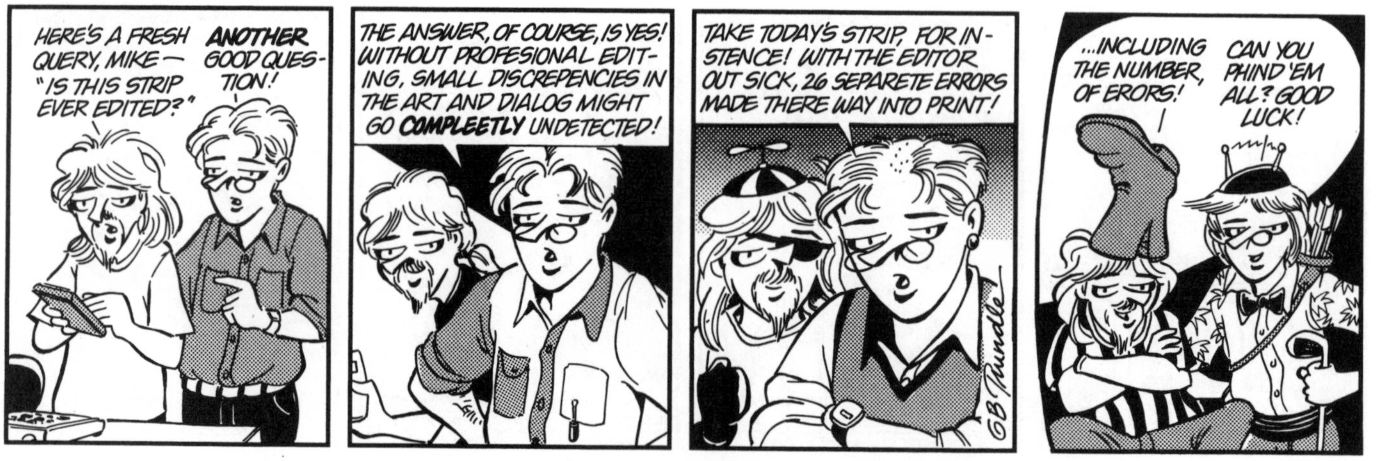
HERE'S A FRESH QUERY, MIKE— "IS THIS STRIP EVER EDITED?"
ANOTHER GOOD QUES-TION!
THE ANSWER, OF COURSE, IS YES! WITHOUT PROFESIONAL EDIT-ING, SMALL DISCREPENCIES IN THE ART AND DIALOG MIGHT GO COMPLEETLY UNDETECTED!
TAKE TODAY'S STRIP, FOR IN-STENCE! WITH THE EDITOR OUT SICK, 26 SEPARETE ERRORS MADE THERE WAY INTO PRINT!
...INCLUDING THE NUMBER OF ERORS!
CAN YOU PHIND 'EM ALL? GOOD LUCK!

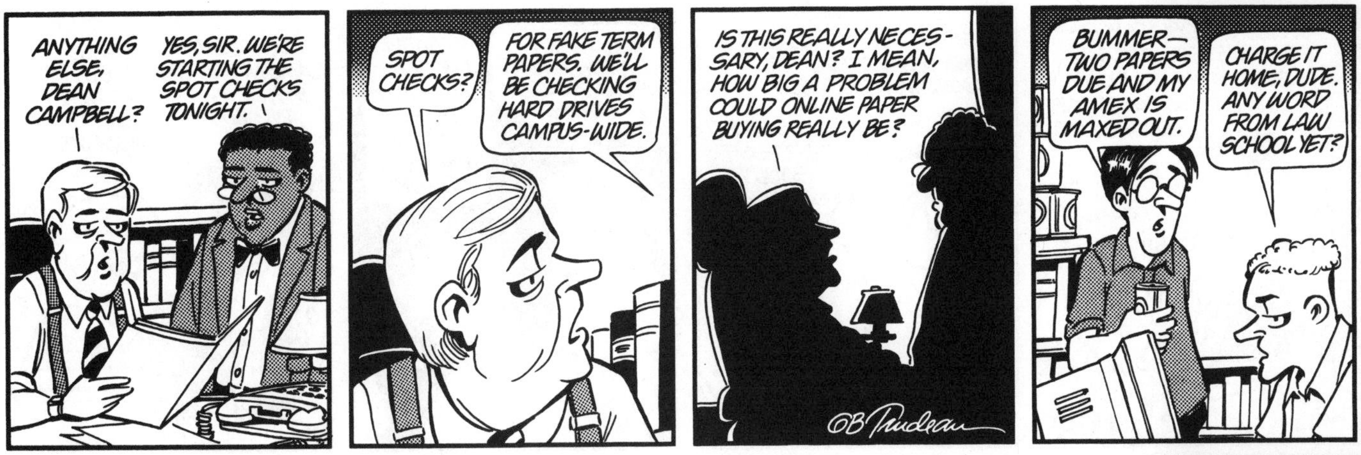
ANYTHING ELSE, DEAN CAMPBELL?
YES, SIR. WE'RE STARTING THE SPOT CHECKS TONIGHT.
SPOT CHECKS?
FOR FAKE TERM PAPERS. WE'LL BE CHECKING HARD DRIVES CAMPUS-WIDE.
IS THIS REALLY NECES-SARY, DEAN? I MEAN, HOW BIG A PROBLEM COULD ONLINE PAPER BUYING REALLY BE?
BUMMER—TWO PAPERS DUE AND MY AMEX IS MAXED OUT.
CHARGE IT HOME, DUDE. ANY WORD FROM LAW SCHOOL YET?

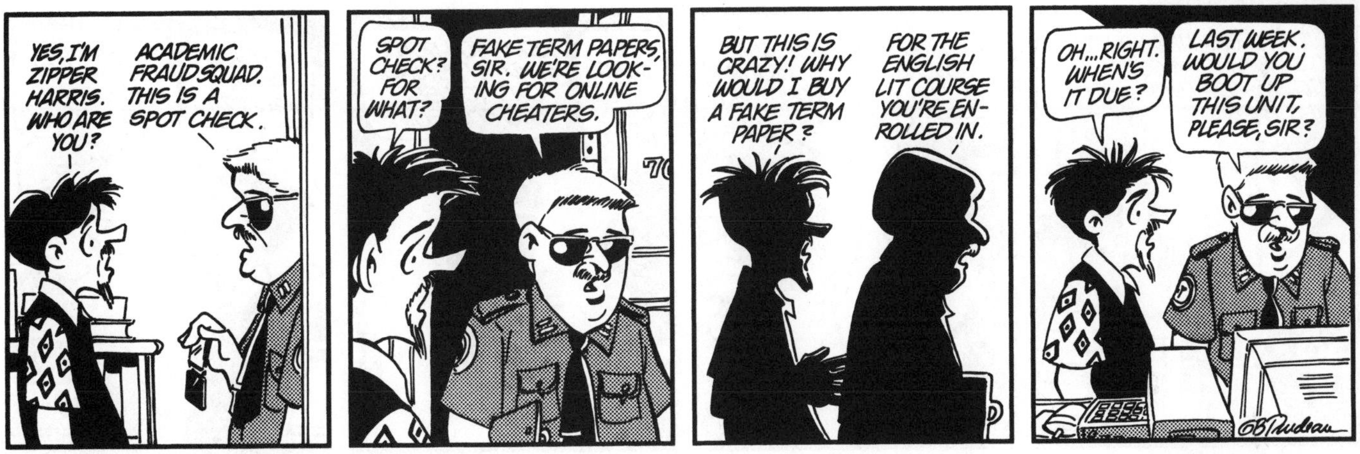
YES, I'M ZIPPER HARRIS. WHO ARE YOU?
ACADEMIC FRAUD SQUAD. THIS IS A SPOT CHECK.
SPOT CHECK? FOR WHAT?
FAKE TERM PAPERS, SIR. WE'RE LOOK-ING FOR ONLINE CHEATERS.
BUT THIS IS CRAZY! WHY WOULD I BUY A FAKE TERM PAPER?
FOR THE ENGLISH LIT COURSE YOU'RE EN-ROLLED IN.
OH... RIGHT. WHEN'S IT DUE?
LAST WEEK. WOULD YOU BOOT UP THIS UNIT, PLEASE, SIR?

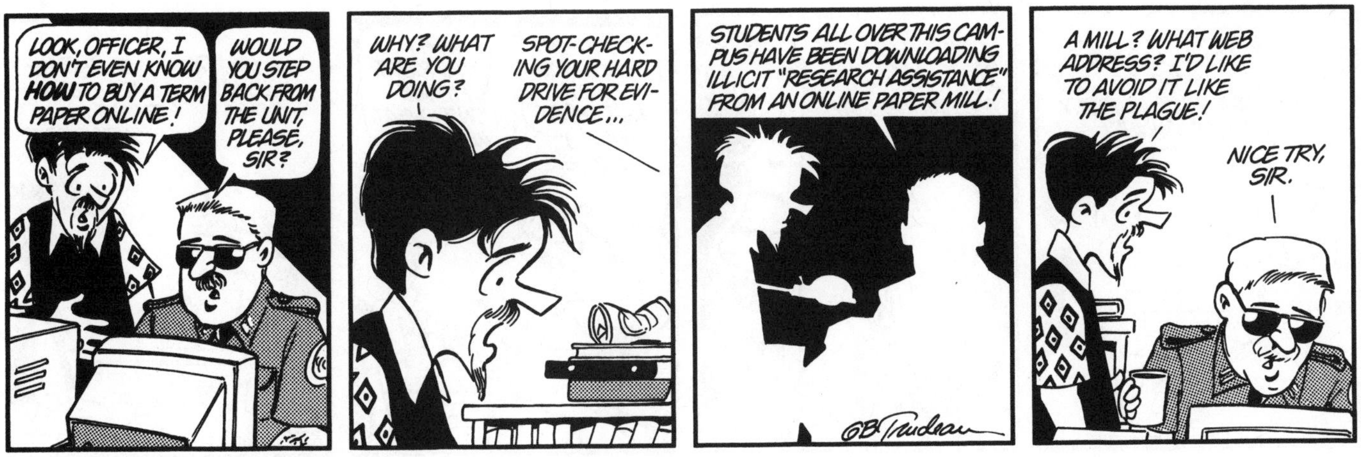
LOOK, OFFICER, I DON'T EVEN KNOW HOW TO BUY A TERM PAPER ONLINE!
WOULD YOU STEP BACK FROM THE UNIT, PLEASE, SIR?
WHY? WHAT ARE YOU DOING?
SPOT-CHECK-ING YOUR HARD DRIVE FOR EVI-DENCE...
STUDENTS ALL OVER THIS CAM-PUS HAVE BEEN DOWNLOADING ILLICIT "RESEARCH ASSISTANCE" FROM AN ONLINE PAPER MILL!
A MILL? WHAT WEB ADDRESS? I'D LIKE TO AVOID IT LIKE THE PLAGUE!
NICE TRY, SIR.

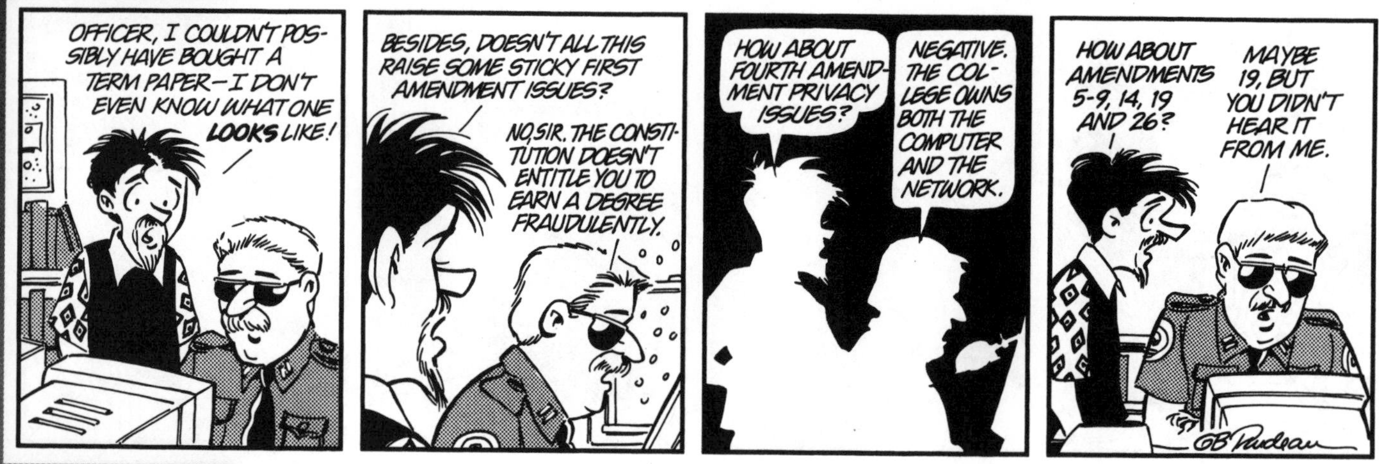
OFFICER, I COULDN'T POSSIBLY HAVE BOUGHT A TERM PAPER—I DON'T EVEN KNOW WHAT ONE **LOOKS** LIKE!
BESIDES, DOESN'T ALL THIS RAISE SOME STICKY FIRST AMENDMENT ISSUES?
NO, SIR. THE CONSTITUTION DOESN'T ENTITLE YOU TO EARN A DEGREE FRAUDULENTLY.
HOW ABOUT FOURTH AMENDMENT PRIVACY ISSUES?
NEGATIVE. THE COLLEGE OWNS BOTH THE COMPUTER AND THE NETWORK.
HOW ABOUT AMENDMENTS 5-9, 14, 19 AND 26?
MAYBE 19, BUT YOU DIDN'T HEAR IT FROM ME.
GB Trudeau

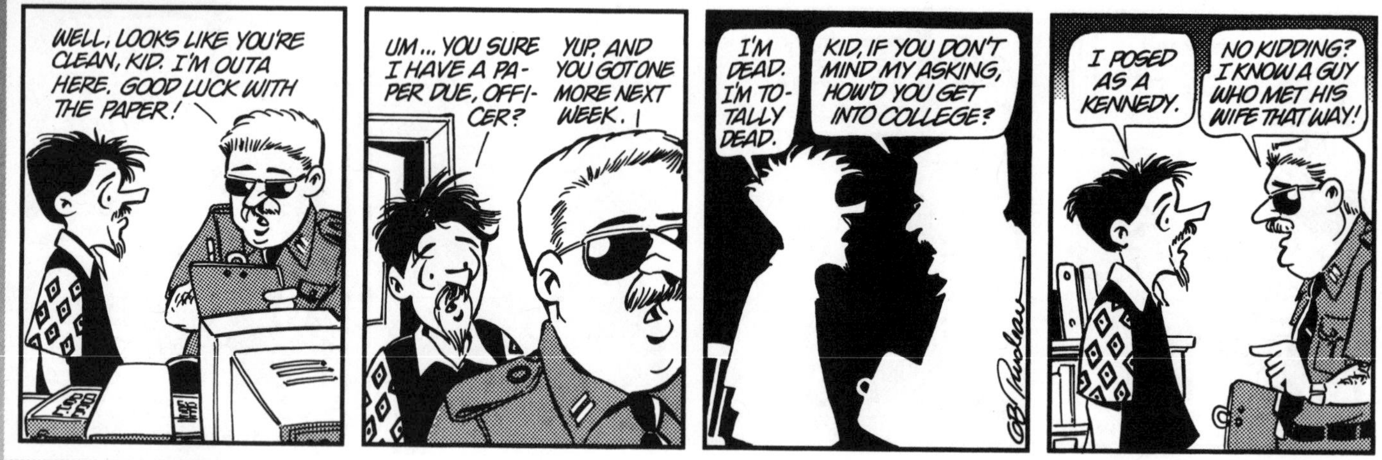
WELL, LOOKS LIKE YOU'RE CLEAN, KID. I'M OUTA HERE. GOOD LUCK WITH THE PAPER!
UM... YOU SURE I HAVE A PAPER DUE, OFFICER?
YUP. AND YOU GOT ONE MORE NEXT WEEK.
I'M DEAD. I'M TOTALLY DEAD.
KID, IF YOU DON'T MIND MY ASKING, HOW'D YOU GET INTO COLLEGE?
GB Trudeau
I POSED AS A KENNEDY.
NO KIDDING? I KNOW A GUY WHO MET HIS WIFE THAT WAY!

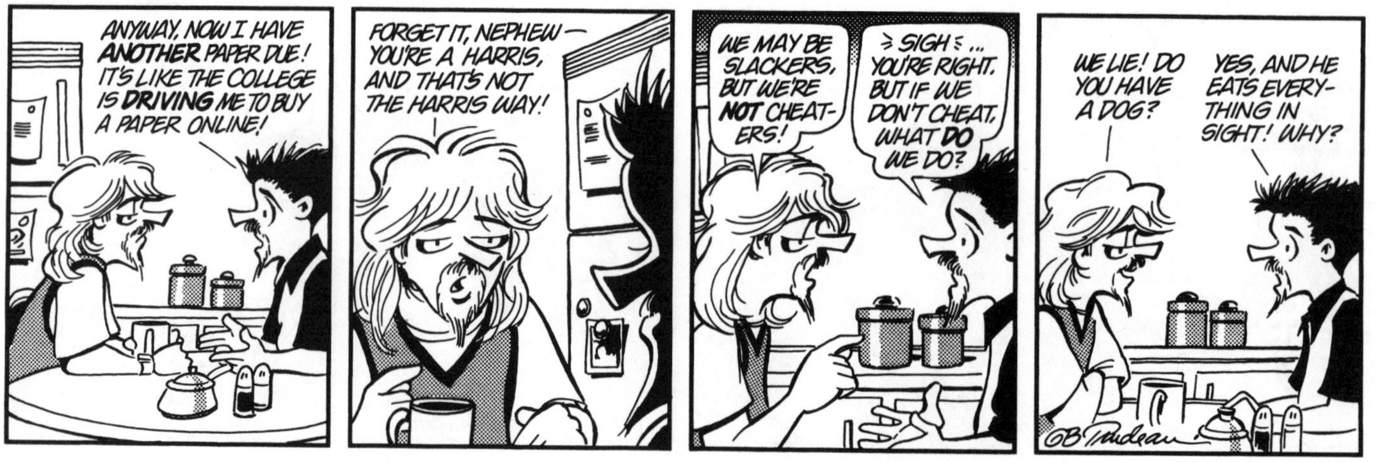
ANYWAY, NOW I HAVE **ANOTHER** PAPER DUE! IT'S LIKE THE COLLEGE IS **DRIVING** ME TO BUY A PAPER ONLINE!
FORGET IT, NEPHEW—YOU'RE A HARRIS, AND THAT'S NOT THE HARRIS WAY!
WE MAY BE SLACKERS, BUT WE'RE **NOT** CHEATERS!
SIGH... YOU'RE RIGHT. BUT IF WE DON'T CHEAT, WHAT **DO** WE DO?
WE LIE! DO YOU HAVE A DOG?
YES, AND HE EATS EVERYTHING IN SIGHT! WHY?
GB Trudeau

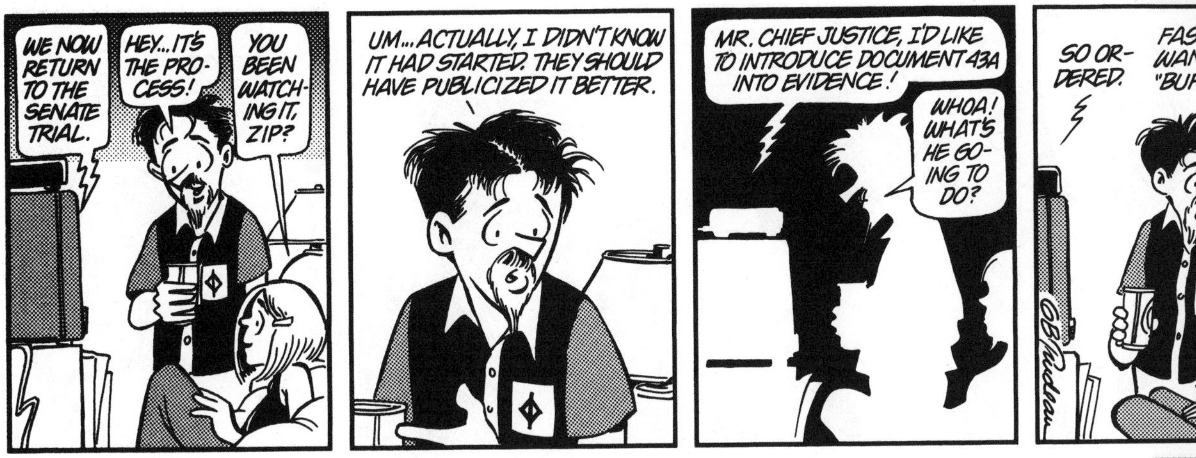
WE NOW RETURN TO THE SENATE TRIAL.
HEY... IT'S THE PROCESS!
YOU BEEN WATCHING IT, ZIP?
UM... ACTUALLY, I DIDN'T KNOW IT HAD STARTED. THEY SHOULD HAVE PUBLICIZED IT BETTER.
MR. CHIEF JUSTICE, I'D LIKE TO INTRODUCE DOCUMENT 43A INTO EVIDENCE!
WHOA! WHAT'S HE GOING TO DO?
SO ORDERED.
FASCINATING. WANT TO WATCH "BUFFY" NOW?
OKAY.

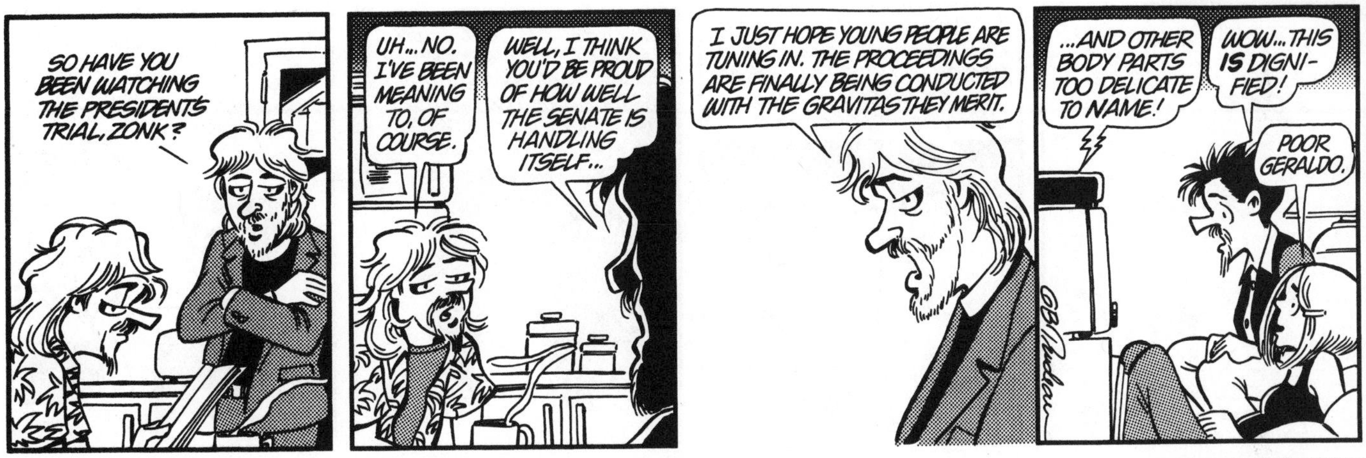
SO HAVE YOU BEEN WATCHING THE PRESIDENT'S TRIAL, ZONK?
UH... NO. I'VE BEEN MEANING TO, OF COURSE.
WELL, I THINK YOU'D BE PROUD OF HOW WELL THE SENATE IS HANDLING ITSELF...
I JUST HOPE YOUNG PEOPLE ARE TUNING IN. THE PROCEEDINGS ARE FINALLY BEING CONDUCTED WITH THE GRAVITAS THEY MERIT.
...AND OTHER BODY PARTS TOO DELICATE TO NAME!
WOW... THIS IS DIGNIFIED!
POOR GERALDO.

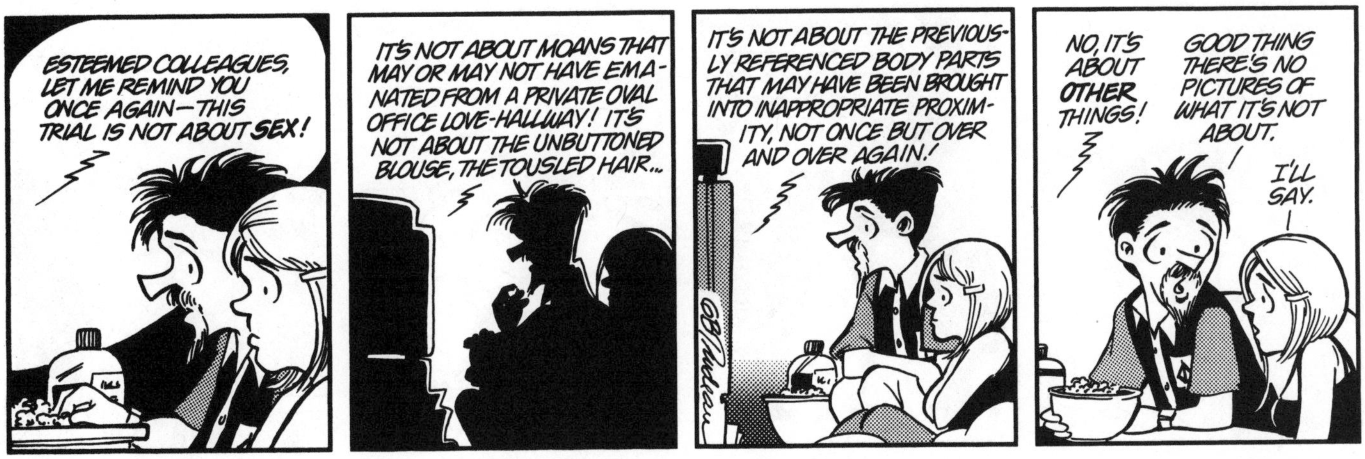
ESTEEMED COLLEAGUES, LET ME REMIND YOU ONCE AGAIN—THIS TRIAL IS NOT ABOUT SEX!
IT'S NOT ABOUT MOANS THAT MAY OR MAY NOT HAVE EMANATED FROM A PRIVATE OVAL OFFICE LOVE-HALLWAY! IT'S NOT ABOUT THE UNBUTTONED BLOUSE, THE TOUSLED HAIR...
IT'S NOT ABOUT THE PREVIOUSLY REFERENCED BODY PARTS THAT MAY HAVE BEEN BROUGHT INTO INAPPROPRIATE PROXIMITY, NOT ONCE BUT OVER AND OVER AGAIN!
NO, IT'S ABOUT OTHER THINGS!
GOOD THING THERE'S NO PICTURES OF WHAT IT'S NOT ABOUT.
I'LL SAY.

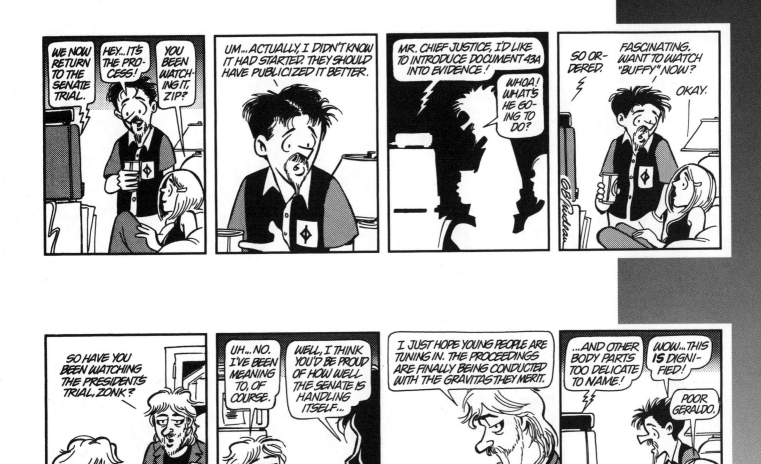

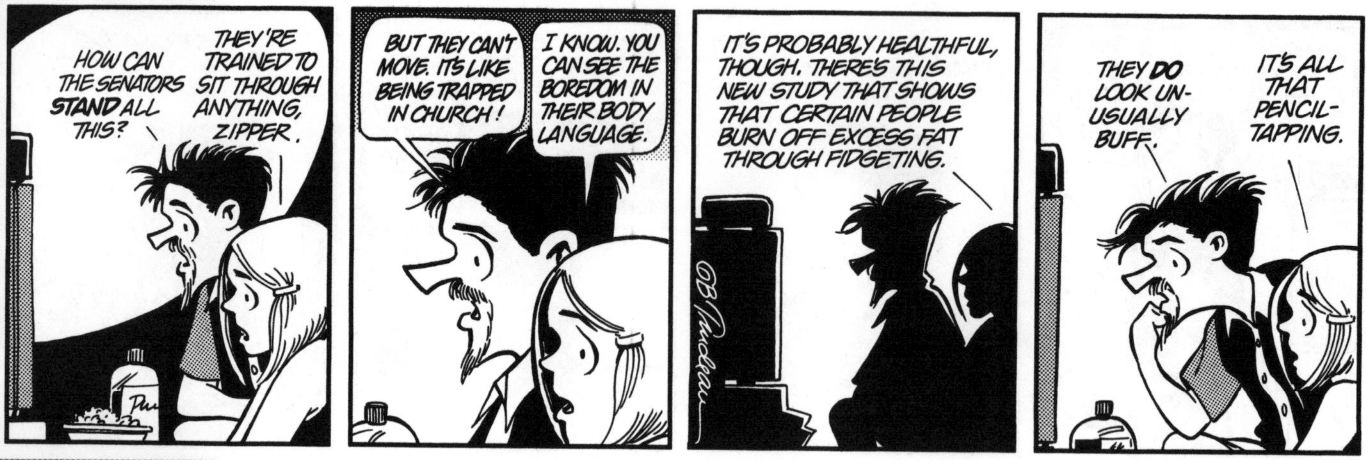
HOW CAN THE SENATORS STAND ALL THIS?
THEY'RE TRAINED TO SIT THROUGH ANYTHING, ZIPPER.
BUT THEY CAN'T MOVE. IT'S LIKE BEING TRAPPED IN CHURCH!
I KNOW. YOU CAN SEE THE BOREDOM IN THEIR BODY LANGUAGE.
IT'S PROBABLY HEALTHFUL, THOUGH. THERE'S THIS NEW STUDY THAT SHOWS THAT CERTAIN PEOPLE BURN OFF EXCESS FAT THROUGH FIDGETING.
THEY DO LOOK UNUSUALLY BUFF.
IT'S ALL THAT PENCIL-TAPPING.

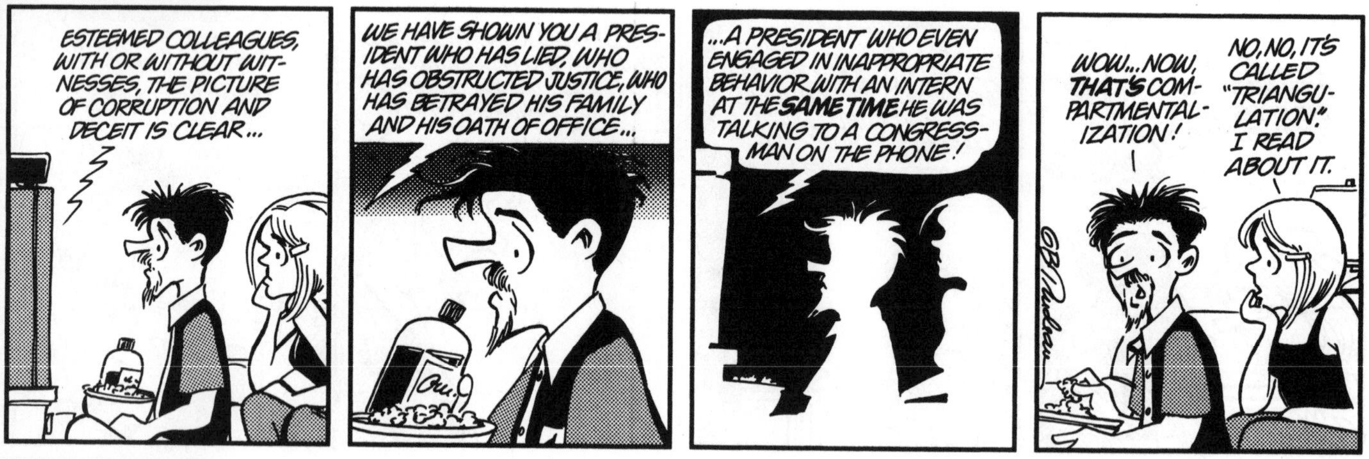
ESTEEMED COLLEAGUES, WITH OR WITHOUT WITNESSES, THE PICTURE OF CORRUPTION AND DECEIT IS CLEAR...
WE HAVE SHOWN YOU A PRESIDENT WHO HAS LIED, WHO HAS OBSTRUCTED JUSTICE, WHO HAS BETRAYED HIS FAMILY AND HIS OATH OF OFFICE...
...A PRESIDENT WHO EVEN ENGAGED IN INAPPROPRIATE BEHAVIOR WITH AN INTERN AT THE SAME TIME HE WAS TALKING TO A CONGRESSMAN ON THE PHONE!
WOW... NOW, THAT'S COMPARTMENTALIZATION!
NO, NO, IT'S CALLED "TRIANGULATION." I READ ABOUT IT.

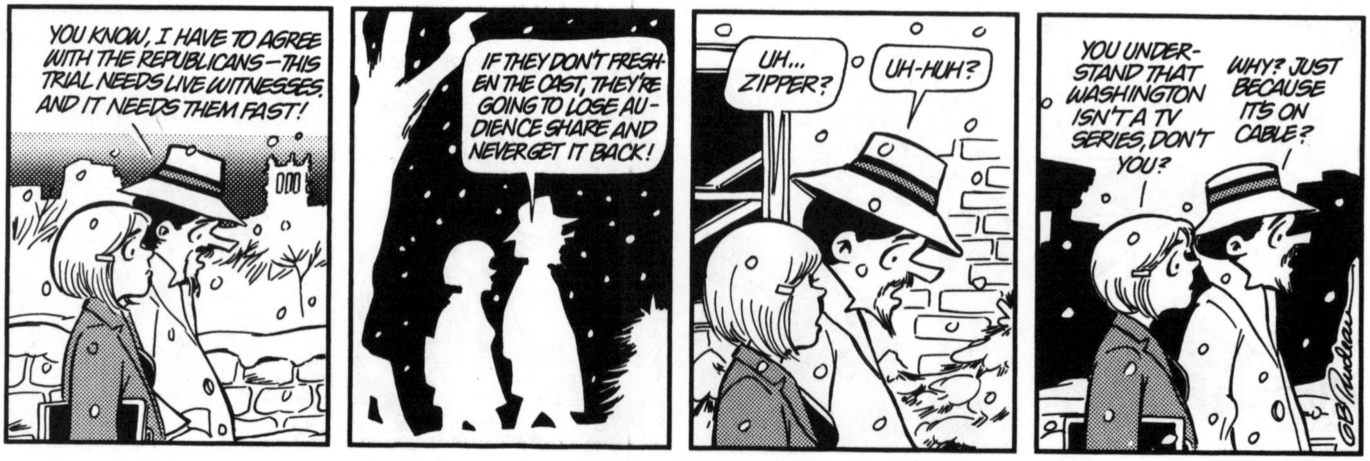
YOU KNOW, I HAVE TO AGREE WITH THE REPUBLICANS—THIS TRIAL NEEDS LIVE WITNESSES, AND IT NEEDS THEM FAST!
IF THEY DON'T FRESHEN THE CAST, THEY'RE GOING TO LOSE AUDIENCE SHARE AND NEVER GET IT BACK!
UH... ZIPPER?
UH-HUH?
YOU UNDERSTAND THAT WASHINGTON ISN'T A TV SERIES, DON'T YOU?
WHY? JUST BECAUSE IT'S ON CABLE?

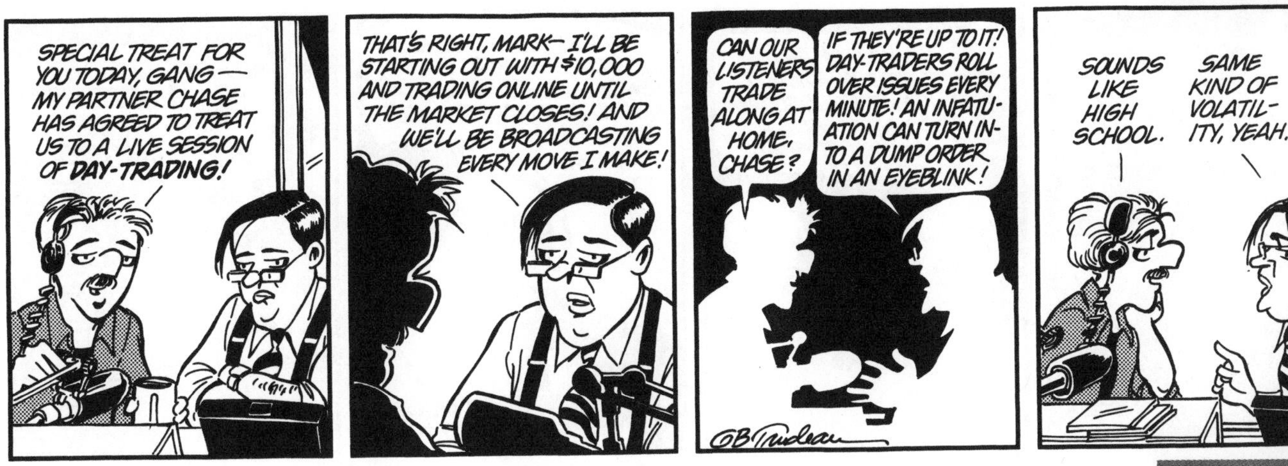
SPECIAL TREAT FOR YOU TODAY, GANG — MY PARTNER CHASE HAS AGREED TO TREAT US TO A LIVE SESSION OF **DAY-TRADING**!
THAT'S RIGHT, MARK— I'LL BE STARTING OUT WITH $10,000 AND TRADING ONLINE UNTIL THE MARKET CLOSES! AND WE'LL BE BROADCASTING EVERY MOVE I MAKE!
CAN OUR LISTENERS TRADE ALONG AT HOME, CHASE?
IF THEY'RE UP TO IT! DAY-TRADERS ROLL OVER ISSUES EVERY MINUTE! AN INFATUATION CAN TURN INTO A DUMP ORDER IN AN EYEBLINK!
SOUNDS LIKE HIGH SCHOOL.
SAME KIND OF VOLATILITY, YEAH.

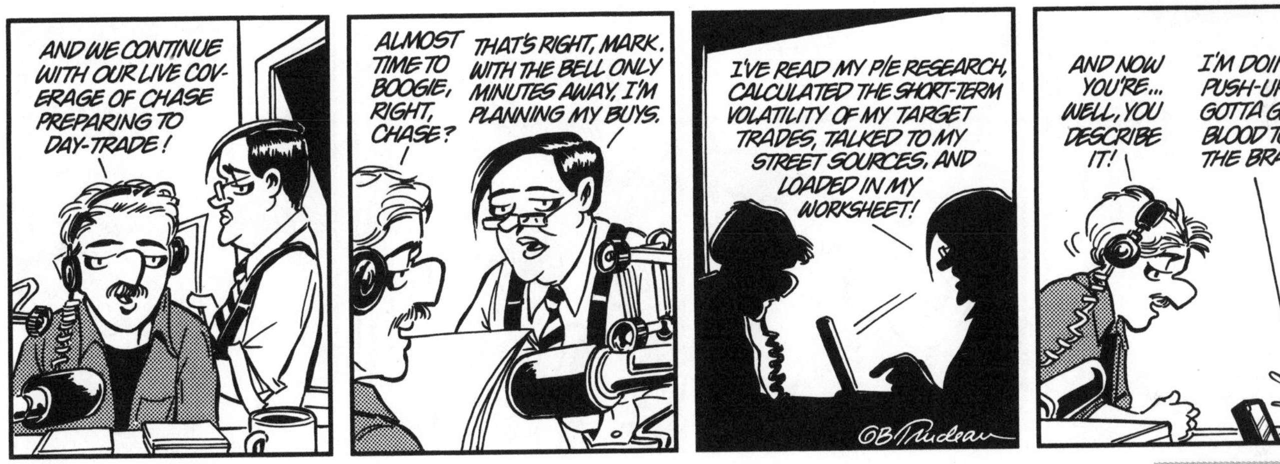
AND WE CONTINUE WITH OUR LIVE COVERAGE OF CHASE PREPARING TO DAY-TRADE!
ALMOST TIME TO BOOGIE, RIGHT, CHASE?
THAT'S RIGHT, MARK. WITH THE BELL ONLY MINUTES AWAY, I'M PLANNING MY BUYS.
I'VE READ MY P/E RESEARCH, CALCULATED THE SHORT-TERM VOLATILITY OF MY TARGET TRADES, TALKED TO MY STREET SOURCES, AND LOADED IN MY WORKSHEET!
AND NOW YOU'RE... WELL, YOU DESCRIBE IT!
I'M DOING PUSH-UPS! GOTTA GET BLOOD TO THE BRAIN!

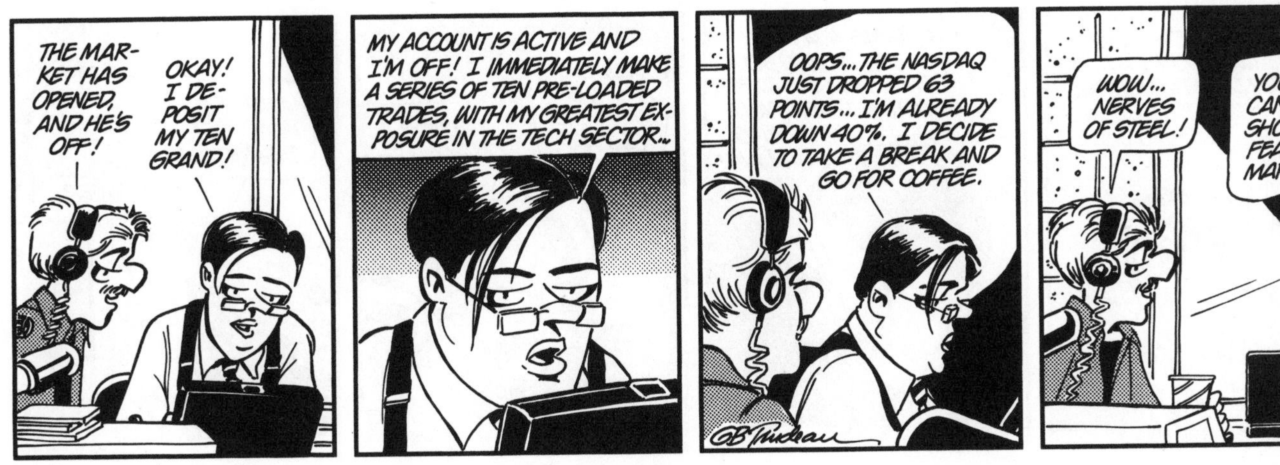
THE MARKET HAS OPENED, AND HE'S OFF!
OKAY! I DEPOSIT MY TEN GRAND!
MY ACCOUNT IS ACTIVE AND I'M OFF! I IMMEDIATELY MAKE A SERIES OF TEN PRE-LOADED TRADES, WITH MY GREATEST EXPOSURE IN THE TECH SECTOR...
OOPS... THE NASDAQ JUST DROPPED 63 POINTS... I'M ALREADY DOWN 40%. I DECIDE TO TAKE A BREAK AND GO FOR COFFEE.
WOW... NERVES OF STEEL!
YOU CAN'T SHOW FEAR, MARK...

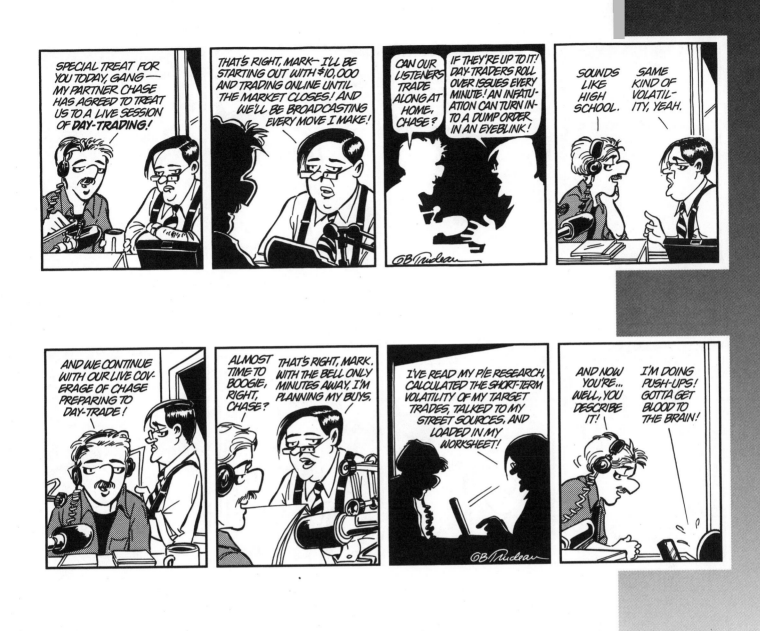

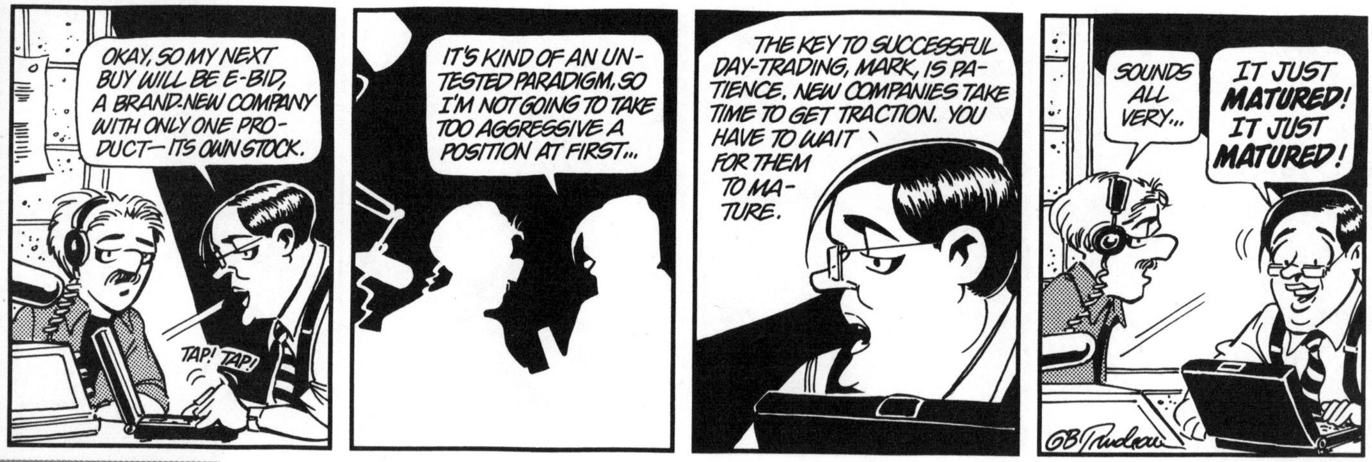
OKAY, SO MY NEXT BUY WILL BE E-BID, A BRAND-NEW COMPANY WITH ONLY ONE PRODUCT— ITS OWN STOCK.
TAP! TAP!
IT'S KIND OF AN UNTESTED PARADIGM, SO I'M NOT GOING TO TAKE TOO AGGRESSIVE A POSITION AT FIRST...
THE KEY TO SUCCESSFUL DAY-TRADING, MARK, IS PATIENCE. NEW COMPANIES TAKE TIME TO GET TRACTION. YOU HAVE TO WAIT FOR THEM TO MATURE.
SOUNDS ALL VERY...
IT JUST MATURED! IT JUST MATURED!
©B Trudeau

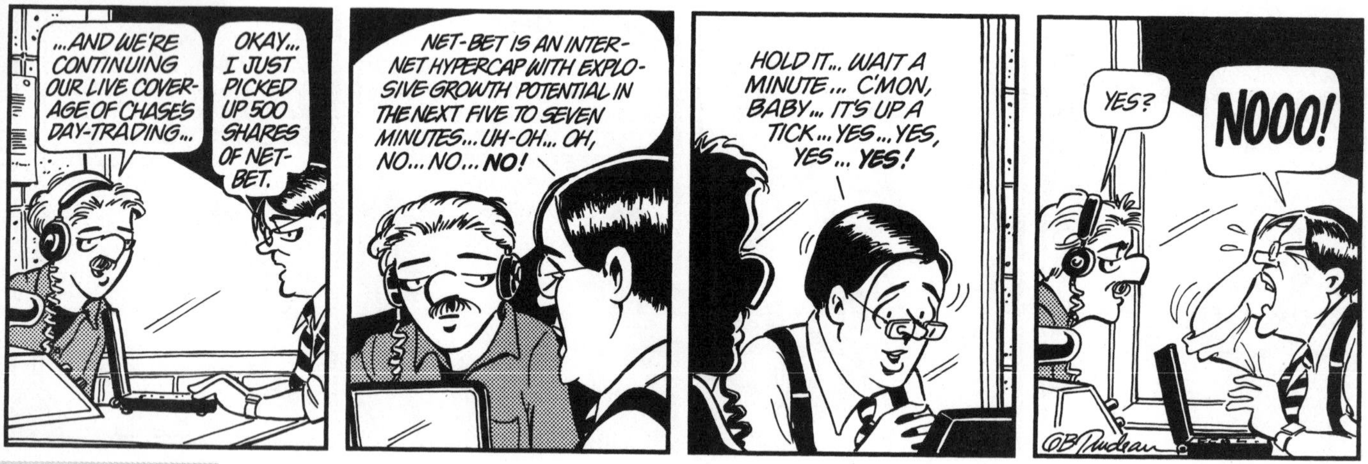
...AND WE'RE CONTINUING OUR LIVE COVERAGE OF CHASE'S DAY-TRADING...
OKAY... I JUST PICKED UP 500 SHARES OF NET-BET.
NET-BET IS AN INTERNET HYPERCAP WITH EXPLOSIVE GROWTH POTENTIAL IN THE NEXT FIVE TO SEVEN MINUTES... UH-OH... OH, NO... NO... NO!
HOLD IT... WAIT A MINUTE... C'MON, BABY... IT'S UP A TICK... YES... YES, YES... YES!
YES?
NOOO!
©B Trudeau

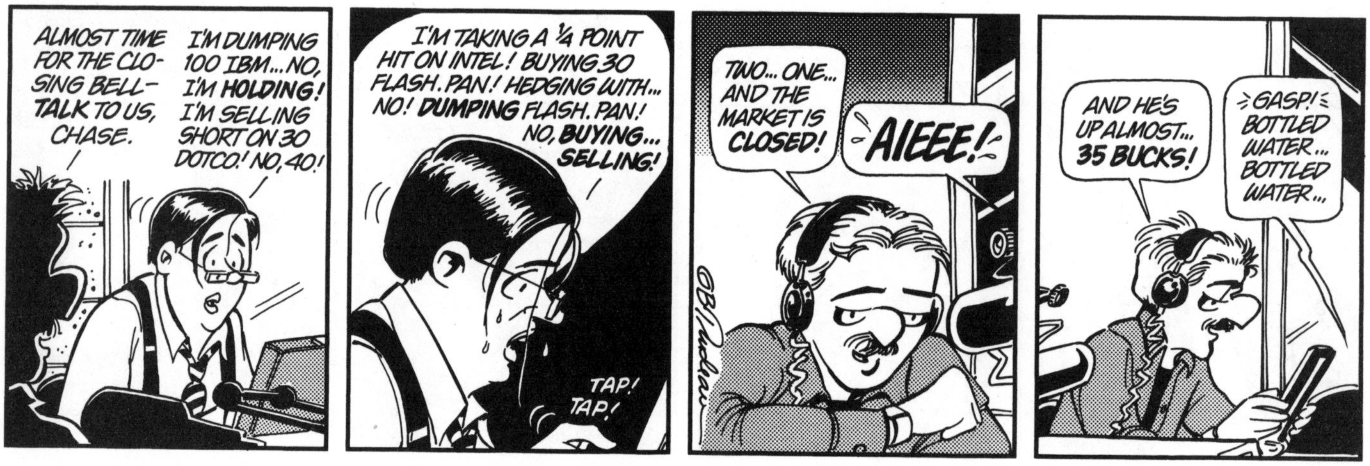
ALMOST TIME FOR THE CLOSING BELL– TALK TO US, CHASE.
I'M DUMPING 100 IBM... NO, I'M HOLDING! I'M SELLING SHORT ON 30 DOTCO! NO, 40!
I'M TAKING A 1/4 POINT HIT ON INTEL! BUYING 30 FLASH. PAN! HEDGING WITH... NO! DUMPING FLASH. PAN! NO, BUYING... SELLING!
TAP! TAP!
TWO... ONE... AND THE MARKET IS CLOSED!
AIEEE!
©B Trudeau
AND HE'S UP ALMOST... 35 BUCKS!
GASP! BOTTLED WATER... BOTTLED WATER...

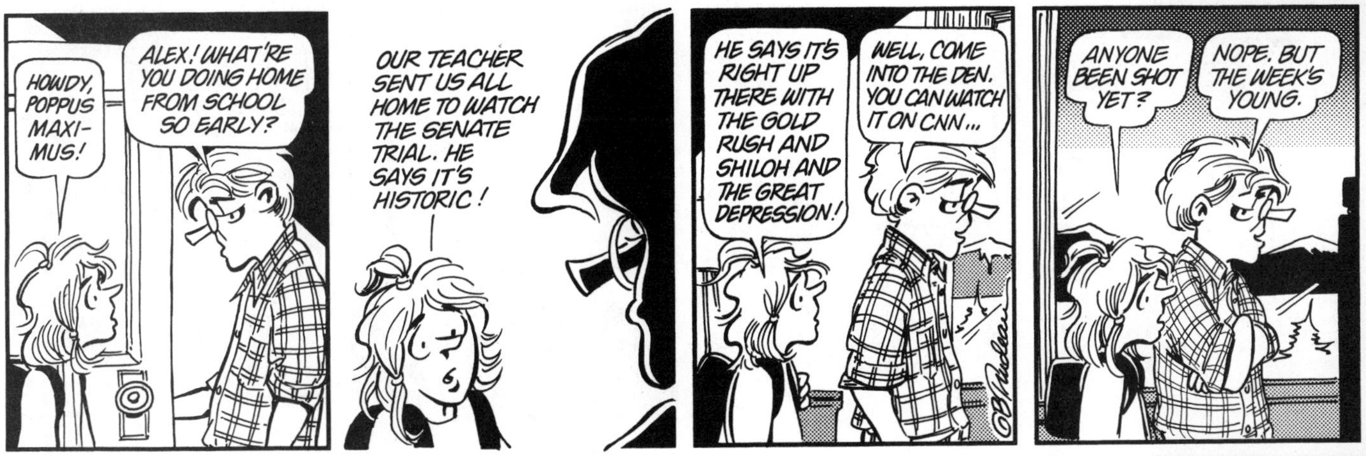
HOWDY, POPPUS MAXI-MUS!
ALEX! WHAT'RE YOU DOING HOME FROM SCHOOL SO EARLY?
OUR TEACHER SENT US ALL HOME TO WATCH THE SENATE TRIAL. HE SAYS IT'S HISTORIC!
HE SAYS IT'S RIGHT UP THERE WITH THE GOLD RUSH AND SHILOH AND THE GREAT DEPRESSION!
WELL, COME INTO THE DEN. YOU CAN WATCH IT ON CNN...
ANYONE BEEN SHOT YET?
NOPE. BUT THE WEEK'S YOUNG.

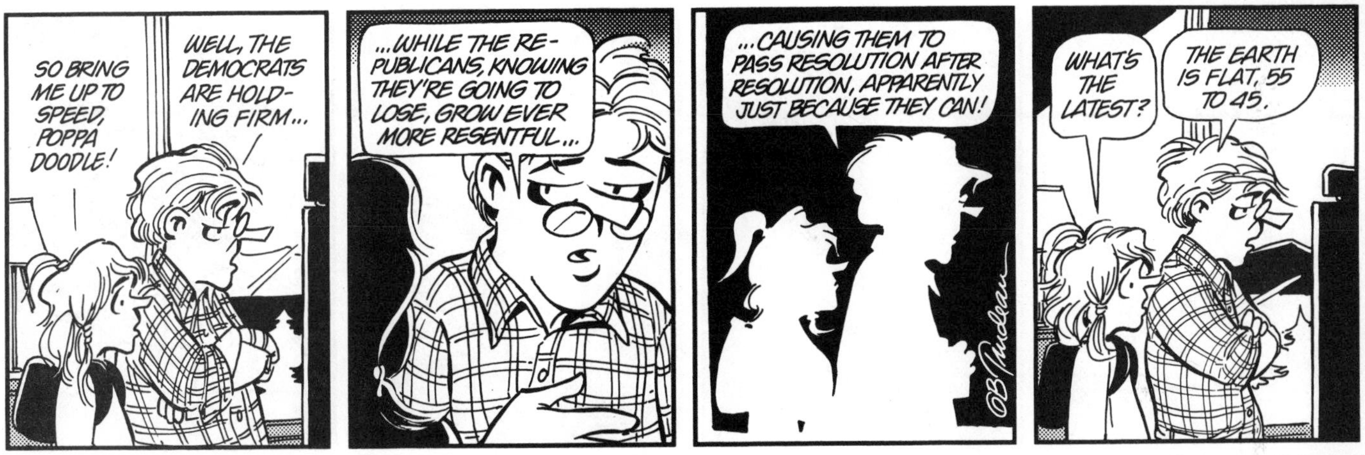
SO BRING ME UP TO SPEED, POPPA DOODLE!
WELL, THE DEMOCRATS ARE HOLD-ING FIRM...
...WHILE THE RE-PUBLICANS, KNOWING THEY'RE GOING TO LOSE, GROW EVER MORE RESENTFUL...
...CAUSING THEM TO PASS RESOLUTION AFTER RESOLUTION, APPARENTLY JUST BECAUSE THEY CAN!
WHAT'S THE LATEST?
THE EARTH IS FLAT, 55 TO 45.

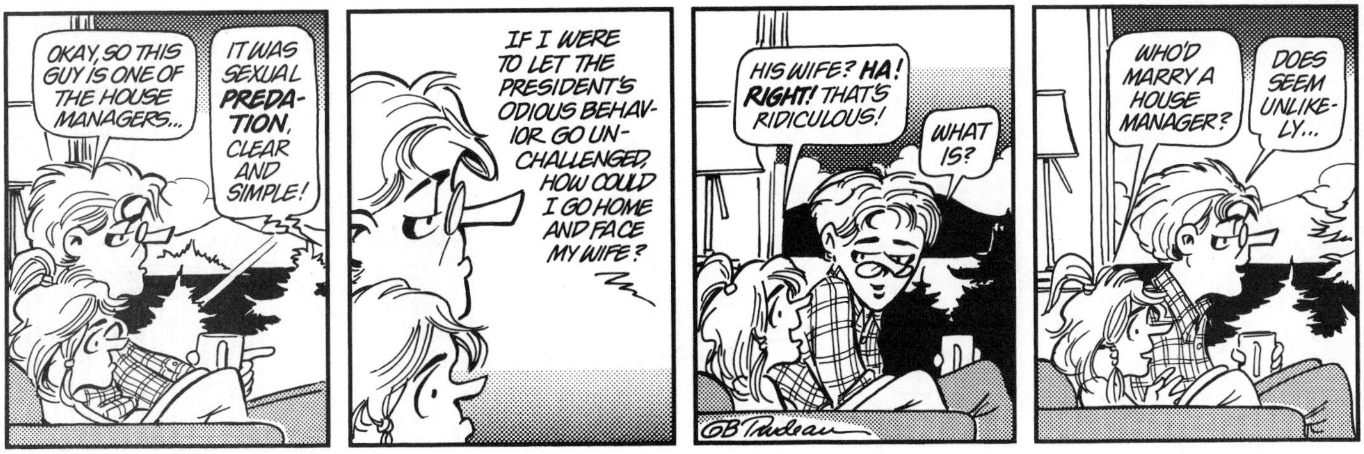
OKAY, SO THIS GUY IS ONE OF THE HOUSE MANAGERS...
IT WAS SEXUAL PREDA-TION, CLEAR AND SIMPLE!
IF I WERE TO LET THE PRESIDENT'S ODIOUS BEHAV-IOR GO UN-CHALLENGED, HOW COULD I GO HOME AND FACE MY WIFE?
HIS WIFE? HA! RIGHT! THAT'S RIDICULOUS!
WHAT IS?
WHO'D MARRY A HOUSE MANAGER?
DOES SEEM UNLIKE-LY...

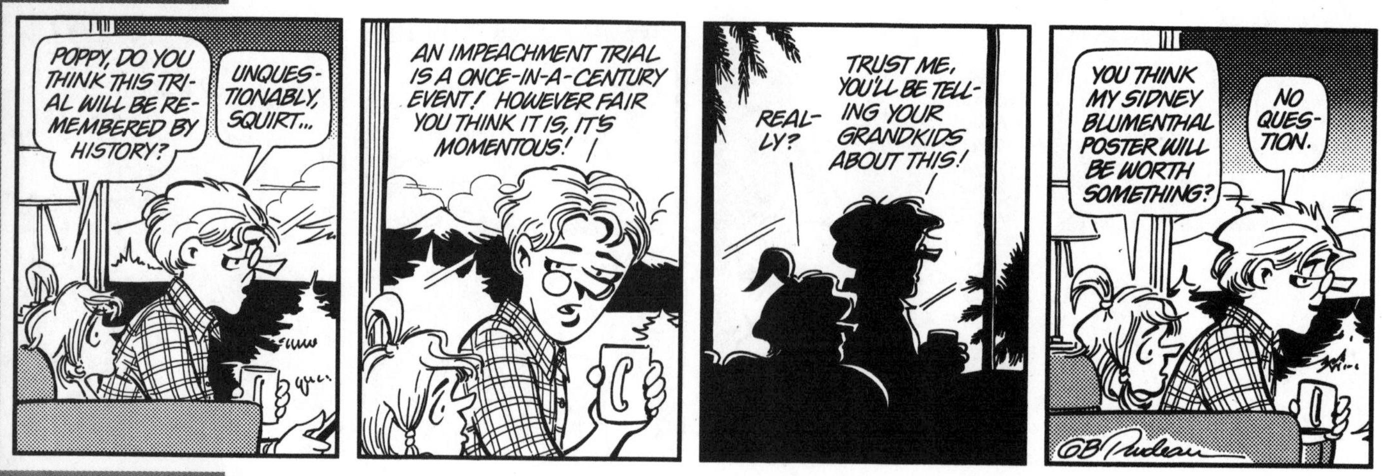
POPPY, DO YOU THINK THIS TRIAL WILL BE REMEMBERED BY HISTORY?
UNQUESTIONABLY, SQUIRT...
AN IMPEACHMENT TRIAL IS A ONCE-IN-A-CENTURY EVENT! HOWEVER FAIR YOU THINK IT IS, IT'S MOMENTOUS!
REALLY?
TRUST ME, YOU'LL BE TELLING YOUR GRANDKIDS ABOUT THIS!
YOU THINK MY SIDNEY BLUMENTHAL POSTER WILL BE WORTH SOMETHING?
NO QUESTION.
©B Trudeau

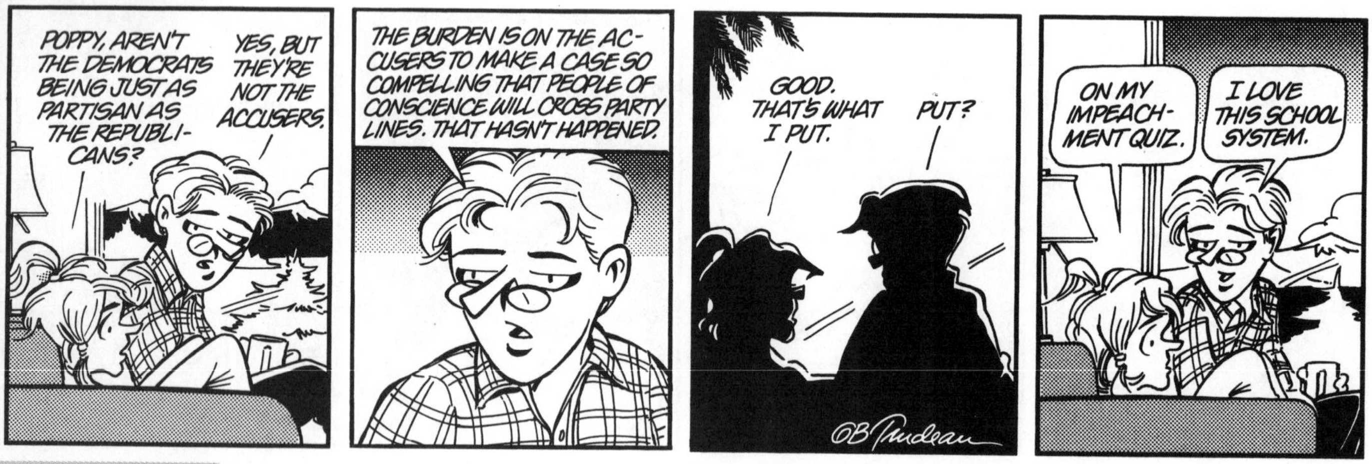
POPPY, AREN'T THE DEMOCRATS BEING JUST AS PARTISAN AS THE REPUBLICANS?
YES, BUT THEY'RE NOT THE ACCUSERS.
THE BURDEN IS ON THE ACCUSERS TO MAKE A CASE SO COMPELLING THAT PEOPLE OF CONSCIENCE WILL CROSS PARTY LINES. THAT HASN'T HAPPENED.
GOOD. THAT'S WHAT I PUT.
PUT?
©B Trudeau
ON MY IMPEACHMENT QUIZ.
I LOVE THIS SCHOOL SYSTEM.

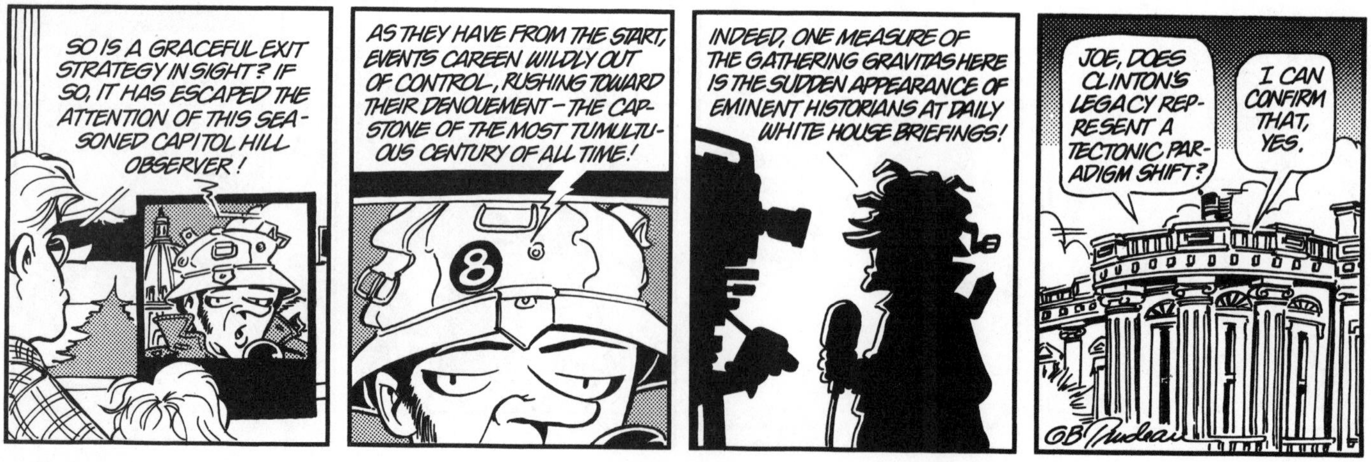
SO IS A GRACEFUL EXIT STRATEGY IN SIGHT? IF SO, IT HAS ESCAPED THE ATTENTION OF THIS SEASONED CAPITOL HILL OBSERVER!
AS THEY HAVE FROM THE START, EVENTS CAREEN WILDLY OUT OF CONTROL, RUSHING TOWARD THEIR DENOUEMENT – THE CAPSTONE OF THE MOST TUMULTUOUS CENTURY OF ALL TIME!
INDEED, ONE MEASURE OF THE GATHERING GRAVITAS HERE IS THE SUDDEN APPEARANCE OF EMINENT HISTORIANS AT DAILY WHITE HOUSE BRIEFINGS!
JOE, DOES CLINTON'S LEGACY REPRESENT A TECTONIC PARADIGM SHIFT?
I CAN CONFIRM THAT, YES.
©B Trudeau

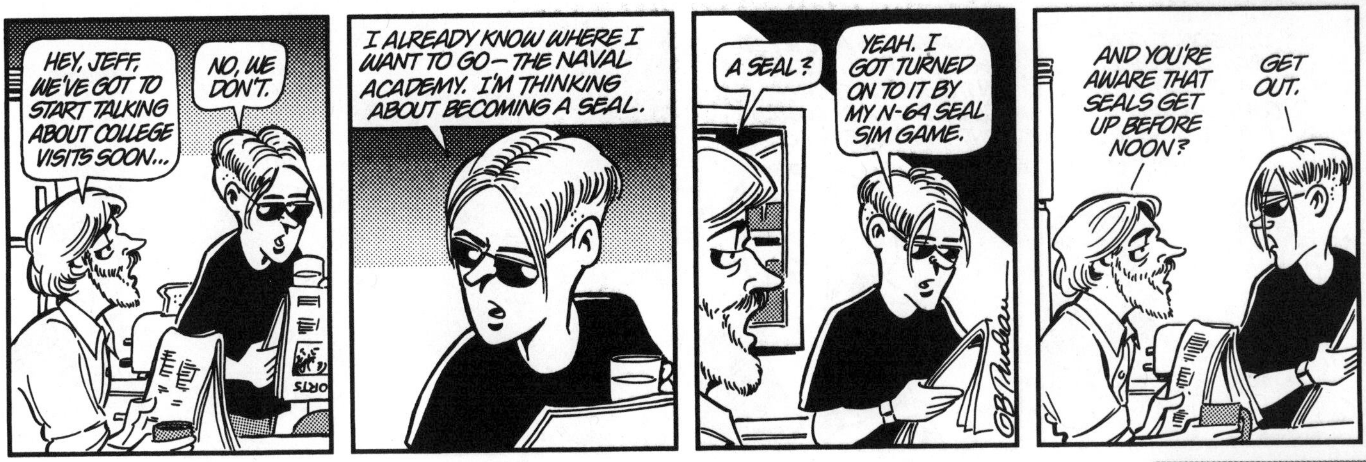
HEY, JEFF, WE'VE GOT TO START TALKING ABOUT COLLEGE VISITS SOON...
NO, WE DON'T.
I ALREADY KNOW WHERE I WANT TO GO – THE NAVAL ACADEMY. I'M THINKING ABOUT BECOMING A SEAL.
A SEAL?
YEAH. I GOT TURNED ON TO IT BY MY N-64 SEAL SIM GAME.
AND YOU'RE AWARE THAT SEALS GET UP BEFORE NOON?
GET OUT.

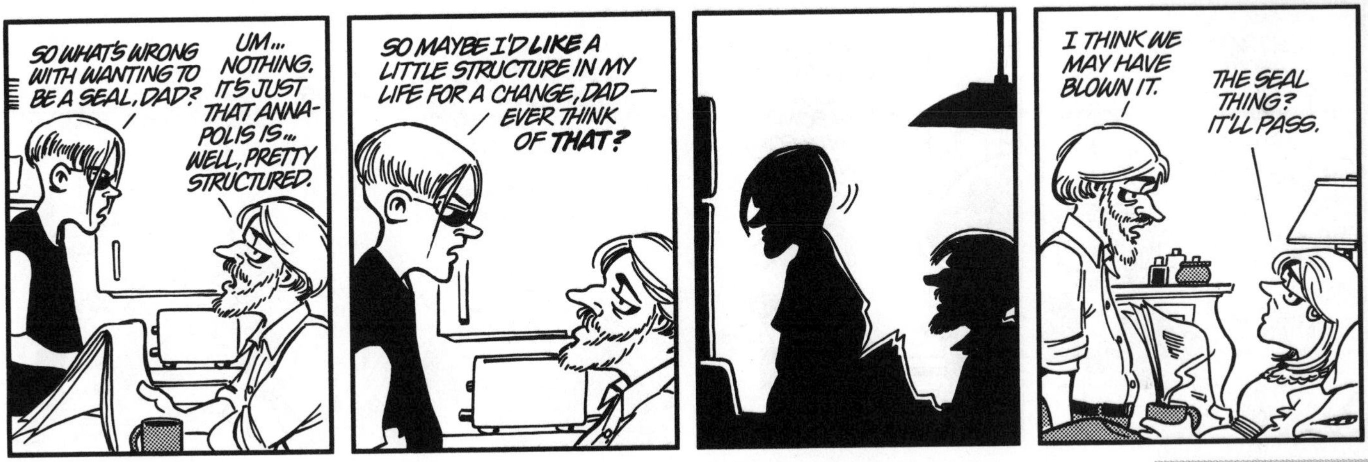
SO WHAT'S WRONG WITH WANTING TO BE A SEAL, DAD?
UM... NOTHING. IT'S JUST THAT ANNA-POLIS IS... WELL, PRETTY STRUCTURED.
SO MAYBE I'D LIKE A LITTLE STRUCTURE IN MY LIFE FOR A CHANGE, DAD – EVER THINK OF THAT?
I THINK WE MAY HAVE BLOWN IT.
THE SEAL THING? IT'LL PASS.

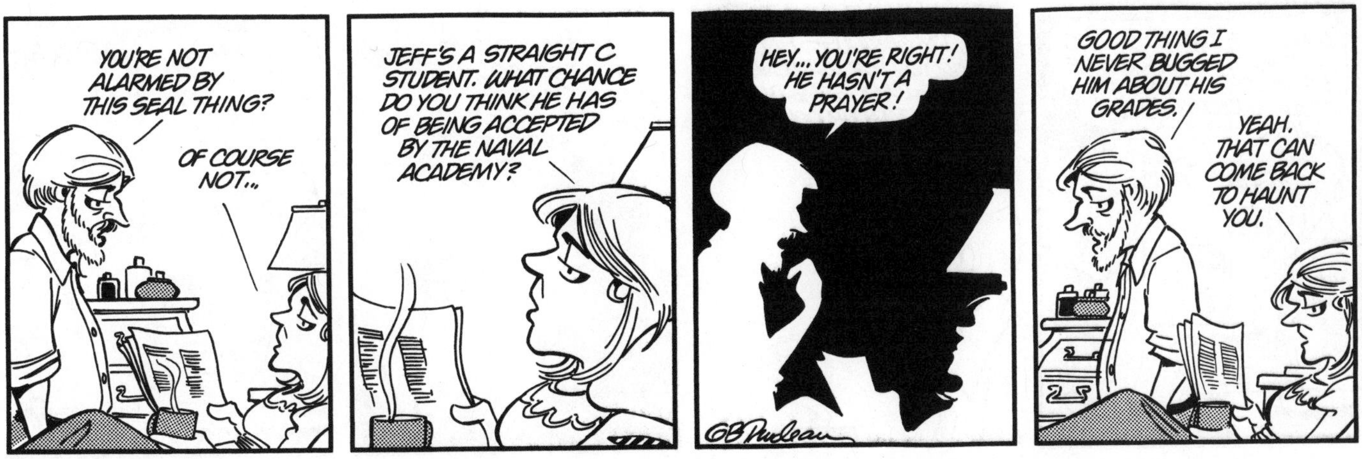
YOU'RE NOT ALARMED BY THIS SEAL THING?
OF COURSE NOT...
JEFF'S A STRAIGHT C STUDENT. WHAT CHANCE DO YOU THINK HE HAS OF BEING ACCEPTED BY THE NAVAL ACADEMY?
HEY... YOU'RE RIGHT! HE HASN'T A PRAYER!
GOOD THING I NEVER BUGGED HIM ABOUT HIS GRADES.
YEAH. THAT CAN COME BACK TO HAUNT YOU.

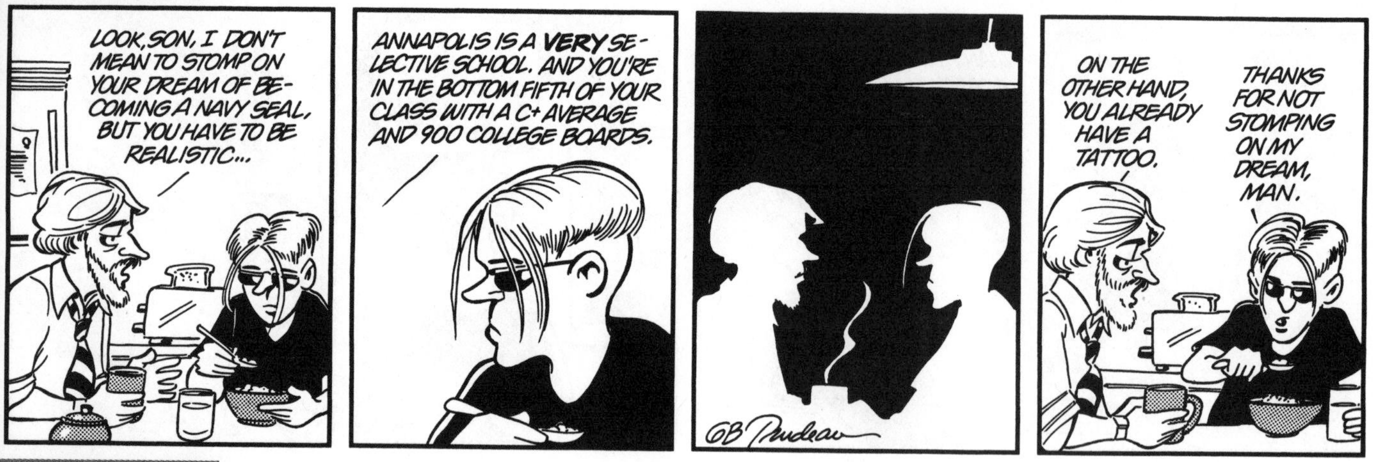
LOOK, SON, I DON'T MEAN TO STOMP ON YOUR DREAM OF BECOMING A NAVY SEAL, BUT YOU HAVE TO BE REALISTIC...
ANNAPOLIS IS A **VERY** SELECTIVE SCHOOL. AND YOU'RE IN THE BOTTOM FIFTH OF YOUR CLASS WITH A C+ AVERAGE AND 900 COLLEGE BOARDS.
ON THE OTHER HAND, YOU ALREADY HAVE A TATTOO.
THANKS FOR NOT STOMPING ON MY DREAM, MAN.

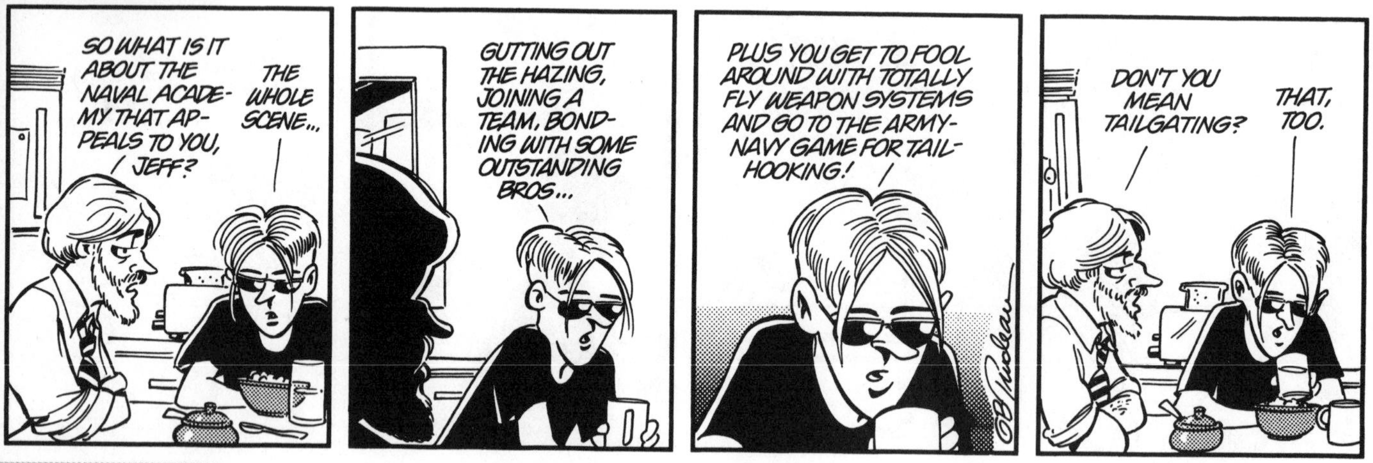
SO WHAT IS IT ABOUT THE NAVAL ACADEMY THAT APPEALS TO YOU, JEFF?
THE WHOLE SCENE...
GUTTING OUT THE HAZING, JOINING A TEAM, BONDING WITH SOME OUTSTANDING BROS...
PLUS YOU GET TO FOOL AROUND WITH TOTALLY FLY WEAPON SYSTEMS AND GO TO THE ARMY-NAVY GAME FOR TAILHOOKING!
DON'T YOU MEAN TAILGATING?
THAT, TOO.

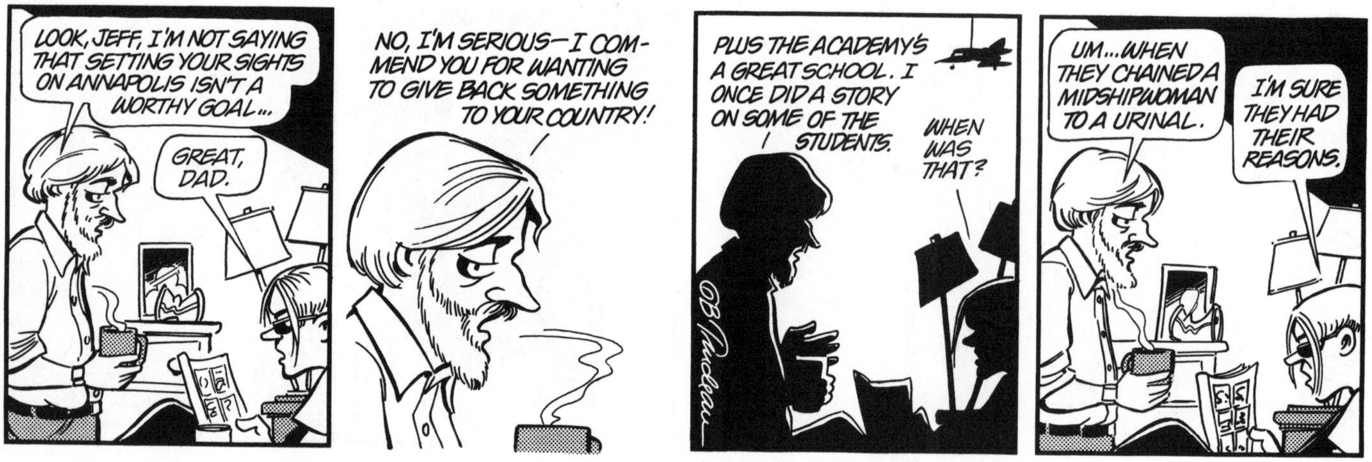
LOOK, JEFF, I'M NOT SAYING THAT SETTING YOUR SIGHTS ON ANNAPOLIS ISN'T A WORTHY GOAL...
GREAT, DAD.
NO, I'M SERIOUS—I COMMEND YOU FOR WANTING TO GIVE BACK SOMETHING TO YOUR COUNTRY!
PLUS THE ACADEMY'S A GREAT SCHOOL. I ONCE DID A STORY ON SOME OF THE STUDENTS.
WHEN WAS THAT?
UM...WHEN THEY CHAINED A MIDSHIPWOMAN TO A URINAL.
I'M SURE THEY HAD THEIR REASONS.

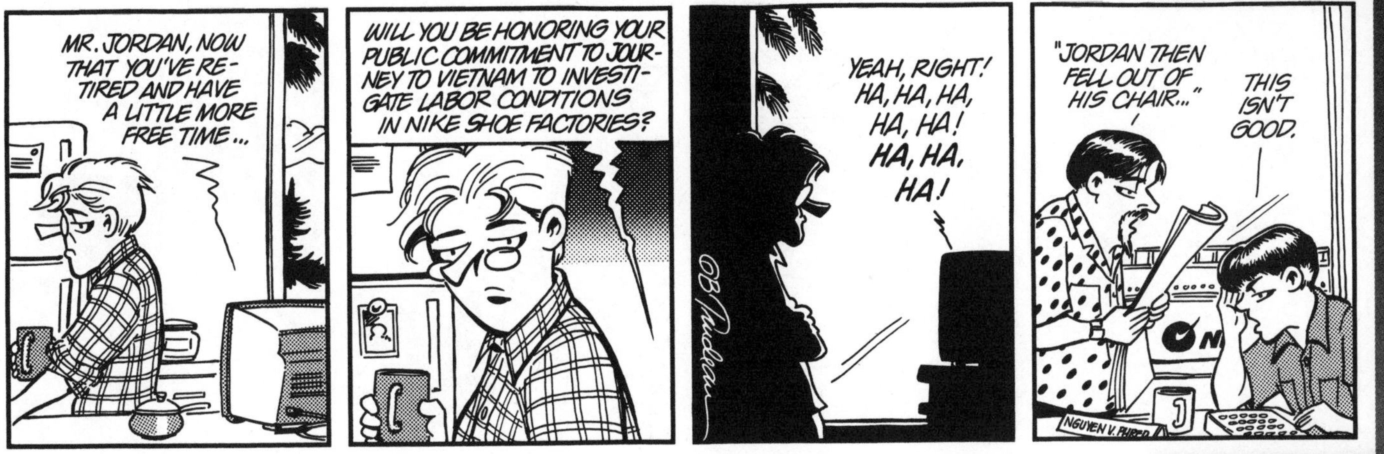
MR. JORDAN, NOW THAT YOU'VE RETIRED AND HAVE A LITTLE MORE FREE TIME...
WILL YOU BE HONORING YOUR PUBLIC COMMITMENT TO JOURNEY TO VIETNAM TO INVESTIGATE LABOR CONDITIONS IN NIKE SHOE FACTORIES?
YEAH, RIGHT! HA, HA, HA, HA, HA! HA, HA, HA!
"JORDAN THEN FELL OUT OF HIS CHAIR..."
THIS ISN'T GOOD.

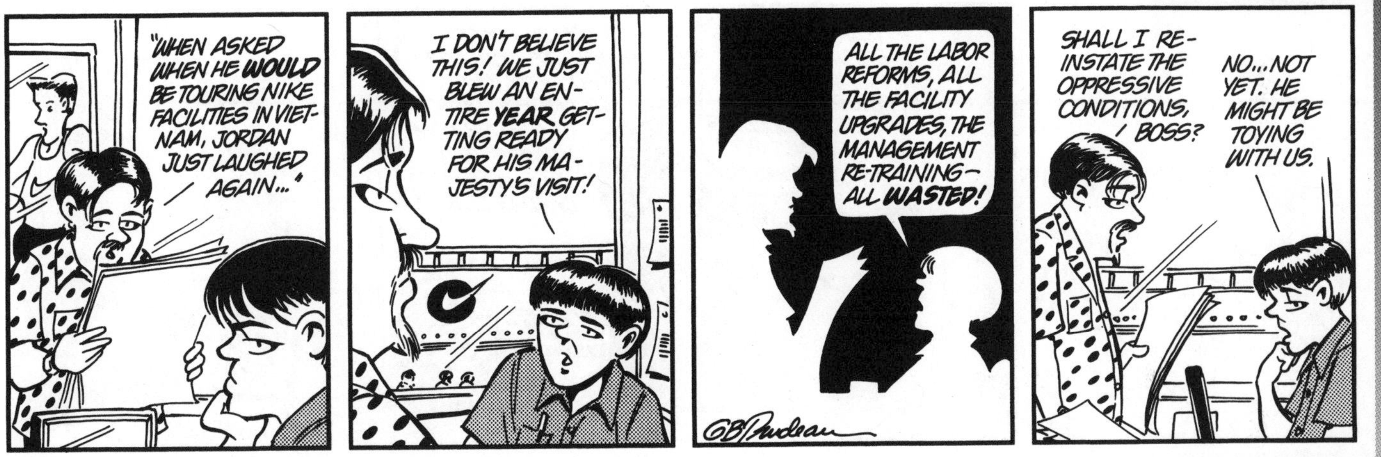
"WHEN ASKED WHEN HE WOULD BE TOURING NIKE FACILITIES IN VIETNAM, JORDAN JUST LAUGHED AGAIN..."
I DON'T BELIEVE THIS! WE JUST BLEW AN ENTIRE YEAR GETTING READY FOR HIS MAJESTY'S VISIT!
ALL THE LABOR REFORMS, ALL THE FACILITY UPGRADES, THE MANAGEMENT RE-TRAINING— ALL WASTED!
SHALL I REINSTATE THE OPPRESSIVE CONDITIONS, BOSS?
NO... NOT YET. HE MIGHT BE TOYING WITH US.

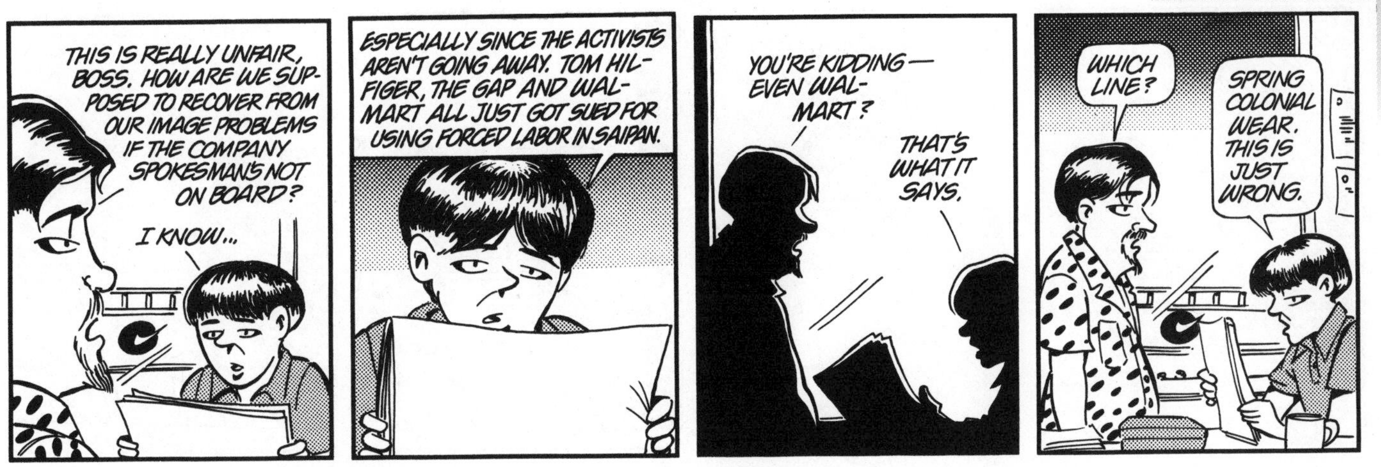
THIS IS REALLY UNFAIR, BOSS. HOW ARE WE SUPPOSED TO RECOVER FROM OUR IMAGE PROBLEMS IF THE COMPANY SPOKESMAN'S NOT ON BOARD?
I KNOW...
ESPECIALLY SINCE THE ACTIVISTS AREN'T GOING AWAY. TOM HILFIGER, THE GAP AND WAL-MART ALL JUST GOT SUED FOR USING FORCED LABOR IN SAIPAN.
YOU'RE KIDDING — EVEN WAL-MART?
THAT'S WHAT IT SAYS.
WHICH LINE?
SPRING COLONIAL WEAR. THIS IS JUST WRONG.

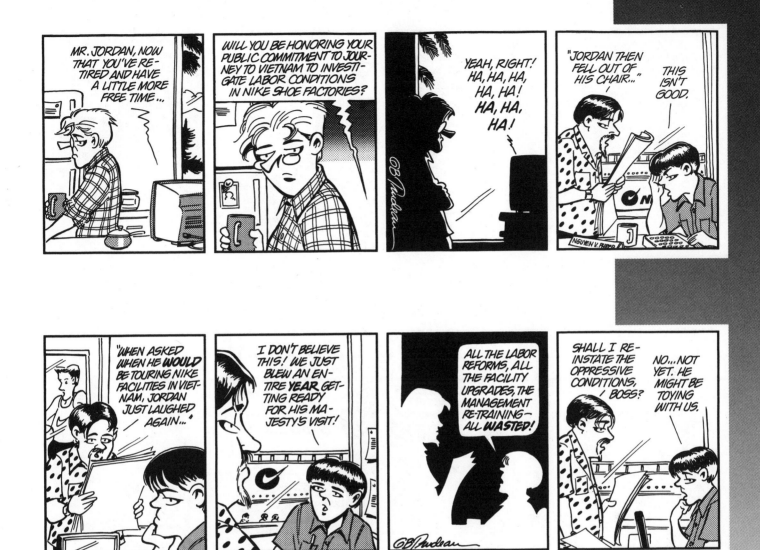

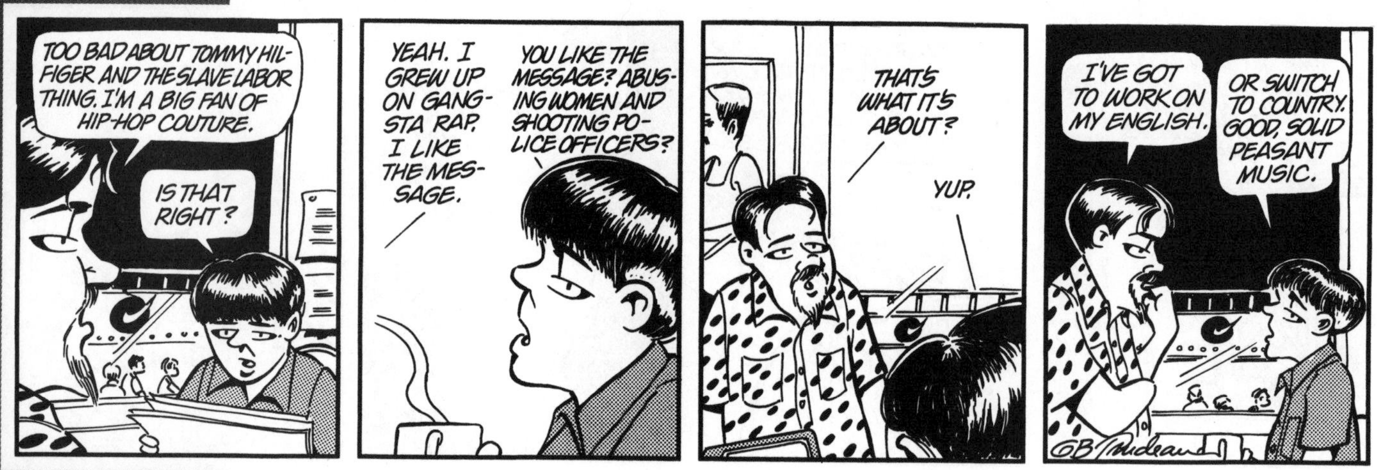
TOO BAD ABOUT TOMMY HILFIGER AND THE SLAVE LABOR THING. I'M A BIG FAN OF HIP-HOP COUTURE.
IS THAT RIGHT?
YEAH. I GREW UP ON GANGSTA RAP. I LIKE THE MESSAGE.
YOU LIKE THE MESSAGE? ABUSING WOMEN AND SHOOTING POLICE OFFICERS?
THAT'S WHAT IT'S ABOUT?
YUP.
I'VE GOT TO WORK ON MY ENGLISH.
OR SWITCH TO COUNTRY. GOOD, SOLID PEASANT MUSIC.

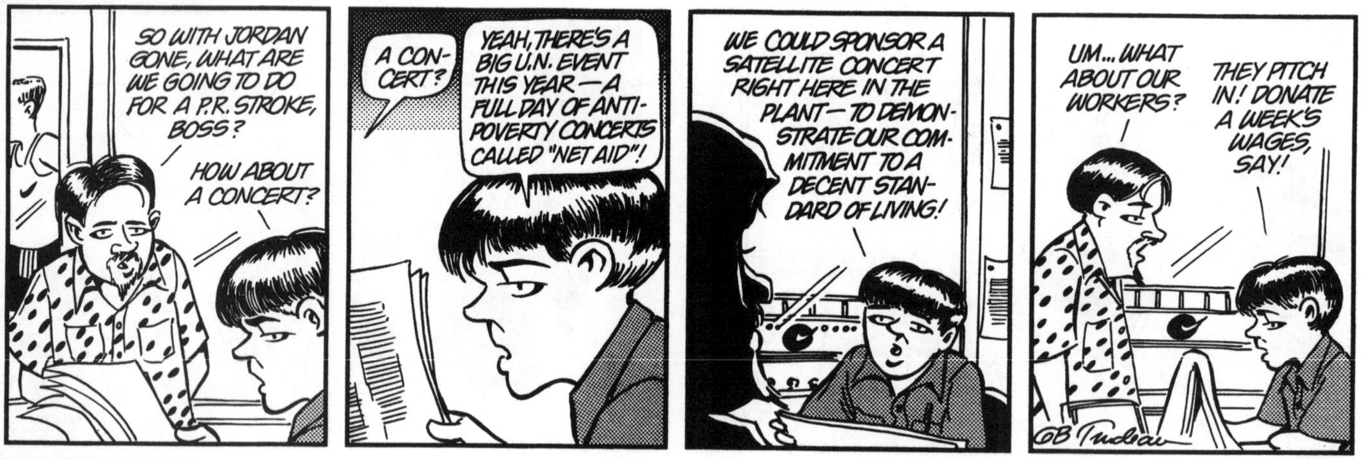
SO WITH JORDAN GONE, WHAT ARE WE GOING TO DO FOR A P.R. STROKE, BOSS?
HOW ABOUT A CONCERT?
A CONCERT?
YEAH, THERE'S A BIG U.N. EVENT THIS YEAR — A FULL DAY OF ANTI-POVERTY CONCERTS CALLED "NET AID"!
WE COULD SPONSOR A SATELLITE CONCERT RIGHT HERE IN THE PLANT — TO DEMONSTRATE OUR COMMITMENT TO A DECENT STANDARD OF LIVING!
UM... WHAT ABOUT OUR WORKERS?
THEY PITCH IN! DONATE A WEEK'S WAGES, SAY!

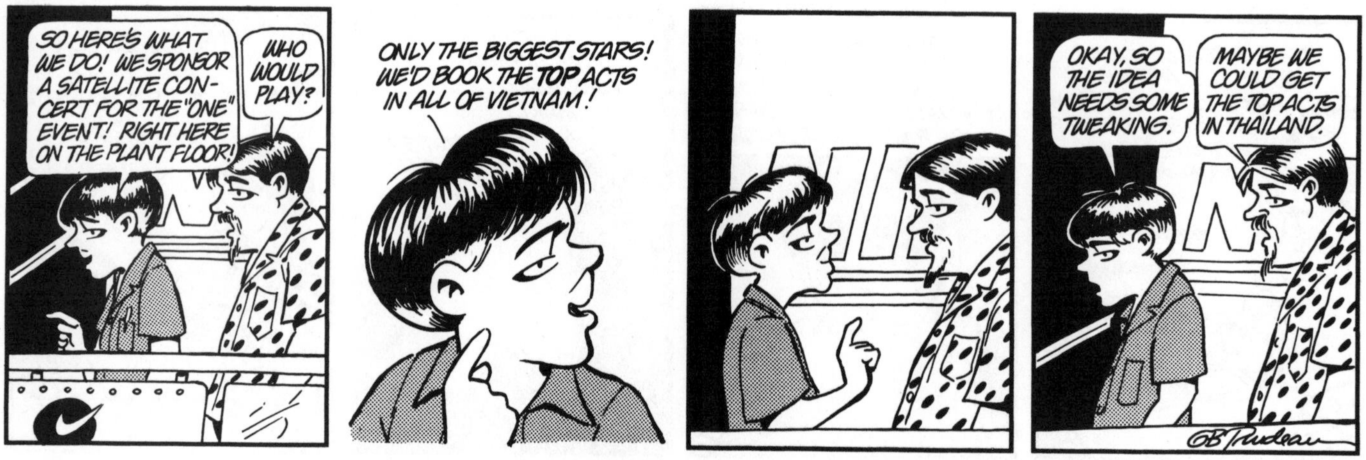
SO HERE'S WHAT WE DO! WE SPONSOR A SATELLITE CONCERT FOR THE "ONE" EVENT! RIGHT HERE ON THE PLANT FLOOR!
WHO WOULD PLAY?
ONLY THE BIGGEST STARS! WE'D BOOK THE TOP ACTS IN ALL OF VIETNAM!
OKAY, SO THE IDEA NEEDS SOME TWEAKING.
MAYBE WE COULD GET THE TOP ACTS IN THAILAND.

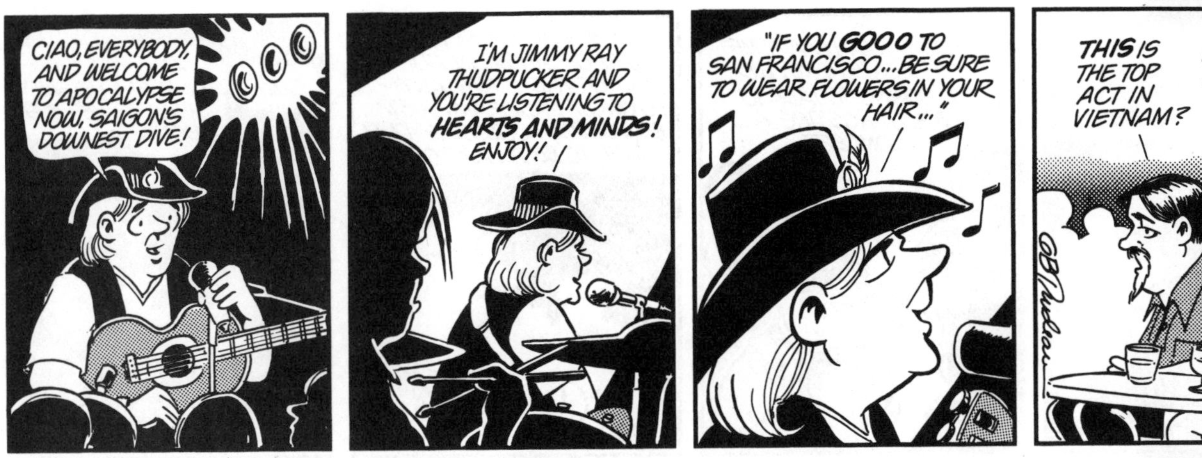
CIAO, EVERYBODY, AND WELCOME TO APOCALYPSE NOW, SAIGON'S DOWNEST DIVE!
I'M JIMMY RAY THUDPUCKER AND YOU'RE LISTENING TO **HEARTS AND MINDS**! ENJOY!
"IF YOU **GOOO** TO SAN FRANCISCO... BE SURE TO WEAR FLOWERS IN YOUR HAIR..."
THIS IS THE TOP ACT IN VIETNAM?
BE PATIENT– HE DOES A KILLER "MANDY."

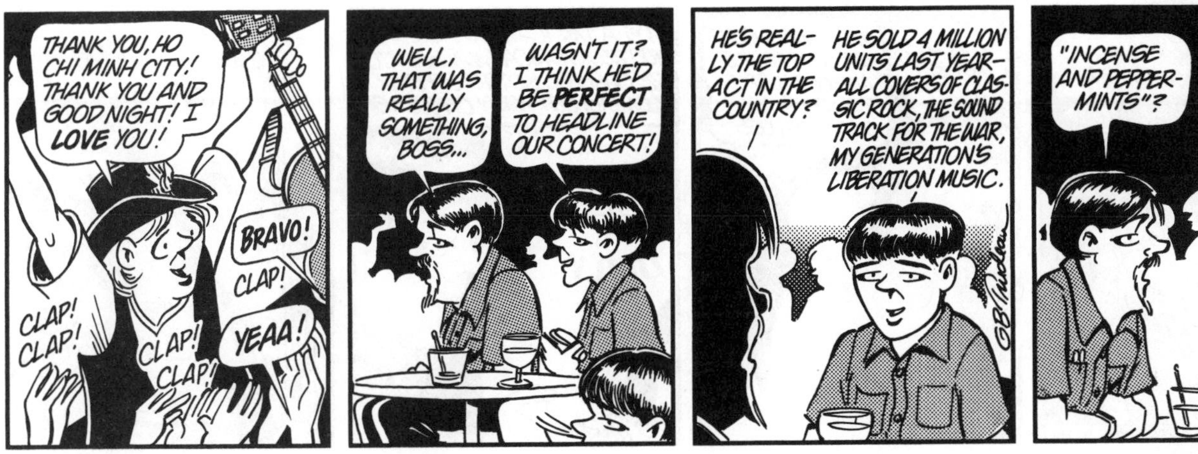
THANK YOU, HO CHI MINH CITY! THANK YOU AND GOOD NIGHT! I **LOVE** YOU!
BRAVO!
CLAP!
CLAP! CLAP!
CLAP! CLAP!
YEAA!
WELL, THAT WAS REALLY SOMETHING, BOSS...
WASN'T IT? I THINK HE'D BE **PERFECT** TO HEADLINE OUR CONCERT!
HE'S REALLY THE TOP ACT IN THE COUNTRY?
HE SOLD 4 MILLION UNITS LAST YEAR– ALL COVERS OF CLASSIC ROCK, THE SOUND TRACK FOR THE WAR, MY GENERATION'S LIBERATION MUSIC.
"INCENSE AND PEPPERMINTS"?
IT WAS PLAYING AT A CAFÉ I BLEW UP.

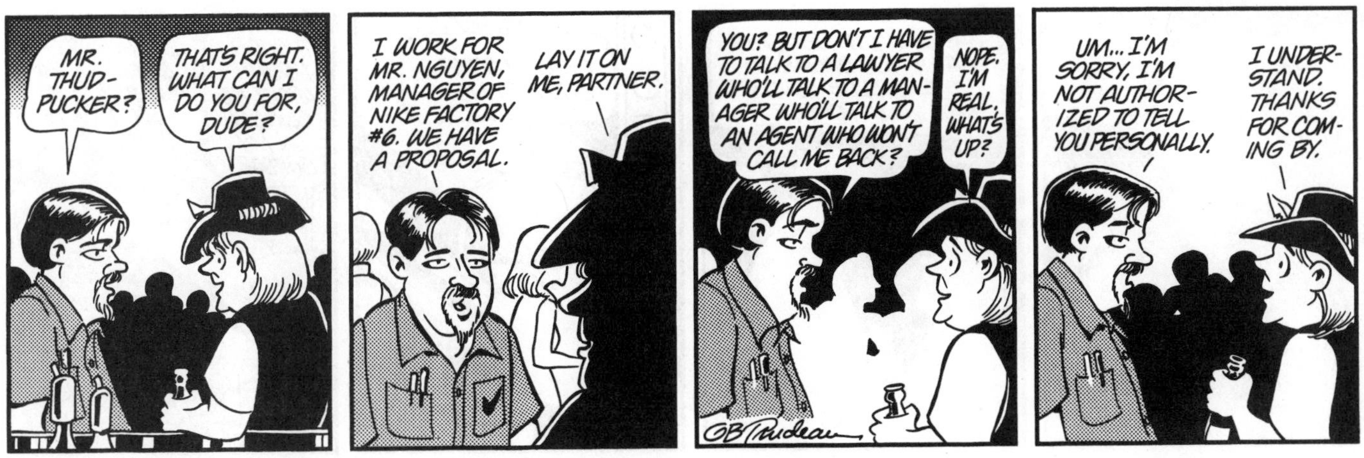
MR. THUDPUCKER?
THAT'S RIGHT. WHAT CAN I DO YOU FOR, DUDE?
I WORK FOR MR. NGUYEN, MANAGER OF NIKE FACTORY #6. WE HAVE A PROPOSAL.
LAY IT ON ME, PARTNER.
YOU? BUT DON'T I HAVE TO TALK TO A LAWYER WHO'LL TALK TO A MANAGER WHO'LL TALK TO AN AGENT WHO WON'T CALL ME BACK?
NOPE. I'M REAL. WHAT'S UP?
UM... I'M SORRY, I'M NOT AUTHORIZED TO TELL YOU PERSONALLY.
I UNDERSTAND. THANKS FOR COMING BY.

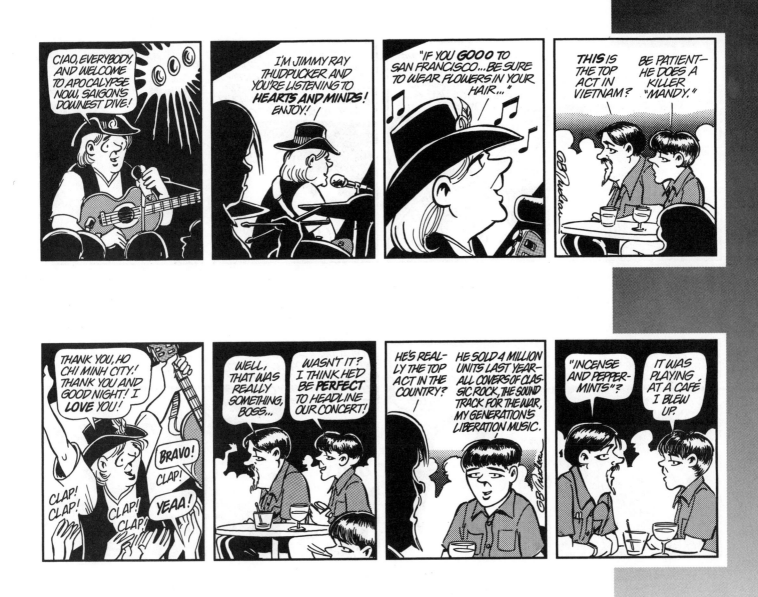

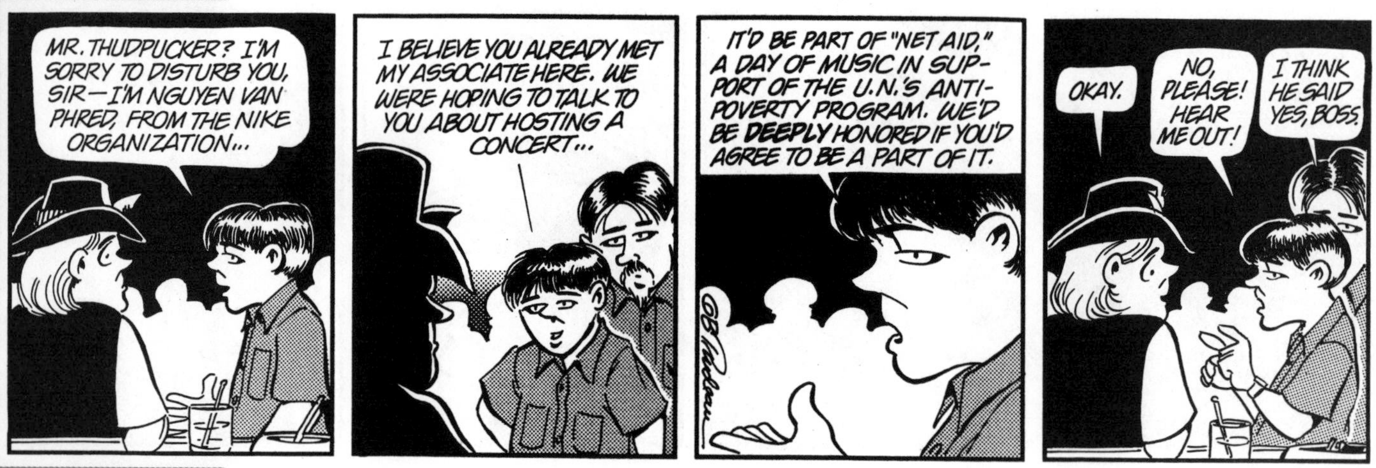
MR. THUDPUCKER? I'M SORRY TO DISTURB YOU, SIR—I'M NGUYEN VAN PHRED, FROM THE NIKE ORGANIZATION...
I BELIEVE YOU ALREADY MET MY ASSOCIATE HERE. WE WERE HOPING TO TALK TO YOU ABOUT HOSTING A CONCERT...
IT'D BE PART OF "NET AID," A DAY OF MUSIC IN SUPPORT OF THE U.N.'S ANTI-POVERTY PROGRAM. WE'D BE DEEPLY HONORED IF YOU'D AGREE TO BE A PART OF IT.
OKAY.
NO, PLEASE! HEAR ME OUT!
I THINK HE SAID YES, BOSS.

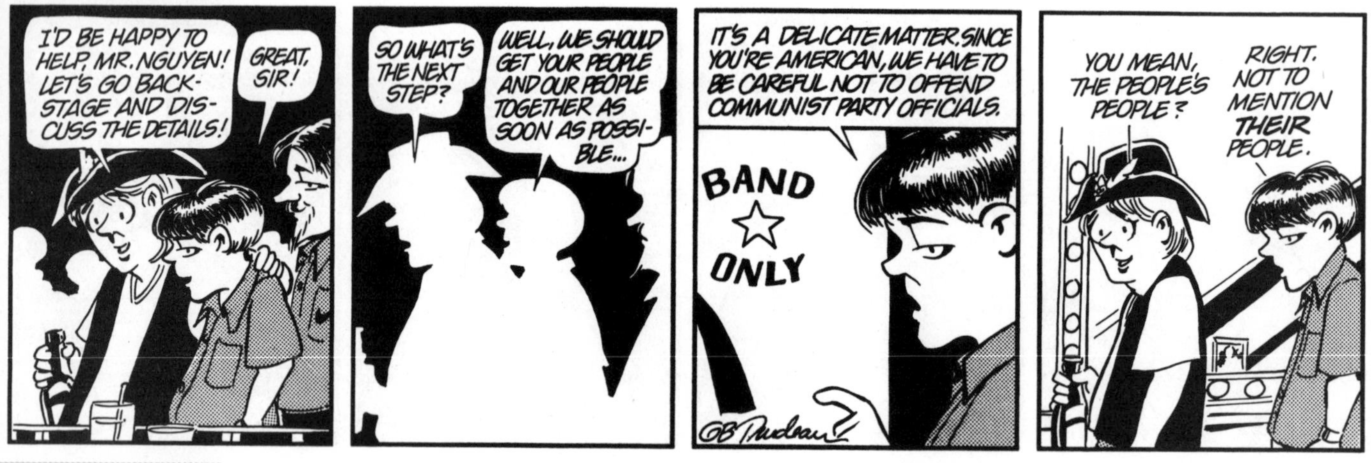
I'D BE HAPPY TO HELP, MR. NGUYEN! LET'S GO BACKSTAGE AND DISCUSS THE DETAILS!
GREAT, SIR!
SO WHAT'S THE NEXT STEP?
WELL, WE SHOULD GET YOUR PEOPLE AND OUR PEOPLE TOGETHER AS SOON AS POSSIBLE...
IT'S A DELICATE MATTER. SINCE YOU'RE AMERICAN, WE HAVE TO BE CAREFUL NOT TO OFFEND COMMUNIST PARTY OFFICIALS.
BAND ☆ ONLY
YOU MEAN, THE PEOPLE'S PEOPLE?
RIGHT. NOT TO MENTION THEIR PEOPLE.

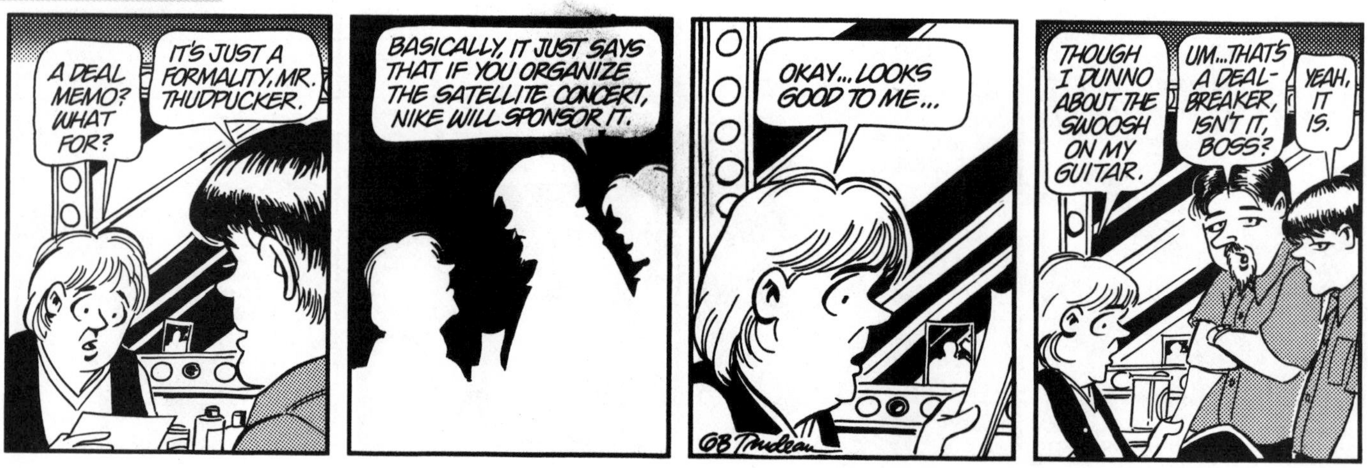
A DEAL MEMO? WHAT FOR?
IT'S JUST A FORMALITY, MR. THUDPUCKER.
BASICALLY, IT JUST SAYS THAT IF YOU ORGANIZE THE SATELLITE CONCERT, NIKE WILL SPONSOR IT.
OKAY... LOOKS GOOD TO ME...
THOUGH I DUNNO ABOUT THE SWOOSH ON MY GUITAR.
UM... THAT'S A DEAL-BREAKER, ISN'T IT, BOSS?
YEAH, IT IS.

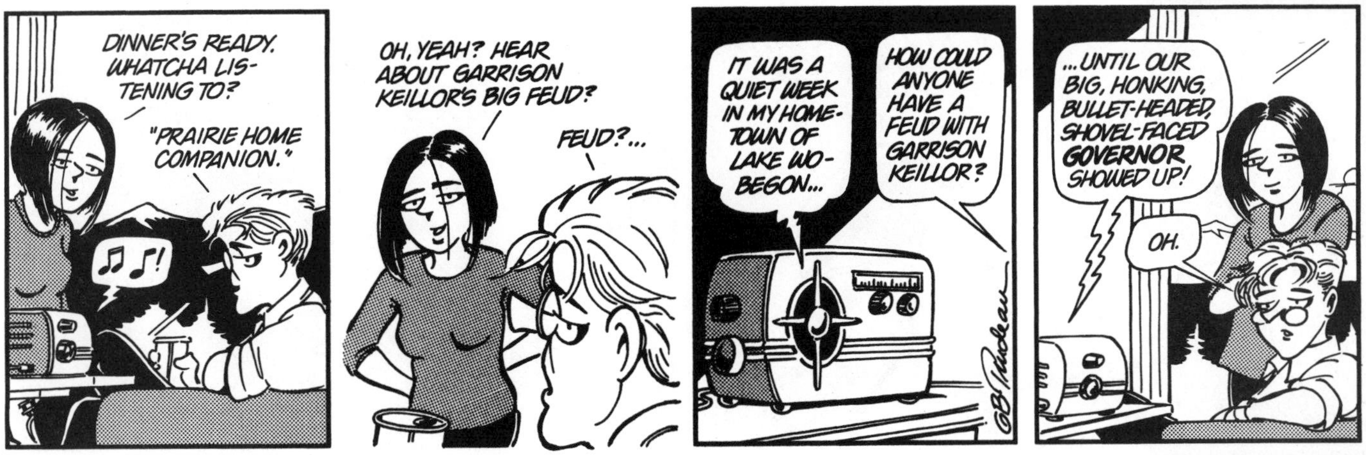
DINNER'S READY. WHATCHA LISTENING TO?
"PRAIRIE HOME COMPANION."
♫♪!
OH, YEAH? HEAR ABOUT GARRISON KEILLOR'S BIG FEUD?
FEUD?...
IT WAS A QUIET WEEK IN MY HOMETOWN OF LAKE WOBEGON...
HOW COULD ANYONE HAVE A FEUD WITH GARRISON KEILLOR?
...UNTIL OUR BIG, HONKING, BULLET-HEADED, SHOVEL-FACED **GOVERNOR** SHOWED UP!
OH.
GB Trudeau

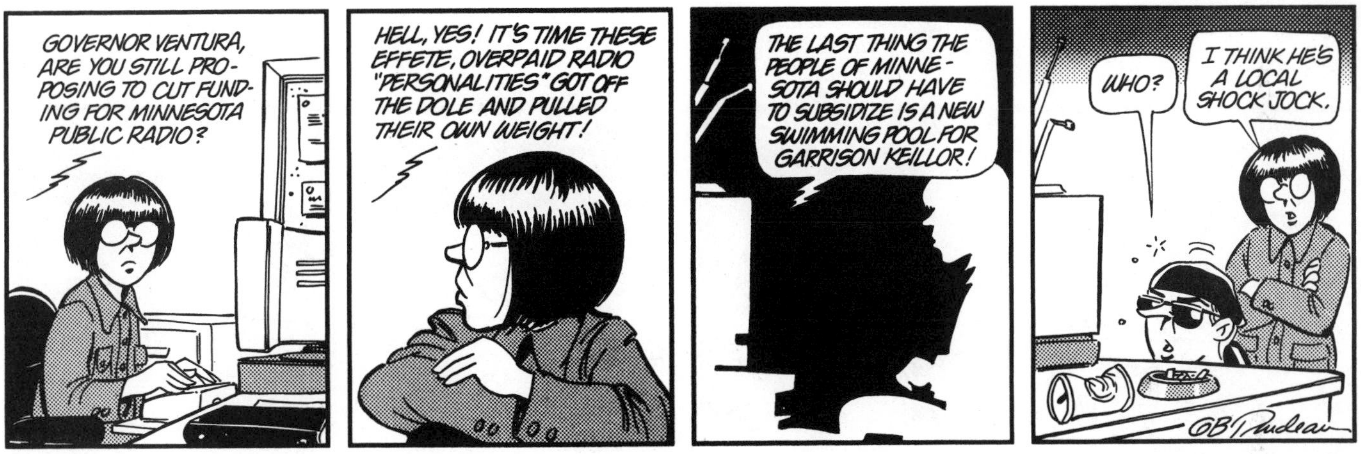
GOVERNOR VENTURA, ARE YOU STILL PROPOSING TO CUT FUNDING FOR MINNESOTA PUBLIC RADIO?
HELL, YES! IT'S TIME THESE EFFETE, OVERPAID RADIO "PERSONALITIES" GOT OFF THE DOLE AND PULLED THEIR OWN WEIGHT!
THE LAST THING THE PEOPLE OF MINNESOTA SHOULD HAVE TO SUBSIDIZE IS A NEW SWIMMING POOL FOR GARRISON KEILLOR!
WHO?
I THINK HE'S A LOCAL SHOCK JOCK.
GB Trudeau

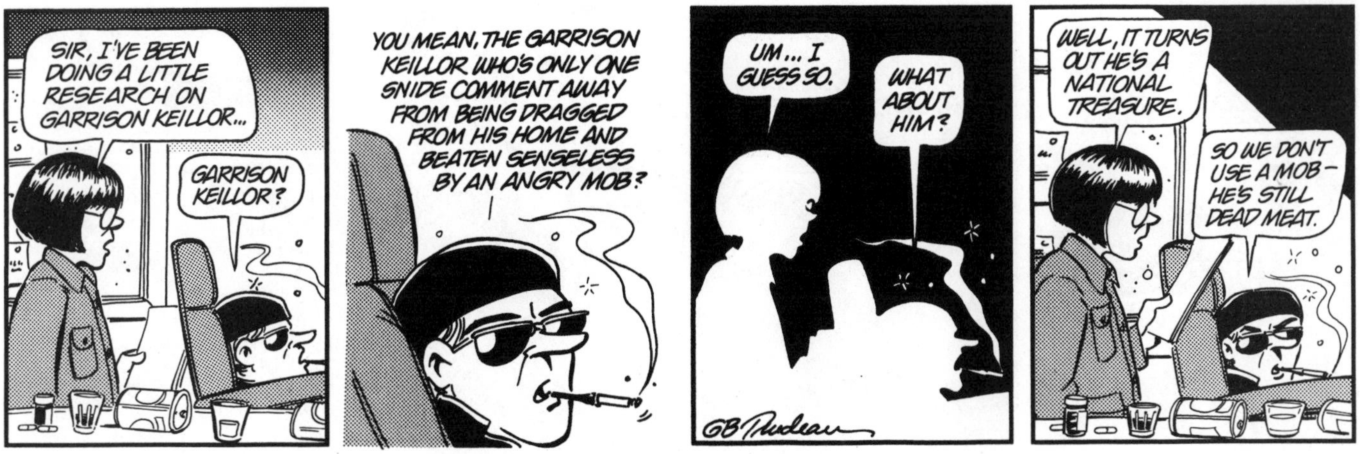
SIR, I'VE BEEN DOING A LITTLE RESEARCH ON GARRISON KEILLOR...
GARRISON KEILLOR?
YOU MEAN, THE GARRISON KEILLOR WHO'S ONLY ONE SNIDE COMMENT AWAY FROM BEING DRAGGED FROM HIS HOME AND BEATEN SENSELESS BY AN ANGRY MOB?
UM... I GUESS SO.
WHAT ABOUT HIM?
GB Trudeau
WELL, IT TURNS OUT HE'S A NATIONAL TREASURE.
SO WE DON'T USE A MOB – HE'S STILL DEAD MEAT.

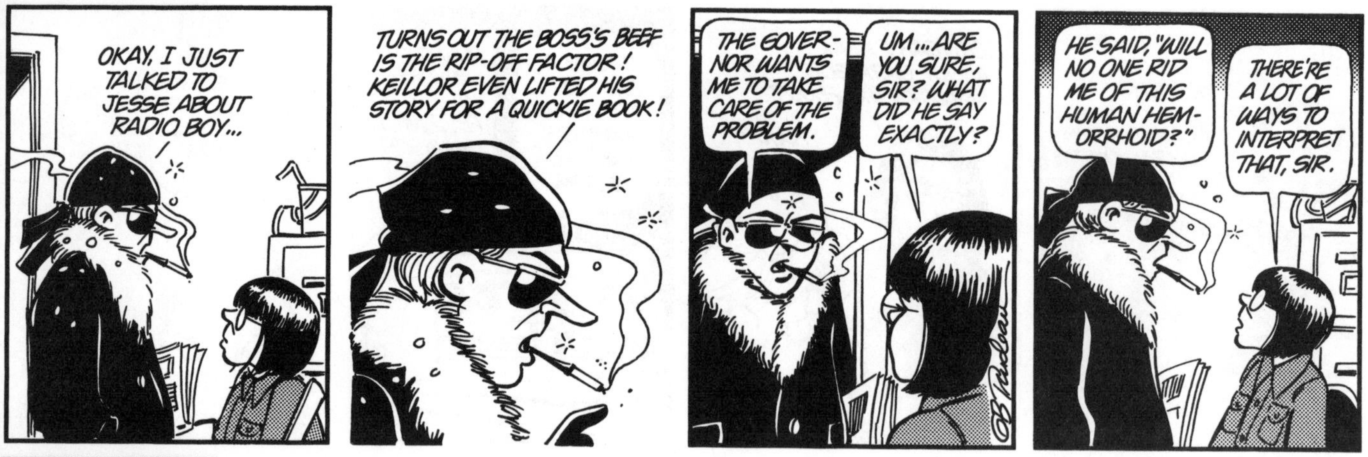
OKAY, I JUST TALKED TO JESSE ABOUT RADIO BOY...
TURNS OUT THE BOSS'S BEEF IS THE RIP-OFF FACTOR! KEILLOR EVEN LIFTED HIS STORY FOR A QUICKIE BOOK!
THE GOVERNOR WANTS ME TO TAKE CARE OF THE PROBLEM.
UM...ARE YOU SURE, SIR? WHAT DID HE SAY EXACTLY?
HE SAID, "WILL NO ONE RID ME OF THIS HUMAN HEMORRHOID?"
THERE'RE A LOT OF WAYS TO INTERPRET THAT, SIR.

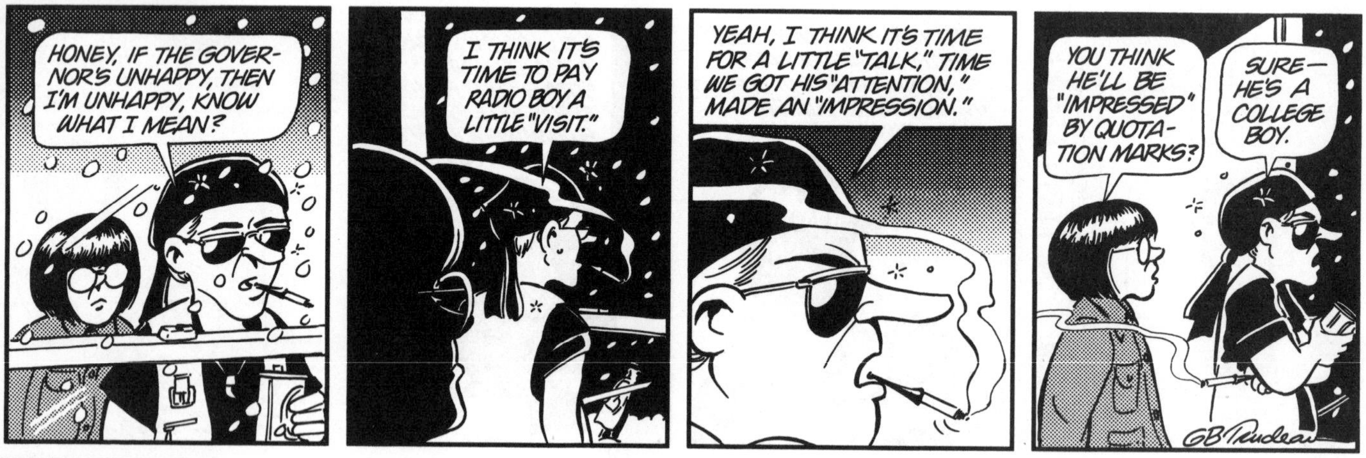
HONEY, IF THE GOVERNOR'S UNHAPPY, THEN I'M UNHAPPY, KNOW WHAT I MEAN?
I THINK IT'S TIME TO PAY RADIO BOY A LITTLE "VISIT."
YEAH, I THINK IT'S TIME FOR A LITTLE "TALK," TIME WE GOT HIS "ATTENTION," MADE AN "IMPRESSION."
YOU THINK HE'LL BE "IMPRESSED" BY QUOTATION MARKS?
SURE— HE'S A COLLEGE BOY.

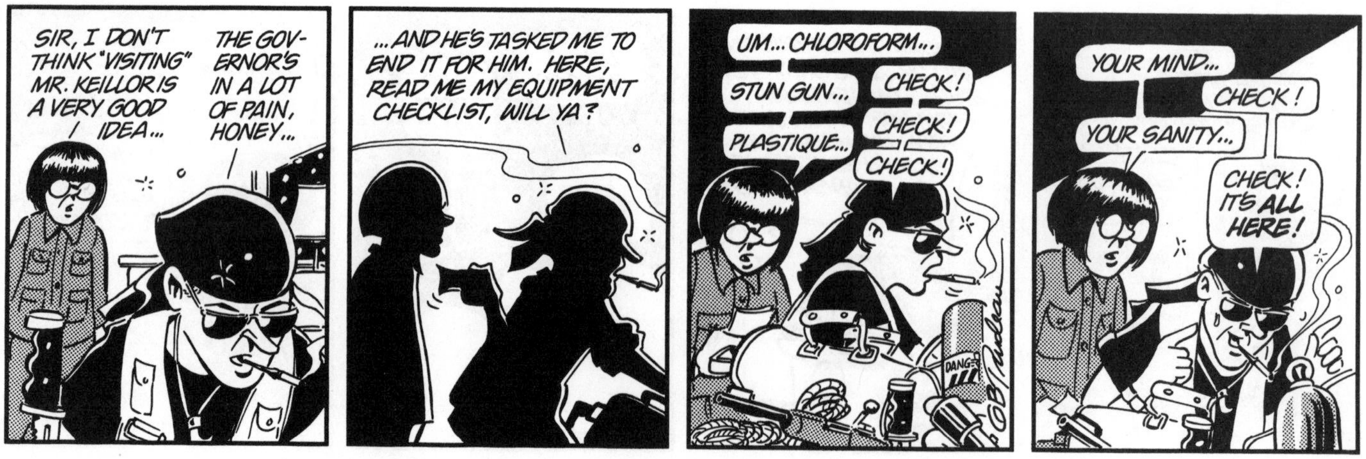
SIR, I DON'T THINK "VISITING" MR. KEILLOR IS A VERY GOOD IDEA...
THE GOVERNOR'S IN A LOT OF PAIN, HONEY...
...AND HE'S TASKED ME TO END IT FOR HIM. HERE, READ ME MY EQUIPMENT CHECKLIST, WILL YA?
UM... CHLOROFORM...
STUN GUN...
CHECK!
PLASTIQUE...
CHECK!
CHECK!
YOUR MIND...
CHECK!
YOUR SANITY...
CHECK! IT'S ALL HERE!

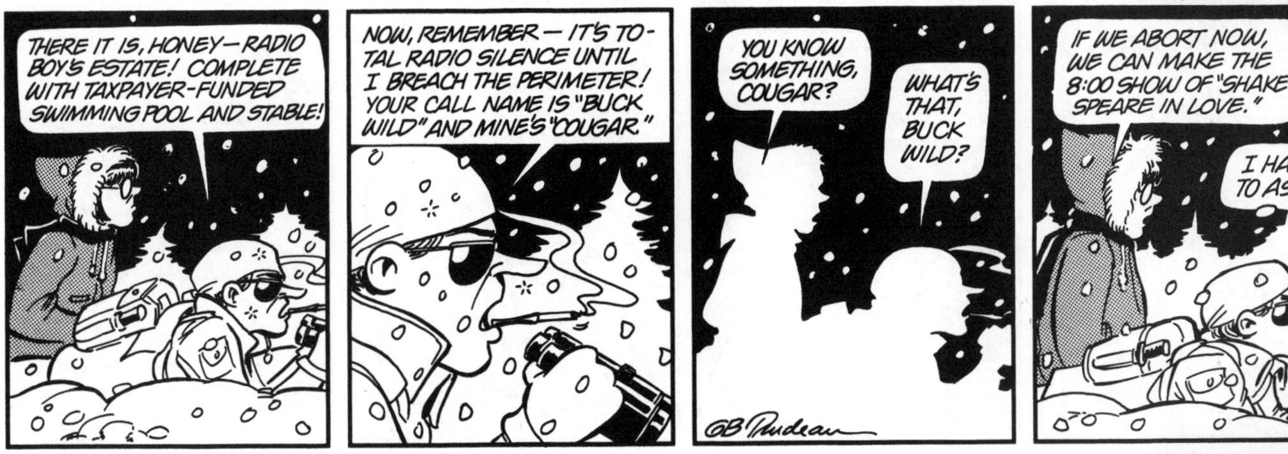
THERE IT IS, HONEY—RADIO BOY'S ESTATE! COMPLETE WITH TAXPAYER-FUNDED SWIMMING POOL AND STABLE!
NOW, REMEMBER — IT'S TOTAL RADIO SILENCE UNTIL I BREACH THE PERIMETER! YOUR CALL NAME IS "BUCK WILD" AND MINE'S "COUGAR."
YOU KNOW SOMETHING, COUGAR?
WHAT'S THAT, BUCK WILD?
IF WE ABORT NOW, WE CAN MAKE THE 8:00 SHOW OF "SHAKESPEARE IN LOVE."
I HAD TO ASK.

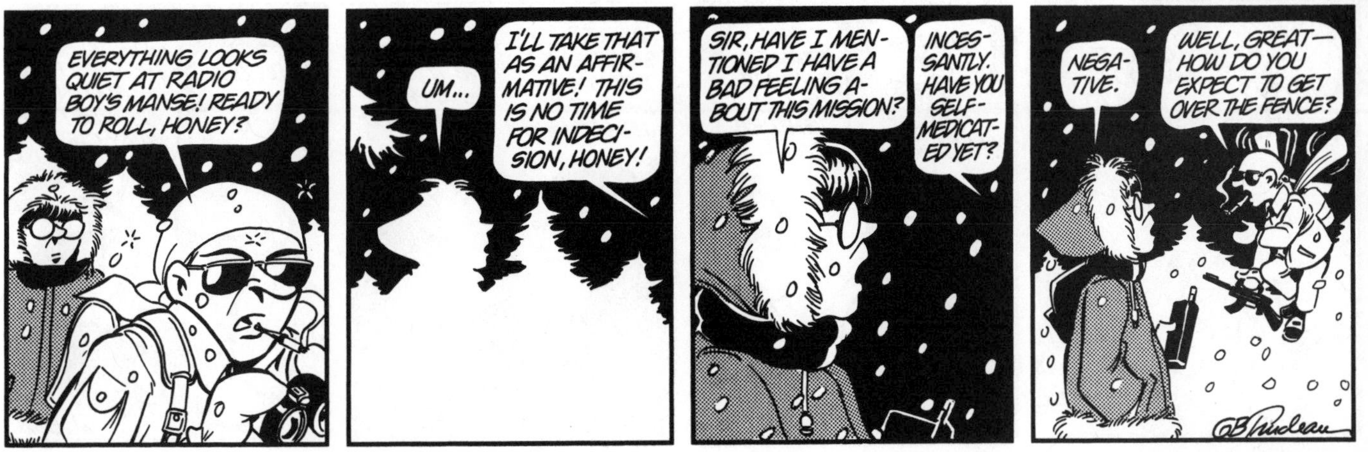
EVERYTHING LOOKS QUIET AT RADIO BOY'S MANSE! READY TO ROLL, HONEY?
UM...
I'LL TAKE THAT AS AN AFFIRMATIVE! THIS IS NO TIME FOR INDECISION, HONEY!
SIR, HAVE I MENTIONED I HAVE A BAD FEELING ABOUT THIS MISSION?
INCESSANTLY. HAVE YOU SELF-MEDICATED YET?
NEGATIVE.
WELL, GREAT—HOW DO YOU EXPECT TO GET OVER THE FENCE?

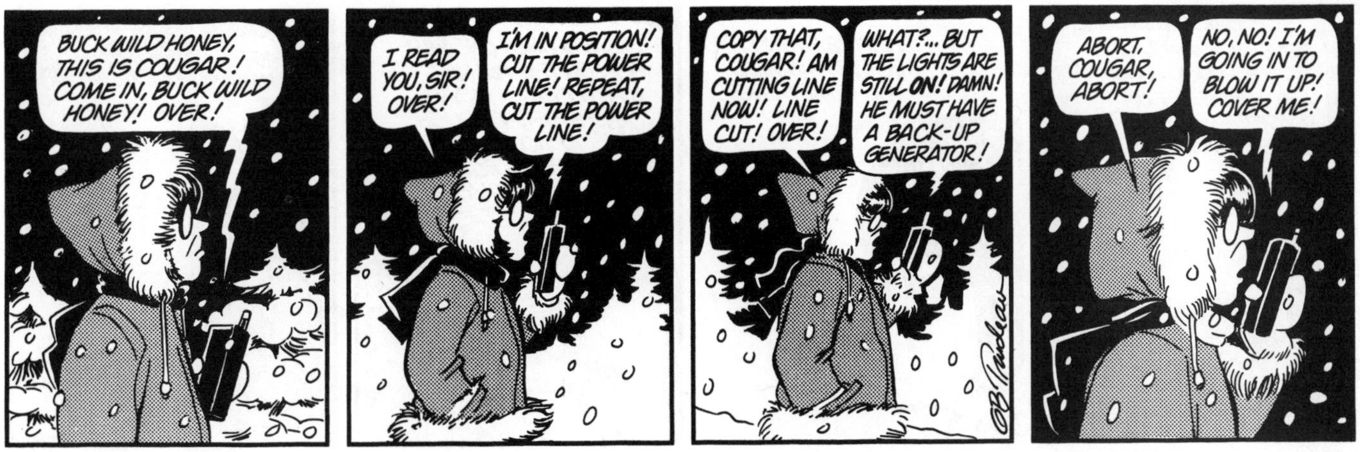
BUCK WILD HONEY, THIS IS COUGAR! COME IN, BUCK WILD HONEY! OVER!
I READ YOU, SIR! OVER!
I'M IN POSITION! CUT THE POWER LINE! REPEAT, CUT THE POWER LINE!
COPY THAT, COUGAR! AM CUTTING LINE NOW! LINE CUT! OVER!
WHAT?... BUT THE LIGHTS ARE STILL ON! DAMN! HE MUST HAVE A BACK-UP GENERATOR!
ABORT, COUGAR, ABORT!
NO, NO! I'M GOING IN TO BLOW IT UP! COVER ME!

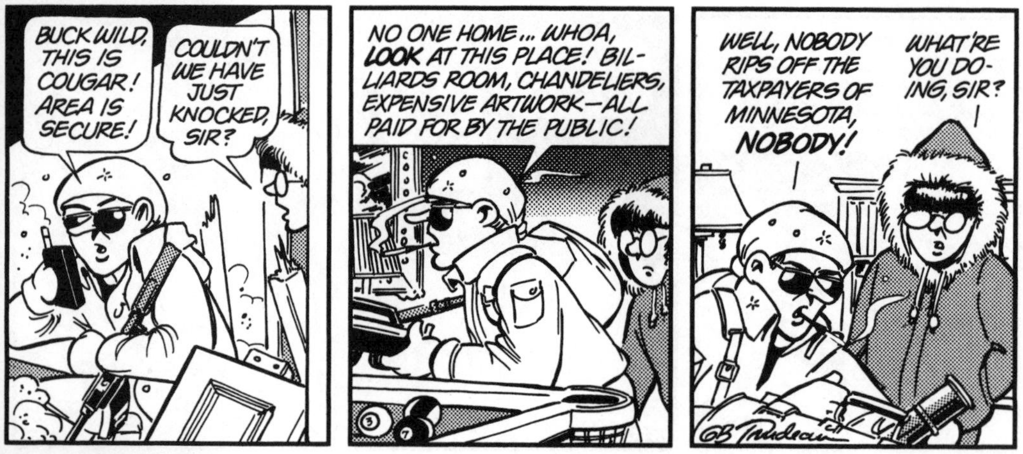
BUCK WILD, THIS IS COUGAR! AREA IS SECURE!
COULDN'T WE HAVE JUST KNOCKED, SIR?
NO ONE HOME... WHOA, LOOK AT THIS PLACE! BILLIARDS ROOM, CHANDELIERS, EXPENSIVE ARTWORK—ALL PAID FOR BY THE PUBLIC!
WELL, NOBODY RIPS OFF THE TAXPAYERS OF MINNESOTA, NOBODY!
WHAT'RE YOU DOING, SIR?
TIME TO RE-DECORATE, RADIO BOY!
I'LL JUST WAIT OUTSIDE, SIR.

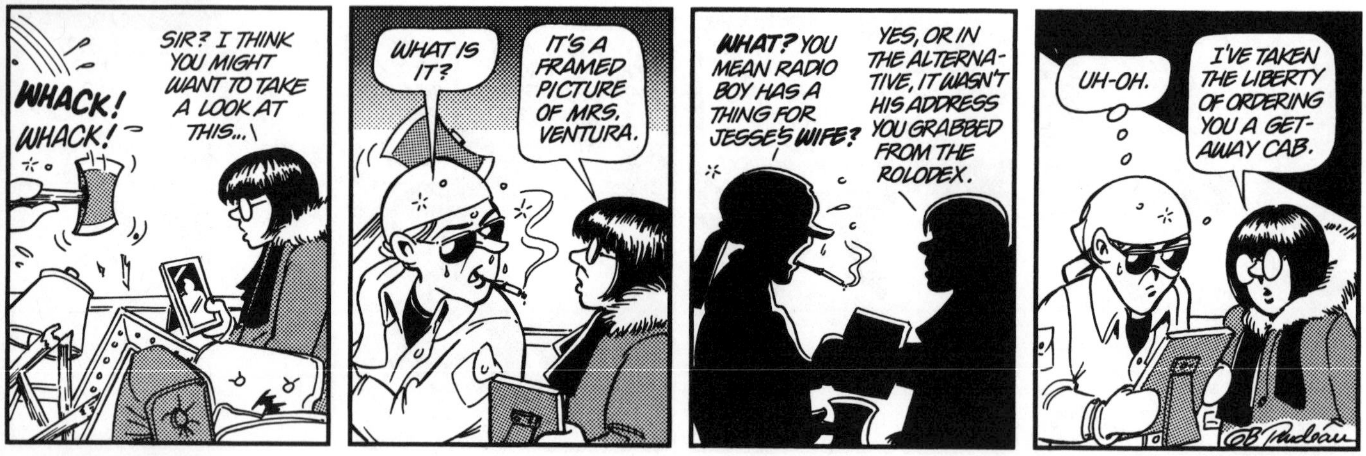
WHACK! WHACK!
SIR? I THINK YOU MIGHT WANT TO TAKE A LOOK AT THIS...
WHAT IS IT?
IT'S A FRAMED PICTURE OF MRS. VENTURA.
WHAT? YOU MEAN RADIO BOY HAS A THING FOR JESSE'S WIFE?
YES, OR IN THE ALTERNATIVE, IT WASN'T HIS ADDRESS YOU GRABBED FROM THE ROLODEX.
UH-OH.
I'VE TAKEN THE LIBERTY OF ORDERING YOU A GETAWAY CAB.

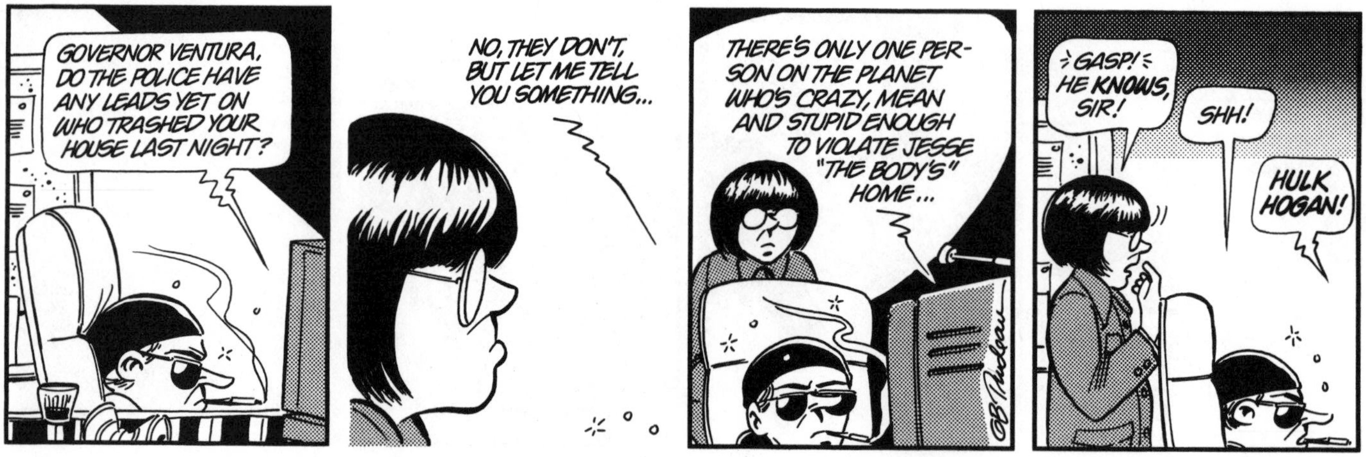
GOVERNOR VENTURA, DO THE POLICE HAVE ANY LEADS YET ON WHO TRASHED YOUR HOUSE LAST NIGHT?
NO, THEY DON'T, BUT LET ME TELL YOU SOMETHING...
THERE'S ONLY ONE PERSON ON THE PLANET WHO'S CRAZY, MEAN AND STUPID ENOUGH TO VIOLATE JESSE "THE BODY'S" HOME...
GASP! HE KNOWS, SIR!
SHH!
HULK HOGAN!

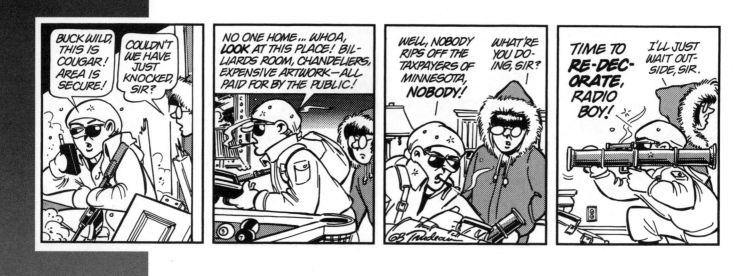

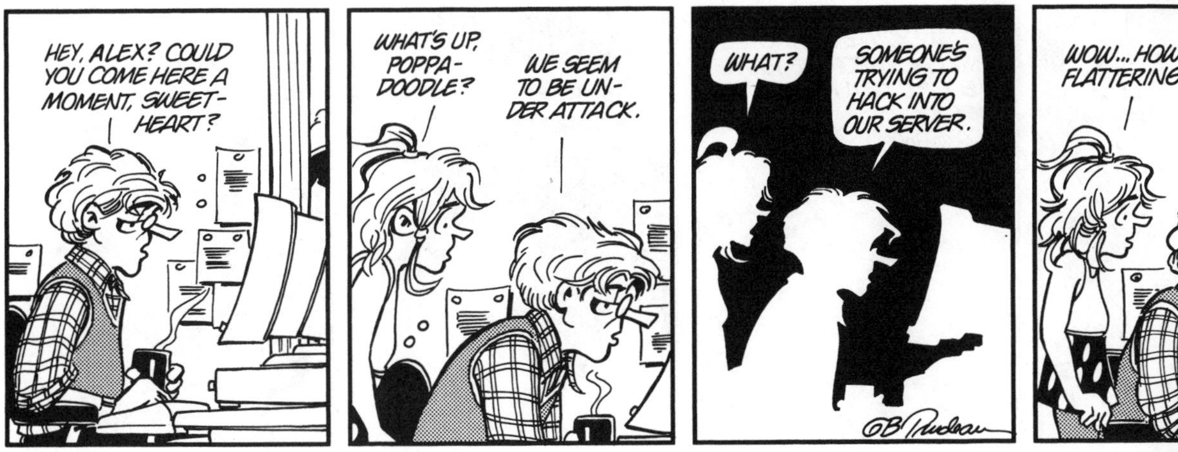
HEY, ALEX? COULD YOU COME HERE A MOMENT, SWEET-HEART?
WHAT'S UP, POPPA-DOODLE?
WE SEEM TO BE UN-DER ATTACK.
WHAT?
SOMEONE'S TRYING TO HACK INTO OUR SERVER.
WOW... HOW FLATTERING!
I KNOW. THERE MUST BE SOME MISTAKE.
©B Trudeau

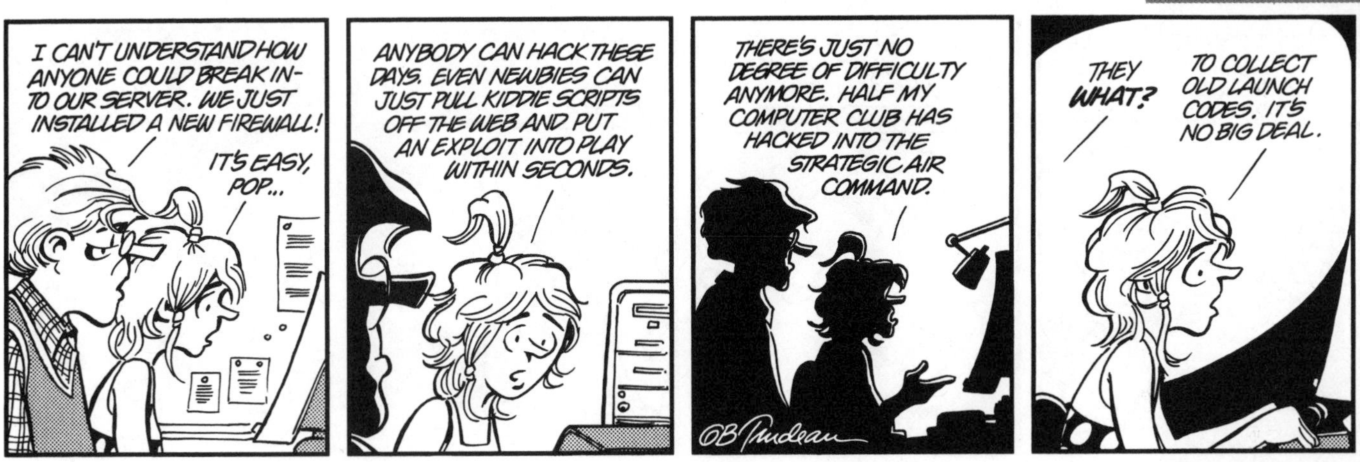
I CAN'T UNDERSTAND HOW ANYONE COULD BREAK IN-TO OUR SERVER. WE JUST INSTALLED A NEW FIREWALL!
IT'S EASY, POP...
ANYBODY CAN HACK THESE DAYS. EVEN NEWBIES CAN JUST PULL KIDDIE SCRIPTS OFF THE WEB AND PUT AN EXPLOIT INTO PLAY WITHIN SECONDS.
THERE'S JUST NO DEGREE OF DIFFICULTY ANYMORE. HALF MY COMPUTER CLUB HAS HACKED INTO THE STRATEGIC AIR COMMAND.
©B Trudeau
THEY WHAT?
TO COLLECT OLD LAUNCH CODES. IT'S NO BIG DEAL.

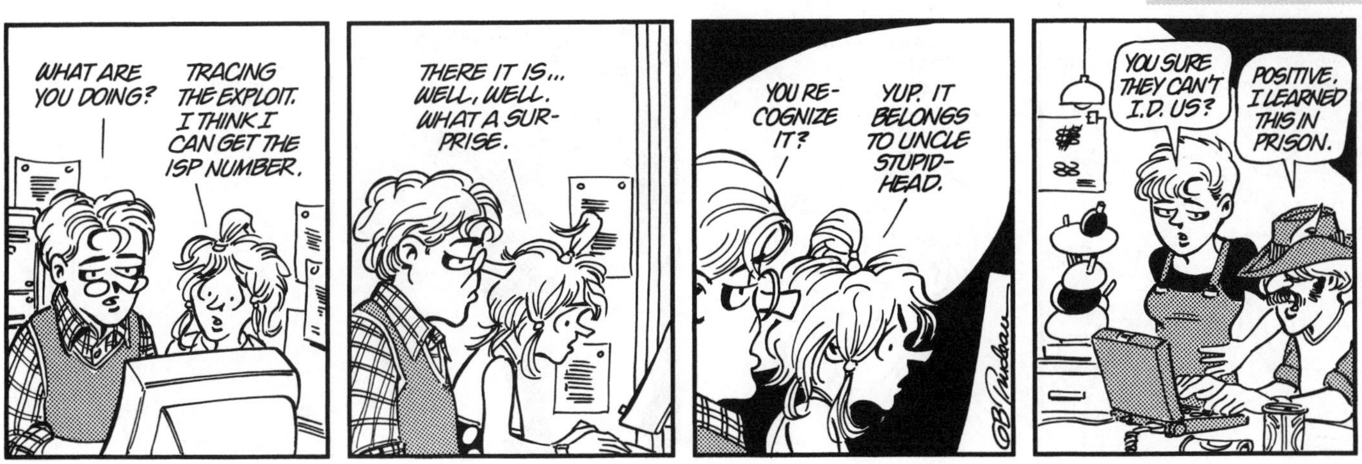
WHAT ARE YOU DOING?
TRACING THE EXPLOIT. I THINK I CAN GET THE ISP NUMBER.
THERE IT IS... WELL, WELL. WHAT A SUR-PRISE.
YOU RE-COGNIZE IT?
YUP. IT BELONGS TO UNCLE STUPID-HEAD.
©B Trudeau
YOU SURE THEY CAN'T I.D. US?
POSITIVE. I LEARNED THIS IN PRISON.

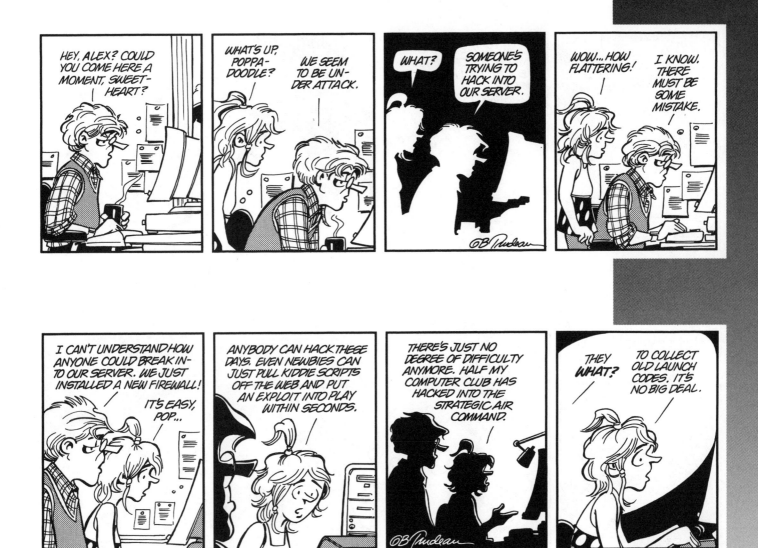

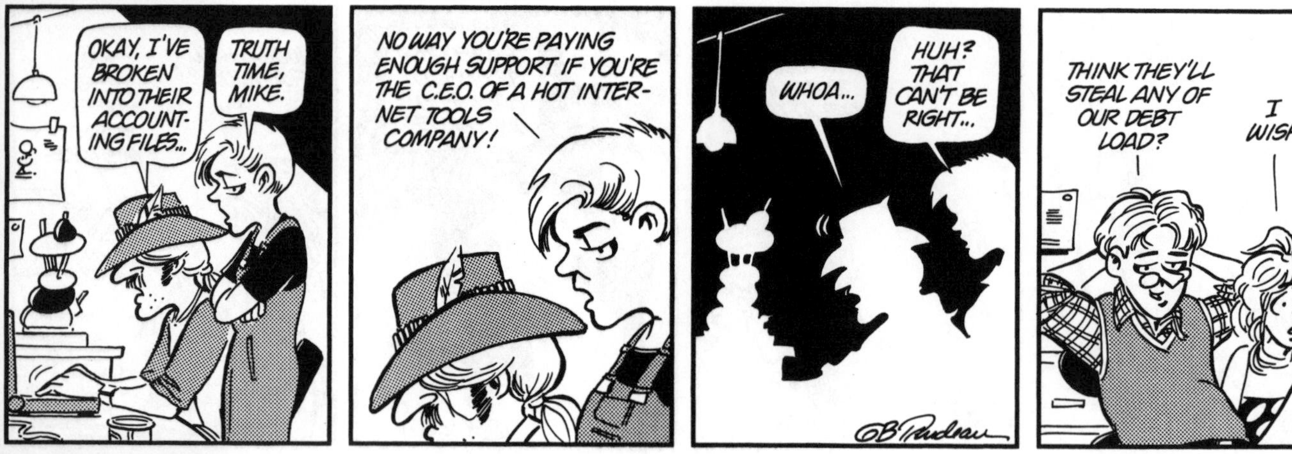
OKAY, I'VE BROKEN INTO THEIR ACCOUNTING FILES...
TRUTH TIME, MIKE.
NO WAY YOU'RE PAYING ENOUGH SUPPORT IF YOU'RE THE C.E.O. OF A HOT INTERNET TOOLS COMPANY!
WHOA...
HUH? THAT CAN'T BE RIGHT...
THINK THEY'LL STEAL ANY OF OUR DEBT LOAD?
I WISH.

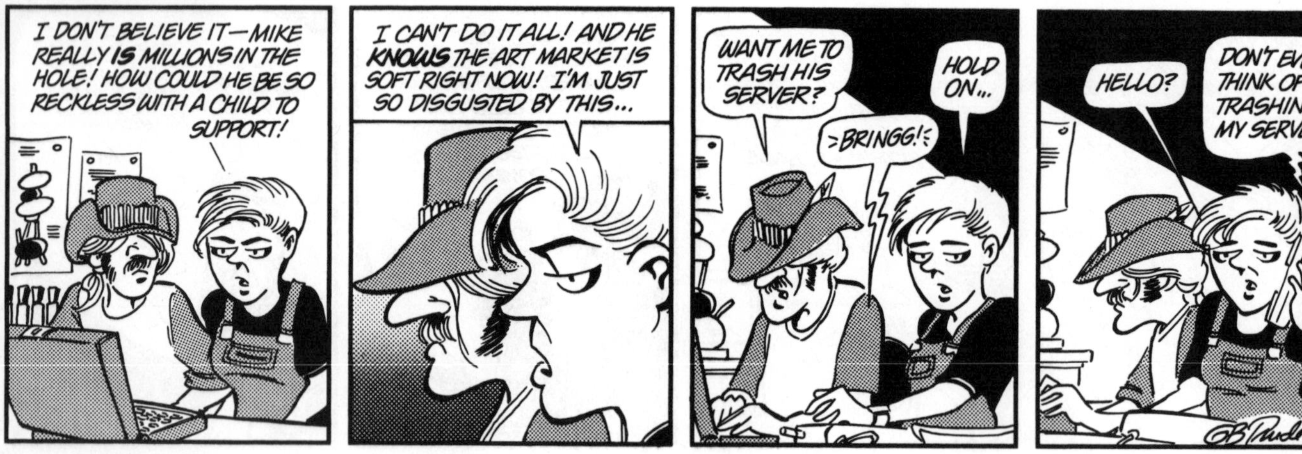
I DON'T BELIEVE IT—MIKE REALLY IS MILLIONS IN THE HOLE! HOW COULD HE BE SO RECKLESS WITH A CHILD TO SUPPORT!
I CAN'T DO IT ALL! AND HE KNOWS THE ART MARKET IS SOFT RIGHT NOW! I'M JUST SO DISGUSTED BY THIS...
WANT ME TO TRASH HIS SERVER?
BRINGG!
HOLD ON...
HELLO?
DON'T EVEN THINK OF TRASHING MY SERVER.

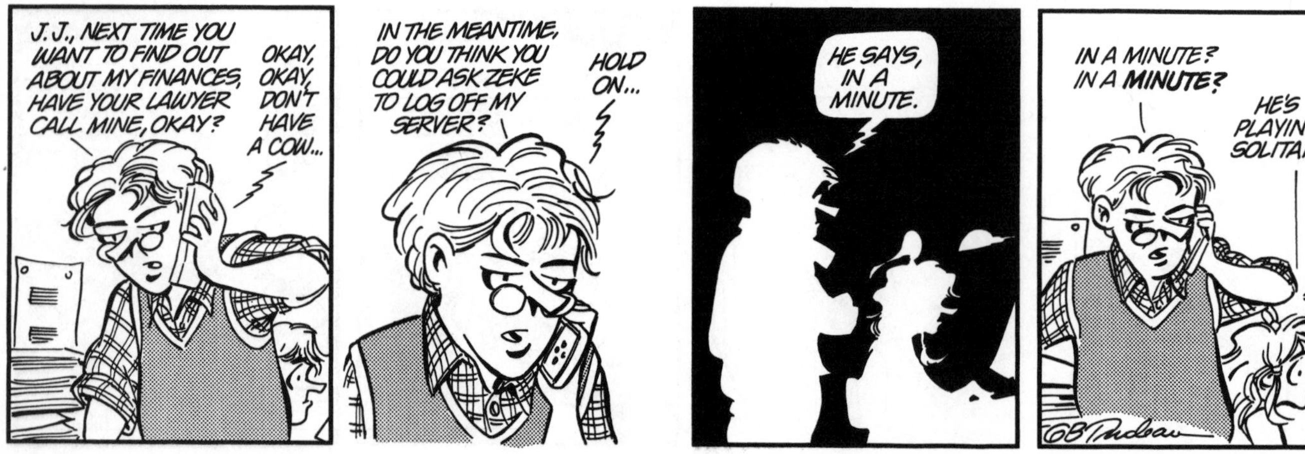
J. J., NEXT TIME YOU WANT TO FIND OUT ABOUT MY FINANCES, HAVE YOUR LAWYER CALL MINE, OKAY?
OKAY, OKAY, DON'T HAVE A COW...
IN THE MEANTIME, DO YOU THINK YOU COULD ASK ZEKE TO LOG OFF MY SERVER?
HOLD ON...
HE SAYS, IN A MINUTE.
IN A MINUTE? IN A MINUTE?
HE'S PLAYING SOLITAIRE.

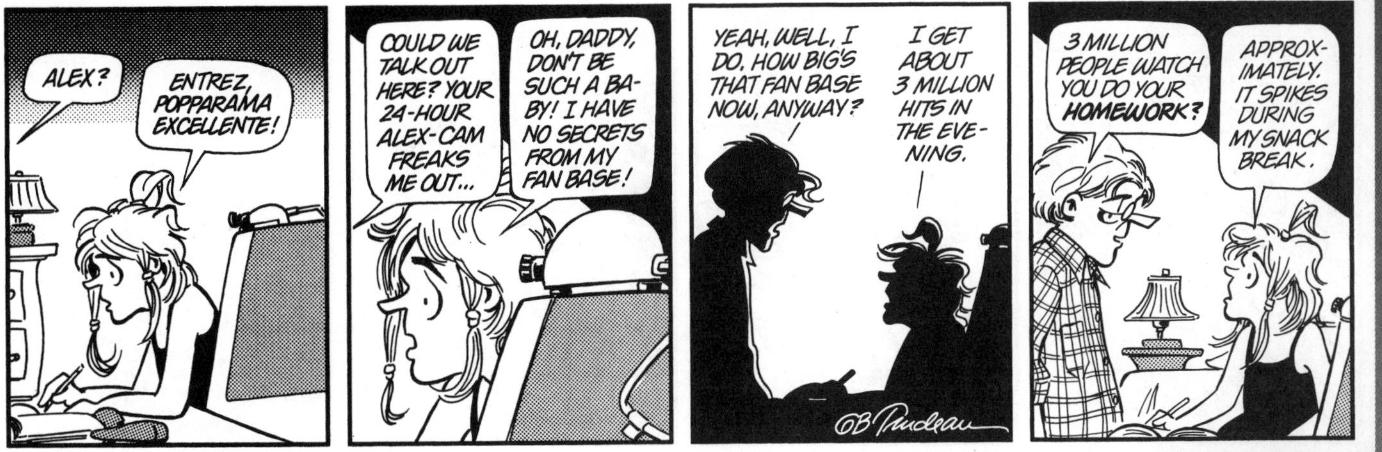
ALEX?
ENTREZ, POPPARAMA EXCELLENTE!
COULD WE TALK OUT HERE? YOUR 24-HOUR ALEX-CAM FREAKS ME OUT...
OH, DADDY, DON'T BE SUCH A BABY! I HAVE NO SECRETS FROM MY FAN BASE!
YEAH, WELL, I DO. HOW BIG'S THAT FAN BASE NOW, ANYWAY?
I GET ABOUT 3 MILLION HITS IN THE EVENING.
3 MILLION PEOPLE WATCH YOU DO YOUR **HOMEWORK?**
APPROXIMATELY. IT SPIKES DURING MY SNACK BREAK.

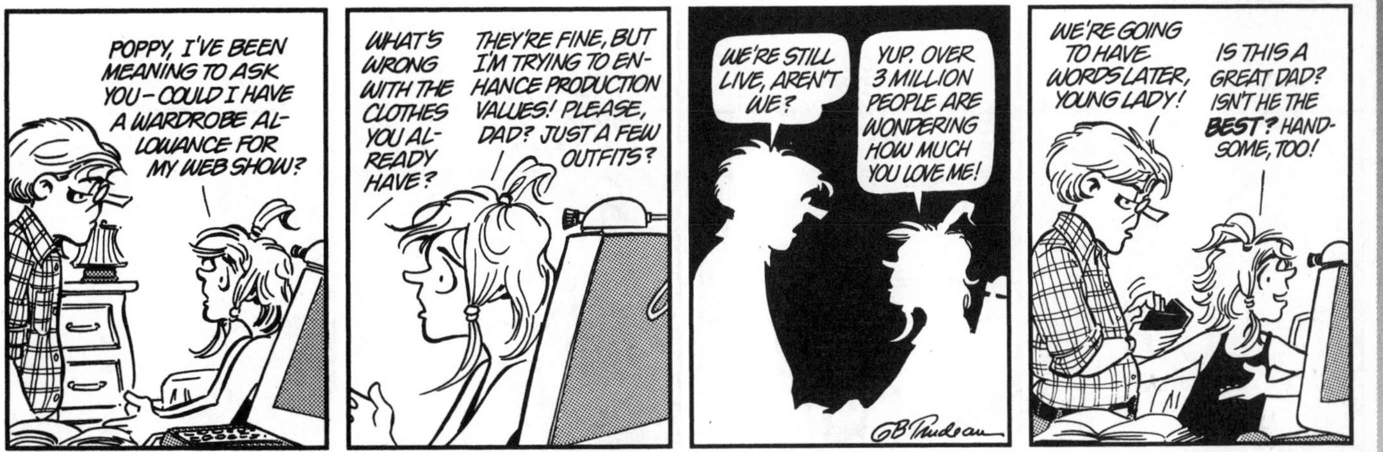
POPPY, I'VE BEEN MEANING TO ASK YOU—COULD I HAVE A WARDROBE ALLOWANCE FOR MY WEB SHOW?
WHAT'S WRONG WITH THE CLOTHES YOU ALREADY HAVE?
THEY'RE FINE, BUT I'M TRYING TO ENHANCE PRODUCTION VALUES! PLEASE, DAD? JUST A FEW OUTFITS?
WE'RE STILL LIVE, AREN'T WE?
YUP. OVER 3 MILLION PEOPLE ARE WONDERING HOW MUCH YOU LOVE ME!
WE'RE GOING TO HAVE WORDS LATER, YOUNG LADY!
IS THIS A GREAT DAD? ISN'T HE THE **BEST?** HANDSOME, TOO!

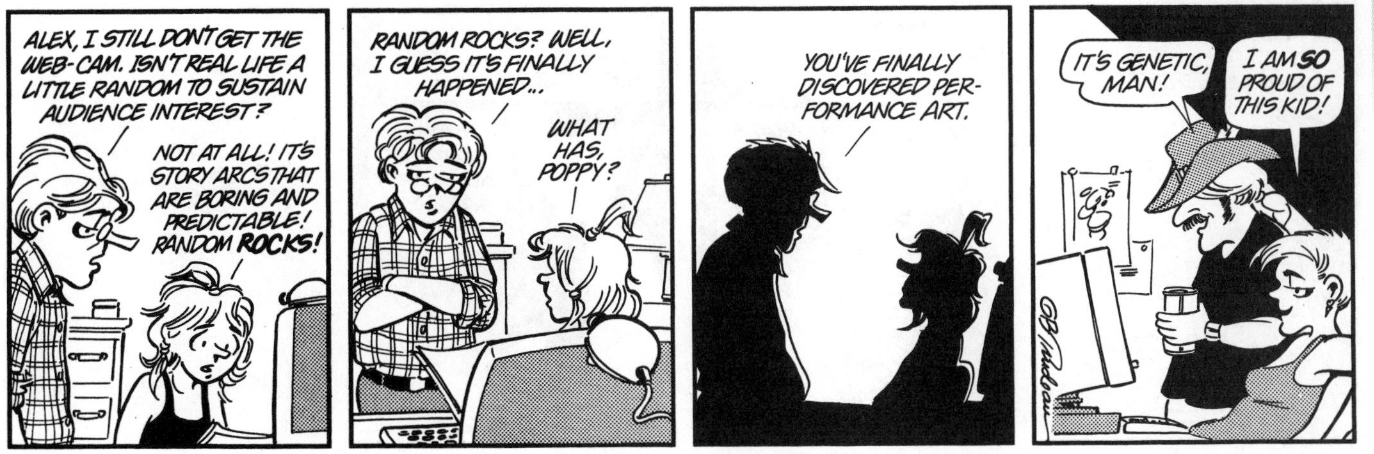
ALEX, I STILL DON'T GET THE WEB-CAM. ISN'T REAL LIFE A LITTLE RANDOM TO SUSTAIN AUDIENCE INTEREST?
NOT AT ALL! IT'S STORY ARCS THAT ARE BORING AND PREDICTABLE! RANDOM **ROCKS!**
RANDOM ROCKS? WELL, I GUESS IT'S FINALLY HAPPENED...
WHAT HAS, POPPY?
YOU'VE FINALLY DISCOVERED PERFORMANCE ART.
IT'S GENETIC, MAN!
I AM **SO** PROUD OF THIS KID!

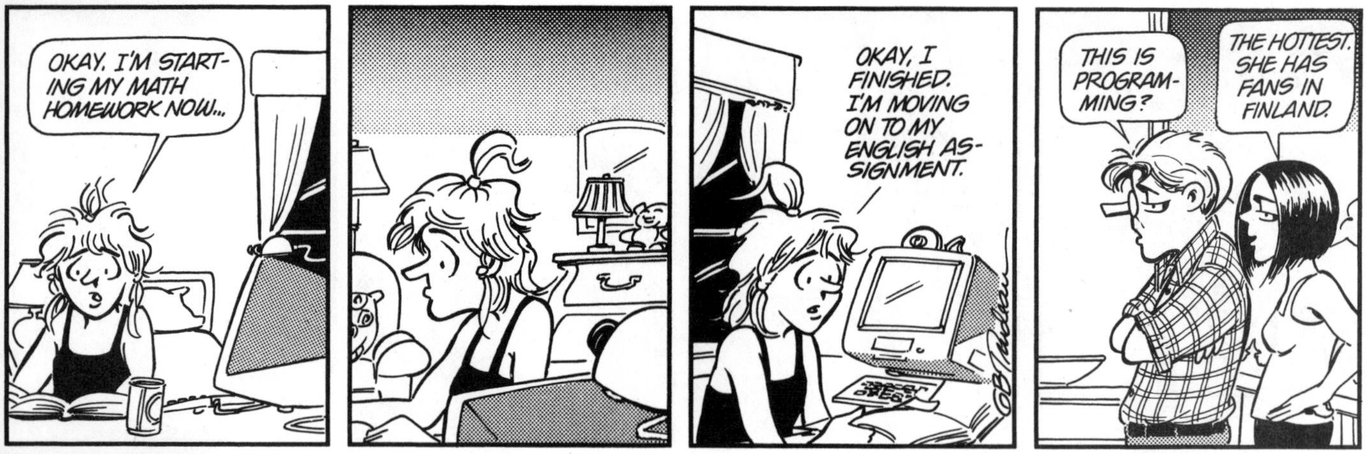
OKAY. I'M STARTING MY MATH HOMEWORK NOW...
OKAY, I FINISHED. I'M MOVING ON TO MY ENGLISH ASSIGNMENT.
THIS IS PROGRAMMING?
THE HOTTEST. SHE HAS FANS IN FINLAND.

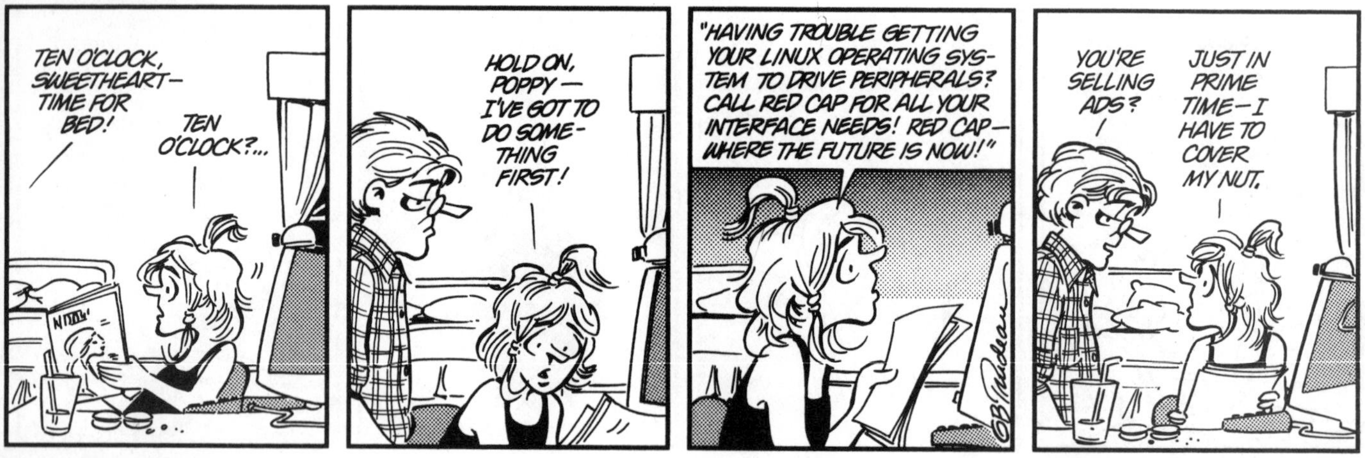
TEN O'CLOCK, SWEETHEART—TIME FOR BED!
TEN O'CLOCK?...
HOLD ON, POPPY—I'VE GOT TO DO SOMETHING FIRST!
"HAVING TROUBLE GETTING YOUR LINUX OPERATING SYSTEM TO DRIVE PERIPHERALS? CALL RED CAP FOR ALL YOUR INTERFACE NEEDS! RED CAP—WHERE THE FUTURE IS NOW!"
YOU'RE SELLING ADS?
JUST IN PRIME TIME—I HAVE TO COVER MY NUT.

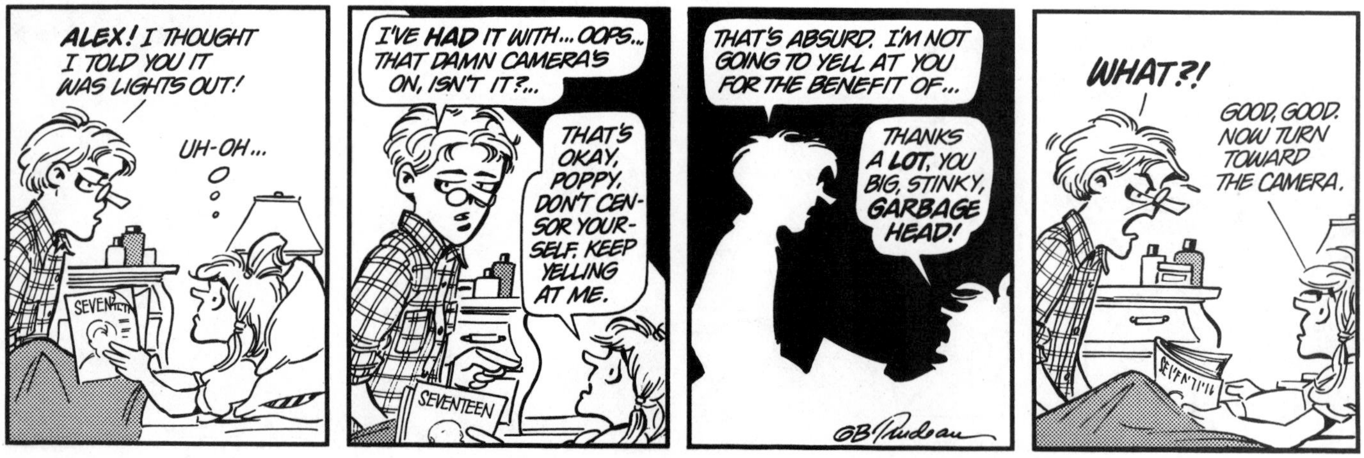
ALEX! I THOUGHT I TOLD YOU IT WAS LIGHTS OUT!
UH-OH...
I'VE HAD IT WITH... OOPS... THAT DAMN CAMERA'S ON, ISN'T IT?...
THAT'S OKAY, POPPY. DON'T CENSOR YOURSELF. KEEP YELLING AT ME.
SEVENTEEN
THAT'S ABSURD. I'M NOT GOING TO YELL AT YOU FOR THE BENEFIT OF...
THANKS A LOT, YOU BIG, STINKY, GARBAGE HEAD!
WHAT?!
GOOD, GOOD. NOW TURN TOWARD THE CAMERA.

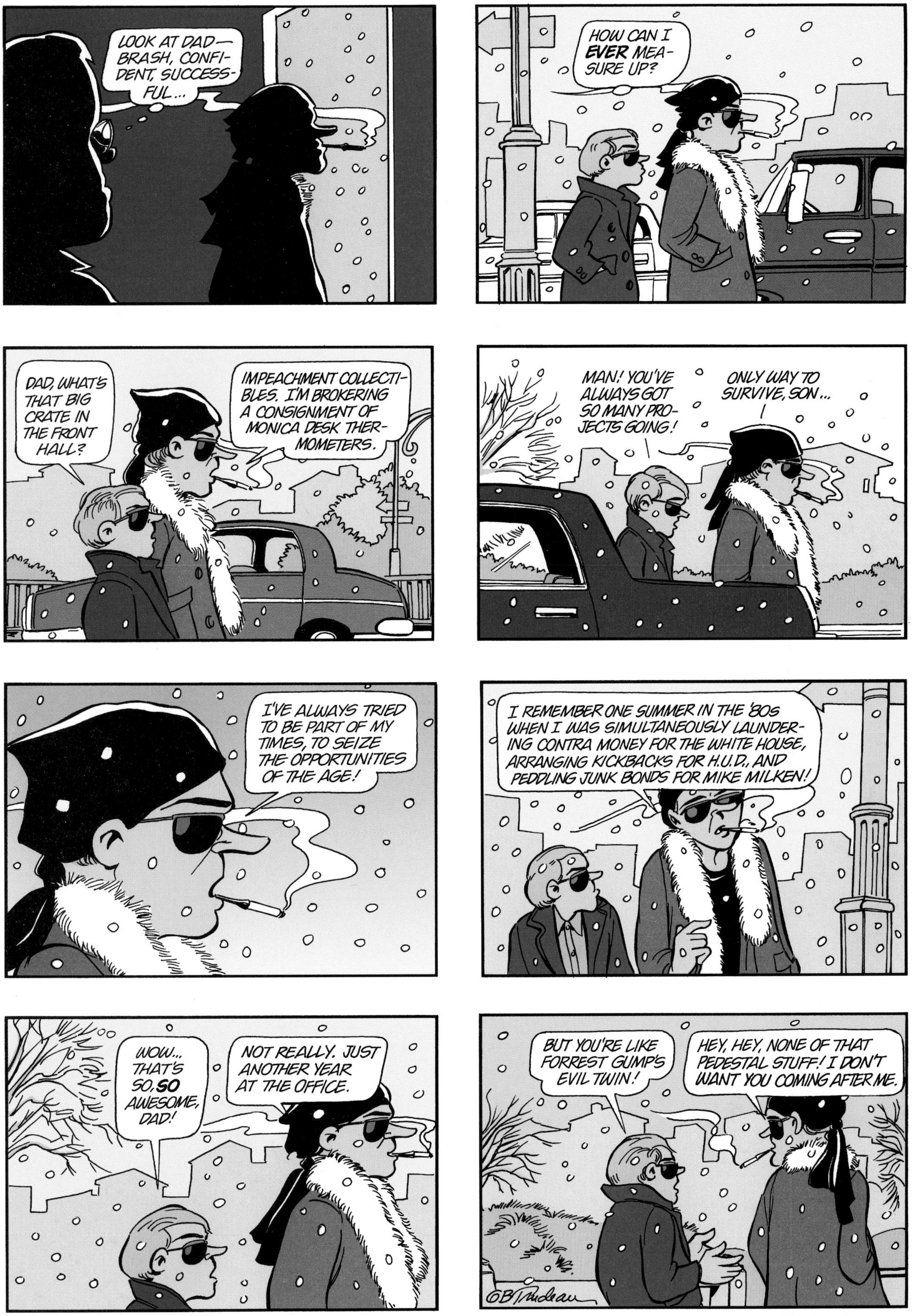
LOOK AT DAD— BRASH, CONFIDENT, SUCCESSFUL...
HOW CAN I **EVER** MEASURE UP?
DAD, WHAT'S THAT BIG CRATE IN THE FRONT HALL?
IMPEACHMENT COLLECTIBLES. I'M BROKERING A CONSIGNMENT OF MONICA DESK THERMOMETERS.
MAN! YOU'VE ALWAYS GOT SO MANY PROJECTS GOING!
ONLY WAY TO SURVIVE, SON...
I'VE ALWAYS TRIED TO BE PART OF MY TIMES, TO SEIZE THE OPPORTUNITIES OF THE AGE!
I REMEMBER ONE SUMMER IN THE '80s WHEN I WAS SIMULTANEOUSLY LAUNDERING CONTRA MONEY FOR THE WHITE HOUSE, ARRANGING KICKBACKS FOR H.U.D., AND PEDDLING JUNK BONDS FOR MIKE MILKEN!
WOW... THAT'S SO, **SO** AWESOME, DAD!
NOT REALLY. JUST ANOTHER YEAR AT THE OFFICE.
BUT YOU'RE LIKE FORREST GUMP'S EVIL TWIN!
HEY, HEY, NONE OF THAT PEDESTAL STUFF! I DON'T WANT YOU COMING AFTER ME.
©GBTrudeau

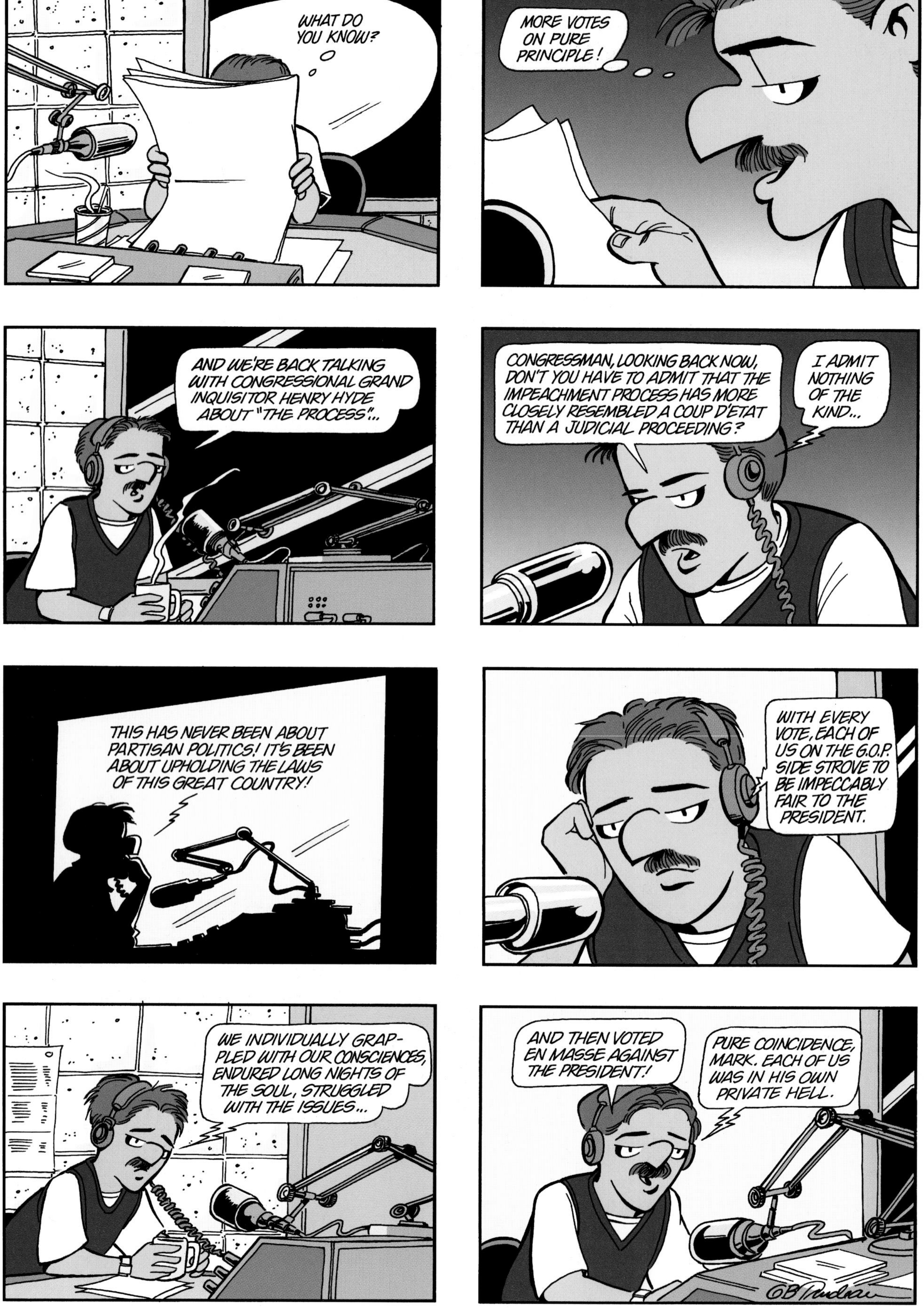
WHAT DO YOU KNOW?
MORE VOTES ON PURE PRINCIPLE!
AND WE'RE BACK TALKING WITH CONGRESSIONAL GRAND INQUISITOR HENRY HYDE ABOUT "THE PROCESS"...
CONGRESSMAN, LOOKING BACK NOW, DON'T YOU HAVE TO ADMIT THAT THE IMPEACHMENT PROCESS HAS MORE CLOSELY RESEMBLED A COUP D'ETAT THAN A JUDICIAL PROCEEDING?
I ADMIT NOTHING OF THE KIND...
THIS HAS NEVER BEEN ABOUT PARTISAN POLITICS! IT'S BEEN ABOUT UPHOLDING THE LAWS OF THIS GREAT COUNTRY!
WITH EVERY VOTE, EACH OF US ON THE G.O.P. SIDE STROVE TO BE IMPECCABLY FAIR TO THE PRESIDENT.
WE INDIVIDUALLY GRAPPLED WITH OUR CONSCIENCES, ENDURED LONG NIGHTS OF THE SOUL, STRUGGLED WITH THE ISSUES...
AND THEN VOTED EN MASSE AGAINST THE PRESIDENT!
PURE COINCIDENCE, MARK. EACH OF US WAS IN HIS OWN PRIVATE HELL.

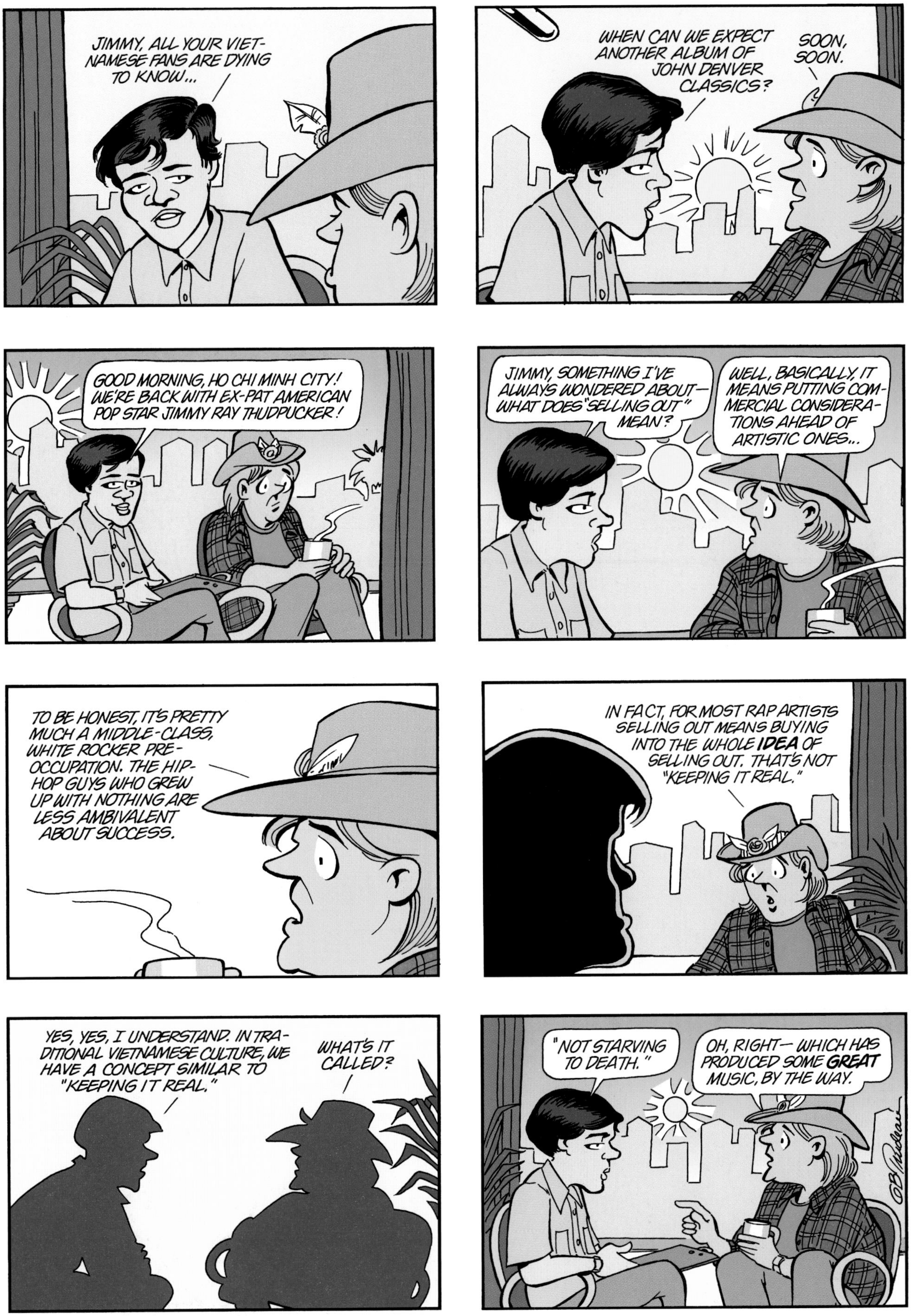
JIMMY, ALL YOUR VIET-NAMESE FANS ARE DYING TO KNOW...
WHEN CAN WE EXPECT ANOTHER ALBUM OF JOHN DENVER CLASSICS?
SOON, SOON.
GOOD MORNING, HO CHI MINH CITY! WE'RE BACK WITH EX-PAT AMERICAN POP STAR JIMMY RAY THUDPUCKER!
JIMMY, SOMETHING I'VE ALWAYS WONDERED ABOUT— WHAT DOES "SELLING OUT" MEAN?
WELL, BASICALLY, IT MEANS PUTTING COMMERCIAL CONSIDERATIONS AHEAD OF ARTISTIC ONES...
TO BE HONEST, IT'S PRETTY MUCH A MIDDLE-CLASS, WHITE ROCKER PRE-OCCUPATION. THE HIP-HOP GUYS WHO GREW UP WITH NOTHING ARE LESS AMBIVALENT ABOUT SUCCESS.
IN FACT, FOR MOST RAP ARTISTS SELLING OUT MEANS BUYING INTO THE WHOLE IDEA OF SELLING OUT. THAT'S NOT "KEEPING IT REAL."
YES, YES, I UNDERSTAND. IN TRADITIONAL VIETNAMESE CULTURE, WE HAVE A CONCEPT SIMILAR TO "KEEPING IT REAL."
WHAT'S IT CALLED?
"NOT STARVING TO DEATH."
OH, RIGHT— WHICH HAS PRODUCED SOME GREAT MUSIC, BY THE WAY.

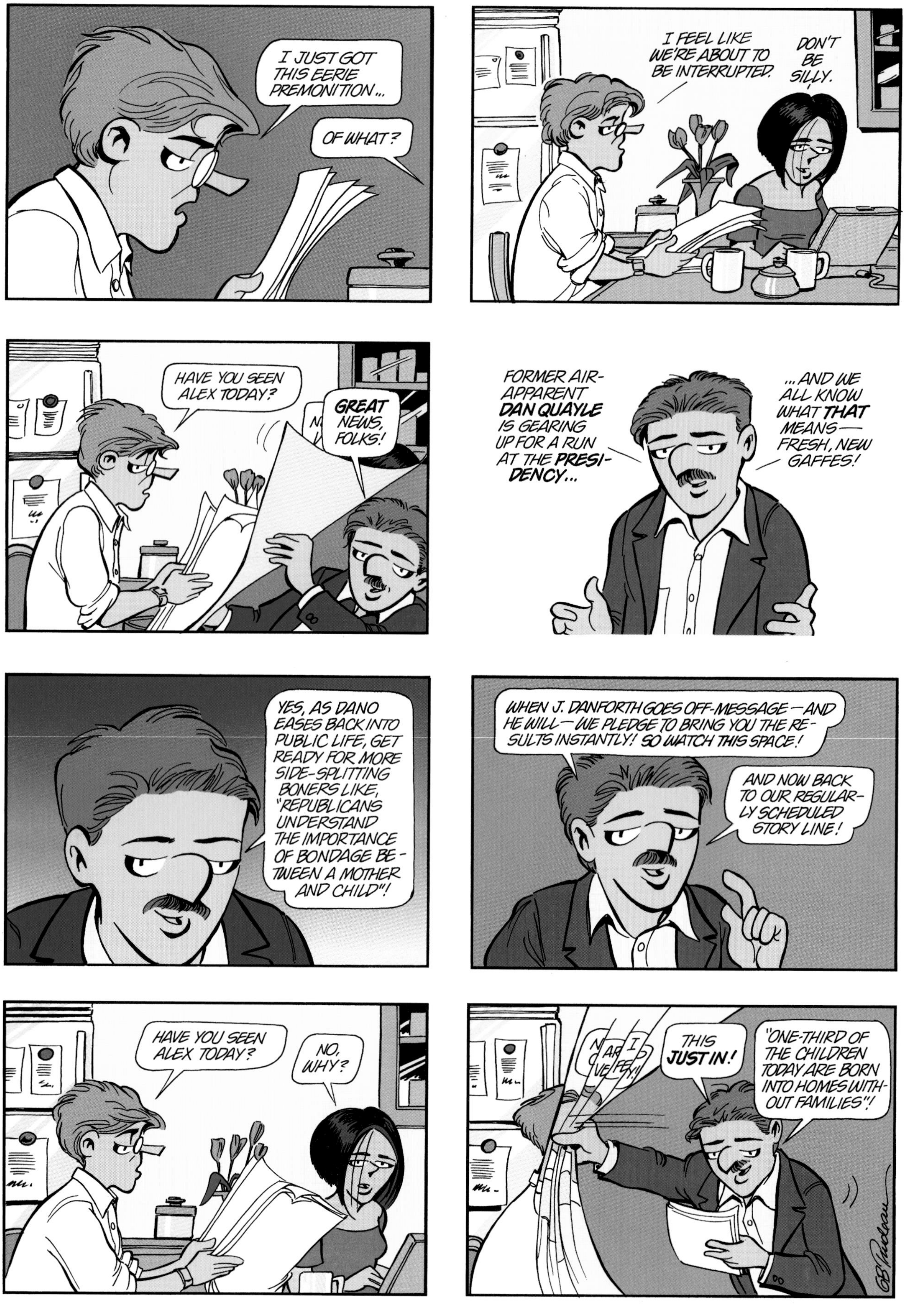

I JUST GOT THIS EERIE PREMONITION...
OF WHAT?
I FEEL LIKE WE'RE ABOUT TO BE INTERRUPTED.
DON'T BE SILLY.
HAVE YOU SEEN ALEX TODAY?
GREAT NEWS, FOLKS!
FORMER AIR-APPARENT DAN QUAYLE IS GEARING UP FOR A RUN AT THE PRESIDENCY...
...AND WE ALL KNOW WHAT THAT MEANS— FRESH, NEW GAFFES!
YES, AS DANO EASES BACK INTO PUBLIC LIFE, GET READY FOR MORE SIDE-SPLITTING BONERS LIKE, "REPUBLICANS UNDERSTAND THE IMPORTANCE OF BONDAGE BETWEEN A MOTHER AND CHILD"!
WHEN J. DANFORTH GOES OFF-MESSAGE—AND HE WILL—WE PLEDGE TO BRING YOU THE RESULTS INSTANTLY! SO WATCH THIS SPACE!
AND NOW BACK TO OUR REGULARLY SCHEDULED STORY LINE!
HAVE YOU SEEN ALEX TODAY?
NO, WHY?
THIS JUST IN!
"ONE-THIRD OF THE CHILDREN TODAY ARE BORN INTO HOMES WITHOUT FAMILIES"!
GBTrudeau

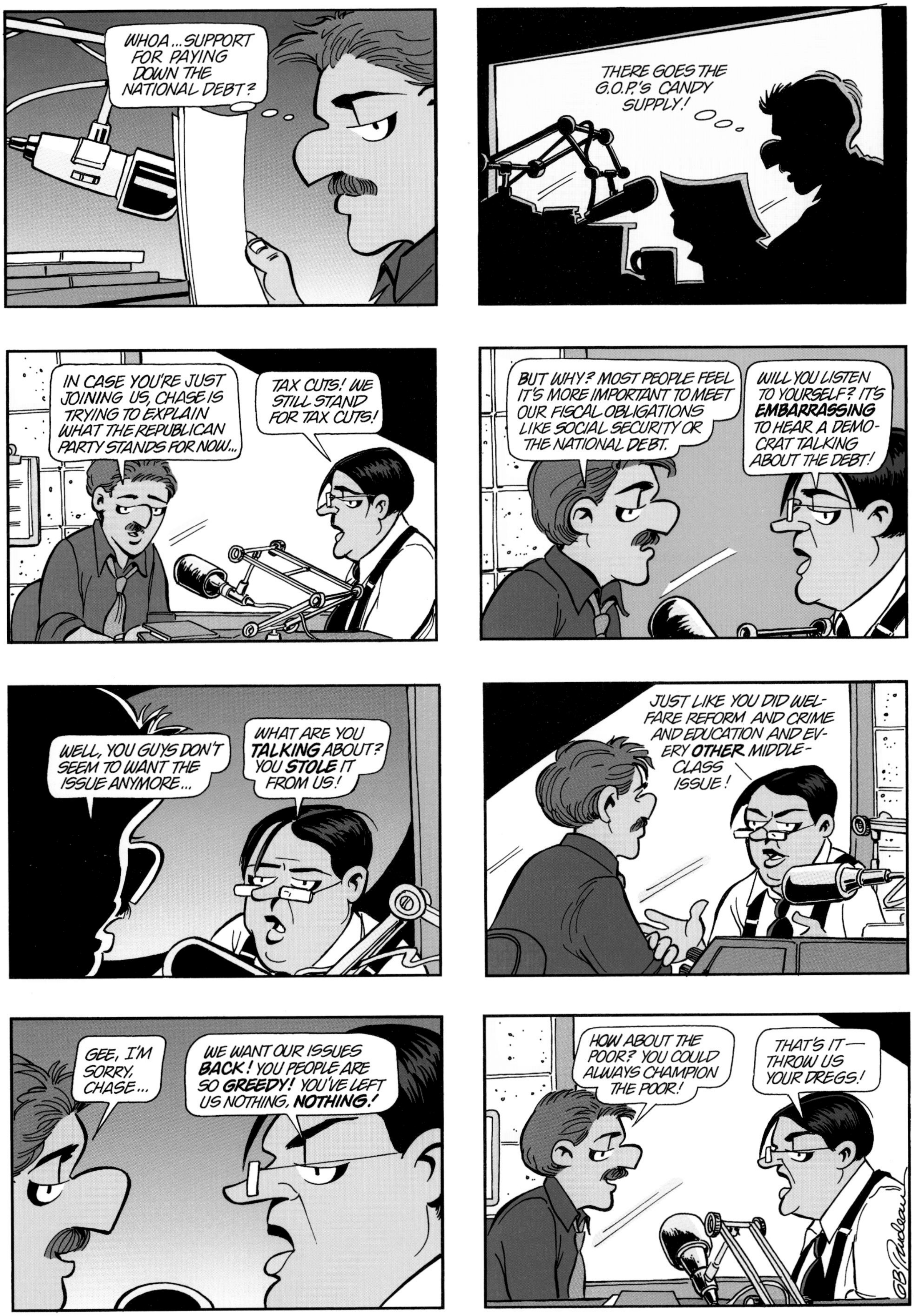
WHOA...SUPPORT FOR PAYING DOWN THE NATIONAL DEBT?
THERE GOES THE G.O.P.'s CANDY SUPPLY!
IN CASE YOU'RE JUST JOINING US, CHASE IS TRYING TO EXPLAIN WHAT THE REPUBLICAN PARTY STANDS FOR NOW...
TAX CUTS! WE STILL STAND FOR TAX CUTS!
BUT WHY? MOST PEOPLE FEEL IT'S MORE IMPORTANT TO MEET OUR FISCAL OBLIGATIONS LIKE SOCIAL SECURITY OR THE NATIONAL DEBT.
WILL YOU LISTEN TO YOURSELF? IT'S **EMBARRASSING** TO HEAR A DEMOCRAT TALKING ABOUT THE DEBT!
WELL, YOU GUYS DON'T SEEM TO WANT THE ISSUE ANYMORE...
WHAT ARE YOU **TALKING** ABOUT? YOU **STOLE** IT FROM US!
JUST LIKE YOU DID WELFARE REFORM AND CRIME AND EDUCATION AND EVERY **OTHER** MIDDLE-CLASS ISSUE!
GEE, I'M SORRY, CHASE...
WE WANT OUR ISSUES **BACK**! YOU PEOPLE ARE SO **GREEDY**! YOU'VE LEFT US NOTHING, **NOTHING**!
HOW ABOUT THE POOR? YOU COULD ALWAYS CHAMPION THE POOR!
THAT'S IT— THROW US YOUR DREGS!
GB Trudeau

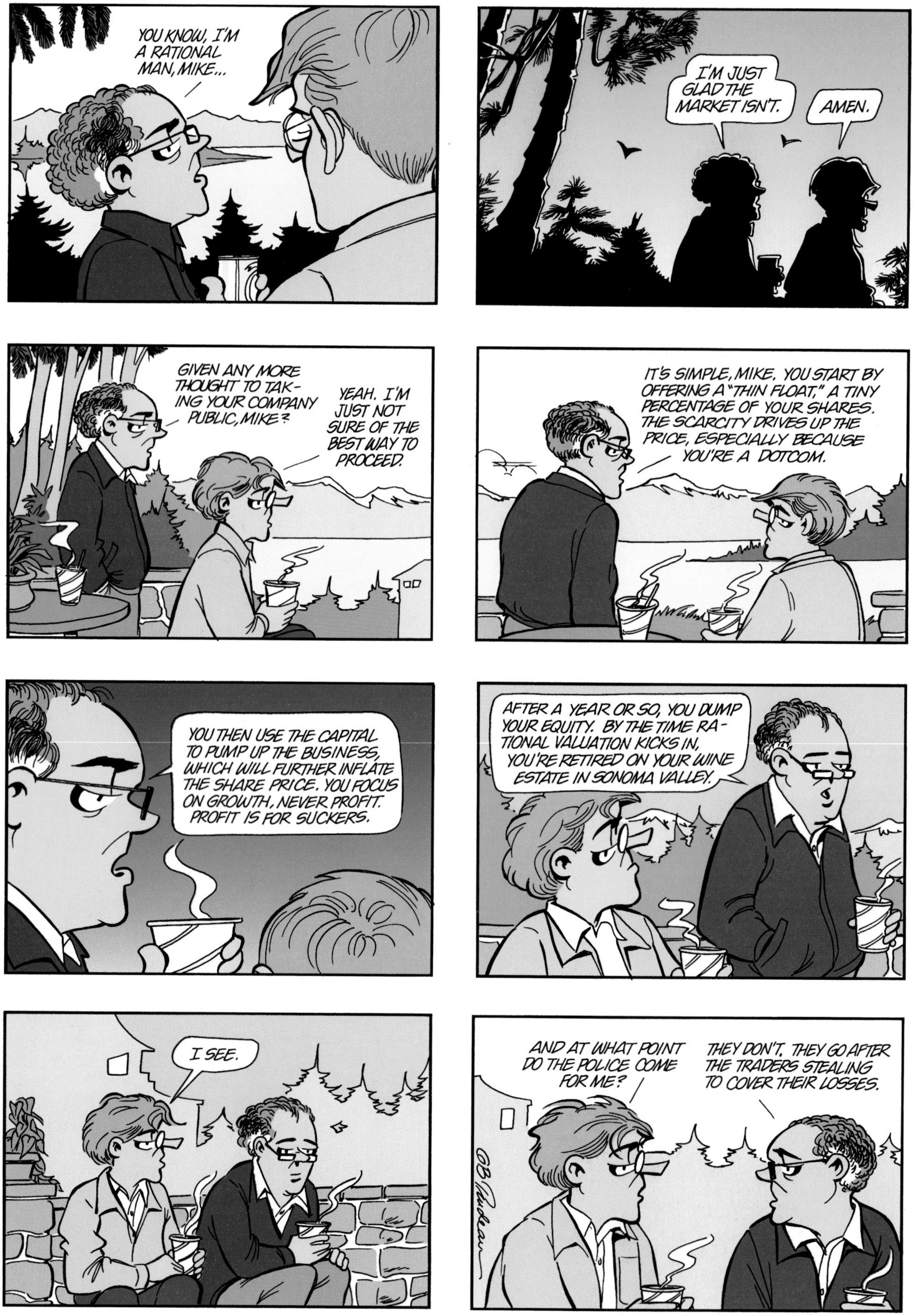
YOU KNOW, I'M A RATIONAL MAN, MIKE...
I'M JUST GLAD THE MARKET ISN'T.
AMEN.
GIVEN ANY MORE THOUGHT TO TAKING YOUR COMPANY PUBLIC, MIKE?
YEAH. I'M JUST NOT SURE OF THE BEST WAY TO PROCEED.
IT'S SIMPLE, MIKE. YOU START BY OFFERING A "THIN FLOAT," A TINY PERCENTAGE OF YOUR SHARES. THE SCARCITY DRIVES UP THE PRICE, ESPECIALLY BECAUSE YOU'RE A DOTCOM.
YOU THEN USE THE CAPITAL TO PUMP UP THE BUSINESS, WHICH WILL FURTHER INFLATE THE SHARE PRICE. YOU FOCUS ON GROWTH, NEVER PROFIT. PROFIT IS FOR SUCKERS.
AFTER A YEAR OR SO, YOU DUMP YOUR EQUITY. BY THE TIME RATIONAL VALUATION KICKS IN, YOU'RE RETIRED ON YOUR WINE ESTATE IN SONOMA VALLEY.
I SEE.
AND AT WHAT POINT DO THE POLICE COME FOR ME?
THEY DON'T. THEY GO AFTER THE TRADERS STEALING TO COVER THEIR LOSSES.

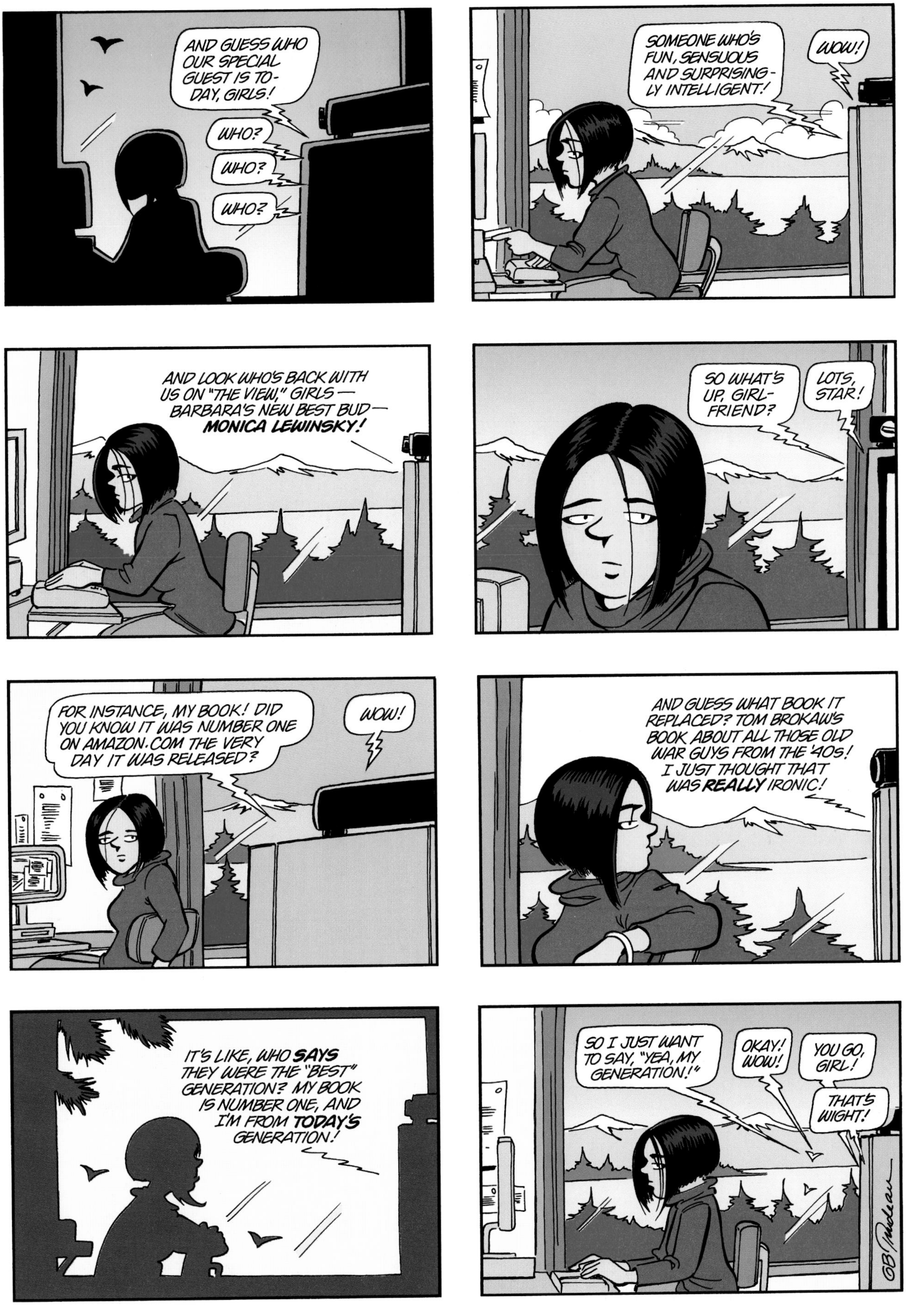
AND GUESS WHO OUR SPECIAL GUEST IS TO-DAY, GIRLS!
WHO?
WHO?
WHO?
SOMEONE WHO'S FUN, SENSUOUS AND SURPRISING-LY INTELLIGENT!
WOW!
AND LOOK WHO'S BACK WITH US ON "THE VIEW," GIRLS — BARBARA'S NEW BEST BUD — MONICA LEWINSKY!
SO WHAT'S UP, GIRL-FRIEND?
LOTS, STAR!
FOR INSTANCE, MY BOOK! DID YOU KNOW IT WAS NUMBER ONE ON AMAZON.COM THE VERY DAY IT WAS RELEASED?
WOW!
AND GUESS WHAT BOOK IT REPLACED? TOM BROKAW'S BOOK ABOUT ALL THOSE OLD WAR GUYS FROM THE '40s! I JUST THOUGHT THAT WAS REALLY IRONIC!
IT'S LIKE, WHO SAYS THEY WERE THE "BEST" GENERATION? MY BOOK IS NUMBER ONE, AND I'M FROM TODAY'S GENERATION!
SO I JUST WANT TO SAY, "YEA, MY GENERATION!"
OKAY! WOW!
YOU GO, GIRL!
THAT'S WIGHT!
GBTrudeau

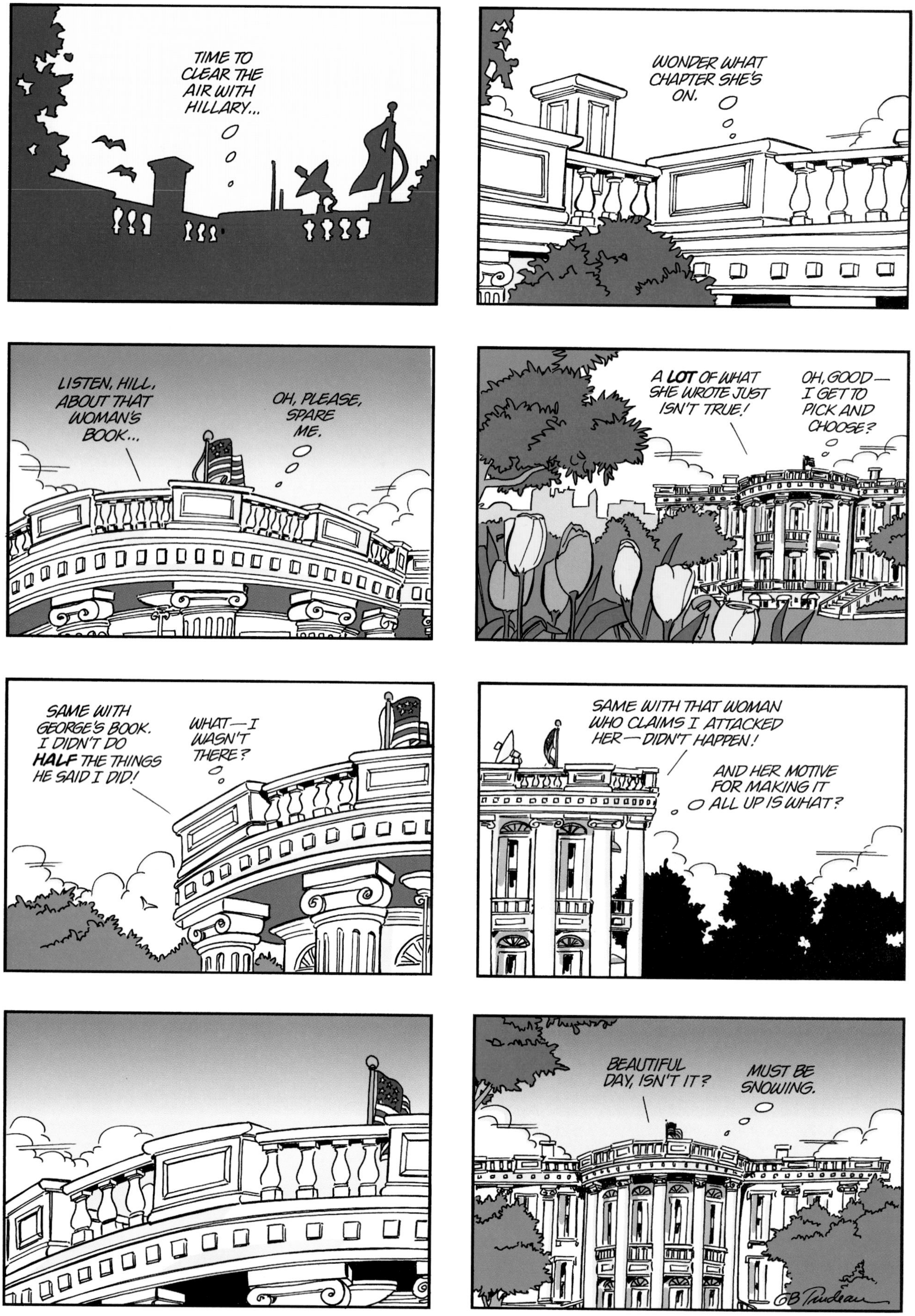
TIME TO CLEAR THE AIR WITH HILLARY...
WONDER WHAT CHAPTER SHE'S ON.
LISTEN, HILL, ABOUT THAT WOMAN'S BOOK...
OH, PLEASE, SPARE ME.
A **LOT** OF WHAT SHE WROTE JUST ISN'T TRUE!
OH, GOOD— I GET TO PICK AND CHOOSE?
SAME WITH GEORGE'S BOOK. I DIDN'T DO **HALF** THE THINGS HE SAID I DID!
WHAT—I WASN'T THERE?
SAME WITH THAT WOMAN WHO CLAIMS I ATTACKED HER—DIDN'T HAPPEN!
AND HER MOTIVE FOR MAKING IT ALL UP IS WHAT?
BEAUTIFUL DAY, ISN'T IT?
MUST BE SNOWING.
GB Trudeau

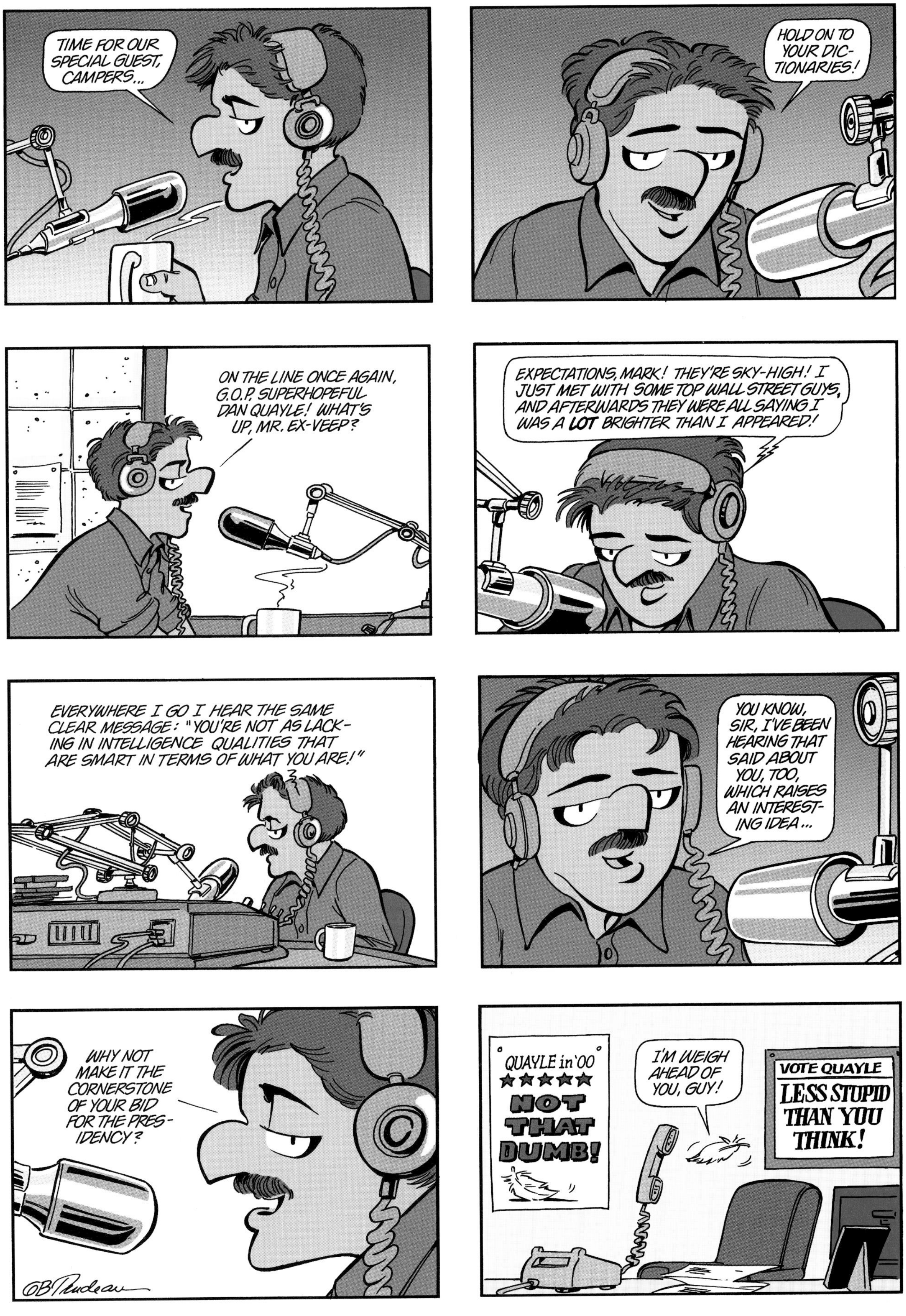
TIME FOR OUR SPECIAL GUEST, CAMPERS...
HOLD ON TO YOUR DICTIONARIES!
ON THE LINE ONCE AGAIN, G.O.P. SUPERHOPEFUL DAN QUAYLE! WHAT'S UP, MR. EX-VEEP?
EXPECTATIONS, MARK! THEY'RE SKY-HIGH! I JUST MET WITH SOME TOP WALL STREET GUYS, AND AFTERWARDS THEY WERE ALL SAYING I WAS A **LOT** BRIGHTER THAN I APPEARED!
EVERYWHERE I GO I HEAR THE SAME CLEAR MESSAGE: "YOU'RE NOT AS LACKING IN INTELLIGENCE QUALITIES THAT ARE SMART IN TERMS OF WHAT YOU ARE!"
YOU KNOW, SIR, I'VE BEEN HEARING THAT SAID ABOUT YOU, TOO, WHICH RAISES AN INTERESTING IDEA...
WHY NOT MAKE IT THE CORNERSTONE OF YOUR BID FOR THE PRESIDENCY?
QUAYLE in '00
NOT THAT DUMB!
I'M WEIGH AHEAD OF YOU, GUY!
VOTE QUAYLE
LESS STUPID THAN YOU THINK!

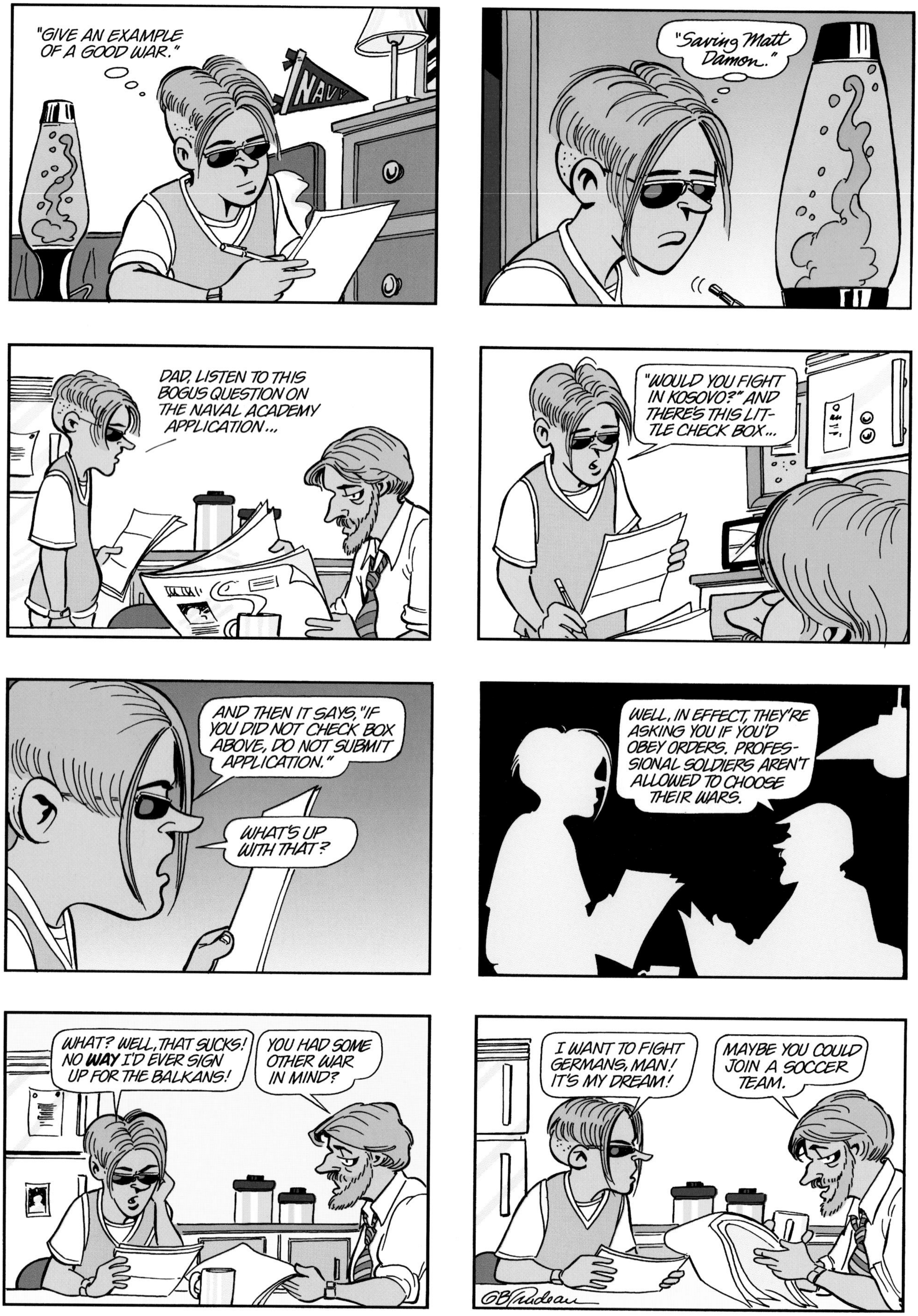
"GIVE AN EXAMPLE OF A GOOD WAR."
NAVY
"Saving Matt Damon."
DAD, LISTEN TO THIS BOGUS QUESTION ON THE NAVAL ACADEMY APPLICATION...
"WOULD YOU FIGHT IN KOSOVO?" AND THERE'S THIS LITTLE CHECK BOX...
AND THEN IT SAYS, "IF YOU DID NOT CHECK BOX ABOVE, DO NOT SUBMIT APPLICATION."
WHAT'S UP WITH THAT?
WELL, IN EFFECT, THEY'RE ASKING YOU IF YOU'D OBEY ORDERS. PROFESSIONAL SOLDIERS AREN'T ALLOWED TO CHOOSE THEIR WARS.
WHAT? WELL, THAT SUCKS! NO **WAY** I'D EVER SIGN UP FOR THE BALKANS!
YOU HAD SOME OTHER WAR IN MIND?
I WANT TO FIGHT GERMANS, MAN! IT'S MY DREAM!
MAYBE YOU COULD JOIN A SOCCER TEAM.

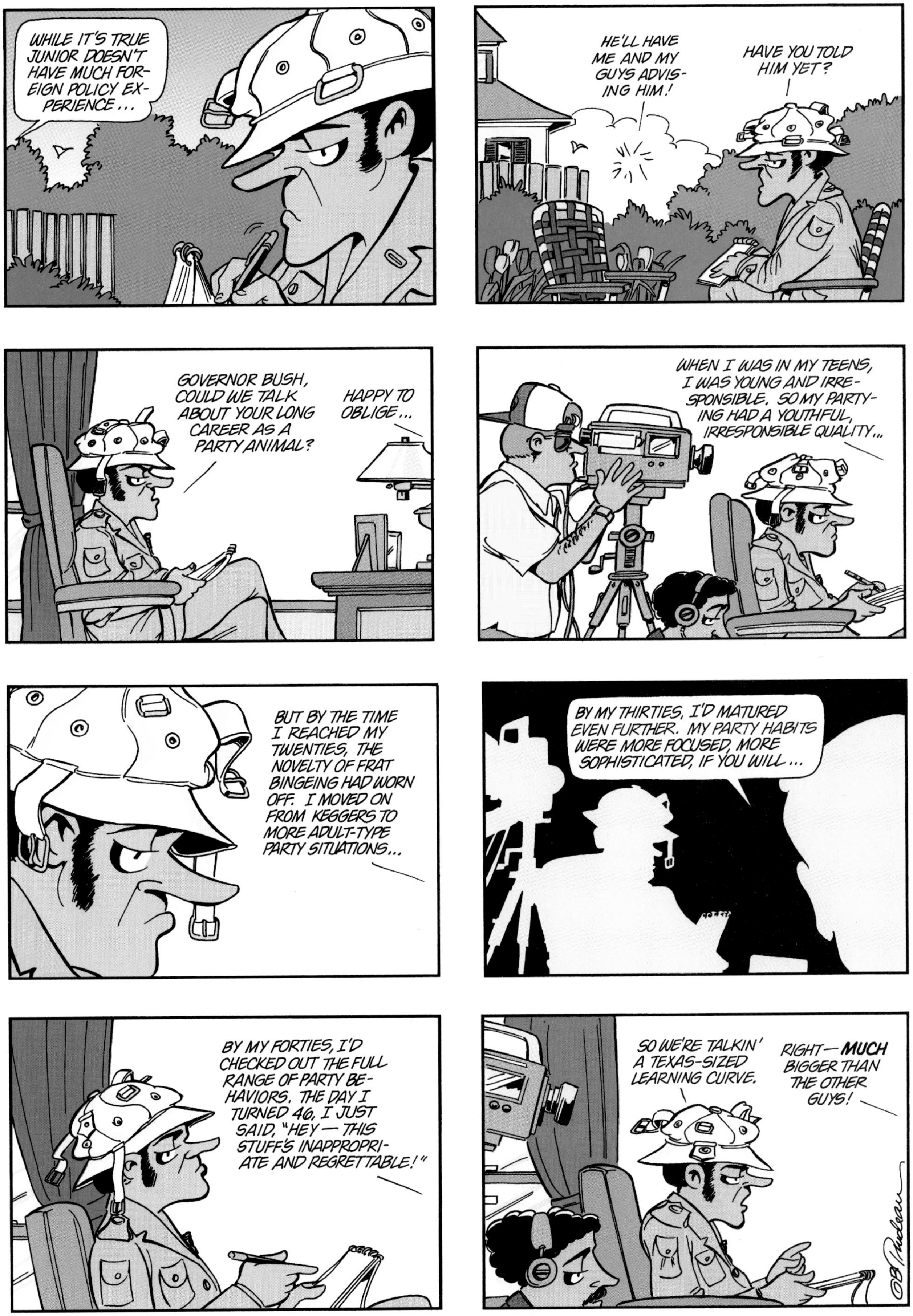
WHILE IT'S TRUE JUNIOR DOESN'T HAVE MUCH FOREIGN POLICY EXPERIENCE...
HE'LL HAVE ME AND MY GUYS ADVISING HIM!
HAVE YOU TOLD HIM YET?
GOVERNOR BUSH, COULD WE TALK ABOUT YOUR LONG CAREER AS A PARTY ANIMAL?
HAPPY TO OBLIGE...
WHEN I WAS IN MY TEENS, I WAS YOUNG AND IRRESPONSIBLE. SO MY PARTYING HAD A YOUTHFUL, IRRESPONSIBLE QUALITY...
BUT BY THE TIME I REACHED MY TWENTIES, THE NOVELTY OF FRAT BINGEING HAD WORN OFF. I MOVED ON FROM KEGGERS TO MORE ADULT-TYPE PARTY SITUATIONS...
BY MY THIRTIES, I'D MATURED EVEN FURTHER. MY PARTY HABITS WERE MORE FOCUSED, MORE SOPHISTICATED, IF YOU WILL...
BY MY FORTIES, I'D CHECKED OUT THE FULL RANGE OF PARTY BEHAVIORS. THE DAY I TURNED 46, I JUST SAID, "HEY — THIS STUFF'S INAPPROPRIATE AND REGRETTABLE!"
SO WE'RE TALKIN' A TEXAS-SIZED LEARNING CURVE.
RIGHT — **MUCH** BIGGER THAN THE OTHER GUYS!

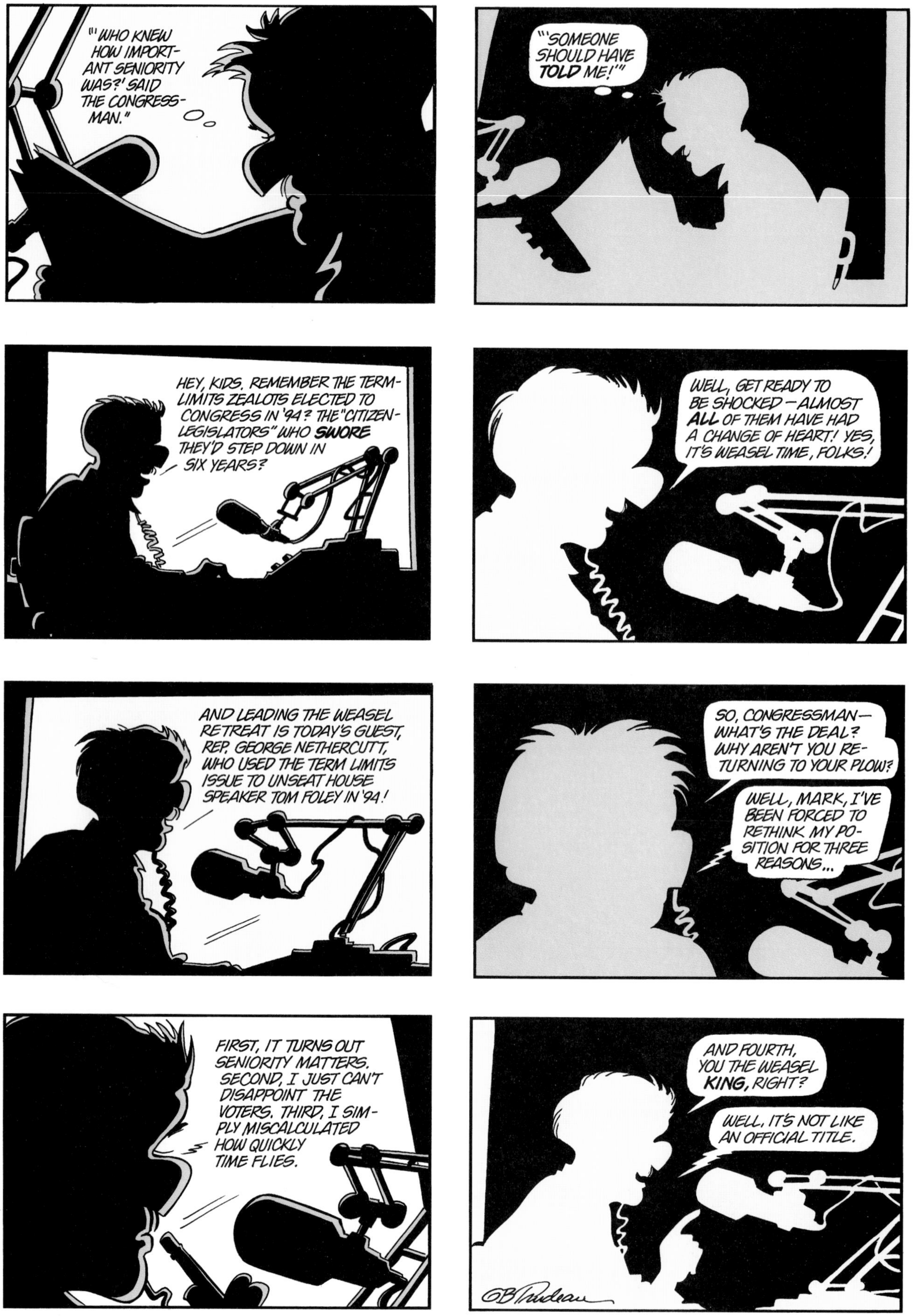
"'WHO KNEW HOW IMPORTANT SENIORITY WAS?' SAID THE CONGRESSMAN."
"'SOMEONE SHOULD HAVE **TOLD** ME!'"
HEY, KIDS, REMEMBER THE TERM-LIMITS ZEALOTS ELECTED TO CONGRESS IN '94? THE "CITIZEN-LEGISLATORS" WHO **SWORE** THEY'D STEP DOWN IN SIX YEARS?
WELL, GET READY TO BE SHOCKED—ALMOST **ALL** OF THEM HAVE HAD A CHANGE OF HEART! YES, IT'S WEASEL TIME, FOLKS!
AND LEADING THE WEASEL RETREAT IS TODAY'S GUEST, REP. GEORGE NETHERCUTT, WHO USED THE TERM LIMITS ISSUE TO UNSEAT HOUSE SPEAKER TOM FOLEY IN '94!
SO, CONGRESSMAN—WHAT'S THE DEAL? WHY AREN'T YOU RETURNING TO YOUR PLOW?
WELL, MARK, I'VE BEEN FORCED TO RETHINK MY POSITION FOR THREE REASONS...
FIRST, IT TURNS OUT SENIORITY MATTERS. SECOND, I JUST CAN'T DISAPPOINT THE VOTERS. THIRD, I SIMPLY MISCALCULATED HOW QUICKLY TIME FLIES.
AND FOURTH, YOU THE WEASEL **KING**, RIGHT?
WELL, IT'S NOT LIKE AN OFFICIAL TITLE.
©B Trudeau

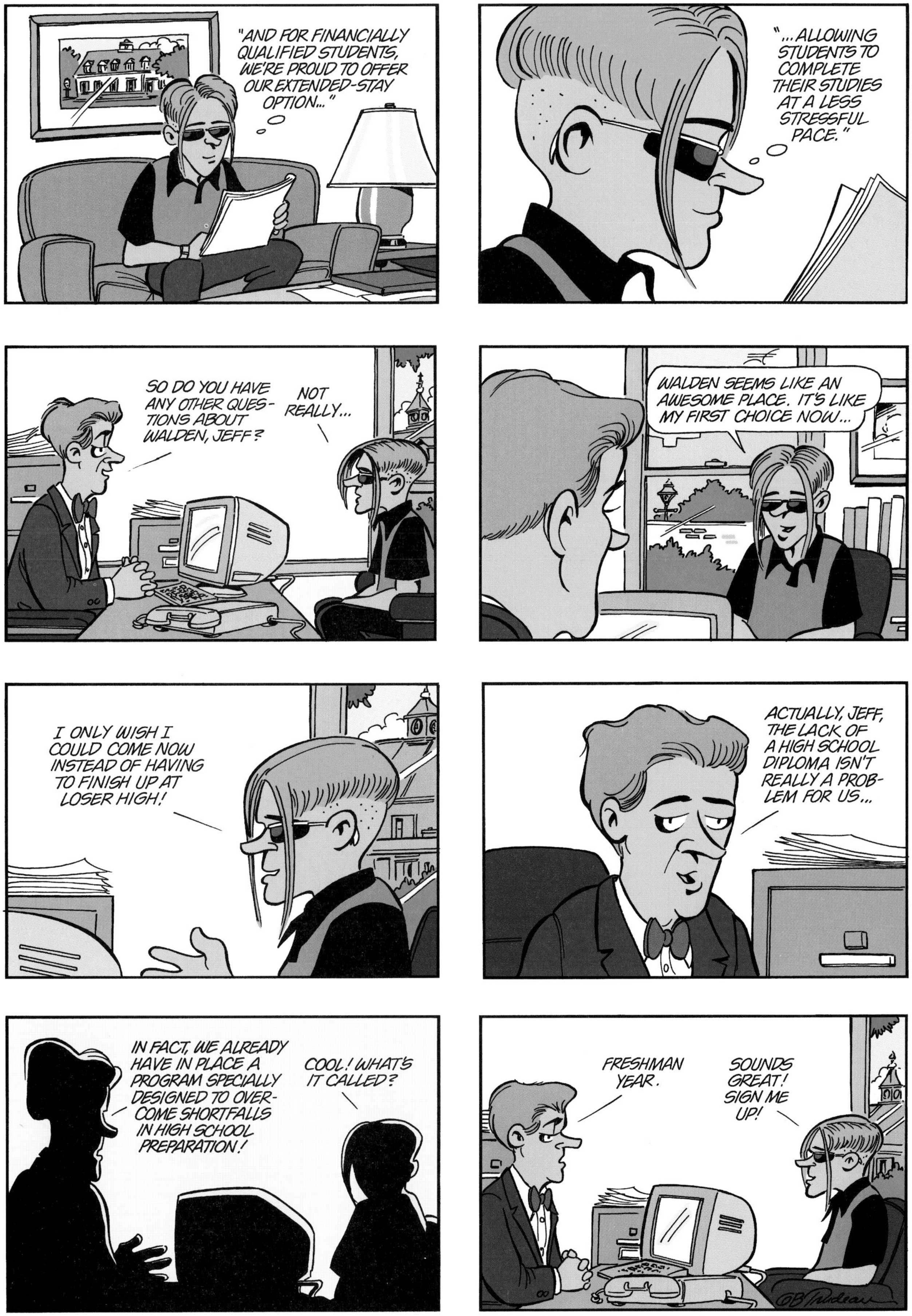
"AND FOR FINANCIALLY QUALIFIED STUDENTS, WE'RE PROUD TO OFFER OUR EXTENDED-STAY OPTION..."
"...ALLOWING STUDENTS TO COMPLETE THEIR STUDIES AT A LESS STRESSFUL PACE."
SO DO YOU HAVE ANY OTHER QUES-TIONS ABOUT WALDEN, JEFF?
NOT REALLY...
WALDEN SEEMS LIKE AN AWESOME PLACE. IT'S LIKE MY FIRST CHOICE NOW...
I ONLY WISH I COULD COME NOW INSTEAD OF HAVING TO FINISH UP AT LOSER HIGH!
ACTUALLY, JEFF, THE LACK OF A HIGH SCHOOL DIPLOMA ISN'T REALLY A PROB-LEM FOR US...
IN FACT, WE ALREADY HAVE IN PLACE A PROGRAM SPECIALLY DESIGNED TO OVER-COME SHORTFALLS IN HIGH SCHOOL PREPARATION!
COOL! WHAT'S IT CALLED?
FRESHMAN YEAR.
SOUNDS GREAT! SIGN ME UP!
GBTrudeau

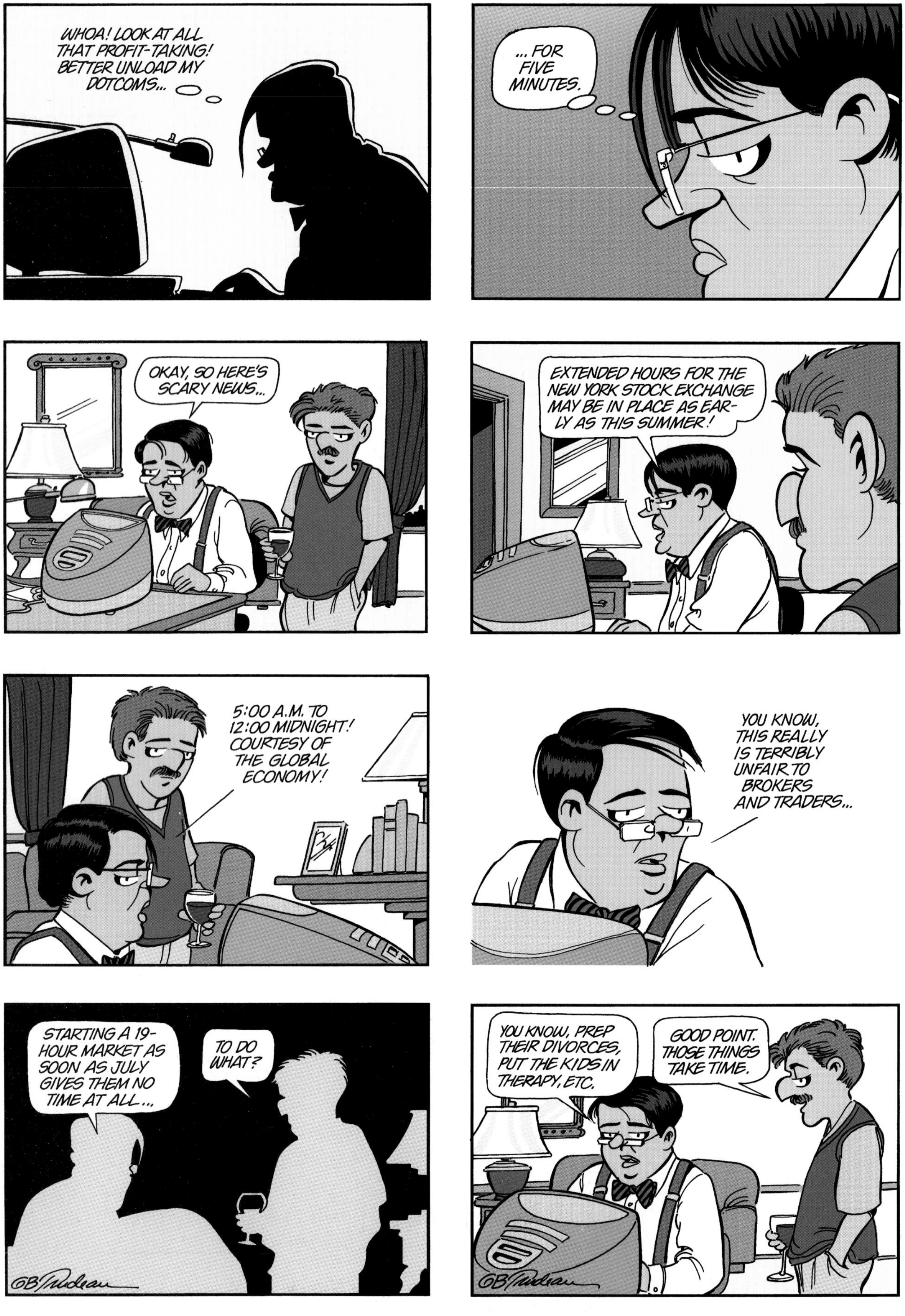
WHOA! LOOK AT ALL THAT PROFIT-TAKING! BETTER UNLOAD MY DOTCOMS...
...FOR FIVE MINUTES.
OKAY, SO HERE'S SCARY NEWS...
EXTENDED HOURS FOR THE NEW YORK STOCK EXCHANGE MAY BE IN PLACE AS EARLY AS THIS SUMMER!
5:00 A.M. TO 12:00 MIDNIGHT! COURTESY OF THE GLOBAL ECONOMY!
YOU KNOW, THIS REALLY IS TERRIBLY UNFAIR TO BROKERS AND TRADERS...
STARTING A 19-HOUR MARKET AS SOON AS JULY GIVES THEM NO TIME AT ALL...
TO DO WHAT?
YOU KNOW, PREP THEIR DIVORCES, PUT THE KIDS IN THERAPY, ETC.
GOOD POINT. THOSE THINGS TAKE TIME.
©B Trudeau
©B Trudeau

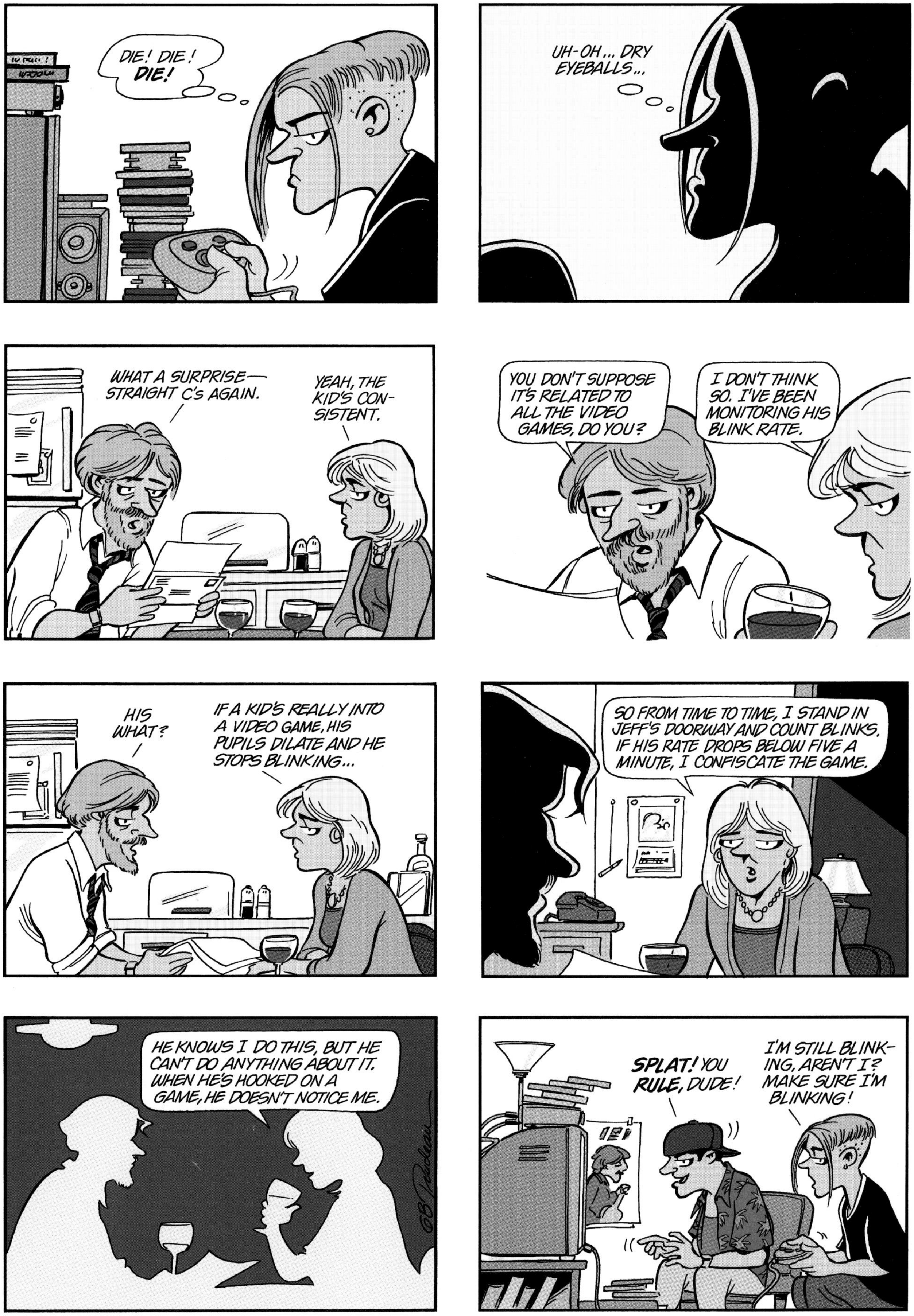
DIE! DIE! DIE!
UH-OH... DRY EYEBALLS...
WHAT A SURPRISE— STRAIGHT C's AGAIN.
YEAH, THE KID'S CONSISTENT.
YOU DON'T SUPPOSE IT'S RELATED TO ALL THE VIDEO GAMES, DO YOU?
I DON'T THINK SO. I'VE BEEN MONITORING HIS BLINK RATE.
HIS WHAT?
IF A KID'S REALLY INTO A VIDEO GAME, HIS PUPILS DILATE AND HE STOPS BLINKING...
SO FROM TIME TO TIME, I STAND IN JEFF'S DOORWAY AND COUNT BLINKS. IF HIS RATE DROPS BELOW FIVE A MINUTE, I CONFISCATE THE GAME.
HE KNOWS I DO THIS, BUT HE CAN'T DO ANYTHING ABOUT IT. WHEN HE'S HOOKED ON A GAME, HE DOESN'T NOTICE ME.
SPLAT! YOU RULE, DUDE!
I'M STILL BLINKING, AREN'T I? MAKE SURE I'M BLINKING!

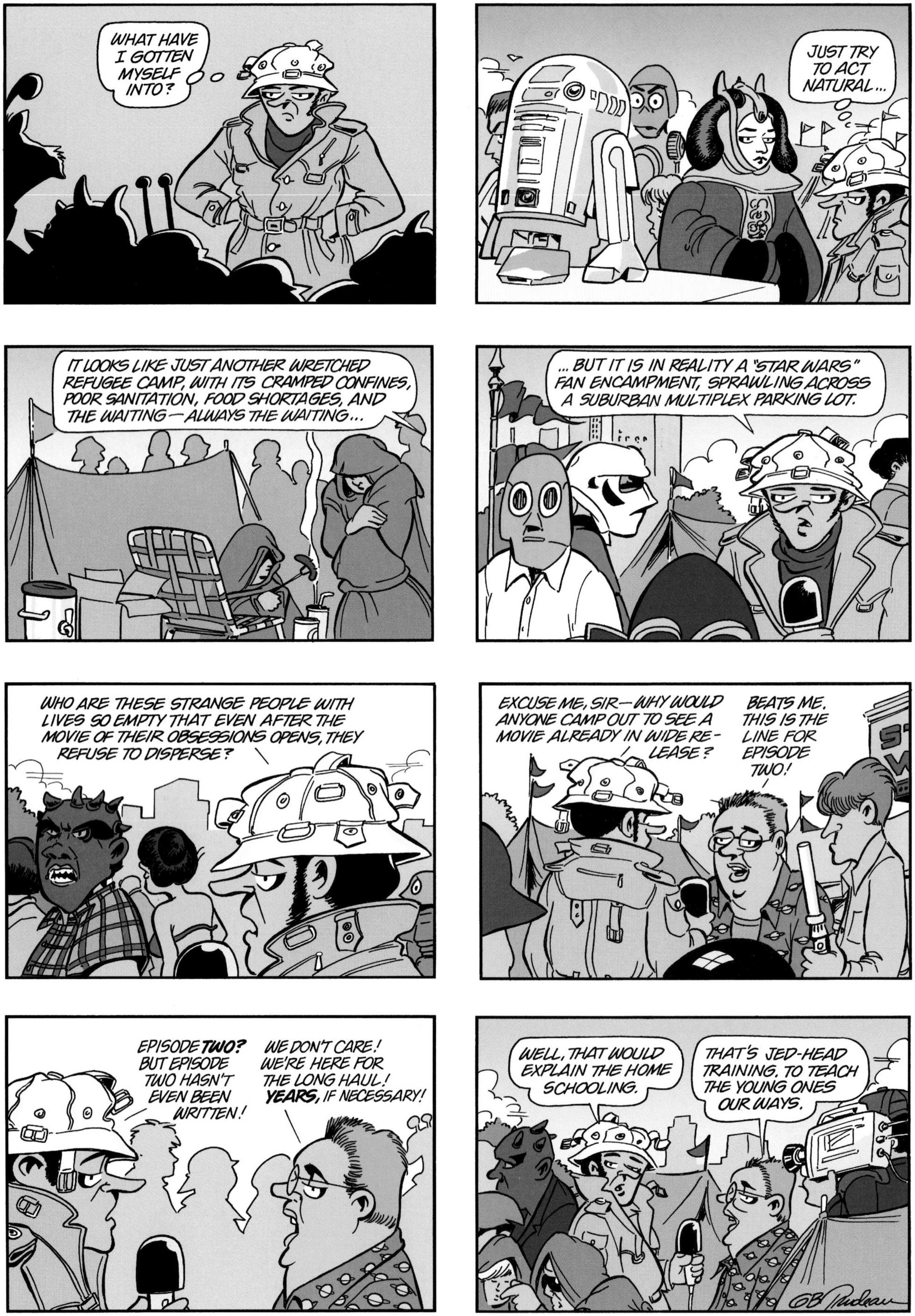
WHAT HAVE I GOTTEN MYSELF INTO?
JUST TRY TO ACT NATURAL...
IT LOOKS LIKE JUST ANOTHER WRETCHED REFUGEE CAMP, WITH ITS CRAMPED CONFINES, POOR SANITATION, FOOD SHORTAGES, AND THE WAITING—ALWAYS THE WAITING...
... BUT IT IS IN REALITY A "STAR WARS" FAN ENCAMPMENT, SPRAWLING ACROSS A SUBURBAN MULTIPLEX PARKING LOT.
WHO ARE THESE STRANGE PEOPLE WITH LIVES SO EMPTY THAT EVEN AFTER THE MOVIE OF THEIR OBSESSIONS OPENS, THEY REFUSE TO DISPERSE?
EXCUSE ME, SIR—WHY WOULD ANYONE CAMP OUT TO SEE A MOVIE ALREADY IN WIDE RE-LEASE?
BEATS ME. THIS IS THE LINE FOR EPISODE TWO!
EPISODE **TWO?** BUT EPISODE TWO HASN'T EVEN BEEN WRITTEN!
WE DON'T CARE! WE'RE HERE FOR THE LONG HAUL! **YEARS,** IF NECESSARY!
WELL, THAT WOULD EXPLAIN THE HOME SCHOOLING.
THAT'S JED-HEAD TRAINING, TO TEACH THE YOUNG ONES OUR WAYS.

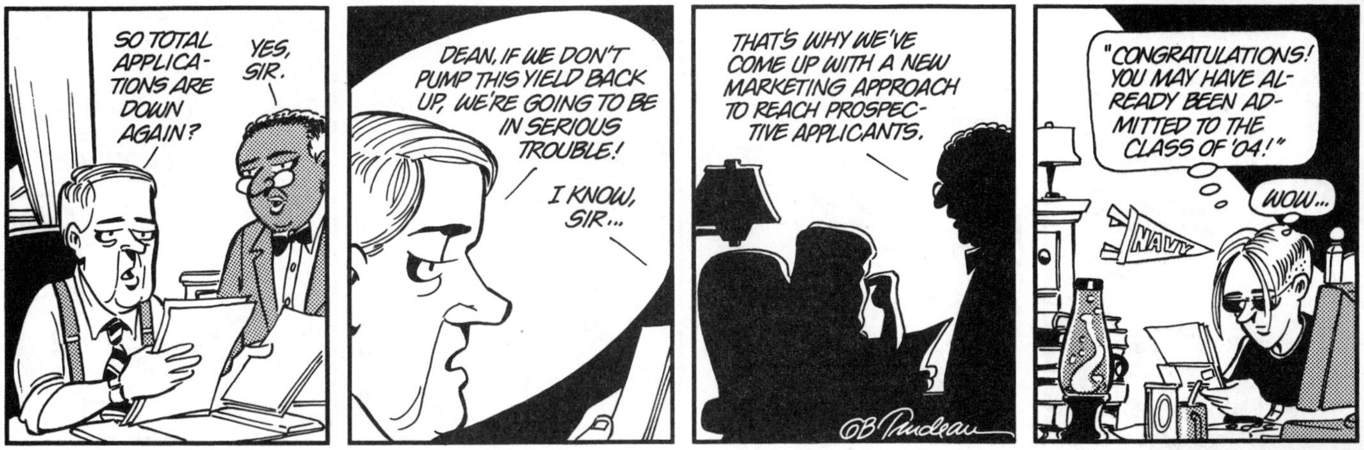
SO TOTAL APPLICATIONS ARE DOWN AGAIN?
YES, SIR.
DEAN, IF WE DON'T PUMP THIS YIELD BACK UP, WE'RE GOING TO BE IN SERIOUS TROUBLE!
I KNOW, SIR...
THAT'S WHY WE'VE COME UP WITH A NEW MARKETING APPROACH TO REACH PROSPECTIVE APPLICANTS.
"CONGRATULATIONS! YOU MAY HAVE ALREADY BEEN ADMITTED TO THE CLASS OF '04!"
NAVY
WOW...

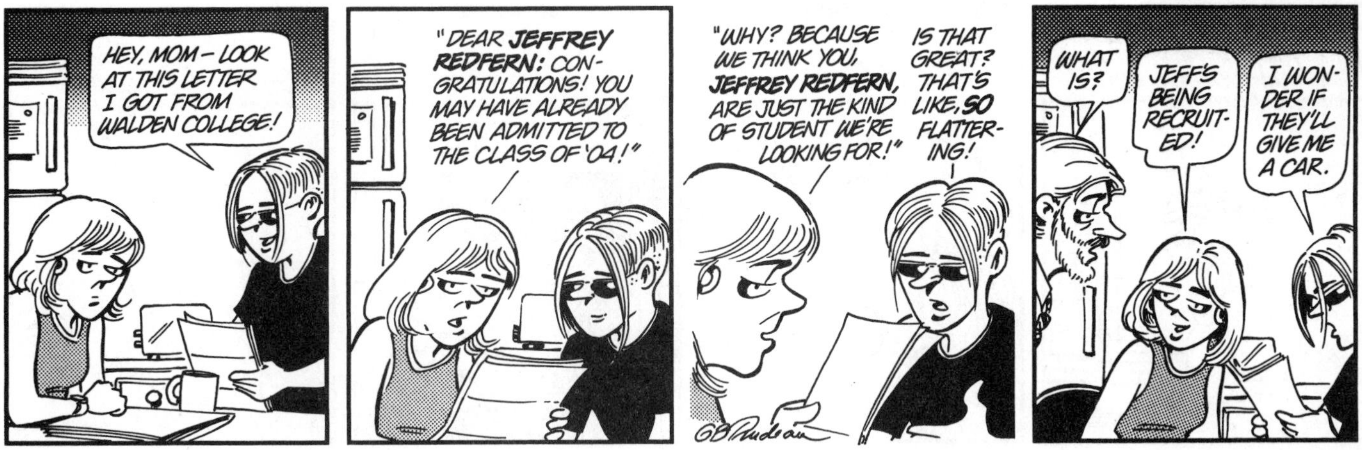
HEY, MOM – LOOK AT THIS LETTER I GOT FROM WALDEN COLLEGE!
"DEAR **JEFFREY REDFERN:** CONGRATULATIONS! YOU MAY HAVE ALREADY BEEN ADMITTED TO THE CLASS OF '04!"
"WHY? BECAUSE WE THINK YOU, **JEFFREY REDFERN,** ARE JUST THE KIND OF STUDENT WE'RE LOOKING FOR!"
IS THAT GREAT? THAT'S LIKE, **SO** FLATTERING!
WHAT IS?
JEFF'S BEING RECRUITED!
I WONDER IF THEY'LL GIVE ME A CAR.

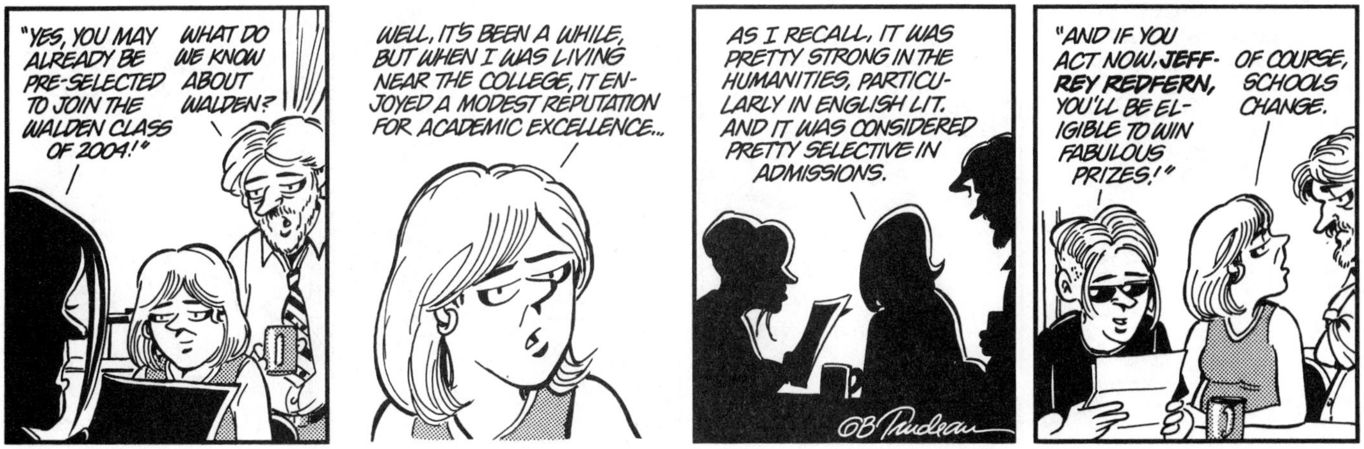
"YES, YOU MAY ALREADY BE PRE-SELECTED TO JOIN THE WALDEN CLASS OF 2004!"
WHAT DO WE KNOW ABOUT WALDEN?
WELL, IT'S BEEN A WHILE, BUT WHEN I WAS LIVING NEAR THE COLLEGE, IT ENJOYED A MODEST REPUTATION FOR ACADEMIC EXCELLENCE...
AS I RECALL, IT WAS PRETTY STRONG IN THE HUMANITIES, PARTICULARLY IN ENGLISH LIT. AND IT WAS CONSIDERED PRETTY SELECTIVE IN ADMISSIONS.
"AND IF YOU ACT NOW, **JEFFREY REDFERN,** YOU'LL BE ELIGIBLE TO WIN FABULOUS PRIZES!"
OF COURSE, SCHOOLS CHANGE.

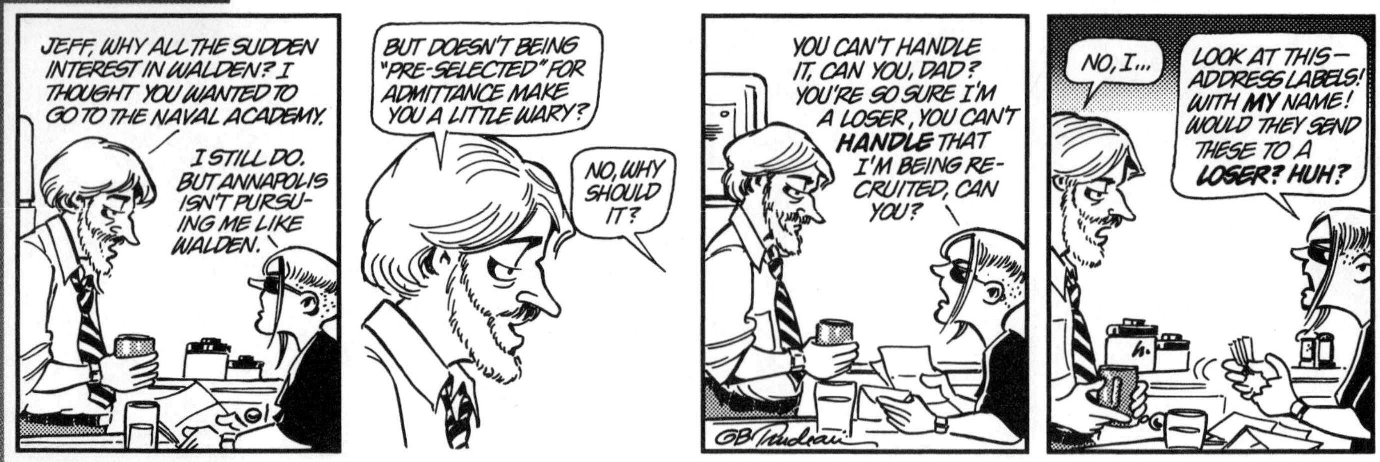
JEFF, WHY ALL THE SUDDEN INTEREST IN WALDEN? I THOUGHT YOU WANTED TO GO TO THE NAVAL ACADEMY.
I STILL DO. BUT ANNAPOLIS ISN'T PURSU-ING ME LIKE WALDEN.
BUT DOESN'T BEING "PRE-SELECTED" FOR ADMITTANCE MAKE YOU A LITTLE WARY?
NO, WHY SHOULD IT?
YOU CAN'T HANDLE IT, CAN YOU, DAD? YOU'RE SO SURE I'M A LOSER, YOU CAN'T **HANDLE** THAT I'M BEING RE-CRUITED, CAN YOU?
NO, I...
LOOK AT THIS— ADDRESS LABELS! WITH **MY** NAME! WOULD THEY SEND THESE TO A **LOSER? HUH?**

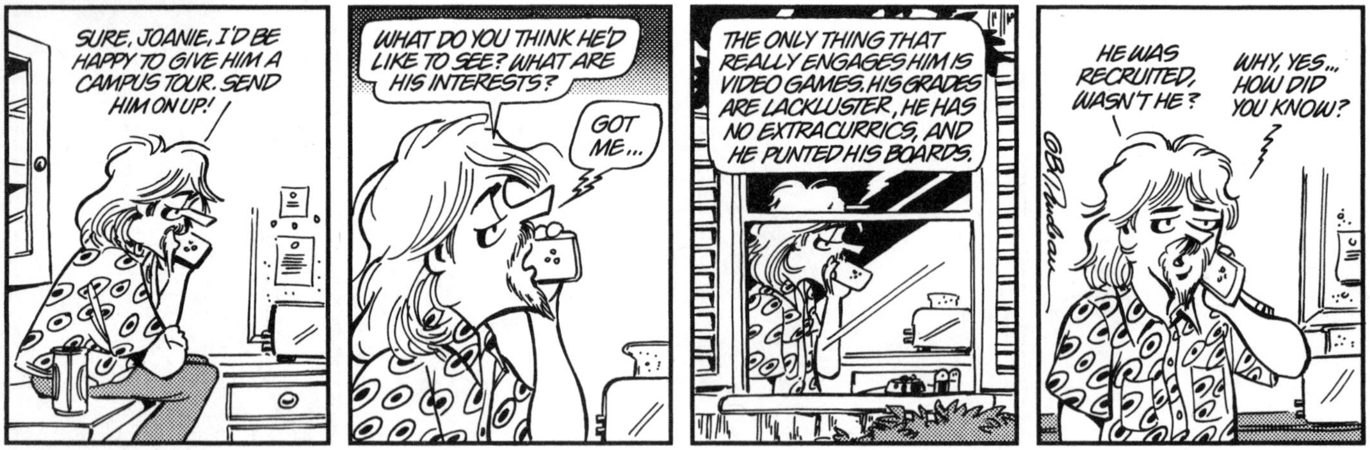
SURE, JOANIE, I'D BE HAPPY TO GIVE HIM A CAMPUS TOUR. SEND HIM ON UP!
WHAT DO YOU THINK HE'D LIKE TO SEE? WHAT ARE HIS INTERESTS?
GOT ME...
THE ONLY THING THAT REALLY ENGAGES HIM IS VIDEO GAMES. HIS GRADES ARE LACKLUSTER, HE HAS NO EXTRACURRICS, AND HE PUNTED HIS BOARDS.
HE WAS RECRUITED, WASN'T HE?
WHY, YES... HOW DID YOU KNOW?

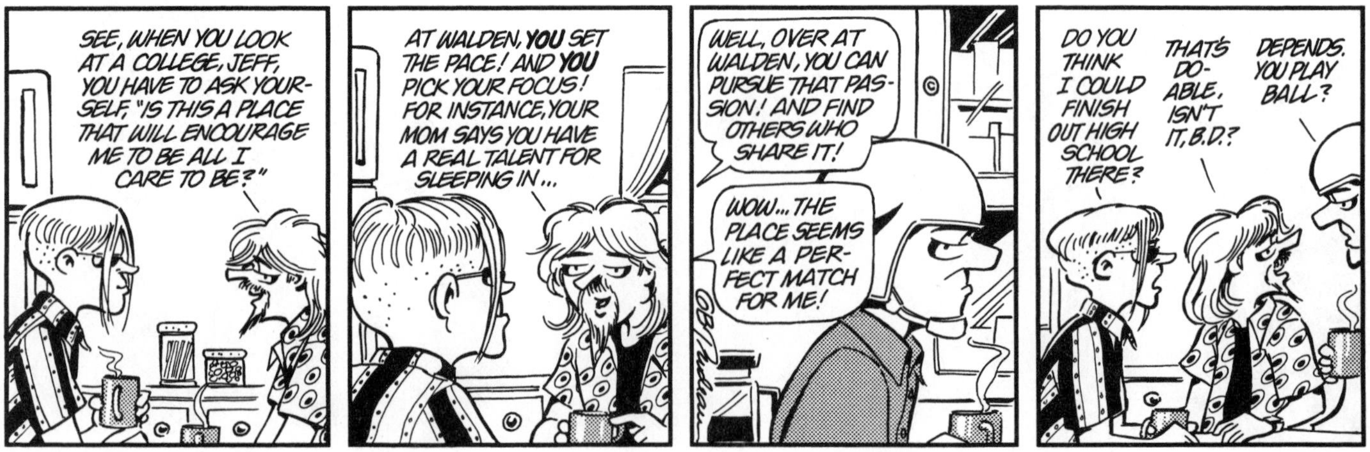
SEE, WHEN YOU LOOK AT A COLLEGE, JEFF, YOU HAVE TO ASK YOUR-SELF, "IS THIS A PLACE THAT WILL ENCOURAGE ME TO BE ALL I CARE TO BE?"
AT WALDEN, **YOU** SET THE PACE! AND **YOU** PICK YOUR FOCUS! FOR INSTANCE, YOUR MOM SAYS YOU HAVE A REAL TALENT FOR SLEEPING IN...
WELL, OVER AT WALDEN, YOU CAN PURSUE THAT PAS-SION! AND FIND OTHERS WHO SHARE IT!
WOW... THE PLACE SEEMS LIKE A PER-FECT MATCH FOR ME!
DO YOU THINK I COULD FINISH OUT HIGH SCHOOL THERE?
THAT'S DO-ABLE, ISN'T IT, B.D.?
DEPENDS. YOU PLAY BALL?

HEY, EVERYBODY, MY NAME'S ZIPPER HARRIS, AND I'LL BE YOUR WALDEN COLLEGE TOUR GUIDE TODAY!
WHAT YOU ARE ABOUT TO SEE MAY IMPRESS YOU OR SHOCK YOU, MAKE YOU SMILE OR MAKE YOU WEEP! BUT YOU **WILL** NOT FORGET IT!
ANYONE HERE HAVE ANY SPECIAL MEDICAL CONDITION? NO? THEN LET'S GET ROLLING! AND REMEMBER, TIPPING **IS** PERMITTED!
COOL TOUR GUIDE.
THANKS. HE'S FAMILY.
GB Trudeau

BEFORE WE START THE TOUR, LET ME FIRST CONGRATULATE YOU...
AS YOU KNOW FROM YOUR MAILING, ALL OF YOU HAVE BEEN "PRE-SELECTED" FOR ADMISSION INTO WALDEN COLLEGE!
ARE THERE ANY QUESTIONS ABOUT THE COLLEGE'S EXCITING, NO-OBLIGATION OFFER?
GB Trudeau
YEAH, DO WE HAVE TO BUY THE MAGAZINE SUBSCRIPTIONS?
ABSOLUTELY NOT! I FELL FOR THAT, TOO.

I'D NOW LIKE TO DRAW YOUR ATTENTION TO THIS STATUE OF OUR FOUNDER, **THADDEUS ELI WALDEN**!
WALDEN WAS A HARVARD DROP-OUT WHO VOWED TO FOUND A COLLEGE WHERE ACADEMIC MEDIOCRITY WOULD BE VALUED AND CHERISHED...
IN WALDEN COLLEGE, HIS DREAM WAS REALIZED, AND TO THIS DAY, ELI WALDEN IS KNOWN AS THE PATRON SAINT OF THE GENTLEMAN'S "C"!
NOW **THAT'S** AN EDUCATOR, MAN!
YUP! AND THIS WAS BEFORE GRADE INFLATION!
GB Trudeau

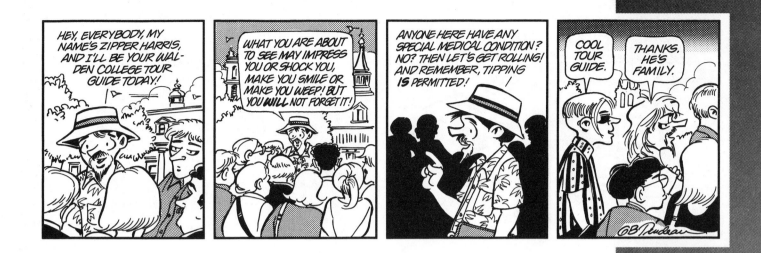

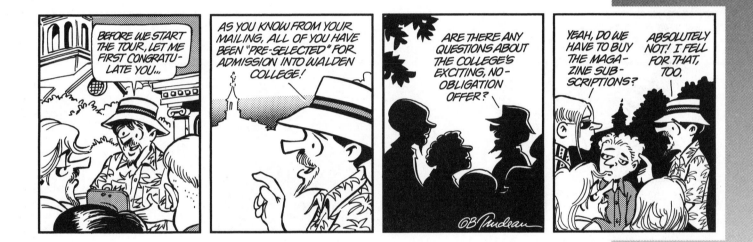

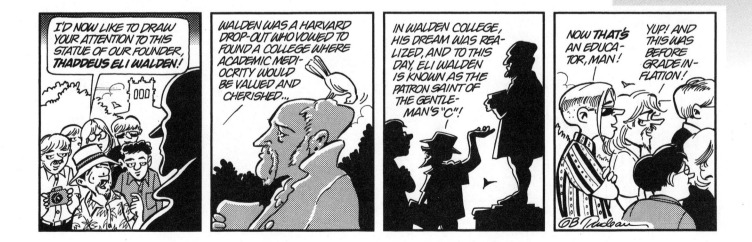

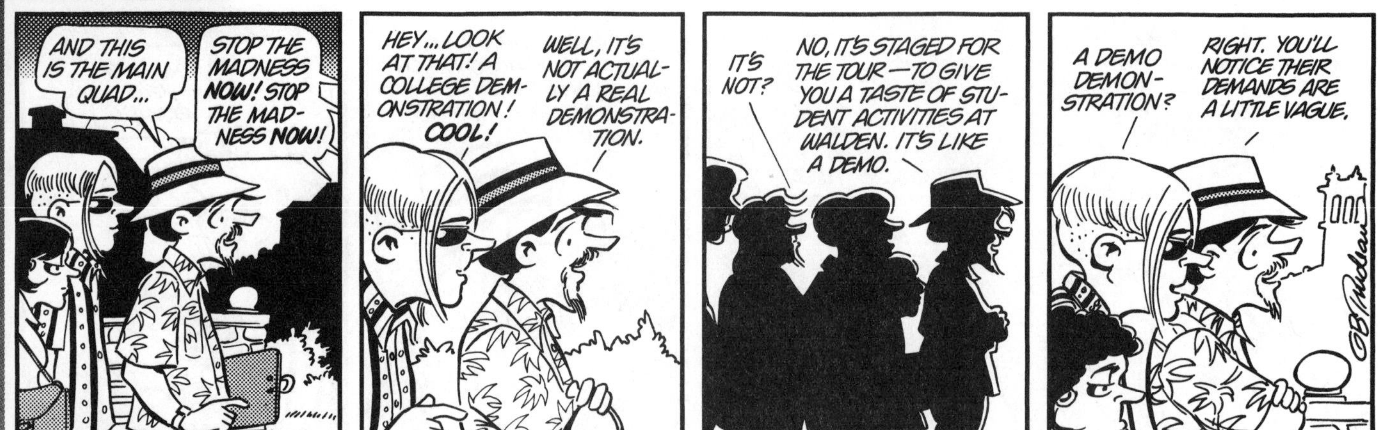
AND THIS IS THE MAIN QUAD...
STOP THE MADNESS NOW! STOP THE MADNESS NOW!
HEY... LOOK AT THAT! A COLLEGE DEMONSTRATION! COOL!
WELL, IT'S NOT ACTUALLY A REAL DEMONSTRATION.
IT'S NOT?
NO, IT'S STAGED FOR THE TOUR—TO GIVE YOU A TASTE OF STUDENT ACTIVITIES AT WALDEN. IT'S LIKE A DEMO.
A DEMO DEMONSTRATION?
RIGHT. YOU'LL NOTICE THEIR DEMANDS ARE A LITTLE VAGUE.
©B Trudeau

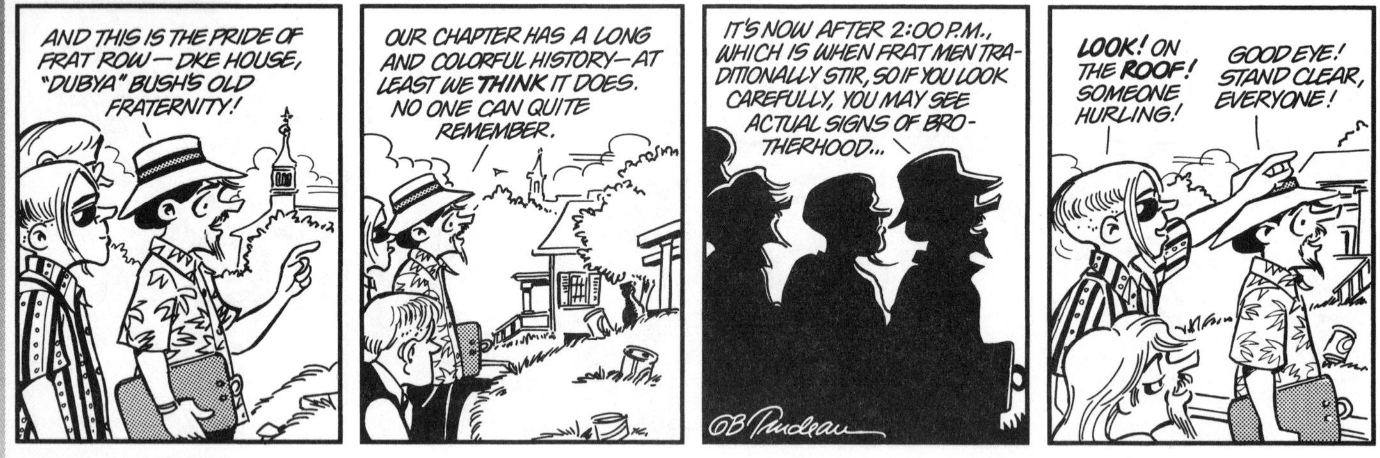
AND THIS IS THE PRIDE OF FRAT ROW—DKE HOUSE, "DUBYA" BUSH'S OLD FRATERNITY!
OUR CHAPTER HAS A LONG AND COLORFUL HISTORY—AT LEAST WE THINK IT DOES. NO ONE CAN QUITE REMEMBER.
IT'S NOW AFTER 2:00 P.M., WHICH IS WHEN FRAT MEN TRADITIONALLY STIR, SO IF YOU LOOK CAREFULLY, YOU MAY SEE ACTUAL SIGNS OF BROTHERHOOD...
©B Trudeau
LOOK! ON THE ROOF! SOMEONE HURLING!
GOOD EYE! STAND CLEAR, EVERYONE!

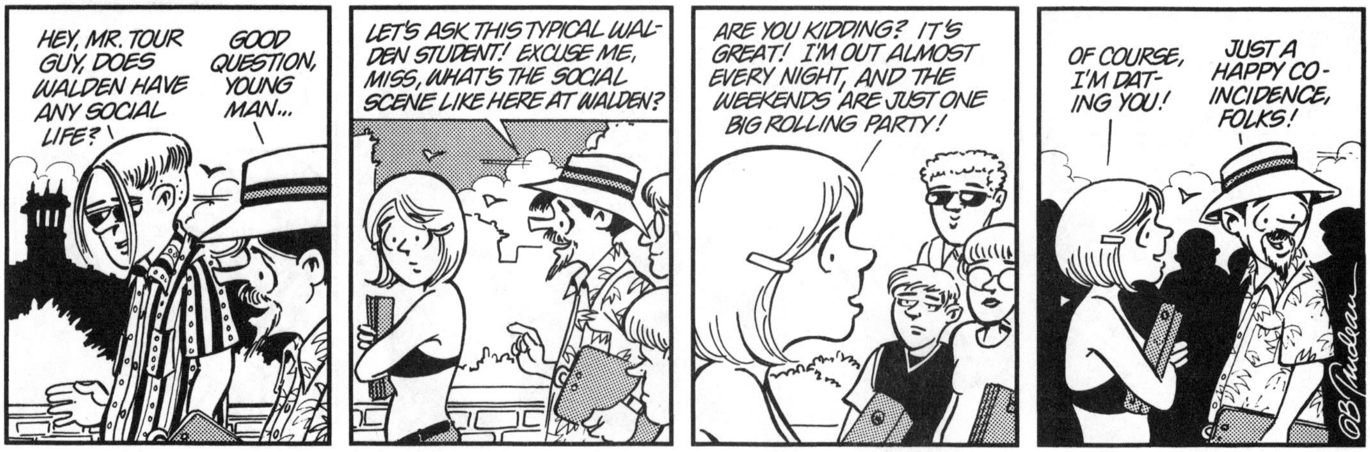
HEY, MR. TOUR GUY, DOES WALDEN HAVE ANY SOCIAL LIFE?
GOOD QUESTION, YOUNG MAN...
LET'S ASK THIS TYPICAL WALDEN STUDENT! EXCUSE ME, MISS, WHAT'S THE SOCIAL SCENE LIKE HERE AT WALDEN?
ARE YOU KIDDING? IT'S GREAT! I'M OUT ALMOST EVERY NIGHT, AND THE WEEKENDS ARE JUST ONE BIG ROLLING PARTY!
OF COURSE, I'M DATING YOU!
JUST A HAPPY COINCIDENCE, FOLKS!
©B Trudeau

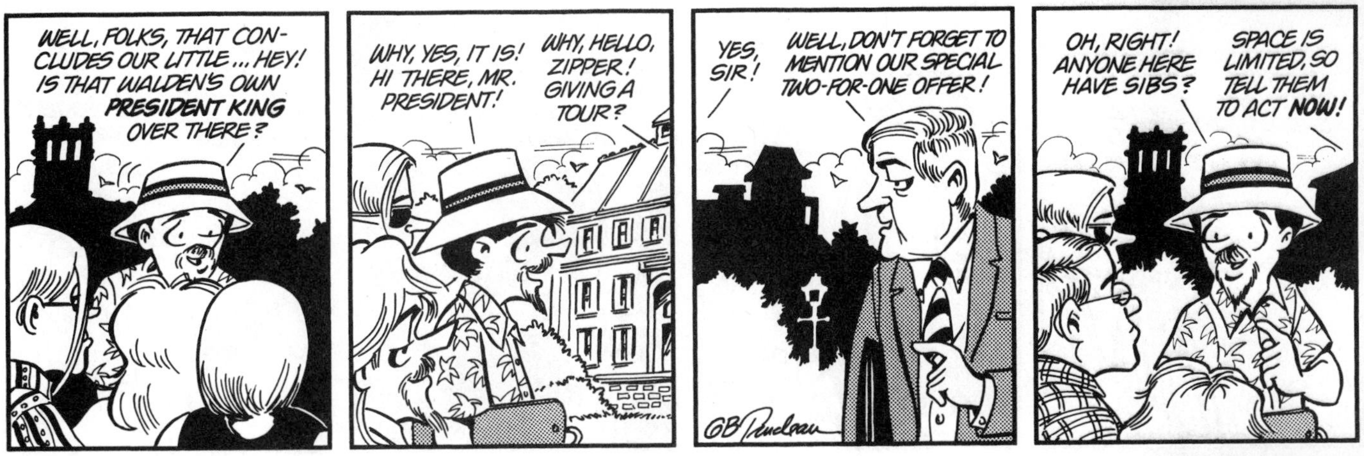
WELL, FOLKS, THAT CONCLUDES OUR LITTLE ... HEY! IS THAT WALDEN'S OWN **PRESIDENT KING** OVER THERE?
WHY, YES, IT IS! HI THERE, MR. PRESIDENT!
WHY, HELLO, ZIPPER! GIVING A TOUR?
YES, SIR!
WELL, DON'T FORGET TO MENTION OUR SPECIAL TWO-FOR-ONE OFFER!
OH, RIGHT! ANYONE HERE HAVE SIBS?
SPACE IS LIMITED, SO TELL THEM TO ACT **NOW!**
GB Trudeau

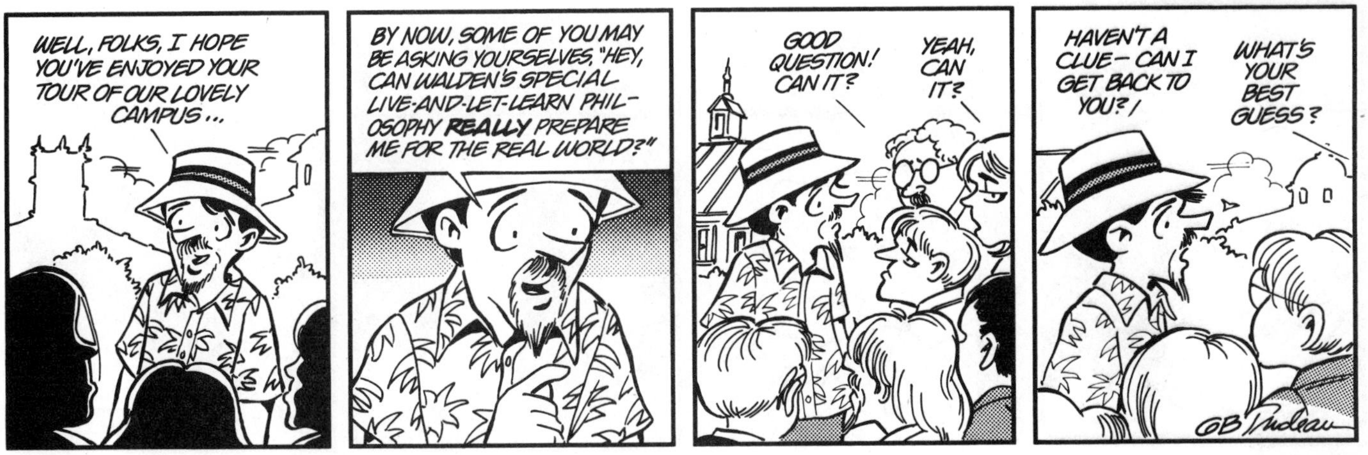
WELL, FOLKS, I HOPE YOU'VE ENJOYED YOUR TOUR OF OUR LOVELY CAMPUS...
BY NOW, SOME OF YOU MAY BE ASKING YOURSELVES, "HEY, CAN WALDEN'S SPECIAL LIVE-AND-LET-LEARN PHILOSOPHY **REALLY** PREPARE ME FOR THE REAL WORLD?"
GOOD QUESTION! CAN IT?
YEAH, CAN IT?
HAVEN'T A CLUE — CAN I GET BACK TO YOU?!
WHAT'S YOUR BEST GUESS?
GB Trudeau

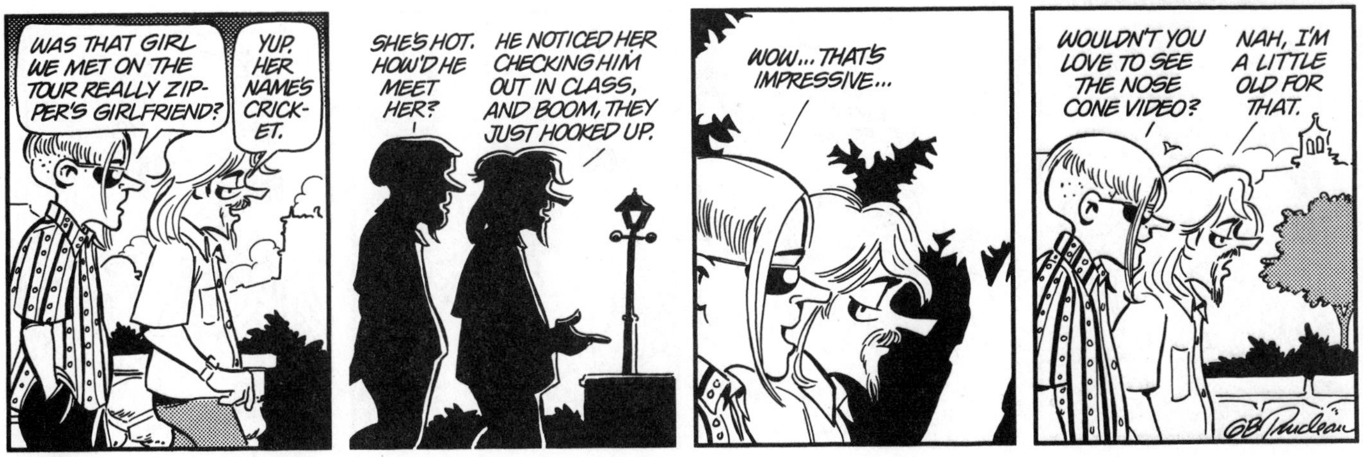
WAS THAT GIRL WE MET ON THE TOUR REALLY ZIPPER'S GIRLFRIEND?
YUP. HER NAME'S CRICKET.
SHE'S HOT. HOW'D HE MEET HER?
HE NOTICED HER CHECKING HIM OUT IN CLASS, AND BOOM, THEY JUST HOOKED UP.
WOW... THAT'S IMPRESSIVE...
WOULDN'T YOU LOVE TO SEE THE NOSE CONE VIDEO?
NAH, I'M A LITTLE OLD FOR THAT.
GB Trudeau

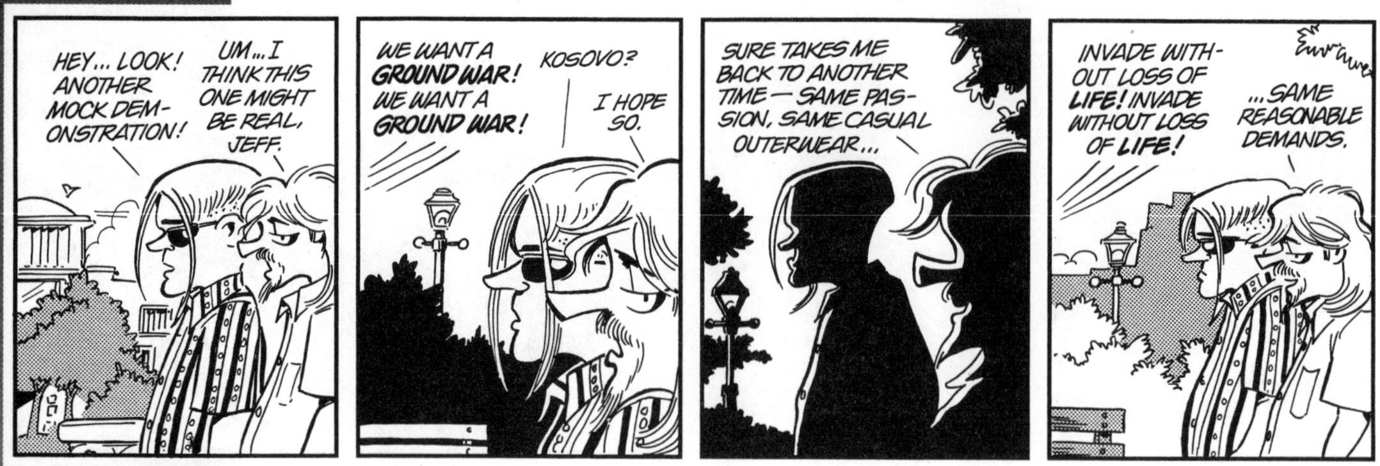
HEY... LOOK! ANOTHER MOCK DEMONSTRATION!
UM... I THINK THIS ONE MIGHT BE REAL, JEFF.
WE WANT A **GROUND WAR!** WE WANT A **GROUND WAR!**
KOSOVO?
I HOPE SO.
SURE TAKES ME BACK TO ANOTHER TIME — SAME PASSION, SAME CASUAL OUTERWEAR...
INVADE WITHOUT LOSS OF **LIFE!** INVADE WITHOUT LOSS OF **LIFE!**
...SAME REASONABLE DEMANDS.

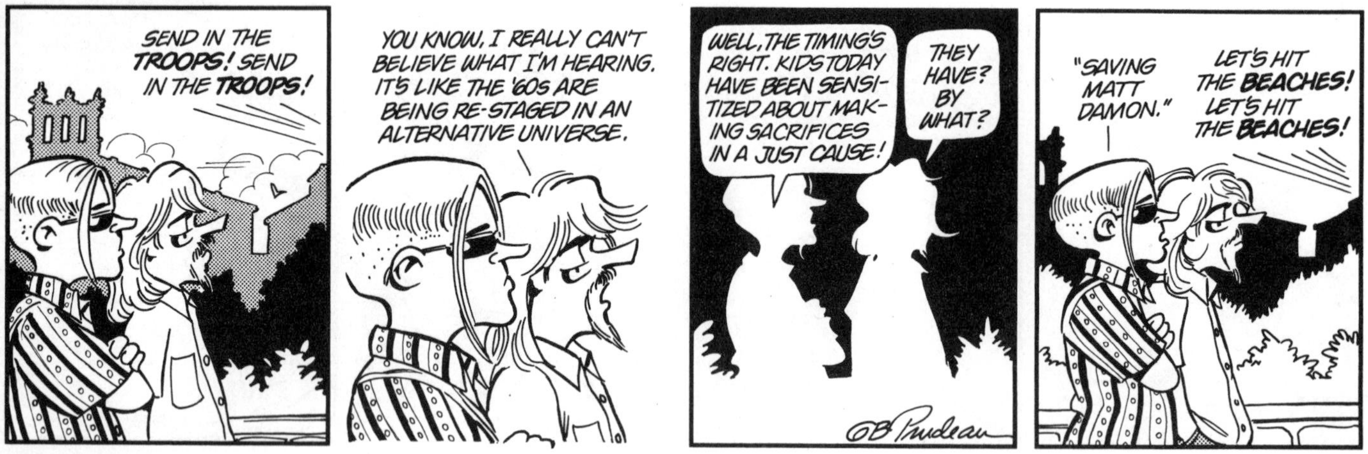
SEND IN THE **TROOPS!** SEND IN THE **TROOPS!**
YOU KNOW, I REALLY CAN'T BELIEVE WHAT I'M HEARING. IT'S LIKE THE '60s ARE BEING RE-STAGED IN AN ALTERNATIVE UNIVERSE.
WELL, THE TIMING'S RIGHT. KIDS TODAY HAVE BEEN SENSITIZED ABOUT MAKING SACRIFICES IN A JUST CAUSE!
THEY HAVE? BY WHAT?
"SAVING MATT DAMON."
LET'S HIT THE **BEACHES!** LET'S HIT THE **BEACHES!**

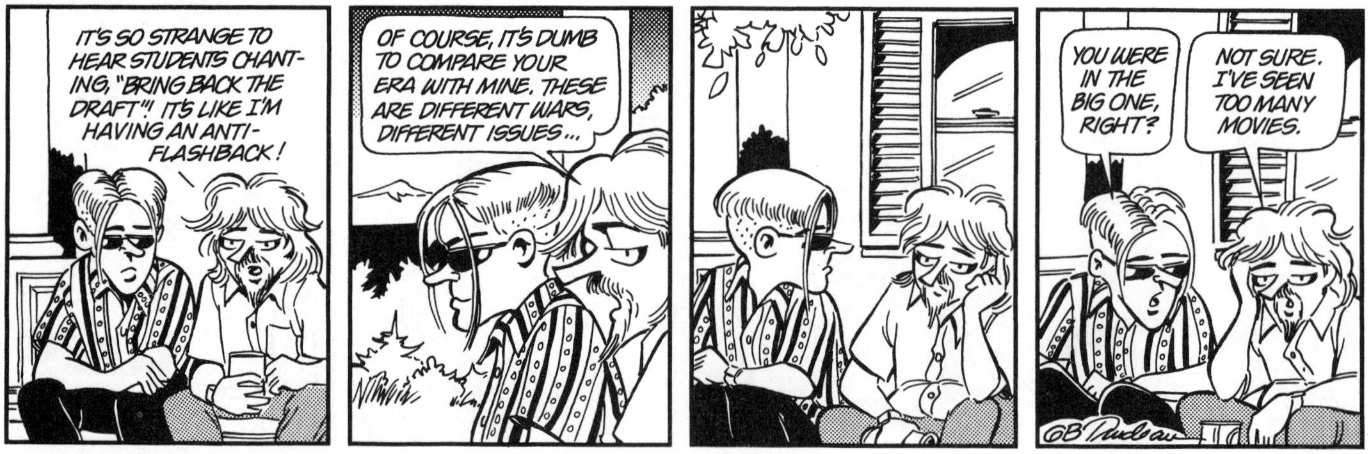
IT'S SO STRANGE TO HEAR STUDENTS CHANTING, "BRING BACK THE DRAFT"! IT'S LIKE I'M HAVING AN ANTI-FLASHBACK!
OF COURSE, IT'S DUMB TO COMPARE YOUR ERA WITH MINE. THESE ARE DIFFERENT WARS, DIFFERENT ISSUES...
YOU WERE IN THE BIG ONE, RIGHT?
NOT SURE. I'VE SEEN TOO MANY MOVIES.

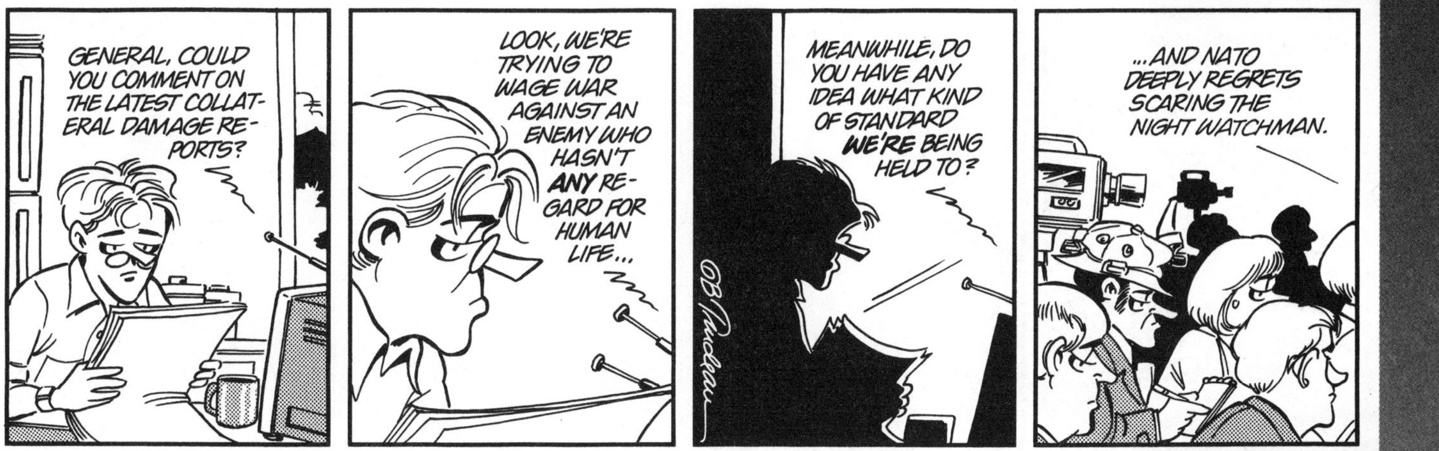
GENERAL, COULD YOU COMMENT ON THE LATEST COLLATERAL DAMAGE REPORTS?
LOOK, WE'RE TRYING TO WAGE WAR AGAINST AN ENEMY WHO HASN'T ANY REGARD FOR HUMAN LIFE...
MEANWHILE, DO YOU HAVE ANY IDEA WHAT KIND OF STANDARD WE'RE BEING HELD TO?
...AND NATO DEEPLY REGRETS SCARING THE NIGHT WATCHMAN.

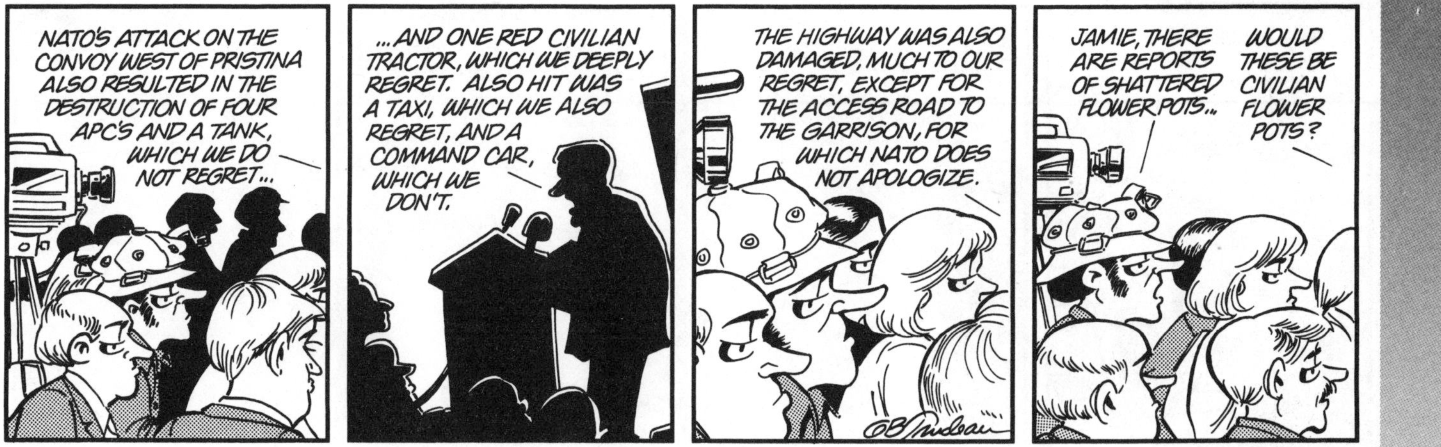
NATO'S ATTACK ON THE CONVOY WEST OF PRISTINA ALSO RESULTED IN THE DESTRUCTION OF FOUR APC'S AND A TANK, WHICH WE DO NOT REGRET...
...AND ONE RED CIVILIAN TRACTOR, WHICH WE DEEPLY REGRET. ALSO HIT WAS A TAXI, WHICH WE ALSO REGRET, AND A COMMAND CAR, WHICH WE DON'T.
THE HIGHWAY WAS ALSO DAMAGED, MUCH TO OUR REGRET, EXCEPT FOR THE ACCESS ROAD TO THE GARRISON, FOR WHICH NATO DOES NOT APOLOGIZE.
JAMIE, THERE ARE REPORTS OF SHATTERED FLOWER POTS...
WOULD THESE BE CIVILIAN FLOWER POTS?

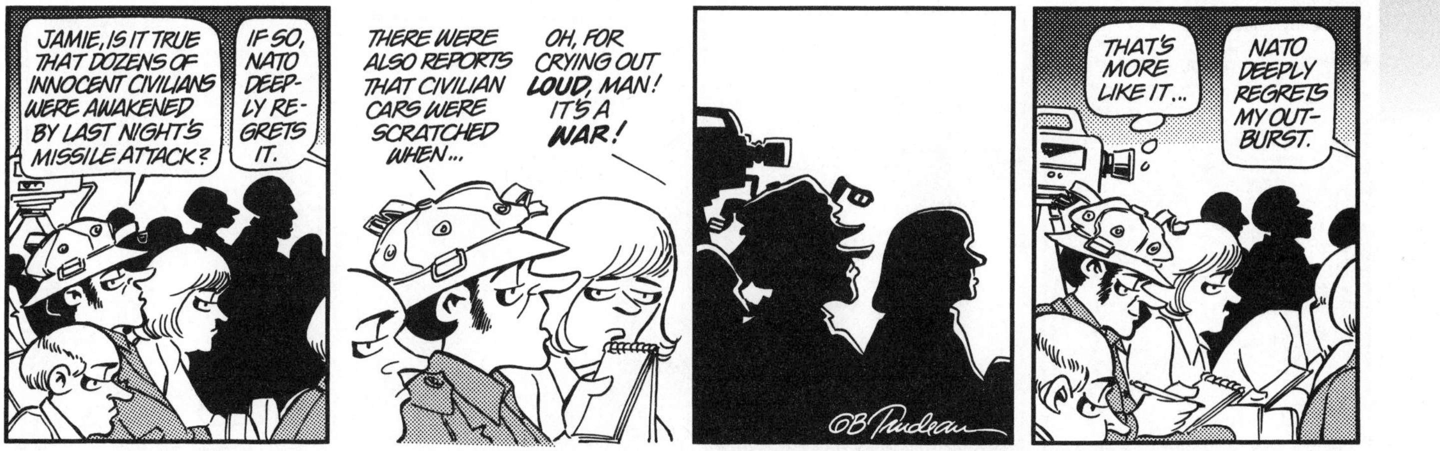
JAMIE, IS IT TRUE THAT DOZENS OF INNOCENT CIVILIANS WERE AWAKENED BY LAST NIGHT'S MISSILE ATTACK?
IF SO, NATO DEEPLY REGRETS IT.
THERE WERE ALSO REPORTS THAT CIVILIAN CARS WERE SCRATCHED WHEN...
OH, FOR CRYING OUT LOUD, MAN! IT'S A WAR!
THAT'S MORE LIKE IT...
NATO DEEPLY REGRETS MY OUTBURST.

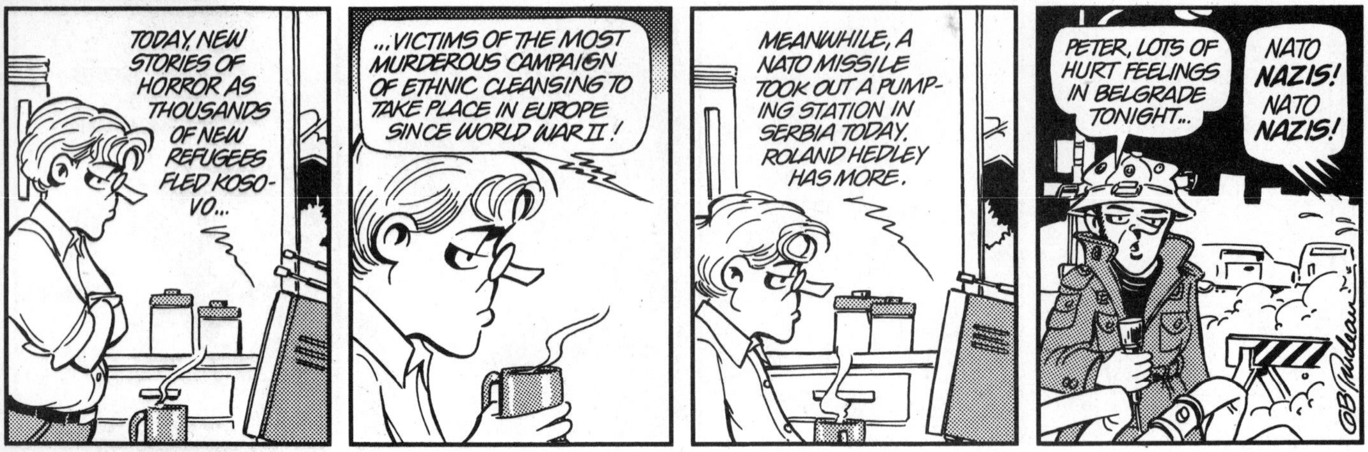
TODAY, NEW STORIES OF HORROR AS THOUSANDS OF NEW REFUGEES FLED KOSOVO...
...VICTIMS OF THE MOST MURDEROUS CAMPAIGN OF ETHNIC CLEANSING TO TAKE PLACE IN EUROPE SINCE WORLD WAR II!
MEANWHILE, A NATO MISSILE TOOK OUT A PUMPING STATION IN SERBIA TODAY. ROLAND HEDLEY HAS MORE.
PETER, LOTS OF HURT FEELINGS IN BELGRADE TONIGHT...
NATO NAZIS! NATO NAZIS!
GB Trudeau

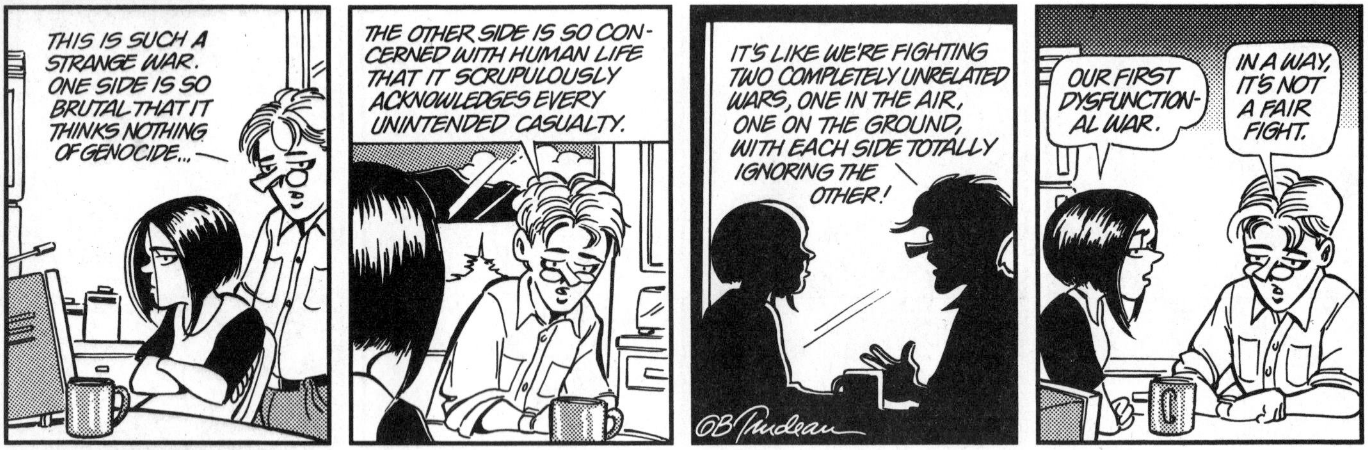
THIS IS SUCH A STRANGE WAR. ONE SIDE IS SO BRUTAL THAT IT THINKS NOTHING OF GENOCIDE...
THE OTHER SIDE IS SO CONCERNED WITH HUMAN LIFE THAT IT SCRUPULOUSLY ACKNOWLEDGES EVERY UNINTENDED CASUALTY.
IT'S LIKE WE'RE FIGHTING TWO COMPLETELY UNRELATED WARS, ONE IN THE AIR, ONE ON THE GROUND, WITH EACH SIDE TOTALLY IGNORING THE OTHER!
GB Trudeau
OUR FIRST DYSFUNCTIONAL WAR.
IN A WAY, IT'S NOT A FAIR FIGHT.

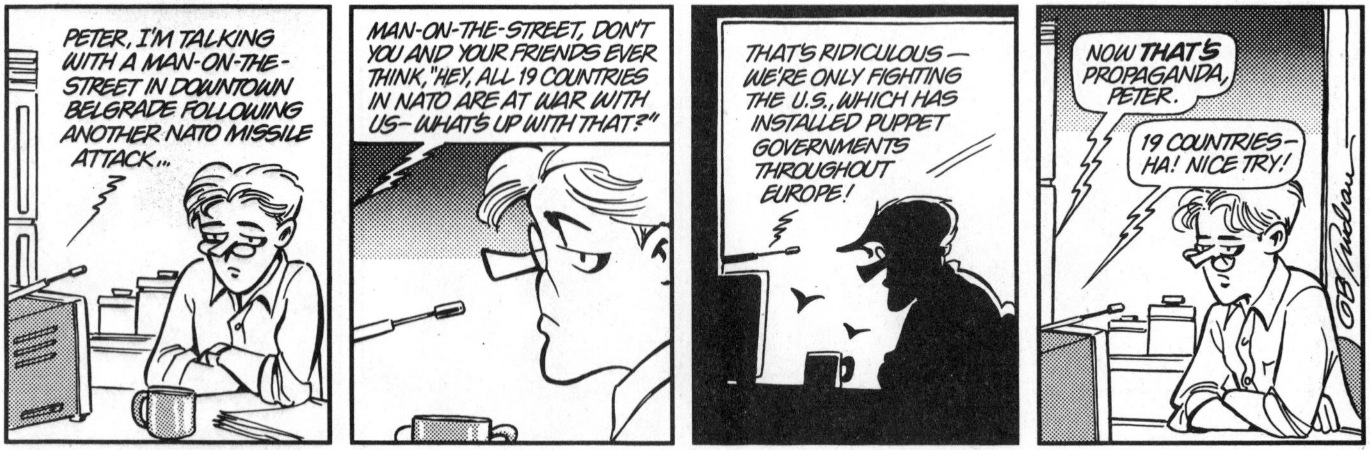
PETER, I'M TALKING WITH A MAN-ON-THE-STREET IN DOWNTOWN BELGRADE FOLLOWING ANOTHER NATO MISSILE ATTACK...
MAN-ON-THE-STREET, DON'T YOU AND YOUR FRIENDS EVER THINK, "HEY, ALL 19 COUNTRIES IN NATO ARE AT WAR WITH US– WHAT'S UP WITH THAT?"
THAT'S RIDICULOUS — WE'RE ONLY FIGHTING THE U.S., WHICH HAS INSTALLED PUPPET GOVERNMENTS THROUGHOUT EUROPE!
NOW THAT'S PROPAGANDA, PETER.
19 COUNTRIES– HA! NICE TRY!
GB Trudeau